Inspiring | Educating | Creating | Entertaining

Brimming with creative inspiration, how-to projects, and useful information to enrich your everyday life, Quarto Knows is a favorite destination for those pursuing their interests and passions. Visit our site and dig deeper with our books into your area of interest: Quarto Creates, Quarto Cooks, Quarto Homes, Quarto Lives, Quarto Drives, Quarto Explores, Quarto Gifts, or Quarto Kids.

10 9 8 7 6 5 4 3 2

ISBN: 978-0-7603-5786-6

Library of Congress Cataloging-in-Publication Data

Title: The Brew your own big book of clone recipes : featuring 300 homebrew recipes
    from your favorite breweries / editors of Brew Your Own.
Other titles: Big book of clone recipes | Brew your own.
Description: Minneapolis, MN, USA : Voyageur Press, an imprint of
    The Quarto Group, [2018] | Includes bibliographical references and index.
Identifiers: LCCN 2017046466 | ISBN 9780760357866 (sc)
Subjects: LCSH: Beer. | Brewing. | Brewing--Amateurs' manuals. |
    LCGFT: Cookbooks.
Classification: LCC TP577 .B7393 2018 | DDC 641.87/3--dc23
    LC record available at https://lccn.loc.gov/2017046466

Acquiring Editor: Thom O'Hearn
Project Manager: Alyssa Bluhm
Art Director: James Kegley
Cover Designer: Faceout Studios
Layout: Diana Boger

Printed in China

THE

Brew® YOUR OWN

BiG BOOK OF

CLONE

RECIPES

FEATURING

300

- HOMEBREW RECIPES FROM YOUR -
FAVORITE BREWERIES

VOYAGEUR
PRESS

CONTENTS

WELCOME TO THE WORLD OF CLONES!

FOR MORE THAN TWENTY YEARS, *Brew Your Own* magazine has been invited into living rooms, kitchens, backyards, and garages to lend a hand as readers enjoy the greatest (and most rewarding) hobby on Earth. We take pride in being the go-to resource for homebrewers at every level and in providing approachable, reliable, and current information to help you improve your brewing. While our focus includes all aspects of the hobby and community that embodies it—ingredients, techniques, equipment, activities/events, and everything in between—the feedback from our readers has always confirmed that popularity of one important part of every issue: the recipes.

We love coming up with our own recipes and enjoy brewing new styles. We enjoy altering a previous batch to get it just right. Even the excitement of testing new ingredients never seems to fade—in fact it often becomes even more enjoyable with the experience and understanding that is gained.

All that said, brewing proven clone recipes of our favorite commercial beers will always hold a special place in our hearts. These are the recipes that made most of us fall in love with craft beer, and they likely played a hand in making us believe that we too can brew our own beer at home. It may be a classic such as Sierra Nevada Pale Ale, a newer favorite such as the Alchemist's Heady Topper, a hard-to-find beer from a Trappist brewery, or even a little-known recipe from the brewpub one town over . . . whichever beer changed your life, it will not be forgotten. But why stop at reminiscing about that beer? You're a homebrewer! All you need is a recipe and the right ingredients, and soon you can have a whole batch of your own to share with others and compare to the original.

In this book, we have fully updated three hundred of our favorite clone recipes (and we threw in a few new ones!). These recipes came from your letters asking for advice from the Replicator (*BYO*'s regular column where we work with your favorite craft breweries to pull together the clone recipes that aren't available anywhere else), were selected by our editors as great examples of styles, and were picked by our trusted authors as beers that have changed their own lives. Our hope is that you'll find some of your favorites and be introduced to new favorites as well.

What sets these recipes apart from the thousands of clone recipes that circulate online is that these recipes have all been formulated in collaboration with, and in some instances have come directly from, the brewers who made the beers famous in the first place. They have been carefully researched, tested, and tweaked so the resulting beer will most closely resemble the beer that you are buying and trying to re-create. We are proud to put our name behind this book, which is the most extensive collection of clone beer recipes available on the market today.

These recipes are approachable for homebrewers at every level, no matter your experience or the equipment you brew on. Almost every one is formatted in both all-grain and extract-based versions.

Of course, we could not have done any of this without our many authors and the tremendous brewers who shared their notes, advice, and recipes with us for the purpose of spreading the love of brewing. To that, we say cheers!

—Dawson Raspuzzi, editor, *Brew Your Own*

BREWING
INDEED
COMPANY

MEXICAN
HONEY
IMPERIAL
LAGER

PRODUCT OF THE USA

LAGER BREWED WITH MEXICAN ORANGE BL

CLONING BASICS & RECIPE STANDARDS

CLONING—brewing a near-exact replica of a commercial beer—has a time-honored place among homebrewers. For one thing, it's a great risk-aversion technique: If you're brewing something new and you're worried about getting a dog of a recipe, a simple way to increase your odds of getting a decent recipe is to use a clone recipe. Someone must think it's okay, right? People pay to drink that beer! Then again, maybe you just love a certain beer. There's nothing wrong with brewing an homage to one of your favorites—especially if you can't get it regularly where you live. Those are both good reasons to clone, but they ignore the best one: Clone brewing will make you a more competent, more confident brewer. You'll build your brewing skills by not only executing a recipe but by adjusting it to your system and fine-tuning it. Cloning requires that you not only engage your brewing skills but also your ingredient and process acumen. Of course, tasting is an important part of the process as well, so you'll flex your sensory evaluation muscles. Cloning is like cross-training for brewers!

So, you've decided to clone a beer. How do you go about it?

TAKE DEAD AIM

Step one is to find your target. This goes far beyond picking the beer you want to clone. By "find your target," we mean you should get a bottle, can, or growler of that beer and start picking it apart using your senses: organoleptic evaluation time! Specifically, you want to note any and all flavor perceptions that stand out. What makes this beer unique? It might only be one thing—Old Speckled Hen is a pretty ordinary English pale ale . . . except for what tastes like a pound of butter in every bottle. You'll find that any beer you're trying to clone has one or two sensory "hooks"

that really stand out and make it memorable. Those are the flavors you want to focus on. You can miss your gravity by a few points or produce a beer that's two shades darker than its original version, but you need to nail its one or two defining features. For example, if you make a Schlenkerla Marzen clone that doesn't smell like a grilled sausage, then you've failed. Find that one thing and then, as golfer Harvey Penick said, take dead aim.

You want those other elements too, though. Take note of every detail you can suss out. They'll eventually be what turns a good clone into a great one.

BREW YOUR OWN BEER

One you've done your analysis and selected your recipe, it's time to brew it. While the recipe will include specific parameters to achieve specific goals, you alone know your brewing system. This means that at times you'll need to change what the brewery does, or what the recipe directs you to do, in favor of what you know will work. Every system is unique. You want to produce your "typical" beer in terms of process, because it will help minimize variability when you go back to fine-tune this beer. If you're switching up your brewing process, you are adding to the possibilities of things that can go wrong.

Now if a certain method is essential to the cloning effort, do it (if you're making a lager, don't put the beer on your back porch in summer just because you "usually" do it that way). However, if your normal mash is at 152°F (66°C) and the brewery mashes at 154°F (68°C) but doesn't give you a reason to follow suit, then stick with your way. Likewise, adjust the grain bill to match your system's efficiency.

There are a few processes to pay attention to time and again, as departures in any one of them can significantly affect your final product:

- Add mash/first wort/boil/whirlpool hops at the recommended times.
- Follow the fermentation schedule (e.g., "Five days at 52°F/11°C, then increase over the next week to 72°F/22°C").
- Dry hop or add specialty ingredients (spices, fruit, etc.) when the brewery recommends, using the same method, for the same length of time.
- Carbonate to the same level.

EVALUATE, ADJUST & REPEAT

Okay, you now have a beer. Hopefully it's a good one and maybe even a close clone. However, if it's actually a perfect clone from one brew day, you're either lying to yourself or you've gotten very lucky. Why? Because there's so much variability from one brew system, water profile, ingredients supplier, and process to the next that the odds of you hitting the exact center of the target the first time out is unlikely. You should be in the ballpark, but you'll almost always need at least one more brew day to lock in your recipe.

That means it's time to evaluate your beer. Take this part seriously: Don't just buy a sample and crack it open next to yours. Buy a bottle as fresh as you can get it—if you can get it right from the brewery, even better. You want to know with as much certainty as possible what the exact age is because you're going to "sync" their ages. Take your brewery bottle and put it in cold storage (near freezing, which will drastically slow its aging process). Then leave your sample at room temperature (pick a warm room too) for X number of days until they're both roughly the same age. Then, and only then, put them in the same fridge at service temperature. Once they equalize, pop them open and evaluate. To remove any bias, have a friend pour you three samples—yours, the brewery's, and a third cup with either a second pour of one of the beers or a blended sample. Try to pick out the "odd" beer and/or note any differences.

Once your blinders are off and you know which sample was which, look at your notes and work back to the beer you were trying to clone. If yours was too bitter, make a note to reduce IBUs. If it wasn't as smooth, look at your water chemistry or consider adding some wheat or flaked barley. If the alcohol presence tastes "hot," reduce your fermentation temperature to prevent fusels. Enlist your friends to help taste and your fellow homebrewers to help tweak the recipe. Take two more bottles and taste them warm to pull out even more detail. Continue to take detailed notes to bring back to your recipe and your process—then go again!

Once you've repeated this process and you're convinced you have your clone locked in, do one last check: Brew the same recipe again, and compare your new batch to the last batch to the original brewery's beer—all three should be very, very similar, and in blind tastings you should have trouble identifying which is which.

Congratulations: You've cloned your beer.

DEVELOP YOUR OWN CLONE RECIPE

While there are hundreds of recipes to choose from in this book—enough to keep any brewer busy for a few years—we often get questions about how to go about creating a clone recipe. Here's our advice.

The first step is to scour the beer world for existing information about what goes into that beer. You may get lucky and find that the brewery already published the recipe, in a publication (thanks, *BYO* "Replicator!"), on the brewery's website, or in an interview. If not, go ahead and stop by the brewery or email and tell them what you're up to. Many will happily share the recipe, or at least provide guidance or hints based on your own best guess. If so, you're well on your way. If not, look around for any information about the beer. Even breweries that don't publish the whole recipe outright will often post vital stats (OG, SRM, IBUs), information about the ingredients (certain hops or malts, water profile information, yeast and fermentation characteristics), or process information. Even if you find a recipe online, look up this information. There's a sliver of historian and archaeologist in every clone brewer: you're looking for independent confirmation. I can't tell you how many times we've received information direct from the brewery that contradicts what was listed on their own website (for example, one recipe was off on SRM by more than ten points). Figure out which version is the current recipe, and make sure the current recipe is the beer you love. It will save you time and frustration once you get brewing!

At the same time, look for assistance from other homebrewers. Jump online and search for others' clone recipe attempts and feedback. You're trying to create a composite recipe that gets you as close as possible (the patent features you should have pulled out of your own analysis).

Also, if you can source the beer, go ahead and measure the final gravity; if you know a bit about the style, this can give you a good idea of what the original gravity might be. If you really focus on the core flavors from water, malt, hops, and yeast, you can come up with a pretty good guess of what may be in the beer. This can be further honed if you know some of the tricks of the style.

When you feel that you've exhausted all the angles, sit down with your notes and your research, and build your recipe—again, giving special attention to whatever unique and essential flavors define the beer.

Ordinarily, we don't hold ourselves to that high of a standard. We taste a beer and decide if we like it or not, whether it's good enough or not, if we think it would do well in competition; those, though, are poor forms of evaluation and development. By cloning, we aim for a specific target, and we know almost immediately whether we've hit it or not. In many ways, it's the ultimate test of your control over your system and process. Can you make what you want — or do you just make what you make?

Pick your favorite beer, and let's find out.

BYO RECIPE STANDARDIZATION

A note on recipes in this book: You may notice variations in language from recipe to recipe. Various brewers and writers provided the original recipes, and we left the recipes as close as possible to the original text. We also left intact any recommendations from the brewer, even if those recommendations are not strictly necessary. For example, a recipe may advise you to oxygenate your wort with pure oxygen, adjust the water chemistry, use a specific size of yeast starter, etc. If you're not familiar with some of the more advanced techniques, you can skip them and brew as you normally would. Likewise, if you are a more advanced brewer and have a feel for what does and doesn't work in your homebrewery, feel free to make adjustments that work for your setup. Then taste, adjust, and refine your clone!

EXTRACT EFFICIENCY: 65%
(i.e., 1 pound of 2-row pale malt—which has a potential extract value of 1.037 in 1 US gallon of water—would yield a wort of 1.024.)

EXTRACT VALUES FOR MALT EXTRACT:
Liquid Malt Extract (LME) = 1.033–1.037
Dried Malt Extract (DME) = 1.045

POTENTIAL EXTRACT FOR GRAINS:
- 2-row base malts = 1.037–1.038
- wheat malt = 1.037
- 6-row base malts = 1.035
- Munich malt = 1.035
- Vienna malt = 1.035
- crystal malts = 1.033–1.035
- chocolate malts = 1.034
- dark roasted grains = 1.024–1.026
- flaked maize and rice = 1.037–1.038

HOPS:
We calculate IBUs based on 25 percent hop utilization for a 1-hour boil of pellet hops at specific gravities (SG) less than 1.050. For post-boil hop stands, we calculate IBUs based on 10 percent hop utilization for 30-minute hop stands at specific gravities less than 1.050. Increase the hop dosage by 10 percent if using whole-leaf hops.

ASSUMPTIONS:
We use US gallons whenever gallons are mentioned.

All mashes are single-infusion at the temperature indicated in the recipe and at 1.25 quarts per pound, unless otherwise specified.
- Collect enough wort to boil 6.5 gallons (25 liters) unless otherwise specified.
- A 1-liter yeast starter should be made in advance if using liquid yeast, or dried yeast should be rehydrated prior to pitching, unless otherwise specified.
- Aerate your wort before pitching yeast.
- Unless otherwise specified, the fermentation temperature matches the temperature to which you should chill the beer before pitching yeast.

CHAPTER

ONE

PALE ALES

BEER PICTURED ON LEFT; SEE PAGE 17

THE ALCHEMIST
MOOSE KNUCKLE
‹‹‹‹‹‹‹-
**(5 gallons/19 L, all-grain) OG = 1.054 FG = 1.013
IBU = 60 SRM = 5 ABV = 5.5%**

This is an American pale ale recipe pulled from the files of the Alchemist Pub & Brewery, prior to the devastating 2011 flood from Hurricane Irene, which forced the closure of the original brewpub property in Waterbury, Vermont.

INGREDIENTS

11 lb. (4.3 kg) Thomas Fawcett Maris Otter malt

3.5 AAU Warrior hops (60 min.) (0.25 oz./7 g at 14% alpha acids)

4.75 AAU Centennial hops (5 min.) (0.5 oz./14 g at 9.5% alpha acids)

3.5 AAU Cascade hops (5 min.) (0.5 oz./14 g at 7% alpha acids)

1 oz. (28 g) Centennial hops (0 min.)

1 oz. (28 g) Cascade hops (0 min.)

1.5 oz. (43 g) Centennial hops (dry hop)

1.5 oz. (43 g) Cascade hops (dry hop)

The Yeast Bay (Vermont Ale) or GigaYeast GY054 (Vermont IPA) or East Coast Yeast ECY29 (North East Ale) or Omega Yeast Labs (DIPA Ale) yeast

¾ cups (150 g) dextrose (if priming)

STEP BY STEP

Crush the malt and add it to 4 gallons (15 liters) of strike water to achieve a stable mash temperature at 160°F (71°C). Raise the temperature to mash out and begin to lauter. Boil for 60 minutes, adding hops as indicated. After you turn off the heat, stir the wort to create a whirlpool, and let it settle for 30 minutes with the lid on. After 30 minutes, chill the wort rapidly to 68°F (20°C) and pitch the yeast. Ferment at 68°F (20°C). After fermentation is complete, add the dry hops and let the beer sit on the hops for 3 to 4 days. Bottle with priming sugar or keg and force carbonate to 2.4 volumes CO_2.

EXTRACT WITH GRAINS OPTION: Substitute the Maris Otter malt in the all-grain recipe with 7.5 pounds (3.4 kilograms) Maris Otter liquid malt extract. Heat 5 gallons (19 liters) of soft water up to boil. As soon as the water begins to boil, remove the brewpot from the heat and stir in the liquid malt extract. Stir until all the extract is dissolved, then return the wort to a boil. Boil for 60 minutes. Follow the remaining portion of the all-grain recipe.

TIPS FOR SUCCESS

Floor malted Maris Otter grains will help lay a solid malt backbone. But don't be afraid to mash on the hotter end of the spectrum to maximize the alpha amylase enzymes, which can help build the body of the beer. The Cascade and Centennial hops add nice grapefruit and orange qualities, which pair nicely with the slight fruitiness that the Alchemist's yeast strain adds. As always with hop-forward beers, pay special attention to oxygen uptake post fermentation as the hop aroma can quickly degrade if you are not careful. The Alchemist's beers are brewed with very soft water. If you get a water report and find that your water has a solid mineral base you might consider diluting your mash or using a distilled water (or at least use something bottled that's softer than yours!). You may also want to add 1 to 2 teaspoons sulfates if using reverse osmosis or soft water low in permanent hardness. Also, John Kimmich is a very technique-oriented brewer with all of his beers, so don't be afraid to experiment with your dry hopping to try and find the best flavor profile. Bagging your hops in a muslin brewing bag commonly used for steeping grains can make them easier to retrieve when you are ready to remove them from the beer. If you bag your dry hops, however, keep in mind that it can reduce the hops exposure to the beer and possibly disturb the blanket of CO_2. Remedy this by making sure you don't pack the bag of hops too tightly.

BASS BREWERS LIMITED
PALE ALE
‹‹‹‹‹‹‹-
**(5 gallons/19 L, all-grain) OG = 1.049 FG = 1.010
IBU = 32 SRM = 11 ABV = 5%**

The famous beerhunter Michael Jackson claims that Bass uses a single addition of Northdown hops. He's probably right, but we think two Northern Brewer additions best captures the minty flavor and aroma of Bass's hop presence in a homebrew clone. Note, though, that this clone is for the bottled version of Bass Pale Ale available in the United States.

INGREDIENTS

8 lb. (3.6 kg) English pale ale malt

1 lb. (0.45 kg) flaked barley

1 lb. (0.45 kg) crystal malt (60 °L)

0.5 oz. (14 g) roasted barley (500 °L)

8 AAU Northern Brewer hops (60 min.) (0.89 oz./25 g at 9% alpha acids)

2 AAU Northern Brewer hops (15 min.) (0.22 oz./6.3 g at 9% alpha acids)

2.6 AAU Challenger hops (5 min.) (0.35 oz./10 g at 7.5% alpha acids)

1 tsp. Irish moss (15 min.)

¼ tsp. yeast nutrients (15 min.)

Wyeast 1098 (British Ale) or White Labs WLP007 (Dry English Ale) yeast

¾ cup (150 g) dextrose (if priming)

STEP BY STEP

Make 13 gallons (49 liters) of brewing liquor with 100 to 150 ppm Ca^{2+} and a slightly lower level of carbonates. If you start with very soft, distilled, or reverse osmosis (RO) water, use 5 teaspoons of gypsum and 4 teaspoons of chalk (calcium carbonate) for your 13 gallons (49 liters). (Yes, Burton upon Trent's water is harder than this, but you don't need "extra chunky" water for a great clone.) On brew day, mash the grains and maize at 152°F (67°C) and rest for 1 hour. Vorlauf until runnings are clear and sparge, collecting around 6.5 gallons (25 liters), and boil for 90 minutes. Add hops, Irish moss, and yeast nutrients at times indicated in the ingredients list. After the boil, turn off the heat and chill the wort rapidly to 68°F (20°C). Aerate the wort well and pitch the yeast. Ferment at 68°F (20°C). When the beer has reached final gravity, transfer to a bottling bucket for priming and bottling, or transfer to a keg.

EXTRACT WITH GRAINS OPTION: Omit the flaked barley. Scale the 2-row pale malt down to 1 pound (0.45 kilogram), and add 0.5 pound (0.23 kilogram) Muntons light dried malt extract, 3 pounds 12 ounces (1.7 kilograms) Alexander's pale liquid malt extract (late addition), and 1 pound 6 ounces (0.62 kilogram) corn sugar. Before brewing, make the brewing liquor: Add 6 gallons (23 liters) of soft, distilled, or RO water to a clean brewing bucket and add 1 teaspoon of gypsum and 0.5 teaspoon of chalk to make your brewing liquor. Place crushed grains in a nylon steeping bag. Heat 3 quarts (2.9 liters) of brewing liquor to 163°F (73°C) and submerge the bag. Steep the grains at 152°F (67°C) for 45 minutes, then pull the bag out and let it drain over the pot in a colander. Rinse the grains with 1 quart (~1 liter) of water at 170°F (77°C). Add brewing liquor to the steeped "grain tea" to make 3 gallons (11 liters) of wort. Add the dried malt extract and corn sugar to the pot and bring to a boil. Add the first charge of hops and boil for 60 minutes. Add other hops, Irish moss, and yeast nutrients at times indicated. With 15 minutes left in boil, shut off heat and stir in the liquid malt extract. Resume heating and finish the boil. Cool wort and transfer to fermenter. Top up to 5 gallons (19 liters) with brewing liquor, aerate the wort well, and pitch the yeast. Ferment at 68°F (20°C).

DESCHUTES BREWING COMPANY
GLUTEN FREE NWPA

(5 gallons/19 L, extract only) OG = 1.051 FG = 1.010 IBU = 43 SRM = 13 ABV = 5.4%

This hop-forward, gluten-free pale ale is cleverly brewed with brown rice syrup and Belgian candi syrup. The goal was a beer that gluten-free and non-gluten-free drinkers can all enjoy at Deschutes' Portland Public House in Oregon.

INGREDIENTS

6 lb. (2.7 kg) brown rice syrup

1 lb. 1 oz. (0.5 kg) dark Belgian candi syrup (90 °L)

6 oz. (170 g) honey (0 min.)

9.8 AAU Nugget hops (60 min.) (0.75 oz./21 g at 13% alpha acids)

1.8 AAU Crystal hops (30 min.) (0.5 oz./14 g at 3.5% alpha acids)

0.5 oz. (14 g) Nugget hops (0 min.)

0.5 oz. (14 g) Crystal hops (0 min.)

1 tsp. Irish moss (15 min.)

Wyeast 1187 (Ringwood Ale) or White Labs WLP005 (British Ale) yeast

5 g gypsum ($CaSO_4$) (if using reverse osmosis water)

¾ cup (150 g) dextrose (if priming)

STEP BY STEP

Heat approximately 5 gallons (19 liters) of water to boiling. Turn off the heat, add the brown rice syrup and candi syrup, and stir until completely dissolved. Top up if necessary to obtain 6 gallons (23 liters) of wort and add optional minerals. Boil for 60 minutes, adding hops and finings according to the ingredients list. Turn off the heat, add the honey, stir until it is completely dissolved, and then chill the wort to slightly below fermentation temperature, about 61°F (16°C). Aerate wort and pitch yeast. Ferment at 63°F (17°C). Once at terminal gravity (approximately 7 days total), bottle or keg the beer and carbonate.

TIPS FOR SUCCESS

Brown rice syrup can sometimes be difficult to find at local homebrew shops. A few online suppliers carry it if your local homebrew supplier doesn't, but you also may want to experiment with pale rice malt or the dry equivalent, which is rice syrup solids. To use the pale rice malt, swap out the brown rice syrup with 15 pounds (6.8 kilograms) rice malt and be sure to add amylase enzyme to the mash. To use the rice syrup solids, simply swap the brown rice syrup with 5.25 pounds (2.4 kilograms) rice syrup solids, but expect a slightly lighter color in the finished beer.

- - - - - - - - - - - - - - - - - - -

DESCHUTES BREWING COMPANY
MIRROR POND PALE ALE

**(5 gallons/19 L, all-grain) OG = 1.053 FG = 1.015
IBU = 40 SRM = 10 ABV = 5%**

Deschutes has been brewing Mirror Pond since 1988. In this classic pale ale, they lean on Cascade hops for lots of floral and citrus notes but keep it a classic pale with subtle hints of caramel. They say it's an "everyday ale" and clearly many beer drinkers agree.

INGREDIENTS

8.5 lb. (3.9 kg) US 2-row malt

1.5 lb. (0.68 kg) US caramel malt (40 °L)

9 oz. (250 g) Carapils malt

9 oz. (250 g) US Munich malt (10 °L)

5.6 AAU Cascade hops (60 min.) (1.25 oz./35 g at 4.5% alpha acids)

2.3 AAU Cascade hops (30 min.) (0.5 oz./14 g at 4.5% alpha acids)

2.3 AAU Cascade hops (15 min.) (0.5 oz./14 g at 4.5% alpha acids)

0.5 oz. (14 g) Cascade hops (0 min.)

0.5 oz. (14 g) Cascade hops (dry hop)

Whirlfloc or Irish moss (15 min.)

Wyeast 1187 (Ringwood Ale) or White Labs WLP005 (British Ale) yeast

5 g gypsum (CaSO₄) (if using reverse osmosis water)

¾ cup (150 g) dextrose (if priming)

STEP BY STEP

Mill grains and mix with 3.5 gallons (13.2 liters) of 163°F (73°C) strike water and optional minerals to reach a mash temperature of 152°F (67°C). Hold this temperature for 60 minutes. Vorlauf until your runnings are clear. Sparge the grains with enough 168°F (76°C) water to collect 6.5 gallons (25 liters) of 1.040 SG wort. Boil for 90 minutes, adding hops and finings according to the ingredients list. Turn off the heat and chill the wort to slightly below fermentation temperature, about 61°F (16°C). Aerate the wort with pure oxygen or filtered air and pitch yeast. Ferment at 63°F (17°C). Once you reach terminal gravity (approximately 7 days total), add dry hops and wait an additional 5 to 7 days. Bottle or keg the beer and carbonate.

EXTRACT WITH GRAINS OPTION: Substitute the 2-row pale malt and Munich malt in the all-grain recipe with 6 pounds (2.7 kilograms) golden liquid malt extract. Place the milled grains in a muslin bag and steep in 5.25 quarts (6 liters) of 151°F (66°C) water for 15 minutes. Remove the grain and rinse with 1 gallon (3.8 liters) of hot water. Add water to reach a volume of 5.5 gallons (20.8 liters), add optional minerals, and heat to boiling. Turn off the heat, add the liquid malt extract, and stir until completely dissolved. Top up if necessary to obtain 6 gallons (23 liters) of 1.044 SG wort. Follow the remaining portion of the all-grain recipe.

- - - - - - - - - - - - - - - - - - -

EDDYLINE BREWERY
RIVER RUNNERS PALE ALE

**(5 gallons/19 L, all-grain) OG = 1.052 FG = 1.013
IBU = 40 SRM = 5 ABV = 5.3%**

River Runners Pale Ale is a classic American pale. It's bright, summery, fresh, fruity, and very easy-drinking.

INGREDIENTS

9 lb. (4.1 kg) 2-row pale malt

1 lb. (0.45 kg) crystal malt (10 °L)

1 lb. (0.45 kg) Carapils malt

6.6 AAU Magnum hops (60 min.) (0.5 oz./14 g at 13.2% alpha acids)

3.5 AAU Cascade hops (10 min.) (0.5 oz./14 g at 7% alpha acids)

7.5 AAU El Dorado hops (10 min.) (0.5 oz./14 g at 15% alpha acids)

4.5 AAU Amarillo hops (0 min.) (0.5 oz./14 g at 9% alpha acids)

0.5 oz. (14 g) Amarillo hops (dry hop)

0.5 oz. (14 g) El Dorado hops (dry hop)

White Labs WLP017 (Whitbread Ale) or Wyeast 1099 (Whitbread Ale) yeast

¾ cup (150 g) dextrose (if priming)

STEP BY STEP

Mill the grains and mix with 3.5 gallons (13.25 liters) of 165°F (74°C) strike water to reach a mash temperature of 153°F (67°C). Hold this temperature for 60 minutes. Vorlauf until your runnings are clear. Sparge the grains with 3.1 gallons (11.7 liters) and top up as necessary to obtain 6 gallons (23 liters) of wort. Boil for 75 minutes, adding hops according to the ingredient list. After the boil, turn off heat and whirlpool for 15 minutes. Then chill the wort to slightly below fermentation temperature, about 65°F (18°C). Aerate the wort with pure oxygen or filtered air and pitch yeast. Ferment at 69°F (21°C) for 6 days. Add the dry hops and hold at 69°F (21°C) for 4 more days. Once the beer reaches terminal gravity, bottle or keg the beer and carbonate to approximately 2.5 volumes. You may want to cold-crash the beer prior to packaging to 35°F (2°C) for 48 hours to improve the beer's clarity.

EXTRACT WITH GRAINS OPTION: Substitute the 2-row pale malt in the all-grain recipe with 6 pounds (2.7 kilograms) extra light liquid malt extract. Bring 5.6 gallons (21.2 liters) of water to approximately 162°F (72°C) and hold there. Steep the milled specialty grains in grain bags for 15 minutes. Remove the grain bags, and let drain fully. Add liquid extract while stirring, and stir until completely dissolved. Bring the wort to a boil. Boil for 60 minutes, adding hops according to the ingredient list. Follow the remaining portion of the all-grain recipe.

LAGUNITAS BREWING COMPANY NEW DOGTOWN PALE ALE

(5 gallons/19 L, all-grain) OG = 1.060 FG = 1.012 IBU = 60 SRM = 8 ABV = 6.4%

Lagunitas first brewed its pale ale in 1993 to much fanfare, but the recipe has since been revised to more align with twenty-first-century pale ales. New Dogtown retains the bready, biscuit malt character of the original but with much more hop character, primarily through mid-boil and flame-out hopping, along with a limited dry hopping regimen.

INGREDIENTS

10.25 lb. (4.7 kg) 2-row pale malt

1 lb. (0.45 kg) Vienna malt

0.5 lb. (0.23 kg) aromatic malt

0.5 lb. (0.23 kg) Victory malt

0.25 lb. (113 g) Briess special roast malt

12 AAU Warrior hops (60 min.) (0.75 oz./21 g at 16% alpha acids)

4 AAU Amarillo hops (20 min.) (0.5 oz./14 g at 8% alpha acids)

4 AAU Cascade hops (20 min.) (0.5 oz./14 g at 8% alpha acids)

4 AAU Amarillo hops (0 min.) (0.5 oz./14 g at 8% alpha acids)

4 AAU Cascade hops (0 min.) (0.5 oz./14 g at 8% alpha acids)

0.5 oz. (14 g) Amarillo hops (dry hop)

0.25 oz. (7 g) Simcoe hops (dry hop)

Wyeast 1335 (British Ale II) or Lallemand Nottingham Ale yeast

⅔ cup (133 g) dextrose (if priming)

STEP BY STEP

Mill the grains, then mix with 15.6 quarts (14.8 liters) of 163°F (73°C) strike water to reach a mash temperature of 152°F (67°C). Hold this temperature for 60 minutes. Vorlauf until your runnings are clear and lauter. Sparge the grains with 3.7 gallons (14.1 liters) and top up as necessary to obtain 6 gallons (23 liters) of wort. Boil for 60 minutes, adding hops according to the ingredient list and Irish moss if desired. Chill to 66°F (19°C), aerate, and pitch yeast. Ferment at 67°F (19°C) for 7 days, then free rise to 72°F (22°C) until the completion of primary fermentation. Once the beer completes fermentation, reduce temperature to 32°F (0°C), add dry hops, and wait 5 days (or to taste). Then bottle or keg the beer and carbonate to approximately 2.25 volumes.

PARTIAL MASH OPTION: Substitute the 2-row pale malt in the all-grain recipe with 6.6 pounds (3 kilograms) pale liquid malt extract and increase the Vienna malt to 1.5 pounds (0.68 kilogram). Bring 1 gallon (4 liters) of water to approximately 165°F (74°C) and submerge the crushed malts in grain bags for 45 minutes. Remove the grain bag, and wash grains with 1 gallon (4 liters) of hot water. Add malt extract while stirring, and stir until completely dissolved and top up to 6 gallons (23 liters). Boil for 60 minutes. Follow the remaining portion of the all-grain recipe.

NEW ALBION BREWING
NEW ALBION ALE

(5 gallons/19 L, all-grain) OG = 1.055 FG = 1.011
IBU = 30 SRM = 4 ABV = 5.7%

This recipe aims to re-create the very first microbrewed American ale. It has a deep gold appearance and a subtle malty character. The Cascade hops give it a spicy pine hop profile—perhaps tame now but unheard of when New Albion Brewing launched in 1976.

INGREDIENTS

11.5 lb. (5.2 kg) Great Western premium 2-row malt

3.6 AAU Cascade hops (60 min.) (0.6 oz./17 g at 6% alpha acids)

3.6 AAU Cascade hops (30 min.) (0.6 oz./17 g at 6% alpha acids)

3.6 AAU Cascade hops (15 min.) (0.6 oz./17 g at 6% alpha acids)

1 tsp. Irish moss (15 min.)

Wyeast 1028 (London Ale) or White Labs WLP013 (London Ale) yeast (1.4 qt./1.3 L yeast starter)

1 cup (200 g) dextrose (for priming)

STEP BY STEP

Mash at 148°F (64°C) for 1 hour in 16 quarts (15 liters) of brewing liquor. Sparge with 170°F (77°C) water over 90 minutes to collect 6 gallons (23 liters) of wort (or however much pre-boil wort will yield 5 gallons (19 liters) after a 1-hour boil). Boil wort for 60 minutes, adding hops at times indicated. Chill the wort rapidly to 68°F (20°C), aerate, and pitch the yeast. Ferment at 68°F (20°C). Bottle or keg as usual.

PARTIAL MASH OPTION: Reduce the amount of 2-row malt to 2 pounds (0.91 kilogram) and add 5 pounds (2.3 kilograms) of light dried malt extract. Steep grains at 148°F (64°C) for 45 minutes in 3 quarts of water (2.8 liters). Add roughly ⅓ of the malt extract and add water to make at least 3 gallons (11 liters). Boil for 60 minutes, adding hops as indicated. Add remaining malt extract in final 15 minutes of the boil. Cool wort and top up to 5 gallons (19 liters). Follow the remaining portion of the all-grain recipe

---

ODELL BREWING COMPANY
5 BARREL
PALE ALE

(5 gallons/19 L, all-grain) OG = 1.052 FG = 1.013
IBU = 38 SRM = 7 ABV = 5.2%

Named for the 5 hop additions the brewers use throughout the brewing process, this pale ale is refreshing. Odell describes it as having a lively hop flavor and aroma.

INGREDIENTS

8 lb. (3.6 kg) English pale ale malt

1.75 lb. (0.79 kg) Gambrinus ESB malt

0.75 lb. (0.34 kg) dark Munich malt (20 °L)

9.5 AAU Willamette hops (90 min.) (0.75 oz./21 g at 5.5% alpha acids)

2.3 AAU Crystal hops (45 min.) (0.5 oz./14 g at 4.6% alpha acids)

2.75 AAU Willamette hops (15 min.) (0.5 oz./14 g at 5.5% alpha acids)

2.75 AAU Willamette hops (0 min.) (0.5 oz./14 g at 5.5% alpha acids)

4.6 AAU Crystal hops (0 min.) (1 oz./28 g at 4.6% alpha acids)

1 oz. (28 g) Crystal whole hops (hopback)

1 oz. (28 g) Willamette whole hops (hopback)

1 oz. (28 g) Crystal hops (dry hop)

1 oz. (28 g) Willamette hops (dry hop)

White Labs WLP007 (Dry English Ale) or Wyeast 1098 (British Ale) yeast

¾ cup (150 g) dextrose (if priming)

STEP BY STEP

Mash the grains at 152°F (67°C). Mash out, vorlauf, and then sparge at 170°F (77°C) to collect about 7 gallons (27 liters) of wort. Boil 90 minutes, adding hops as directed. After the boil is complete, give the wort a stir to create a whirlpool, then let settle for 20 minutes. If you don't have a hopback device, add the hopback hops during the final couple minutes of the whirlpool, just prior to chilling. Then chill and pitch yeast. After primary fermentation, add dry hops 3 to 5 days and then chill to as close to 32°F (0°C) as you can for 1 to 2 weeks. Bottle or keg as usual.

EXTRACT WITH GRAINS OPTION: Omit pale ale malt. Replace with 1.75 pounds (0.8 kilogram) light dried malt extract added at beginning of boil and 3.3 pounds (1.5 kilograms) Maris Otter liquid malt extract added at the end of the boil. Place crushed grains in a nylon steeping bag and steep at 155°F (68°C) in 3.5 quarts (3.3 liters) of water for 45 minutes. Rinse grains with 1.5 quarts (1.4 liters) of water at 170°F (77°C). Add water (to save time, preferably boiling water) to "grain tea" to make 3 gallons (11 liters), stir in dried malt extract, and bring to a boil. Boil for 60 minutes, adding hops at times indicated. Stir in liquid malt extract with 15 minutes remaining in boil. Follow the remaining portion of the all-grain recipe, topping off to 5 gallons (19 liters) after cooling.

out, vorlauf, and then sparge at 170°F (77°C). Collect 6.5 gallons (25 liters) of wort. (Check that the final runnings do not drop below SG 1.010.) Boil 90 minutes, adding the hops at the times indicated. Pitch the yeast and ferment at 68°F (20°C) until final gravity is reached. Bottle or keg as usual.

PARTIAL MASH OPTION: Scale the 2-row pale malt down to 1 pound 5 ounces (0.60 kilogram) and add 1.75 pounds (0.80 kilogram) light dried malt extract and 4 pounds (0.79 kilogram) light liquid malt extract. Place the crushed grains in a steeping bag. Steep the grains at 155°F (68°C) in 3 quarts (2.9 liters) of water. Remove the bag and place in a colander over the brewpot. Rinse the grains with 2 quarts (2 liters) of 170°F (77°C) water. Add water to the brewpot to make at least 3 gallons (11 liters) of wort. Stir in the dried malt extract and boil the wort for 90 minutes, adding the hops at the times indicated. Keep some boiling water handy and do not let the boil volume dip below 3 gallons (11 liters). Add the liquid malt extract during the final 15 minutes of the boil. Chill the wort and transfer to your fermenter. Top up the fermenter to 5 gallons (19 liters). Follow the remaining portion of the all-grain recipe.

SIERRA NEVADA BREWING COMPANY
PALE ALE

(5 gallons/19 L, all-grain) OG = 1.052
FG = 1.011 IBU = 38 SRM = 10 ABV = 5.4%

This signature American pale ale was originally dreamed up as a homebrew recipe. Now, decades later, it has launched thousands of homebrewers in its wake. It's a crisp, hoppy classic by which all American pale ales are measured.

INGREDIENTS

10 lb. 2 oz. (4.6 kg) 2-row pale malt

11 oz. (0.3 kg) caramel malt (60 °L)

4.4 AAU Perle hops (90 min.) (0.5 oz./14 g at 8.8% alpha acids)

6 AAU Cascade hops (45 min.) (1 oz./28 g at 6% alpha acids)

1.5 oz. (43 g) Cascade hops (0 min.)

Wyeast 1056 (American Ale), White Labs WLP001 (California Ale), or Fermentis Safale US-05 yeast (1 qt./1 L yeast starter)

1 cup (200 g) dextrose (for priming)

STEP BY STEP

Two or 3 days before brew day, make a yeast starter, aerating the wort thoroughly (preferably with oxygen) before pitching the yeast. Mash the grains at 155°F (68°C). Mash

SQUATTERS PUB BREWERY
FULL SUSPENSION PALE ALE

(5 gallons/19 L, all-grain) OG = 1.043 FG = 1.012
IBU = 39 SRM = 8 ABV = 4%

This rich, Northwest-style pale ale is all about balance and sessionability. Maybe that's why it won gold at the Great American Beer Festival (GABF) two years in a row! Brew it if you're looking for an addictive, low-ABV beer.

INGREDIENTS

8 lb. (3.6 kg) 2-row pale malt

1 lb. (0.45 kg) caramel Munich malt (45 °L)

10 AAU Nugget hops (60 min.) (0.6 oz./17 g at 14% alpha acids)

10 AAU Columbus hops (5 min.) (0.77 oz./22 g at 13% alpha acids)

10 AAU Columbus hops (0 min.) (0.77 oz./22 g at 13% alpha acids)

1 tsp. Irish moss (15 min.)

White Labs WLP001 (California Ale) or Wyeast 1056 (American Ale) yeast (1.5 qt./~1.5 L yeast starter)

¾ cup (150 g) dextrose (if priming)

STEP BY STEP

Use 12.5 quarts (11.8 liters) of mash water and mash grains at 152°F (67°C) for 60 minutes. Mash out, vorlauf, and then sparge with 170°F (77°C) water to collect 5 gallons (19 liters) of wort. Add 1.5 gallons (5.7 liters) of water and boil wort for 90 minutes, adding hops at times indicated in ingredient list. After the boil is complete, turn off heat, give wort a stir for one minute, and then cover and leave alone for 15 minutes to whirlpool. Cool, aerate, and pitch yeast. Ferment at 68°F (20°C). After fermentation is complete, bottle or keg as usual.

EXTRACT WITH GRAINS OPTION: Substitute the pale malt in the all-grain recipe with 6.6 pounds (3 kilograms) Coopers light liquid malt extract. Steep crushed malts in 1.5 quarts (1.5 liters) of water at 150°F (66°C) for 30 minutes. Rinse grains with 0.75 quarts (750 milliliters) of water at 170°F (77°C). Add water to make 3 gallons (11 liters), stir in dried malt extract, and bring to a boil. Add hops as indicated and liquid malt extract with 15 minutes remaining. Top off to 5 gallons (19 liters) after cooling. Follow the remaining portion of the all-grain recipe.

SUMMIT BREWING COMPANY
SUMMIT EXTRA PALE ALE

(5 gallons/19 L, all-grain) OG = 1.049 FG = 1.010
IBU = 49 SRM = 12 ABV = 5.2%

First brewed in 1984, this English-style pale ale is bronze in color with caramel, biscuity malts balanced by an earthy hop bite and juicy, citrus flavors. This remains a popular beer on tap in Minneapolis and beyond.

INGREDIENTS

9.25 lb. (4.2 kg) 2-row pale malt

4 oz. (113 g) Weyermann Caramunich III malt (57 °L)

12 oz. (0.34 kg) crystal malt (90 °L)

7 AAU Horizon pellet hops (60 min.) (¾ 0.7 oz./20 g at 13% alpha acids)

2.4 AAU Fuggle pellet hops (30 min.) (0.5 oz./14 g at 4.75% alpha acids)

2.9 AAU Cascade pellet hops (30 min.) (0.5 oz./14 g at 5.75% alpha acids)

2.9 AAU Cascade pellet hops (0 min.) (0.5 oz./14 g at 5.75% alpha acids)

½ tsp. Irish moss (15 min.)

White Labs WLP001 (California Ale) or Wyeast 1056 (American Ale) yeast

¾ cup (150 g) dextrose (if priming)

STEP BY STEP

This is a single-infusion mash. Mix the crushed grain with 3.5 gallons (13.2 liters) of 170°F (77°C) water to stabilize at 152°F (67°C) for 60 minutes. Sparge slowly with 175°F (79°C) water. Collect approximately 6 gallons (23 liters) of wort runoff to boil for 60 minutes. Add hops and Irish moss at times indicated. Cool, aerate, and pitch yeast. Ferment at 68°F (20°C). After fermentation is complete, bottle or keg as usual.

EXTRACT WITH GRAINS OPTION: Substitute the 2-row pale malt in the all-grain recipe with 3.3 pounds (1.5 kilograms) Briess light liquid malt extract and 2.5 pounds (1.13 kilograms) light dried malt extract, and decrease both crystal malts by 2 ounces (57 grams). Steep the crushed grain in 5 gallons (19 liters) of water at 152°F (67°C) for 30 minutes. Remove grains from the wort and rinse with 1 quart (1 liter) of 175°F (79°C) water. Add malt extracts and bring to a boil. Follow the remaining portion of the all-grain recipe.

TERRAPIN BEER COMPANY
RYE PALE ALE

(5 gallons/19 L, all-grain) OG = 1.054 FG = 1.013
IBU = 38 SRM = 8 ABV = 5.6%

Terrapin won a gold medal at GABF with this beer in their early days, and they've never looked back. Rye Pale Ale remains a year-round staple, and it's easy to see why. Rye combines with other character malts for a distinctive base beer. Fuggle and East Kent Golding hops, often not seen in American pales, also set the beer apart.

INGREDIENTS

8.6 lb. (3.9 kg) 2-row pale malt

1 lb. (0.45 kg) rye malt

1 lb. (0.45 kg) Munich malt (10 °L)

0.5 lb. (0.23 kg) Victory malt (30 °L)

6 oz. (170 g) Gambrinus honey malt

7 AAU Magnum hops (60 min.) (0.5 oz./14 g at 14% alpha acids)

2.5 AAU Fuggle hops (30 min.) (0.5 oz./14 g at 5% alpha acids)

2.38 AAU East Kent Golding hops (10 min.) (0.5 oz./14 g at 4.75% alpha acids)

3.4 AAU Cascade hops (3 min.) (0.5 oz./14 g at 6.8% alpha acids)

2 oz. (57 g) Amarillo leaf hops (dry hop)

1 tsp. Irish moss (15 min.)

White Labs WLP051 (California Ale V) or Wyeast 1272 (American Ale II) yeast

¾ cup (150 g) dextrose (if priming)

STEP BY STEP

Mash the grains at 155°F (68°C) for 60 minutes. Mash out, vorlauf, and then sparge at 170°F (77°C) to collect enough wort to result in 5 gallons (19 liters) after a 90-minute boil. Boil 90 minutes, adding hops at times indicated. Cool, aerate, and pitch yeast. Ferment at 70°F (21°C). After fermentation is complete, add dry hops for 4 days and then bottle or keg as usual.

PARTIAL MASH OPTION: Substitute the 2-row pale malt in the all-grain recipe with 3.3 pounds (1.5 kilograms) Briess light liquid malt extract and 2 pounds (0.91 kilogram) Briess extra light dried malt extract. Place the crushed grains in a large grain bag. Submerge the grains in 1 gallon (4 liters) of water at 155°F (68°C) for 60 minutes. Remove the grain bag and place in a colander over the brewpot. Slowly wash the grains with 1 gallon (4 liters) of hot water. Stir in the liquid and dried malt extracts, then top off to 6 gallons (23 liters). Bring wort to a boil for 60 minutes. Follow the remaining portion of the all-grain recipe.

THREE FLOYDS BREWING COMPANY
ALPHA KING

**(5 gallons/19 L, all-grain) OG = 1.062 FG = 1.016
IBU = 68 SRM = 8 ABV = 6%**

Three Floyds pushes the boundaries of pale ale with this beer, their flagship. It's bold yet balanced with a slight caramel sweetness that plays against the admittedly aggressive level of citrusy hops.

INGREDIENTS

6 lb. (2.7 kg) American 2-row malt

6 lb. 6 oz. (2.9 kg) Belgian pale ale malt

1.5 oz. (43 g) Carapils malt

1.5 oz. (43 g) melanoidin malt

1.5 oz. (43 g) Weyermann Caramunich II malt

3.5 oz. (99 g) caramel malt (60 °L)

1.5 oz. (43 g) Special B malt

8 AAU Warrior hops (90 min.) (0.5 oz./14 g at 16% alpha acids)

8.5 AAU Centennial hops (90 min.) (0.7 oz./20 g at 12% alpha acids)

2 oz. (57 g) Cascade hops (0 min.)

1 oz. (28 g) Cascade hops (dry hop)

1 oz. (28 g) Columbus hops (dry hop)

1 oz. (28 g) Centennial hops (dry hop)

1 tsp. Irish moss (15 min.)

Wyeast 1056 (American Ale) or White Labs WLP001 (California Ale) yeast (2 qt./~2 L yeast starter)

¾ cup (150 g) dextrose (if priming)

STEP BY STEP

Mash the grains in 17 quarts (16 liters) of water to get a single-infusion mash temperature of 154°F (68°C) for 45 minutes. Sparge with hot water of 170°F (77°C) and collect 7 gallons (26 liters) of wort. Boil for 90 minutes and add hops and Irish moss at times indicated. Cool, aerate, and pitch yeast. Ferment at 68°F (20°C) until active fermentation ceases, then rack to secondary with dry hops for 1 more week. Bottle or keg and leave at fermentation temperature for a few days. Drop the temperature to 40°F (4°C) for 1 week, then (if possible) go to 34°F (1°C) for yet another week.

EXTRACT WITH GRAINS OPTION: Omit the 2-row pale malt, the Belgian pale ale malt, and the Carapils malt in the all-grain recipe. Add 1.4 pounds (0.64 kilogram) light dried malt extract and 6.6 pounds (3 kilograms) light liquid malt extract. Place crushed malts in a nylon steeping bag and steep in 5 gallons (19 liters) of water at 154°F (68°C) for 30 minutes. Rinse grains with 1.25 quarts (1.25 liters) of water at 170°F (77°C). Bring to a boil and add extracts. Boil for 75 minutes. Follow the remaining portion of the all-grain recipe.

TRILLIUM
BREWING COMPANY
FORT POINT
PALE ALE

–≪≪≪≪≪≪–

(5 gallons/19 L, all-grain) OG = 1.063 FG = 1.013
IBU = 45 SRM = 5 ABV = 6.6%

Trillium describes this beer as having "layers of hops-derived aromas and flavors," and we have to agree. This beer is well loved for its citrus zest and tropical fruit character. It's dangerously drinkable thanks to a soft mouthfeel from the wheat and a dry finish.

INGREDIENTS

10 lb. (0.45 kg) 2-row pale malt

1.5 lb. (0.68 kg) wheat malt

12 oz. (0.34 kg) dextrin malt

4 oz. (113 g) British pale crystal malt (22 °L)

3.5 AAU Columbus hops (60 min.) (0.25 oz./7 g at 14% alpha acids)

10.5 AAU Columbus hops (10 min.) (0.75 oz./21 g at 14% alpha acids)

2 oz. (57 g) Columbus hops (hop stand)

4 oz. (113 g) Citra hops (dry hop)

1 oz. (28 g) Columbus hops (dry hop)

½ Whirlfloc tablet (10 min.)

White Labs WLP007 (Dry English Ale) or Wyeast 1098 (British Ale) or GigaYeast GY054 (Vermont IPA) yeast

¾ cup (150 g) dextrose (if priming)

STEP BY STEP

Crush the malt and add to 4 gallons (15 liters) strike water to achieve a stable mash temperature at 150°F (65.5°C) until enzymatic conversion is complete. Sparge slowly with 170°F (77°C) water, collecting wort until the pre-boil kettle volume is 6 gallons (23 liters). Boil the wort for 60 minutes, adding the hops as indicated. After the boil is finished, cool the wort to 180°F (82°C) and then add the hop stand addition. Stir the wort, then let settle for 30 minutes before chilling the wort down to yeast-pitching temperature. Now transfer to the fermenter and pitch the yeast. Ferment at 68°F (20°C). As the kräusen begins to fall, typically day 4 or 5, add the dry hops to the fermenter, and let the beer sit on the hops for 5 days. Bottle with priming sugar or keg and force carbonate to 2.4 volumes CO_2.

EXTRACT WITH GRAINS OPTION: Replace the 2-row pale malt and wheat malt in the all-grain recipe with 6.6 pounds (3 kilograms) golden liquid malt extract and 1 pound (0.45 kilogram) wheat dried malt extract. Reduce the dextrin malt to 4 ounces (113 grams). Place the crushed malt in a muslin bag. Steep the grains in 1 gallon (4 liters) of water at 160°F (71°C) for 20 minutes. Remove the grain bag and wash with 2 quarts (2 liters) of hot water. Top off the kettle to 5 gallons (19 liters) and heat up to boil. As soon as the water begins to boil, remove the brewpot from the heat and stir in the dried and liquid malt extracts. Stir until all the extract is dissolved then return the wort to a boil. Boil the wort for 60 minutes. Follow the remaining portion of the all-grain recipe.

TIPS FOR SUCCESS

Trillium Head Brewer JC Tetreault suggests building a water profile for this beer starting with soft water. "Supplement the mash with gypsum and calcium chloride to about a 2:1 ratio. This ensures sufficiently assertive hop character but still provides a softer finish." I think maybe a 100:50 ppm ratio would be a good starting point, and you can adjust from there. Handling the post fermentation beer with the utmost care to avoid introducing oxygen in any form is key to retaining those precious hop oils that Trillium Brewing Co. has become known for. JC adds his dry hops while primary fermentation is nearing completion "to ensure good aromatic pre-cursor bioconversion. Ideally, dry hop in a keg under a little head pressure to avoid blowing off aromatics with the escaping carbonation. We strongly recommend force carbonating hop forward beers. Purge the keg with CO_2 and add the dry hops in a fine mesh bag along with some sanitized stainless weights or glass marbles. Tie the fine mesh bag to the lid with some Teflon floss (i.e., Glide) to suspend the hops off the bottom of the keg." Beware of "beer volcanoes" when adding hops to the primary fermenter before terminal gravity, as the hops can create a nucleation point to release dissolved CO_2, creating a volcano effect on the beer that can lead to significant beer loss and create a giant mess. JC is also well known for having hop variations on base beer recipes. Don't be afraid to substitute out Citra in the dry hop for Mosaic, Galaxy, or El Dorado. He will also at times double dry hop his beers, so splitting the dry hops may help add a new dimension.

–––––––––––––––––––––

INDIA PALE ALES (IPAs)

Beer Pictured on Left; see page 28

ALESMITH BREWING COMPANY
ALESMITH IPA

~~~~~~~~~~

**(5 gallons/19 L, all-grain) OG = 1.066 FG = 1.011
IBU = 73 SRM = 5 ABV = 7.3%**

This West Coast IPA is a San Diego classic. It's filled with aromas of grapefruit and tangerine, fresh pine, and tropical fruit.

INGREDIENTS

13.5 lb. (6.1 kg) 2-row pale malt

2 oz. (57 g) crystal malt (15 °L)

2 oz. (57 g) Carapils malt (6 °L)

2 oz. (57 g) Gambrinus honey malt

7 AAU Columbus hops (first wort hop) (0.5 oz./14 g at 14% alpha acids)

3.25 AAU Columbus hops (60 min.) (0.23 oz./6.5 at 14% alpha acids)

1.33 AAU Amarillo hops (30 min.) (0.17 oz./4.8 g at 8% alpha acids)

2.25 AAU Simcoe hops (15 min.) (0.17 oz./4.8 g at 13% alpha acids)

2.66 AAU Columbus hops (10 min.) (0.19 oz./5.4 g at 14% alpha acids)

5.2 AAU Simcoe hops (5 min.) (0.4 oz./11 g at 5% alpha acids)

5 AAU Cascade hops (1 min.) (1 oz./28 g at 5% alpha acids)

0.5 oz. (14 g) Columbus hops (dry hop)

0.5 oz. (14 g) Amarillo hops (dry hop)

0.5 oz. (14 g) Cascade hops (dry hop)

0.25 oz. (7.1 g) Simcoe hops (dry hop)

0.25 oz. (7.1 g) Chinook hops (dry hop)

1 tsp. Irish moss (15 min.)

White Labs WLP001 (California Ale), Wyeast 1056 (American Ale), or Fermentis Safale US-05 yeast

¾ cup (150 g) dextrose (if priming)

STEP BY STEP

Mash at 152°F (67°C) for 60 minutes. Mash out, vorlauf, and then add the first wort hops before sparging at 170°F (77°C) to collect enough wort to result in 5 gallons (19 liters) after a 90-minute boil. Boil for 90 minutes, following the hop addition schedule. Whirlpool wort and let sit for 15 minutes before you begin cooling. Ferment at 68°F (20°C). After fermentation is complete, bottle or keg as usual.

PARTIAL MASH OPTION: Reduce the 2-row pale malt in the all-grain recipe to 1 pound (0.45 kilogram) and add 6.75 pounds (3.1 kilograms) light dried malt extract. Steep crushed grains in 2 quarts (2 liters) of water at 152°F (67°C) for 45 minutes. Add the first wort hops as the wort is heating up to a boil. Boil for 90 minutes. Follow the remaining portion of the all-grain recipe.

BALE BREAKER BREWING COMPANY
TOPCUTTER IPA

~~~~~~~~~~

**(5 gallons/19 L, all-grain) OG = 1.058 FG = 1.008
IBU = 70 SRM = 6 ABV = 6.6%**

With a name that references the farm equipment responsible for removing hop vines from their trellis, Bale Breaker's flagship IPA doesn't disappoint. It is a decidedly West Coast IPA that boasts a complex floral and citrus aroma.

INGREDIENTS

10.75 lb. (4.9 kg) 2-row pale malt

12 oz. (0.34 kg) Munich malt (8 °L)

4 oz. (0.11 kg) Vienna malt

4 oz. (0.11 kg) Carapils (dextrin) malt

4 oz. (0.11 kg) caramel malt (40 °L)

4.6 AAU Simcoe pellet hops (first wort hop) (0.35 oz./10 g at 13.2% alpha acids)

9.6 AAU Warrior pellet hops (60 min.) (0.6 oz./17 g at 16% alpha acids)

6.6 AAU Simcoe pellet hops (15 min.) (0.5 oz./14 g at 13.2% alpha acids)

0.75 oz. (21 g) Simcoe pellet hops (0 min.)

0.75 oz. (21 g) Citra pellet hops (0 min.)

0.75 oz. (21 g) Mosaic pellet hops (0 min.)

1 oz. (28 g) Citra pellet hops (dry hop)

1 oz. (28 g) Ahtanum pellet hops (dry hop)

½ tsp. Irish moss (30 min.)

½ tsp. yeast nutrient (15 min.)

White Labs WLP001 (California Ale), Wyeast 1056 (American Ale), or Fermentis Safale US-05 yeast

⅔ cup (133 g) dextrose (if priming)

STEP BY STEP

Mix all the crushed grains with 4 gallons (15 liters) of 170°F (77°C) water to stabilize at 149°F (65°C) for 60 minutes. Sparge slowly with 175°F (79°C) water. Collect 6 gallons (23 liters) of wort runoff to boil 60 minutes. Boil 60 minutes, adding ingredients as per the schedule. Cool the wort to 75°F (24°C) and pitch your yeast. Hold at 68°F (20°C) until fermentation is complete. Transfer to a carboy, add the dry hops, allow the beer to condition for 1 week, and then bottle or keg.

PARTIAL MASH OPTION: Reduce the 2-row pale malt in the all-grain recipe to 1.75 pounds (0.79 kilogram) and add 3.3 pounds (1.5 kilograms) Briess light liquid malt extract and 2 pounds (0.9 kilogram) light dried malt extract. Steep the crushed grain at 149°F (65°C) in 5 gallons (19 liters) for 30 minutes. Remove grains from the wort and rinse with 2 quarts (1.8 liters) of hot water. Boil 60 minutes. Follow the remaining portion of the all-grain recipe.

PARTIAL MASH OPTION: Reduce the 2-row pale malt in the all-grain recipe to 1 pound (0.45 kilogram) and add 5.5 pounds (2.5 kilograms) extra light dried malt extract. Steep crushed grains in 2.25 gallons (8.5 liters) of water at 152°F (67°C) for 45 minutes. Wash grains with 2 gallons (7.6 liters) of hot water. Top off brewpot to 6.5 gallons (25 liters). Boil for 90 minutes. Follow the remaining portion of the all-grain recipe.

BEAR REPUBLIC BREWING COMPANY
HOP ROD RYE

(5 gallons/19 L, all-grain) OG = 1.076 FG = 1.015
IBU = 80 SRM = 15 ABV = 8%

This high-gravity IPA is brewed with nearly 20 percent rye malt, which provides an earthy, spicy character to play with the sweeter malts and the floral hop aroma.

INGREDIENTS

11 lb. (5 kg) 2-row pale malt

3 lb. (1.4 kg) rye malt

1.15 lb. (0.52 kg) Munich malt

0.63 lb. (0.28 kg) crystal malt (60 °L)

0.63 lb. (0.28 kg) Carapils malt

1.75 oz. (50 g) black malt

10.5 AAU Tomahawk hops (60 min.) (0.75 oz./21 g at 14% alpha acids)

4.7 AAU Centennial hops (30 min.) (0.43 oz./12 g at 11% alpha acids)

23.8 AAU Tomahawk hops (0 min.) (1.7 oz./49 g at 14% alpha acids)

0.75 oz. (21 g) Amarillo hops (dry hop)

1 oz. (28 g) Centennial hops (dry hop)

1 tsp. Irish moss (15 min.)

Wyeast 1272 (American Ale II) or White Labs WLP051 (California V) yeast

¾ cup (150 g) dextrose (if priming)

STEP BY STEP

Mash in at 145°F (63°C), then ramp temperature to 152°F (67°C) for conversion. Mash out to 170°F (77°C). Boil for 90 minutes, adding hops and Irish moss at the times indicated in the ingredient list. Whirlpool the wort after the boil is complete and let it sit for 15 minutes prior to cooling. Aerate, pitch yeast, and ferment at 68°F (20°C). After fermentation is complete, add dry hops for 3 to 5 days and then bottle or keg as normal.

BEAR REPUBLIC BREWING COMPANY
RACER 5 IPA

(5 gallons/19 L, all-grain) OG = 1.070 FG = 1.013
IBU = 75 SRM = 6 ABV = 7.5%

This full-bodied West Coast IPA is one of America's most medal-winning IPAs. No crazy experimental hops required; it's built on a base of the good old American "C" hops.

INGREDIENTS

13 lb. (5.9 kg) 2-row pale malt

0.63 lb. (0.28 kg) crystal malt (15 °L)

0.4 lb. (0.19 kg) dextrose (corn sugar)

0.2 lb. (95 g) Carapils malt

6 AAU Chinook hops (90 min.) (0.5 oz./14 g at 12% alpha acids)

5 AAU Cascade hops (60 min.) (1 oz./28 g at 5% alpha acids)

7.5 AAU Cascade hops (0 min.) (1.5 oz./43 g at 5% alpha acids)

4.5 AAU Centennial hops (0 min.) (0.5 oz./14 g at 9% alpha acids)

7 AAU Columbus hops (0 min.) (0.5 oz./14 g at 14% alpha acids)

0.4 oz. (11 g) Centennial hops (dry hop)

0.4 oz. (11 g) Chinook hops (dry hop)

1 oz. (28 g) Cascade hops (dry hop)

1 oz. (28 g) Columbus hops (dry hop)

Wyeast 1272 (American Ale II) or White Labs WLP051 (California V) yeast

¾ cup (150 g) dextrose (if priming)

STEP BY STEP

Mash in at 145°F (63°C), then ramp temperature to 152°F (67°C) for conversion. Mash out to 170°F (77°C). Boil for 90 minutes, adding hops at the times indicated in the ingredient list. After the boil is finished, remove from heat and add the final hop addition. Stir the brewpot into a whirlpool and let stand for 30 minutes before chilling.

Ferment at 68°F (20°C). After primary fermentation is complete, add the dry hops and wait 5 to 7 days before bottling or kegging.

PARTIAL MASH OPTION: Reduce the 2-row pale malt in the all-grain recipe to 0.33 pounds (0.15 kilogram) and add 6 pounds (2.7 kilograms) dried malt extract. Steep crushed grains in 1 gallon (3.8 liters) of water at 152°F (67°C) for 45 minutes. Bring grains up to 170°F (77°C), then remove the grains and place in a colander. Wash the grains with 1 gallon (3.8 liters) of hot water. Top off the 5 gallons, then boil for 90 minutes. Follow the remaining portion of the all-grain recipe.

- - - - - - - - -

BELL'S BREWERY
TWO HEARTED ALE

««««««-

**(5 gallons/19 L, all-grain)   OG = 1.064   FG = 1.013
IBU = 56   SRM = 8   ABV = 7%**

Bell's flagship IPA might be named after the Two Hearted River in Michigan's Upper Peninsula. However, it's brewed with 100 percent Centennial hops from the Pacific Northwest. If you really want to clone this beer, you'll have to culture Bell's house strain, but the yeast substitutes listed here will get you close.

INGREDIENTS

10.5 lb. (4.8 kg) 2-row pale malt

2 lb. (0.91 kg) Vienna malt

0.5 lb. (0.23 kg) crystal malt (40 °L)

0.33 lb. (0.15 kg) Carapils malt

11 AAU Centennial hops (45 min.) (1 oz./28 g at 11% alpha acids)

11 AAU Centennial hops (30 min.) (1 oz./28 g at 11% alpha acids)

0.5 oz. (14 g) Centennial hops (0 min.)

3 oz. (85 g) Centennial hops (dry hop)

0.5 tsp. Irish moss (15 min.)

Wyeast 1272 (American Ale II), White Labs WLP051 (California Ale V) or yeast cultured from a bottle of this beer

¾ cup (150 g) dextrose (for priming)

STEP BY STEP

Mash the grains at 152°F (67°C) for 60 minutes. Vorlauf until your runnings are clear, sparge, and boil the wort for 75 minutes, adding hops and Irish moss at the times indicated in the ingredients list. After the boil, turn off the heat and chill the wort rapidly to just below fermentation

temperature, about 68°F (20 C). Aerate the wort well and pitch the yeast. Ferment at 70°F (21°C). Dry hop for 3 days in a secondary, then bottle or keg as usual.

PARTIAL MASH OPTION: Replace the 2-row malt with 4.5 pounds (2 kilograms) dried malt extract and 1 pound (0.45 kilogram) 2-row malt. Steep the crushed grains in 1.2 gallons (4.6 liters) of water at 152°F (67°C) for 45 minutes. Pull the grain bag out and drain over the pot in a colander. Rinse the grains with 1.5 quarts (~1.5 liters) of water at 170°F (66°C). Add water to make 3 gallons (11 liters), stir in the dried malt extract, and bring to a boil. Boil for 60 minutes, adding the hops and Irish moss at time indicated in the ingredients list. After the boil, cool the wort, transfer to a fermenter, and top up with cool water to make 5 gallons (19 liters). Aerate the wort and pitch the yeast. Follow the remainder of the all-grain recipe.

- - - - - - - - - - - - - - - - - -

DOGFISH HEAD BREWERY
60 MINUTE IPA

««««««-

**(5 gallons/19 L, all-grain)   OG = 1.064   FG = 1.019
IBU = 60   SRM = 6   ABV = 6%**

This innovative IPA employs Dogfish Head's pioneering method of adding hops continuously over the entire boil. Showcasing a big US Northwest hop bill, 60-Minute is the lower-gravity sister of 90-Minute IPA (see page 46).

INGREDIENTS

13 lb. (5.9 kg) 2-row pale malt

6.4 oz. (0.18 kg) Thomas Fawcett amber malt (35 °L)

11.2 AAU Warrior hops (60–35 min.) (0.7 oz./20 g at 16% alpha acids)

3.6 AAU Simcoe hops (35–0 min.) (0.7 oz./20 g at 13% alpha acids)

5.6 AAU Amarillo hops (35–0 min.) (0.7 oz./20 g at 8% alpha acids)

0.7 oz. (20 g) Amarillo hops (0 min.)

1 oz. (28 g) Amarillo hops (dry hop)

0.5 oz. (14 g) Simcoe hops (dry hop)

1 tsp. Irish moss (15 min.)

Wyeast 1187 (Ringwood Ale) or White Labs WLP005 (British Ale) yeast (1.5 qt./~1.5 L starter @ SG 1.030)

⅞ cup (175 g) dextrose (if priming)

STEP BY STEP

Mash the grains at 152°F (67°C) for 60 minutes. Mash out, vorlauf, and then sparge at 170°F (77°C). Boil wort for 60 minutes. Begin hopping wort with a continuous stream of Warrior hops at a rate of 0.28 ounces (7.9 grams) per 10 minutes. Warrior should run out with 35 minutes left in boil. Refill hopper with Simcoe and Amarillo hops and resume hopping until the end of the boil. Add Irish moss with 15 minutes remaining. Add the 0-minute hops after boil and begin cooling. Aerate cooled wort and pitch yeast. Ferment initially at 71°F (22°C), but let temperature rise to 74°F (23°C) toward the end of fermentation. Warm condition for 3 days (to remove diacetyl), then cool beer and add dry hops, allowing 10 to 14 days contact time. Bottle or keg as usual.

PARTIAL MASH OPTION: Reduce the 2-row pale malt in the all-grain recipe to 1.5 pounds (0.68 kilogram) and add 4 pounds (1.8 kilograms) Muntons light dried malt extract and 2 pounds 14 ounces (1.3 kilograms) Muntons light liquid malt extract. Steep crushed malt at 152°F (67°C) in 2.25 quarts (2.1 liters) of water. After 45 minutes, rinse grains with 1 quart (1 liter) of 170°F (77°C) water. Add water to "grain tea" to make 4 gallons (15 liters). To save time, heat 3.5 gallons/13 liters of water during steep. Stir in the dried malt extract and bring to a boil. During the boil, do not let wort volume drop below 3.5 gallons (13 liters). Add boiling water if wort volume dips near this mark. Follow the hopping schedule in the all-grain version, adding the liquid malt extract with 15 minutes remaining in the boil. Follow the remaining portion of the all-grain recipe.

- - - - - - - - - - - - - - - - - - - -

FIRESTONE WALKER BREWING COMPANY
UNION JACK

««««««

(5 gallons/19 L, all-grain) OG = 1.070 FG = 1.015
IBU = 70 SRM = 7 ABV = 7.2%

This aggressively hopped West Coast IPA was named with a nod to the colonial origins of the IPA style—and to the British expatriate who cofounded the brewery. Double dry hopped and smooth, this beer delivers bold grapefruit, tangerine, and citrus flavors.

INGREDIENTS

- 12 lb. 5 oz. (5.6 kg) Rahr Standard 2-row malt
- 1 lb. 6 oz. (0.6 kg) Great Western Munich malt (10 °L)
- 11 oz. (310 g) Carapils malt
- 5 oz. (140 g) UK light crystal malt (38 °L)
- 11.4 AAU German Magnum hops (60 min.) (1.04 oz./29 g at 11% alpha acids)
- 1.9 AAU Cascade hops (30 min.) (0.4 oz./11 g at 4.5% alpha acids)
- 3.6 AAU Centennial hops (30 min.) (0.4 oz./11 g at 8.5% alpha acids)
- 1.9 AAU Cascade hops (10 min.) (0.4 oz./11 g at 4.5% alpha acids)
- 3.6 AAU Centennial hops (10 min.) (0.4 oz./11 g at 8.5% alpha acids)
- 1 oz. (28 g) Cascade hops (first dry hop)
- 1 oz. (28 g) Centennial hops (first dry hop)
- 0.4 oz. (11 g) Amarillo hops (second dry hop)
- 0.4 oz. (11 g) Citra hops (second dry hop)
- 0.4 oz. (11 g) Chinook hops (second dry hop)
- 0.4 oz. (11 g) Simcoe hops (second dry hop)
- 3.5 g calcium chloride (if using reverse osmosis water)
- 3.5 g gypsum (if using reverse osmosis water)
- White Labs WLP002 (English Ale) or Wyeast 1968 (London ESB Ale) yeast
- ¾ cup (150 g) dextrose (if priming)

STEP BY STEP

Mill grains and mix with 5.5 gallons (21 liters) of 156°F (69°C) strike water and optional brewing salts to reach a mash temperature of 145°F (63°C). Hold this temperature for 15 minutes. Raise the temperature to 155°F (68°C) and hold for 30 minutes. Raise the temperature to a mash out of 168°F (75°C). Vorlauf until your runnings are clear. Sparge the grains with enough 168°F (75°C) water to collect 6 gallons (23 liters) of 1.058 SG wort. Boil for 60 minutes, adding hops according to the ingredients list. After the boil, turn off the heat and chill the wort to 66°F (19°C). Aerate the wort with pure oxygen or filtered air and pitch the yeast. Ferment at 68°F (20°C). After 4 days add the first dry hop addition. After 7 days add the second dry hop addition. Once at terminal gravity (~10 days), bottle or keg the beer and carbonate.

EXTRACT WITH GRAINS OPTION: Substitute the 2-row pale malt and Munich malt in the all-grain recipe with 6 pounds (2.7 kilograms) golden liquid malt extract and 3.3 pounds (1.5 kilograms) Briess Munich liquid malt extract, and reduce the Carapils addition to 6 ounces (310 grams). Place the milled grains in a muslin bag and steep in 5 quarts (4.7 liters) of 149°F (65°C) water for 15 minutes. Remove the grain and rinse with 1 gallon (3.8 liters) of hot water. Add water to reach a volume of 5.4 gallons (20.4 liters) and boil. Turn off the heat, add the malt extract and brewing salts, and stir until dissolved. Top up to 6 gallons (23 liters) of 1.058 SG wort. Follow the remaining portion of the all-grain recipe.

FORT GEORGE BREWERY
SUICIDE SQUEEZE IPA

‹‹‹‹‹‹‹

(5 gallons/19 L, all-grain) OG = 1.044 FG = 1.008
IBU = 48 SRM = 6 ABV = 4.7%

If you're curious about the unusual name, this beer was brewed as a collaboration with Seattle's Suicide Squeeze Records. It is packed with Mosaic, Amarillo, and Citra hops. It pairs well with rock, pop, and metal.

INGREDIENTS

8.4 lb. (3.8 kg) 2-row pale malt

0.25 lb. (113 g) crystal malt (40 °L)

0.5 lb. (0.23 kg) flaked oats

2.8 AAU Mosaic pellet hops (60 min.) (0.25 oz./7 g at 11% alpha acids)

8.3 AAU Mosaic pellet hops (15 min.) (0.75 oz./21 g at 11% alpha acids)

6.5 AAU Citra pellet hops (15 min.) (0.5 oz./14 g at 13% alpha acids)

2 oz. (57 g) Mosaic pellet hops (0 min.)

2.5 oz. (71 g) Mosaic pellet hops (dry hop)

0.25 oz. (7 g) Citra pellet hops (dry hop)

½ tsp. Irish moss (30 min.)

Wyeast 1968 (London ESB Ale), White Labs WLP002 (English Ale), or Lallemand London ESB Ale

⅔ cup (133 g) dextrose (if priming)

STEP BY STEP

This is a single-infusion mash, mashing at 154 to 156°F (68 to 69°C) to create a fuller-bodied beer. Mix all the crushed grains with 3.5 gallons (13 liters) of 170°F (77°C) water and stabilize the mash at 156°F (68°C) for 60 minutes. Raise your mash temperature to 165°F (74°C) and sparge with enough 175°F (79°C) water to collect approximately 6 gallons (23 liters) of wort. Boil wort for 60 minutes. Add hops and Irish moss as indicated. At the end of the boil, add 0-minute hop addition and immediately begin cooling your wort. You would like to have these hops in the wort with the temperature between boiling and around 150°F (66°C) for close to 5 minutes. When you have cooled the wort to about 80°F (27°C), you can strain the wort into a fermenter. Aerate the wort and pitch the yeast. Ferment at 70°F (21°C). When fermentation is complete, rack the beer off the trub and add the dry hops. Allow the beer to absorb the dry hop flavors for about 4 days. Bottle or keg as usual.

EXTRACT WITH GRAINS OPTION: Substitute the 2-row pale malt in the all-grain recipe with 3.3 pounds (1.5 kilograms) Briess Pilsen liquid malt extract and 2 pounds (0.9 kilogram) Briess light dried malt extract. Steep the crushed grains in 2.5 gallons (9.5 liters) of water at 155°F (68°C) for 30 minutes. Remove the grains from the wort and rinse with hot water, bringing the brewpot volume up to 5.5 gallons (21 liters). Add the malt extracts and boil for 60 minutes. Follow the remaining portion of the all-grain recipe.

TIPS FOR SUCCESS

Flaked grains such as flaked oats (as used in this recipe) or flaked wheat can provide extra mouthfeel, which can help balance a beer with higher hops and lower alcohol. Flaked grains technically should be mashed or partial mashed to convert the starch. In the extract with grains version of this recipe, the grains are steeped at 155°F (68°C). This will not convert the starch in the grains, but it will still increase the mouthfeel (and may also leave some haze behind).

HARPOON BREWERY
HARPOON IPA

‹‹‹‹‹‹‹

(5 gallons/19 L, all-grain) OG = 1.057 FG = 1.013
IBU = 42 SRM = 7 ABV = 5.9%

This Harpoon classic started out as a summer seasonal in 1993. Today, it is one of the brewery's biggest sellers year-round. It is a crisp, clean, fairly traditional English IPA that will always be in style.

INGREDIENTS

10 lb. (4.5 kg) 2-row pale malt

1.5 lb. (0.68 kg) Munich malt (10 °L)

0.5 lb. (0.23 kg) Briess Victory malt

7.8 AAU Columbus hops (60 min.) (0.6 oz./17 g at 13% alpha acids)

5 AAU Cascade hops (10 min.) (1 oz./28 g at 5% alpha acids)

5 AAU Cascade hops (0 min.)
(1 oz./28 g at 5% alpha acids)

1.5 oz. (43 g) Cascade hops
(dry hop)

1 tsp. Irish moss (15 min.)

White Labs WLP007 (Dry English
Ale), Wyeast 1098 (British Ale),
or Lallemand Nottingham Ale
yeast

¾ cup (150 g) dextrose
(if priming)

STEP BY STEP

Mash grains for 60 minutes at 152°F (67°C) in 4 gallons (15 liters) of mash water. Mash out, vorlauf, and then sparge at 170°F (77°C) to collect 6.5 gallons (25 liters). Boil for 90 minutes. Add hops and Irish moss according to the schedule. When done boiling, let the wort settle for 10 minutes, then begin cooling. Aerate wort and pitch yeast. Ferment at 68°F (20°C) until complete (7 to 10 days). After fermentation is complete, transfer beer to secondary and add dry hops. Let these hops sit in the beer for about 1 week to enhance the hop aroma, then separate the hops from the beer and bottle or keg as usual.

PARTIAL MASH OPTION: Substitute the 2-row pale malt in the all-grain recipe with 2.7 pounds (1.2 kilograms) light dried malt extract and 3.3 pounds (1.5 kilograms) light liquid malt extract. Place crushed malts in a nylon steeping bag and steep in 3 quarts (2.8 liters) of water at 152°F (67°C) for 30 minutes. Rinse grains with 1.5 quarts (1.5 liters) of water at 170°F (77°C). Add water to make 3 gallons (11 liters), stir in dried malt extract, and bring to a boil. Add hops according to the schedule and Irish moss and liquid malt extract with 15 minutes left in the boil. Follow the remaining portion of the all-grain recipe.

ITHACA BEER COMPANY
FLOWER POWER IPA

**(5 gallons/19 L, all-grain) OG = 1.072 FG = 1.015
IBU = 75 SRM = 6 ABV = 7.5%**

Out of the trippy yellow-labeled bottle pours a beer with a honey-colored hue. The brewery calls this beer simultaneously punchy and soothing, with aromas of pineapple and grapefruit.

INGREDIENTS

14 lb. (6.35 kg) 2-row pale malt

6.6 oz. (0.19 kg) honey malt

6.6 oz. (0.19 kg) acidulated malt

3.3 AAU Chinook pellet hops
(60 min.) (0.25 oz./7 g at 13%
alpha acids)

9.8 AAU Simcoe pellet hops
(10 min.) (0.75 oz./21 g at
13% alpha acids)

6 AAU Citra pellet hops (10 min.)
(0.5 oz./14 g at 12% alpha
acids)

5 AAU Centennial pellet hops
(10 min.) (0.5 oz./14 g at 10%
alpha acids)

3 AAU Ahtanum pellet hops
(10 min.) (0.5 oz./14 g at 6%
alpha acids)

9.8 AAU Simcoe pellet hops
(0 min.) (0.75 oz./21 g at 13%
alpha acids)

9 AAU Citra pellet hops (0 min.)
(0.75 oz./21 g at 12% alpha
acids)

7.5 AAU Centennial pellet hops
(0 min.) (0.75 oz./21 g at 10%
alpha acids)

4.5 AAU Ahtanum pellet hops
(0 min.) (0.75 oz./21 g at 6%
alpha acids)

1 oz. (28 g) Simcoe pellet hops
(dry hop for 7 days)

1 oz. (28 g) Centennial pellet
hops (dry hop for 7 days)

1 oz. (28 g) Amarillo pellet hops
(dry hop for 7 days)

0.25 oz. (7 g) Simcoe pellet hops
(dry hop for 3 days)

0.25 oz. (7 g) Centennial pellet
hops (dry hop for 3 days)

0.25 oz. (7 g) Amarillo pellet
hops (dry hop for 3 days)

½ tsp. yeast nutrient (15 min.)

½ Whirlfloc tablet (15 min.)

White Labs WLP007 (Dry English
Ale) or Wyeast 1098 (British
Ale) yeast

½ cup (100 g) dextrose
(if priming)

STEP BY STEP

Mill the grains and mix with 5.1 gallons (19.3 liters) of 162°F (72°C) strike water to reach a mash temperature of 150°F (68°C). Hold at this temperature for 60 minutes. Vorlauf until your runnings are clear. Sparge the grains with 3.2 gallons (12.1 liters) of 168°F (75.5°C) water until 6.5 gallons (24.6 liters) of 1.059 SG wort is collected in your boil kettle. Boil for 60 minutes, adding hops, yeast nutrient, and kettle finings according to the ingredients list. After the boil, turn off the heat and add the 0-minute hop additions. Whirlpool the kettle by gently stirring the wort for 2 minutes, and then let it rest for an additional 23 minutes. Chill the wort to 65°F (20°C), aerate, and pitch the yeast. The recommended pitch rate is 240 billion yeast cells, which can be obtained by using 1 vial/packet after making a 1-liter stir plate starter, by using 1 vial/packet after making a 2.75-liter non-stir plate starter, or by using 2.5 vials/packets without a starter. Ferment between 65°F (18°C) and 66°F (19°C) for the first 3 days, then ramp up to 69°F (20.5°C) for the remainder of primary fermentation. On day 8, add your first round of dry hops directly to the primary

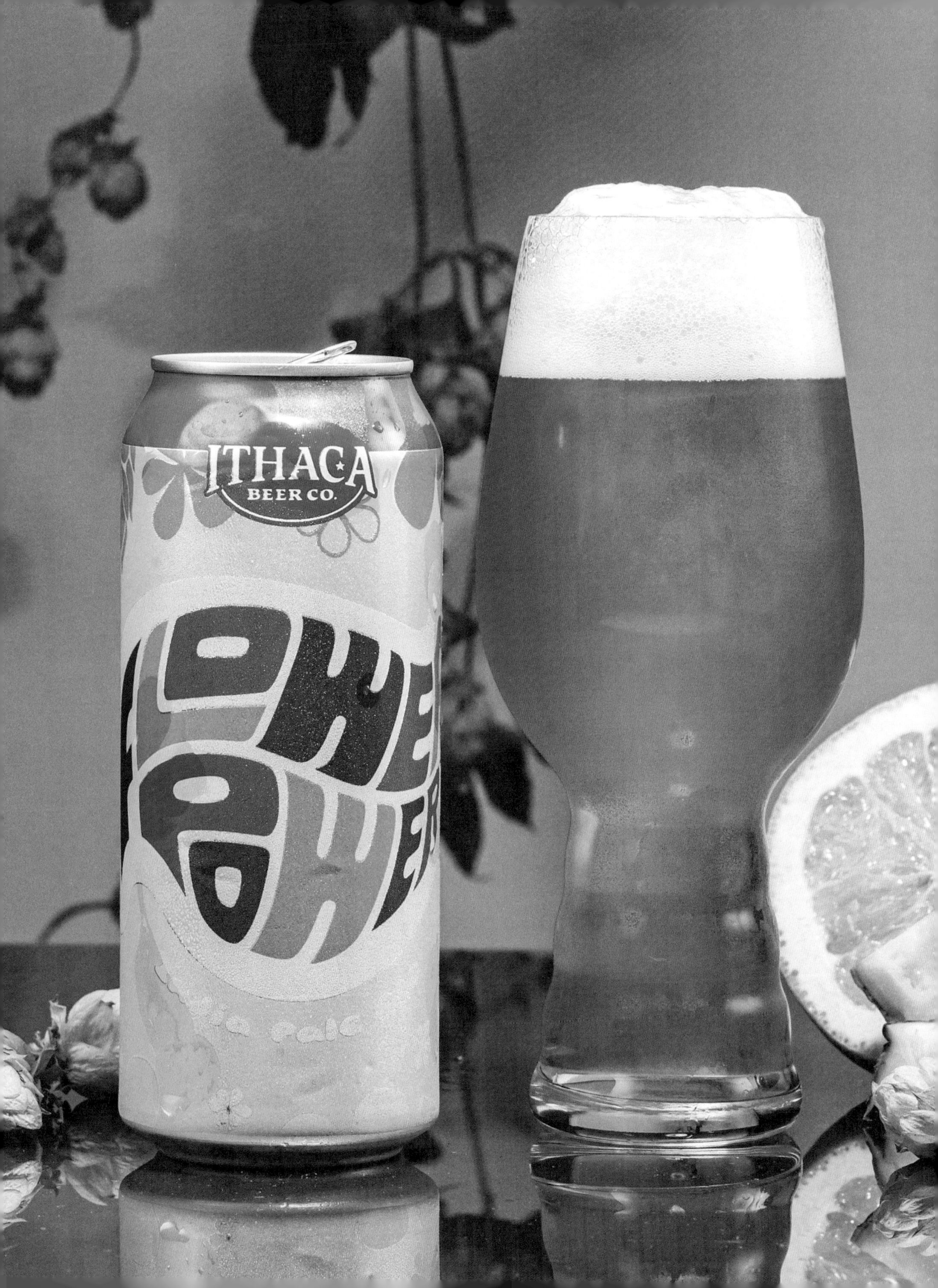
ITHACA
BEER CO.

fermenter. On day 12, add your second round of dry hops to the primary fermenter. On day 15, begin to slowly crash cool the fermenter down at the rate of 5°F (2.7°C) per day for 7 days until the beer reaches 34°F (1°C), and then bottle or keg the beer. Carbonate to between 2.2 and 2.3 volumes of CO_2 and enjoy!

EXTRACT WITH GRAINS OPTION: Substitute the grain bill in the all-grain recipe with 9.75 pounds (4.4 kilograms) golden light liquid malt extract, 4 ounces (0.11 kilogram) honey malt, and 1 teaspoon (5 milliliters) 88 percent lactic acid. Steep the honey malt in 2 gallons (7.5 liters) of 150°F (66°C) water, along with the lactic acid, for 20 to 30 minutes while you continue to heat the water up to no hotter than 170°F (77°C) to avoid extracting tannins. Remove grains and top off to 6.5 gallons (24.6 liters). Boil for 60 minutes. Follow the remaining portion of the all-grain recipe.

LAGUNITAS
BREWING COMPANY
LAGUNITAS IPA

**(5 gallons/19 L, all-grain) OG = 1.061 FG = 1.014
IBU = 67 SRM = 9 ABV = 6.2%**

Lagunitas built their brewery on the strength of this IPA. It's a well-rounded West Coast version with lots of hop complexity and a sweet, malty balance.

INGREDIENTS

9.4 lb. (4.3 kg) 2-row pale malt

1.3 lb. (0.59 kg) crystal malt (10 °L)

13 oz. (0.37 kg) wheat malt

13 oz. (0.37 kg) light Munich malt (6 °L)

9 oz. (0.25 kg) crystal malt (60 °L)

8.25 AAU Horizon hops (60 min.) (0.75 oz./21 g at 11% alpha acids)

4.5 AAU Summit hops (60 min.) (0.25 oz./7 g at 18% alpha acids)

4.5 AAU Willamette hops (30 min.) (0.9 oz./26 g at 5% alpha acids)

2.4 AAU Centennial hops (30 min.) (0.25 oz./7 g at 9.5% alpha acids)

7.5 AAU Cascade hops (0 min.) (1.5 oz./43 g at 5% alpha acids)

1 oz. (28 g) Cascade hops (dry hop)

1 oz. (28 g) Centennial hops (dry hop)

1 tsp. Irish moss (15 min.)

Wyeast 1056 (American Ale), White Labs WLP001 (California Ale), or Fermentis Safale US-05 yeast

¾ cup (150 g) dextrose (if priming)

STEP BY STEP

Mash grains at 160°F (71°C). Mash out, vorlauf, and then sparge at 170°F (77°C) to collect enough wort to result in 5 gallons (19 liters) after a 90-minute boil. Boil for 90 minutes, adding ingredients as indicated in the ingredient list. After the boil, let the wort sit for 15 minutes before cooling. Ferment at 70°F (21°C). When fermentation slows, add dry hops for 5 to 7 days. Bottle or keg as usual.

PARTIAL MASH OPTION: Reduce the 2-row pale malt in the all-grain recipe to 1 pound (0.45 kilogram) and add 4.5 pounds (2 kilograms) light dried malt extract. Steep crushed grains in 1 gallon (3.8 liters) of water at 160°F (71°C) for 45 minutes. Remove grain bag and rinse with at least 2 gallons (8 liters) of hot water over your brewpot. Boil for 60 minutes. Follow the remaining portion of the all-grain recipe.

MAYFLOWER
BREWING COMPANY
MAYFLOWER IPA

**(5 gallons/19 L, all-grain) OG = 1.062 FG = 1.014
IBU = 72 SRM = 6 ABV = 6.5%**

This IPA strives for balance, with plenty of malt to even out the 70+ IBU. There's a nod to the British IPAs with the yeast selection as well, which creates a more rounded, fruity beer than American strains.

INGREDIENTS

11.5 lb. (5.2 kg) 2-row pale malt

18 oz. (0.51 kg) Munich malt (8 °L)

10 oz. (0.28 kg) Weyermann CaraRed malt (20 °L)

7.8 AAU Nugget pellet hops (60 min.) (0.6 oz./17 g at 13% alpha acids)

12.8 AAU Simcoe pellet hops (30 min.) (1 oz./28 g at 12.8% alpha acids)

5 AAU Amarillo pellet hops (5 min.) (0.5 oz./14 g at 10% alpha acids)

5 AAU Amarillo pellet hops (0 min.) (0.5 oz./14 g at 10% alpha acids)

1 oz. (28 g) Glacier pellet hops (dry hop)

½ tsp. Irish moss (30 min.)

½ tsp. yeast nutrient (15 min.)

White Labs WLP002 (English Ale), Wyeast 1099 (Whitbread Ale), or Fermentis Safale S-04 yeast

¾ cup (150 g) dextrose (if priming)

STEP BY STEP

This is a single-infusion mash. Mix all the crushed grains with 5 gallons (19 liters) of 171°F (77°C) water to stabilize at 150°F (66°C) for 60 minutes. Sparge slowly with 175°F (79°C) water. Collect approximately 6 gallons (23 liters) of wort runoff to boil for 60 minutes. Add hops, Irish moss, and yeast nutrients according to the schedule. Cool the wort to 75°F (24°C). Pitch your yeast and aerate the wort heavily. Allow the beer to cool to 68°F (20°C). Hold at that temperature until fermentation is complete. Transfer to a carboy, avoiding any splashing. Add the dry hops and allow the beer to condition for 1 week, and then bottle or keg.

PARTIAL MASH OPTION: Reduce the 2-row pale malt in the all-grain recipe to 1.5 pounds (0.68 kilogram) and add 6.6 pounds (3 kilograms) Coopers light liquid malt extract. Steep the crushed grain in 2 gallons (7.6 liters) of water at 150°F (66°C) for 30 minutes. Remove grains from the wort and rinse with 2 quarts (1.8 liters) of hot water. Add the liquid malt extract and boil for 60 minutes. Add the hops, Irish moss, and yeast nutrient as per the schedule. Add the wort to 2 gallons (7.6 liters) of cold water in the sanitized fermenter and top off with cold water up to 5 gallons (19 liters). Follow the remaining portion of the all-grain recipe.

MODERN TIMES BEER
SOUTHERN LANDS IPA

ᕦᕦᕦᕦᕦᕦᕦ-

**(5 gallons/19 L, all-grain) OG = 1.065 FG = 1.008
IBU = 60 SRM = 5 ABV = 7.5%**

This IPA is thoroughly modern. It features an intense tropical pineapple character from a combination of the hops and a 100 percent *Brett Trois* fermentation. It also uses hop extract for bittering and a touch of acidulated malt for additional complexity.

INGREDIENTS

10.7 lb. (4.9 kg) 2-row pale malt

2 lb. (0.9 kg) white wheat malt

6.4 oz. (180 g) acidulated malt

6.4 oz. (180 g) dextrin malt

2 oz. (57 g) crystal malt (60 °L)

3 mL HopShot extract (60 min.) (~30 IBU)

20 AAU Centennial hops (1 min.) (2 oz./57 g at 10% alpha acids)

14 AAU Calypso hops (1 min.) (1 oz./28 g at 14% alpha acids)

2 oz. (57 g) Centennial hops (dry hop)

1.5 oz. (43 g) Calypso hops (dry hop)

½ tsp. yeast nutrient (15 min.)

1 Whirlfloc tablet (5 min.)

White Labs WLP648 (*Brettanomyces bruxellensis Trois Vrai*) yeast

⅔ cup (133 g) dextrose (if priming)

STEP BY STEP

Mill the grains and dough-in with 16 quarts (15 liters) water for a mash ratio of about 1.25 quarts per pound of grain. Target a mash temperature of 156°F (69°C) and hold for 60 minutes. Sparge slowly with 170°F (77°C) water. Collect approximately 6.3 gallons (23.8 liters) of wort runoff and bring to a boil. Add bittering hops and boil for 60 minutes. After the boil, add the flameout hops and whirlpool for 30 minutes before cooling. Cool the wort to room temperature, pitch yeast, and ferment at 68 to 72°F (20 to 22°C). Dry hop for 7 days before bottling or kegging.

EXTRACT WITH GRAINS OPTION: Substitute the 2-row, white wheat, acidulated, and dextrin malt in the all-grain recipe with 3.3 pounds (1.5 kilograms) Pilsen light liquid malt extract, 3 pounds (1.4 kilograms) golden light dried malt extract, and 1.5 pounds (0.68 kilogram) wheat dried malt extract. Increase the crystal malt to 4 ounces (0.11 kilogram). Steep the crushed grains in 2 gallons (7.6 liters) of water as it warms to about 150°F (65.5°C) or for approximately 20 minutes. Remove grains from the wort and rinse with 4 quarts (3.8 liters) of hot water. Add the liquid to reach a total of 3 gallons (11.3 liters) and bring to a boil. Turn off heat, add malt extract, and stir until completely dissolved. Return to heat and boil 60 minutes. Follow the remaining portion of the all-grain recipe.

OSKAR BLUES BREWERY
IPA

ᕦᕦᕦᕦᕦᕦᕦ-

**(5 gallons/19 L, all-grain) OG = 1.059 FG = 1.010
IBU = 70 SRM = 6 ABV = 6.4%**

OB IPA takes the crisp, refreshing West Coast IPA style and injects it with a unique flavor from Down Under. Pleasant and drying bitterness brings citrus, melon, pepper, and wine grape aromas and flavors alive in this exclusively Australian-hopped IPA.

INGREDIENTS

11.4 lb. (5.2 kg) North American 2-row pale malt (1.8 °L)

1.32 lb. (600 g) pale wheat malt (2 °L)

0.33 lb. (152 g) Simpsons Premium English Caramalt (25 °L)

4.5 AAU Vic Secret hops (first wort hop) (0.25 oz./7 g at 18% alpha acids)

10.8 AAU Vic Secret hops (80 min.) (0.6 oz./16.8 g at 18% alpha acids)

4.5 AAU Vic Secret hops (25 min.) (0.25 oz./7 g at 18% alpha acids)

8.6 AAU Vic Secret hops (10 min.) (0.48 oz./13.4 g at 18% alpha acids)

0.9 oz. (25 g) Galaxy hops (0 min.)

0.45 oz. (12.6 g) Ella hops (0 min.)

1.2 oz. (34 g) Enigma hops (dry hop)

1 oz. (28 g) Galaxy hops (dry hop)

0.8 oz. (22.4 g) Ella hops (dry hop)

1 tsp. yeast nutrient (Servomyces recommended) (5 min.)

½ Whirlfloc tablet (5 min.)

White Labs WLP001 (California Ale), Wyeast 1056 (American Ale), or Safale US-05 yeast

¾ cup (150 g) corn sugar (if priming)

STEP BY STEP

Mill the grains and dough-in targeting a mash of around 1.3 quarts of water to 1 pound of grain (2.7 liters/kilograms) and a temperature of 156°F (69°C). Hold the mash at 156°F (69°C) until enzymatic conversion is complete. Sparge slowly with 168°F (75.5°C) water, collecting wort until the pre-boil kettle volume is 7 gallons (25.6 liters). Add the first wort hops as soon as wort covers the bottom of the kettle.

Total boil time is 90 minutes, targeting 5.5 gallons (20 liters) hot wort at the end of boil. Add Whirlfloc and yeast nutrient with 5 minutes left in the boil. After the boil, give the wort a long stir to create a whirlpool, then add the flameout hops. Let the wort settle for 10 minutes, then chill the wort to 65°F (18°C) and aerate thoroughly. Pitch rate is 1 M cells per mL per degree Plato. Regulate the fermentation temperature at 68°F (20°C). At the end of active fermentation, ~5 days, rack the beer onto the dry hops in purged secondary vessel. Let rest for 9 more days at 68°F (20°C), longer if showing fermentation activity. Then lower temperature to 32°F (0°C). Once beer is clarified, rack the beer and carbonate it to around 2.55 volumes of CO_2. If bottling conditioning, you may consider pitching fresh yeast at bottling.

EXTRACT WITH GRAINS OPTION: Replace the 2-row pale malt and pale wheat malt with 6.6 pounds (3 kilograms) of golden liquid malt extract and 1.5 pounds (0.68 kilograms) wheat dried malt extract. Place the crushed grains in a muslin bag and submerge bag in 5 gallons (19 liters) water as it heats up to 160°F (71°C). Remove the grain bag and allow to drip back into the kettle. Add the liquid and dried malt extract as well as the first wort hops and stir until extracts are fully dissolved. Bring wort to a boil. Follow the remaining portion of the all-grain recipe.

SAMUEL SMITH OLD BREWERY
INDIA ALE

(5 gallons/19 L, all-grain) OG = 1.060   FG = 1.015
IBU = 50   SRM = 13   ABV = 6.1%

If your clone of this beer doesn't taste exactly like the bottled version, it might be because this classic is still brewed with well water from the Samuel Smith Old Brewery. The well was sunk in 1758!

INGREDIENTS

10 lb. (4.5 kg) British pale ale malt

1 lb. (0.45 kg) pale ale malt (toasted)

0.75 lb. (0.34 kg) crystal malt (60 °L)

0.5 lb. (0.23 kg) malted wheat

7.25 AAU Northdown hops (60 min.) (0.8 oz./23 g at 9% alpha acids)

6 AAU Kent Golding hops (30 min.) (1.5 oz./43 g at 4% alpha acids)

4 AAU Bramling Cross hops (15 min.) (1 oz./28 g at 4% alpha acids)

1 oz. (28 g) Fuggle hops (dry hop)

Wyeast 1098 (British Ale) or White Labs WLP007 (Dry English Ale) yeast (1.75 qt./1.75 L yeast starter)

¾ cup (150 g) dextrose (if priming)

STEP BY STEP

Toast the 1 pound (0.45 kilogram) pale ale malt on a baking sheet in oven set at 350°F (177°C) for 15 minutes. Heat 15 quarts (~15 liters) water to 164°F (73°C), crush grains, mix into liquor. Hold mash at 153°F (67°C) for 60 minutes. Collect around 6.5 gallons (25 liters) of wort and bring to a boil. Boil 90 minutes total, adding hops at times indicated in recipe. Cool wort to 70°F (21°C), aerate, and pitch yeast. Ferment at 72°F (22°C), transfer to secondary, add dry hops, and condition at 50°F (10°C) for 2 weeks. Rack and bottle or keg, and then age 4 to 6 weeks.

PARTIAL MASH OPTION: Replace the 10 pounds (4.5 kilograms) British pale ale malt with 2.25 pounds (1 kilogram) light dried malt extract and 4.5 pounds (2 kilograms) Maris Otter liquid malt extract. Toast the 1-pound (0.45 kilogram) pale ale malt on a baking sheet in oven set at 350°F (177°C) for 15 minutes. Steep toasted pale, crystal, and wheat malts in 3.4 quarts (3.2 liters) of water at 153°F (67°C) for 45 minutes. Rinse grains with 1.5 gallons (5.7 liters) of water at 170°F (77°C). Add water to make 3 gallons (11.4 liters) of wort, stir in the dried malt extract, and bring to a boil. Add hops at times indicated in recipe. Add the liquid malt extract with 15 minutes left in boil. Cool wort, transfer to fermenter, and top up to 5 gallons (19 liters) with water. Aerate wort and pitch yeast. Ferment and bottle as described in all-grain recipe.

- - - - - - - - - - - - - - - - -

SIERRA NEVADA BREWING COMPANY
CELEBRATION ALE

꜀꜀꜀꜀꜀꜀-

**(5 gallons/19 L, all-grain) OG = 1.064 FG = 1.012
IBU = 65 SRM = 12 ABV = 6.8%**

First brewed in 1981, Celebration Ale is one of the earliest examples of an American-style IPA. It remains one of the few hop-forward holiday beers to this day.

INGREDIENTS

12.5 lb. (5.7 kg) 2-row pale malt

15 oz. (0.43 kg) caramel malt (60°L)

9 AAU Chinook hops (100 min.) (0.75 oz./21 g at 12% alpha acids)

5 AAU Centennial hops (100 min.) (0.5 oz./14 g at 10% alpha acids)

7.5 AAU Cascade hops (10 min.) (1.5 oz./43 g at 5% alpha acids)

0.66 oz. (19 g) Centennial hops (0 min.)

1.33 oz. (38 g) Cascade hops (0 min.)

1.33 oz. (38 g) Cascade hops (dry hop)

0.66 oz. (19 g) Centennial hops (dry hop)

Wyeast 1056 (American Ale), White Labs WLP001 (California Ale), or Fermentis Safale US-05 yeast (1.5 qt./1.5 L yeast starter)

1 cup (200 g) dextrose (for priming)

STEP BY STEP

Mash at 157.5°F (69.7°C) in 17 quarts (16 liters) of water. Hold at this temperature for 60 minutes. Mash out, vorlauf, and then sparge at 170°F (77°C). Boil the wort for 100 minutes, adding the hops at times indicated. Pitch the yeast and ferment at 68°F (20°C). Dry hop in secondary for 5 days. Bottle or keg as usual.

EXTRACT WITH GRAINS OPTION: Replace the 12.5 pounds (5.7 kilograms) 2-row pale malt in the all-grain recipe with 1 pound 1 ounce (0.48 kilogram) 2-row pale malt, 2.5 pounds (1.13 kilograms) light dried malt extract, and 5 pounds (2.27 kilograms) light liquid malt extract. Steep the grains at 157.5°F (69.7°C) in 3 quarts (2.9 liters) of water. Rinse the grains with 2 quarts (2 liters) of 170°F (77°C) water. Add water to the brewpot to make at least 3 gallons (11 liters) of wort. Stir in the dried malt extract and boil the wort for 100 minutes, adding hops at times indicated. Keep some boiling water handy and do not let the boil volume dip below 3 gallons (11 liters). Add the liquid malt extract during the final 15 minutes of the boil. Stir thoroughly to avoid scorching. Chill the wort, transfer to your fermenter, and top up with filtered water to 5 gallons (19 liters). Follow the remaining portion of the all-grain recipe.

- - - - - - - - - - - - - - - - -

STONE BREWING COMPANY
STONE RUINATION IPA 1.0

꜀꜀꜀꜀꜀꜀-

**(5 gallons/19 L, all-grain) OG = 1.074 FG = 1.012
IBU = 100+ SRM = 6 ABV = 8.2%**

This recipe is for the original formulation of Stone Ruination, a West Coast IPA that defined the style with resinous pine, a big malt backbone, and a lovely orange amber color. For many, it is a nostalgic IPA.

INGREDIENTS

14.5 lb. (6.6 kg) 2-row pale malt

1 lb. (0.45 kg) Briess crystal malt (15 °L)

36 AAU Magnum hops (90 min.) (2.25 oz./64 g at 16% alpha acids)

16 AAU Centennial hops (0 min.) (1.5 oz./43 g at 10.5% alpha acids)

6.5 AAU Chinook hops (0 min.) (0.5 oz./14 g at 13% alpha acids)

2 oz. (57 g) Centennial whole hops (dry hop)

1 tsp. Irish moss (15 min.)

White Labs WLP002 (English Ale) or Wyeast 1968 (London ESB Ale) yeast (2 qt./2 L yeast starter)

⅞ cup (175 g) dextrose (for priming)

STEP BY STEP

Mash your grains at 149°F (65°C) for 60 minutes. Mash out, vorlauf, and then sparge at 170°F (77°C) to collect enough wort to result in 5 gallons (19 liters) after a 90-minute boil. Boil 90 minutes, adding hops at times indicated. At the end of the boil, remove the wort from heat and add the flameout hop addition. Stir the wort to create a whirlpool, then let settle for 15 minutes or more before chilling. Ferment at 68°F (20°C). After primary fermentation is complete, add Centennial hops and dry hop for 3 to 5 days. Add priming sugar, and bottle or keg.

EXTRACT WITH GRAINS OPTION: Substitute the 2-row pale malt in the all-grain recipe with 7.75 pounds (3.5 kilograms) light dried malt extract. Place the crushed grain in a muslin bag. Steep in 6 gallons (23 liters) of water as the water warms to a boil. Remove grains from wort once the temperature reaches about 160°F (71°C). Remove your brewpot from the burner and add malt extract. Return to burner and boil for 60 minutes, adding hops at the times indicated. Follow the remaining portion of the all-grain recipe.

SURLY BREWING COMPANY
FURIOUS IPA

~~~~~~

(5 Gallons/19 L, all-grain) OG = 1.060 FG = 1.014
IBU = 99 SRM = 15 ABV = 6.2%

Surly brought big West Coast IPAs to the Midwest with Furious. As you can tell by the IBUs, it has a refreshingly bitter finish.

INGREDIENTS

8 lb. (3.6 kg) North American 2-row pale malt

3 lb. (1.4 kg) Bairds or Simpsons Golden Promise malt

10 oz. (0.28 kg) Belgian aromatic malt (25 °L)

12 oz. (0.34 kg) crystal malt (60 °L)

2 oz. (57 g) roasted barley (480 °L)

3 AAU Ahtanum pellet hops (first wort hop) (0.5 oz./14 g at 6% alpha acids)

24 AAU Warrior pellet hops (60 min.) (1.5 oz./43 g at 16% alpha acids)

9.6 AAU Warrior pellet hops (2 min.) (0.6 oz./17 g at 16% alpha acids)

3 AAU Ahtanum pellet hops (2 min.) (0.5 oz./14 g at 6% alpha acids)

5 AAU Amarillo pellet hops (2 min.) (0.5 oz./14 g at 10% alpha acids)

6.4 AAU Simcoe pellet hops (2 min.) (0.5 oz./14 g at 12.8% alpha acids)

0.5 oz. (14 g) Ahtanum whole leaf hops (dry hop)

0.5 oz. (14 g) Amarillo whole leaf hops (dry hop)

0.5 oz. (14 g) Simcoe whole leaf hops (dry hop)

0.2 oz. (6 g) Warrior whole leaf hops (dry hop)

½ tsp. Irish moss (30 min.)

½ tsp. yeast nutrient (15 min.)

Wyeast 1335 (British Ale II) or White Labs WLP007 (Dry English Ale) yeast

¾ cup (150 g) dextrose (if priming)

STEP BY STEP

Mix the crushed grains with 3.75 gallons (14 liters) of 170°F (77°C) water to stabilize at 153°F (67°C) for 60 minutes. Sparge slowly with 175°F (79°C) water, adding the first wort hops to the brewpot. Collect approximately 6 gallons (23 liters) of wort runoff to boil for 60 minutes. Add hops, Irish moss, and yeast nutrient at times indicated. After the boil is complete, give the wort a stir and let the wort settle for 5 minutes. Cool the wort to 75°F (24°C). Pitch your yeast and aerate the wort heavily. Allow the beer to cool to 68°F (20°C). Hold at that temperature until fermentation is complete. Transfer to a carboy, avoiding any splashing to prevent aerating the beer, and add the dry hops. Allow the beer to condition for 1 week and then bottle or keg.

EXTRACT WITH GRAINS OPTION: Reduce the Golden Promise malt in the all-grain recipe to 1.5 pounds (0.68 kilogram) and replace the 2-row pale malt with 6.6 pounds (3 kilograms) Muntons light unhopped liquid malt extract. Steep the crushed grain in 2 gallons (7.6 liters) of water at 153°F (67°C) for 30 minutes. Remove grains from the wort and rinse with 2 quarts (1.9 liters) of hot water. Add the liquid malt extract plus the first wort hop addition and boil for 60 minutes. Follow the remaining portion of the all-grain recipe.

TREE HOUSE BREWING COMPANY
JULIUS

cccccc

**(5 gallons/19 L, all-grain) OG = 1.061 FG = 1.014
IBU = 75 SRM = 8 ABV = 6.5%**

This New England–style IPA is clouded with yeast and resin from American hops. Fans love its mango, passion fruit, and citrus aroma.

INGREDIENTS

11 lb. (5 kg) UK pale ale malt

1 lb. (0.45 kg) oat malt

5 oz. (142 g) honey malt

5 oz. (142 g) Carapils malt

5 oz. (142 g) flaked oats

8 oz. (227 g) turbinado sugar (15 min.)

8 mL HopShot (60 min.)

2 oz. (57 g) Citra hops (hop stand)

2 oz. (57 g) Mosaic hops (hop stand)

1 oz. (28 g) Simcoe hops (hop stand)

2.5 oz. (71 g) Citra hops (dry hop)

2 oz. (57 g) Mosaic hops (dry hop)

1.5 oz. (43 g) Simcoe hops (dry hop)

Wyeast 1318 (London Ale III), White Labs WLP022 (Essex Ale), or Wyeast 1335 (British Ale II) yeast

¾ cup (150 g) dextrose (if priming)

STEP BY STEP

This recipe is designed for homebrewers to achieve 5.5 gallons (21 liters) wort in their fermenter on brew day. This will help offset the loss of volume to the heavy hopping rate of this beer. Build your water profile to achieve a 100:200 ppm sulfate:chloride profile. Crush the malt and add to 4.5 gallons (17 liters) strike water to achieve a stable mash temperature at 154°F (68°C). After 60 minutes, begin to lauter. Collect 7 gallons (26.5 liters) of wort in the kettle. Boil for 60 minutes, adding the hop extract after the wort comes to a boil and the turbinado sugar with 15 minutes left in the boil. After the boil, chill the wort down to 180°F (82°C) and then add the hop stand addition. Stir the wort, then let settle for 30 minutes before cooling to yeast pitching temperature. Ferment at 68°F (20°C). As the kräusen begins to fall, typically day 4 or 5, add the dry hops and spunding valve. Let the beer sit on the hops for 3 days. Bottle with priming sugar or keg and force carbonate to 2.4 volumes of CO_2.

EXTRACT WITH GRAINS OPTION: Substitute the pale ale malt in the all-grain recipe with 6 pounds (2.7 kilograms) extra light dried malt extract. Place the crushed malt in a muslin bag. Steep the grains in 1 gallon (4 liters) water at 154°F (68°C) for 45 minutes. Remove the grain bag and wash with 2 quarts (2 liters) of hot water. Top off the kettle to 6.5 gallons (25 liters), stir in the dried malt extract, and heat up to boil. Follow the remaining portion of the all-grain recipe.

TRILLIUM BREWING COMPANY
SLEEPER STREET

cccccc

**(5 gallons/19 L, all-grain) OG = 1.066 FG = 1.013
IBU = 75 SRM = 5 ABV = 7.2%**

Trillium brewers describe this nearly opaque IPA as having floral aromas with notes of lime zest, grapefruit peel, pine sap, and candied orange.

INGREDIENTS

11 lb. (5 kg) 2-row pale malt

1.5 lb. (0.68 kg) wheat malt

12 oz. (0.34 kg) dextrin malt

4 oz. (113 g) pale crystal malt (15 °L)

12 oz. (0.34 kg) dextrose sugar

14 AAU Columbus hops (60 min.) (1 oz./28 g at 14% alpha acids)

14 AAU Columbus hops (10 min.) (1 oz./28 g at 14% alpha acids)

2.5 oz. (71 g) Columbus hops (hop stand)

5 oz. (142 g) El Dorado hops (dry hop)

1.5 oz. (43 g) Columbus hops (dry hop)

½ Whirlfloc tablet (10 min.)

White Labs WLP007 (Dry English Ale), Wyeast 1098 (British Ale), or GigaYeast GY054 (Vermont IPA) yeast

¾ cup (150 g) dextrose (if priming)

STEP BY STEP

This recipe is designed for homebrewers to achieve 5.5 gallons (21 liters) wort in their fermenter on brew day. This will help offset the loss of volume to the heavy hopping rate of this beer. Build your water profile, starting with either very soft or RO water. Target a water profile of 200:100 ppm sulfate:chloride. Crush the malt and add to 4 gallons (15 liters) strike water to achieve a stable mash temperature at

150°F (65.5°C). After 60 minutes, begin to lauter. Boil for 60 minutes, adding the first hop addition after the wort comes to a boil and a second hop addition with 10 minutes left in the boil. After the boil, chill the wort to 180°F (82°C) and then add the hop stand addition. Stir the wort, then let settle for 30 minutes before cooling to yeast pitching temperature. Ferment at 68°F (20°C). As the kräusen begins to fall, typically day 4 or 5, transfer to a keg with the dry hops and add a spunding valve. Let the beer sit on the hops for 4 to 5 days, then transfer to a serving keg or bottling bucket. You may want to cold-crash the beer prior to the transfer by dropping the temperature of the beer to 35°F (2°C) for 24 hours. Bottle with priming sugar or force carbonate the serving keg to 2.4 volumes CO_2.

EXTRACT WITH GRAINS OPTION: Substitute the 2-row pale malt and wheat malt in the all-grain recipe with 6.6 pounds (3 kilograms) golden liquid malt extract and 2 pounds (0.91 kilogram) wheat dried malt extract, and reduce the dextrin malt addition to 4 ounces (113 grams). Place the crushed malt in a muslin bag. Steep the grains in 6 gallons (23 liters) water at 160°F (71°C) for 20 minutes. Remove the grain bag and wash with 2 quarts (2 liters) of hot water. Be sure to remove the wort from heat, then stir in the dried and liquid malt extracts. Stir until all the extract is dissolved, then return the wort to a boil. Boil for 60 minutes. Follow the remaining portion of the all-grain recipe.

Dogfish Head

Indian Brown

DARK IPA

Our boisterous brown ale meets well-hopped IPA is brewed with aromatic dark malt, organic brown sugar & dry-hopped liberally for your pleasure.

12 FL. OZ. | 7.2% ALC. BY VOL.

THREE

SPECIALTY IPAS

BEER PICTURED ON LEFT; SEE PAGE 46

THE ALCHEMIST
FOCAL BANGER
cccccc-

**(5 gallons/19 L, all-grain) OG = 1.063 FG = 1.012
IBU = 80 SRM = 5 ABV = 7%**

The Alchemist specializes in fresh, unfiltered IPAs. Focal Banger is reputed to change over the years, but the Citra/Mosaic hop combination has been a constant. However, if you can't track down the Pearl malt, pilsner malt has been known to be part of the grain bill for some formulations.

INGREDIENTS

12 lb. (5.4 kg) Thomas Fawcett Pearl malt

1.2 lb. (0.54 kg) corn sugar (15 min.)

4 mL HopShot (60 min.)

1.5 oz. (43 g) Citra hops (0 min.)

2.5 oz. (71 g) Mosaic hops (0 min.)

2.5 oz. (71 g) Citra hops (dry hop)

1.5 oz. (43 g) Mosaic hops (dry hop)

The Yeast Bay (Vermont Ale), GigaYeast GY054 (Vermont IPA), East Coast Yeast ECY29 (North East Ale), or Omega Yeast Labs (DIPA Ale) yeast

¾ cup (150 g) dextrose (if priming)

STEP BY STEP

This recipe is designed for homebrewers to achieve 5.5 gallons (21 liters) wort in their fermenter on brew day. This will help offset the loss of volume to the heavy hopping rate of this beer. Build your water profile, starting with either very soft water or RO water. Target a water profile of 250:100 ppm sulfate:chloride. Crush the malt and add to 4 gallons (15 liters) strike water to achieve a stable mash temperature at 154°F (68°C). Raise to mash out and begin to lauter. Boil for 60 minutes, adding the HopShot addition after the wort comes to a boil and the corn sugar with 15 minutes left in the boil. After you turn off the heat, add the final addition of hops, then stir the wort and let settle for 30 minutes with the lid on before cooling to yeast pitching temperature. Ferment at 68°F (20°C). As fermentation nears completion, transfer the beer to a keg, add the dry hops, and attach a spunding valve. Let the beer sit on the hops for 3 to 4 days, then transfer to a serving keg or bottling bucket. Bottle with priming sugar or force carbonate the serving keg to 2.4 volumes CO_2.

EXTRACT WITH GRAINS OPTION: Substitute the Thomas Fawcett Pearl malt in the all-grain recipe with 6.6 pounds (3 kilograms) Maris Otter liquid malt extract and 1.2 pounds

(0.54 kilogram) Pilsen dried malt extract. Heat 5 gallons (19 liters) soft or RO water up to boil. As soon as the water begins to boil, remove from heat and stir in the liquid and dried malt extracts. Stir until all the extract is dissolved then return the wort to a boil. Boil for 60 minutes. Follow the remaining portion of the all-grain recipe.

THE ALCHEMIST
HEADY TOPPER
cccccc-

**(5.5 gallons/21 L, all-grain) OG = 1.076 FG = 1.014
IBU = 100+ SRM = 6 ABV = 8%**

While every beer from the Alchemist has a tendency to sell out quickly, there's no doubt that Heady Topper is the brewery's crown jewel. Featuring a proprietary blend of six hops, this double IPA boasts a complex and unique bouquet of hop flavor without any astringent bitterness.

INGREDIENTS

15 lb. (6.8 kg) British 2-row pale malt

6 oz. (170 g) Caravienne malt

1 lb. (0.45 kg) turbinado sugar (10 min.)

7 AAU Magnum hops (60 min.) (0.5 oz./14 g at 14% alpha acids)

13 AAU Simcoe hops (30 min.) (1 oz./28 g at 13% alpha acids)

5.75 AAU Cascade hops (0 min.) (1 oz./28 g at 5.75% alpha acids)

8.6 AAU Apollo hops (0 min.) (0.5 oz./14 g at 17.2% alpha acids)

13 AAU Simcoe hops (0 min.) (1 oz./28 g at 13% alpha acids)

10.5 AAU Centennial hops (0 min.) (1 oz./28 g at 10.5% alpha acids)

7 AAU Columbus hops (0 min.) (0.5 oz./14 g at 14% alpha acids)

1 oz. (28 g) Chinook hops (primary dry hop)

1 oz. (28 g) Apollo hops (primary dry hop)

1 oz. (28 g) Simcoe hops (primary dry hop)

1.25 oz. (35 g) Centennial hops (secondary dry hop)

1.25 oz. (35 g) Simcoe hops (secondary dry hop)

1 tbsp. polyclar

The Yeast Bay (Vermont Ale), GigaYeast GY054 (Vermont IPA), East Coast Yeast ECY29 (North East Ale), White Labs WLP095 (Burlington Ale), or Omega Yeast Labs (DIPA Ale) yeast (as a 3 L yeast starter)

⅔ cup (130 g) dextrose (if priming)

STEP BY STEP

Mash the grains at 153°F (67°C). Mash out, vorlauf, and then sparge at 170°F (77°C). Collect at least 6.5 gallons (25 liters) of wort. Boil for 60 minutes, adding the hops as instructed. After the boil is complete, begin a whirlpool in the kettle and let the knockout hops rest in the hot wort for at least 30 minutes before chilling. Chill the wort, pitch the yeast, and ferment at 68°F (20°C) for 1 week. After final gravity has been achieved, add a clarifying agent such as polyclar. Three days later, add your first set of dry hops to the primary fermenter. After 7 days, rack the beer off the dry hops and yeast cake into a keg or secondary fermenter. Purge with carbon dioxide if available. Add the second set of dry hops to the keg or secondary fermenter. After 5 days, add the priming sugar, and bottle or keg.

EXTRACT WITH GRAINS OPTION: Substitute the British 2-row pale malt with 9.9 pounds (4.5 kilograms) light liquid malt extract and 1 pound (0.45 kilogram) extra light dried malt extract. Steep the crushed grains in 2 quarts (1.9 liters) water for 20 minutes at 155°F (68°C). Rinse the grain with hot water, and add water to achieve 6.5 gallons (25 liters) in your kettle. Turn off the heat, add the malt extract to your kettle, and stir until fully dissolved. Turn the heat back on and boil for 60 minutes, adding the hops as instructed. After the boil is complete, begin a whirlpool in the kettle and let the knockout hops rest in the hot wort for at least 30 minutes before chilling. Follow the remaining portion of the all-grain recipe.

- - - - - - - - - - - - - - - - - -

THE ALCHEMIST, NINKASI BREWING COMPANY, AND STONE BREWING COMPANY
MORE BROWN THAN BLACK IPA

❦❦❦❦❦❦

(5 gallons/19 L, all-grain) OG = 1.066 FG = 1.016
IBU = 100+ SRM = 19 ABV = 6.9%

This collaboration combines the expertise of three breweries all known for making excellent IPAs. With big aroma hops such as Nelson Sauvin, Galaxy, Citra, and Delta, expect a very interesting aroma with fruity, spicy, and herbal notes.

INGREDIENTS

12 lb. (5.4 kg) Maris Otter pale ale malt

1 lb. (0.45 kg) light Munich malt

5.6 oz. (159 g) Weyermann Carafa Special III malt (525 °L)

4.6 oz. (130 g) Weyermann Carahell malt (9 °L)

0.34 oz. (10 mL) CO_2 extracted hop extract (~100 IBUs)

1.9 oz. (55 g) Delta hops (0 min.)

1.9 oz. (55 g) Nelson Sauvin hops (0 min.)

1.9 oz. (55 g) Citra hops (dry hop)

1.9 oz. (55 g) Galaxy hops (dry hop)

White Labs WLP090 (San Diego Super) yeast (2.75 qts./2.75 L yeast starter)

¾ cup (150 g) dextrose (if priming)

STEP BY STEP

You will need 4.25 gallons (16 liters) of strike water. Infusion mash at 152°F (67°C) for 60 minutes, then raise temperature to 165°F (74°C) for mash out. Recirculate wort, then run off and sparge to yield about 6.5 gallons (25 liters) of wort. Use sparge water hot enough to maintain grain bed temperature at around 170°F (77°C) but not over. Boil wort for 90 minutes, adding hops at times indicated. Chill wort and transfer to fermenter. Aerate well and pitch sediment from yeast starter. Ferment at 68°F (20°C). At end of fermentation, dry hop and hold warm for 3 days, then chill to 34°F (1.1°C) and age for 1 week. Bottle or keg as usual.

EXTRACT WITH GRAINS OPTION: Substitute the pale and Munich malts in the all-grain recipe with 2.25 pounds (1 kilogram) light dried malt extract and 6 pounds (2.7 kilograms) Maris Otter liquid malt extract. Place grains in a steeping bag and steep at 152°F (67°C) for 20 minutes in 2.7 quarts (2.6 liters) of water. Begin heating at least 3 gallons (11 liters) of water in your brewpot as the grains steep. Rinse grains with 1.5 quarts (1.4 liters) of 170°F (77°C) water, and add "grain tea" to water in brewpot. Stir in dried malt extract and bring wort to a boil. Boil for 60 minutes, adding hops at times indicated. Stir in liquid malt extract during the final 15 minutes of the boil. Follow the remaining portion of the all-grain recipe.

TIPS FOR SUCCESS

If you are unable to source the hop extract in this recipe, try substituting any neutral high-alpha hop that will get you to about 100 theoretical IBUs—for example, 1.6 ounces (45 grams) of Summit hops, at 17.5 percent alpha acids (for 28 AAU total), boiled for 60 minutes. For this beer, adjust your water's chemistry to an appropriate residual alkalinity (RA) for the color and the right amount of sulfates (and sulfate-to-chloride ratio) for a bitter or very bitter beer. When brewing this beer, gypsum is your friend.

- - - - - - - - - - - - - - - - - -

BASE CAMP
BREWING COMPANY
IN-TENTS IPL

❮❮❮❮❮❮

(5 gallons/19 L, all-grain) OG = 1.066 FG = 1.014
IBU = 62 SRM = 9 ABV = 6.8%

This is a labor-intensive beer to produce, utilizing a triple batch sparge, kräusening, a 3-week bulk lagering period, and oak chip aging. The result is a malty and firmly hopped, oak-aged lager softened by natural carbonation. The lager yeast allows the piney and floral aromatics to shine while the oak chips heighten the maltiness of the brew.

INGREDIENTS

12.5 lb. (5.7 kg) Vienna malt

1 lb. (0.45 kg) Simpsons Golden Naked Oats malt

1 lb. (0.45 kg) melanoidin malt

17.5 AAU Summit pellet hops (60 min.) (1.15 oz./32 g at 15.2% alpha acids)

0.75 oz. (21 g) Nugget pellet hops (dry hop)

0.75 oz. (21 g) Mt. Hood pellet hops (dry hop)

0.75 oz. (21 g) Fuggle pellet hops (dry hop)

0.75 oz. (21 g) Centennial pellet hops (dry hop)

0.25 oz. (7 g) dark toasted American oak chips (added during dry hop)

½ tsp. yeast nutrients (15 min.)

1 Whirlfloc tablet (15 min.)

Kräusen beer (*see step by step*) 8 oz. (0.23 kilogram) pale dried malt extract

2.5 g Summit pellet hops

White Labs WLP802 (Czech Budejovice Lager) or Wyeast 2278 (Czech Pils) yeast

¾ cup (150 g) dextrose (if priming)

STEP BY STEP

Several days before your brew day, be sure to make a yeast starter. It is recommended that you pitch 468 billion yeast cells for this recipe. Mill the grains and mix with 3.9 gallons (14.7 liters) of 154°F (68°C) strike water to reach a mash temperature of 142°F (61°C). Hold at this temperature for 75 minutes. Step the mash (increase the temperature) to 158°F (70°C) and hold for an additional 15 minutes before performing an optional mash out at 168°F (76°C) for 10 minutes. Vorlauf until your runnings are clear. You will need 5.2 gallons (19.7 liters) of 170°F (77°C) sparge water. The sparge water is divided across a triple batch sparge as follows. Drain the mash tun then refill first with 1.6 gallons (6.1 liters). Drain the mash tun then refill a second time with 2.6 gallons (9.8 liters). Drain the mash tun again and add the final 1 gallon (3.8 liters) until 7 gallons (26.5 liters) of 1.050

SG wort is collected. Boil for 90 minutes, adding hops, yeast nutrient, and kettle finings according to the ingredients list. After the boil, turn off the heat and whirlpool the kettle by gently stirring for 2 minutes. Let rest for an additional 13 minutes. Chill the wort to 55°F (13°C), aerate, and pitch yeast. Ferment at 57°F (14°C) for 7 days, then lower to 45°F (7°C) and hold for 4 more days. Transfer the beer to a secondary vessel that contains the dry hops and oak chips. Harvest and store about 2 fluid ounces (60 milliliters) worth of yeast slurry from the primary fermenter yeast cake, and allow the beer to rise back up to 57°F (14°C) in the secondary fermenter. Make a small amount of kräusen beer by boiling 8 ounces (0.23 kilogram) of pale dried malt extract with 0.4 gallons (1.5 liters) of water for roughly 45 minutes, until you reduce it down to about 0.26 gallons (1 liters) of 1.068 specific gravity wort. Add 2.5 grams of Summit hops (15.2% alpha acids) at flameout, cool, and transfer to a growler (or small carboy). Pitch 2 fluid ounces (60 milliliters) worth of yeast slurry and add an airlock. When active fermentation is present, transfer the kräusen beer into the secondary vessel that your main batch is in. Hold the secondary vessel at 57°F (14°C) for 3 days after adding the kräusen beer, then slowly cool to lagering temperature (35 to 45°F/2 to 7°C), depending on activity levels of yeast strain. Lager for 3 weeks at this temperature. Bottle or keg as usual.

EXTRACT WITH GRAINS OPTION: Substitute the Vienna and melanoidin malts in the all-grain recipe with 8 pounds (3.6 kilograms) Briess Vienna liquid malt extract and 1 pound (0.45 kilogram) Weyermann CaraRed malt (20 °L). Steep grains in 2 gallons (7.5 liters) of 150°F (66°C) water for 20 to 30 minutes while you continue to heat the water up to no hotter than 170°F (77°C) to avoid extracting tannins. Remove the grain bag, top your kettle up with enough preheated water to reach a total pre-boil volume of 7 gallons (26.5 liters), and turn your heat source back on. Once you reach a boil, add your malt extract and hops according to the ingredients list during a 90-minute boil. Follow the remaining portion of the all-grain recipe.

TIPS FOR SUCCESS

Base Camp Brewing Company brewers recommend using extremely soft base water and adding 2 grams of gypsum ($CaSO_4$) plus 1 gram of calcium chloride to the mash for this recipe. This beer is very flexible with regards to base malt. Brewers are encouraged to substitute the listed Vienna malt for other darker pale malts, such as Maris Otter, Golden

Promise, ESB malt, etc. If you are an extract brewer, you can substitute with Maris Otter liquid malt extract.

BEND BREWING COMPANY
HOPHEAD

(5 gallons/19 L, all-grain) OG = 1.073 FG = 1.013 IBU = 100 SRM = 6 ABV = 8%

Bend Brewing's award-winning imperial IPA is available year-round on draft and in 22- ounce bottles, but with limited distribution. Now you can brew it fresh and enjoy the big aroma from Cascade hops anytime.

INGREDIENTS

14 lb. 10 oz. (6.6 kg) 2-row pale malt

8 oz. (0.23 kg) crystal malt (30 °L)

4.4 AAU Saaz hops (FWH) (1.1 oz./31 g at 4% alpha acids)

19 AAU Chinook hops (90 min.) (1.6 oz./44 g at 12% alpha acids)

1.8 oz. (51 g) Northern Brewer hops (5 min.)

1.8 oz. (51 g) Cascade hops (0 min.)

1.5 oz. (43 g) Cascade hops (dry hop)

Wyeast 1968 (London ESB Ale) or White Labs WLP002 (English Ale) yeast (2.5 qt./~2.5 L yeast starter)

¾ cup (150 g) dextrose (if priming)

STEP BY STEP

Mash the grains at 155°F (68°C) for 60 minutes. Vorlauf until your runnings are clear, sparge, and then boil the wort for 90 minutes. Add the hops at the times indicated in the ingredients list. After the boil, turn off the heat and add the 0-minute hops. Give the wort a stir to create a whirlpool and let stand for 15 minutes. Chill the wort rapidly to 68°F (20°C). Aerate the wort well and pitch the yeast. Ferment at 68°F (20°C). When fermentation has finished, add the dry hops and let sit for 3 to 7 days. Carbonate the beer to 2.5 volumes CO_2.

EXTRACT WITH GRAINS OPTION: Omit the 2-row pale malt and add 2.5 pounds (1.1 kilograms) light dried malt extract and 3.3 pounds (1.5 kilograms) light liquid malt extract (late addition). Place the crushed malts in a nylon steeping bag and steep in 3 quarts (2.8 liters) of water at 152°F (67°C) for 30 minutes. Rinse grains with 1.5 quarts (~1.5 liters) of water at 170°F (77°C). Add water to the brewpot to total 3 gallons (11 liters), stir in dried malt extract, and bring to a boil. Add the hops at the times indicated in the ingredients list. After the boil, cool the wort and top fermenter up to 5 gallons (19) with cool water. Add yeast, aerate, and ferment at 55 to 58°F (13 to 14°C). Follow the remaining portion of the all-grain recipe.

BOULEVARD
BREWING COMPANY
POP-UP
SESSION IPA

(5 gallons/19 L, all-grain) OG = 1.042 FG = 1.010 IBU = 41 SRM = 5 ABV = 4.2%

This easy-drinking hoppy ale has a balanced bitterness and aroma. The hops shine, but there's also a slight caramel malt character.

INGREDIENTS

8.25 lb. (3.7 kg) British pale ale malt

0.25 lb. (113 g) amber malt

4 AAU Australian Topaz pellet hops (60 min.) (0.25 oz./7 g at 16% alpha acids)

2.5 oz. (71 g) Cascade pellet hops (0 min.)

1.5 oz. (43 g) Citra pellet hops (0 min.)

1.5 oz. (43 g) Mosaic pellet hops (0 min.)

1 oz. (28 g) Amarillo pellet hops (dry hop)

1 oz. (28 g) Cascade pellet hops (dry hop)

0.25 oz. (7 g) Citra pellet hops (dry hop)

0.25 oz. (7 g) Centennial pellet hops (dry hop)

½ tsp. Irish moss (30 min.)

Wyeast 1098 (British Ale), White Labs WLP007 (Dry English Ale), Fermentis Safale S-04, Mangrove Jack's M07 (British Ale), or Lallemand Nottingham Ale Yeast

⅔ cup (133 g) dextrose (if priming)

STEP BY STEP

This is a single-infusion mash, mashing at 154°F to 156°F (68°C to 69°C) to create a fuller-bodied beer. Mix all the crushed grains with 3.5 gallons (13 liters) of 170°F (77°C) water and stabilize the mash at 156°F (68°C) for 60 minutes. Raise the mash temperature to 165°F (74°C) and sparge with enough 175°F (79°C) water to collect approximately 6 gallons (23 liters) of wort. Boil the wort for 60 minutes. Add the first hop addition of Topaz at the beginning of the boil and the Irish moss for the last 30 minutes. Turn off the burner and add the first Cascade, Mosaic, and Citra hop additions and stir. After about 3 to 4 minutes, use your wort chiller to drop the temperature of the wort to 170°F (77°C) and hold for 15 minutes. Then chill to yeast-pitching temperature. When you reach about 80°F (27°C), strain the wort into a fermenter. Aerate the wort and pitch the yeast. Ferment at 68°F (20°C). When fermentation is complete, rack the beer off the trub, add the dry hop additions, and dry hop for 4 days. Bottle or keg as usual.

EXTRACT WITH GRAINS OPTION: Substitute the British pale ale malt in the all-grain recipe with 3.3 pounds (1.5 kilograms) Briess light liquid malt extract and 2 pounds (0.9 kilogram) Briess light dried malt extract. Steep the crushed amber malt in 2.5 gallons (9.5 liters) of water at 155°F (68°C) for 30 minutes. Remove the grains from the wort and rinse as you top your brewpot up to 5.5 gallons (21 liters). Add the malt extracts and boil for 60 minutes. Follow the remaining portion of the all-grain recipe.

DOGFISH HEAD
CRAFT BREWERY
90 MINUTE IPA

**(5 gallons/19 L, all-grain) OG = 1.085 FG = 1.016
IBU = 90 SRM = 13 ABV = 9%**

While many think 60 Minute IPA (page 28) came first, 90 Minute IPA was the first beer that Dogfish Head brewed using their continuous hopping technique—adding hops throughout the boil. *Esquire* magazine has called this double IPA "perhaps the best IPA in America."

INGREDIENTS

16 lbs. (7.3 kg) 2-row pale malt

0.5 lbs. (0.68 kg) dark Munich malt (20 °L)

16 AAU Amarillo hops (90–0 min.) (2 oz./57 g at 8% alpha acids)

8 AAU Simcoe hops (90–0 min.) (0.62 oz./17 g at 13% alpha acids)

8 AAU Warrior hops (90–0 min.) (0.53 oz./15 g at 15% alpha acids)

1 oz. (28 g) Amarillo hops (dry hop)

0.5 oz. (14 g) Simcoe hops (dry hop)

0.5 oz. (14 g) Glacier hops (dry hop)

1 tsp. Irish moss (15 min.)

Wyeast 1187 (Ringwood Ale) or Fermentis Safale S-04 yeast

¾ cup (150 g) dextrose (if priming)

STEP BY STEP

Mash in at 122°F (50°C), then raise the temperature to 149°F (65°C) until conversion is complete. Mash out at

170°F (77°C). Boil the wort for 105 minutes. Starting with 90 minutes left in the boil, begin slowly and evenly adding hops to the kettle. (This works out to a little over 0.25 ounce (7 grams) of hops every 7.5 minutes.) Start fermentation at 71°F (22°C) and let rise to 74°F (23°C). Dry hop in secondary at 71°F for 3 to 5 days, then cool to 32°F (0°C). Bottle or keg as usual.

PARTIAL MASH OPTION: Reduce the 2-row pale malt in the all-grain recipe to 1.75 pounds (0.8 kilogram) and add 7.6 pounds (3.45 kilograms) extra light dried malt extract. Steep crushed grains in 1.1 gallons (4 liters) of water at 150°F (66°C) for 45 minutes, then remove grains and wash with 1 gallon (3.8 liters) of hot water. Top off the brewpot to 7 gallons (26.5 liters) and add all the dried malt extract. Boil the wort for 105 minutes. Starting with 90 minutes left in the boil, begin slowly and evenly adding hops to the kettle. (This works out to a little over 0.25 oz./7 g of hops every 7.5 minutes.) Start fermentation at 71°F (22°C) and let rise to 74°F (23°C). Dry hop in secondary at 71°F for 3 to 5 days, then cool to 32°F (0°C). Bottle or keg as usual.

DOGFISH HEAD
CRAFT BREWERY
INDIAN BROWN

**(5 gallons/19 L, all-grain) OG = 1.070 FG = 1.016
IBU = 50 SRM = 18 ABV = 7.2%**

This dark IPA is available year-round. It's actually dry hopped similarly to Dogfish Head's 60 Minute and 90 Minute IPAs. However, because it is roasty, it has a milder hop bitterness.

INGREDIENTS

10.75 lb. (4.88 kg) pilsner malt

15.2 oz. (0.43 kg) flaked maize

10.9 oz. (0.31 kg) amber malt

10.8 oz. (0.31 kg) crystal malt (60 °L)

6.5 oz. (0.18 kg) coffee malt

2.2 oz. (62 g) roasted barley

6 oz. (0.17 kg) dark brown sugar

11.5 AAU Warrior hops (60–10 min.) (0.72 oz./20 g at 16% alpha acids)

6 AAU Golding hops (10–0 min.) (1.2 oz./34 g at 5% alpha acids)

6 AAU Liberty hops (0 min.) (1.33 oz./38 g at 4.5% alpha acids)

1 oz. (28 g) Amarillo hops (dry hop)

0.5 oz. (14 g) Simcoe hops (dry hop)

0.5 oz. (14 g) Glacier hops (dry hop)

White Labs WLP005 (British Ale) or Wyeast 1187 (Ringwood Ale) yeast

¾ cup (150 g) dextrose (for priming)

STEP BY STEP

Mix half a cup of water to the brown sugar and slowly caramelize the sugar in a small pot. Be sure not to scorch. Mash the grains at 152°F (67°C) in 3.75 gallons (14 liters) of water. Vorlauf until your runnings are clear, sparge, add the caramelized sugar, and then boil the wort for 60 minutes. Begin hopping the wort with a continuous stream of Warrior hops. When you run out of Warrior hops, refill hopper with Golding hops and resume hopping until the end of the boil. Add the 0-minute hops after boil and stir wort to create a whirlpool. Allow wort to settle for 15 minutes then begin cooling. Aerate cooled wort and pitch yeast. Ferment at 70°F (21°C). Add the dry hops after final gravity is reached, and leave them in contact with the beer for 3 to 5 days. Bottle or keg as usual.

EXTRACT WITH GRAINS OPTION: Scale the pilsner malt down to 1 pound (0.45 kilogram). Add 1.25 pounds (0.57 kilogram) Muntons light dried malt extract and 5.25 pounds (2.3 kilograms) Muntons light liquid malt extract (late addition). Omit the flaked maize and add 15.2 ounces (0.43 kilogram) brewer's corn syrup. In your brewpot, add just enough water to the brown sugar to dissolve it. Heat to a boil and caramelize sugar (without scorching it). Then, add 4.3 quarts (4.1 liters) of water to your brewpot and heat to 163°F (73°C). Place the crushed grains in a steeping bag and steep grains at around 152°F (67°C) for 45 minutes. During the steep, heat 3.2 quarts (3.1 liters) of sparge water to 170°F (77°C) in a separate pot. After steep, rinse grains, add water to make at least 2.5 gallons (9.5 liters) of "grain tea" (wort), and bring to a boil. Add dried malt extract and corn syrup and boil for 60 minutes, adding hops as indicated in the all-grain recipe. Add liquid malt extract with 15 minutes left in boil. Cool wort and transfer to fermenter. Top up to 5 gallons (19 liters) with water, aerate, and pitch the yeast. Follow the remainder of the all-grain recipe.

FIRESTONE WALKER BREWING COMPANY
WOOKEY JACK

(5 gallons/19 L, all-grain) OG = 1.076 FG = 1.013
IBU = 75 SRM = 33 ABV = 8.3%

This black rye IPA was one of the originals in Firestone Walker's Proprietor's Reserve Series. It is now slated for only occasional appearances, either in original recipe form or in variations.

INGREDIENTS

13 lb. 3 oz. (6 kg) Rahr Standard 2-row malt

1 lb. 6 oz. (0.63 kg) rye malt

9 oz. (255 g) Weyermann CaraRye malt (70 °L)

6 oz. (170 g) caramel malt (80 °L)

6 oz. (170 g) Briess Midnight Wheat malt

6 oz. (170 g) Weyermann Carafa Special III malt

9.1 AAU German Magnum hops (60 min.) (0.8 oz./22 g at 11% alpha acids)

6.3 AAU Citra hops (30 min.) (0.4 oz./11 g at 15% alpha acids)

3.6 AAU Amarillo hops (30 min.) (0.4 oz./11 g at 9% alpha acids)

6.3 AAU Citra hops (10 min.) (0.4 oz./11 g at 15% alpha acids)

3.6 AAU Amarillo hops (10 min.) (0.4 oz./11 g at 9% alpha acids)

0.4 oz. (11 g) Citra hops (first dry hop)

0.4 oz. (11 g) Amarillo hops (first dry hop)

0.4 oz.(11 g) Citra hops (second dry hop)

0.4 oz. (11 g) Amarillo hops (second dry hop)

3.5 g calcium chloride (if using RO water)

3.5 g gypsum (if using RO water)

White Labs WLP002 (English Ale) or Wyeast 1968 (London ESB Ale) yeast

¾ cup (150 g) dextrose (if priming)

STEP BY STEP

Mill grains and mix with 6 gallons (23 liters) of 156°F (69°C) strike water and optional brewing salts to reach a mash temperature of 145°F (63°C). Hold this temperature for 15 minutes. Raise the temperature to 155°F (68°C) and hold for 30 minutes. Raise the temperature to a mash out of 168°F (75°C). Vorlauf until your runnings are clear. Sparge the grains with enough 168°F (75°C) water to collect 6 gallons (23 liters) of 1.063 SG wort. Boil for 60 minutes, adding hops according to the ingredients list. Turn off the heat and chill the wort to slightly below fermentation temperature, about 66°F (19°C). Aerate the wort with pure oxygen or filtered air and pitch the yeast. Ferment at 68°F (20°C). After 4 days of fermentation add the first dry hop addition. After 7 days fermentation add the second dry hop addition. Once at terminal gravity (approximately 10 days), bottle or keg the beer and carbonate.

PARTIAL MASH OPTION: Substitute the 2-row malt in the all-grain recipe with 7 pounds (3.2 kilograms) extra light dried malt extract. Place the milled rye malt in a muslin bag and steep in 4 quarts (3.8 liters) of 149°F (65°C) water for 45 minutes. Remove the grain and rinse with 1 gallon (3.8 liters) of hot water. Add the roasted and caramel malts in a second bag and steep for 15 minutes. Remove that grain bag, then add water to reach a volume of 5.4 gallons (20.4 liters) and heat to boiling. Turn off the heat, add the liquid malt extract and optional brewing salts, and stir until completely dissolved. Top up if necessary to obtain 6 gallons (23 liters) of 1.063 wort. Boil 60 minutes, and follow the remainder of the all-grain recipe.

FORTSIDE BREWING COMPANY
BLACK RYEPA

**(5 gallons/19 L, all-grain) OG = 1.076 FG = 1.020
IBU = 71 SRM = 35 ABV = 7.6%**

This black IPA is enhanced with two forms of rye malt. It pours a very dark brownish-black color with a billowing light tan head. Expect big tropical fruit and citrus rind aromas mixed with sweet brown sugar and subtle rye notes. The silky body creates a great mouthfeel that showcases the rye and roasted malts.

INGREDIENTS

12 lb. (5.4 kg) 2-row pale malt

2 lb. (0.9 kg) rye malt

1.5 lb. (0.7 kg) flaked rye

1 lb. (0.45 kg) wheat malt

1 lb. (0.45 kg) Munich malt (10 °L)

1 lb. (0.45 kg) black malt

14 AAU Columbus leaf hops (60 min.) (1 oz./28 g at 14% alpha acids)

8.5 AAU Amarillo leaf hops (30 min.) (1 oz./28 g at 8.5% alpha acids)

14 AAU Columbus leaf hops (5 min.) (1 oz./28 g at 14% alpha acids)

4.25 AAU Amarillo leaf hops (0 min.) (0.5 oz./14 g at 8.5% alpha acids)

10 AAU Centennial pellet hops (dry hop) (1 oz./28 g at 10% alpha acids)

White Labs WLP051 (California Ale V) or Wyeast 1272 (American Ale II) yeast

¾ cup (150 g) dextrose (if priming)

STEP BY STEP

This is a single-infusion mash. Mix the crushed grains with 5.8 gallons (22 liters) of water at 161°F (72°C), stabilizing at 150°F (66°C) for 60 minutes. Raise the temperature of the mash to 168°F (76°C) with approximately 3.7 gallons (14 liters) of 200°F (93°C) water, and then collect 7 gallons

(26.5 liters) of wort to begin your 60-minute boil. Add hops as indicated. At the end of the boil, you should have about 5.5 gallons (21 liters) wort in your kettle. Chill your wort, pitch your yeast when the temperature of the wort is less than 75°F (24°C), and allow it to cool to 68°F (20°C) for fermenting. Because this is a relatively high-gravity beer, make a yeast starter or use multiple packages of beer yeast. Dry hop with 1 ounce (28 grams) of Centennial pellets after about 4 days of fermentation. When fermentation is complete, wait about 3 more days for a diacetyl rest, and then bottle or keg your beer.

PARTIAL MASH OPTION: Reduce the 2-row pale malt in the all-grain recipe to 1 pound (0.45 kilogram) and add 6.6 pounds (3 kilograms) pale liquid malt extract and 0.5 pound (0.23 kilogram) light dried malt extract. Mash the crushed grains in 3 gallons (11.3 liters) of 150 to 160°F (66 to 71°C) water for 30 minutes, stirring the grain just prior to removing. Remove the grain from the hot water with a colander, then wash the grains with 1 gallon (4 liters) of hot water. Bring wort to a boil and add dried malt extract, stirring to dissolve. Boil for 60 minutes, adding hops at times indicated. At the end of the boil, turn off the heat and add the liquid malt extract, stirring until all malt is dissolved. Strain the hot wort into a fermenter filled with approximately 2.5 gallons (9.5 liters) of cold water and top off to 5.5 gallons (21 liters) mark. Follow the remaining portion of the all-grain recipe.

FOUNDATION BREWING COMPANY
EPIPHANY

**(5 gallons/19 L, all-grain) OG = 1.073 FG = 1.012
IBU = 85 SRM = 7 ABV = 8.1%**

Foundation Head Brewer and Co-Owner Joel Mahaffey says this beer delivers on the hallmarks of a Maine IPA: It has a soft body and a modest but solid malt backbone, low bitterness (though enough to avoid cloying sweetness), and a dominating hop flavor and aroma. The aroma is heavier on fruit, but it does have notes of pine and resin. The strength puts it in double IPA territory.

INGREDIENTS

7.25 lb. (3.3 kg) pilsner malt

5.5 lb. (2.5 kg) 2-row pale malt

2 lb. (0.91 kg) Simpsons Golden Naked Oats malt

- 1 lb. (0.45 kg) corn sugar (10 min.)
- 7.25 AAU Columbus hops (first wort hop) (0.5 oz./14 g at 14.5% alpha acids)
- 7 AAU Cascade hops (10 min.) (1 oz./28 g at 7% alpha acids)
- 14.5 AAU Columbus hops (10 min.) (1 oz./21 g at 14.5% alpha acids)
- 0.5 oz. (14 g) Columbus hops (0 min.)
- 0.5 oz. (14 g) Cascade hops (0 min.)
- 1 oz. (28 g) Citra hops (0 min.)
- 0.75 oz. (21 g) Mosaic hops (0 min.)
- 0.75 oz. (21 g) Ella hops (0 min.)
- 2 oz. (57 g) Citra hops (dry hop)
- 1 oz. (28 g) Mosaic hops (dry hop)
- 1 oz. (28 g) Ella hops (dry hop)
- Wyeast 1318 (London Ale III), White Labs WLP013 (London Ale), or Wyeast 1028 (London Ale) yeast
- ¾ cup (150 g) dextrose (if priming)

STEP BY STEP

This recipe is designed for homebrewers to achieve 5.5 gallons (21 liters) wort in their fermenter on brew day. This will help offset the loss of volume to the heavy hopping rate of this beer. Build your water profile to achieve a 100:100 ppm sulfate:chloride profile. Crush the malt and add to 5 gallons (19 liters) strike water to achieve a stable mash temperature at 154°F (68°C). After 60 minutes, begin to lauter. Collect approximately 7 gallons (26.5 liters) of wort in the kettle. Boil for 60 minutes, adding the first hop addition and corn sugar with 10 minutes left in the boil. After the boil, remove from heat then add the second hop addition. Stir the wort, then let settle for 30 minutes before cooling to yeast pitching temperature. Ferment at 68°F (20°C). As the kräusen begins to fall, typically day 4 or 5, add the dry hops and let the beer sit on the hops for 3 days. Bottle with priming sugar or keg and force carbonate to 2.4 volumes CO_2.

PARTIAL MASH OPTION: Substitute the pilsner and 2-row malts in the all-grain recipe with 4 pounds (1.8 kilograms) Pilsen dried malt extract and 3.3 pounds (1.5 kilograms) light liquid malt extract, and increase the corn sugar addition to 1.3 pounds (0.6 kilogram). Place the crushed malt in a large muslin bag. Soak the grains in 1.5 gallons (6 liters) water at 154°F (68°C) for 60 minutes. Remove the grain bag and wash with 2 quarts (2 liters) of hot water. Top off the kettle to 6 gallons (23 liters) and heat up to boil. As soon as the water begins to boil, remove from heat and stir in the dried and liquid malt extracts. Stir until all the extract is dissolved, then return the wort to a boil. Follow the remaining portion of the all-grain recipe.

GRUMPY TROLL BREW PUB
BELGIAN IPA

(5 gallons/19 L, all-grain) OG = 1.093 FG = 1.024 IBU = 44 SRM = 6 ABV = 9.2%

At close to 10 percent alcohol, this is a big double IPA. It's further set apart by its Belgian yeast, which the brewers use to add complexity to the hoppy aroma. The result is a unique yet satisfyingly drinkable brew.

INGREDIENTS

- 17 lb. (7.7 kg) Belgian pilsner malt
- 1 lb. (0.45 kg) clear Belgian candi sugar
- 8 oz. (0.23 kg) acidulated malt
- 5.5 AAU Target hops (80 min.) (0.5 oz./14 g at 11% alpha acids)
- 7.5 AAU Styrian Aurora hops (30 min.) (1 oz./28 g at 7.5% alpha acids)
- 14 AAU Columbus hops (3 min.) (1 oz./28 g at 14% alpha acids)
- 1 oz. (28 g) Cascade hops (0 min.)
- 1 oz. (28 g) Columbus hops (dry hop)
- 1 oz. (28 g) Cascade hops (dry hop)
- Wyeast 3522 (Belgian Ardennes) or White Labs WLP550 (Belgian Ale) yeast
- ¾ cup (150 g) dextrose (if priming)

STEP BY STEP

Mill the grains and mix with 5.5 gallons (20.7 liters) of 164°F (73°C) strike water to reach a mash temperature of 152°F (67°C). Hold this temperature for 60 minutes. Vorlauf until your runnings are clear and lauter into the kettle. Sparge the grains with 4 gallons (15 liters) and top up as necessary to obtain 6.5 gallons (25 liters) of wort. Add half of the Belgian candi sugar to the wort and boil for 90 minutes, adding hops according to the ingredient list. When the boil is complete, turn off heat and whirlpool for at least 5 minutes. Then chill to 65°F (18°C), aerate, and pitch yeast. Ferment at 66°F (19°C) for 7 days, adding the remaining Belgian candi sugar after 1 to 2 days. At 7 days, allow the beer to free rise to 80°F (27°C), add dry hops, and age for 7 more days. Once the beer reaches terminal gravity, bottle or keg the beer and carbonate to approximately 2.5 volumes. You may want to cold-crash the beer to 35°F (2°C) for 48 hours prior to packaging to improve clarity.

EXTRACT ONLY OPTION: Substitute all the grains in the all-grain recipe with 9.5 pounds (4.3 kilograms) Pilsen dried malt extract and 1 teaspoon lactic acid (88 percent solution). Bring 5.2 gallons (19.7 liters) of water to a boil. Remove from heat, then add dried malt extract and stir until completely dissolved. Add half of the Belgian candi sugar and lactic acid to the wort and boil for 60 minutes. Follow the remaining portion of the all-grain recipe.

TIPS FOR SUCCESS

Brewmaster Mark Knoebl notes that because Belgian yeast strains tend to scrub out a lot of kettle hop flavors and aromas, it's important to use a healthy dose of dry hops. Also, because this is a rather high-octane beer, it is important to manage your fermentation processes and temperatures to ensure full attenuation and minimize hot alcohols.

- - - - - - - - - - - - - - - - - -

HAIR OF THE DOG BREWING COMPANY
BLUE DOT DOUBLE IPA

cccccc

**(5 gallons/19 L, all-grain) OG = 1.072 FG = 1.010
IBU = 100+ SRM = 6 ABV = 8%**

Named for planet Earth and brewed in honor of Earth Day, this double IPA combines organic malts with a variety of intense hops. It packs lots of herbal, floral, citrus, grapefruit, raw honey, and fresh mint hop aromas.

INGREDIENTS

13.15 lb. (6 kg) organic pilsner malt

1.75 lb. (0.8 kg) organic flaked rye

64 AAU Warrior hops (75 min.) (4 oz./113 g at 16% alpha acids)

56 AAU Magnum hops (40 min.) (4 oz./113 g at 14% alpha acids)

48 AAU Columbus hops (10 min.) (4 oz./113 g at 12% alpha acids)

5 oz. (142 g) Warrior hops (dry hop)

5 oz. (142 g) Amarillo hops (dry hop)

Wyeast 1728 (Scottish Ale) or White Labs WLP028 (Edinburgh Scottish Ale) yeast (2 qt./2 L yeast starter)

¾ cup (150 g) dextrose (if priming)

STEP BY STEP

This is a single-infusion mash. Achieve a target mash temperature of 155°F (68°C). Mash out, vorlauf, and

then sparge at 170°F (77°C) to collect roughly 8 gallons (30 liters) of wort in your brewpot. Boil for a total of 180 minutes, adding the hops at the times indicated in the ingredient list. After the boil, cool, aerate, and ferment at 68°F (20°C). After fermentation is complete, dry hop for 5 to 7 days, and then bottle or keg.

PARTIAL MASH OPTION: Reduce the pilsner malt in the all-grain recipe to 2.25 pounds (1 kilogram) and add 2 pounds (0.91 kilogram) Briess organic light dried malt extract and 5 pounds (2.3 kilograms) Briess organic light liquid malt extract. Steep grains for 45 minutes at 155°F (68°C) in 5 quarts (4.7 liters) of water. Add dried malt extract to wort and bring wort volume to 6.5 gallons (25 liters) and boil for 90 minutes. Add hops as per ingredient list and liquid malt extract for final 15 minutes of boil. Follow the remaining portion of the all-grain recipe.

- - - - - - - - - - - - - - - - - -

HILL FARMSTEAD BREWERY
ABNER

cccccc

**(5.5 gallons/21 L, all-grain) OG = 1.075 FG = 1.014
IBU = 100+ SRM = 6 ABV = 8.2%**

Part of Hill Farmstead's Ancestral Series, Abner is a double IPA named for brewmaster Shaun Hill's great-grandfather, who once owned the land where the brewery now stands. Described as "aromatic and flowery, bursting with notes of citrus and pine," Abner is just one of the reasons why so many beer lovers make the pilgrimage to Vermont's Northeast Kingdom to visit the brewery each year.

INGREDIENTS

15 lb. (6.8 kg) 2-row pale malt

0.75 lb. (0.34 kg) caramalt (12°L)

1 lb. (0.45 kg) dextrose (10 min.)

15.5 AAU Warrior hops (60 min.) (1 oz./28 g at 15.5% alpha acids)

10.5 AAU Columbus hops (30 min.) (0.75 oz./21 g at 14% alpha acids)

13 AAU Simcoe hops (0 min.) (1 oz./28 g at 13% alpha acids)

10 AAU Centennial hops (0 min.) (1 oz./28 g at 10% alpha acids)

6.5 AAU Chinook hops (0 min.) (0.5 oz./14 g at 13% alpha acids)

7 AAU Columbus hops (0 min.) (0.5 oz./14 g at 14% alpha acids)

3 oz. (84 g) Centennial hops
(dry hop)

2 oz. (56 g) Simcoe hops
(dry hop)

Wyeast 1028 (London Ale), White
Labs WLP013 (London Ale),
or Lallemand Nottingham Ale
yeast (~2 L starter)

1 tbsp. polyclar

⅔ cup (130 g) dextrose
(if priming)

STEP BY STEP

Mash the grains at 149°F (65°C) for 45 minutes. Mash out, vorlauf, and then sparge at 170°F (77°C) to collect about 7 gallons (27 liters) of wort (the goal is to get 5.5 gallons (21 liters) into your fermenter). Boil for 75 minutes, adding the hops as instructed. After the boil is complete, begin a whirlpool in the kettle and let the knockout hops rest in the hot wort for at least 30 minutes before chilling. Pitch the yeast and ferment at 68°F (20°C) until the final gravity is reached, about 1 week. Add a fining agent to clear yeast from beer. Add the dry hops and let the beer sit on the dry hops for an additional 7 to 10 days. Bottle or keg as usual.

EXTRACT WITH GRAINS OPTION: Substitute 9.9 pounds (4.5 kilograms) light liquid malt extract and 0.5 pound (0.23 kilogram) extra light dried malt extract for the 2-row pale malt. Steep the crushed caramalt in 2 quarts (1.9 liters) water at 155°F (68°C) for 20 minutes. Top off kettle to 7 gallons (27 liters). Turn off the heat, add the liquid and dried malt extract, and bring to a boil. Boil for 75 minutes, adding the hops and corn sugar as instructed in the ingredients list. Follow the remaining portion of the all-grain recipe.

- - - - - - - - - - - - - - - - - - -

HOPWORKS
URBAN BREWERY
SECESSION
CASCADIAN
DARK ALE

ᙅᙅᙅᙅᙅᙅ

(5 gallons/19 L, all-grain) OG = 1.064 FG = 1.014
IBU = 70 SRM = 29 ABV = 6.8%

Hopworks is an "eco-brewpub" well known for their sustainability initiatives and IPAs. According to the brewery, this beer features an alliance of Northwest hop flavors "as formidable as the Cascade Mountain Range" with roasted malts "as dark as a moonless night."

INGREDIENTS

11.5 lb. (5.2 kg) pilsner malt

12 oz. (0.34 kg) crystal malt
(60 °L)

8 oz. (0.23 kg) black barley malt
(530 °L)

4 oz. (113 g) chocolate malt
(350 °L)

8.4 AAU Magnum hops (60 min.)
(0.6 oz./17 g at 14% alpha
acids)

6.5 AAU Mt. Hood hops (30 min.)
(1 oz./28 g at 6.5% alpha
acids)

3 AAU Amarillo hops (30 min.)
(0.3 oz./8.5 g at 10% alpha
acids)

3.8 AAU Simcoe hops (30 min.)
(0.3 oz./8.5 g at 12.8% alpha
acids)

0.75 oz. (21 g) Cascade hops
(0 min.)

0.4 oz. (11 g) Amarillo hops
(0 min.)

0.4 oz. (11 g) Simcoe hops
(0 min.)

0.5 oz. (14 g) Amarillo hops
(dry hop)

0.5 oz. (14 g) Cascade hops
(dry hop)

0.3 oz. (8.5 g) Simcoe hops
(dry hop)

½ tsp. yeast nutrient (15 min.)

½ tsp. Irish moss (30 min.)

White Labs WLP013 (London
Ale) or Wyeast 1318 (London
Ale III) yeast

¾ cup (150 g) dextrose
(if priming)

STEP BY STEP

This is a single-infusion mash. Mix the crushed grains with 17 quarts (16 liters) of 163°F (73°C) water to stabilize at 152°F (67°C) for 60 minutes. Sparge slowly with 170°F (77°C) water. Collect approximately 6.5 gallons (23 liters) of wort runoff to boil for a total of 90 minutes, adding hops and other ingredients as per the ingredient schedule. Cool the wort to 68°F (20°C). Pitch your yeast and aerate the wort heavily. Hold at that temperature until fermentation is complete. Transfer to a carboy, avoiding any splashing to prevent aerating the beer, and add the dry hops. Allow the beer to condition for 1 week, and then bottle or keg.

EXTRACT WITH GRAINS OPTION: Substitute the pilsner malt in the all-grain recipe with 6.6 pounds (3 kilograms) Pilsen liquid malt extract. Steep the crushed grain in 2 gallons (7.6 liters) of water at 152°F (67°C) for 30 minutes. Remove grains from the wort and rinse with 2 quarts (1.8 liters) of hot water. Add the dried malt extract and boil for 60 minutes. While boiling, add the hops, Irish moss, and yeast nutrient as per the schedule. With 15 minutes remaining in the boil add the liquid malt extract and stir until completely dissolved to avoid scorching the extract. After the boil is complete, add the wort to 2 gallons (7.6 liters) of cold water in the sanitized fermenter and top off with cold water up to 5 gallons (19 liters). Follow the remaining portion of the all-grain recipe.

- - - - - - - - - - - - - - - - - - -

ITHACA BEER COMPANY
IPABBEY

(5 gallons/19 L, all-grain) OG = 1.072 FG = 1.008
IBU = 76 SRM = 9 ABV = 8.3%

This unusual offering from Ithaca throws Saaz into the mix with the classic hop combination of Simcoe/Amarillo. Then the whole IPA gets a remix from the Abbey Ale yeast. This just might be what they'd serve at an Abbey that grew its own hops!

INGREDIENTS

8 lb. (3.6 kg) pilsner malt

4 lb. (1.8 kg) 2-row pale malt

0.4 lb. (0.18 kg) Gambrinus honey malt (if unavailable, substitute dark Munich malt)

1.6 lb. (0.72 kg) powdered dextrose (30 min.)

11.7 AAU Simcoe pellet hops (90 min.) (0.9 oz./26 g at 13% alpha acids)

6.6 AAU Amarillo pellet hops (90 min.) (0.9 oz./26 g at 7.3% alpha acids)

3.2 AAU Saaz pellet hops (90 min.) (0.9 oz./26 g at 3.5% alpha acids)

4.9 AAU Saaz pellet hops (10 min.) (1.4 oz./40 g at 3.5% alpha acids)

18.2 AAU Simcoe pellet hops (5 min.) (1.4 oz./40 g at 13% alpha acids)

10 AAU Amarillo pellet hops (0 min.) (1 oz./28 g at 10% alpha acids)

1 oz. (28 g) Simcoe whole leaf hops (dry hop)

1 oz. (28 g) Amarillo whole leaf hops (dry hop)

1 oz. (28 g) Saaz whole leaf hops (dry hop)

½ tsp. yeast nutrient (15 min.)

White Labs WLP530 (Abbey Ale), Wyeast 3787 (Trappist High Gravity), or Lallemand Abbaye Belgian Ale yeast

¾ cup (150 g) dextrose (if priming)

STEP BY STEP

This is a single-infusion mash. Mix the crushed grain with 4 gallons (15 liters) of 170°F (77°C) water to stabilize at 149°F (65°C) for 60 minutes. Sparge slowly with 175°F (79°C) water. Collect approximately 6.5 gallons (25 liters) of wort runoff to boil for 90 minutes. While boiling, add the hops, dextrose, and yeast nutrient as per the schedule. Cool the wort to 80°F (27°C). Pitch your yeast and aerate the wort heavily. Allow the beer to cool to 75°F (24°C). Hold at that temperature until fermentation is complete. Add the dry hops and let the beer condition for 1 week. Bottle or keg as usual.

EXTRACT WITH GRAINS OPTION: Substitute the pilsner and 2-row pale malts in the all-grain recipe with 6.6 pounds (3 kilograms) pilsner liquid malt extract and 1.6 pounds (0.73 kilogram) light dried malt extract. Steep the crushed grain in 2 quarts (1.8 liters) of water at 149°F (65°C) for 30 minutes. Remove grains from the wort and rinse with 2 quarts (1.8 liters) of hot water. Add the liquid and dry malt extracts, then top off the 3.5 gallons (13.2 liters) and bring to a boil. While boiling, add the hops, powdered dextrose, and yeast nutrient as per the schedule. After the boil, add the wort to 2 gallons (7.6 liters) of cold water in the fermenter and top off with cold water up to 5 gallons (19 liters). Follow the remaining portion of the all-grain recipe.

JACK'S ABBY BREWING
HOPONIUS UNION

(5 gallon/19 L, all-grain) OG = 1.063 FG = 1.012
IBU = 65 SRM = 6 ABV = 6.7%

Hoponius Union is an India Pale Lager that features a blend of popular American hops, creating a huge tropical fruit and citrusy hop aroma. A dry finish accentuates the pleasant bitterness and hop profile.

INGREDIENTS

10.5 lb. (4.5 kg) 2-row pale malt

1.6 lb. (0.73 kg) Munich malt (9 °L)

9 oz. (255 g) Weyermann CaraBelge malt (12 °L)

9 oz. (255 g) spelt berries

3.3 AAU Magnum pellet hops (60 min.) (0.25 oz./7 g at 13% alpha acids)

16.5 AAU Centennial pellet hops (5 min.) (1.5 oz./43 g at 11% alpha acids)

22 AAU Centennial pellet hops (0 min.) (2 oz./57 g at 11% alpha acids)

26 AAU Citra pellet hops (0 min.) (2 oz./57 g at 13% alpha acids)

1.5 oz. (43 g) Centennial pellet hops (dry hop)

1.5 oz. (43 g) Citra pellet hops (dry hop)

White Labs WLP830 (German Lager), Wyeast 2124 (Bohemian Lager), White Labs WLP029 (German Ale/Kölsch), or Wyeast 2565 (Kölsch) yeast

¾ cup (150 g) dextrose (if priming)

STEP BY STEP

Mash the grains at 148°F (64°C) for 90 minutes. Mash out, vorlauf, and then sparge at 168°F (76°C). Boil for 60 minutes, adding hops at the times indicated. At the end of the boil, remove from heat and add the 0-minute hops. Begin a whirlpool and let settle for about 20 minutes. At the end of the 20 minutes, cool the wort to yeast pitching temperature,

65°F (18°C) if using a Kölsch strain or 50°F (10°C) if using the lager strain. Pitch the yeast and ferment at 65°F (18°C) for the Kölsch strain and 50 to 55°F (10 to 12°C) for the lager strain. Dry hop at the same temperature and then lager at 32°F (0°C) for 3 weeks. Bottle or keg as usual.

PARTIAL MASH OPTION: Substitute 7 pounds (3.2 kilograms) golden light liquid malt extract for the 2-row malt and scale the Weyermann CaraBelge malt down to 8 ounces (227 grams). Place the crushed grains in a large nylon bag. Mix grains with 1 gallon of 158°F (70°C) water to achieve a stable mash temperature at 148°F (64°C) and hold for 60 minutes. Raise temperature of the mash, either by direct heat or adding boiling water to 168°F (76°C), and hold for 5 minutes. Remove the grain bag and place in a colander. Slowly pour 1 gallon (3.8 liters) of hot water over the grains. Add the liquid malt extract off heat, then add water in your brewpot until you have about 6 gallons (23 liters) of wort in your kettle, then bring up to a boil. Boil for 60 minutes. Follow remaining portion of all-grain recipe.

- - - - - - - - - - - - - - - - - -

LAWSON'S FINEST LIQUIDS
DOUBLE SUNSHINE IPA

(5 gallons/19 L, all-grain) OG = 1.074 FG = 1.013
IBU = 100+ SRM = 6 ABV = 8%

Double Sunshine is a sought-after Vermont-style double IPA. It's packed with juicy tropical fruit flavors and bright herbal aromas thanks to the abundance of US-grown Citra hops.

INGREDIENTS

9.5 lb. (4.3 kg) 2-row pale malt

2.5 lb. (1.1 kg) Vienna malt

1 lb. (0.45 kg) flaked oats

12 oz. (0.34 kg) Carapilsen malt (7–9 °L)

6 oz. (0.17 kg) Caramunich-type malt (20–30 °L)

1 lb. (0.45 kg) dextrose (10 min.)

10.5 AAU Columbus hops (60 min.) (0.75 oz./21 g at 14% alpha acids)

12.5 AAU Citra hops (20 min.) (1 oz./21 g at 12.5% alpha acids)

37.5 AAU Citra hops (5 min.) (3 oz./84 g at 12.5% alpha acids)

37.5 AAU Citra hops (knockout) (3 oz./84 g at 12.5% alpha acids)

3 oz. (84 g) Citra hops (dry hop)

Fermentis Safale US-05, Lallemand BRY-97, Wyeast 1056 (American Ale), or White Labs WLP001 (California Ale) yeast (as a 3.5 L yeast starter)

¾ cup (150 g) dextrose (for priming)

STEP BY STEP

A few days before brew day, make a yeast starter. You will need 254 billion healthy yeast cells. Mash at 152°F (67°C) for 45 minutes. Mash out, vorlauf, and then sparge at 170°F (77°C). Boil for 60 minutes, adding the hops as instructed and the dextrose with 10 minutes left in the boil. After the boil is complete, begin a whirlpool in the kettle and let the knockout hops rest in the hot wort for at least 30 minutes before chilling. Chill the wort, pitch the yeast, and ferment at 68°F (18°C) for 1 week. Cool to 55°F (13°C) to settle the yeast. Dump the yeast from the bottom of fermenter or rack to a clean, sanitized vessel. Add the dry hops and let the beer sit for an additional 4 to 7 days at 55 to 57°F (13 to 14°C). Bottle or keg as usual.

EXTRACT WITH GRAINS OPTION: Substitute the 2-row pale malt in the all-grain recipe with 6.6 pounds (3 kilograms) light liquid malt extract, skip the carapilsen malt, and boost the dextrose up to 1.5 pounds (0.68 kilogram) (versus 1 pound/0.45 kilogram in the all-grain recipe). Mix the crushed Vienna-style malt, flaked oats, and Caramunich-type malts into 2 gallons (7.6 liters) water to achieve a temperature of 152°F (67°C), then hold at this temperature for 45 minutes. Rinse the grains with 2.5 quarts (2.4 liters) of hot water, add the liquid extract, and bring to a boil. Top off the kettle to 6.5 gallons (25 liters). Boil for 60 minutes. Follow the remaining portion of the all-grain recipe.

- - - - - - - - - - - - - - - - - -

LAWSON'S FINEST LIQUIDS
SUPER SESSION IPA #2

(5 gallons/19 L, all-grain) OG = 1.050 FG = 1.017
IBU = 47 SRM = 5 ABV = 4.3%

Sean Lawson designed Super Session to be a hoppy, flavorful beer with low alcohol for those times when you are having more than one. With a big aroma from over a half-pound of hops per 5-gallon batch, this fits the bill.

INGREDIENTS

8.6 lb. (3.9 kg) 2-row pale ale malt

1 lb. (0.45 kg) Carapils malt

6 oz. (170 g) crystal malt (10°L)

6 oz. (170 g) Munich malt (10°L)

2.5 AAU Amarillo pellet hops (60 min.) (0.25 oz./7 g at 10% alpha acids)

5 oz. (142 g) Amarillo pellet hops
(0 min.)

3 oz. (85 g) Amarillo pellet hops
(dry hop)

½ tsp. Irish moss (30 min.)

Wyeast 1056 (American Ale),
White Labs WLP001 (California
Ale), Lallemand BRY-97,
Fermentis Safale US-05, or
Mangrove Jack's M44 (US
West Coast) yeast

⅔ cup (130 g) dextrose
(if priming)

STEP BY STEP

Mash the grains at 158°F (70°C) for 60 minutes. Raise the mash temperature to 165°F (74°C) and sparge with enough 175°F (79°C) water to collect approximately 6 gallons (23 liters) of wort. Boil the wort for 60 minutes. Add the first Amarillo hop addition at the beginning of the boil, primarily as a foam inhibitor. Add the Irish moss for the last 30 minutes. Turn off the burner at the end of the boil and remove the pot from the heat source (if you're brewing on an electric burner). Add 5 ounces (142 grams) of Amarillo hops and stir. After about 3 to 4 minutes, begin using your wort chiller to drop the temperature of the wort to pitching temperature. This addition is a bit tricky, but the goal is to have the large amount of hops in your wort for about 5 minutes after the wort has finished boiling but hasn't yet cooled to below approximately 150°F (66°C). This extracts a small amount of hop bitterness and a large amount of hop flavor. When you have cooled the wort to about 80°F (27°C), you can strain the wort into a fermenter. Aerate the wort and pitch the yeast. Ferment at 68 to 70°F (20 to 21°C) to help hold the aromatics in the beer. When fermentation is complete, rack the beer off the trub and add the remaining Amarillo dry hop addition. Allow the beer to absorb the dry hop flavors for about 4 days. Bottle or keg as usual.

EXTRACT WITH GRAINS OPTION: Substitute the 2-row pale ale malt with 3.3 pounds (1.5 kilograms) Briess light unhopped liquid malt extract and 2.1 pounds (0.95 kilogram) Briess light dried malt extract. Steep the crushed malts in 2.5 gallons (9.5 liters) of water at 155°F (68°C) for 30 minutes. Remove the grains from the wort. Add the malt extracts, stir well to incorporate, and boil for 60 minutes (see the all-grain recipe for notes on hop additions). Chill the wort, transfer to your fermenter, and top up with filtered water to 5 gallons (19 liters). Follow the remaining portion of the all-grain recipe.

LEFT HAND
BREWING COMPANY
TWIN SISTERS

**(5 gallons/19 L, all-grain) OG = 1.084 FG = 1.012
IBU = 80 SRM = 10 ABV = 9.6%**

This double IPA, named for Colorado's front range, contains approximately double the hops and double the malt of Left Hand's normal IPAs.

INGREDIENTS

15 lb. (6.8 kg) Castle pale ale malt

1.5 lb. (0.68 kg) rye malt

0.5 lb. (0.23 kg) flaked barley

0.5 lb. (0.23 kg) crystal rye malt (75 °L)

13.8 AAU Tomahawk hops (60 min.) (0.92 oz./26 g at 15% alpha acids)

7.5 AAU Glacier hops (45 min.) (0.63 oz./18 g at 12% alpha acids)

3.8 AAU Cascade hops (30 min.) (0.75 oz./21 g at 5% alpha acids)

11.3 AAU Glacier hops (5 min.) (0.94 oz./27 g at 12% alpha acids)

3 AAU Willamette hops (5 min.) (0.75 oz./21 g at 4% alpha acids)

1.25 oz. (35 g) Cascade hops (dry hop)

Wyeast 1272 (American Ale II) or White Labs WLP005 (California Ale V) yeast (3 qt./~3 L yeast starter)

¾ cup (150 g) dextrose (if priming)

STEP BY STEP

Mash at 152°F (67°C) for 45 minutes. Mash out, vorlauf, and then sparge at 170°F (77°C) to collect enough wort to result in 5 gallons (19 liters) after a 90-minute boil. Boil 90 minutes, adding hops at times indicated. Cool, aerate, and pitch yeast. Ferment at 68°F (20°C). Dry hop for 5 days just before bottling or kegging.

PARTIAL MASH OPTION: Reduce the pale ale malt in the all-grain recipe to 1.75 pounds (0.8 kilogram) and add 2 pounds (0.91 kilogram) Muntons light dried malt extract and 6.6 pounds (3 kilograms) Muntons light liquid malt extract. In your brewpot, heat 1.5 gallons (5.7 liters) of water to 163°F (73°C). Add crushed grains to a nylon steeping bag and steep for 45 minutes at 152°F (67°C). While grains are steeping, heat 1.5 quarts (1.4 liters) of sparge water to 170°F (77°C). After the grains are done steeping, put a colander over your brewpot and put the grain bag in it. Rinse grains with 170°F (77°C) sparge water. Add water to brewpot to make 5.5 gallons (21 liters). Bring "grain tea" and water to a boil and add dried and liquid malt extracts. Boil for 60 minutes, adding hops at times indicated in the ingredient list. Follow the remaining portion of the all-grain recipe.

- - - - - - - - - - - - - - - - - - -

MAINE BEER COMPANY
DINNER

«««««-

(5 gallons/19 L, all-grain) OG = 1.070 FG = 1.007
IBU = 92 SRM = 8 ABV = 8.2%

Maine Beer Company's iconic double IPA is all about the aroma: Citrus, grapefruit, tropical fruit, lemon, and pine keep drinkers coming back for seconds of Dinner.

INGREDIENTS

14 lb. (6.35 kg) 2-row pale malt

6 oz. (0.17 kg) dextrin malt

3 oz. (85 g) crystal malt (40 °L)

13 oz. (0.37 kg) dextrose sugar (15 min.)

8.3 AAU Falconer's Flight hops (30 min.) (0.75 oz./21 g at 11% alpha acids)

9.8 AAU Simcoe hops (30 min.) (0.75 oz./21 g at 13% alpha acids)

8.3 AAU Citra hops (5 min.) (0.75 oz./26 g at 11% alpha acids)

8.3 AAU Falconer's Flight hops (5 min.) (0.75 oz./21 g at 11% alpha acids)

9 AAU Mosaic hops (5 min.) (0.75 oz./21 g at 12% alpha acids)

22 AAU Citra hops (0 min.) (2 oz./57 g at 11% alpha acids)

2 oz. (57 g) Mosaic hops (dry hop)

2 oz. (57 g) Falconer's Flight hops (dry hop)

2 oz. (57 g) Simcoe hops (dry hop)

Wyeast 1056 (American Ale), White Labs WLP001 (California Ale), or Fermentis Safale US-05 yeast

¾ cup (150 g) dextrose (if priming)

STEP BY STEP

Mill the grains and mix with 4.8 gallons (18.2 liters) of 160°F (71°C) strike water to reach a mash temperature of 148°F (64°C). Hold this temperature for 60 minutes. Vorlauf until your runnings are clear. Sparge the grains with 3.6 gallons (11.7 liters) and top up as necessary to obtain 6.5 gallons (25 liters) of wort. Boil for 60 minutes, adding hops according to the ingredient list. After the boil, turn off heat and begin a whirlpool of the hot wort. Let stand for 20 minutes, then chill the wort to slightly below fermentation temperature, about 65°F (18°C). There should be 5.5 gallons (21 liters) of wort in your kettle. Aerate the wort with pure oxygen or filtered air and pitch yeast. Ferment at 67°F

(19°C) for 7 days. Add the dry hops and raise to 72°F (22°C) for 3 more days. Once the beer reaches terminal gravity, bottle or keg the beer and carbonate to approximately 2.5 volumes. You may want to cold-crash the beer to 35°F (2°C) for 48 hours prior to packaging to improve the clarity.

EXTRACT WITH GRAINS OPTION: Substitute the 2-row pale malt and dextrin malt in the all-grain recipe with 9 pounds (4.1 kilograms) extra light liquid malt extract. Bring 5.4 gallons (20 liters) of water to approximately 162°F (72°C) and steep milled specialty grains in grain bags for 15 minutes. Remove the grain bags, and let drain fully. Add liquid extract while stirring, and stir until completely dissolved. Boil for 60 minutes. Follow the remaining portion of the all-grain recipe.

TIPS FOR SUCCESS

Maine Beer Company keeps a tight hold on the "official" recipe for Dinner, which is only brewed in small batches and at not-quite-regular intervals. Their website states that they use 6 pounds (2.7 kilograms) of dry hops per barrel of Dinner. That translates to roughly 1 pound (0.45 kilogram) of dry hops per 5-gallon (19-liter) batch of beer. On a homebrew scale this could be detrimental to your beer. Oxidation and vegetal qualities from the hops are the main causes for concern. Consensus among the *BYO* staff was that 6 ounces (170 grams) would be better on a homebrew scale, but feel free to experiment by adding more. Needless to say, late and dry hopping is essential to Dinner's success. Maine Beer Company utilizes a hop-burst type technique for Dinner, so feel free to substitute your favorite hop-burst schedule here. Dry hop only after fermentation has completed. Three days with a free addition of pellets seems sufficient to mirror the hop aroma on Dinner; utilize 7 days if you are using whole leaf hops.

- - - - - - - - - - - - - - - - - - -

OAKSHIRE
BREWING COMPANY
O'DARK:30

«««««-

(5 gallons/19 L, all-grain) OG = 1.060 FG = 1.012
IBU = 70 SRM = 25 ABV = 6.4%

This black IPA from the Pacific Northwest boasts a rich malty backbone and a burst of Cascade and Centennial hops.

INGREDIENTS

10.5 lb. (4.8 kg) 2-row pale malt

1.5 lb. (0.68 kg) wheat malt

11 oz. (0.31 kg) Weyermann Carafa II malt (425 °L)

16.4 AAU Nugget pellet hops (60 min.) (1.4 oz./40 g at 11.7% alpha acids)

2.9 AAU Cascade pellet hops (15 min.) (0.5 oz./14 g at 5.75% alpha acids)

2.9 AAU Cascade pellet hops (0 min.) (0.5 oz./14 g at 5.75% alpha acids)

0.5 oz. (14 g) Centennial pellet hops (dry hop)

0.5 oz. (14 g) Cascade pellet hops (dry hop)

½ tsp. Irish moss (15 min.)

½ tsp. yeast nutrient (15 min.)

White Labs WLP001 (California Ale), Wyeast 1056 (American Ale), or Fermentis Safale US-05 yeast

¾ cup (150 g) dextrose (if priming)

STEP BY STEP

This is a single-infusion mash. Mix the crushed grains with 3.7 gallons (14 liters) of 172°F (78°C) water to stabilize at 153°F (67°C) for 60 minutes. Sparge slowly with 175°F (79°C) water. Collect approximately 6 gallons (23 liters) of wort runoff to boil for 60 minutes, adding hops at the times indicated. Cool the wort to 75°F (24°C). Pitch your yeast and aerate the wort heavily. Allow the beer to cool to 68°F (20°C). Hold at that temperature until fermentation is complete. Transfer to a carboy, avoiding any splashing to prevent aerating the beer, and add the dry hops. Allow the beer to condition for 1 week, and then bottle or keg.

PARTIAL MASH OPTION: Reduce the 2-row pale malt in the all-grain recipe to 1.5 pounds (0.68 kilogram) and add 6.6 pounds (3 kilograms) light liquid malt extract and 12 ounces (0.34 kilogram) light dried malt extract. Steep the crushed grain in 2 gallons (7.6 liters) of water at 153°F (67°C) for 30 minutes. Remove grains from the wort and rinse with 2 quarts (1.8 liters) of hot water. Add the malt extracts and boil for 60 minutes. Add the hops, Irish moss, and yeast nutrient as per the schedule. Now add the wort to 2 gallons (7.6 liters) of cold water and top off with cold water up to 5 gallons (19 liters). Follow the remaining portion of the all-grain recipe.

RIGHT BRAIN BREWERY
BLACK EYE PA

(5 gallons/19 L, all-grain) OG = 1.058 FG = 1.013
IBU = 55 SRM = 31 ABV = 6.2%

Right Brain's Black Eye PA was an early pioneer of the black IPA style. It is a traditional American IPA darkened with toasted malts for a bit of chocolate character.

INGREDIENTS

10.75 lb. (5.4 kg) 2-row pale malt

13.7 oz. (388 g) Briess Midnight Wheat malt

11.4 oz. (323 g) crystal malt (45 °L)

4.6 oz. (130 g) flaked oats

14 AAU Summit hops (60 min.) (0.78 oz./22 g at 14.2% alpha acids)

8.5 AAU Simcoe hops (30 min.) (0.68 oz./19 g at 12.3% alpha acids)

3.5 AAU Summit hops (15 min.) (0.25 oz./7 g at 14.2% alpha acids)

0.78 oz. (22 g) Simcoe hops (0 min.)

1.28 oz. (36 g) Simcoe hops (dry hop)

White Labs WLP001 (California Ale), Wyeast 1056 (American Ale), or Fermentis Safale US-05 yeast

¾ cup (150 g) dextrose (if priming)

STEP BY STEP

This is a single-infusion mash. Mix the crushed grains with 4 gallons (15.1 liters) of water at 162°F (72°C), stabilizing at 151°F (66°C) for 60 minutes. Raise the temperature of the mash to 168°F (76°C) and begin to lauter. Collect 6.5 gallons (24.6 liters) of wort to begin your 60-minute boil, adding hops at times indicated. After the boil is complete, rapidly chill your wort to 68°F (20°C) for fermenting, aerate the wort well, then pitch the yeast. Dry hop after primary fermentation is complete. Wait 3 to 5 days, then transfer the beer to a bottling bucket for priming and bottling, or transfer to a keg. Carbonate to approximately 2 volumes.

EXTRACT WITH GRAINS OPTION: Substitute the 2-row pale malt and flaked oats in the all-grain recipe with 5.75 pounds (2.6 kilograms) extra light dried malt extract. Steep crushed grains in 3 gallons (11.3 liters) of 150 to 160°F (66 to 71°C) water for 20 minutes, stirring the grain just prior to removing. Remove the grain from the hot water with a colander, then wash the grains with 1 gallon (4 liters) of hot water. Bring wort to a boil and add dried malt extract. Follow the remaining portion of the all-grain recipe.

ROCK ART BREWERY
LIMITED ACCESS

‹‹‹‹‹‹‹-

**(5 gallons/19 L, all-grain) OG = 1.070 FG = 1.013
IBU = 75 SRM = 7 ABV = 7.5%**

While Rock Art uses the clean American/California Ale strain in this beer, the unfiltered double IPA still has a glowing haze thanks to the huge late bursting of hops and a high dry hopping rate.

INGREDIENTS

13.5 lb. (6.12 kg) 2-row pale malt

1.1 lb. (500 g) wheat malt (40 °L)

12 oz. (340 g) Carapils malt

12 oz. (340 g) aromatic malt

1.3 AAU Chinook hops (first wort hop) (0.1 oz./3 g at 12.8% alpha acids)

4.6 AAU Chinook hops (20 min.) (0.35 oz./10 g at 12.8% alpha acids)

7.8 AAU Simcoe hops (10 min.) (0.6 oz./17 g at 13% alpha acids)

0.5 oz. (14 g) Citra hops (5 min.)

0.5 oz. (14 g) Simcoe hops (5 min.)

0.5 oz. (14 g) Galaxy hops (5 min.)

1 oz. (28 g) Citra hops (0 min.)

1 oz. (28 g) Simcoe hops (0 min.)

1 oz. (28 g) Galaxy hops (0 min.)

0.75 oz. (21 g) Citra hops (dry hop)

1 oz. (28 g) Galaxy hops (dry hop)

0.75 oz. (21 g) Cascade hops (dry hop)

0.75 oz. (21 g) Falconer's Flight hops (dry hop)

0.75 oz. (21 g) Simcoe hops (dry hop)

Wyeast 1056 (American Ale), White Labs WLP001 (California Ale), or Fermentis Safale US-05 yeast

¾ cup (150 g) dextrose (if priming)

STEP BY STEP

This recipe is designed to achieve 5.5 gallons (21 liters) wort in the fermenter on brew day. This will help offset the loss of volume to the heavy hopping rate of this beer. Build your water profile to achieve a 300:150 ppm sulfate:chloride profile. Mill the grains and mix with 5 gallons (19 liters) of 167°F (71°C) strike water to reach a mash temperature of 155°F (68°C), targeting a mash pH of 5.2. Hold this temperature for 60 minutes. Vorlauf until your runnings are clear. Sparge with enough water to obtain 7 gallons (25 liters) of wort, and add the first wort hops while the sparge is ongoing. Boil for 60 minutes, adding hops according to the ingredients list. After the boil, turn off heat and begin a whirlpool of the hot wort. Let stand for 20 minutes, then

chill the wort to 65°F (18°C). There should be 5.5 gallons (21 liters) of wort in your kettle. Aerate with pure oxygen or filtered air, and pitch yeast. Ferment at 67°F (19°C) for 7 days. Add the dry hops and raise to 72°F (22°C) for 3 more days. Once the beer reaches terminal gravity, bottle or keg and carbonate to approximately 2.5 volumes. You can cold-crash the beer to 35°F (2°C) for 48 hours prior to packaging to improve clarity.

PARTIAL MASH OPTION: Substitute the 2-row pale malt in the all-grain recipe with 9 pounds (4.1 kilograms) extra light liquid malt extract. Bring 1 gallon (4 liters) of water to approximately 155°F (68°C) and hold there. Place the milled grains in grain bags, and steep for 45 minutes. Remove the grain bags and place in a colander. Wash the grains with 1 gallon (4 liters) of hot water. Add liquid extract while stirring, and stir until dissolved, then top off to 7 gallons (26.5 liters). Boil for 60 minutes. Follow the remaining portion of the all-grain recipe.

RUSSIAN RIVER
BREWING COMPANY
PLINY THE ELDER

‹‹‹‹‹‹‹-

**(5 gallons/19 L, all-grain) OG = 1.074 FG = 1.014
IBU = 100+ SRM = 6 ABV = 8%**

Originally brewed to be part of a first-ever Double IPA festival in 2000, Pliny has become the standard by which many modern double IPAs are measured. As with any hop-heavy beer, Pliny is best enjoyed fresh, while the massive hop aroma is at its peak.

INGREDIENTS

12.8 lb. (5.8 kg) 2-row pale malt

0.28 lb. (0.13 kg) crystal malt (45 °L)

0.86 lb. (0.39 kg) Carapils malt

1 lb. (0.45 kg) dextrose

42.9 AAU Warrior hops (90 min.) (2.75 oz./78 g at 15.6% alpha acids)

6.1 AAU Chinook hops (90 min.) (0.5 oz./14 g at 12.2% alpha acids)

14.3 AAU Columbus hops (45 min.) (1 oz./28 g at 14.3% alpha acids)

12 AAU Simcoe hops (30 min.) 1 oz./28 g at 12% alpha acids)

20.5 AAU Centennial hops (0 min.) (2.25 oz./64 g at 9.1% alpha acids)

12 AAU Simcoe hops (0 min.) (1 oz./28 g at 12% alpha acids)

3.25 oz. (92 g) Columbus hops (dry hop)

1.75 oz. (50 g) Centennial hops (dry hop)

1.75 oz. (50 g) Simcoe hops (dry hop)

1 tsp. Irish moss (15 min.)

White Labs WLP001 (California Ale), Wyeast 1056 (American Ale), or Fermentis Safale US-05 yeast

¾ cup (150 g) dextrose (if priming)

STEP BY STEP

Mash the grains at 150 to 152°F (66 to 67°C). Hold this temperature for 60 minutes. Mash out, vorlauf, and sparge. Boil the wort for 90 minutes, adding hops at the time indicated in the ingredients list. Chill the wort and pitch the yeast. Ferment at 68°F (20°C). Dry hop 2 weeks after primary fermentation slows for 5 days. Bottle or keg as usual.

EXTRACT WITH GRAINS OPTION: Replace the 12.8 pounds (5.8 kilograms) 2-row pale malt with 6.7 pounds (3 kilograms) extra light dried malt extract. Steep the crushed grains in 1 gallon (3.8 liters) of water at 151°F (66°C) for 30 minutes. Rinse the grains with 2 quarts (2 liters) of 170°F (77°C) water. Top up the kettle to 5.5 gallons and stir in the dried malt extract. Follow the remaining portion of the all-grain recipe.

SAMUEL ADAMS BREWING COMPANY
DOUBLE AGENT IPL

‹‹‹‹‹‹‹-

**(5 gallons/19 L, all-grain) OG = 1.053 FG = 1.015
IBU = 43 SRM = 10 ABV = 5%**

Perhaps it's no surprise that a company that's known for their lager would put a lager twist on the IPA. Sam Adams's crack at it is impressive, with the hops shining bright thanks to the lager yeast.

INGREDIENTS

7.7 lb. (3.5 kg) 2-row pale malt (2 °L)

3.5 lb. (1.6 kg) Munich malt (10 °L)

6.3 AAU Zeus pellet hops (60 min.) (0.4 oz./11 g at 15.8% alpha acids)

1.4 AAU Citra pellet hops (15 min.) (0.1 oz./3 g at 13.7% alpha acids)

1.3 AAU Simcoe pellet hops (15 min.) (0.1 oz./3 g at 12.8% alpha acids)

1.9 AAU Ahtanum pellet hops (15 min.) (0.4 oz./11 g at 4.7% alpha acids)

3.8 AAU Simcoe pellet hops (5 min.) (0.3 oz./9 g at 12.8% alpha acids)

2.5 AAU Cascade pellet hops (5 min.) (0.4 oz./11 g at 6.3% alpha acids)

0.5 tsp. yeast nutrients (15 min.)

0.5 oz. (14 g) Centennial pellet hops (dry hop)

0.5 oz. (14 g) Simcoe pellet hops (dry hop)

0.5 oz. (14 g) Nelson Sauvin pellet hops (dry hop)

0.5 oz. (14 g) Cascade pellet hops (dry hop)

White Labs WLP830 (German Lager), Wyeast 2206 (Bavarian Lager) or Mangrove Jack's Bohemian Lager yeast (~4 qts./3.9 L starter, or 2 sachets dry yeast)

⅔ cup (133 g) dextrose (if priming)

STEP BY STEP

Mix the crushed grains with 4.5 gallons (17 liters) of 165°F (74°C) strike water to stabilize the mash at 153°F (67°C). Hold at this temperature for 45 minutes. Vorlauf for 15 minutes, then begin sparge. Run off into kettle to collect enough wort for a pre-boil gravity of 1.042 (about 6 gallons/23 liters). Boil for 60 minutes. Add hops and yeast nutrients according to the ingredients list. Turn off the heat, stir the wort for a minute to create a whirlpool, and let settle for 15 minutes. Cool the wort to around 53 to 55°F (12 to 13°C), aerate, and pitch yeast. Ferment at 57°F (14°C) for 2 weeks or until signs of fermentation slow down. Rack to a secondary, and lager for 3 weeks at 40°F (5°C). Add the dry hops for the final week of the lagering phase. If signs of diacetyl are apparent during racking, a diacetyl rest is recommended. Give the beer 2 days at 70°F (21°C) to allow the yeast to process any diacetyl before racking over to the secondary vessel. After the lager period is complete, bottle or keg and carbonate to 2.4 volumes of CO_2.

EXTRACT ONLY OPTION: Substitute both of the malts in the all-grain recipe with 3.3 pounds (1.5 kilograms) light liquid malt extract, 3.3 pounds (1.5 kilograms) Munich liquid malt extract, and 0.7 pound (0.32 kilogram) extra light dried malt extract. Heat 6 gallons (23 liters) soft water in your brew kettle. If you have hard water (>150 ppm calcium carbonate), you can soften by boiling the water for half an hour and decanting off the precipitated chalk or by cutting your tap water with distilled or RO water. Just before the water reaches boil, remove from heat and stir in the malt extract until all extract is dissolved. Boil for 60 minutes. Follow the remaining portion of the all-grain recipe.

SIERRA NEVADA BREWING COMPANY
TORPEDO EXTRA IPA

ecccccc-

(5 gallons/19 L, all-grain) OG = 1.070 FG = 1.015
IBU = 70 SRM = 8 ABV = 7.2%

Sierra Nevada designed this beer to showcase their innovative "hop torpedo," a dry hopping device that controls how much hop aroma is imparted into the beer without adding additional bitterness. It has a citrus, pine, and tropical fruit hop profile.

INGREDIENTS

14 lb. (6.4 kg) pale malt

11 oz. (0.31 kg) caramel malt (60 °L)

17 AAU Magnum leaf hops (60 min.) (1.2 oz./34 g at 14% alpha acids)

14 AAU Magnum leaf hops (5 min.) (1 oz./28 g at 14% alpha acids)

4.6 AAU Crystal leaf hops (5 min.) (1 oz./28 g at 4.6% alpha acids)

0.67 oz. (19 g) Magnum leaf hops (dry hop)

0.67 oz. (19 g) Crystal leaf hops (dry hop)

0.67 oz. (19 g) Citra leaf hops (dry hop)

1 tsp. Irish moss (15 min.)

Wyeast 1056 (American Ale), White Labs WLP001 (California Ale), or Fermentis Safale US-05 yeast

¾ cup (150 g) dextrose (if priming)

STEP BY STEP

Mash the grains at 152°F (67°C) for 60 minutes. Mash out, vorlauf, and then sparge at 170°F (77°C) to collect enough wort to result in 5 gallons (19 liters) after a 90-minute boil. Boil 90 minutes, adding hops at times indicated. Cool, aerate, and pitch yeast. Ferment at 68°F (20°C). When fermentation slows, dry hop for 10 to 14 days or use a CO_2-flushed closed dry hop recirculation system for 4 to 24 hours to add hop character. Bottle or keg as usual.

EXTRACT WITH GRAINS OPTION: Substitute the pale malt in the all-grain recipe with 5 pounds (2.3 kilograms) extra light dried malt extract and 3.3 pounds (1.5 kilograms) light liquid malt extract. Steep crushed grains in 6 gallons (23 liters) of water at 152°F (67°C) for 45 minutes. Bring to a boil and stir in dried malt extract and liquid malt extract. Boil 90 minutes. Follow the remaining portion of the all-grain recipe.

SMUTTYNOSE BREWING COMPANY
FRANKENLAGER

ecccccc-

(5 gallons/19 L, all-grain) OG = 1.060 FG = 1.015
IBU = 61 SRM = 4 ABV = 6.1%

Frankenlager is Smuttynose's interpretation of what would happen if an IPA were decoction-mashed and fermented like the classic lagers of Europe. It's crisp and refined, but certainly not meek or mild.

INGREDIENTS

12.5 lb. (5.7 kg) US 2-row pale malt

50 AAU German Magnum pellet hops (60 min.) (1 oz./28 g at 14% alpha acids)

1.8 AAU Saphir pellet hops (20 min.) (0.5 oz./14 g at 3.5% alpha acids)

3.4 AAU Saphir pellet hops (10 min.) (0.75 oz./21 g at 3.5% alpha acids)

3.5 AAU Saphir pellet hops (0 min.) (1 oz./28 g at 3.5% alpha acids)

5 oz. (140 g) Saphir pellet hops (dry hop)

½ tsp. yeast nutrient (15 min.)

½ Whirlfloc tablet (15 min.)

White Labs WLP920 (Old Bavarian Lager) or White Labs WLP833 (German Bock Lager) yeast

⅔ cup (133 g) dextrose (if priming)

STEP BY STEP

This is either single or double decoction mash, so build in some extra time in your brew day to account for the added steps. Mill the grains and mix with 4.7 gallons (17.8 liters) of 158°F (70°C) strike water to reach a mash temperature of 147°F (64°C). Hold at this temperature for 40 minutes. Remove 1 gallon (3.8 liters) of the grist and bring it to a boil (decoction), then add it back to the mash tun. This should step the mash up to 162°F (72°C) where you hold again for 20 minutes. Direct fire (or double decoct) up to 170°F (77°C) and hold for 10 minutes if you wish to perform a mash out. Vorlauf until your runnings are clear. Sparge the grains with approximately 3.5 gallons (13.25 liters) of 170°F (77°C) water until 6.5 gallons (24.6 liters) of 1.046 SG wort is collected in your boil kettle. Boil for 60 minutes, adding hops, yeast nutrient, and kettle finings according to the ingredients list. After the boil, create a whirlpool by gently stirring with a mash paddle for 2 minutes, and then let rest for an additional 13 minutes. Chill the wort to 50°F (10°C), aerate, and pitch yeast. It is recommended that you pitch 424 billion yeast cells, which can be obtained by using either 1 fresh vial after making a 2.3-liter stir plate starter, 2 fresh vials after making a 4.35-liter non-stir plate starter, or 5 fresh vials without a starter.

Ferment at 50°F (10°C) until you reach terminal gravity. Add dry hops and dry hop at 50°F (10°C) for 1 week. Crash cool for 2 days, and then package. Carbonate to between 2.4 and 2.5 volumes of CO_2.

EXTRACT ONLY OPTION: Substitute the 2-row pale malt in the all-grain recipe with 8.5 pounds (3.9 kilograms) golden light liquid malt extract. Bring 6.5 gallons (24.6 liters) of water up to a boil. Remove from heat, and add your malt extract and stir until fully dissolved. Return to a boil for 60 minutes. Follow the remaining portion of the all-grain recipe.

THREE FLOYDS BREWING COMPANY
DREADNAUGHT

**(5 gallons/19 L, all-grain) OG = 1.084 FG = 1.014
IBU = 100+ SRM = 11 ABV = 9.3%**

This unforgettable imperial IPA features an intense citrus hop aroma and a huge malt body. The hops and yeast selection set it apart from many of the big New England–style IPAs.

INGREDIENTS

16.25 lb. (7.4 kg) American 2-row pale malt

1.25 lb. (0.57 kg) Melanoidin malt (27 °L)

8 AAU Warrior hops (60 min.) (0.53 oz./15 g at 15% alpha acids)

8 AAU Simcoe hops (60 min.) (0.62 oz./17 g at 13% alpha acids)

8 AAU Centennial hops (45 min.) (0.72 oz./20 g at 11% alpha acids)

8 AAU Centennial hops (30 min.) (0.72 oz./20 g at 11% alpha acids)

8 AAU Cascade hops (0 min.) (1.6 oz./45 g at 5% alpha acids)

1.5 oz. (43 g) Cascade whole hops (dry hop)

0.75 oz. (21 g) Simcoe hops (dry hop)

0.75 oz. (21 g) Centennial hops (dry hops)

1 tsp. Irish moss (15 min.)

Wyeast 1056 (American Ale), White Labs WLP001 (California Ale), or Safale US-05 yeast

¾ cup (150 g) dextrose (if priming)

STEP BY STEP

Mash the grains at 159°F (71°C) for 60 minutes. Mash out, vorlauf, and then sparge at 170°F (77°C) to collect enough wort to result in 5 gallons (19 liters) after a 90-minute boil. Boil the wort 90 minutes, adding hops at the times indicated in the ingredient list. After the boil, cool, aerate, and pitch yeast. Ferment at 68°F (20°C). Add dry hops after fermentation slows for 4 to 7 days. Bottle or keg as usual.

PARTIAL MASH OPTION: Reduce the 2-row pale malt in the all-grain recipe to 1.33 pounds (0.6 kilogram) and add 8 pounds (3.6 kilograms) extra light dried malt extract. Steep crushed grains in 3.2 quarts (3 liters) of water at 159°F (71°C) for 45 minutes. Wash the grains with 1 gallon (4 liters) of hot water. Top off brewpot to 6.5 gallons (25.6 liters). Boil the wort 60 minutes, adding hops at the times indicated. Follow the remaining portion of the all-grain recipe.

URBAN FAMILY BREWING COMPANY
LIMESICLE

**(5 gallons/19 L, all-grain) OG = 1.074 FG = 1.020
IBU = 14 SRM = 4 ABV = 7.2%**

This is a "milkshake" IPA using lactose and lime zest. Head brewer Isaac Koski says the dry hop addition in this beer rotates among citrusy hop varieties, including Citra, Simcoe, and Motueka: "These are interchangeable in my mind based on availability and how they are smelling."

INGREDIENTS

11 lb. (5 kg) 2-row pale malt

2.5 lb. (1.13 kg) flaked oats

1 lb. (0.45 kg) rice hulls

4 oz. (113 g) acidulated malt

1.75 lb. (0.79 kg) lactose powder

4.75 AAU Centennial hops (60 min.) (0.5 oz./14 g at 9.5% alpha acids)

4 oz. (113 g) Citra hops (dry hop)

1–2 limes, zested

1 vanilla bean, split and chopped

White Labs WLP002 (English Ale) or Wyeast 1968 (London ESB Ale) or substitute favorite English strain

¾ cup (150 g) dextrose (if priming)

STEP BY STEP

Mash in with a standard mash at 1.25 quarts/pound (2.6 L/ kilograms) at 155°F (68°C) until fully converted, about 60 minutes. Sparge with enough water to collect 6.5 gallons (24.6 liters) of wort in the kettle. Boil 60 minutes, adding sole hop addition at the beginning of the boil. Add the lactose powder to the boil at any point. Chill, then ferment at 67°F (19°C) with your favorite English ale strain. On brew day, zest the lime and chop the vanilla bean. Add vodka to bowl to just cover the zest and bean, then cover with plastic wrap. Let soak in vodka during active fermentation. Dry hop in secondary with a citrus-forward hops such as Citra, but you can substitute in Simcoe, Motueka, or another favorite citrusy hop. Add tincture of lime zest and vanilla bean at the same time as the dry hop addition. After achieving the desired dry hop character, cold-crash and package.

PARTIAL MASH OPTION: Reduce the 2-row pale malt in the all-grain recipe to 2.5 pounds (1.13 kilograms) and add 4.75 pounds (2.2 kilograms) extra light dried malt extract. The rice hulls are not needed in partial mash brewing. Place crushed malt in a muslin bag. Mash the grains in 6.6 quarts (6.2 liters) water at 155°F (68°C) until fully converted, about 60 minutes. Remove grain bag, place in a large colander, and wash with 2 quarts (2 liters) of hot water. Top off the kettle to 5 gallons (19 liters) and raise to a boil. Upon reaching a boil, remove kettle from heat and stir in the dried malt extract and the lactose, stirring vigorously until fully dissolved. Once dissolved, return kettle to a boil and add hops. Boil for 60 minutes. Follow the remaining portion of the all-grain recipe.

- - - - - - - - - - - - - - - -

WIDMER BROTHERS BREWING
PITCH BLACK IPA

**(5 gallons/19 L, all-grain) OG = 1.064 FG = 1.014
IBU = 65 SRM = 26 ABV = 6.8%**

This dark IPA from Widmer is meant as a winter treat; it is available from January through April. It pours a bright black color and backs it up with notes of chocolate. The dry hop is on the tame side, with just a bit of Cascade and Warrior for complexity.

INGREDIENTS

- 10.5 lb. (4.8 kg) 2-row pale malt
- 1.5 lb. (0.68 kg) caramel malt (10 °L)
- 12 oz. (0.34 kg) Weyermann Carafa Special II (dehusked) malt (450 °L)
- 10 oz. (0.28 kg) Briess special roast malt (50 °L)
- 16 AAU Warrior hops (75 min.) (1 oz./28 g at 16% alpha acids)
- 1.5 AAU Cascade hops (2 min.) (0.25 oz./7 g at 5.8% alpha acids)
- 12 AAU Warrior hops (2 min.) (0.75 oz./21 g at 16% alpha acids)
- 0.25 oz. (7 g) Warrior hops (dry hop)
- 0.5 oz. (14 g) Cascade hops (dry hop)
- ½ tsp. Irish moss (30 min.)
- ½ tsp. yeast nutrient (15 min.)
- White Labs WLP001 (California Ale), Wyeast 1056 (American Ale), or Fermentis Safale US-05 yeast
- ¾ cup (150 g) dextrose (if priming)

STEP BY STEP

This is a single-infusion mash. Mix the crushed grains with 4 gallons (15 liters) of 161°F (72°C) water to stabilize at 150°F (66°C) for 60 minutes. Sparge slowly with 170°F (77°C) water. Collect approximately 6.5 gallons (25 liters) of wort runoff to boil for 75 minutes. While boiling, add the hops, Irish moss, and yeast nutrient as per the schedule. Cool the wort to 75°F (24°C). Pitch your yeast and aerate the wort heavily. Allow the beer to cool to 68°F (20°C). Hold at that temperature until fermentation is complete. Transfer to a carboy and add the dry hops. Allow the beer to condition for 1 week, and then bottle or keg.

EXTRACT WITH GRAINS OPTION: Substitute the 2-row pale malt in the all-grain recipe with 7.75 pounds (3.5 kilograms) Briess light liquid malt extract. Steep the crushed grains in 2 gallons (7.6 liters) of water at 150°F (66°C) for 30 minutes. Remove grains from the wort and rinse with 2 quarts (1.8 liters) of hot water. Add the liquid malt extract, and boil for 75 minutes. Follow the remaining portion of the all-grain recipe.

- - - - - - - - - - - - - - - -

AMBER ALES & LAGERS

BEER PICTURED ON LEFT; SEE PAGE 66

ALASKAN BREWING COMPANY
AMBER

⟨⟨⟨⟨⟨⟨-

**(5 gallons/19 L, all-grain) OG = 1.054 FG = 1.015
IBU = 18 SRM = 15 ABV = 5.1%**

A classic amber, this beer is richly malty and long on the palate with just enough hop backing. It undergoes a cool, slow fermentation to help condition the flavors, contributing to its overall balance and smoothness.

INGREDIENTS

9.5 lb. (4.3 kg) pale ale malt

1 lb. (0.45 kg) crystal malt (40 °L)

0.66 lb. (0.3 kg) crystal malt (60 °L)

0.33 lb. (0.14 kg) crystal malt (90 °L)

3.3 AAU Cascade hops (60 min.) (0.66 oz./18 g at 5% alpha acids)

3.33 AAU Saaz hops (15 min.) (1.1 oz./31 g at 3% alpha acids)

1 tsp. Irish moss (15 min.)

Wyeast 1007 (German Ale) or White Labs WLP029 (German Ale/Kölsch) yeast (1.5 qt./ ~1.5 L yeast starter)

¾ cup (150 g) dextrose (if priming)

STEP BY STEP

Mash the grains in 14 quarts (13 liters) of water at 152°F (67°C). Mash out, vorlauf, and then sparge at 170°F (77°C) to collect 6 gallons (23 liters) of wort. Add 2 quarts (1.9 liters) of water and boil 90 minutes, adding hops and Irish moss at times indicated. Cool, aerate, and pitch yeast. Ferment at 68°F (20°C). After fermentation is complete, bottle or keg as usual.

EXTRACT WITH GRAINS OPTION: Replace the pale ale malt in the all-grain recipe and add 2.5 pounds (1.13 kilograms) light dried malt extract and 3.3 pounds (1.5 kilograms) light liquid malt extract. Bring 5.5 gallons (21 liters) of water to approximately 162°F (72°C) and hold there. Steep grains for 15 minutes, then remove bag and allow to drain into the wort. Add malt extracts while stirring and stir until completely dissolved. Boil for 60 minutes. Follow the remaining portion of the all-grain recipe.

CAMBRIDGE BREWING COMPANY
CAMBRIDGE AMBER

⟨⟨⟨⟨⟨⟨-

**(5 gallons/19 L, all-grain) OG = 1.048 FG = 1.012
IBU = 24 SRM = 14 ABV = 4.7%**

Medium-bodied, with a deep amber-red color, this beer's complex palate covers all the bases. A malty caramel sweetness is followed by notes of chocolate and a dry, slightly roasty finish, complemented by a touch of fruity, spicy hops.

INGREDIENTS

8.5 lb. (3.9 kg) 2-row pale malt

1 lb. (0.45 kg) British crystal malt (45 °L)

0.5 lb. (0.23 kg) US crystal malt (40 °L)

1.33 oz. (37 g) chocolate malt

0.66 oz. (16 g) black patent malt

1 tsp. Irish moss

4.5 AAU Willamette hops (60 min.) (1 oz./28 g at 4.5% alpha acids)

2.25 AAU Willamette hops (45 min.) (0.5 oz./14 g at 4.5% alpha acids)

4.7 AAU Yakima Golding hops (0 min.) (1 oz./28 g at 4.7% alpha acids)

2.25 AAU Willamette hops (0 min.) (0.5 oz./14 g at 4.5% alpha acids)

1 tsp. Irish moss (15 min.)

White Labs WLP001 (California Ale) or Wyeast 1056 (American Ale) yeast

¾ cup (150 g) dextrose (if priming)

STEP BY STEP

Mash all the crushed grains for 60 minutes at 152°F (67°C). Vorlauf until your runnings are clear, sparge, and then boil the wort for 60 minutes, adding hops and Irish moss as directed in the ingredients list. After the boil, turn off the heat and chill the wort rapidly to 68°F (20°C). Aerate the wort well and pitch the yeast. Ferment at 68°F (20°C). When the beer has reached final gravity, bottle or keg as normal.

EXTRACT WITH GRAINS OPTION: Omit the 2-row pale malt. Replace with 3.3 pounds (1.5 kilograms) Coopers light liquid malt extract and 1.85 pounds (0.84 kilogram) Coopers light dried malt extract. Steep the crushed grains in 3 gallons (11 liters) water at 152°F (67°C) for 30 minutes. Remove grains from wort, add the malt extracts, and bring to a boil. Boil for 60 minutes. Add the hops at the times indicated in the ingredients list. Now cool the wort, transfer to a sanitary fermenter, and top off with cool water to 5.5 gallons (21 liters). Aerate the wort and pitch your yeast. Follow the remainder of the all-grain recipe.

EPIC BREWING COMPANY
IMPERIAL RED ALE

**(5 gallons/19 L, all-grain) OG = 1.072 FG = 1.014
IBU = 52 SRM = 21 ABV = 7.7%**

This bold double red ale features a big American hop profile and a sweet caramel maltiness. It's especially big among ambers, packing an ABV close to 8 percent!

INGREDIENTS

9 lb. (4.1 kg) Maris Otter 2-row pale malt

4.2 lb. (1.9 kg) Briess 2-row pale malt

17 oz. (0.48 kg) crystal malt (60 °L)

17 oz. (0.48 kg) Weyermann Caramunich III malt (55 °L)

7 oz. (0.19 kg) Weyermann CaraAroma malt (130 °L)

2 oz. (56 g) roasted barley (450 °L)

10.5 AAU Columbus pellet hops (60 min.) (0.75 oz./21 g at 14.2% alpha acids)

3.25 AAU Mt. Hood pellet hops (40 min.) (0.5 oz./14 g at 6.5% alpha acids)

1.44 AAU Cascade pellet hops (10 min.) (0.25 oz./7 g at 5.75% alpha acids)

5.25 AAU Centennial pellet hops (0 min.) (0.5 oz./14 g at 10.5% alpha acids)

1 oz. (28 g) Centennial pellet hops (dry hop)

½ tsp. Irish moss (last 30 min.)

½ tsp. yeast nutrient (last 15 min.)

White Labs WLP001 (California Ale), Wyeast 1056 (American Ale), or Fermentis Safale US-05 yeast

¾ cup (150 g) dextrose (if priming)

STEP BY STEP

This is a single-infusion mash. Mix all the crushed grains with 6 gallons (23 liters) of 173°F (78°C) water to stabilize at 152°F (67°C) for 60 minutes. Sparge slowly with 175°F (79°C) water. Collect approximately 6 gallons (23 liters) of wort runoff to boil for 60 minutes. Add hops, Irish moss, and yeast nutrient as indicated. Cool the wort to 75°F (24°C). Pitch your yeast and aerate the wort heavily. Allow the beer to cool to 68°F (20°C). Hold at that temperature until fermentation is complete. Transfer to a carboy, avoiding any

splashing to prevent aerating the beer. Add the dry hops and allow the beer to condition for 1 week, and then bottle or keg.

PARTIAL MASH OPTION: Substitute the two varieties of 2-row pale malts in the all-grain recipe with 6.6 pounds (3 kilograms) Muntons Maris Otter light liquid malt extract, 1 pound 6 ounces (0.62 kilogram) light dried malt extract, and 1 pound (0.45 kilogram) Briess 2-row pale malt. Steep the crushed grain in 2 gallons (7.6 liters) of water at 152°F (66°C) for 30 minutes. Remove grains from the wort and rinse with 2 quarts (1.8 liters) of hot water. Add the liquid and dried malt extracts, and boil for 60 minutes. While boiling, add the hops, Irish moss, and yeast nutrient as per the schedule. Now add the wort to 2 gallons (7.6 liters) of cold water in the sanitized fermenter, and top off with cold water up to 5 gallons (19 liters). Follow the remaining portion of the all-grain recipe.

FULL SAIL
BREWING COMPANY
AMBER ALE

**(5 gallons/19 L, all-grain) OG = 1.057 FG = 1.014
IBU = 31 SRM = 16 ABV = 6%**

Full Sail's flagship Amber Ale has earned the brewery multiple awards, including more than 20 gold medals in brewing competitions. It is a sweet, malty, medium-bodied ale with a spicy, floral hop finish. If you're looking to start with a classic, look no further.

INGREDIENTS

10.5 lb. (4.8 kg) 2-row pale malt

1.5 lb. (0.68 kg) crystal malt (60 °L)

2 oz. (57 g) chocolate malt

3.3 AAU Mt. Hood hops (45 min.) (0.66 oz./19 g at 5% alpha acids)

3.3 AAU Cascade hops (45 min.) (0.66 oz./19 g at 5% alpha acids)

1 oz. (28 g) Mt. Hood hops (10 min.)

1 oz. (28 g) Cascade hops (10 min.)

1 tsp. Irish moss (15 min.)

Wyeast 1028 (London Ale), Wyeast 1318 (London Ale III), White Labs WLP013 (London Ale), or WLP023 (Burton Ale) yeast

¾ cup (150 g) dextrose (if priming)

STEP BY STEP

Mash grains for at least 45 minutes at 150°F (66°C). Sparge as normal and collect enough wort for a 60-minute boil. Boil wort for 60 minutes, adding the hops and Irish moss at times indicated in the ingredients list. After the boil, chill the wort to pitching temperature, aerate well, and pitch the yeast. Ferment at 68°F (20°C). Bottle or keg as usual.

PARTIAL MASH OPTION: Replace 2-row pale malt with 1.5 pounds (0.68 kilogram) Muntons light dried malt extract, 4 pounds 2 ounces (1.9 kilograms) Alexander's pale liquid malt extract, and 1 pound (0.45 kilogram) 2-row pale malt. Steep the grains at 150°F (66°C) in 4.75 quarts (~4.5 liters) of water for 45 minutes. Add water to make 3 gallons (11 liters), add the dried malt extract, and boil for 60 minutes, adding the hops and Irish moss at the times indicated in the ingredients list. Add liquid malt extract with 15 minutes left in boil. After the boil, chill the wort to pitching temperature, aerate well, and pitch the yeast. Follow the remainder of the all-grain recipe.

- - - - - - - - - - - - - - - - - -

MILLSTREAM BREWING COMPANY
SCHILD BRAU AMBER

≪≪≪≪≪≪≫

**(5 Gallons/19 L, all-grain) OG = 1.054 FG = 1.015
IBU = 16 SRM = 11 ABV = 5%**

This Vienna lager is Millstream's flagship brew, and it mimics the classic German style. It features a balanced malty sweetness and a firm bitterness. Try brewing it after you brew an amber ale to really home in on the different character of lager yeast.

INGREDIENTS

8.5 lb. (3.85 kg) 2-row pale malt	1.6 AAU Mt. Hood pellet hops (30 min.) (0.25 oz./7 g at 6.5% alpha acids)
1.5 lb. (0.68 kg) Vienna malt	
14 oz. (0.39 kg) Munich malt (20 °L)	½ tsp. yeast nutrient (15 min.)
	½ tsp. Irish moss (30 min.)
14 oz. (0.39 kg) crystal malt (60 °L)	White Labs WLP830 (German Lager) or Wyeast 2206 (Bavarian Lager) yeast
2.6 AAU Magnum pellet hops (60 min.) (0.2 oz./5.7 g at 12.8% alpha acids)	¾ cup (150 g) dextrose (if priming)

STEP BY STEP

This is a single-infusion mash. Mix the crushed grains with 4 gallons (15 liters) of 170°F (77°C) water to stabilize at 152°F (67°C) for 60 minutes. Sparge slowly with 175°F (79°C) water. Collect approximately 6 gallons (23 liters) of wort runoff to boil for 60 minutes. While boiling, add the hops, Irish moss, and yeast nutrient as per the schedule. Cool the wort to 75°F (24°C). Pitch your yeast and aerate the wort. Allow the beer to cool over the next few hours to 65°F (19°C). When evidence of fermentation is apparent, drop the temperature to 52°F (11°C). Hold at that temperature until fermentation is complete (approximately 10 days). Transfer to a carboy, avoiding any splashing to prevent aerating the beer. Condition for 2 weeks at 42°F (5°C) and then bottle or keg. Allow to carbonate and age for 4 weeks.

EXTRACT WITH GRAINS OPTION: Substitute the 2-row pale malt in the all-grain recipe with 3.3 pounds (1.5 kilograms) Muntons light liquid malt extract and 1.75 pounds (0.79 kilogram) light dried malt extract. Steep the crushed grain in 2.5 gallons (9.5 liters) of water at 152°F (67°C) for 30 minutes. Remove grains from the wort and rinse with 2 quarts (1.8 liters) of hot water. Add the malt extracts and boil for 60 minutes. While boiling, add the hops, Irish moss, and yeast nutrient as per the schedule. After the boil is complete, add the wort to 2 gallons (7.6 liters) of cold water in a sanitized fermenter and top off with cold water up to 5 gallons (19 liters). Cool the wort to 75°F (24°C). Pitch your yeast and aerate the wort. Follow the remaining portion of the all-grain recipe.

- - - - - - - - - - - - - - - - - -

NEW BELGIUM BREWING COMPANY
FAT TIRE

≪≪≪≪≪≪≫

**(5 gallons/19 L, all-grain) OG = 1.050 FG = 1.013
IBU = 19 SRM = 14 ABV = 4.7%**

True, there are older amber beer recipes out there, but perhaps none is more iconic than New Belgium's Fat Tire. Whether you're enjoying one after a long bike ride or a long day of work, it's the perfect thirst-quenching beer for those who demand more taste than a macro lager can deliver.

INGREDIENTS

8 lb. 10 oz. (3.9 kg) pale malt

1 lb. (0.45 kg) Munich malt

6 oz. (0.17 kg) Victory malt

8 oz. (0.23 kg) crystal malt (80 °L)

4.4 AAU Nugget hops (60 min.) (0.4 oz./11 g at 11% alpha acids)

2.5 AAU Willamette hops (10 min.) (0.5 oz./14 g at 5% alpha acids)

0.5 oz. (14 g) Golding hops (0 min.)

Wyeast 1792 (Fat Tire Ale), Wyeast 1272 (American Ale II), or White Labs WLP051 (California Ale V) yeast

¾ cup (150 g) dextrose (if priming)

STEP BY STEP

Mash the grains at 154°F (68°C) in 13 quarts (12 liters) of water for 45 minutes. Mash out, vorlauf, and then sparge at 170°F (77°C) to collect 6 gallons (23 liters) of wort. Add 0.5 gallon (1.9 liters) of water and boil for 60 minutes, adding the hops at the times indicated in ingredient list. Add the Irish moss with 15 minutes left in the boil. Pitch the yeast and ferment at 68°F (20°C) until final gravity is reached (7 to 10 days). Bottle or keg with dextrose. (Try lowering the amount of priming sugar to mimic the low carbonation level of Fat Tire.) Lay the beer down for at least a few months to mellow and mature for best results.

EXTRACT WITH GRAINS OPTION: Omit the 2-row pale malt and instead use 2 pounds 3 ounces (1 kilogram) Coopers light dried malt extract and 3.3 pounds (1.5 kilograms) Coopers light liquid malt extract (late addition). Place the crushed malts in a nylon steeping bag and steep in 3 quarts (2.8 liters) of water at 154°F (68°C) for 30 minutes. Rinse the grains with 1.5 quarts (about 1.5 liters) of water at 170°F (77°C). Add water to make 3 gallons (11 liters), stir in the dried malt extract, and bring to a boil. Boil for 60 minutes, adding the hops at the times indicated in ingredient list. Add the liquid malt extract and Irish moss with 15 minutes left in the boil. Chill the wort, transfer to your fermenter, and top up with filtered water to 5 gallons (19 liters). Follow the remaining portion of the all-grain recipe.

NINKASI BREWING COMPANY
RACIN' MASON IRISH RED ALE

◄◄◄◄◄◄

(5 gallons/19 L, all-grain) OG = 1.052 FG = 1.014 IBU = 40 SRM = 17 ABV = 5.1%

On the darker side for this chapter, Ninkasi's classic Irish red has a seductive dark red/copper color. It delivers plenty of flavor as well, with a sweet caramel and toasted malt profile.

INGREDIENTS

10 lb. (4.5 kg) 2-row pale malt

8 oz. (0.22 kg) Carapils malt

8 oz. (0.22 kg) crystal malt (40 °L)

8 oz. (0.22 kg) crystal malt (75 °L)

3 oz. (85 g) biscuit malt

2 oz. (57 g) chocolate malt (350 °L)

1 oz. (28 g) black malt (600 °L)

7.1 AAU East Kent Golding pellet hops (60 min.) (1.5 oz./43 g at 4.75% alpha acids)

3.6 AAU Fuggle pellet hops (30 min.) (0.75 oz./21 g at 4.75% alpha acids)

4.13 AAU Perle pellet hops (0 min.) (0.5 oz./14 g at 8.25% alpha acids)

½ tsp. yeast nutrient (15 min.)

½ tsp. Irish moss (30 min.)

White Labs WLP002 (English Ale) or Wyeast 1968 (London ESB Ale) yeast

¾ cup (150 g) dextrose (if priming)

STEP BY STEP

This is a single-infusion mash. Mix the crushed grains with 3.7 gallons (14 liters) of 170°F (77°C) water to stabilize at 150°F (66°C) for 60 minutes. Sparge slowly with 175°F (79°C) water. Collect approximately 6 gallons (23 liters) of wort runoff to boil for 60 minutes. While boiling, add the hops, Irish moss, and yeast nutrient. After the boil is complete, add the wort to 2 gallons (7.6 liters) of cold water in the sanitized fermenter and top off with cold water up to 5 gallons (19 liters). Follow the remaining portion of the all-grain recipe.

PARTIAL MASH OPTION: Reduce the 2-row pale malt from the all-grain version to 1 pound (0.45 kilogram) and add 3.3 pounds (1.5 kilograms) Briess light liquid malt extract and 2 pounds (0.9 kilogram) light dried malt extract. Steep the crushed grain in 2 gallons (7.6 liters) of water at 150°F (66°C) for 30 minutes. Remove grains from the wort and rinse with 2 quarts (1.8 liters) of hot water. Add the liquid

and dried malt extracts and boil for 60 minutes. While boiling, add the hops, Irish moss, and yeast nutrient. After the boil is complete, add the wort to 2 gallons (7.6 liters) of cold water in the sanitized fermenter and top off with cold water up to 5 gallons (19 liters). Follow the remaining portion of the all-grain recipe.

SANTAN BREWING COMPANY
EPICENTER ALE

**(5 gallons/19 L, all-grain) OG = 1.056 FG = 1.014
IBU = 21 SRM = 14 ABV = 5.7%**

Described by the brewery as a "gateway ale" for those new to craft beer, this amber ale is still plenty interesting. It has an enjoyable toasted malt character and a crisp dry finish.

INGREDIENTS

9 lb. (4.1 kg) 2-row pale malt

13 oz. (0.37 kg) caramel malt (80 °L)

8 oz. (0.23 kg) Munich malt (20 °L)

8 oz. (0.23 kg) wheat malt

8 oz. (0.23 kg) Victory malt

8 oz. (0.23 kg) Vienna malt

1 oz. (28 g) roasted barley

5 AAU Fuggle hops (60 min.) (1 oz./28 g at 5% alpha acids)

1 Whirlfloc tablet (10 min.)

White Labs WLP001 (California Ale), Wyeast 1056 (American Ale), or Fermentis Safale US-05 yeast (as a 1.5 qt./1.5 L yeast starter)

¾ cup (150 g) dextrose (if priming)

STEP BY STEP

Mash the grains at 152°F (67°C) in 16 quarts (15 liters) of water and hold for 60 minutes. Mash out, vorlauf, and then sparge at 170°F (77°C) to collect 7 gallons (26.5 liters) of wort. Boil wort for 90 minutes, adding hops and Whirlfloc at times indicated. Pitch the yeast and ferment at 70°F (21°C) until final gravity is reached. Bottle or keg as usual.

EXTRACT WITH GRAINS OPTION: Substitute all the grains in the all-grain version with the exception of the roasted barley, and replace with 4 pounds 5 ounces (2 kilograms) Briess gold dried malt extract, 6 ounces (0.17 kilogram) Briess amber dried malt extract, 1 pound 4 ounces (0.56 kilogram) Briess dark dried malt extract, and 3 ounces (85 grams) Briess wheat dried malt extract. Stir the malt extracts into 3 gallons (11 liters) of water in your brewpot. Heat to a boil, steeping roasted barley until temperature

reaches 160°F (71°C). Remove the barley and boil wort for 60 minutes, adding hops at beginning. Follow the remaining portion of the all-grain recipe.

SHORT'S BREWING COMPANY
THE MAGICIAN

**(5 gallons/19 L, all-grain) OG = 1.058 FG = 1.012
IBU = 22 SRM = 17 ABV = 5.8%**

The Magician is a lustrous, dark-red, London-style red ale with a rich grain bill. The grain combination lends complex notes of toasted caramel, raisins, chocolate, and roasted toffee. Very light hop additions let the true malt characters show throughout this beer.

INGREDIENTS

8.5 lb. (3.85 kg) 2-row pale malt

6 oz. (170 g) Carapils malt

12 oz. (0.34 kg) Munich malt

4 oz. (113 g) crystal malt (60 °L)

12 oz. (0.34 kg) crystal malt (80 °L)

2 oz. (57 g) roasted barley (450 °L)

3.4 AAU Cascade pellet hops (60 min.) (0.65 oz./18 g at 5.25% alpha acids)

2.6 AAU Cascade pellet hops (30 min.) (0.5 oz./14 g at 5.25% alpha acids)

1.3 AAU Cascade pellet hops (5 min.) (0.25 oz./7 g at 5.25% alpha acids)

½ tsp. yeast nutrient (15 min.)

½ tsp. Irish moss (30 min.)

White Labs WLP013 (London Ale) or Wyeast 1028 (London Ale) yeast

¾ cup (150 g) dextrose (if priming)

STEP BY STEP

This is a single-infusion mash. Mix the crushed grains with 3.75 gallons (14 liters) of 168°F (76°C) water to stabilize at 150°F (66°C) for 60 minutes. Sparge slowly with 175°F (79°C) water. Collect approximately 6 gallons (27.3 liters) of wort runoff to boil for 60 minutes. Cool the wort to 75°F (24°C). Pitch the yeast and aerate heavily. Ferment at 68°F (20°C). Transfer to a carboy, avoiding any splashing. Condition for 1 week, and then bottle or keg.

EXTRACT WITH GRAINS OPTION: Substitute the 2-row pale malt in the all-grain recipe with 6.6 pounds (3 kilograms) Briess light liquid malt extract. Steep the crushed grain in 2 gallons (7.6 liters) of water at 150°F (66°C) for 30 minutes. Remove grains and rinse with 2 quarts (1.8 liters) of hot water. Add the malt extract and boil for 60 minutes. Add the hops, Irish moss, and yeast nutrient as per the recipe. Add the wort to 2 gallons (7.6 liters) of cold water and top off with cold water up to 5 gallons (19 liters). Follow the remaining portion of the all-grain recipe.

SPRECHER
BREWING COMPANY
SPECIAL AMBER

**(5 gallons/19 L, all-grain) OG = 1.052 FG = 1.013
IBU = 19 SRM = 10 ABV = 5.1%**

A delicate balance of toasted malt and fresh hops gives this medium-bodied German-style lager an intriguing, complex flavor. You'll find it noticeably different from the amber ales in this chapter.

INGREDIENTS

9 lb. (4.1 kg) pilsner malt

0.5 lb. (0.23 kg) dark Munich malt (20 °L)

0.5 lb. (0.23 kg) Belgian Caravienna malt

0.5 lb. (0.23 kg) crystal malt (120 °L)

5.5 AAU Cascade hops (60 min.) (1.1 oz./25 g at 5% alpha acids)

4 AAU Mt. Hood hops (2 min.) (1 oz./28 g at 4% alpha acids)

1 tsp. Irish moss (15 min.)

Wyeast 2206 (Bavarian Lager) or White Labs WLP830 (German Lager) yeast

¾ cup (150 g) dextrose (if priming)

STEP BY STEP

Sprecher does a two-step mash when brewing Special Amber. Mash all your grains at 122°F (50°C) for 30 minutes, then raise the temperature to 155°F (68°C) for 45 minutes. Mash out, vorlauf, and then sparge at 170°F (77°C) to collect 6 gallons (23 liters) of wort. Add 2 quarts (1.9 liters) of water and boil for 90 minutes. Add hops at times indicated. Cool, aerate, and pitch yeast. Ferment at 50°F (10°C). After fermentation is complete, bottle or keg as usual.

EXTRACT WITH GRAINS OPTION: Substitute the pilsner malt in the all-grain recipe with 2 pounds 2 ounces (0.96 kilogram) Briess light dried malt extract and 4 pounds (1.8 kilograms) Alexander's pale liquid malt extract. Place crushed malts in a nylon steeping bag and steep in 2.3

quarts (2.1 liters) of water at 150°F (66°C) for 30 minutes. Rinse grains with 1.3 quarts (1.3 liters) of water at 170°F (77°C). Add water to make 3 gallons (11 liters), stir in dried malt extract, and bring to a boil. Add hops at times indicated and liquid malt extract and Irish moss for last 15 minutes. Top off to 5 gallons (19 liters) after cooling. Follow the remaining portion of the all-grain recipe.

TEMPEST
BREWING COMPANY
UNFORGIVEN
RED RYE

**(5 gallons/19 L, all-grain) OG = 1.053 FG = 1.013
IBU = 28 SRM = 18 ABV = 5.4%**

Tempest Brewing Company was established in 2010 in Tweedbank, Scotland, and has been churning out tasty, unique brews ever since. This beer is hard to classify. It features a healthy dose of beech-smoked malt, a bit of spicy rye, some darker character malts, and new British hops that add a whiff of stone fruit and spice character.

INGREDIENTS

9 lb. (4.1 kg) beech-smoked malt

1 lb. (0.45 kg) rye malt

0.75 lb. (0.34 kg) crystal rye malt (75 °L)

2 oz. (57 g) crystal malt (40 °L)

2 oz. (57 g) crystal malt (120 °L)

2 oz. (57 g) Special B malt

2 oz. (57 g) roasted barley

3.5 AAU First Gold hops (60 min.) (0.5 oz./14 g at 7% alpha acids)

7 AAU First Gold hops (20 min.) (1 oz./28 g at 7% alpha acids)

Wyeast 1056 (American Ale), White Labs WLP001 (California Ale), or Fermentis Safale US-05 yeast

⅔ cup (133 g) dextrose (if priming)

STEP BY STEP

Mill the grains and mix with 4 gallons (15 liters) of 165°F (74°C) strike water to reach a mash temperature of 152°F (67°C). Hold this temperature for 60 minutes. Vorlauf until your runnings are clear and lauter. Sparge the grains with 2.9 gallons (11 liters) and top up as necessary to obtain 6 gallons (23 liters) of wort. Boil for 60 minutes, adding hops according to the ingredient list and Irish moss as desired. Chill to 66°F (19°C), aerate, and pitch yeast. Ferment at 68°F (20°C) for the first 3 days, then allow temperature to rise to 70°F (21°C). Hold there until fermentation is complete, and then bottle or keg the beer and carbonate to approximately 2.25 volumes. You may want to cold-crash the beer to 35°F (2°C) for 48 hours prior to packaging to improve clarity.

PARTIAL MASH OPTION: Reduce the beech-smoked malt in the all-grain recipe to 1 pound (0.45 kilogram) and add 5.5 pounds (2.5 kilograms) pale liquid malt extract. Bring 1.25 gallons (4.6 liters) of water to approximately 165°F (74°C), steeping the smoked malt and specialty malts in grain bags for 45 minutes. Remove the grain bags and let drain fully. Add malt extract and stir until completely dissolved. Top up to 6 gallons (23 liters) and bring the wort to a boil for 60 minutes. Follow the remaining portion of the all-grain recipe.

TRÖEGS INDEPENDENT BREWING
HOPBACK AMBER ALE

ᒪᒪᒪᒪᒪᒪ

(5 gallons/19 L, all-grain) OG=1.063 FG=1.017
IBU = 55 SRM= 11 ABV = 6%

More than a fun name, HopBack is named for the 12-foot-tall HopBack vessel used to deliver whole flower hops into this beer at Tröegs. A gold-medal winner at the Great American Beer Festival, this beer is an amber with big presence in the glass.

INGREDIENTS

10.3 lb. (4.7kg) Briess pilsner malt

2.5 lb. (1.1 kg) Munich malt (20 °L)

0.25 lb. (113 g) crystal malt (20 °L)

0.25 lb. (113 g) crystal malt (90 °L)

13 AAU Nugget hops (60 min.) (1 oz./28 g at 13% alpha acids)

6.5 AAU Cascade hops (0 min.) (1 oz./28 g at 6.5% alpha acids)

2.4 AAU Willamette hops (0 min.) (0.5 oz./14 g at 4.8% alpha acids)

0.5 oz. (14 g) Nugget hops (hopback)

0.5 oz. (14 g) Crystal hops (hopback)

Wyeast 1056 (American Ale), White Labs WLP001 (California Ale), or Fermentis Safale US-05 yeast

¾ cup (150 g) dextrose (if priming)

STEP BY STEP

Mash the grains at 152°F (67°C) for 60 minutes. Collect approximately 7 gallons (26 liters) of wort to boil for 90 minutes and have a 5.5-gallon (21-liter) yield. Add hops at times indicated during the boil. After the boil, give the wort a long stir to create a whirlpool and let settle for 15 minutes. For the hopback addition, you have two options. If you have a hopback, then utilize the hopback prior to sending the wort into your chiller. If you do not have a hopback, add these hops with 5 minutes remaining in the whirlpool. Cool the wort to 75°F (24°C), aerate the beer, and pitch your yeast. Allow the beer to cool over the next few hours to 68°F (20°C), and hold at this temperature until the beer has finished fermenting. Bottle or keg as usual.

EXTRACT WITH GRAINS OPTION: Substitute the pilsner and Munich malt in the all-grain recipe with 3.3 pounds (1.5 kilograms) Briess Pilsen light liquid malt extract, 3.3 pounds (1.5 kilograms) Briess Sparkling Amber liquid malt extract, and 1.5 pounds (0.91 kilogram) Munich dried malt extract. Steep the crushed malts in 5 gallons (19 liters) of water at 152°F (67°C) for 30 minutes. Remove grains from wort, add all the malt extracts, and bring to a boil for 60 minutes. Follow the remaining portion of the all-grain recipe.

TRÖEGS INDEPENDENT BREWING
NUGGET NECTAR

ᒪᒪᒪᒪᒪᒪ

(5 gallons/19 L, all-grain) OG = 1.071 FG = 1.015
IBU = 91 SRM = 8 ABV = 7.4%

Released each fall after the hop harvest, Nugget Nectar is an imperial amber ale featuring an explosion of pine, resin, and mango hop flavors and aromas. If you brewed HopBack and came looking for its big brother, you've found it.

INGREDIENTS

11.5 lb. (5.2 kg) Vienna malt (3.5 °L)

2 lb. (0.91 kg) Munich malt (6 °L)

2 lb. (0.91 kg) pilsner malt

16 AAU Warrior pellet hops (90 min.) (1 oz./28 g at 16% alpha acids)

7.5 AAU Columbus pellet hops (20 min.) (0.5 oz./14 g at 15% alpha acids)

6.2 AAU Palisade pellet hops (10 min.) (0.75 oz./21 g at 8.25% alpha acids)

13 AAU Nugget pellet hops (1 min.) (1 oz./28 g at 13% alpha acids)

21 AAU Simcoe pellet hops (1 min.) (1.5 oz./43 g at 14% alpha acids)

7.5 AAU Columbus pellet hops (1 min.) (0.5 oz./14 g at 15% alpha acids)

0.25 oz. (7 g) Columbus pellet hops (dry hop)

1 oz. (28 g) Nugget pellet hops (dry hop)

1 oz. (28 g) Simcoe pellet hops (dry hop)

½ tsp. Irish moss (30 min.)

½ tsp. yeast nutrient (15 min.)

White Labs WLP001 (California Ale), Wyeast 1056 (American Ale), or Fermentis Safale US-05 yeast

¾ cup (150 g) dextrose (if priming)

STEP BY STEP

Mix the crushed grains with 5 gallons (19 liters) of 168°F (76°C) water to stabilize at 152°F (67°C) for 60 minutes. Sparge with 175°F (79°C) water. Collect 6 gallons (23 liters) of wort runoff to boil for 60 minutes. Add the hops, Irish moss, and yeast nutrient as per the schedule. Cool the wort to 75°F (24°C). Pitch the yeast and aerate the wort heavily. Allow the beer to cool to 68°F (20°C). Hold at that temperature until fermentation is complete. Transfer to a carboy, avoiding any splashing to prevent aerating the beer, and add the dry hops. Condition for 1 week and then bottle or keg.

EXTRACT ONLY OPTION: Substitute all the malts listed in the all-grain recipe with 6.6 pounds (3 kilograms) Briess Goldpils Vienna liquid malt extract, 1.3 pounds (0.59 kilogram) Munich dried malt extract, and 1.3 pounds (0.59 kilogram) Pilsen dried malt extract. Bring 5 gallons of water up to 200°F (93°C). Remove from heat and add the liquid and dried malt extracts and the Warrior hop addition. Stir until all the extract has dissolved, then continue to heat to a boil. Boil for 60 minutes, adding the remaining hops as indicated. Follow the remaining portion of the all-grain recipe.

CHAPTER FIVE

BROWN ALES

Beer Pictured on Left; see page 78

ABITA BREWING COMPANY
TURBODOG
~~~~~~~
**(5 gallons/19 L, all-grain) OG = 1.054 FG = 1.014
IBU = 32 SRM = 30 ABV = 5.5%**

Turbodog, one of Abita's flagship brews, is a dark brown ale with a rich body and a sweet chocolate and toffee-like flavor.

INGREDIENTS

9.75 lb. (4.4 kg) 2-row pale malt

1.25 lb. (0.57 kg) Muntons crystal malt (150 °L)

0.5 lb. (0.23 kg) Muntons chocolate malt

7 AAU Chinook hops (90 min.) (0.6 oz./17 g at 12% alpha acids)

5 AAU Willamette hops (5 min.) (1.25 oz./35 g at 4% alpha acids)

6 AAU Willamette hops (0 min.) (1.5 oz./43 g at 4% alpha acids)

White Labs WLP036 (Düsseldorf Alt) or Wyeast 1007 (German Ale) yeast

¾ cup (150 g) dextrose (for priming)

STEP BY STEP

Heat 3.6 gallons (14 liters) to 160°F (71°C) in a brewpot and slowly mix in milled malt. Hold at 152°F (67°C) for 45 minutes, then heat the thick mash to 172°F (78°C) and hold for 5 minutes. Transfer to lauter unit and runoff first wort (should hit 1.070). Sparge with 3.75 gallons (14.25 liters) at 172°F (78°C). Bring wort to boil and add the hops at the times indicated in the ingredients list. Chill the wort rapidly to 65 to 68°F (18 to 20°C), aerate well, and pitch the yeast. Ferment at 65 to 68°F (18 to 20°C). When primary fermentation is complete, cool to around 45°F (7°C) and condition for 1 week before bottling or kegging as usual.

EXTRACT WITH GRAINS OPTION: Omit the 2-row pale malt and add 2.5 pounds (1.1 kilograms) light dried malt extract and 3.3 pounds (1.5 kilograms) light liquid malt extract (late addition). Place the crushed malts in a nylon steeping bag and steep in 3 quarts (2.8 liters) of water at 152°F (67°C) for 30 minutes. Rinse grains with 1.5 quarts (~1.5 liters) of water at 170°F (77°C). Add water to the brewpot to total 3 gallons (11 liters), stir in dried malt extract, and bring to a boil. Add the hops at the times indicated in the ingredients list. After the boil, cool the wort and top fermenter up to 5 gallons (19) with cool water. Add yeast, aerate, and ferment at 55 to 58°F (13 to 14°C). Follow the remaining portion of the all-grain recipe.

BELL'S BREWERY
BEST BROWN ALE
~~~~~~~
**(5 gallons/19 L, all-grain) OG = 1.060 FG = 1.017
IBU = 30 SRM = 18 ABV = 5.8%**

Bell's Best Brown is a smooth, toasty brown ale with aromas of caramel and cocoa. A seasonal release in the fall, it's meant to pair with the cooler weather without being as heavy as wintertime beers.

INGREDIENTS

10 lb. (4.5 kg) 2-row pale malt

14 oz. (0.39 kg) Briess Victory malt

14 oz. (0.39 kg) Briess special roast malt

14 oz. (0.39 kg) Briess crystal malt (60 °L)

2 oz. (57 g) Briess chocolate malt

5 AAU Cascade hops (45 min.) (1 oz./28 g at 5% alpha acids)

2.5 AAU Nugget hops (45 min.) (0.19 oz./5 g at 13% alpha acids)

1.2 AAU Fuggle hops (15 min.) (0.25 oz./7 g at 4.7% alpha acids)

2.4 AAU Fuggle hops (2 min.) (0.5 oz./14 g at 4.7% alpha acids)

1 tsp. Irish moss (15 min.)

White Labs WLP001 (California Ale) or Wyeast 1056 (American Ale) yeast (1 qt./~1 L yeast starter)

¾ cup (150 g) of dextrose (if priming)

STEP BY STEP

Mash your grains at 155°F (68°C). Vorlauf until your runnings are clear, sparge, and then boil the wort for 75 minutes. Add the hops according to the times indicated in the ingredients list. After the boil, turn off the heat and chill the wort rapidly to 68°F (20°C). Aerate the wort well and pitch the yeast. Ferment at 68°F (20°C). When the beer has reached final gravity, bottle or keg as normal. Age for 2 to 3 weeks before serving.

EXTRACT WITH GRAINS OPTION: Substitute the 2-row pale malt with 7 pounds 14 ounces (3.6 kilograms) Briess light liquid malt extract. Place the crushed malts in a steeping bag and steep in 4 quarts (3.7 liters) of water at 150°F (66°C) for 30 minutes. Pull the grain bag out and drain over the pot in a colander. Rinse the grains with 2 quarts (1.9 liters) of water at 170°F (77°C). Add water to the pot to make 3 gallons (11 liters), add the liquid malt extract, and bring to a boil. Add the hops and Irish moss according to the ingredients list. After the boil, cool the wort, transfer to a fermenter, cool to 80°F (27°C), and top up with cool water to make 5 gallons (19 liters). Aerate the wort and pitch the yeast. Follow the remainder of the all-grain recipe.

BIG SKY BREWING COMPANY
MOOSE DROOL

(5 gallons/19 L, all-grain) OG = 1.052 FG = 1.012
IBU = 26 SRM = 22 ABV = 5.3%

This is the beer that put Montana craft beer on the map! Released shortly after Big Sky opened in 1995, Moose Drool has taken home many medals. It has great drinkability and complexity, with subtle coffee and cocoa notes balanced with a pleasant bitterness.

INGREDIENTS

9.75 lb. (4.4 kg) 2-row pale malt

18 oz. (0.5 kg) crystal malt (75 °L)

6 oz. (0.17 kg) chocolate malt (350 °L)

0.5 oz. (14 g) black barley (450 °L)

4.3 AAU East Kent Golding pellet hops (60 min.) (0.9 oz./26 g at 4.75% alpha acids)

2 AAU Liberty pellet hops (30 min.) (0.5 oz./14 g at 4% alpha acids)

2.5 AAU Willamette pellet hops (0 min.) (0.5 oz./14 g at 5% alpha acids)

½ tsp. yeast nutrient (15 min.)

½ tsp. Irish moss (15 min.)

White Labs WLP013 (London Ale) or Wyeast 1028 (London Ale) yeast

¾ cup (150 g) dextrose (if priming)

STEP BY STEP

Mash the crushed grains with 3.75 gallons (14 liters) of 172°F (78°C) water to stabilize at 154°F (68°C) for 60 minutes. Sparge slowly with 175°F (79°C) water. Collect approximately 6 gallons (23 liters) of wort runoff to boil for 60 minutes. Add the hops, Irish moss, and yeast nutrient per the schedule. Cool the wort to 75°F (24°C), aerate, and pitch your yeast. Allow the beer to cool to 68°F (20°C) and hold there until fermentation is complete. Allow the beer to condition for 1 week, and then bottle or keg.

EXTRACT WITH GRAINS OPTION: Reduce the 2-row pale malt in the all-grain recipe to 1 pound (0.45 kilogram) and add 3.3 pounds (1.5 kilograms) Muntons light unhopped malt extract and 2 pounds (0.9 kilogram) light dried malt extract. Steep the crushed grains in 6 gallons (23 liters) of water at 154°F (68°C) for 30 minutes. Remove grains and drain. Add the liquid malt extract and boil for 60 minutes. Follow the remaining portion of the all-grain recipe.

CAPITAL BREWERY
BROWN ALE

(5 gallons/19 L, all-grain) OG = 1.048 FG = 1.012
IBU = 20 SRM = 20 ABV = 4.7%

This brown ale, an early staple of Wisconsin-based Capital Brewery, has since been retired. That's no reason to skip it, though. It has an English bent straight from the malts to the hops to the yeast.

INGREDIENTS

8 lb. (3.6 kg) Maris Otter pale ale malt

1 lb. (0.45 kg) Crisp Caramalt (15 °L)

10 oz. (0.28 kg) crystal malt (90 °L)

4.5 oz. (0.13 kg) black patent malt

5.4 AAU Fuggle hops (60 min.) (1.1 oz./31 g at 5% alpha acids)

Wyeast 1028 (London Ale) or White Labs WLP013 (London Ale) yeast

¾ cup (150 g) dextrose (if priming)

STEP BY STEP

Mash at 154°F (68°C). Vorlauf until your runnings are clear, sparge, and then boil the wort for 60 minutes, adding the hops at the time indicated in the ingredients list. After the boil, turn off the heat and chill the wort rapidly to just below fermentation temperature, about 68°F (20°C). Aerate the wort well and pitch the yeast. Ferment at 70°F (21°C). When final gravity is reached, bottle or keg as normal.

EXTRACT WITH GRAINS OPTION: Omit the Maris Otter pale ale malt. Add 1.7 pounds (0.77 kilogram) Muntons light dried malt extract and 3.3 pounds (1.5 kilograms) Maris Otter light liquid malt extract (late addition). Steep the crushed grains in a nylon bag at 154°F (68°C) in 5 quarts (4.8 liters) of water for 30 minutes. At the end of the steep, remove the bag from the steeping pot, place it in a colander, and let drip dry into the brewpot. Rinse the grains with 3.8 quarts (3.6 liters) of 170°F (77°C) water. Now add enough water to the brewpot to make at least 2.5 gallons (9.5 liters). Boil for 60 minutes, adding the hops according to the ingredients list. Add liquid malt extract with 15 minutes left in boil. After the boil, cool the wort and transfer to fermenter. Top up to 5 gallons (19 liters), aerate, and pitch the yeast. Follow the remainder of the all-grain recipe.

FREE WILL
BREWING COMPANY
C.O.B. (COFFEE OATMEAL BROWN)

cccccc

(5 gallons/19 L, all-grain) OG = 1.082 FG = 1.020
IBU = 26 SRM = 20 ABV = 8.3%

A popular seasonal for Free Will, this ale is on the strong side for a brown. It has a big, delicious malt character and is aged in coconut and unique cocoa nibs from Ghana. The nibs are essential to replicate the exact flavor, but other nib varietals will be equally delicious.

INGREDIENTS

13 lb. (5.9 kg) Maris Otter pale malt

1.5 lb. (0.68 kg) Briess Carabrown malt

1.5 lb. (0.68 kg) flaked oats

0.5 lb. (0.23 kg) UK brown malt

0.25 lb. (0.11 kg) British crystal malt (45 °L)

0.25 lb. (0.11 kg) pale chocolate malt

6.5 AAU Pilgrim hops (90 min.) (0.5 oz./14 g at 11% alpha acids)

2.75 AAU Pilgrim hops (5 min.) (0.25 oz./7 g at 11% alpha acids)

5 oz. (142 g) ground coffee

2 lb. (0.9 kg) Baker's shaved coconut (secondary)

1 lb. (0.45 kg) Ghana cocoa nibs or 0.5 lb. (0.23 kg) unsweetened cocoa powder (secondary)

Wyeast 1968 (London ESB Ale), White Labs WLP002 (English Ale), or Lallemand London ESB Ale yeast

⅔ cup (133 g) dextrose (if priming)

STEP BY STEP

Mill the grains and mix with 5.3 gallons (20 liters) of 164°F (73°C) strike water to reach a mash temperature of 152°F (67°C). Hold this temperature for 60 minutes. Vorlauf until your runnings are clear. Sparge the grains with 3 gallons (11.3 liters) water and top up as necessary to obtain 6 gallons (23 liters) of wort. Boil for 90 minutes, adding hops according to the ingredient list. Chill the wort to 65°F (18°C), aerate, and pitch yeast. Ferment at 68°F (20°C) for 7 days, then drop the temperature to 60°F (16°C) for 24 hours. Add the cocoa nibs and coconut, and age for 14 days. Crash the beer to 36°F (2°C) for 48 hours, adding the ground coffee after 12 hours, bottle or keg the beer, and carbonate to approximately 2.25 volumes.

PARTIAL MASH OPTION: Reduce the pale malt in the all-grain recipe to 3.5 pounds (1.6 kilograms) and add 6.6 pounds (3 kilograms) pale liquid malt extract. Mill the grains and place in one or more grain bags. Mix with 2.3 gallons (8.9 liters) of 164°F (73°C) strike water to reach a mash temperature of 152°F (67°C). Hold this temperature for 60 minutes. Remove the grain bags and place into a colander. Wash the grains with 2 gallons (7.6 liters) of hot water and let drain fully. Add liquid extract and stir until completely dissolved and top off to 6 gallons (23 liters) of wort. Bring to a boil and boil for 90 minutes. Follow the remaining portion of the all-grain recipe.

TIPS FOR SUCCESS

Brewmaster John Stemler notes that the brewery, when adding the coconut and cocoa to the beer, bags and autoclaves the ingredients—but due to standard food processing requirements it is highly likely that you can add them directly from unopened containers without fear of infection! For the coffee addition, he states, "We get fresh roasted Colombian and have it ground coarse like for a French press. Post fermentation we crash the beer to 36°F (2°C) in the fermenter and just drop the coffee in the top of the tank. It stays in contact for 36 hours, then gets strained to the bright. We dose at a rate of 1 pound (0.45 kilogram) per barrel, so about 0.5 ounce (14 grams) per gallon (4 liters). I'd do 1 ounce (28 grams) per gallon (4 liters) for homebrew scale batches, I think. The short contact is key to not getting the vegetable off flavors from coffee."

THE MITTEN
BREWING COMPANY
LABEL UP

cccccc

(5 gallons/19 L, all-grain) OG = 1.050 FG = 1.012
IBU = 25 SRM = 23 ABV = 5%

While there's no indicator in the name, this brown ale is set apart from the rest with an addition of pure maple extract and crushed pecans. Together with the flavorful malt bill, this is an ale that swings above its 5% weight.

INGREDIENTS

- 7.5 lb. (3.4 kg) British pale ale malt
- 1 lb. (0.45 kg) Munich malt
- 0.5 lb. (0.23 kg) caramel malt (60 °L)
- 0.5 lb. (0.23 kg) Thomas Fawcett brown malt
- 0.25 lb. (113 g) pale chocolate malt
- 0.25 lb. (113 g) roasted barley (500 °L)
- 6 oz. (170 g) crushed pecans (toasted)

- Maple extract (to taste)
- 5.5 AAU Magnum hops (60 min.) (0.5 oz./14 g at 11% alpha acids)
- 2 AAU Fuggle hops (15 min.) (0.5 oz./14 g at 4% alpha acids)
- 0.5 oz. (14 g) Fuggle hops (0 min.)
- Wyeast 1056 (American Ale) or White Labs WLP001 (California Ale) yeast
- ⅔ cup (133 g) dextrose (if priming)

STEP BY STEP

Mill the grains, add the toasted pecans, and mix with 3.1 gallons (11.8 liters) of 167°F (75°C) strike water to reach a mash temperature of 154°F (68°C). Hold this temperature for 60 minutes. Vorlauf until your runnings are clear and lauter. Sparge the grains with 3.8 gallons (14.4 liters) of water and top up as necessary to obtain 6 gallons (23 liters) of wort. Boil for 60 minutes, adding hops according to the ingredient list and Irish moss as desired. Chill to 66°F (19°C), aerate, and pitch yeast. Ferment at 68°F (20°C) for 14 days or until fermentation is complete. Once the beer completes fermentation, add maple extract to taste (see TIPS FOR SUCCESS), then bottle or keg the beer and carbonate to approximately 2.25 volumes. You may want to cold-crash the beer to 35°F (2°C) for 48 hours prior to packaging to improve clarity.

EXTRACT WITH GRAINS OPTION: Substitute the pale ale malt in the all-grain recipe with 5 pounds (2.3 kilograms) pale liquid malt extract. Bring 5.4 gallons (20.4 liters) of water to approximately 165°F (74°C) and hold there, steeping the toasted pecans and specialty malts in grain bags for 15 minutes. Remove the grain bags and let drain fully. Add malt extract while stirring, and stir until completely dissolved. Bring the wort to a boil for 60 minutes. Follow the remaining portion of the all-grain recipe.

TIPS FOR SUCCESS

Focus on dialing in the maple and pecan flavors in your finished beer. If either method (mashing for all-grain, steeping for extract) does not yield noticeable pecan character, try increasing the amount of pecan used and/or adding a second charge of crushed/toasted pecans in the secondary. As for the maple extract—use it cautiously and taste as you add. It is a powerful flavor and a little goes a long way. Too much will dramatically increase the perception of sweetness, and we want to avoid that. This may call for a bit of trial and error! There are many maple extracts available and all are not created equally. For what it's worth, The Mitten uses a maple extract from Beanilla, a local company out of Rockford, Michigan.

NØGNE Ø DET KOMPROMISSLØSE BRYGGERI A/S
IMPERIAL BROWN ALE

༺༺༺༺༺༺

(5 gallons/19 L, all-grain) OG = 1.079 FG = 1.021
IBU = 40 SRM = 17 ABV = 7.5%

Nøgne Ø is a Norwegian brewery that has taken their craft seriously since they were founded in 2002. They now export some of their beers, including this unique imperial brown ale. It's a take on a dark brown English-style ale that turns the volume up and combines classic English malts with some New World hops.

INGREDIENTS

- 11 lb. (5 kg) Thomas Fawcett Maris Otter pale malt
- 1 lb. 11 oz. (0.77 kg) wheat malt
- 1 lb. 11 oz. (0.77 kg) Munich malt
- 1 lb. (0.45 kg) CaraMalt malt
- 6.3 oz. (0.18 kg) amber malt
- 3.2 oz. (90 g) brown malt
- 3.2 oz. (90 g) chocolate malt
- 9 AAU Chinook hops (90 min.) (0.75 oz./21 g at 12% alpha acids)

- 11 AAU East Kent Golding hops (5 min.) (2.3 oz./65 g at 4.75% alpha acids)
- 1.6 oz. (45 g) Columbus hops (0 min.)
- White Labs WLP007 (Dry English Ale) or Wyeast 1098 (British Ale) yeast
- ¾ cup (150 g) dextrose (if priming)

STEP BY STEP

Mash in at 151°F (66°C) for 45 minutes; raise to 162°F (72°C) for 15 minutes to finish saccharification. Or, you can just hold the mash at 151°F (66°C) for the duration of the 60 minutes. Mash out, vorlauf, and then sparge at 170°F (77°C) to collect approximately 6.5 gallons (24.5 liters) wort. Boil for 90 minutes, adding hops at times indicated. Cool, aerate, and pitch yeast at 68°F (20°C). Maintain that temperature through primary fermentation. Age for ideally 6 months after packaging before consumption.

PARTIAL MASH OPTION: Replace pale malt with 2 pounds (0.91 kilogram) light dried malt extract and 5.75 pounds (2.6 kilograms) light liquid malt extract. Mash grains in 6.5 quarts (6.2 liters) of water at 151°F (66°C) for 45 minutes. Rinse grains with ~4 quarts (~4 liters) of 170°F (77°C) water. Dissolve dried malt extract into wort and bring to a boil. Boil wort for 90 minutes, adding hops at times indicated and stirring in liquid malt extract for the final 10 minutes of the boil. Cool wort and transfer to fermenter. Add water to top up to 5 gallons (19 liters). Follow the remaining portion of the all-grain recipe.

PEEKSKILL BREWERY
MALT BALLS BROWN ALE

««««««-

**(5 gallons/19 L, all-grain) OG = 1.064 FG = 1.013
IBU = 51 SRM = 22 ABV = 6.7%**

Malt Balls Brown Ale is a decidedly hop-forward American brown ale. The addition of Midnight Wheat adds a unique character and darker color than many brown ales.

INGREDIENTS

10 lbs. (4.5 kg) Maris Otter pale malt

2 lbs. (0.91 kg) Briess aromatic malt (20 °L)

15 oz. (0.42 kg) flaked barley

5 oz. (0.14 kg) Briess Midnight Wheat malt (550 °L)

22.4 AAU Centennial hops (15 min.) (2 oz./57 g at 11.2% alpha acids)

11.2 AAU Centennial hops (5 min.) (1 oz./28 g at 11.2% alpha acids)

11.2 AAU Centennial hops (0 min.) (1 oz./28 g at 11.2% alpha acids)

1/2 tsp. Irish moss (15 min.)

1/2 tsp. yeast nutrient (10 min.)

White Labs WLP001 (California Ale), Wyeast 1056 (American Ale), or Safale US-05 yeast

3/4 cup (150 g) corn sugar (if priming)

STEP BY STEP

This is a single step infusion mash. Mix all of the crushed grains with 4.6 gallons (17.4 liters) of 156°F (69°C) water to stabilize at 145°F (63°C). This is a medium thin mash using 1.4 quarts (2.9 liters/kilograms) of strike water per pound of grain. This ratio will help to increase maximum fermentability. A more fermentable wort is also created by the low mash temperature. After 90 minutes, check to be sure starch conversion is complete. When complete, slowly sparge with 170°F (77°C) water. Collect approximately 6 gallons (22.7 liters) of wort runoff. Boil for 60 minutes, adding the hops, Irish moss, and yeast nutrient as per the schedule. Cool the wort to 75°F (24°C). Pitch your yeast and aerate the wort heavily. Allow the beer to cool to 68°F (20°C). Hold at that temperature until fermentation is complete. This may take 6 to 8 days. Gently transfer to a carboy, avoiding any splashing to prevent aerating the beer. Allow the beer to condition for an additional week. Prime and bottle condition or keg and force carbonate to 2.4 volumes CO_2.

PARTIAL MASH OPTION: Reduce the Maris Otter pale malt to 1 pound (0.45 kilogram) and add 6.6 pounds (3 kilograms) Muntons Maris Otter unhopped liquid malt extract. Steep the milled grains in 2 gallons (7.5 liters) of water at 145°F (63°C) for 90 minutes. Remove grains from the wort and rinse with 1 gallon (4 liters) of hot water. Top up kettle to 6 gallons (23 liters) and bring to a boil. Remove kettle from eat and stir in malt extract, then return to a boil for 60 minutes. Follow the remaining portion of the all-grain recipe.

ROGUE ALES
HAZELNUT BROWN NECTAR

**(5 gallons/19 L, all-grain) OG = 1.056 FG = 1.014
IBU = 33 SRM = 22 ABV = 5.7%**

Leave it to Rogue to put a nutty twist on a traditional European brown ale. Dark brown in color, this beer has a noticeable hazelnut aroma, a rich nutty flavor, and a smooth malty finish.

INGREDIENTS

8 lb. (3.6 kg) pale malt

1.5 lb. (0.68 kg) Munich malt (10 °L)

9 oz. (0.25 kg) Hugh Baird brown malt

5.6 oz. (0.15 kg) crystal malt (15 °L)

1 lb. 3 oz. (0.54 kg) crystal malt (75 °L)

5.6 oz. (0.15 kg) crystal malt (120 °L)

3.8 oz. (0.11 kg) pale chocolate malt (187 °L)

7.8 AAU Perle hops (60 min.) (0.86 oz./24 g at 9% alpha acids)

1.75 AAU Saaz hops (30 min.) (0.5 oz./14 g at 3.5% alpha acids)

⅛ oz. hazelnut flavoring

1 tsp. Irish moss

Wyeast 1764 (Rogue Pacman Ale) (1.5 qt./~1.5 L yeast starter)

¾ cup (150 g) dextrose (if priming)

STEP BY STEP

Mash in 15 quarts (~14 liters) of water to get a single-infusion mash temperature of 153°F (~67°C) for 45 minutes. Sparge with hot water of 170°F (77°C) and collect 6.5 gallons (24.5 liters) of wort. Boil for 90 minutes. Add hops at times indicated and Irish moss with 15 minutes left in the boil. Cool wort to 70°F (21°C), transfer to fermenter, and top up to 5 gallons (19 liters). Aerate well and pitch yeast. Ferment cool (60°F/16°C) until complete (about 7 to 10 days). Add hazelnut flavoring, and then bottle or keg as normal.

PARTIAL MASH OPTION: Substitute the pale malt in the all-grain recipe with 1.5 pounds (0.68 kilogram) Coopers light dried malt extract and 3.3 pounds (1.5 kilograms) Coopers light liquid malt extract. Place crushed malts in a nylon steeping bag and steep in 6.3 quarts (5.9 liters) of water at 154°F (68°C) for 30 minutes. Rinse grains with 3.2 quarts (3 liters) of water at 170°F (77°C). Add water to make 3 gallons (11 liters), stir in dried malt extract, and bring to

a boil. Add hops at times indicated and liquid malt extract with 15 minutes remaining. Cool and top off to 5 gallons (19 liters). Follow the remaining portion of the all-grain recipe.

SCOTTISH AND NEWCASTLE BREWING COMPANY
NEWCASTLE BROWN ALE

**(5 gallons/19 L, all-grain) OG = 1.046 FG = 1.009
IBU = 22 SRM = 17 ABV = 4.7%**

INGREDIENTS

7.5 lb. (3.4 kg) British 2-row pale ale malt

1 lb. (0.45 kg) flaked barley

4 oz. (113 g) caramalt (22 °L)

4 oz. (113 g) British medium crystal malt (55 °L)

4 oz. (113 g) British dark crystal malt (80 °L)

1.5 oz. (43 g) British chocolate malt (450 °L)

1.5 oz. (43 g) roasted barley (500 °L)

1/2 tsp. Irish moss (15 min.)

1/2 tsp. yeast nutrients (15 min.)

6.25 AAU Fuggle hops (60 min.) (1.25 oz./35 g at 5% alpha acids)

Wyeast 1099 (Whitbread ale), White Labs WLP017 (Whitbread Ale), or Mangrove Jack's M15 (Empire Ale) yeast

¾ cup (150 g) corn sugar (if priming)

STEP BY STEP

Heat 12 quarts (11.4 liters) of water to 163°F (73°C). Mash grains at 152°F (67°C) for 60 minutes. Collect 6.5 gallons (24.6 liters) of wort. Boil wort for 90 minutes, adding hops and kettle additions at the times indicated in ingredients list. The goal is to have 5.25 gallons (20 liters) at the end of the boil. Cool, aerate, and pitch yeast. Ferment at 70°F (21°C). Rack to secondary and let condition in a cool place.

PARTIAL MASH OPTION: Reduce the 2-row pale malt in the all-grain recipe to 1 pound (0.45 kilogram). Replace with 1 pound (0.45 kilogram) extra light dried malt extract and 3.3 pounds (1.5 kilograms) Maris Otter liquid malt extract. Place crushed pale ale malt with the flaked barley in a nylon steeping bag. Heat 4 quarts (3.8 liters) of brewing liquor to 163°F (73°C) and submerge bag. Steep grains at 152°F (67°C) for 45 minutes. Place the roasted and crystal malts in a second nylon grain bag and submerge in the mash. Steep for 15 more minutes. Rinse both grain bags with 4 quarts (3.8 liters) of water at 170°F (77°C). Add water to "grain tea" to make 3 gallons (11 liters) of wort. Add dried malt extract and bring to a boil. Bring to a boil, adding ingredients at times indicated and the liquid malt extract with 15 minutes remaining. After the boil, chill the wort then top off to 5 gallons (19 liters) and follow the remaining portion of the all-grain recipe.

SURLY BREWING COMPANY
BENDER

**(5 gallons/19 L, all-grain) OG = 1.057 FG = 1.015
IBU = 43 SRM = 27 ABV = 5.5%**

Bender is a category-bending American brown ale, now a mainstay at their pubs and in cans. It's built on a foundation of British pale malt, but from there Surly puts their own spin on the brown. The resulting flavor is crisp and lightly hoppy but with a velvety sleekness from the oats. Tasting notes include cocoa, bitter coffee, caramel, and hints of cream.

INGREDIENTS

7.5 lb. (3.4 kg) 2-row British pale malt

2 lb. (0.9 kg) Belgian aromatic malt

0.75 lb. (0.34 kg) British medium crystal malt (55 °L)

0.75 lb. (0.34 kg) Belgian Special B malt (135 °L)

0.63 lb. (0.28 kg) Simpsons Golden Naked Oats (10 °L)

4 oz. (113 g) British chocolate malt (425 °L)

1.25 AAU Willamette hops (first wort hop) (0.25 oz./7 g at 5% alpha acids)

10.5 AAU Columbus hops (60 min.) (0.75 oz./21 g at 13% alpha acids)

2.5 oz. (71 g) Willamette hops (0 min.)

Wyeast 1335 (British Ale II) or White Labs WLP022 (Essex Ale) yeast

⅝ cup (125 g) dextrose (if priming)

STEP BY STEP

Mash the grains at 152°F (67°C) and hold for 60 minutes. Vorlauf until your runnings are clear, and add the Willamette first wort hops to the kettle. Sparge the grains and top up with as much water necessary to obtain 6 gallons (23 liters) of wort. Boil the wort for 60 minutes, adding the Columbus hops at the beginning of the boil and the second Willamette addition at the end. After the boil, turn off the heat and chill the wort rapidly to slightly below fermentation temperature,

about 65°F (18°C). Aerate the wort with pure oxygen or filtered air and pitch the yeast. Ferment at 67°F (19°C) for 7 days. Increase the temperature to 72°F (22°C) for an additional 3 days. Once the beer reaches final gravity, transfer the beer to a bottling bucket for priming and bottling or transfer to a keg. Carbonate to approximately 2 volumes.

PARTIAL MASH OPTION: Scale the British 2-row pale malt down to 1 pound (0.45 kilogram) and add 4.5 pounds (2 kilograms) golden light liquid malt extract. Bring 2 gallons (7.6 liters) of water to approximately 165°F (74°C) to stabilize the mash at 152°F (67°C). Add the milled grains in grain bags to the brewpot to mash for 60 minutes. Remove the grain bags and wash the grains with 1 gallon (4 liters) of hot water. Top off to 5.5 gallons (20 liters) with water. Remove the brewpot from the heat and add the liquid extract while stirring. Stir until completely dissolved. Add the Willamette first wort hops addition, put your pot back on the heat, and bring the wort to a boil. Boil for 60 minutes, adding the Columbus hops at the beginning of the boil and then the second Willamette addition at the end. Follow the remaining portion of the all-grain recipe.

TIPS FOR SUCCESS

There are times when substituting one grain for another based on availability, national origin, or even SRM, is a perfectly acceptable practice. This beer isn't one of those times. Bender relies to a significant degree on the use of British (note the British medium crystal) and Belgian (note the aromatic and Special B) malts to develop its unique malt characteristics and set off the floral and earthy notes of the king of aroma hops (note the large and late Willamette addition). This recipe is a significant determinant of success for this beer—don't stray too far on this one.

Simpsons Golden Naked Oats is a huskless oat crystal malt from Simpsons Malt that is added for a subtle, nutty flavor that adds a smooth oaty mouthfeel and a creamy head to your beer. Because they are "crystal" malts, they have been gently cooked during the malting process, which initiates the enzymatic conversion of the starch into fermentable sugars. Thus they do not need to be mashed (extract brewers can steep them).

TOMMYKNOCKER BREWERY
IMPERIAL NUT BROWN ALE

**(5 gallons/19 L, all-grain) OG = 1.080 FG = 1.016
IBU = 56 SRM = 23 ABV = 8.4%**

If you tried Label Up (page 81) but wanted something bigger, perhaps it's time to brew this imperial nut brown! This rich ale gets its complexity from pure maple syrup as well as the chocolate and crystal malts.

INGREDIENTS

12 lb. 13 oz. (5.81 kg) 2-row pale malt

1 lb. 9.5 oz. (0.72 kg) Munich malt

1 lb. 2 oz. (0.51 kg) crystal malt (40 °L)

7.5 oz. (0.21 kg) chocolate malt

10.5 oz. (0.3 kg) maple syrup

15 AAU Willamette hops (60 min.) (3 oz./85 g at 5% alpha acids)

Wyeast 1056 (American Ale) yeast or White Labs WLP001 (California Ale) yeast

¾ cup (150 g) dextrose (if priming)

STEP BY STEP

Mash the grains at 154°F (68°C) for 60 minutes. Mash out, vorlauf, and then sparge at 170°F (77°C) to collect enough wort to result in 5 gallons (19 liters) after a 2-hour boil. Boil 2 hours, adding hops with 60 minutes remaining and the maple syrup at knockout. Cool, aerate, and pitch yeast. Ferment at 72°F (22°C). After fermentation is complete, bottle or keg as usual.

EXTRACT WITH GRAINS OPTION: Substitute the 2-row pale malt and the Munich malt in the all-grain recipe with 2.4 pounds (1.1 kilograms) Munich dried malt extract and 6.6 pounds (3 kilograms) Coopers light liquid malt extract. In your brewpot, heat 5 gallons (19 liters) of water to 165°F (74°C). Place crushed grain in a steeping bag and steep for 20 minutes. After the 20 minutes, remove the grain bag and add the liquid and dried malt extracts. Stir until completely dissolved, then bring the wort up to a boil. Boil for 60 minutes, adding hops at the times indicated. Cool and top off to 5 gallons (19 liters). Follow the remaining portion of the all-grain recipe.

TRIPLE ROCK BREWERY
DRAGON'S MILK BROWN ALE

**(5 gallons/19 L, all-grain) OG = 1.067 FG = 1.016
IBU = 49 SRM = 27 ABV = 6.7%**

This ale, fit for a knight, is a strong American-style brown ale with complex notes of roasted barley and chocolate.

INGREDIENTS

12.25 lb. (5.6 kg) 2-row pale malt

1.5 lb. (0.68 kg) crystal malt (75 °L)

0.25 lb. (0.11 kg) chocolate malt

0.25 lb. (0.11 kg) roasted barley (450 °L)

11.2 AAU Magnum hops (60 min.) (0.7 oz./20 g at 14% alpha acids)

4.3 AAU Cascade hops (30 min.) (0.75 oz./21 g at 5.75% alpha acids)

0.25 oz. (7 g) Chinook hops (0 min.)

0.25 oz. (7 g) Simcoe hops (0 min.)

½ tsp. yeast nutrient (15 min.)

½ tsp. Irish moss (15 min.)

White Labs WLP001 (California Ale) or Wyeast 1056 (American Ale) yeast

¾ cup (150 g) dextrose (if priming)

STEP BY STEP

Mix the crushed grains with 4.5 gallons (17 liters) of 165°F (74°C) water to stabilize at 150°F (65.5°C) for 60 minutes. Sparge slowly with 175°F (79°C) water. Collect approximately 6 gallons (23 liters) of wort runoff to boil for 60 minutes. Add hops at times indicated. Cool the wort to 75°F (24°C). Pitch your yeast and aerate the wort heavily. Allow the beer to cool to 65°F (18°C). Hold at that temperature until fermentation is complete. Allow the beer to condition for 1 week, and then bottle or keg.

EXTRACT WITH GRAINS OPTION: Substitute the 2-row pale malt in the all-grain recipe with 6.6 pounds (3 kilograms) Briess light liquid malt extract and 1.2 pounds (0.54 kilogram) Briess extra light dried malt extract. Steep the crushed grain in 5 gallons (19 liters) of water at 150°F (66°C) for 30 minutes. Remove grains from the wort and rinse with 2 quarts (1.8 liters) of hot water. Add the liquid and dried malt extracts and bring to a boil for 60 minutes. Follow the remaining portion of the all-grain recipe.

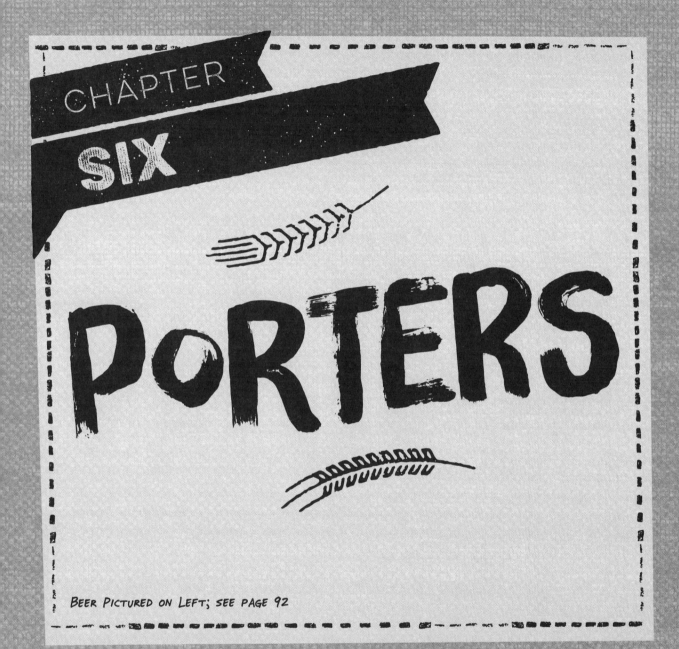

CHAPTER SIX

PORTERS

BEER PICTURED ON LEFT; SEE PAGE 92

ALASKAN BREWING COMPANY
SMOKED PORTER

eeeeee-

**(5 gallons/19 L, all-grain) OG = 1.065 FG = 1.015
IBU = 45 SRM = 58 ABV = 6.5%**

Dark, robust, and smoky when young, this porter develops notes of sherry, Madeira, and raisin as it ages. It has a chewy malt character and is chocolaty with a smoky, oily finish.

INGREDIENTS

8.25 lb. (3.74 kg) 2-row pale malt

4 lb. (1.81 kg) Munich malt

12 oz. (0.34 kg) crystal malt (45 °L)

11 oz. (0.31 kg) chocolate malt

7 oz. (0.20 kg) black patent malt

10.75 AAU Chinook hops (60 min.) (0.90 oz./25 g at 12% alpha acids)

3.75 AAU Willamette hops (15 min.) (0.75 oz./21 g at 5% alpha acids)

Wyeast 1968 (London ESB Ale) or White Labs WLP002 (English Ale) yeast

¾ cup (150 g) dextrose (for priming)

STEP BY STEP

Before brew day, smoke 1 pound (0.45 kilogram) of the Munich malt with alder wood. (Alaskan Brewing Company actually has its grains smoked at Taku Smokeries, a local Juneau smokehouse.) On brew day, mash the grains at 154°F (68°C). Mash out, vorlauf, and then sparge at 170°F (77°C). Boil for 90 minutes, adding the hops at the times indicated in the ingredients list. Pitch the yeast and ferment at 68°F (20°C) until final gravity is reached. Bottle or keg as normal.

PARTIAL MASH OPTION: Replace the 2-row pale and Munich malts with 2.25 pounds (1 kilogram) dried malt extract, 4.75 pounds (1.25 kilograms) liquid malt extract, and 1.25 pounds (0.56 kilogram) Munich malt. Smoke 1 pound (0.45 kilogram) of the Munich malt. Heat 4.7 quarts (4.4 liters) water to 165°F (74°C). Steep the crushed grains at 154°F (68°C) for 45 minutes. Rinse with 3.5 quarts (3.3 liters) of water at 170°F (77°C). Add the dried malt extract and water to make 2.5 gallons (9.5 liters) of wort. Boil for 60 minutes, adding the hops at the times indicated in the ingredients list and liquid malt extract with 15 minutes remaining. Cool the wort, transfer to your fermenter, and top up with filtered water to 5 gallons (19 liters). Follow the remaining portion of the all-grain recipe.

BIG TIME BREWERY
GODDESS PORTER

eeeeee-

**(5 gallons/19 L, all-grain) OG = 1.060 FG = 1.018
IBU = 33 SRM = 31 ABV = 5.5%**

Big Time's former brewmaster Billy Jenkins, who developed this recipe, says that the porter style has a good amount of latitude. He aims to find balance between the subtle sweetness and dark malt character. He advocates a low amount of finishing hops.

INGREDIENTS

9 lb. 10 oz. (4.5 kg) 2-row pale malt

1 lb. (0.45 kg) Munich malt

9 oz. (0.26 kg) flaked barley

9 oz. (0.26 kg) chocolate malt

3.6 oz. (100 g) crystal malt (15 °L)

3.6 oz. (100 g) crystal malt (75 °L)

3.6 oz. (100 g) roasted barley

1.8 oz. (51 g) black malt

8.2 AAU Chinook hops (60 min.) (0.63 oz./18 g at 13% alpha acids)

0.75 oz. (21 g) Centennial hops (0 min.)

Wyeast 1028 (London Ale) or White Labs WLP013 (London Ale) yeast (1 quart/~1 L yeast starter)

¾ cup (150 g) dextrose (if priming)

STEP BY STEP

Mash the grains at 154°F (68°C) for 45 minutes in 4 gallons (15 liters) of water. Boil for 90 minutes, adding hops at times indicated in ingredient list. After the boil, turn off the heat and chill the wort rapidly to 68°F (20°C). Aerate the wort well and pitch the yeast. Ferment at 68°F (20°C). When the beer has reached final gravity, bottle or keg as normal.

EXTRACT WITH GRAINS OPTION: Omit the 2-row pale malt. Add 2 pounds (0.91 kilogram) light dried malt extract and 4.5 pounds (2 kilograms) light liquid malt extract (late addition). Place the crushed malts in a nylon steeping bag and steep in 4.5 quarts (4.2 liters) of water at 154°F (68°C) for 30 minutes. Pull the grain bag out and drain over the pot in a colander. Rinse the grains with 1.5 quarts (~1.5 liters) of water at 170°F (66°C). Add water to make 3 gallons (11 liters), stir in the dried malt extract, and bring to a boil. Boil for 60 minutes, adding the hops at time indicated in the ingredients list. Add the liquid malt extract with 15 minutes left in the boil. After the boil, cool the wort, transfer to a fermenter, and top up with cool water to make 5 gallons (19 liters). Aerate the wort and pitch the yeast. Follow the remainder of the all-grain recipe.

BRIDGEPORT BREWING COMPANY
PUB PORTER

~~~~~~~

**(5 gallons/19 L, all-grain) OG = 1.055 FG = 1.013
IBU = 35 SRM = 41 ABV = 5.6%**

Some beers are just better on draft, and BridgePort's dark and malty porter is one of those beers. While it's only sold at their Portland, Oregon, pub, you can now keep it on draft at home (or in bottles, if you must).

INGREDIENTS

9.5 lb. (4.3 kg) British pale ale malt

0.75 lb. (0.34 kg) crystal malt (60 °L)

0.5 lb. (0.23 kg) chocolate malt

0.75 lb. (0.34 kg) roasted black barley

8.7 AAU Magnum hops (60 min.) (0.67 oz./18.8 g at 13% alpha acids)

3.7 AAU Kent Golding hops (5 min.) (1 oz./28 g at 3.7% alpha acids)

White Labs WLP051 (California V Ale) or Wyeast 1272 (American Ale II) yeast

¾ cup (150 g) dextrose (if priming)

STEP BY STEP

Mash the grains at 152°F (67°C). Vorlauf until your runnings are clear, sparge, and then boil the wort for 60 minutes. Add the hops at the times indicated in the ingredients list. After the boil, turn off the heat and chill the wort rapidly to 68°F (20°C). Aerate the wort well and pitch the yeast. Ferment at 68 to 70°F (20 to 21°C). When the beer has reached final gravity, bottle or keg as normal.

EXTRACT WITH GRAINS OPTION: Omit the British pale ale and crystal (60 °L) malts. Add 6.6 pounds (3 kilograms) Coopers amber liquid malt extract and 1 pound (0.45 kilogram) Muntons amber dried malt extract. Steep the crushed chocolate malt and roasted black barley in 2 quarts (~2 liters) of water at 150°F (66°C) for 30 minutes. Remove the bag, and add water to the pot to make 3 gallons (11 liters). Add the dried malt extract to the wort and bring to a boil. Boil for 60 minutes, trying to keep the wort topped up to 3 gallons (11 liters). Add the hops at the times indicated in the ingredients list. Add the liquid malt extract for last 15 minutes of boil. After the boil, cool the wort, transfer to a fermenter, and top off with cool water to reach 5 gallons (19 liters). Aerate and pitch yeast. Follow the remainder of the all-grain recipe.

CAPTURED BY PORCHES BREWING COMPANY
PUNCTURED BY CORPSES UNDEAD PORTER

~~~~~~~

**(5 gallons/19 L, all-grain) OG = 1.064 FG = 1.015
IBU = 29 SRM = 26 ABV = 6.3%**

This porter has an unusually heavy body and mouthfeel, thanks to the high percentage of unmalted grains, and a nose that accents hints of coffee and caramel. Chocolate dominates the flavor with just enough hops to prevent the finish from being too sweet.

INGREDIENTS

7.5 lb. (3.4 kg) 2-row pale malt

1.25 lb. (0.56 kg) crystal malt (30 °L)

7 oz. (0.19 kg) crystal malt (60 °L)

12 oz. (0.34 kg) chocolate malt

1 lb. 6 oz. (0.62 kg) flaked wheat

1 lb. 1 oz. (0.48 kg) flaked rye

1 lb. 1 oz. (0.48 kg) flaked oats

9 AAU Saaz pellet hops (first wort hop) (2.25 oz./64 g at 4% alpha acids)

5 AAU Saaz pellet hops (0 min.) (1.25 oz./35 g at 4% alpha acids)

½ tsp. yeast nutrient (15 min.)

½ tsp. Irish moss (30 min.)

White Labs WLP001 (California Ale) or Wyeast 1056 (American Ale) yeast

¾ cup (150 g) dextrose (if priming)

STEP BY STEP

Mix the crushed and flaked grains with 4.5 gallons (17 liters) of 176°F (80°C) water to stabilize at 156°F (69°C) for 60 minutes. Sparge slowly with 175°F (79°C) water. Collect approximately 6 gallons (23 liters) of wort runoff to boil for 60 minutes. Add hops, Irish moss, and yeast nutrient as per the schedule. Cool the wort to 75°F (24°C). Pitch your yeast and aerate the wort heavily. Allow the beer to cool to 68°F (20°C). Hold at that temperature until fermentation is complete. Allow the beer to condition for 1 week, and then bottle or keg.

EXTRACT WITH GRAINS OPTION: Reduce the 2-row pale malt in the all-grain recipe to 1 pound (0.45 kilogram), the flaked wheat to 10 ounces (0.28 kilogram), the flaked rye to 5 ounces (0.14 kilogram), and the flaked oats to

5 ounces (0.14 kilogram). Steep the crushed and flaked grains in 5.5 gallons (21 liters) of water at 156°F (69°C) for 45 minutes. Remove grains from the wort and rinse with 2 quarts (1.8 liters) of hot water. Add the liquid and dried malt extracts and boil for 60 minutes. Follow the remaining portion of the all-grain recipe.

- - - - - - - - - - - - - - -

DESCHUTES BREWING COMPANY
BLACK BUTTE PORTER

**(5 gallons/19 L, all-grain) OG = 1.058 FG = 1.016
IBU = 31 SRM = 32 ABV = 5.5%**

This is the recipe for Deschutes's flagship beer—the one that started it all! A rich, creamy mouthfeel complements a layered depth, revealing distinctive chocolate and coffee notes.

INGREDIENTS

9 lb. (4.1 kg) US 2-row malt

1 lb. (0.45 kg) US chocolate malt (350 °L)

1 lb. (0.45 kg) Carapils malt

12 oz. (340 g) US caramel malt (80 °L)

8 oz. (225 g) wheat malt

6 AAU Bravo hops (60 min.) (0.4 oz./11 g at 15% alpha acids)

1.1 AAU German Tettnang hops (30 min.) (0.25 oz./7 g at 4.5% alpha acids)

2.3 AAU Cascade hops (15 min.) (0.5 oz./14 g at 4.5% alpha acids)

0.5 oz. (14 g) Cascade hops (0 min.)

Whirlfloc or Irish moss (15 min.)

Wyeast 1187 (Ringwood Ale) or White Labs WLP005 (British Ale) yeast

5 g gypsum (CaSO4) (if using RO water)

¾ cup (150 g) dextrose (if priming)

STEP BY STEP

Mill grains and mix with 3.8 gallons (14.4 liters) of 162°F (72°C) strike water and optional minerals to reach a mash temperature of 151°F (66°C). Hold this temperature for 60 minutes. Vorlauf until your runnings are clear. Sparge the grains with enough 168°F (76°C) water to collect 6.5 gallons (25 liters) of 1.044 SG wort. Boil for 90 minutes, adding hops and finings according to the ingredients list. Turn off the heat and chill the wort to slightly below fermentation temperature, about 61°F

(16°C). Aerate the wort with pure oxygen or filtered air and pitch the yeast. Ferment at 63°F (17°C). Once at terminal gravity (approximately 7 days total), bottle or keg the beer and carbonate.

EXTRACT WITH GRAINS OPTION: Omit the 2-row malt and substitute with 6.5 pounds (3 kilograms) golden liquid malt extract. Place the milled grains in a muslin bag and steep in 6.5 quarts (7.4 liters) of 151°F (66°C) water for 15 minutes. Remove the grain and rinse with 1 gallon (3.8 liters) of hot water. Add water to the kettle to reach a volume of 5.5 gallons (20.8 liters), add optional minerals, and heat the wort to boiling. When you reach a boil, turn off the heat, add the liquid malt extract, and stir until completely dissolved. Top up if necessary to obtain 6 gallons (23 liters) of 1.048 SG wort. Boil for 60 minutes, adding hops and finings according to the ingredients list. Follow the remainder of the all-grain recipe.

- - - - - - - - - - - - - - -

FLYING DOG BREWERY
GONZO IMPERIAL PORTER

**(5 gallons/19 L, all-grain) OG = 1.088 FG = 1.019
IBU = 75 SRM = 57 ABV = 9.02%**

Brewed in honor of Hunter S. Thompson, this beer, the brewery says, is "big, bold, and beautiful." It features notes of roasted chocolate, coffee, and vanilla malt flavors.

INGREDIENTS

15 lb. (6.8 kg) 2-row pale malt

2.5 lb. (1.1 kg) crystal malt (120 °L)

1 lb. (0.45 kg) black malt

0.5 lb. (0.23 kg) chocolate malt

5.5 AAU Warrior hops (90 min.) (0.34 oz./9.7 g at 16% alpha acids)

9.4 AAU Northern Brewer hops (60 min.) (1 oz./28 g at 9% alpha acids)

9.4 AAU Northern Brewer hops (30 min.) (1 oz./28 g at 9% alpha acids)

3 oz. (85 g) Cascade hops (0 min.)

4 oz. (114 g) Cascade hops (dry hop)

Wyeast 1056 (American Ale) or White Labs WLP001 (California Ale) yeast (3 qt./~3 L yeast starter)

¾ cup (150 g) dextrose (for priming)

STEP BY STEP

Crush the grains and mash at 152°F (67°C) for 60 minutes. Mash out, vorlauf, and then sparge at 170°F (77°C) to collect enough wort to result in 5 gallons (19 liters) after a 2-hour boil. Boil 2 hours, adding the hops as directed. Cool, aerate, and pitch yeast. Ferment at 70°F (21°C). After fermentation is complete, bottle or keg as usual.

EXTRACT WITH GRAINS OPTION: Substitute the 2-row pale malt in the all-grain recipe with 3 pounds (1.4 kilograms) Briess light dried malt extract and 6.75 pounds (3.1 kilograms) Alexander's pale liquid malt extract. Heat 5.5 quarts (5.2 liters) of water to 166°F (74°C) and pour into 2-gallon (7.6-liter) beverage cooler. Place crushed specialty grains in a nylon steeping bag and submerge. Stir grains well, tie off bag lightly, and seal cooler. Let grains steep, starting at 155°F (68°C), for 30 minutes. While grains are steeping, heat 2 gallons (7.6 liters) of water to a boil in your brewpot and 2.5 quarts (2.4 liters) of water to 180°F (82°C) in a large kitchen pot. Run off "grain tea" and add to boiling water in brewpot. Add the 2.5 quarts (2.4 liters) of 180°F (82°C) water to the cooler, untie bag, stir grains, and let sit for 5 minutes. Run off remaining "grain tea" and add to brewpot. Add dried malt extract and bring to a boil. Add first charge of hops and boil for 60 minutes, adding other hops at times indicated in the ingredient list. With 15 minutes left in boil, stir in half of the liquid malt extract; add the remaining half at the end of the boil. Let wort sit 15 minutes before cooling. Cool wort and transfer to fermenter. Add water to make 5 gallons (19 liters). Follow the remaining portion of the all-grain recipe.

FULLER, SMITH & TURNER PLC
FULLER'S LONDON PORTER

(5 gallons/19 L, all-grain) OG = 1.054 FG = 1.014
IBU = 30 SRM = 33 ABV = 5.4%

Fuller's brewery describes their classic London porter as their take on the nineteenth-century style of porter. They say it "recaptures the brooding beauty of pre-Victorian London."

INGREDIENTS

8.27 lb. (3.75 kg) Muntons pale ale malt

1 lb. (0.45 kg) English crystal malt (75 °L)

1.5 lb. (0.68 kg) brown malt

0.75 lb. (0.34 kg) chocolate malt

6.25 AAU Fuggle hops (60 min.) (1.3 oz./37 g at 4.7% alpha acids)

3.15 AAU Fuggle hops (15 min.) (0.67 oz./19 g at 4.7% alpha acids)

Wyeast 1968 (London ESB Ale) or White Labs WLP002 (English Ale) yeast

¾ cup (150 g) dextrose (if priming)

STEP BY STEP

Crush the grains and mash at 153°F (67°C) for 60 minutes at mash thickness of 1.3 quarts per pound. Mash out, vorlauf, and then sparge at 170°F (77°C) to collect enough wort to result in 5 gallons (19 liters) after a 60-minute boil. Boil for 60 minutes, adding hops at times indicated. Cool, aerate, and pitch yeast. Ferment at 62°F (17°C). After fermentation is complete, bottle or keg as usual.

PARTIAL MASH OPTION: Reduce the pale ale malt in the all-grain recipe to 1 pound (0.45 kilogram) and add 1 pound (0.45 kilogram) Muntons light dried malt extract and 4 pounds (1.8 kilograms) Muntons light liquid malt extract. Mash grains at 153°F (67°C) for 45 minutes. Collect wort and add water to make 3 gallons (11 liters). Stir in dried malt extract and bring to a boil. Boil 60 minutes, adding hops at times indicated. With 15 minutes left in boil, remove from heat and add liquid malt extract. Stir well to dissolve, then resume heating. At the end of the boil, cool wort and transfer to fermenter, adding enough water to make 5 gallons (19 liters). Follow the remaining portion of the all-grain recipe.

GREAT LAKES BREWING COMPANY
EDMUND FITZGERALD PORTER

‹‹‹‹‹‹‹‹-

**(5 gallons/19 L, all-grain) OG = 1.060 FG = 1.015
IBU = 37 SRM = 34 ABV = 5.8%**

A rich, robust, complex ale that was brewed as a tribute to the legendary freighter's fallen crew. This beer has won a dozen medals over the years from the World Beer Championships (including World Champion) and five medals at the Great American Beer Festival (including gold).

INGREDIENTS

11 lb. (5 kg) 2-row pale malt

12 oz. (0.34 kg) crystal malt (60 °L)

8 oz. (0.22 kg) chocolate malt (350 °L)

8 oz. (0.22 kg) roasted barley (450 °L)

6.75 AAU Northern Brewer pellet hops (60 min.) (0.75 oz./21 g at 9% alpha acids)

2.4 AAU Fuggle pellet hops (30 min.) (0.5 oz./14 g at 4.75% alpha acids)

2.9 AAU Cascade pellet hops (0 min.) (0.5 oz./14 g at 5.75% alpha acids)

½ tsp. Yeast nutrient (15 min.)

White Labs WLP013 (London Ale) or Wyeast 1028 (London Ale) yeast

¾ cup (150 g) dextrose (if priming)

STEP BY STEP

Mix the crushed grains with 3.75 gallons (14 liters) of 170°F (77°C) water to stabilize at 155°F (68°C) for 60 minutes. Sparge slowly with 175°F (79°C) water. Collect approximately 6 gallons (23 liters) of wort runoff to boil for 60 minutes. Add the hops as indicated. After the boil, cool the wort to 75°F (24°C). Pitch your yeast and aerate the wort heavily. Allow the beer to cool to 68°F (20°C). Hold at that temperature until fermentation is complete. Transfer to a carboy, avoiding any splashing. Condition for 1 week and then bottle or keg. Allow the beer to carbonate and age for 2 weeks.

EXTRACT WITH GRAINS OPTION: Substitute the 2-row pale malt in the all-grain recipe with 6.6 pounds (3 kilograms) Coopers light unhopped malt extract and 1.1 pounds (0.49 kilogram) light dried malt extract. Steep the crushed grains

in 1.5 gallons (5.6 liters) of water at 155°F (68°C) for 30 minutes. Remove grains from the wort and rinse with 2 quarts (1.8 liters) of hot water. Add the liquid and dried malt extracts and bring to a boil. While boiling, add the hops and yeast nutrient as per the schedule. Now add the wort to 2 gallons (7.6 liters) of cold water in a sanitized fermenter and top off with cold water up to 5 gallons (19 liters). Follow the remaining portion of the all-grain recipe.

‹‹--‹--‹--‹--‹---‹--

HILL FARMSTEAD BREWERY
EVERETT

‹‹‹‹‹‹‹-

**(5 gallons/19 L, all-grain) OG = 1.088 FG = 1.030
IBU = 38 SRM = 55 ABV = 7.5%**

This porter is brewed using American malted barley, English and German roasted malts, American hops, and the Hill Farmstead's house ale yeast. It features deep dark flavors of coffee and chocolate.

INGREDIENTS

13.5 lb. (6.1 kg) 2-row pale malt

1 lb. (0.45 kg) dextrin malt

1.25 lb. (0.57 kg) CaraMalt (37 °L)

0.5 lb. (0.23 kg) crystal malt (90 °L)

1 lb. (0.45 kg) chocolate malt (300 °L)

1.25 lb. (0.57 kg) roasted barley (500 °L)

11 AAU Columbus hops (60 min.) (0.8 oz./23 g at 14% alpha acids)

Wyeast 1028 (London Ale), White Labs WLP013 (London Ale), or Lallemand Nottingham Ale yeast (~2.5 L starter)

¾ cup (150 g) dextrose (for priming)

STEP BY STEP

When crushing the grains, keep the dark roasted grains (crystal 90 °L, chocolate malt, and roasted barley) separate from the other grains. Mash the 2-row pale malt, dextrin malt, and caramalt at 159°F (71°C) in 5 gallons (19 liters) of water for 20 minutes, then mix in the darker grains. Hold for 5 minutes, then mash out, vorlauf, and sparge at 170°F (77°C). Boil for 60 minutes, adding the Columbus hops at the beginning of the boil. Pitch the yeast and ferment at 68°F (20°C) until the final gravity is reached, about 1 week. Allow the beer to condition for an additional week at 52°F (11°C) before packaging. Bottle or keg as usual.

EXTRACT WITH GRAINS OPTION: Replace the 2-row pale malt with 9.9 pounds (4.5 kilograms) light liquid malt extract. Crush the caramalt, crystal malt, chocolate malt, and roasted barley and place them in a muslin brewing bag. Steep the crushed specialty grains in 2 gallons (7.8 liters) water at 155°F (68°C) for 20 minutes. Rinse the grains with 3 quarts (2.8 liters) of hot water and allow it to drip into the kettle for about 15 minutes. To prevent extracting harsh tannins from the grain husks, be sure not to squeeze the bag. Add the malt extract to the brewpot with the heat turned off and stir well to avoid scorching or boil-overs. Top off the kettle to 6 gallons (23 liters). Follow the remaining portion of the all-grain recipe.

THE KERNEL BREWERY
EXPORT INDIA PORTER

(5 gallons/19 L, all-grain) OG = 1.060 FG = 1.015
IBU = 48 SRM = 40 ABV = 6%

This recipe is based on some of the Barclay Perkins (1855) and Whitbread (1856) porters that were sent out from England to India nearly two hundred years ago. Of course, elements of the ingredients, equipment, and processes are different, and tastes have also changed over time, so in keeping with The Kernel's philosophy, they have made a beer that contemporary beer drinkers want to drink, rather than a blindly faithful copy of a nineteenth-century recipe.

INGREDIENTS

9.6 lb. (4.3 kg) Maris Otter pale ale malt (2.4 °L)

0.9 lb. (0.4 kg) brown malt (38 °L)

0.9 lb. (0.4 kg) chocolate malt (330 °L)

0.9 lb. (0.4 kg) crystal malt (60 °L)

0.4 lb. (0.2 kg) black malt (500 °L)

5.6 AAU Bramling Cross hops (first wort hop) (0.7 oz./20 g at 8% alpha acids)

5.6 AAU Bramling Cross hops (15 min.) (0.7 oz./20 g at 8% alpha acids)

8 AAU Bramling Cross hops (10 min.) (1 oz./30 g at 8% alpha acids)

11.2 AAU Bramling Cross hops (5 min.) (1.4 oz./40 g at 8% alpha acids)

2.8 oz. (80 g) Bramling Cross hops (dry hop)

½ Whirlfloc tablet (10 min.)

White Labs WLP013 (London Ale) or Wyeast 1028 (London Ale) yeast

½ cup (100 g) dextrose (if priming)

STEP BY STEP

Mill the grains and dough-in targeting a mash of around 1.3 quarts of strike water to 1 pound of grain (2.7 L/kg) and a temperature of 154°F (68°C). Hold the mash at 154°F (68°C) until enzymatic conversion is complete. Sparge slowly with 171°F (77°C), collecting wort until the pre-boil kettle volume is 6 gallons (23 liters). Add the first wort hops during the sparging process. Total boil time is 60 minutes, adding the remaining hops at the times indicated. Add Whirlfloc with 10 minutes left in the boil. Chill the wort to 68°F (20°C) and aerate thoroughly. Pitch the yeast. Ferment at 68°F (20°C) until fermentation is complete. Dry hop 3 days before bottling or kegging. Carbonate the beer to around 2.4 volumes of CO_2. Condition at 59 to 68°F (15 to 20°C), allowing time for the beer to carbonate fully.

EXTRACT WITH GRAINS OPTION: Substitute the Maris Otter pale malt in the all-grain recipe with 6.6 pounds (3 kilograms) Maris Otter liquid malt extract. Steep the crushed grains in 6 gallons (23 liters) of 154°F (68°C) water for 30 minutes. Remove steeping bag and add liquid malt extract with the heat source off. Stir until completely dissolved. Add the first wort hops and bring wort to a boil for 60 minutes. Follow the remaining portion of the all-grain recipe.

TIPS FOR SUCCESS

Chocolate malt and crystal malt have replaced some of the black malt, which can sometimes produce burnt or astringent flavors. This recipe calls for lots of late hops and dry hopping, and The Kernel Brewery experiments with a number of different varieties. Bramling Cross (used here) gives a traditional British character, but Columbus can also work well if you want more of a New World character.

KISSMEYER BEER & BREWING
BALTIC PORTER

(5 gallons/19 L, all-grain) OG = 1.072 FG = 1.012
IBU = 45 SRM = 27 ABV = 8%

This big Baltic porter comes out of Denmark. The brewery describes it as medium-bodied with a crisp lager background. Expect the dominant flavors to come from the dark, roasty malts, with a hint of smokiness from the home-smoked malt.

INGREDIENTS

9 lb. 14 oz. (4.5 kg) pilsner malt

1.3 lb. (0.58 kg) dark Munich malt

1 lb. (0.45 kg) hand smoked lager malt (using alder as the wood, maximum smoke intensity)

0.5 lb. (0.23 kg) dark crystal malt

6 oz. (0.17 kg) pale wheat malt

6 oz. (0.17 kg) chocolate malt

4 oz. (0.11 kg) black malt

1 lb. (0.45 kg) local honey (0 min.)

0.035 oz. (1 g) raw licorice root (0 min.)

12 AAU Perle hops (60 min.) (1.7 oz./49 g at 7% alpha acids)

1 AAU East Kent Golding hops (30 min.) (0.2 oz./5.7 g at 5% alpha acids)

1 AAU East Kent Golding hops (15 min.) (0.2 oz./5.7 g at 5% alpha acids)

0.2 oz. (5.7 g) East Kent Golding hops (0 min.)

0.2 oz. (5.7 g) Styrian Golding hops (0 min.)

White Labs WLP830 (German Lager) or Wyeast 2124 (Bohemian Lager) yeast (12 qt./11 L yeast starter)

¾ cup (150 g) dextrose (if priming)

STEP BY STEP

Adjust your water to 60 ppm of calcium using calcium chloride ($CaCl_2$). Mash in at 122°F (50°C) before raising to a saccharification rest at 147°F (64°C) for 45 minutes, then 158°F (70°C) for 15 minutes before mashing out at 172°F (78°C). Alternatively, a single-infusion mash at 151°F (66°C) for 60 minutes is sufficient. Boil 60 minutes with hop additions as specified. Add the honey and raw licorice at the end of the boil. Cool wort to 57°F (14°C), aerate, pitch yeast, and then ferment at 57°F (14°C) until fermentation is complete (7 to 10 days). Cool beer to 41 to 46°F (5 to 8°C), leave at this temperature until all traces of sulfur and diacetyl are eliminated (5 to 10 days), then cool to just under 32°F (0°C) and cold lager for as long as possible (4 weeks will do, 8 weeks is better, 12 weeks is nice, 16 weeks near optimal). Aim for a carbonation level close to 2.5 volumes of CO_2.

PARTIAL MASH OPTION: Reduce the pilsner malt in the all-grain recipe to 3.2 ounces (91 grams) and add 2 pounds (0.91 kilogram) pilsner dried malt extract and 4.5 pounds (2 kilograms) pilsner liquid malt extract. Place the crushed grains in a large steeping bag and mash the crushed grains in 5.5 quarts (5.2 liters) of water at 151°F (66°C) for 60 minutes. Recirculate (if possible) until wort runs clear, then begin running off wort. Rinse grain bed with hot water (around 180 to 190°F/82 to 88°C, but don't let the grain bed exceed 170°F/77°C) until you have collected roughly 9 quarts (8.5 liters) of wort. Add liquid and dried malt extract and water to make 5.5 gallons (21 liters). Boil 60 minutes. Follow the remaining portion of the all-grain recipe.

MAUI BREWING COMPANY
COCONUT HIWA PORTER

(5 gallons/19 L, all-grain) OG = 1.057 FG = 1.014
IBU = 32 SRM = 26 ABV = 5.8%

Maui Brewing Co.'s flagship porter has gained a huge following thanks to a solid base beer recipe and the addition of fresh toasted coconut. Black and creamy, the chocolaty malts play perfectly with the coconut, with a touch of hoppy spice in the finish.

INGREDIENTS

8 lb. (3.6 kg) Maris Otter pale malt

12 oz. (0.34 kg) pale chocolate malt

4 oz. (113 g) caramel malt (80 °L)

4 oz. (113 g) Special B malt

2 oz. (57 kg) chocolate malt

8 oz. (0.23 kg) dark candi syrup (15 min.)

1 lb. (0.45 kg) corn sugar (15 min.)

8.3 AAU Golding pellet hops (60 min.) (1.15 oz./33 g at 7.2% alpha acids)

1 lb. (0.45 kg) shredded coconut, toasted (secondary)

Wyeast 2007 (Pilsen Lager) or Wyeast 1272 (American Ale II) yeast

¾ cup (150 g) dextrose (if priming)

STEP BY STEP

On brew day, prepare your ingredients: Mill the grain, measure your hops, and prepare your water. This recipe uses RO water. Add 1 teaspoon gypsum ($CaSO_4$), ½ teaspoon calcium chloride ($CaCl_2$), and 2 teaspoons calcium carbonate ($CaCO_3$) to the mash per 10 gallons of RO water. Heat to 3.5 gallons (13.3 liters) strike water to achieve a stable mash temperature at 152°F (67°C). Raise to mash out and begin to lauter. Boil for 90 minutes, adding the hops after 30 minutes at a boil and the corn sugar and dark candi syrup with 15 minutes left in the boil. After you turn off the heat, chill the wort to yeast pitching temperature and oxygenate heavily. Ferment at 50 to 55°F (10 to 13°C) if using the lager strain and 60 to 65°F

(16 to 18°C) if using the ale strain. After fermentation is complete, toast the shredded coconut (nonsweetened, no preservative) at low oven temperature (~250°F/121°C), flipping often to avoid burning, until golden brown. The reaction may take as little as 10 to 15 minutes or as much as 25 to 30 minutes. Add the coconut to secondary in a sanitized bag. Age on the coconut for 24 hours to 4 days. If flavor is lacking, follow up with coconut extract at packaging time. It is recommended to lager the beer for a couple weeks before drinking to clarify and help remove coconut solids. Bottle with priming sugar or force carbonate the serving keg to 2.4 volumes CO_2.

EXTRACT WITH GRAINS OPTION: Substitute the Maris Otter pale malt in the all-grain recipe with 4.5 pounds (2 kilograms) dark dried malt extract (17 °L). Prepare water as described in the all-grain recipe. Heat 5.5 gallons (21 liters) brewing water and place the crushed grain in a muslin bag. Steep the grains in the brewing water for 20 minutes as the water heats up. Remove the grain bag when the temperature reaches 170°F (77°C). Remove from heat and stir in the dried malt extract. Once the extract is fully dissolved, bring the wort to a boil and boil for 60 minutes. Follow the remaining portion of the all-grain recipe.

TIPS FOR SUCCESS

Instead of directly adding coconut, you could use a homemade extract. To do this, the day before brew day fill a 1-gallon (3.8-liter) glass jar with shredded coconut and a moderate quality vodka. Let the coconut steep in the vodka until your beer is finished fermenting, and then add the extract to the finished beer to taste.

ODELL BREWING COMPANY
CUTHROAT PORTER

eeeeeee

(5 gallons/19 L, all-grain) OG = 1.052 FG = 1.015
IBU = 43 SRM = 36 ABV = 5%

This London-style porter was named after Colorado's state fish: the Cutthroat Trout. With notes of chocolate and coffee, the beer, as Odell describes it, is smooth and robust but "not quite a stout."

INGREDIENTS

9 lb. (4.1 kg) 2-row pale ale malt

8 oz. (227 g) caramalt

6 oz. (170 g) crystal malt (40 °L)

4 oz. (113 g) amber or brown malt

4 oz. (113 g) Munich malt

8 oz. (227 g) chocolate malt

2 oz. (57 g) roasted barley

0.07 oz. (2 g) gypsum

0.04 oz. (1 g) calcium carbonate

11.25 AAU Fuggle hops (60 min.) (2.5 oz./71 g at 4.5% alpha acids)

0.5 oz. (14 g) Kent Golding hops (1 min.)

0.25 oz. (7 g) Kent Golding hops (1 min.)

0.25 oz. (7 g) Northern Brewer hops (0 min.)

1 pkg. of your favorite ale yeast (not an estery strain)

⅞ cup (175 g) dextrose (if priming)

STEP BY STEP

Mill all the grains and mash with the gypsum and calcium carbonate to achieve a 155°F (68°C) mash temperature. You will need 3.4 gallons (13 liters) of strike water at around 166°F (74°C) to do this. Let the mash rest for 40 minutes. Recirculate until the drawn off wort is fairly clear. Sparge with 170°F (77°C) water. Bring wort to a boil, starting at a level of 5.8 gallons (22 liters). Boil 60 minutes, adding hops as directed. Chill the wort, aerate, pitch yeast, and ferment at the appropriate temperature for your favorite ale yeast. Once fermentation is complete, chill the beer to as close to 36°F (2°C) as you can and age for 10 to 14 days. Bottle or keg and enjoy.

EXTRACT WITH GRAINS OPTION: Substitute the 2-row pale malt in the all-grain recipe with 2 pounds 6 ounces (1.1 kilograms) Muntons light dried malt extract and 3.3 pounds (1.5 kilograms) Muntons light liquid malt extract. Place crushed grains in a nylon steeping bag and steep at 155°F (68°C) in 3 quarts (2.8 liters) of water for 45 minutes. Rinse grains with 1.5 quarts (1.4 liters) of water at 170°F (77°C). Add water (to save time, preferably boiling water) to "grain tea" to make 3 gallons (11 liters), stir in dried malt extract, and bring to a boil. Boil for 60 minutes, adding hops at times indicated in the ingredient list. Stir in liquid malt extract with 15 minutes remaining in boil. After the boil, top off to 5 gallons (19 liters) and follow the remaining portion of the all-grain recipe.

OSKAR BLUES BREWERY
DEATH BY COCONUT

ссссссс-

(5 gallons/19 L, all-grain) OG = 1.067 FG = 1.017
IBU = 25 SRM = 40 ABV = 6.5%

This porter is packed full of intense malt flavor and then infused with pure liquid cacao and loads of dried coconut. A balance of intensities!

INGREDIENTS

12 lb. (5.4 kg) North American 2-row pale malt (1.8 °L)

4.6 oz. (132 g) Munich malt (10 °L)

12.5 oz. (354 g) Simpsons extra dark crystal malt (175 °L)

7.4 oz. (209 g) Simpsons coffee (brown) malt (200 °L)

7.7 oz. (218 g) chocolate malt (400 °L)

4.7 oz. (132 g) Carafa Special III malt (500 °L)

7.8 AAU Columbus hops (80 min.) (0.6 oz./16.8 g at 13% alpha acids)

1 tsp. yeast nutrient (Servomyces recommended) (5 min.)

½ Whirlfloc tablet (5 min.)

1.3 lb. (0.59 kg) dried coconut

750 mL Cholaca pure liquid cacao

White Labs WLP001 (California Ale), Wyeast 1056 (American Ale), or Safale US-05 yeast

¾ cup (150 g) dextrose (if priming)

STEP BY STEP

Mill the grains and dough-in targeting a mash of around 1.3 quarts of water to 1 pound of grain (2.7 liters/kilograms) and a mash temperature of 153°F (67°C). Hold the mash at 153°F (67°C) until enzymatic conversion is complete. Sparge slowly with 168°F (76°C) water, collecting wort until the pre-boil kettle volume is 6.5 gallons (24.6 liters).

Total boil time is 90 minutes. Add hops at times indicated and the Whirlfloc and yeast nutrient when 5 minutes are left in the boil. After the boil is complete, give the wort a long stir to create a whirlpool, and let settle for 10 minutes. Chill the wort to 65°F (18°C) and aerate thoroughly. Pitch rate is 1 million cells per mL per degree Plato. Regulate the fermentation temperature at 68°F (20°C). At the end of fermentation activity (~5 days), let rest for 5 more days at 68°F (20°C). Then lower temperature to 32°F (0°C). Once beer is clarified, rack the beer into secondary. Add the pure liquid cacao and dried coconut (bag the dried coconut). Hold for 1 week at 32°F (0°C) and then rack and carbonate the beer to around 2.55 volumes of CO_2. If bottling conditioning, you may consider pitching fresh yeast at bottling.

EXTRACT WITH GRAINS OPTION: Replace the 2-row pale malt and Munich malt with 6.6 pounds (3 kilograms) golden liquid malt extract and 1.5 pounds (0.68 kilograms) Munich dried malt extract. Place the crushed grains in a muslin bag and submerge bag in 5 gallons (19 liters) water as it heats up to 160°F (71°C). Remove the grain bag and allow to drip back into the kettle. Add the liquid and dried malt extract and stir until extracts are fully dissolved. Bring wort to a boil. Boil for 80 minutes, adding hops as the wort comes to a boil. Follow the remaining portion of the all-grain recipe.

OSKAR BLUES BREWERY
OLD CHUB SCOTCH ALE

ссссссс-

(5 gallons/19 L, all-grain) OG = 1.078 FG = 1.020
IBU = 35 SRM = 32 ABV = 7.4%

Oskar Blues proved it can make beers for malt lovers with this mega-malty Scottish strong ale. It's brewed with a variety of specialty malts, including a touch of smoked malt for added depth. It features flavors of cocoa and coffee with just a bit of that smoke.

INGREDIENTS

13 lb. 10 oz. (6.2 kg) North American 2-row pale malt

18 oz. (0.52 kg) English dark crystal malt

12 oz. (0.34 kg) Munich malt (10 °L)

3.5 oz. (99 g) English chocolate malt

6 oz. (0.17 kg) Special B malt

4.5 oz. (0.13 kg) Weyermann smoked malt

9.6 AAU Nugget hops (60 min.) (0.8 oz./23 g at 12% alpha acids)

Wyeast 1056 (American Ale), White Labs WLP001 (California Ale), or Fermentis Safale US-05 yeast (3.5 qt./3.5 L yeast starter)

½ cup (100 g) dextrose (if priming)

STEP BY STEP

If possible, make a smaller beer 2 to 4 weeks prior to brewing this beer and use the yeast from the small beer to pitch into this beer. Otherwise, make a 3.5-quart (3.5-liter) yeast starter several days prior to brew day. Mash the grains at 155°F (68°C). Boil for 90 minutes, adding the hops with 60 minutes left in the boil. Pitch the yeast and ferment at 69°F (21°C) until final gravity is reached. Bottle or keg, then cold condition the beer for at least 3 weeks at or below 50°F (10°C) before serving.

PARTIAL MASH OPTION: Scale down the North American 2-row pale malt to 8 ounces (0.23 kilogram) and add 3 pounds (1.4 kilograms) Muntons light dried malt extract and 5.5 pounds (2.5 kilograms) Muntons light liquid malt extract to the ingredients list. Steep the grains at 155°F (68°C) in 5 quarts (4.7 liters) of water. Rinse the grains and add water to the "grain tea" to make at least 3.5 gallons (13 liters). Add the dried malt extract and bring to a boil. Boil for 60 minutes, adding the hops at the beginning of the boil. Stir in the liquid malt extract near the end of the boil. Cool the wort and transfer to your fermenter. Top up to 5 gallons (19 liters) with filtered water. Follow the remaining portion of the all-grain recipe.

SAMUEL ADAMS BREWING COMPANY HOLIDAY PORTER

(5 gallons/19 L, all-grain) OG = 1.063 FG = 1.020
IBU = 40 SRM = 30 ABV = 5.8%

This seasonal release features a deep dark color with rich chocolate and coffee flavors. It's the ideal dark beer for sipping fireside over a winter break.

INGREDIENTS

- 10.1 lb. (4.6 kg) 2-row pale malt (2 °L)
- 1.4 lb. (0.64 kg) Munich malt (10 °L)
- 1.2 lb. (0.54 kg) caramel malt (60 °L)
- 0.5 lb. (0.23 kg) Weyermann Carafa Special III malt (525 °L)
- 0.3 lb. (0.14 kg) flaked oats
- 4.25 AAU Spalt pellet hops (60 min.) (1.25 oz./35 g at 3.4% alpha acids)
- 1.25 AAU UK Fuggle pellet hops (60 min.) (0.25 oz./7 g at 5% alpha acids)
- 6 AAU Spalt pellet hops (5 min.) (1.75 oz./50 g at 3.4% alpha acids)
- 4.4 AAU East Kent Golding pellet hops (5 min.) (0.75 oz./21 g at 5.8% alpha acids)
- 0.5 tsp. yeast nutrients (15 min.)
- White Labs WLP001 (California Ale), Wyeast 1056 (American Ale), Fermentis Safale US-05, or Lallemand BRY-97 yeast
- ¾ cup (150 g) dextrose (if priming)

STEP BY STEP

This is a single-infusion mash. Mix the crushed grains with 5 gallons (19 liters) of 167°F (75°C) strike water to stabilize the mash at 155°F (68°C). Hold at this temperature for 45 minutes. Vorlauf for 15 minutes then begin sparge. Run off into kettle to achieve volume and pre-boil gravity around 1.051 SG. Boil for 60 minutes, adding hops and yeast nutrients according to the ingredients list. Once you turn off the heat, give the wort a stir for about a minute to create a whirlpool and let that spin and settle out for about 15 minutes before beginning to chill the wort. Cool the wort down to slightly below fermentation temperature, about 65°F (18°C). Aerate the wort with filtered air or pure O_2 and pitch yeast. Ferment at 68°F (20°C) for 1 week or until signs of fermentation have died down. Rack to a secondary vessel and cool beer to 60°F (16°C). Condition for an additional 1 to 2 weeks. Bottle or keg and carbonate to 2.2 volumes of CO_2.

PARTIAL MASH OPTION: Replace the Munich malt and reduce the 2-row pale malt in the all-grain recipe to 1.5 pounds (0.68 kilogram) and add 3.3 pounds (1.5 kilograms) light liquid malt extract and 3.3 pounds (1.5 kilograms) Munich liquid malt extract. Place crushed grains in a muslin bag and steep in 1.5 gallons (5.7 liters) water at 155°F (68°C) for 45 minutes. Remove the grain bag and slowly wash the grains with 1 gallon (3.8 liters) of hot water. Transfer wort to brew kettle and top off to 6 gallons (23 liters). Just before the water reaches boil, remove from heat and stir in the malt extract until dissolved. Your pre-boil gravity should be around 1.051 SG. Boil for 60 minutes. Follow the remaining portion of the all-grain recipe.

STONE BREWING COMPANY SMOKED PORTER

(5 gallons/19 L, all-grain) OG = 1.064 FG = 1.018
IBU = 53 SRM = 36 ABV = 6%

Stone is known for their bold personality and bold flavors—but that doesn't mean they go over the top. This smoky porter is a good example. It's brewed with chocolate malt, crystal malt, and just a hint of lightly peated malt.

INGREDIENTS

11.5 lb. (5.2 kg) 2-row pale malt

12 oz. (0.34 kg) crystal malt (75 °L)

1.25 lb. (0.57 kg) chocolate malt

1 oz. (28 g) lightly peated malt

12.5 AAU Perle hops (90 min.) (1.8 oz./51 g at 7% alpha acids)

0.5 oz. (14 g) Mt. Hood hops (15 min.)

White Labs WLP002 (English Ale) or Wyeast 1968 (London ESB Ale) yeast (1.5 qt./1.5 L yeast starter)

⅞ cup (175 g) dextrose (for priming)

STEP BY STEP

Crush the grains and mash at 154°F (68°C) for 60 minutes. Mash out, vorlauf, and then sparge at 170°F (77°C) to collect enough wort to result in 5 gallons (19 liters) after a 90-minute boil. Boil for 90 minutes, adding hops at times directed. Cool, aerate, and pitch yeast. Ferment at 68°F (20°C). After fermentation is complete, bottle or keg as usual.

EXTRACT WITH GRAINS OPTION: Substitute the 2-row pale malt in the all-grain recipe with 3 pounds (1.4 kilograms) light dried malt extract and 4.25 pounds (1.9 kilograms) light liquid malt extract. Steep the crushed grains in 3 quarts (3 liters) of water at 154°F (68°C) for 45 minutes. Remove grains and add water to make 3.5 gallons (13 liters) of wort. Add dried malt extract and bring to a boil for 60 minutes. Follow the remaining portion of the all-grain recipe.

VERMONT PUB & BREWERY
VERMONT SMOKED PORTER

(5 gallons/19 L, all-grain) OG = 1.055 FG = 1.016
IBU = 47 SRM = 33 ABV = 5.7%

Vermont Pub & Brewery smokes their own malts over apple, maple, and hickory woodchips to re-create this seventeenth-century-style robust ale. You can smoke your own malts or buy rauchmalt as an alternative.

INGREDIENTS

8 lb. 14 oz. (4 kg) 2-row pale malt

2 lb. (0.91 kg) smoked malt

0.5 lb. (0.23 kg) black patent malt

0.5 lb. (0.23 kg) chocolate malt

12 AAU Chinook hops (65 min.) (1 oz./28 g at 12% alpha acids)

3 AAU Golding hops (5 min.) (0.75 oz./21 g at 4% alpha acids)

Wyeast 1098 (British Ale) or White Labs WLP007 (Dry English Ale) yeast (1.5 qt./ ~1.5 L yeast starter)

¾ cup (150 g) dextrose (if priming)

STEP BY STEP

Mash the grains at 152°F (67°C) for 60 minutes. Mash out, vorlauf, and then sparge at 170°F (77°C) to collect enough wort to result in 5 gallons (19 liters) after a 90-minute boil. Boil 90 minutes, adding hops at times indicated. Cool, aerate, and pitch yeast. Ferment at 65°F (18°C). After fermentation is complete, rack to secondary and condition 3 weeks at 55°F (13°C). Bottle or keg and condition for another 3 weeks at 45°F (7°C).

PARTIAL MASH OPTION: Reduce the 2-row pale malt in the all-grain recipe to 2 pounds (0.9 kilogram) and add 1.25 pounds (0.56 kilogram) light dried malt extract and 3.3 pounds (1.5 kilograms) light liquid malt extract. Heat 2 gallons (7.6 liters) water to 163°F (73°C). Crush grains, mix into liquor, and hold 75 minutes at 152°F (67°C). Sparge grains with 1.5 gallons (5.7 liters) at 168°F (76°C). Add the dried malt extract, mix well. Raise to boiling, add hops as indicated and liquid malt extract with 15 minutes left in boil. Cool and top off to 5 gallons (19 liters). Follow the remaining portion of the all-grain recipe.

CHAPTER SEVEN

STOUTS

BEER PICTURED ON LEFT; SEE PAGE 107

ANDERSON VALLEY BREWING COMPANY
BARNEY FLATS OATMEAL STOUT

⋘⋘⋘-

(5 gallons/19 L, all-grain) OG = 1.060 FG = 1.017
IBU = 14 SRM = 34 ABV = 5.8%

Anderson Valley describes Barney Flats Oatmeal Stout as having "aromas of freshly baked bread, espresso, and dried cherries meld seamlessly with rich toffee flavors and a creamy mouthfeel."

INGREDIENTS

8.75 lb. (4 kg) 2-row pale malt

12 oz. (0.34 kg) crystal malt (40 °L)

12 oz. (0.34 kg) crystal malt (80 °L)

12 oz. (0.34 kg) Munich malt (20 °L)

1.3 oz. (37 g) roasted barley

14 oz. (0.39 kg) chocolate malt

15 oz. (0.42 kg) flaked oats

3.9 AAU Columbus hops (60 min.) (0.28 oz./8 g at 14% alpha acids)

0.25 oz. (7 g) Northern Brewer hops (0 min.)

Wyeast 1968 (London ESB Ale) or White Labs WLP002 (English Ale) yeast (2 qt./2 L yeast starter)

¾ cup (150 g) dextrose (if priming)

STEP BY STEP

Mash at 154°F (68°C) in 18 quarts (17 liters) of water. Collect wort until last runnings dip below original gravity 1.012. Adjust pre-boil volume to have enough for a 90-minute boil. Add hops at times indicated. After the boil, cool to 68°F (20°C), aerate, pitch yeast, and ferment at that temperature. Bottle or keg as usual.

PARTIAL OPTION: Substitute the 2-row pale malt in the all-grain recipe with 4.5 pounds (2 kilograms) extra light dried malt extract and increase the amount of Munich malt to 1 pound (0.45 kilogram). Place the crushed Munich malt and flaked oats in 1 muslin bag and the crystal and roasted grains in a separate bag. Mash the crushed Munich malt and flaked oats at 154°F (68°C) in 6 quarts (6 liters) of water for 45 minutes. Add the second bag to the mash and steep for an additional 15 minutes. Remove both bags and place in a colander. Wash all the grains with 1 gallon (4 liters) of hot water. Top off to 6 gallons (23 liters) and heat to a boil. Follow the remaining portion of the all-grain recipe.

BEAMISH
GENUINE IRISH STOUT

⋘⋘⋘-

(5 gallons/19 L, all-grain) OG = 1.039 FG = 1.008
IBU = 26 SRM = 40 ABV = 4.0%

Beamish describes their classic Irish dry stout as having a rich, roasted flavor with coffee and dark chocolate undertones. Note the low target FG when cloning this recipe.

INGREDIENTS

5.88 lb. (2.65 kg) 2-row pale ale malt

8 oz. (226 g) wheat malt

6 oz. (170 g) cane sugar

4 oz. (0.11 kg) crystal malt (60 °L)

6 oz. (170 g) chocolate malt

4.5 oz. (128 g) roasted barley (500 °L)

1.5 oz. (43 g) black patent malt (500 °L)

3.5 AAU Challenger hops (60 min.) (0.5 oz./14 g at 7% alpha acids)

3 AAU Kent Golding hops (60 min.) (0.6 oz./17 g at 5% alpha acids)

1 AAU Hallertau-Hersbrücker hops (15 min.) (0.25 oz./7 g at 4% alpha acids)

1 tsp. Irish moss (15 min.)

Wyeast 1968 (London ESB Ale) or White Labs WLP002 (English Ale) yeast (1 qt./~1 L yeast starter)

⅔ cup (130 g) dextrose (if priming)

STEP BY STEP

Mash the grains at 149°F (65°C) for 60 minutes. Vorlauf until your runnings are clear, sparge, and collect 4 gallons (~15 liters) of wort. Add 2.5 gallons (9.4 liters) of water and boil wort for 90 minutes, adding hops at times indicated in the ingredients list. Add sugar and Irish moss for final 15 minutes of boil. After the boil, turn off the heat and chill the wort rapidly to just below fermentation temperature, about 68°F (20°C). Aerate the wort well and pitch the yeast. Ferment at 70°F (21°C). When the beer has reached final gravity, bottle or keg as normal.

EXTRACT WITH GRAINS OPTION: Scale the 2-row pale malt down to 0.5 pound (0.23 kilogram) and the wheat malt up to 0.5 pound (0.23 kilogram). Add 0.5 pound (0.23 kilogram) light dried malt extract and 3.3 pounds (1.5 kilograms) light liquid malt extract (late addition). Place the crushed malts in a nylon steeping bag and steep in 3 quarts (2.8 liters) of water at 149°F (65°C) for 30 minutes. Pull the grain bag out and drain over the pot in a colander. Rinse the grains with 1.5 quarts (~1.5 liters) of water at 170°F (66°C). Add water to make 3 gallons (11 liters), stir in the dried malt extract, and bring to a boil. Boil for 60 minutes, adding the hops at time indicated in the ingredients list. Add the liquid malt extract and Irish moss with 15 minutes left in the boil. After the boil, cool the wort, transfer to a fermenter, and top up with cool water to make 5 gallons (19 liters). Aerate the wort and pitch the yeast. Follow the remainder of the all-grain recipe.

BISON BREWING COMPANY
ORGANIC CHOCOLATE STOUT

**(5 gallons/19 L, all-grain) OG = 1.058 FG = 1.020
IBU = 25 SRM = 40 ABV = 5.1%**

Bison Organic Chocolate Stout is rich and roasty with charismatic flavors of dark chocolate and espresso. It's creamy but with a drier finish than its FG would suggest.

INGREDIENTS

7.5 lb. (3.4 kg) organic 2-row pale malt

1.5 lb. (0.68 kg) organic Munich malt

2 lb. (0.91 kg) organic Caramunich malt (45 °L)

1 lb. (0.45 kg) organic chocolate malt (350 °L)

0.5 lb. (0.23 kg) organic roasted barley (300 °L)

1 oz. (28 g) cocoa powder

6 AAU Pacific Gem hops (60 min.) (0.5 oz./14 g at 12% alpha acids)

2 AAU Pacific Gem hops (2 min.) (0.4 oz./11 g at 5% alpha acids)

White Labs WLP011 (European Ale) or Wyeast 2565 (Kölsch) yeast (1.5 qt./1.5 L yeast starter)

¾ cup (150 g) dextrose (if priming)

STEP BY STEP

Mash at 152°F (67°C) for 60 minutes. To mash in, add ⅓ of the grains and stir in cocoa. Layer remaining ⅔ of grain bed over this. Mash out, vorlauf, and then sparge at 170°F (77°C) to collect enough wort in the kettle to account for an extended boil. Boil for 75 to 90 minutes, adding hops as per the ingredient schedule. Following the boil, cool, aerate, and pitch yeast. Ferment at 70°F (21°C). After fermentation is complete, bottle or keg as usual.

PARTIAL MASH OPTION: Substitute the 2-row pale malt in the all-grain recipe with 4 pounds (1.8 kilograms) Briess Maltoferm organic light dried malt extract. Mash crushed Munich grains for 45 minutes at 152°F (67°C) in 4 quarts (4 liters) of water. Stir in the Caramunich, chocolate malt, roasted barley, and cocoa along with 4 quarts (4 liters) more of hot water and steep for an additional 15 minutes. Remove the grains and add dried malt extract to wort to bring wort volume to 3 gallons (11.4 liters) and boil for 60 minutes. Add hops according to the ingredient list. Cool wort and transfer to fermenter, topping off to 5 gallons (19 liters). Follow the remaining portion of the all-grain recipe.

BROUWERIJ DE DOLLE BROUWER
DE DOLLE EXTRA EXPORT STOUT

**(5 gallons/19 L, all-grain) OG = 1.086 FG = 1.018
IBU = 53 SRM = 70 ABV = 9%**

This Belgian stout is a deep, dark-colored beer with lots of coffee and chocolate flavors.

INGREDIENTS

10 lb. (4.5 kg) Dingemans pale ale malt (4 °L)

1 lb. (0.45 kg) Special B malt (125 °L)

0.5 lb. (0.23 kg) chocolate malt

1.25 lb. (0.57 kg) roasted barley (450 °L)

3 lb. (1.4 kg) Belgian dark candi sugar (15 min.)

14 AAU Nugget hops (60 min.) (1 oz./28 g at 14% alpha acids)

7 AAU Nugget hops (20 min.) (0.5 oz./14 g at 14% alpha acids)

White Labs WLP510 (Bastogne Belgian Ale) or Wyeast 3942 (Belgian Wheat) yeast

¾ cup (150 g) dextrose (if priming)

STEP BY STEP

Step mash at 125°F (52°C) for 15 minutes, 145°F (63°C) for 35 minutes, 165°F (74°C) for 25 minutes, and 172°F (78°C) for 5 minutes. Collect wort and boil for 60 minutes, adding hops at times indicated. Cool the wort, aerate, and pitch yeast. Ferment at 72°F (22°C). Once fermentation is complete, bottle or keg as usual.

PARTIAL MASH OPTION: Reduce the pale ale malt in the all-grain recipe to 3 pounds (1.4 kilograms) and add 3.3 pounds (1.5 kilograms) Maris Otter liquid malt extract and 1 pound (0.45 kilogram) extra light dried malt extract. Heat 5.5 quarts (5.2 liters) of soft water to 163°F (73°C) in a large kitchen pot. Stir ½ teaspoon gypsum ($CaSO_4$) or calcium chloride into this water. In another pot, heat 2.5 quarts (2.4 liters) of soft water to around 163°F (73°C). Stir 1 teaspoon calcium carbonate (chalk) or ½ teaspoon sodium bicarbonate (baking soda) into this water. In your brewpot, begin heating a half-gallon (2 liters) of water to around 170°F (77°C). Place crushed pale malt and Special B in 1 grain bag and place in mash tun. Put remaining dark grains (crushed) in the other bag. Add the 5.5 quarts (5.2 liters) of water to the pale grains in the mash tun and stir it in. Let this mash, starting at 152°F (67°C), for 45 minutes. Likewise, steep the specialty grains in the pot of carbonate-rich water for 45 minutes (around 152°F/67°C). While grains mash and steep, heat 2 gallons (7.6 liters) of water to 180°F (82°C). When mashing and steeping is complete, scoop 1 quart (1 liter) of 170°F (77°C) water from your brewpot. Lift the specialty grains out of their pot and place in a colander over your brewpot. Pour the "grain tea" through the grain bag and then rinse the grains with the water pulled from your brewpot. Start heating this "grain tea" while you collect the wort from the cooler. To collect wort from mash, recirculate about 2.5 quarts (2.4 liters) of wort, then add 180°F (82°C) water to cooler until it is full. Draw off wort and add to brewpot until the liquid level in the cooler is just above the grain bed. Add 180°F (82°C) water to fill cooler again. Repeat this process until you have collected 2 gallons (7.6 liters) of wort. Add dried malt extract and bring wort to a boil for 60 minutes, adding hops at times indicated. Stir in liquid malt extract and Belgian candi sugar for the final 15 minutes of the boil. Cool wort to 72°F (22°C) and transfer to fermenter, topping off to 5 gallons 919 liters). Follow the remaining portion of the all-grain recipe.

FIRESTONE WALKER BREWING COMPANY
VELVET MERLIN

ccccccc-

(5 gallons/19 L, all-grain) OG = 1.061
FG = 1.020 IBU = 29 SRM = 44 ABV = 5.6%

This seasonal oatmeal stout is named in honor of Firestone Walker's brewmaster Matt "Merlin" Brynildson, who earned the nickname because of his magical ability to rack up top honors at prestigious beer competitions. This is a rich beer with dark chocolate and roasted coffee flavors. It boasts a truly creamy mouthfeel and dry finish.

INGREDIENTS

8.75 lb. (4 kg) Rahr Standard 2-Row malt

1 lb. 9 oz. (0.71 kg) flaked oats

1 lb. 9 oz. (0.71 kg) Briess roasted barley (300 °L)

14 oz. (400 g) caramel malt (120 °L)

5 oz. (140 g) Carapils malt

4 oz. (113 g) caramel malt (80 °L)

4 oz. (113 g) Weyermann Carafa Special III malt

3.8 AAU Fuggle hops (60 min.) (0.85 oz./24 g at 4.5% alpha acids)

3.8 AAU Fuggle hops (30 min.) (0.85 oz./24 g at 4.5% alpha acids)

7 g calcium chloride (if using RO water)

White Labs WLP002 (English Ale) or Wyeast 1968 (London ESB Ale) yeast

¾ cup (150 g) dextrose (if priming)

STEP BY STEP

Mash the grains (and calcium chloride) at 145°F (63°C) for 15 minutes. Raise the mash temperature to 155°F (68°C) and hold for 30 minutes. Raise the temperature to a mash-out of 168°F (76°C). Mash out, vorlauf, and then sparge at 168°F (76°C). You should now have 6 gallons (23 liters) of 1.051 SG wort. Boil for 60 minutes, adding the hops at the times indicated. Chill the wort to slightly below fermentation temperature, about 66°F (19°C). Aerate the wort with pure oxygen or filtered air and pitch the yeast. Ferment at 68°F (20°C) until final gravity is reached. Bottle or keg as usual.

PARTIAL MASH OPTION: Substitute 5 pounds (2.27 kilograms) of golden liquid malt extract and 1.5 pounds (0.68 kilogram) of US 2-row pale malt in place of the Rahr Standard 2-Row malt in the all-grain recipe. Place the milled 2-row pale malt and flaked oats in a muslin bag and steep in 10 quarts (9.5 liters) of 149°F (65°C) water for 45 minutes. Remove the grains and rinse with 1 gallon (3.8 liters) of hot water. Add the remaining crushed grains in a separate muslin bag and steep for an additional 15 minutes. Add water to reach a volume of 5.4 gallons (20.4 liters) and heat to boiling. Turn off the heat, add the liquid malt extract and optional calcium chloride, and stir until completely dissolved. Top up to obtain 6 gallons (23 liters) of 1.051 SG wort. Boil for 60 minutes, adding hops according to the ingredients list. Follow the remaining portion of the all-grain recipe.

GUINNESS
DRAUGHT

⸺⸺⸺

(5 gallons/19 L, all-grain) OG = 1.038 FG = 1.006
IBU = 45 SRM = 36 ABV = 4.2%

Guinness Draught, the kind found in widget cans or bottles, is an Irish dry stout. Side by side, you'll notice it has a sharper roast character and more hop bitterness than Murphy's. The key to making a great clone is using roasted unmalted barley (or black barley) with a color rating around 500 °L.

INGREDIENTS

5 lb. (2.3 kg) English 2-row pale ale malt

2.5 lb. (1.1 kg) flaked barley

1 lb. (0.45 kg) roasted barley (500 °L)

12 AAU East Kent Golding hops (60 min.) (2.4 oz./68 g at 5% alpha acids)

Wyeast 1084 (Irish Ale) or White Labs WLP004 (Irish Ale) yeast (1 qt./1 L yeast starter)

¾ cup (150 g) dextrose (if priming)

STEP BY STEP

Heat 2.66 gallons (10 liters) of water to 161°F (72°C) and stir in crushed grains and flaked barley. Mash at 150°F (66°C) for 60 minutes. Stir boiling water into grain bed until temperature reaches 168°F (76°C) and rest for 5 minutes. Recirculate until wort is clear, then begin running wort off to kettle. Sparge with 170°F (77°C) water. Boil wort for 90 minutes, adding hops with 60 minutes left in boil. Cool wort and transfer to fermenter. Aerate wort and pitch yeast. Ferment at 72°F (22°C). Rack to secondary when fermentation is complete. Bottle a few days later, when beer falls clear. If beer is kegged, consider pushing with a nitrogen (beer gas) blend.

PARTIAL MASH OPTION: Reduce the 2-row pale malt in the all-grain recipe to 1.25 pounds (0.57 kilogram) and reduce the flaked barley to 1.25 pounds (0.57 kilogram), and add 3.3 pounds (1.5 kilograms) Maris Otter liquid malt extract. Place crushed malt and barley in a steeping bag. In a large kitchen pot, heat 4.5 quarts (4.3 liters) of water to 161°F (72°C) and submerge grain bag. Let grains mash for 45 minutes at around 150°F (66°C). While grains are steeping, begin heating 2.1 gallons (7.9 liters) of water in your brewpot. Add in the crushed roasted barley and steep for an additional 15 minutes. When steep is over, remove 1.25 quarts (1.2 liters) of water from brewpot and add to the "grain tea" in steeping pot. Rinse grain bag with diluted grain tea and then bring to a boil. Stir in liquid malt extract off heat, and add hops at the beginning of the 60-minute boil. Top off to 5 gallons (19 liters) at the end of the boil. Follow the remaining portion of the all-grain recipe.

TIPS FOR SUCCESS

To get that "Guinness tang," try this: After pitching the yeast to your stout, siphon 19 ounces of pitched wort to a sanitized 22-ounce bottle. Pitch bottle with a small amount of *Brettanomyces* and *Lactobacillus*. Cover bottle with aluminum foil and let ferment. When beer in bottle is done fermenting, pour it in a saucepan and heat to 160°F (71°C) for 15 minutes. Cool the beer and pour back in the bottle. Cap bottle and refrigerate. Add to stout when bottling or kegging.

- - - - - - - - - - - - - - - -

GUINNESS
FOREIGN EXTRA STOUT

⸺⸺⸺

(5 gallons/19 L, all-grain) OG = 1.075 FG = 1.018
IBU = 40 SRM = 40 ABV = 7.5%

A classic beer from the Guinness lineup, this foreign extra stout defines the style. It boasts a full-bodied roasty character and a dry finish.

INGREDIENTS

12.5 lb. (5.7 kg) 2-row pale ale malt (3 °L)

2 lb. 4 oz. (1 kg) flaked barley

1 lb. 2 oz. (0.5 kg) roasted barley (500 °L)

11.9 AAU Challenger hops (60 min.) (1.7 oz./48 g at 7% alpha acids)

Wyeast 1084 (Irish Ale) or White Labs WLP004 (Irish Ale) yeast (2 qt./2 L starter)

⅔ cup (133 g) dextrose (if priming)

STEP BY STEP

Several days before brewing, make a 2-quart (2-liter) yeast starter. One day prior to brewing, place the starter in a fridge so you can decant the liquid prior to pitching the yeast. Mash grains for 60 minutes at 152°F (67°C) in 5.2 gallons (19.6 liters) of water. Collect about 6.5 gallons (24.6 liters) of wort and boil for 90 minutes, adding hops with 60 minutes left in boil. At the end of the boil, cool wort, siphon to fermenter, aerate, and pitch yeast from your starter. Ferment at 68°F (20°C). Keg or bottle as normal.

PARTIAL MASH OPTION: Reduce the 2-row pale malt in the all-grain recipe to 3 pounds (1.4 kilograms) and add 6.6 pounds (3 kilograms) Maris Otter liquid malt extract. Prepare a yeast starter, as described in the all-grain recipe, prior to brew day. Place the crushed grains in a large muslin bag. Mash the crushed grains for 60 minutes at 152°F (67°C) in 2 gallons (7.6 liters) of water. Place the grain bag in a colander and slowly wash with 1 gallon (4 liters) of hot water. Add the liquid malt extract and top off to about 6.5 gallons (24.6 liters) of wort and boil for 90 minutes. Follow the remaining portion of the all-grain recipe.

KIUCHI BREWERY
HITACHINO NEST SWEET STOUT

**(5 gallons/19 L, all-grain) OG = 1.049 FG = 1.019
IBU = 16 SRM = 42 ABV = 3.9%**

The Kiuchi Brewery's Hitachino Nest Sweet Stout is like a delicately sweetened cappuccino: You'll taste dark roasted coffee with dark fruit notes and the unmistakable aroma and flavor of lactose.

INGREDIENTS

6 lb. (2.7 kg) 2-row pale malt

0.5 lb. (0.23 kg) wheat malt

1 lb. (0.45 kg) crystal malt (55 °L)

1.25 lb. (0.57 kg) roasted barley (450 °L)

1 lb. (0.45 kg) lactose sugar (15 min.)

4.1 AAU Kent Golding hops (60 min.) (0.75 oz./21 g at 5.5% alpha acids)

Wyeast 1099 (Whitbread Ale) or Fermentis Safale S-04 yeast

⅔ cup (133 g) dextrose (if priming)

STEP BY STEP

Mash at 153°F (67°C) in 11 quarts (10.4 liters) of water for 60 minutes. Mash out, vorlauf, and then sparge at 170°F (77°C) to collect 5.5 gallons (21 liters). Boil wort for 60 minutes, adding hops and lactose at times indicated. After the boil, chill the wort to 68°F (20°C) and aerate thoroughly. Ferment at 68°F (20°C). Bottle or keg as usual.

EXTRACT WITH GRAINS OPTION: Substitute the 2-row pale malt and wheat malt in the all-grain recipe with 3.3 pounds (2.7 kilograms) light liquid malt extract and 1

pound (0.45 kilogram) wheat dried malt extract. Place the crushed grains in a muslin bag and steep in 5.5 gallons (21 liters) water as the water heats up. Remove the grain bag when the temperature reaches 170°F (77°C). Add the liquid and dried malt extracts off heat and stir until fully dissolved. Boil for 60 minutes. Follow the remaining portion of the all-grain recipe.

MCMENAMINS BREWERIES
TERMINATOR STOUT

**(5 gallons/19 L, all-grain) OG = 1.065 FG = 1.016
IBU = 27 SRM = 40 ABV = 6.4%**

McMenamins describes Terminator Stout as having "a wide array of toasted, chocolate, nutty, and coffee-like flavors." It's one of the original craft brewery stouts with roots in the 1980s.

INGREDIENTS

10 lb. (4.5 kg) 2-row pale malt

2.25 lb. (1 kg) Munich malt

1 lb. (0.45 kg) crystal malt (40 °L)

1 lb. (0.45 kg) black barley (530 °L)

6.5 AAU Chinook pellet hops (60 min.) (0.5 oz./14 g at 13% alpha acids)

1.4 AAU Cascade pellet hops (30 min.) (0.25 oz./7 g at 5.5% alpha acids)

½ tsp. Irish moss (30 min.)

½ tsp. yeast nutrient (15 min.)

White Labs WLP001 (California Ale), Wyeast 1056 (American Ale), or Fermentis Safale US-05 yeast

¾ cup (150 g) dextrose (if priming)

STEP BY STEP

This is a single-infusion mash. Mix all the crushed grains with 4.75 gallons (18 liters) of 171°F (77°C) water to stabilize at 156°F (69°C) for 60 minutes. Slowly sparge with 175°F (79°C) water. Collect approximately 6 gallons (23 liters) of wort runoff to boil for 60 minutes. While boiling, add other ingredients as per the schedule. Cool the wort to 75°F (24°C). Pitch your yeast and aerate the wort heavily. Allow the beer to cool to 68°F (20°C). Hold at that temperature until fermentation is complete. Transfer to a carboy and allow the beer to condition for 1 week, and then bottle or keg.

PARTIAL MASH OPTION: Substitute the 2-row pale malt in the all-grain recipe with 3.3 pounds (1.5 kilograms) Briess light liquid malt extract and 2.6 pounds (1.2 kilograms) extra light dried malt extract. Steep the crushed grains in 1 gallon (4 liters) of water at 156°F (69°C) for 30 minutes. Then rinse the grains with 2 quarts (1.9 liters) of hot water. Add the extracts, top off to 3 gallons (11 liters), and boil 60 minutes. Follow the remaining portion of the all-grain recipe.

- - - - - - - - - - - - - -

MIKKELLER
BEER GEEK BREAKFAST STOUT

**(5 gallons/19 L, all-grain) OG = 1.080 FG = 1.023
IBU = 86 SRM = 64 ABV = 7.5%**

Beer Geek Breakfast, which adds French press coffee to an oatmeal stout, is the beer that put Mikkeller on the map. It was voted the number one stout on www.Ratebeer.com.

INGREDIENTS

7 lb. (3.2 kg) pilsner malt

2 lb. 3 oz. (1 kg) flaked oats

2 lb. 3 oz. (1 kg) oat malt

1 lb. 2 oz. (0.5 kg) Belgian caramel Munich malt (45 °L)

10 oz. (0.27 kg) smoked malt

1 lb. 2 oz. (0.5 kg) brown malt

12 oz. (0.34 kg) pale chocolate malt

1 lb. 2 oz. (0.5 kg) chocolate malt

1 lb. 2 oz. (0.5 kg) roasted barley (450 °L)

12.3 AAU Centennial hops (90 min.) (1.4 oz./39 g at 8.8% alpha acids)

8.7 AAU Chinook hops (90 min.) (0.7 oz./20 g at 12.4% alpha acids)

2.8 AAU Cascade hops (90 min.) (0.4 oz./11 g at 7% alpha acids)

7 AAU Cascade hops (1 min.) (1 oz./28 g at 7% alpha acids)

1.5 oz. (43 g) ground coffee

Wyeast 1056 (American Ale), White Labs WLP001 (California Ale), or Fermentis Safale US-05 yeast

¾ cup (150 g) dextrose (if priming)

STEP BY STEP

Mash in at 153°F (67°C) and hold for 75 minutes. You may want to add in a handful or two of rice hulls to aid with the lautering process. Lauter slowly to account for the high levels of glucans in the mash. Boil for 90 minutes, adding hops as indicated. Cool, aerate, and pitch yeast, fermenting between 68 to 72°F (20 to 22°C). Two days prior to bottling or kegging, add the ground coffee to a 1-liter French press for hot extraction of the coffee. Press

off and very gently pour into the fermenter. Two days later, bottle or keg as normal.

EDITOR'S NOTE: Due to the high percentage of specialty grains in this recipe, an extract version of this recipe would be very difficult to achieve. It's best to pick another stout recipe!

- - - - - - - - - - - - - -

NINKASI BREWING COMPANY
VANILLA OATIS OATMEAL STOUT

**(5 gallons/19 L, all-grain) OG = 1.072 FG = 1.022
IBU = 50 SRM = 40 ABV = 7%**

Ninkasi describes Vanilla Oatis Oatmeal Stout as having roast up front followed by smooth oats, chocolate, and vanilla thanks to the use of whole vanilla beans. It's a beer with slightly more alcohol, body, and bitterness than a traditional stout.

INGREDIENTS

13 lb. (5.9 kg) 2-row pale malt

1 lb. (0.45 kg) extra dark crystal malt (135–165 °L)

1 lb. (0.45 kg) chocolate malt (350 °L)

1 lb. (0.45 kg) flaked oats

12 oz. (0.34 kg) Vienna malt

6 oz. (170 g) black barley

4 oz. (113 g) rice hulls

2 vanilla beans (added during fermentation)

9.8 AAU Nugget leaf hops (60 min.) (0.75 oz./21 g at 13% alpha acids)

9.8 AAU Nugget leaf hops (30 min.) (0.75 oz./21 g at 13% alpha acids)

½ tsp. Irish moss (15 min.)

Wyeast 1968 (London ESB Ale), White Labs WLP002 (English Ale), or Lallemand Winsor Ale yeast

¾ cup (150 g) dextrose (if priming)

STEP BY STEP

This is a single-infusion mash. Mix the crushed grains with 5.5 gallons (21 liters) of water at 163°F (73°C), stabilizing at 152°F (67°C) for 60 minutes until conversion is complete. Raise the temperature of the mash to 168°F (76°C) with approximately 3.1 gallons (11.7 liters) of 200°F (93°C) water, and then collect 7 gallons (26.5 liters) of wort to begin your 60-minute boil. Add hops and Irish moss at times indicated. At the end of the boil, 5.5 gallons (21 liters) wort should be left in your kettle. Chill the wort rapidly and pitch the yeast when the temperature is less than 75°F (24°C), and allow to cool to 68°F (20°C) for fermenting. Add the 2 vanilla beans to the fermenter after slicing one side of the bean open to expose the inside of the vanilla bean. When fermentation is complete, do a 3-day diacetyl rest, and then bottle or keg. Carbonate to approximately 2 to 2.5 volumes.

PARTIAL MASH OPTION: Substitute the 2-row pale malt in the all-grain recipe with 6.6 pounds (3 kilograms) pale liquid malt extract and 1.5 pounds (0.68 kilogram) extra light dried malt extract. Place the crushed Vienna and flaked oats in a muslin bag and mash in 2 quarts (2 liters) of water at 150 to 160°F (66 to 71°C) for 30 minutes. Then, add 3 gallons (11.4 liters) of 150 to 160°F (66 to 71°C) water and the crystal and roasted grains in a separate muslin bag. Hold for 30 minutes more. Remove both grain bags from the hot water and wash them with 1 gallon (4 liters) of hot water. Bring wort to a boil. When boiling starts, remove pot from the burner and slowly add all the dried malt extract, stirring to dissolve. Return to a boil for 60 minutes, adding the hops and Irish moss as indicated. Top off to 5 gallons (19 liters). Follow the remaining portion of the all-grain recipe.

ROCKY RIVER BREWING COMPANY
CHOCOLATE JITTERS

(5 gallons/19 L, all-grain) OG = 1.071 FG = 1.018
IBU = 21 SRM = 33 ABV = 7.3%

Chocolate Jitters is a combination of Rocky River's Oompa Loompa Chocolate Stout and Merlin's Black Magic Coffee Stout. Brewer Matt Cole suggests adding the melted chocolate in the boil, adding a vanilla bean in the secondary, and using cold-brewed coffee, which is less acidic than traditionally brewed coffee.

INGREDIENTS

10 lb. (4.5 kg) 2-row pale malt

1 lb. (454 g) Munich malt (20 °L)

1 lb. (454 g) Munich malt (10 °L)

0.75 lb. (340 g) aromatic malt

0.44 lb. (200 g) Weyermann Carafa III malt (500 °L)

0.44 lb. (200 g) chocolate malt

0.75 lb. (340 g) lactose (60 min.)

3.3 AAU Tettnanger hops (60 min.) (0.75 oz./21 g at 4.5% alpha acids)

3.3 AAU Tettnanger hops (30 min.) (0.75 oz./21 g at 4.5% alpha acids)

1 AAU Liberty hops (hopback) (0.25 oz./7 g at 4% alpha acids)

2.5 oz. (70 g) Belgian chocolate, melted (0 min.)

½ vanilla bean, chopped (secondary)

20 oz. cold-brewed Jamaican Blue coffee (at bottling)

Wyeast 1007 (German Ale) or White Labs WLP029 (German Ale/Kölsch) yeast

¾ cup (150 g) dextrose (if priming)

STEP BY STEP

Mash the grains together at 152°F (67°C) for 60 minutes. Mash out, vorlauf, and then sparge at 170°F (77°C) to collect approximately 7 gallons (26.5 liters) wort to boil for 90 to 120 minutes and have a 5-gallon (19 liters) yield. Add hops at the times indicated. Near the end, melt the Belgian chocolate in a double boiler and add at the end of the boil. Give the wort a vigorous stir to create a whirlpool and let settle for 15 minutes. If you do not have a hopback device, add the Liberty hops during the final 5 minutes of the whirlpool. Cool, aerate, and pitch yeast. Ferment at 68°F (20°C). Soak the chopped vanilla bean in vodka or neutral spirits for 1 week. When primary fermentation is finished, transfer the beer into a secondary fermenter and add the chopped vanilla bean plus spirits to the beer. Age for 1 more week. Cold brew 20 ounces (590 milliliters) of coffee for 24 hours and then add it to your beer. Bottle or keg.

PARTIAL MASH OPTION: Substitute the 2-row pale malt in the all-grain recipe with 6.6 pounds (3 kilograms) Coopers light unhopped liquid malt extract. Place crushed malts in a large nylon steeping bag and steep in 5.4 quarts (5.2 liters) of water at 150°F (66°C) for 30 minutes. Rinse grains with 2 quarts (1.9 liters) of water at 170°F (77°C). Add water to make 3 gallons (11 liters). Remove grains from wort, add the liquid malt extract and lactose, and bring to a boil. Add hops at times indicated. Near the end, melt the Belgian chocolate in a double boiler and add at the end of the boil. Cool and top off to 5 gallons (19 liters). Follow the remaining portion of the all-grain recipe.

ROGUE ALES
SHAKESPEARE STOUT

(5 gallons/19 L, all-grain) OG = 1.060 FG = 1.016
IBU = 60 SRM = 48 ABV = 5.8%

Rogue's Shakespeare Stout is a classic example of the American stout style. Rogue describes it as an ebony-colored beer with a rich, creamy head; earthy flavor; and a mellow, chocolaty finish.

INGREDIENTS

8.8 lb. (4 kg) Great Western pale malt (2 °L)

1.34 lb. (0.61 kg) flaked oats (2 °L)

1.45 lb. (0.66 kg) Briess chocolate malt (350 °L)

1.34 lb. (0.61 kg) crystal malt (120 °L)

3.17 oz. (90 g) black barley (500 °L)

12.8 AAU Cascade hops (60 min.) (2 oz./57 g at 6.4% alpha acids)

7.2 AAU Cascade pellet hops (15 min.) (1.13 oz./32 g at 6.4% alpha acids)

Wyeast 1764 (Rogue Pacman) or Lallemand Nottingham Ale yeast

¾ cup (150 g) dextrose (if priming)

STEP BY STEP

Mill the grains and mash at 148°F (64°C) until enzymatic conversion is complete, about 60 minutes. Infuse the mash with near boiling water while stirring or with a recirculating mash system to raise the temperature to mash out at 168°F (76°C). Sparge with 170°F (77°C) water, collecting wort until the pre-boil kettle volume is around 6.5 gallons (25 liters) and the gravity is 1.046. Boil for 90 minutes. Add the hops according to the ingredients list. Following the boil, chill the wort to 60°F (16°C) and aerate thoroughly. The proper pitch rate is 2 packages of liquid yeast, 1 package of dry yeast, or 1 package of liquid yeast in a 2-liter starter. Pacman yeast (and Nottingham Ale) ferments well at cold temperatures, but you can let it warm a little as fermentation progresses to ensure complete attenuation. Pitch at 60°F (16°C) and ferment until the yeast drops clear. Allow the brew to mature without pressure for another 2 days after fermentation appears finished. Rack to a keg or bottle. Target a carbonation level of 2.5 volumes.

PARTIAL MASH OPTION: Substitute the pale malt in the all-grain recipe with 4 pounds (1.8 kilograms) extra light dried malt extract and 1.33 pounds (0.61 kilogram) Great Western pale malt (2 °L). Place the crushed pale malt and flaked oats grains in a large muslin bag. Mix in with 7 quarts (6.7 liters) water. Hold the mash at 148°F (64°C) for 60 minutes. Place the crushed crystal and roasted grains in a second muslin bag and add to the mash for 15 minutes longer. Heat the mash up to 168°F (76°C), then remove the bags and wash the grains with 1 gallon (4 liters) of hot water. Stir in the dried malt extract and add water until the pre-boil kettle volume is around 6 gallons (23 liters) and the gravity is 1.050. Boil for 60 minutes. Follow the remaining portion of the all-grain recipe.

SAMUEL ADAMS BREWING COMPANY
CREAM STOUT
‹‹‹‹‹‹-

**(5 gallons/19 L, all-grain) OG = 1.057 FG = 1.020
IBU = 28 SRM = 55 ABV = 4.9%**

This stout was designed as a traditional English sweet stout, with lots of rich, creamy, roasted character.

INGREDIENTS

8 lb. (3.6 kg) 2-row pale malt (2 °L)

1.5 lb. (0.68 kg) white wheat malt (2 °L)

0.9 lb. (0.41 kg) caramel malt (60 °L)

0.9 lb. (0.41 kg) chocolate malt (350 °L)

0.6 lb. (0.27 kg) roasted barley (500 °L)

4 oz. (0.11 kg) Weyermann Carafa I malt (350 °L)

0.7 AAU East Kent Golding pellet hops (60 min.) (0.1 oz./3 g at 6.9% alpha acids)

1.4 AAU East Kent Golding pellet hops (30 min.) (0.2 oz./6 g at 6.9% alpha acids)

0.6 AAU UK Fuggle pellet hops (30 min.) (0.1 oz./3 g at 5.7% alpha acids)

1.1 AAU UK Fuggle pellet hops (15 min.) (0.2 oz./6 g at 5.7% alpha acids)

4.8 AAU East Kent Golding pellet hops (5 min.) (0.7 oz./20 g at 6.9% alpha acids)

½ tsp. yeast nutrients (15 min.)

White Labs WLP001 (California Ale), Wyeast 1056 (American Ale), Fermentis Safale US-05 or Lallemand BRY-97 yeast

⅔ cup (133 g) dextrose (if priming)

STEP BY STEP

This is a single-infusion mash. Mix the crushed grains with 4.5 gallons (17 liters) of 167°F (75°C) strike water to stabilize the mash at 155°F (68°C). Hold at this temperature for 45 minutes. Vorlauf for 15 minutes then begin sparge. Run off into kettle to achieve volume and pre-boil gravity around 1.046 SG. Boil for 60 minutes, adding hops and yeast nutrients according the ingredients list. Once you turn off the heat, give the wort a stir for about a minute to create a whirlpool and let that spin and settle out for about 15 minutes before beginning to chill the wort. Cool the wort down to slightly below fermentation temperature, about 65°F (18°C). Aerate the wort with filtered air or pure O_2 and pitch yeast. Ferment at 68°F (20°C) for 1 week or until signs of fermentation have died down. Cool beer to 60°F (16°C) and condition for an additional 1 to 2 weeks. Bottle or keg and carbonate to 2 volumes of CO_2.

EXTRACT WITH GRAINS OPTION: Omit the 2-row pale and white wheat malt and add 3.3 pounds (1.5 kilograms) light liquid malt extract and 3.3 pounds (1.5 kilograms) liquid wheat malt extract. Place crushed specialty grains in a muslin bag and steep in 1 gallon (3.8 liters) water at 150 to 160°F (66 to 71°C) for 20 minutes. Remove the grain bag and slowly wash the grains with 2 quarts (1.9 liters) of hot water. Transfer the wort to brew kettle and top off to make 6 gallons (23 liters). Just before the water reaches a boil, remove from the heat and stir until all the extract is dissolved. Your pre-boil gravity should be around 1.046 SG. Boil for 60 minutes, adding hops and yeast nutrients according to the ingredients list. Turn off the heat, give the wort a stir for about 1 minute to create a whirlpool, and let that spin and settle out for 15 minutes before beginning to chill the wort. Cool the wort down to about 65°F (18°C). Aerate the wort with filtered air or pure O_2 and pitch yeast. Follow the remainder of the all-grain recipe.

STEP BY STEP

Mash the grains at 150°F (66°C) for 60 minutes. Mash out, vorlauf, and then sparge at 170°F (77°C) to collect approximately 7 gallons (26.5 liters) of wort to boil for 120 minutes so you have a 5-gallon (19-liter) yield. Add hops at times indicated. Cool the wort to 75°F (24°C)—do not aerate (you want a high ending gravity for this beer). Pitch your yeast and allow the beer to cool over the next few hours to 68°F (20°C), and hold at this temperature until the beer has finished fermenting. Then bottle or keg.

PARTIAL MASH OPTION: Substitute the 2-row pale malt in the all-grain recipe with 4.5 pounds (2 kilograms) Briess extra light dried malt extract. Steep the crushed malts in 1.5 gallons (5.8 liters) of water at 150°F (66°C) for 60 minutes. Remove grains from wort and add water to make 5 gallons (19 liters). Add the dried malt extract to your wort and bring to a boil. Follow the remaining portion of the all-grain recipe.

SAND CREEK BREWING COMPANY
OSCAR'S CHOCOLATE OATMEAL STOUT

**(5 gallons/19 L, all-grain) OG = 1.057 FG = 1.016
IBU = 30 SRM = 33 ABV = 5.6%**

The winner of a gold medal in the World Beer Cup, Oscar's Chocolate Oatmeal Stout is full-bodied and smooth, with a complex nutty finish.

INGREDIENTS

8.5 lb. (3.86 kg) Briess 2-row pale malt

1 lb. (0.45 kg) Briess wheat malt

10 oz. (283 g) Briess Munich malt (10 °L)

10 oz. (283 g) Briess roasted barley

10 oz. (283 g) Briess chocolate malt

4 oz. (113 g) caramel malt (80 °L)

10 oz. (283 g) flaked oats

7.1 AAU Golding hops (60 min.) (1.5 oz./42 g at 4.75% alpha acids)

4.75 AAU Golding hops (5 min.) (1 oz./28 g at 4.75% alpha acids)

1 tsp. Irish moss (15 min.)

Wyeast 1968 (London ESB Ale) or White Labs WLP002 (English Ale) yeast

¾ cup (150 g) dextrose (if priming)

SIERRA NEVADA BREWING COMPANY
STOUT

**(5 gallons/19 L, all-grain) OG = 1.064 FG = 1.020
IBU = 50 SRM = 45 ABV = 5.8%**

Sierra Nevada brewers have long counted their stout as a favorite, and they have brewed it consistently for more than thirty years. It's big, rich, bold, and black as night.

INGREDIENTS

9 lb. (4.1 kg) American 2-row pale malt

2 lb. (0.91 kg) Munich malt (10 °L)

0.67 lb. (0.3 kg) crystal malt (60 °L)

8 oz. (23 kg) Weyermann Carafa II malt

8 oz. (23 kg) roasted barley (300 °L)

5 oz. (14 kg) chocolate malt (350 °L)

5 oz. (14 kg) black patent malt (500 °L)

12 AAU Bravo hops (60 min.) (0.75 oz./21 g at 16% alpha acids)

5.75 AAU Cascade hops (10 min.) (1 oz./28 g at 5.75% alpha acids)

2 oz. (57 g) Yakima Golding hops (0 min.)

Wyeast 1056 (American Ale), White Labs WLP001 (California Ale), or Fermentis Safale US-05 yeast

¾ cup (150 g) dextrose (if priming)

STEP BY STEP

Mash 154°F (68°C) for 60 minutes in 16 quarts (15 liters) of water. Mash out, vorlauf, and then sparge at 170°F (77°C) to collect 6 gallons (23 liters) of wort. Boil for 60 minutes, adding hops at times indicated. Cool, aerate, and pitch yeast. Ferment at 68°F (20°C). After fermentation is complete, rack to secondary and condition for 14 days at 68°F (20°C). Bottle or keg as usual.

EXTRACT WITH GRAINS OPTION: Substitute the 2-row pale malt and Munich malt in the all-grain recipe with 3 pounds (1.4 kilograms) Briess extra light dried malt extract and 3.3 pounds (1.5 kilograms) Munich liquid malt extract. Steep the crushed grains in 2 gallons (7.6 liters) of water as the water heats up to 170°F (77°C). Wash the grains with 1 gallon (4 liters) of hot water. Combine grain tea with dried malt extract and add enough water to total at least 3.5 gallons (13 liters). Boil wort for 60 minutes. Add hops as per ingredient list and liquid malt extract with 15 minutes left in boil. Top off to 5 gallons (19 liters) with cold water at the end of the boil. Follow the remaining portion of the all-grain recipe.

- - - - - - - - - - - - - - - - - -

STONE BREWING COMPANY
12TH ANNIVERSARY BITTER CHOCOLATE OATMEAL STOUT

**(5 gallons/19 L, all-grain) OG = 1.094 FG = 1.022
IBU = 45 SRM = 42 ABV = 9.6%**

This beer is bursting with decadent chocolate bitterness thanks to both the chocolate malt and cocoa powder. The dark chocolate is balanced with a big oatmeal mouthfeel.

INGREDIENTS

15 lb. (6.8 kg) 2-row malt	1 lb. (0.45 kg) chocolate malt
0.75 lb. (0.34 kg) Carapils malt	0.25 lb. (113 g) roasted barley
0.75 lb. (0.34 kg) crystal malt (15 °L)	0.25 lb. (113 g) black malt
2 lb. (0.91 kg) flaked oats	

2 AAU Willamette hops (60 min.) (0.4 oz./11 g at 5% alpha acids)

2 AAU Ahtanum hops (60 min.) (0.4 oz./11 g at 5% alpha acids)

4 AAU Galena hops (60 min.) (0.33 oz./9.4 g at 12% alpha acids)

6.5 AAU Summit hops (60 min.) (0.38 oz./11 g at 17% alpha acids)

3.25 oz. (92 g) cocoa powder (15 min.)

White Labs WLP002 (English Ale) or Wyeast 1968 (London ESB Ale) yeast

¾ cup (150 g) dextrose (if priming)

STEP BY STEP

This is a single-infusion mash. Mash in 25 quarts (23.7 liters) of strike water at 150°F (66°C) for 45 minutes then begin the lautering process. Sparge to collect about 7 gallons (26.5 liters) wort. Boil for 90 minutes, adding hops and cocoa at times indicated in the ingredient list. Once the boil is complete, cool, aerate, and pitch yeast. Ferment at 66°F (19°C). After fermentation is complete, bottle or keg as usual.

PARTIAL MASH OPTION: Reduce the 2-row Carapils and crystal malts in the all-grain recipe to 2 pounds (0.91 kilogram) 2-row malt, 0.5 pound (0.23 kilogram) Carapils malt, and 0.5 pound (0.23 kilogram) crystal malt (15 °L). Also add 2 pounds (0.91 kilogram) light dried malt extract and 6.6 pounds (3 kilogram) light liquid malt extract. Mash the crushed grains at 150°F (66°C) for 45 minutes in 9 quarts (8.5 liters) of water. Add water to make 3 gallons (11 liters) of wort, add dried malt extract, and bring to a boil. Boil for 60 minutes, adding the liquid malt extract with 15 minutes remaining, and other ingredients as indicated. Follow the remaining portion of the all-grain recipe.

- - - - - - - - - - - - - - - - - -

SUMMIT BREWING COMPANY
REBELLION STOUT

**(5 gallons/19 L, all-grain) OG = 1.076 FG = 1.014
IBU = 65 SRM = 52 ABV = 8.5%**

This limited-time release foreign extra stout was brewed based loosely on a recipe from 1896 taken from the archives of an old Cork, Ireland, brewery. For a base malt it uses Irish stout malt from the Malting Company of Ireland (also from Cork).

INGREDIENTS

- 13.7 lb. (6.2 kg) Irish stout malt (2 °L)
- 1.5 lb. (0.68 kg) Simpsons black malt (550 °L)
- 1 lb. (0.45 kg) Crisp amber malt (27 °L)
- 7 AAU German Select hops (60 min.) (1.4 oz./40 g at 5% alpha acids)
- 7 AAU German Select hops (25 min.) (1.4 oz./40 g at 5% alpha acids)
- 3.5 AAU German Select hops (10 min.) (0.7 oz./20 g at 5% alpha acids)
- 3.4 AAU UK Phoenix hops (10 min.) (0.7 oz./20 g at 4.8% alpha acids)
- 8.4 AAU UK Progress hops (0 min.) (1.4 oz./40 g at 6% alpha acids)
- 0.7 oz. (20 g) Brewer's Gold hops (dry hop)
- ½ Whirlfloc tablet
- Wyeast 1084 (Irish Ale) yeast or White Labs WLP004 (Irish Ale) yeast
- ⅔ cup (133 g) dextrose (if priming)

STEP BY STEP

Add calcium chloride ($CaCl_2$) to the brewing water for a minimum 100 ppm of calcium (Ca^{2+}). Mash the grains at 144°F (62°C) and hold at this temperature for 30 minutes. Raise grain bed to 151°F (66°C) and hold at this temperature for 30 minutes. Raise grain bed to mash out at 172°F (78°C), then begin the sparge. Sparge until you collect 6 gallons (23 liters) in your kettle or until pre-boil gravity in the kettle reaches about 1.063 specific gravity. Total boil time is 60 minutes, adding hops at the times indicated and Whirlfloc tablet with 10 minutes left in the boil. At 0 minutes, add the last addition of hops, then give the wort a stir for at least 1 minute and let settle for 20 minutes. If your wort pH needs adjusting, add lactic acid to be sure your wort is at 5.2 at this point. Chill the wort to 68°F (20°C), let the cold break settle, pitch the yeast, and aerate. Ferment at 70°F (21°C) for 5 days or until signs of fermentation have subsided. Add dry hops and let the beer sit on the dry hops for 5 days. Drop the temperature to 54°F (12°C) and condition the beer for 3 weeks at this temperature. Rack to a keg and force carbonate or rack to a bottling bucket, add priming sugar, and bottle. Target carbonation levels around 2.4 volumes CO_2.

PARTIAL MASH OPTION: Reduce the Irish stout malt in the all-grain recipe to 1 pound (0.45 kilogram) and add 7 pounds (3.2 kilograms) extra light dried malt extract (2 °L). Place the crushed stout malt and amber malt into a muslin bag for mashing in 1 gallon (~4 liters) of water. Mash the grains at 144°F (62°C). Hold at 144°F (62°C) for 30 minutes. Raise the mash to 151°F (66°C) and hold at this temperature for 30 minutes. Add the black malt, then raise grains to mash out at 172°F (78°C) and hold for 5 minutes. Raise the grains out of the mash water and rinse the grain bag with 1 gallon (4 liters) of hot water. Top off kettle to 6 gallons (23 liters) water and bring to a boil. Once at a boil, remove the kettle from heat and add the dried malt extract, stirring until dissolved. Then return to a boil for 60 minutes. Follow the remaining portion of the all-grain recipe.

WEIRD BEARD BREW COMPANY
BLACK PERLE COFFEE MILK STOUT

**(5 gallons/19 L, all-grain) OG = 1.055 FG = 1.025
IBU = 50 SRM = 44 ABV = 4%**

Black Perle is one of the first beers that Weird Beard of London, England, produced commercially, and it still forms part of their core range in bottles and traditional cask. It takes its name from German Perle, with which it is single-hopped. It's a sweet stout with a rich coffee backbone.

INGREDIENTS

- 7.5 lb. (3.4 kg) Maris Otter pale ale malt (2.8°L)
- 1.1 lb. (0.52 kg) caramel malt (120 °L)
- 0.7 lb. (0.32 kg) roasted barley (525 °L)
- 0.6 lb. (0.28 kg) flaked oats
- 0.5 lb. (0.22 kg) chocolate malt (330 °L)
- 0.2 lb. (0.1 kg) torrified wheat
- 0.2 lb. (0.1 kg) lactose sugar (30 min.)
- 0.4 lb. (0.2 kg) lactose sugar (15 min.)
- 5.6 AAU Perle hops (first wort hop) (0.7 oz./20 g at 8% alpha acids)
- 11.2 AAU Perle hops (20 min.) (1.4 oz./40 g at 8% alpha acids)
- 5.6 AAU Perle hops (5 min.) (0.7 oz./20 g at 8% alpha acids)
- ½ Whirlfloc tablet (10 min.)
- 0.8 oz. (23 g) roasted whole coffee beans (secondary)
- Fermentis Safale US-05 American Ale or Lallemand BRY-97 (American West Coast Ale) yeast
- ⅔ cup (133 g) dextrose (if priming)

STEP BY STEP

Mill the grains and dough-in targeting a mash of around 1.2 quarts of strike water to 1 pound of grain (2.5 L/kilograms) and a temperature of 154°F (68°C). Hold the mash at 154°F (68°C) until enzymatic conversion is complete. Sparge slowly with 171°F (77°C) water, collecting wort until pre-boil kettle volume is 6 gallons (23 liters). Add the first wort hops during the sparging process. Total boil time is 60 minutes, with the hops and the lactose sugar added as indicated. Add Whirlfloc with 10 minutes left in the boil. Chill the wort to 68°F (20°C) and aerate thoroughly. Pitch the yeast and let the temperature free rise to 72°F (22°C). When fermentation is two-thirds complete, let the temperature free rise again to 75°F (24°C). At approximately 2 points away from final gravity, add the coffee beans to the fermenter. Keep it at 75°F (24°C) for 2 days and then cool to 41°F (5°C) for around 5 days. Carbonate the beer to around 2.1 volumes of CO_2, and allow time for the beer to condition fully.

PARTIAL MASH OPTION: Substitute the Maris Otter pale malt in the all-grain recipe with 3.5 pounds (1.6 kilograms) Muntons light dried malt extract and 1 pound (0.45 kilogram) Maris Otter pale ale malt (2.8°L). Place crushed pale ale malt along with flaked oats and torrified wheat in a grain bag. Submerge the grains in 5 quarts of water that has been heated to 164°F (73°C). The mash should rest at a temperature of 154°F (68°C). Hold the mash at 154°F (68°C) for about 45 minutes, then submerge in a second bag the remaining grains. Hold for 15 minutes. Remove both bags and wash with 1 gallon (4 liters) of hot water. Stir in the dried malt extract and top off with water to 6 gallons (23 liters). Add the first wort hops and bring to a boil for 60 minutes. Follow the remaining portion of the all-grain recipe.

WIDMER BROTHERS BREWING COMPANY
SNOWPLOW MILK STOUT

**(5 gallons/19 L, all-grain) OG = 1.070 FG = 1.028
IBU = 31 SRM = 39 ABV = 5.5%**

As you probably guessed from the name, Snowplow Milk Stout is a winter seasonal from Widmer. It was originally a collaboration beer with the Oregon Brew Crew, a local homebrewing club.

INGREDIENTS

5.25 lb. (2.4 kg) 2-row pale malt	1 lb. (0.45 kg) flaked oats
2 lb. (0.91 kg) wheat malt	2.1 lb. (0.95 kg) Carapils malt

2.1 lb. (0.95 kg) crystal malt (60 °L)

13 oz. (0.37 kg) roasted barley

6.5 oz. (0.18 kg) black patent malt

1 lb. (0.45 kg) lactose sugar (15 min.)

7 AAU Magnum hops (60 min.) (0.5 oz./15 g at 14% alpha acids)

2.5 AAU Willamette hops (15 min.) (0.5 oz./14 g at 5% alpha acids)

Wyeast 1187 (Ringwood Ale) yeast or White Labs WLP005 (British Ale)

¾ cup (150 g) dextrose (if priming)

STEP BY STEP

Mash the grains at 156°F (69°C) for 60 minutes. Mash out, vorlauf, and then sparge at 170°F (77°C) to collect 6.5 gallons (25 liters) of wort. Boil 90 minutes, adding hops at times indicated and lactose for the final 15 minutes of the boil. Cool, aerate, and pitch yeast. Ferment at 70°F (21°C). After fermentation is complete, bottle or keg as usual.

PARTIAL MASH OPTION: Eliminate the 2-row pale malt, reduce the wheat malt to 1.5 pounds (0.68 kilogram), and reduce both the Carapils and crystal malts to 1 pound (0.45 kg) each. Add 4 pounds (1.8 kilograms) amber dried malt extract. Heat 2.1 gallons (7.9 liters) of water to 167°F (75°C) in your brewpot. Place the crushed grains in a large grain steeping bag and submerge them in this water. Steep grains at 156°F (69°C) for 30 to 45 minutes. Add dried malt extract and 0.9 gallons (3.4 liters) of water to brewpot and bring to a boil. Follow the remaining portion of the all-grain recipe, topping up to 5 gallons (19 liters) after cooling.

WOLAVER'S ORGANIC BREWING COMPANY
OATMEAL STOUT

**(5 gallons/19 L, all-grain) OG = 1.059 FG = 1.018
IBU = 40 SRM = 35 ABV = 5.4%**

Wolaver's describes its Oatmeal Stout as a "smooth-as-silk stout brimming with darkly roasted malts and rich notes of chocolate and coffee. A mocha-topped, black-as-night body gives way to a surprisingly smooth, full-bodied experience in this unfiltered offering."

INGREDIENTS

9.5 lb. (4.3 kg) organic 2-row malt

1.4 lb. (0.64 kg) organic roasted barley (300 °L)

0.7 lb. (0.32 kg) organic rolled oats

0.5 lb. (0.23 kg) organic crystal malt (120 °L)

0.7 lb. (0.32 kg) organic Munich malt (10 °L)

0.28 lb. (0.13 kg) organic unmalted wheat

9.2 AAU Magnum hops (60 min.) (0.67 oz./19 g at 14% alpha acids)

0.4 AAU organic Hallertau hops (15 min.) (0.1 oz./4 g at 4% alpha acids)

2.5 AAU organic Cascade hops (15 min.) (0.5 oz./14 g at 5% alpha acids)

White Labs WLP036 (Düsseldorf Alt) or Wyeast 1007 (German Ale) yeast (1.5 qt./1.5 L yeast starter)

¾ cup (150 g) dextrose (if priming)

STEP BY STEP

Heat 4.5 gallons (17 liters) water up to 165°F (74°C). If you have soft water, you may want to mix in some dissolved chalk or baking soda. Mash at 152°F (67°C) for 1 hour. Sparge with enough water to collect 7 gallons (26.5 liters) wort in the kettle. Total boil time is 90 minutes, adding hops at times indicated. After the boil is complete, cool, aerate, and ferment at 68°F (20°C). Bottle or keg as usual.

PARTIAL MASH OPTION: Reduce the 2-row pale malt in the all-grain recipe to 0.42 pound (0.19 kilogram) and add 6 pounds (2.7 kilograms) Briess organic light liquid malt extract. Mash the crushed grains for 45 minutes at 152°F (67°C) in 5 quarts (4.7 liters) of water. Bring wort volume to 3 gallons (11.4 liters) and boil for a total of 60 minutes. Add hops according to ingredient list and liquid malt extract for final 15 minutes of the boil. Top off to 5 gallons (19 liters). Follow the remaining portion of the all-grain recipe.

- - - - - - - - - - - - - - - - -

YOUNG'S
DOUBLE CHOCOLATE STOUT

⪡⪡⪡⪡⪡⪡

(5 gallons/19 L, all-grain) OG = 1.053 FG = 1.013
IBU = 28 SRM = 35 ABV = 5.2%

This rich stout is one of the best-known chocolate stouts on both sides of the pond. Young's uses a blend of real dark chocolate and chocolate essence, as well as crystal, chocolate malt, and lactose, to create a beer that is rich, with a luxurious mouthfeel.

INGREDIENTS

7 lb. (3.2 kg) pale ale malt

11 oz. (0.31 kg) English medium crystal malt (55 °L)

20 fl. oz. (591 mL) Cholaca liquid cacao

12 oz. (0.34 kg) lactose sugar (15 min.)

8 oz. (0.23 kg) invert sugar #3 (70 °L) (15 min.)

4 oz. (0.11 kg) cane sugar (15 min.)

6 oz. (0.17 kg) cocoa powder (15 min.)

7 AAU Fuggle hops (60 min.) (1.4 oz./40 g at 5% alpha acids)

1.25 AAU Kent Golding hops (15 min.) (0.25 oz./7 g at 5% alpvha acids)

1 tsp. Irish moss (15 min.)

¼ tsp. yeast nutrients (15 min.)

0.33 oz. (9.4 g) natural chocolate extract (secondary)

Wyeast 1768 (English Special Bitter) or Wyeast 1968 (London ESB Ale) yeast

¾ cup (150 g) dextrose (if priming)

STEP BY STEP

Heat 10.5 quarts (9.9 liters) of water to 164°F (73°C). Stir in crushed grains and mash at 153°F (67°C) for 60 minutes. Collect 6.5 gallons (24.6 liters) of wort and boil for a total of 90 minutes. Add hops at times indicated in ingredient list. Add sugars, Irish moss, and yeast nutrients with 15 minutes remaining in the boil. Dissolve cocoa in hot water and also add with 15 minutes remaining. After the boil is complete, cool wort, aerate, and pitch yeast. Ferment at 68°F (20°C). Add chocolate extract in secondary. Bottle or keg as usual.

EXTRACT WITH GRAINS OPTION: Substitute the pale ale malt in the all-grain recipe with 5 pounds (1.9 kilograms) Maris Otter liquid malt extract. Place crushed grains in a nylon steeping bag. Heat 3 quarts (2.8 liters) water to 164°F (73°C) and steep grains for 45 minutes at 153°F (67°C). Rinse grain bag with 1.5 quarts (~1.5 liters) of water at 170°F (77°C). Add half of the liquid malt extract and water to make 3 gallons (11 liters) of wort and bring to a boil. Boil 60 minutes, adding hops according to the ingredient list. With 15 minutes left, turn off heat and stir in the rest of the liquid malt extract. Add sugars, cocoa powder (dissolved in hot water), Irish moss, and yeast nutrients, and resume boiling. Top off to 5-gallons and follow the remainder of the all-grain recipe.

- - - - - - - - - - - - - - - -

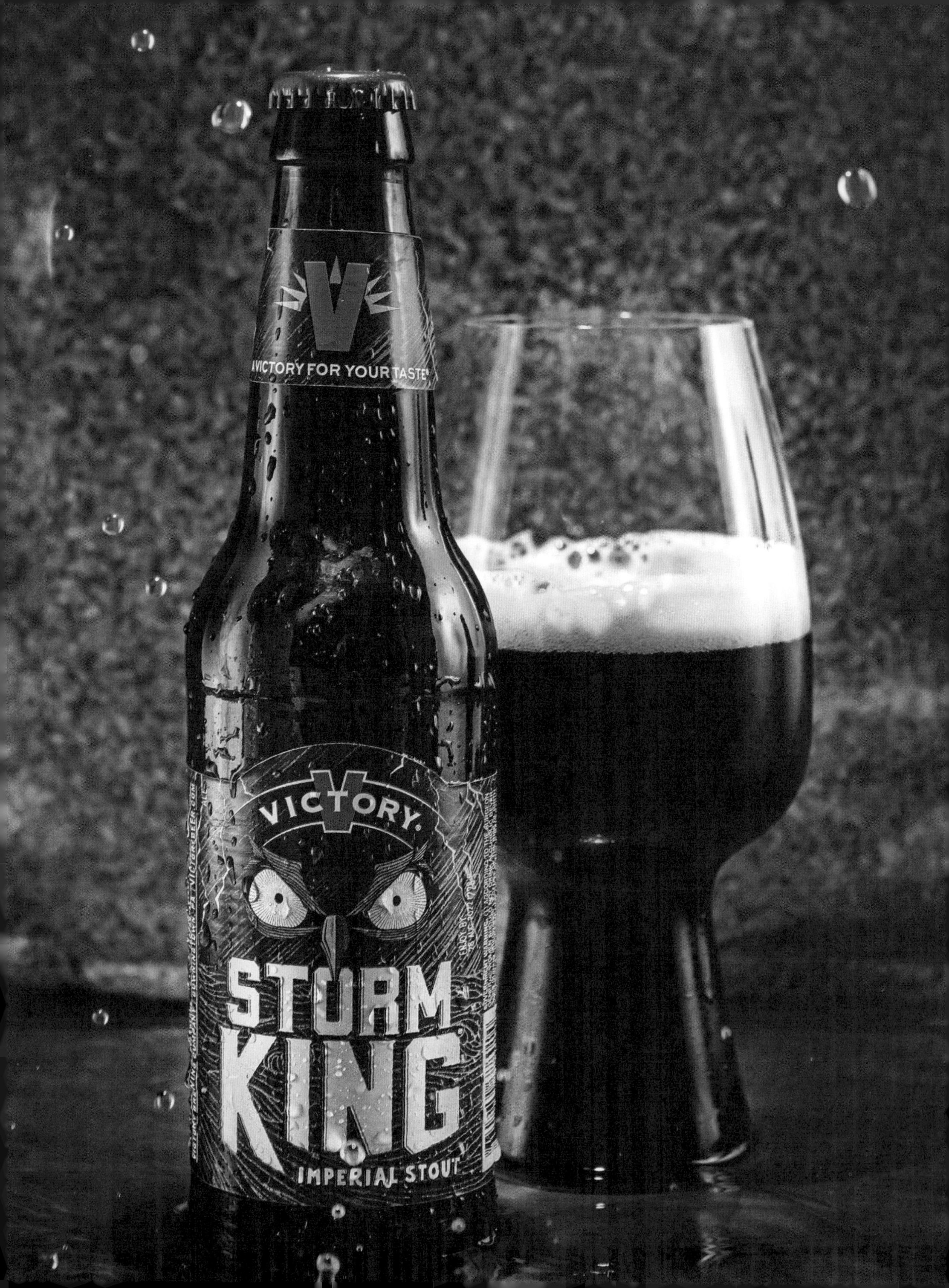
A VICTORY FOR YOUR TASTE®
VICTORY
STORM KING
IMPERIAL STOUT

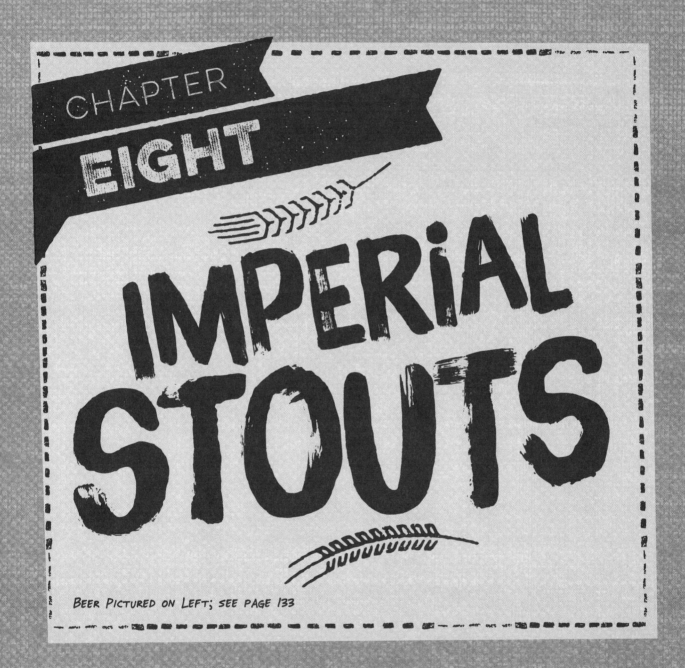

CHAPTER

EIGHT

IMPERIAL STOUTS

BEER PICTURED ON LEFT; SEE PAGE 133

BROOKLYN BREWERY
BLACK OPS
(5 gallons/19 L, all-grain) OG = 1.098 FG = 1.018
IBU = 28 SRM = 43 ABV = 10.7%

At the brewery, this rich imperial stout is aged in bourbon barrels and bottled flat. It is then refermented with Champagne yeast. Whether you take that step or not at home, it should hold up very well to cellar aging.

INGREDIENTS

15 lb. (6.8 kg) 2-row pale malt

1.25 lb. (0.57 kg) British crystal malt (77 °L)

0.5 lb. (0.23 g) black malt

0.5 lb. (0.23 g) British chocolate malt

0.25 lb. (113 g) roasted barley

1.5 lb. (0.68 kg) demerara sugar

½ tsp. yeast nutrient (10 min.)

8 AAU Summit hops (60 min.) (0.5 oz./14 g at 16% alpha acids)

1.5 oz. (43 g) East Kent Golding hops (0 min.)

Wyeast 1968 (London ESB Ale), White Labs WLP002 (English Ale), or Lallemand Winsor Ale yeast

⅞ cup (175 g) dextrose (if priming)

STEP BY STEP

Adjust your brewing water with calcium chloride to reach 2:1 chloride:sulfate ratio. Mill the grains, then mix with 5.5 gallons (20.7 liters) strike water to reach 122°F (50°C) and hold for 10 minutes, then raise to 154°F (68°C) and hold for 45 minutes. Mash out at 170°F (77°C), then proceed to vorlauf and sparge. If you don't want to perform a step mash, you can utilize a single-infusion mash by mixing 5.5 gallons (20.7 liters) of 165°F (74°C) strike water to reach a mash temperature of 152°F (67°C). Hold this temperature for 60 minutes. Vorlauf until your runnings are clear and lauter. Sparge the grains with enough water to obtain 7 gallons (26.5 liters) of wort. Stir in demerara sugar until dissolved. Boil for 90 minutes, adding hops and yeast nutrients according to the ingredient list and Irish moss if desired. After the boil, chill the wort to slightly below fermentation temperature, about 65°F (18°C). Aerate the wort with pure oxygen or filtered air and pitch yeast. Ferment at 66°F (19°C), for the first 7 days, then free rise to 70°F (21°C) and hold there until the completion of primary fermentation. Once the beer completes fermentation, transfer off of yeast. Rack beer into a 5-gallon (19-liter) heat-pasteurized white oak Bourbon barrel. Age for no less than 6 months at cellar temperatures (52°F/11°C). If you don't have an oak barrel, you can alternatively rack beer into a secondary fermenter and add bourbon-soaked medium toast American oak chips (1 oz./5 gallons). Chips should be soaked for 2 weeks, then discard the liquid and add the wet chips to the beer. Age for no less than 6 months at cellar temperatures (52°F/11°C). When complete, rack beer off the oak chips and bottle. Refermentation in the bottle using 10 g/L of dextrose and 1.2 M/cells/mL of either Lallemand CBC-1 or Lalvin EC1118.

EXTRACT WITH GRAINS OPTION: Omit the 2-row pale malt and add 10 pounds (4.54 kilograms) pale liquid malt extract. Bring 5.4 gallons (20.4 liters) of water to approximately 162°F (72°C) and hold there. Steep grains for 15 minutes, then remove bag and allow to drain into the wort. Add all the liquid extract, and add demerara sugar while stirring, and stir until completely dissolved. Bring wort up to a boil and boil for 90 minutes, adding hops and yeast nutrients according to the ingredient list and Irish moss if desired. Now follow the remainder of the all-grain recipe.

TIPS FOR SUCCESS

Brooklyn step mashes this beer, so purists are welcome to do so, but single-infusion mash folks should be able to get similar results with a standard mash. The other major deviation will be in the oak aging step. This may be a good time to invest in a 5-gallon (19-liter) bourbon cask, or procure a standard barrel and brew this one with a number of friends to fill it. If you choose not to, however, you can mimic the barrel-aged flavor using chips or cubes, as noted above. What I would also recommend, though, is aging in a standard bottling bucket. One significant flavor-developer in barrel-aged beers is the slow micro-oxidation of the beer, which a glass- or steel-aged beer might miss out on slightly. Most plastic fermentation buckets, though, are oxygen-permeable and might actually create a more authentic beer.

CAROLINA BREWING COMPANY
GROUNDHOG IMPERIAL STOUT

**(5 gallons/19 L, all-grain) OG= 1.093 FG = 1.022
IBU = 45 SRM = 49 ABV = 9.5%**

This Russian imperial stout is part of Carolina's seasonal offerings. It pours a deep, dark color and features a classic roasted, malty profile.

INGREDIENTS

16 lb. (7.3 kg) 2-row pale malt

2.25 lb. (1 kg) caramel malt (60 °L)

1.3 lb. (0.6 kg) roasted barley (300 °L)

8 oz. (0.23 kg) black malt

12 AAU Nugget hops (90 min.) (1 oz./28 g at 12% alpha acids)

0.25 oz. (7 g) Willamette hops (10 min.)

0.25 oz. (7 g) Willamette hops (5 min.)

0.25 oz. (7 g) Willamette hops (1 min.)

Wyeast 1056 (American Ale), White Labs WLP001 (California Ale), or Fermentis Safale US-05 yeast

¾ cup (150 g) dextrose (if priming)

STEP BY STEP

Mash for 60 minutes at 152°F (67°C). Mash out, vorlauf, and then sparge at 170°F (77°C) to collect enough wort to result in 5 gallons (19 liters) after a 90-minute boil. Boil for 90 minutes, adding hops at times indicated. Cool, aerate, and pitch yeast. Ferment at 68°F (20°C) for 3 weeks, then drop temperature 10°F (5°C) per day until it reaches 30°F (-1.1°C). Hold at 30°F (-1.1°C) for 1 week. Bottle or keg as usual.

PARTIAL MASH OPTION: Substitute the 2-row pale malt in the all-grain recipe with 3.5 pounds (1.6 kilograms) extra light dried malt extract and 6.6 pounds (3 kilograms) golden light liquid malt extract. Place crushed grains in a steeping bag and steep in 5 quarts (4.6 liters) of water at 152°F (67°C) for 45 minutes. Remove grain bag and rinse with 2.5 quarts (2.4 liters) of water at 170°F (77°C). Add water to make 3.5 gallons (13 liters), stir in dried malt extract, and bring to a boil. Boil for 90 minutes, adding hops at the appropriate times. Keep a small pot of boiling water handy and do not let the boil volume drop below 3 gallons (11 liters). Stir in liquid malt extract during final 15 minutes of the boil, stirring until extract has dissolved completely. After the boil, top off to 5 gallons (19 liters) and follow the remaining portion of the all-grain recipe.

DEFIANCE BREWING COMPANY
FUZZY KNUCKLES

**(5 gallons/19 L, all-grain) OG = 1.100 FG = 1.025
IBU = 55 SRM = 43 ABV = 10%**

This impressive imperial stout from Hays, Kansas, is described by the brewer as an approachable, full-bodied beast. Rich roasty malts, earthy English hops, Sumatran coffee, and nutty cocoa nibs blend harmoniously to create Fuzzy Knuckles. They say to think of "wooly mammoths, Bob Vila, and that barista who makes the best lattes."

INGREDIENTS

16.5 lb. (7.5 kg) 2-row pale malt

1.5 lb. (0.68 kg) Munich malt (10 °L)

1.3 lb. (0.6 kg) flaked oats

15 oz. (0.43 kg) chocolate malt

12 oz. (0.34 kg) roasted barley

3 oz. (85 g) caramel malt (120 °L)

3 oz. (85 g) Weyermann Carafa Special III malt

12.5 AAU Columbus pellet hops (90 min.) (0.82 oz./23 g at 15.5% alpha acids)

4.5 AAU Willamette pellet hops (20 min.) (0.82 oz./23 g at 5.5% alpha acids)

8 AAU Willamette pellet hops (0 min.) (1.33 oz./37 g at 5.5% alpha acids)

½ tsp. yeast nutrient (15 min.)

½ Whirlfloc tablet (15 min.)

1.1 oz. (31 g) ground Sumatran coffee (0 min.)

1.2 oz. (34 g) cocoa nibs (0 min.)

White Labs WLP007 (Dry English Ale Yeast), Wyeast 1098 (British Ale), or Lallemand Nottingham Ale yeast

⅔ cup (133 g) dextrose (if priming)

STEP BY STEP

Mill the grains (flaked oats don't need to be milled) and mix with 6 gallons (22.7 liters) of 169°F (76°C) strike water to reach a mash temperature of 154°F (68°C). Hold this temperature for 60 minutes. Vorlauf until your runnings are clear. Now sparge the grains with 3.5 gallons (13.25 liters) of 169°F (76°C) water until 7 gallons (26.5 liters) of 1.068 specific gravity wort are collected in your boil kettle. Boil for 90 minutes, adding hops, yeast nutrient, and kettle finings according to the ingredients list. After the boil, turn off the heat and add the 0-minute hop additions, coffee, and cocoa nibs. Whirlpool the kettle by gently stirring with a mash paddle for 2 minutes and then let rest for an additional 28 minutes to achieve a 30-minute flameout steep. Next, chill the wort to 64°F (18°C) and transfer into a clean and sanitized fermenter. Aerate the wort with pure oxygen for 90 seconds and pitch yeast. Allow fermentation to free rise up to 68°F (20°C) and hold it at that temperature until the beer reaches 60% apparent attenuation (1.035), then ramp fermentation temperature up to 72°F (22°C) and hold at this temperature for an additional 14 days. Begin to slowly crash cool the fermenter down at the rate of 5°F (2.8°C) per day for 8 days until the beer reaches 32°F (0°C), and then bottle or keg the beer. Carbonate to between 2.2 and 2.3 volumes of CO_2.

EXTRACT WITH GRAINS OPTION: Substitute the 2-row pale malt, Munich malt, and flaked oats in the all-grain recipe with 6 ounces (170 grams) CaraFoam malt, 2 pounds (0.9 kilogram) Munich dried malt extract, and 10 pounds (4.5 kilograms) golden light liquid malt extract. Place the crushed grains in a grain bag, then add to 2 gallons (7.6 liters) of 150°F (66°C) water. Allow grains to steep for 20 to 30 minutes while you continue to heat the water up to no hotter than 170°F (77°C) to avoid extracting tannins. Next, remove the grain bag, top your kettle up with enough preheated water to reach a total pre-boil volume of 7 gallons (26.5L), and turn your heat source back on. Once you reach a boil, add your malt extract, hops, yeast nutrient, and kettle finings, according to the ingredients list. Follow the remaining portion of the all-grain recipe.

TIPS FOR SUCCESS

This is a high-gravity beer that will require lots of yeast (about 334 billion total cells) for a healthy fermentation. If you have 1 White Labs vial or 1 Wyeast Activator pack, you will need to make either a 1.75-liter stir plate starter or a 5-liter non-stir plate starter in advance. If you are unable to make a starter, be prepared to pitch at least 3.5 vials/packs of fresh yeast. Oxygenating your wort with pure oxygen for 90 seconds prior to pitching your yeast and (optionally) for an additional 30 seconds 12 to 18 hours after you initially pitch your yeast is recommended to ensure optimal yeast growth. Due to the high gravity and use of ground coffee in

this beer, the extended fermentation and cold conditioning period outlined above is beneficial. It will allow the yeast ample time to ferment the beer completely, reabsorb diacetyl properly, and allow the ground coffee to completely settle before packaging, which helps to avoid creating nucleation points that could lead to "gushers" if bottling.

FOUNDER'S BREWING COMPANY
BREAKFAST STOUT

**(5 gallons/19 L, all-grain) OG = 1.078 FG = 1.020
IBU = 60 SRM = 59 ABV = 7.5%**

Founder's describes this as "the coffee lover's consummate beer." Brewed with flaked oats, bitter and imported chocolate, and two types of coffee, this is indeed like the strong, dark cup of joe you'll want for breakfast—or anytime!

INGREDIENTS

13.2 lb. (6 kg) 2-row pale malt

22 oz. (0.62 kg) flaked oats

1 lb. (0.45 kg) chocolate malt (350 °L)

12 oz. (0.34 kg) roast barley malt (450 °L)

9 oz. (0.25 kg) debittered black malt (530 °L)

7 oz. (0.19 kg) crystal malt (120 °L)

14.3 AAU Nugget pellet hops (60 min.) (1.1 oz./31 g at 13% alpha acids)

2.5 AAU Willamette pellet hops (30 min.) (0.5 oz./14 g at 5% alpha acids)

2.5 AAU Willamette pellet hops (0 min.) (0.5 oz./14 g at 5% alpha acids)

2 oz. (57 g) ground Sumatran coffee

2 oz. (57 g) ground Kona coffee

2.5 oz. (71 g) dark bittersweet chocolate

1.5 oz. (43 g) unsweetened chocolate baking nibs

½ tsp. yeast nutrient (15 min.)

½ tsp. Irish moss (15 min.)

White Labs WLP001 (California Ale) or Wyeast 1056 (American Ale) yeast (as a 3.5 L yeast starter)

¾ cup (150 g) dextrose (for priming)

STEP BY STEP

Mash the crushed grains with 5 gallons (19 liters) of water at 155°F (68°C) for 60 minutes. Vorlauf, then sparge slowly with 175°F (79°C) water. Add the hops and Irish moss according to times indicated in the ingredients list. Add the Sumatran coffee and 2 chocolate varieties at the end of

the boil. Pitch the yeast and ferment at 68°F (20°C) until final gravity is reached. Transfer to a carboy, avoiding any splashing. Add the Kona coffee and condition for 1 week, then bottle or keg. Carbonate and age for 2 weeks.

EXTRACT WITH GRAINS OPTION: Substitute the 2-row pale malt with 6.6 pounds (3.0 kilograms) Briess light unhopped malt extract and 1.7 pounds (0.77 kilogram) light dried malt extract. Steep the crushed grain in 2 gallons (7.6 liters) of water at 155°F (68°C) for 30 minutes. Remove grains from the wort and rinse with 2 quarts (1.8 liters) of hot water. Add the liquid and dried malt extracts and bring to a boil. Add the hops and Irish moss as per the ingredients list. Add the Sumatran coffee and two chocolate varieties at the end of the boil. Add the wort to 2 gallons (7.6 liters) of filtered water in a sanitized fermenter and top up to 5 gallons (19 liters). Follow the remaining portion of the all-grain recipe.

FREETAIL BREWING COMPANY
LA MUERTA IMPERIAL STOUT

‹‹‹‹‹‹‹-

**(5 gallons/19 L, all-grain) OG = 1.092 FG = 1.023
IBU = 50 SRM = 66 ABV = 9.1%**

Freetail brews this beer each year for Día de los Muertos to honor departed family and friends. They say this garnet-black ale with notes of smoke, roast, and chocolate is meant to age for years, so brew it to enjoy now and later.

INGREDIENTS

10 lb. (4.5 kg) 2-row pale malt

4.5 lb. (2 kg) Weyermann smoked barley malt

2 lb. (0.91 kg) chocolate malt (350 °L)

1.4 lb. (0.62 kg) Munich malt

1 lb. (0.45 kg) crystal malt (120 °L)

14 oz. (0.4 kg) roasted barley (450 °L)

15.8 AAU Summit pellet hops (60 min.) (0.9 oz./26 g at 17.5% alpha acids)

½ tsp. Irish moss (15 min.)

½ tsp. yeast nutrient (15 min.)

White Labs WLP007 (Dry English Ale), Wyeast 1335 (British Ale II), or Fermentis Safale S-04 yeast

¾ cup (150 g) dextrose (if priming)

STEP BY STEP

This is a single-infusion mash. Mix all the crushed grains with 6 gallons (23 liters) of 168°F (76°C) water to stabilize at 152°F (67°C) for 60 minutes. Slowly sparge with 175°F (79°C) water. Collect approximately 7 gallons (26.5 liters) of wort runoff to boil for 60 minutes. Add hops, Irish moss, and yeast nutrient as indicated. Cool the wort to 75°F (24°C). Once cooled, pitch your yeast and aerate the wort heavily. Allow the beer to cool to 68°F (20°C). Hold at that temperature until fermentation is complete. Transfer to a secondary fermenter and allow the beer to condition for 1 week, and then bottle or keg.

PARTIAL MASH OPTION: Replace the entire malt bill in the all-grain version with 6.6 pounds (3 kilograms) Briess special dark unhopped liquid malt extract (90 °L), 2.5 pounds (1.1 kilograms) traditional dark dried malt extract (30 °L), 3 pounds (1.36 kilograms) Weyermann smoked barley malt, 1.5 pounds (0.68 kilograms) chocolate malt (350 °L), 4 ounces (113 grams) Munich malt, 2 ounces (57 grams) crystal malt (120 °L), and 2 ounces (57 grams) roasted barley (450 °L). Mash the crushed grain in 2.5 gallons (9.5 liters) of water at 152°F (67°C) for 60 minutes. Remove grains from the wort and rinse with 2 quarts (1.9 liters) of hot water and bring your brewpot volume up to 5.5 gallons (21 liters). Add the liquid and dried malt extracts and boil for 60 minutes. Follow the remaining portion of the all-grain recipe.

LAGUNITAS BREWING COMPANY
CAPPUCCINO STOUT

‹‹‹‹‹‹‹-

**(5 gallons/19 L, all-grain) OG = 1.080 FG = 1.014
IBU = 30 SRM = 45 ABV = 8.9%**

Lagunitas says they use boatloads of coffee in this beer. Lucky for us, this amount is much more manageable on a homebrew scale! They say this full-flavored stout "will leave you wondering whether you are coming or going."

INGREDIENTS

11.6 lb. (5.3 kg) 2-row pale malt

1.75 lb. (0.8 kg) wheat malt

1.25 lb. (0.57 kg) crystal malt (60 °L)

9.5 oz. (0.27 kg) chocolate malt

9.5 oz. (0.27 kg) Weyermann Carafa Special III malt

9.5 oz. (0.27 kg) corn sugar (60 min.)

7.4 AAU Horizon hops (60 min.) (0.67 oz./19 g at 11% alpha acids)

0.72 AAU Willamette hops (30 min.) (0.14 oz./4 g at 5% alpha acids)

2.15 AAU Cascade hops (30 min.) (0.36 oz./10 g at 6% alpha acids)

5 AAU Willamette hops (hop stand) (1 oz./28 g at 5% alpha acids)

6 AAU Cascade hops (hop stand) (1 oz./28 g at 6% alpha acids)

0.07 oz. (2 g) Willamette hops (dry hop)

0.1 oz. (3 g) Cascade hops (dry hop)

3 oz. (85 g) ground coffee (hop stand)

Wyeast 1056 (American Ale), White Labs WLP001 (California Ale), or Fermentis Safale US-05 yeast

¾ cup (150 g) dextrose (if priming)

STEP BY STEP

Mash at 155°F (68°C) for 45 minutes. Collect 6.5 gallons (24.6 liters) of wort in your kettle. Boil 60 minutes, adding corn sugar at beginning of boil. Add hops according to the schedule, waiting on the hop stand additions. After the boil is finished, remove from heat and cool the wort down to 180°F (82°C). Add the hop stand additions along with the ground coffee. Stir the wort into a whirlpool and let settle for 15 minutes. Chill the wort down 68°F (21°C), aerate, and pitch the yeast. Ferment at 70°F (21°C) for 2 weeks. Add the dry hops and let sit 3 to 4 days. If you want more coffee flavor, add some cold-brewed coffee to taste at this time. Bottle or keg as usual.

PARTIAL MASH OPTION: Substitute the 2-row pale malt and wheat in the all-grain recipe with 6.6 pounds (3 kilograms) pale liquid malt extract and 1 pound (0.45 kilogram) wheat dried malt extract. Heat 7 quarts (6.6 liters) of water to 166°F (74°C). Place crushed grains in a steeping bag and steep at 155°F (68°C) for 45 minutes. In a separate pot, heat 5.25 quarts (5 liters) to 170°F (77°C). After done steeping, rinse grains with the 170°F (77°C) water and bring wort volume up to 3 gallons (11.4 liters), then raise to a boil. Add dried malt extract and corn sugar and boil for 60 minutes, adding hops at times indicated in recipe and add liquid malt extract with 15 minutes left in boil. Follow the remaining portion of the all-grain recipe.

NORTH COAST BREWING CO.
OLD RASPUTIN RUSSIAN IMPERIAL STOUT

(5 gallons/19 L, all-grain) OG = 1.090 FG = 1.022 IBU = 85 SRM = 39 ABV = 9%

According to North Coast, this stout was designed to honor the tradition of eighteenth-century English brewers, who supplied the court of Catherine the Great. The distinctive label does indeed picture Rasputin. The phrase in Russian translates to: "A sincere friend is not born instantly."

INGREDIENTS

15.5 lb. (7 kg) Maris Otter pale ale malt

1 lb. (0.45 kg) British light crystal malt (35 °L)

1 lb. (0.45 kg) crystal malt (120 °L)

0.5 lb. (0.23 g) brown malt

0.5 lb. (0.23 g) chocolate malt

0.25 lb. (113 g) roasted barley

22.75 AAU Nugget hops (60 min.) (1.75 oz./50 g at 13% alpha acids)

1 oz. (28 g) Northern Brewer hops (0 min.)

1 oz. (28 g) Centennial hops (0 min.)

Wyeast 1007 (German Ale) or White Labs WLP036 (Düsseldorf Alt) yeast

⅔ cup (133 g) dextrose (if priming)

STEP BY STEP

Mill the grains, then mix with 23.5 quarts (22.2 liters) of 165°F (74°C) strike water to reach a mash temperature of 152°F (67°C). Hold this temperature for 60 minutes. Vorlauf until your runnings are clear and lauter. Sparge the grains with enough water to obtain 6.5 gallons (24.6 liters) of wort. Boil for 60 minutes, adding hops according to the ingredient list and Irish moss if desired. After the boil, chill the wort to slightly below fermentation temperature, about 63°F (17°C). Aerate the wort with pure oxygen or filtered air and pitch yeast. Ferment at 64°F (19°C) for the first 7 days, then free rise to 70°F (21°C) and hold there until the completion of primary fermentation. Once the beer completes fermentation, reduce temperature to 32°F (0°C), then bottle or keg the beer and carbonate to approximately 2.25 volumes.

EXTRACT WITH GRAINS OPTION: Substitute the Maris Otter pale ale malt with 10.6 pounds (4.8 kilograms) Maris Otter liquid malt extract. Bring 5.4 gallons (20.4 liters) of water to approximately 162°F (72°C) and hold there. Steep grains for 15 minutes, then remove bag and allow to drain into the wort. Add liquid extract while stirring, and stir until completely dissolved. Boil for 60 minutes, adding hops according to the ingredient list and Irish moss if desired. Follow the remaining portion of the all-grain recipe.

TIPS FOR SUCCESS

The theme here is "less is more." Rather than going heavy on the chocolate malts, this recipe spreads the wealth and includes healthy additions of light crystal, dark crystal, brown malt, and then drops in an appropriate amount of roast and coffee flavor. It increases its intense, flinty impression through a fairly aggressive bittering regimen, which is then softened a bit by complex herbal and earthy aromas and flavors from the late hops addition. The fermentation temperature starts and stays low through the bulk of the fermentation process, which might entail a slightly longer wait to ensure that the beer is fully attenuated—wait at least 1 week after all visible signs of fermentation have ended before packaging.

ROUND GUYS BREWING CO.
RUSSIAN MESSENGER

(5 gallons/19 L, all-grain) OG = 1.095 FG = 1.024 IBU = 71 SRM = 52 ABV = 9.5%

Round Guys owner Scott Rudich takes a distinctly European approach to this beer. The pilsner and Munich malts that form the bulk of the grist lay down a bready base for the rich brown malt and raisiny crystal to follow.

INGREDIENTS

13.5 lb. (6.1 kg) pilsner malt

3 lb. (1.4 kg) Munich malt

1 lb. (0.45 kg) pale chocolate malt

1 lb. (0.45 kg) brown malt

1 lb. (0.45 kg) roasted barley (500 °L)

0.5 lb. (0.23 kg) crystal malt (120 °L)

12.75 AAU Apollo hops (60 min.) (0.75 oz./21 g at 17% alpha acids)

8.4 AAU Bravo hops (30 min.) (0.6 oz./17 g at 14% alpha acids)

0.6 oz. (17 g) Columbus hops (0 min.)

Fermentis Safale US-05, White Labs WLP001 (California Ale), or Wyeast 1056 (American Ale) yeast

⅔ cup (133 g) dextrose (if priming)

STEP BY STEP

Mill the grains, then mix with 6.25 gallons (23.7 liters) of 163°F (73°C) strike water to reach a mash temperature of 150°F (66°C). Hold this temperature for 60 minutes. Vorlauf until your runnings are clear and begin sparge. Sparge the grains with enough water to obtain 6.5 gallons (24.6 liters) of wort. Boil for 60 minutes, adding hops according to the ingredient list and Irish moss if desired. After the boil, chill the wort to slightly below fermentation temperature, about 63°F (17°C). Aerate the wort with pure oxygen or filtered air and pitch yeast. Ferment at 64°F (17°C), raising by 1°F per day to reach 70°F (21°C), then hold there until the completion of primary fermentation. Once the beer completes fermentation, reduce temperature to 32°F (0°C), then bottle or keg the beer and carbonate to approximately 2.25 volumes.

EXTRACT WITH GRAINS OPTION: Substitute the pilsner malt with 8 pounds (3.6 kilograms) Pilsen liquid malt extract, and the Munich malt with 3.3 pounds (1.5 kilograms) Munich liquid malt extract. Bring 5.4 gallons (20.4 liters) of water to approximately 162°F (72°C) and hold there. Steep grains for 15 minutes, then remove bag and allow to drain into the wort. Add liquid extract while stirring, and stir until completely dissolved. Boil for 60 minutes, adding hops according to the ingredient list and Irish moss if desired. Follow the remaining portion of the all-grain recipe.

SMOG CITY BREWING COMPANY
THE NOTHING

(5 gallons/19 L, all-grain) OG = 1.087 FG = 1.022 IBU = 84 SRM = 50 ABV = 9.3%

Smog City's winter seasonal, a double chocolate stout, is named for the Nothing, a character from the movie *The NeverEnding Story*. The beer is aged in raw cocoa nibs and should have the flavor of a high-quality, dark chocolate bar.

INGREDIENTS

- 6.5 lb. (3 kg) Maris Otter pale ale malt
- 6 lb. (2.7 kg) Rahr 2-row pale malt
- 2 lb. (0.9 kg) flaked oats
- 1 lb. (0.45 kg) flaked barley
- 0.5 lb. (0.23 kg) chocolate wheat malt (375 °L)
- 0.5 lb. (0.23 kg) medium crystal malt (60 °L)
- 0.5 lb. (0.23 kg) Crisp crystal malt (120 °L)
- 0.5 lb. (0.23 kg) pale chocolate malt
- 0.5 lb. (0.23 kg) roasted barley
- 0.25 lb. (113 g) Weyermann Carafa Special III malt
- 0.25 lb. (113 g) dark brown sugar (90 min.)
- 22.5 AAU Summit hops (90 min.) (1.25 oz./35 g at 18% alpha acids)
- 0.7 oz. (20 g) Tcho Ecuador cocoa nibs (crushed)
- 0.7 oz. (20 g) Tcho Ghana cocoa nibs (crushed)
- Wyeast 1056 (American Ale), White Labs WLP001 (California Ale), or Fermentis Safale US-05 yeast
- ⅔ cup (133 g) dextrose (if priming)

STEP BY STEP

Mill the grains, then mix with 5.7 gallons (21.6 liters) of 165°F (74°C) strike water to reach a mash temperature of 152°F (67°C). Hold this temperature for 60 minutes. Vorlauf until your runnings are clear and sparge. Sparge the grains with enough water to obtain 7 gallons (26.5 liters) of wort. Boil for 90 minutes, adding hops and sugar according to the ingredient list and Irish moss if desired. After the boil, chill the wort to slightly below fermentation temperature, about 65°F (18°C). Aerate the wort with pure oxygen or filtered air and pitch yeast. Ferment at 66°F (19°C) for 7 days, then free rise to 72°F (22°C) until the completion of primary fermentation. Add the crushed cocoa nibs to a neutral spirit such as vodka (just enough to cover the nibs) and let soak for 1 week or more. Once the beer completes fermentation, reduce temperature to 32°F (0°C), and add the cocoa nibs with spirits, resting for 10 to 14 days. Then bottle or keg the beer and carbonate to approximately 2.25 volumes.

PARTIAL MASH OPTION: Substitute the Maris Otter pale ale malt with 6.6 pounds (3 kilograms) Maris Otter liquid malt extract, and scale the Rahr 2-row pale malt down to 3 pounds (1.4 kilograms). Bring 11 quarts (10.4 liters) of water to approximately 165°F (74°C). Place crushed 2-row malt, flaked oats, and barley in a large grain bag. Submerge in water, stirring the grains to make sure there are no dry clumps. Steep grains for 45 minutes, trying to maintain the temperature at 152°F (67°C). Place the crushed crystal and dark roasted malts in a second grain bag; submerge

in the mash. Wait an additional 15 minutes, then remove both bags and place in a colander over the kettle. Slowly wash the grains with 2 gallons hot water. Add liquid extract while stirring, and stir until completely dissolved. Top up to 7 gallons (26.5 liters) and boil for 90 minutes, adding hops and sugar according to the ingredient list and Irish moss if desired. Follow the remaining portion of the all-grain recipe.

TIPS FOR SUCCESS

Head brewmaster Jonathan Porter passed on that the first time they brewed The Nothing it took 11 hours to lauter! Now, they mash in all the base malt first, then add the dark and specialty malts on top of the grain bed. If you're concerned about a stuck lauter or sparge (what with all the wheat, flaked barley, and oats), you can take this approach and/or add a pound of rice hulls to ease the process. Porter also noted that the ingredients matter: be sure to source the best cocoa nibs you can find and avoid going overboard on the chocolate/black malts.

SOUTHERN TIER BREWING COMPANY
CRÈME BRÛLÉE

(5 gallons/19 L, all-grain) OG = 1.104 FG = 1.03
IBU = 55 SRM = 55 ABV = 10%

While many imperial stouts are all about recreating chocolate desserts, Southern Tier had another idea: why not crème brûlée? This inventive brew brings all the flavor of the classic hard-coated custard dessert into a creamy, dreamy beer.

INGREDIENTS

- 15.25 lb. (6.9 kg) 2-row pale malt
- 1.5 lb. (0.68 kg) flaked barley
- 1 lb. (0.45 kg) crystal malt (60 °L)
- 1 lb. (0.45 kg) Belgian debittered black malt (600 °L)
- 1 lb. (0.45 kg) lactose sugar (0 min.)
- 12 oz. (0.34 kg) caramelized white cane sugar (0 min.)
- 10.8 AAU Columbus hops (60 min.) (0.75 oz./21 g at 14.5% alpha acids)
- 9.2 AAU Chinook pellet hops (30 min.) (0.75 oz./21 g at 12.3% alpha acids)
- 3 vanilla beans split and deseeded (0 min.)
- 1 tsp. ground cardamom powder (0 min.)
- ½ tsp. yeast nutrient (15 min.)
- ½ tsp. Irish moss (15 min.)
- White Labs WLP007 (Dry English Ale) or Wyeast 1028 (London Ale) yeast
- ⅔ cup (133 g) dextrose (if priming)

STEP BY STEP

This is a single-infusion mash. Mix the crushed grains with 5.5 gallons (21 liters) of 168°F (76°C) water to stabilize at 155°F (68°C) for 60 minutes. Sparge slowly with 175°F (79°C) water. Collect approximately 6.5 gallons (25 liters) of wort runoff to boil for 60 minutes. During the boil you will want to make the caramelized sugar. Mix 12 ounces (0.34 kilogram) sugar in ¾ cup water in a sauce pan over medium heat. Stir constantly until it turns to a thick liquid and becomes a medium amber color. Add to boiling wort immediately before it hardens. Make the other kettle additions as per the schedule. At the end of the boil let the wort rest 20 minutes, and remove the vanilla beans. Cool the wort to 75°F (24°C). Pitch your yeast and aerate the wort heavily. Ferment at 68°F (20°C). After fermentation is complete, transfer to a carboy, and condition for 1 week before you bottle or keg.

EXTRACT WITH GRAINS OPTION: Reduce the 2-row pale malt in the all-grain recipe to 1.5 pounds (0.68 kilograms) and add 9 pounds (4.1 kilograms) light liquid malt extract. Steep the crushed grains in 2 gallons (7.6 liters) of water at 155°F (68°C) for 30 minutes. Remove grains from the wort and rinse with 2 quarts (1.8 liters) of hot water. Add the liquid malt extract and boil for 60 minutes. Follow the remaining portion of the all-grain recipe.

SPEAKEASY ALES & LAGERS
SCARFACE IMPERIAL STOUT

(5 gallons/19 L, all-grain) OG = 1.087 FG = 1.022
IBU = 50 SRM = 36 ABV = 9.3%

Part of Speakeasy's "Infamous" series, this full-bodied imperial stout is ready to take on all comers with notes of burnt caramel, espresso, and smoke. According to the brewery, "this is not a beer to be taken lightly."

INGREDIENTS

14 lb. (6.4 kg) 2-row pale malt

2 lb. (0.9 kg) Weyermann Carahell malt

1 lb. (0.45 kg) flaked oats

0.5 lb. (0.23 kg) Simpsons dark crystal malt (75 °L)

0.5 lb. (0.23 kg) Patagonia Perla Negra (340 °L)

0.5 lb. (0.23 kg) roasted barley

13.6 AAU Columbus hops (90 min.) (0.85 oz./24 g at 16% alpha acids)

0.5 oz. (14 g) Magnum hops (0 min.)

White Labs WLP001 (California Ale), Wyeast 1056 (American Ale), or Fermentis Safale US-05

⅔ cup (133 g) dextrose (if priming)

STEP BY STEP

Mill the grains, then mix with 5.8 gallons (21.9 liters) of 165°F (74°C) strike water to reach a mash temperature of 152°F (67°C). Hold this temperature for 60 minutes. Vorlauf until your runnings are clear and begin to sparge. Sparge the grains with enough water to obtain 7 gallons (25.6 liters) of wort. Boil for 90 minutes, adding hops according to the ingredient list and Irish moss if desired. After the boil, chill the wort to slightly below fermentation temperature, about 65°F (18°C). Aerate the wort with pure oxygen or filtered air, and pitch yeast. Ferment at 66°F (19°C) for 7 days, then free rise to 72°F (22°C) until the completion of primary fermentation. Once the beer completes fermentation, reduce temperature to 32°F (0°C), then bottle or keg the beer and carbonate to approximately 2.25 volumes.

PARTIAL MASH OPTION: Scale the 2-row pale malt down to 2 pounds (0.91 kilograms) and add 8 pounds (3.6 kilograms) pale liquid malt extract. Bring 8 quarts (7.6 liters) of water to approximately 165°F (74°C). Place crushed 2-row malt, Weyermann Carahell, and flaked oats in a large grain bag. Submerge in water, stirring the grains to make sure there are no dry clumps. Steep grains for 45 minutes, trying to maintain the temperature at 152°F (67°C). Place the crushed crystal and dark roasted malts in a second grain bag; submerge in the mash. Wait an additional 15 minutes, then remove both bags and place in a colander over the kettle. Slowly wash the grains with 2 gallons (7.6 liters) of hot water. Add liquid extract while stirring, and stir until completely dissolved. Top up to 7 gallons (26.5 liters) and boil for 90 minutes, adding hops according to the ingredient list and Irish moss if desired. Follow the remaining portion of the all-grain recipe.

TIPS FOR SUCCESS

Brewer Clay Jordan notes that this beer mashes at a slightly lower temperature to help ensure there aren't a lot of long-chain sugars in the wort. To ensure proper conversion, it may be necessary to add a few more minutes to the mash (say, lengthening to 70 minutes), especially if your strike water comes in a little low and you start in the 148 to 150°F (65 to 66°C) range.

TERRAPIN BEER COMPANY
WAKE-N-BAKE COFFEE OATMEAL IMPERIAL STOUT

eeeeeee-

**(5 gallons/19 L, all-grain) OG = 1.086 FG = 1.020
IBU = 50 SRM = 49 ABV = 9.4%**

More than just a fun name, this imperial oatmeal stout is brewed using "Wake-N-Bake" beans from Athens, Georgia's Jittery Joe's coffee. If you want to brew it the way the Terrapin brewers do, get the beans online directly from the source. Otherwise, try this recipe with your local roaster.

INGREDIENTS

12.25 lb. (5.6 kg) UK 2-row pale malt

1.75 lb. (0.79 kg) flaked oats

1.75 lb. (0.79 kg) flaked barley

12 oz. (0.34 kg) Simpsons chocolate malt

12 oz. (0.34 kg) Thomas Fawcett dark crystal malt (85 °L)

9 oz. (0.26 kg) Simpsons roasted barley

9 oz. (0.26 kg) Simpsons black malt

½ tsp. yeast nutrient (15 min.)

½ Whirlfloc tablet (15 min.)

9.6 AAU Nugget pellet hops (60 min.) (0.75 oz./21 g at 12.8% alpha acids)

7.7 AAU Nugget pellet hops (30 min.) (0.6 oz./17 g at 12.8% alpha acids)

2.5 oz. (71 kg) Jittery Joe's "Terrapin Wake-n-Bake" Coffee (coarsely ground)

Wyeast 1272 (American Ale II) or White Labs WLP051 (California Ale V) yeast

½ cup (100 g) dextrose (if priming)

STEP BY STEP

Mill the grains (flaked oats and flaked barley don't need to be milled) and mix with 6 gallons (23 liters) of 165°F (74°C) strike water to reach a mash temperature of 150°F (66°C). Hold at this temperature for 60 minutes. Vorlauf until your runnings are clear. Sparge the grains with 3.5 gallons (13.25 liters) of 169°F (76°C) water until 7 gallons (26.5 liters) of 1.065 gravity wort is collected in your boil kettle. Boil for 75 minutes, adding hops and other additions at times indicated. After the boil, turn off the heat and whirlpool the kettle by gently stirring with a mash paddle for 2 minutes, and then let rest for an additional 8 minutes to achieve a 10-minute flameout steep. Chill the wort to 66°F (19°C) and transfer to your fermenter. Aerate the wort with pure oxygen for 90 seconds and pitch yeast. Recommended pitch rate is 294 billion yeast cells, which can be obtained by using either 1 packet after making a 1.5-liter stir plate starter, 1 packet after making a 4.4-liter non-stir plate starter, or 3 vials/packets of yeast without a starter. Allow fermentation to free rise up to 68°F (20°C), and hold until the beer reaches 60 percent apparent attenuation (1.033 specific gravity). Then ramp fermentation temperature up to 72°F (22°C) and hold at this temperature for an additional 14 days. Slowly crash cool the fermenter down at the rate of 5°F (3°C) per day for about 8 days or until you reach 32°F (0°C). Hold at this temperature for an additional 5 to 7 days. Then rack the beer onto the coarsely ground coffee. After 48 hours on coffee, transfer the beer into a keg or bottling bucket. Carbonate to 2.2 volumes of CO_2.

PARTIAL MASH OPTION: Reduce the 2-row pale malt in the all-grain recipe to 3.5 pounds (1.6 kilograms) and add 6 pounds (2.7 kilograms) golden light liquid malt extract. You will need either a small mash tun or 2 large brew-in-a-bag or paint strainer bags to make this partial mash work. Place the crushed 2-row pale malt, flaked oats, and flaked barley in the first bag. Add the grain bag to 3 gallons (7.5 liters) of 160°F (71°C) water to reach a mash temperature of 150°F (66°C). Hold at this temperature for 45 minutes, then add the crystal, chocolate, barley, and black malt in the second bag. Hold 15 minutes. Remove both grain bags and wash with 2 gallons (7.6 liters) of hot water, then top your kettle up to 7 gallons (26.5 liters). Once you reach a boil, add your malt extract and hops. Boil for 75 minutes. Follow the remaining portion of the all-grain recipe.

TIPS FOR SUCCESS

If opting for North American 2-row malt in the all-grain recipe, which generally has more beta amylase than most British 2-row malt, increase your mash temperature to 154°F (68°C) to properly limit yeast attenuation.

THREE FLOYDS BREWING COMPANY
DARK LORD

eeeeeee-

**(5 gallons/19 L, all-grain) OG = 1.169 FG = 1.054
IBU = 100+ SRM = 73 ABV = 15%**

Dark Lord is a highly sought-after Russian imperial stout brewed with coffee, Mexican vanilla, and Indian sugar. It features notes of mocha and charred fruit, and has a "motor oil–like consistency." Note the extended total boil time. This is not your typical brew session.

INGREDIENTS

- 27.8 lb. (12.6 kg) Great Western Northwestern Pale Ale malt (4 °L)
- 1.7 lb. (0.77 kg) Simpsons Golden Naked Oats malt
- 10.2 oz. (289 g) Simpsons medium crystal malt (55 °L)
- 13.3 oz. (377 g) Crisp extra dark crystal malt (120 °L)
- 1.3 lb. (0.59 kg) pale chocolate malt (200 °L)
- 1.1 lb. (0.5 kg) Simpsons chocolate malt (430 °L)
- 13.6 oz. (385 g) Simpsons black malt (550 °L)
- 9.4 oz. (266 g) flaked oats
- 2.7 lb. (1.2 kg) Jaggery/Panela/Gur sugar (10 °L) (10 min.)
- 18 mL CO_2 hop extract (start of boil) (62% alpha acids)
- 1 tablet Whirlfloc tablet (10 min.)
- 0.5 tsp. Yeastex nutrient (10 min.)
- 2 Mexican vanilla beans
- 2.5–5 oz. (71-142 g) coffee beans
- 2 packs Wyeast 1968 (London ESB Ale) or White Labs WLP002 (English Ale) yeast
- 2 packs Wyeast 1056 (American Ale) or White Labs WLP001 (California Ale) yeast
- Lallemand CBC-1 or other high alcohol tolerant yeast strain (if priming)
- ⅔ cup (133 g) dextrose (if priming)

STEP BY STEP

Before brew day, pitch 2 packs each of Wyeast 1968 and 1056 (White Labs WLP002 and WLP001, respectively) into a 0.8-gallon (3 liters) yeast starter on a stir plate (equates to a pitching rate of 1 million cells per milliliters wort per degree Plato). When yeast flocculates, place the starter in the fridge and store until brew day. The brew day will require 2 mashes, referred to here as Mash #1 and Mash #2. On brew day, mill 16.7 pounds (7.6 kilograms) of pale ale malt and dough-in with 22.25 quarts hot water (21.1 liters), targeting a mash at 159°F (70.6°C) (Mash #1). Hold until enzymatic conversion is complete. If your system allows, raise the mash temperature to 168°F (76°C) and recirculate the wort until clear. Sparge with 170°F (77°C) water to collect 6.5 gallons (25 liters) of wort. If your boil-off volume is greater than 10 percent per hour, adjust the amount of wort you collect accordingly. Take a specific gravity reading and, if needed, add light dried malt extract to reach a specific gravity of 1.065. Heat to a boil and add the hop extract. Boil for 4 hours. Time Mash #2 so that the wort from Mash #1 has boiled for at least 4 hours before you begin to collect the first runnings from Mash #2 into the boil kettle. For Mash #2, mill 11.1 pounds (5 kilograms) of pale ale malt,

along with the remaining grain and dough-in with 22.25 quarts of hot water (21.1 liters), targeting a mash at 159°F (70.6°C). Hold until enzymatic conversion is complete. If your system allows, raise the mash temperature to 168°F (76°C) and recirculate the wort until clear. Collect 3.5 gallons (13.2 liters) of first runnings wort in the boil kettle to reach a total volume of 6.5 gallons (25 liters). If necessary, sparge with 170°F (77°C) water to bring the volume up to 6.5 gallons (25 liters) of wort. The specific gravity of the wort in the kettle at this point should be about 1.124. Boil for 90 minutes, adding Whirlfloc, yeast nutrient, and sugar at 10 minutes. Before cooling, take a specific gravity reading, and, if needed, add light dried malt extract to reach a specific gravity of 1.169 and a final volume of 5.5 gallons (20.7 liters).

Chill the wort to 62°F (16.7°C). Oxygenate with pure oxygen for 90 seconds before pitching the yeast starter (decanting the spent wort first). Ferment at 62 to 64°F (16.7 to 17.8°C). After 12 to 24 hours of fermentation, oxygenate with pure oxygen for 60 seconds. Hold the fermentation temperature at 62 to 64°F (16.7 to 17.8°C) for 7 to 10 days before raising the temperature up to 70°F (21.1°C) for 7 days to perform a diacetyl rest and ensure a complete fermentation (final specific gravity of ~1.055). Rack to secondary fermenter and leave for 1 to 3 weeks. (Due to extreme viscosity, racking this beer can take an incredibly long time.) Before or after racking the beer to the secondary, prepare a vanilla bean tincture: Cut open two Mexican vanilla beans, making sure to scrape out the seeds, and cut the pods into pieces. Place the vanilla seeds and pods into just enough neutral spirit (such as vodka) to cover, and age for 5 days before adding it directly to the secondary fermenter. Age the beer with vanilla bean tincture for a minimum of 3 days. If barrel aging, rack the beer into barrel after secondary fermentation and age to taste. My "brandy barrel aged with vanilla beans" version of this beer was aged in a brandy barrel with an additional vanilla bean tincture for 6 months before kegging (read on). If bottling, add 2.5 to 5 ounces (71 to 142 grams) of whole Intelligentsia Black Cat (pre-2014 Dark Lord) or Dark Matter Unicorn Blood (2014–2015 Dark Lord) coffee beans (in a muslin bag) to the beer in secondary fermenter and age for 24 to 48 hours, preferably at 38°F (3°C). Rack the beer to a bottling bucket and add a fresh packet of yeast to assure proper carbonation. Lallemand CBC-1 and Fermentis Safale US-05 are two good options that can handle the high ABV. Carbonate aiming for a carbonation level of 2 to 2.2 volumes of CO_2. Once carbonated, condition the beer at cellar temperature for several months. If kegging, add 2.5 to 5 ounces (71 to 142 grams) of whole Intelligentsia Black Cat (pre-2014 Dark Lord) or Dark Matter Unicorn Blood (2014–2015 Dark Lord) coffee beans (in a muslin bag) to empty keg and rack the beer into a keg, aging on coffee beans for 24 to 48 hours, preferably at 38°F (3°C). Remove the beans and aim for a carbonation level of 2 to 2.2 volumes of CO_2. Once carbonated, condition at cellar temperature for several months.

PARTIAL MASH OPTION: Substitute the pale ale malt in the all-grain recipe with 14.6 pounds (6.6 kilograms) Briess extra light dried malt extract and 9.4 ounces (266 grams) Weyermann CaraFoam malt. Prepare yeast starter as described in the all-grain recipe. On brew day, crush the steeping grains and place them in 2 steeping bags. Steep the bags at 155°F (68°C) in 20 quarts (18.9 liters) of water for 20 minutes. Rinse the grains with 4 quarts (3.8 liters) of 170°F (77°C) water. Add dried malt extract (DME) and water to achieve a pre-boil volume of 6.5 gallons (25 liters). Boil for 60 minutes, adding the hop extract, sugar, and yeast nutrients at the specified times. Follow the remaining portion of the all-grain recipe.

- - - - - - - - - - - - - - - - -

TWO RIVERS BREWING CO.
ESOTERIK

⟨⟨⟨⟨⟨⟨⟨-

**(5 gallons/19 L, all-grain) OG = 1.099 FG = 1.024
IBU = 49 SRM = 71 ABV = 10%**

Esoterik is a commemorative beer named in honor of Mr. Anthony Marraccini, who has contributed extensively to the work of the arts community of Easton, Pennsylvania. It's quite a tribute: The dark fruit really pops in this recipe, but only if you hold the alcohols in check.

INGREDIENTS

15.5 lb. (7 kg) Muntons Propino Pale malt (pale 2-row)

1.5 lb. (0.68 kg) roasted barley

1 lb. (0.45 kg) Special B malt

0.5 lb. (0.23 kg) Caramunich III malt

0.5 lb. (0.23 kg) chocolate malt

0.5 lb. (0.23 kg) pale chocolate malt

1 lb. (0.45 kg) D2 candi syrup

13 AAU Nugget hops (60 min.) (1 oz./28 g at 13% alpha acids)

2 oz. (57 g) East Kent Golding hops (0 min.)

White Labs WLP095 (Burlington Ale), GigaYeast GY054 (Vermont Ale), or Imperial A04 (Barbarian) yeast

¾ cup (133 g) dextrose (if priming)

STEP BY STEP

Mill the grains, then mix with 24.4 quarts (23.1 liters) of 167°F (75°C) strike water to reach a mash temperature of 154°F (68°C). Hold this temperature for 60 minutes. Vorlauf until your runnings are clear and sparge. Sparge the grains with enough water to obtain 6.5 gallons (24.6 liters) of wort. Remove kettle from heat and stir in Belgian candi syrup until dissolved. Boil for 60 minutes, adding hops according to the ingredient list and Irish moss if desired. After the boil, chill the wort to slightly below fermentation temperature, about 65°F (18°C). Aerate the wort with pure oxygen or filtered air, and pitch yeast. Ferment at 66°F (19°C), for the first 2 days, then free rise to 70°F (21°C) and hold there until the completion of primary fermentation. Once the beer completes fermentation, reduce temperature to 32°F (0°C), then bottle or keg the beer and carbonate to approximately 2.4 volumes.

EXTRACT WITH GRAINS OPTION: Omit the Muntons Propino Pale malt and add 10.75 pounds (4.9 kilograms) Maris Otter liquid malt extract. Bring 5.4 gallons of water to approximately 162°F (72°C) and hold there. Steep grains for 20 minutes, then remove bag and allow to drain into the wort. Add liquid extract and Belgian candi syrup while stirring, and stir until completely dissolved. Boil for 60 minutes, adding hops according to the ingredient list and Irish moss if desired. Now follow the remainder of the all-grain recipe.

TIPS FOR SUCCESS

Head Brewer Josh Bushey recommends pitching more healthy yeast than you think you'll need (and incidentally, if you can't source the Vermont IPA strain from the various yeast providers, any alcohol-tolerant and mildly estery yeast will work too). The relatively high mash temperature will add body, but the candi syrup will balance against that, leaving behind a beer that's intensely flavorful and full but still quite drinkable.

- - - - - - - - - - - - - - - - -

VICTORY BREWING COMPANY
STORM KING IMPERIAL STOUT

ecccccc-

**(5 gallons/19 L, all-grain) OG = 1.089 FG = 1.021
IBU = 82 SRM = 53 ABV = 9.2%**

Victory Brewing Company touts "a thundering hop presence" in this imperial stout. But the hops meet their match with a rich malt bill full of espresso and dark chocolate flavors.

INGREDIENTS

14 lb. (6.4 kg) pilsner malt

2.5 lb. (1.13 kg) Vienna malt

1 lb. (0.45 kg) Weyermann Carafa II malt (425 °L)

1 lb. (0.45 kg) roast barley (450 °L)

20 AAU Centennial hops (60 min.) (1.9 oz./54 g at 10.5% alpha acids)

5.25 AAU Cluster pellet hops (30 min.) (0.75 oz./21 g at 7% alpha acids)

2.9 AAU Cascade pellet hops (5 min.) (0.5 oz./14 g at 5.75% alpha acids)

½ tsp. yeast nutrients (15 min.)

½ tsp. Irish moss (15 min.)

White Labs WLP001 (California Ale), Wyeast 1056 (American Ale), or Fermentis Safale US-05 yeast

¾ cup (150 g) dextrose (if priming)

STEP BY STEP

This is a single-infusion mash. Mix all the crushed grains with 6 gallons (22.7 liters) of 170°F (77°C) water to stabilize at 155°F (68°C) for 60 minutes. Sparge slowly with 175°F (79°C) water. Collect approximately 6 gallons (23 liters) of wort runoff to boil for 60 minutes, adding the hops, Irish moss, and yeast nutrients according to the schedule. After the boil, cool the wort to 75°F (24°C). Pitch your yeast and aerate the wort heavily. Allow the beer to cool to 68°F (20°C). Hold at that temperature until fermentation is complete. Transfer to a carboy, avoiding any splashing to prevent aerating the beer. Condition for 1 week. Bottle or keg.

EXTRACT WITH GRAINS OPTION: Substitute the pilsner malt in the all-grain recipe with 6.6 pounds (3 kilograms) Briess Pilsen unhopped liquid malt extract and 2.5 pounds (1.13 kilograms) Pilsen light dried malt extract. Steep the crushed grain in 2 gallons (7.6 liters) of water at 155°F (68°C) for 30 minutes. Remove grains from the wort and rinse with 2 quarts (1.8 liters) of hot water. Add the liquid and dried malt extracts and boil for 60 minutes. Follow the remaining portion of the all-grain recipe.

WEYERBACHER BREWING COMPANY
FIFTEEN

ecccccc-

**(5 gallons/19 L, all-grain) OG = 1.101 FG = 1.022
IBU = 52 SRM = 74 ABV = 10.8%**

To celebrate their fifteenth anniversary, Weyerbacher brewed an intense imperial stout. The brewery says, "Fifteen has a rich flavor profile, balancing notes of dark roast, burnt toast, and spicy rye with a deep earthy aroma of smoke and wood."

INGREDIENTS

15 lb. (6.8 kg) smoked malt

1.88 lb. (0.85 kg) Weyermann CaraAroma malt (150 °L)

1.25 lb. (0.57 kg) Weyermann Carafa Special II malt (425 °L)

1.25 lb. (0.57 kg) rye malt

1.25 lb. (0.57 kg) pale malt

0.75 lb. (0.34 kg) black malt

0.75 lb. (0.34 kg) roasted barley

15.75 AAU Centennial hops (90 min.) (1.5 oz./43 g at 10.5% alpha aids)

1 oz. (28 g) Fuggle hops (2 min.)

Wyeast 1272 (American Ale II) or White Labs WLP051 (California Ale V) yeast

¾ cup (150 g) dextrose (if priming)

STEP BY STEP

We recommend making a small beer with your yeast to get the yeast count up to an appropriate level to pitch into this beer. You could also make a 1-gallon (4-liter) starter several days in advance then place the starter in the fridge prior to brew day. Decant the liquid once the yeast has properly settled. On brew day, mash in to 130°F (54°C), rest for 20 minutes, then ramp up the mash to 154°F (68°C) and rest for 30 minutes. Raise temperature to 172°F (78°C) to mash out. Collect approximately 7 gallons (27 liters) of wort and boil for 90 minutes, adding the hops as indicated. After the boil is complete, cool and ferment at 68°F (20°C). Condition in a secondary vessel for 4 weeks at 50°F (10°C) prior to bottling or kegging as normal.

EDITOR'S NOTE: Due to the high percentage of smoked malt, an approximate extract version of this recipe would be very difficult to achieve.

GREAT DIVIDE BREWING CO
OLD RUFFIAN
HEFTY Barley Wine-Style Ale HOPPY
BREWED AND BOTTLED BY
GREAT DIVIDE BREWING CO
DENVER, COLORADO

NINE

BARLEY-WINE & STRONG ALES

BEER PICTURED ON LEFT; SEE PAGE 139

7 SEAS BREWING COMPANY
WHEELCHAIR BARLEYWINE

ᥱᥱᥱᥱᥱᥱ-

(5 gallons/19 L, all-grain) OG = 1.107 FG = 1.021
IBU = 38 SRM = 22 ABV = 11.5%

Brewed slightly differently each year, but typically aged a minimum of eight months, 7 Seas barleywines display a reddish-brown hue and exhibit prominent notes of ripe pit fruit, brown sugar, toffee, and a full-bodied, malty mouthfeel.

INGREDIENTS

17 lb. (7.7 kg) Maris Otter pale ale malt

1.25 lb. (0.57 kg) British carastan malt (34 °L)

13 oz. (0.37 kg) Belgian Special B malt (120 °L)

5.7 AAU Glacier pellet hops (60 min.) (1 oz./28 g at 5.7% alpha acids)

5.7 AAU Glacier pellet hops (40 min.) (1 oz./28 g at 5.7% alpha acids)

3.6 AAU East Kent Golding pellet hops (20 min.) (0.75 oz./21 g at 4.75% alpha acids)

2.4 AAU East Kent Golding pellet hops (5 min.) (0.5 oz./14 g at 4.75% alpha acids)

2 lb. (0.91 kg) clover honey (10 min.)

½ tsp. Irish moss (30 min.)

½ tsp. yeast nutrient (15 min.)

White Labs WLP001 (California Ale), Wyeast 1056 (American Ale) yeast, or Fermentis Safale US-05 yeast

¾ cup (150 g) dextrose (if priming)

STEP BY STEP

Mix all the crushed grains with 6.7 gallons (25 liters) of 170°F (77°C) water to stabilize at 151°F (66°C). This is a medium-thin mash using 1.4 quarts. (1.3 liters) of strike water per pound (0.45 kilogram) of grain. This is designed to help achieve maximum fermentability. The lower mash temperature also serves to create a more fermentable wort. Mash for 60 minutes, then slowly sparge with 175°F (79°C) water. Collect approximately 7.5 gallons (28 liters) of wort runoff to boil for 3 hours. While you are boiling the wort, add the hops, Irish moss, yeast nutrient, and honey as the schedule indicates. After the boil is complete, cool the wort to 75°F (24°C) and transfer to your fermenter. Pitch the yeast and aerate the wort heavily. Allow the beer to cool to 68°F (20°C), and then hold at that temperature until fermentation is complete. Gently transfer to a carboy, avoiding any splashing to prevent aerating the beer. Allow the beer to condition for an additional week. Prime and bottle condition or keg and force carbonate to 2.2 volumes CO_2. Allow the beer to age 6 more weeks (or longer) to fully develop the flavors.

EXTRACT WITH GRAINS OPTION: Substitute the pale ale malt in the all-grain recipe with 9.9 pounds (4.5 kilograms) Muntons light malt extract (Maris Otter if possible), 9 ounces (0.25 kilogram) light dried malt extract, and 1.5 pounds (0.68 kilogram) Maris Otter pale ale malt. Steep the milled grain in 2.5 gallons (9.5 liters) of water at 151°F (66°C) for 30 minutes. Remove grains from the wort and rinse with 2 quarts (2 liters) of hot water. Boil for 30 minutes. Add the liquid and dried malt extracts and boil for 60 more minutes. Follow the remaining portion of the all-grain recipe.

ALESMITH
BREWING COMPANY
OLD NUMBSKULL

ᥱᥱᥱᥱᥱᥱ-

(5 gallons/19 L, all-grain) OG = 1.106 FG = 1.023
IBU = 90 SRM = 15 ABV = 11%

There are American barleywines, and then there are West Coast–style American barleywines. In other words, if you like big beers and hops, Old Numbskull doesn't disappoint. Packed with caramel and toffee notes, this copper-colored ale boasts an aggressive bitterness.

INGREDIENTS

16 lb. 13 oz. (7.6 kg) Gambrinus 2-row pale malt

16.3 oz. (0.46 kg) C&H golden brown sugar

9.8 oz. (0.28 kg) Munich dark malt

6.5 oz. (0.19 kg) Crisp crystal malt (45°L)

4.9 oz. (0.14 kg) Crisp Caramalt malt

4.9 oz. (0.14 kg) Gambrinus Honey malt

4.9 oz. (0.14 kg) Simpsons CaraMalt malt

4.9 oz. (0.14 kg) Simpsons CaraMalt Light malt

4.9 oz. (0.14 kg) flaked barley

16 AAU Chinook hops (FWH) (1.5 oz./42 g at 11% alpha acids)

15 AAU Columbus hops (FWH) (1.1 oz./31 g at 14% alpha acids)

9.8 AAU Warrior hops (FWH) (0.65 oz./18 g at 15% alpha acids)

2.3 AAU Simcoe hops (30 min.) (0.19 oz./5.4 g at 12% alpha acids)

1.1 AAU Chinook hops (15 min.) (0.1 oz./2.8 g at 11% alpha acids)

0.6 AAU Cascade hops (5 min.) (0.1 oz./2.8 g at 6% alpha acids)

1.7 AAU Palisade hops (2 min.) (0.28 oz./7.8 g at 6% alpha acids)

1 oz. (28 g) Amarillo hops (dry hop)

1 oz. (28 g) Columbus hops (dry hop)

1 oz. (28 g) Chinook hops (dry hop)

1 oz. (28 g) Simcoe hops (dry hop)

1 oz. (28 g) Palisade hops (dry hop)

1 oz. (28 g) Warrior hops (dry hop)

White Labs WLP001 (California Ale), Wyeast 1056 (American Ale), or Fermentis Safale US-05 yeast (342 billion active cells [~2.75 L starter])

¾ cup (150 g) dextrose (if priming)

STEP BY STEP

Mash the grains at 150°F (66°C). Boil for 90 minutes, adding the hops as indicated in the ingredients list. Pitch the yeast and ferment at 65 to 68°F (18 to 20°C) until final gravity is reached. Bottle or keg as usual.

EXTRACT WITH GRAINS OPTION: Omit the flaked barley. Reduce pale malt to 1 pound (0.45 kilogram). Add 8.66 pounds (3.9 kilogram) of light dried malt extract. Steep the grains at 150°F (66°C). Boil at least 4 gallons (15 liters) of wort. Add the hops at the times indicated in the all-grain ingredients list. Reserve roughly half of the malt extract until 5 minutes before the end of the boil. Chill the wort, transfer to your fermenter, and top up with filtered water to 5 gallons (19 liters). Follow the remaining portion of the all-grain recipe.

ANCHOR BREWING COMPANY
ANCHOR OLD FOGHORN (1ST RUNNINGS)

(5 gallons/19 L, all-grain) OG = 1.099 FG = 1.030
IBU = 43 SRM = 22 ABV = 9.2%

Old Foghorn is brewed using the parti-gyle method, which is brewing two batches of beer by separating the first and second runnings to create two distinct beers—one high gravity, one lower gravity. Old Foghorn is the beer made from the first runnings. Small Beer (recipe on page 162) is the beer made from the second runnings.

INGREDIENTS

22.5 lb. (10.2 kg) 2-row pale malt

5 lb. 3 oz. (2.4 kg) caramel malt (40 °L)

6.8 AAU Cascade pellet hops (60 min.) (1.5 oz./42 g at 4.5% alpha acids)

4.5 AAU Cascade pellet hops (30 min.) (1 oz./28 g at 4.5% alpha acids)

1 oz. (28 g) Cascade pellet hops (dry hop)

White Labs WLP051 (California Ale V) or Wyeast 1272 (American Ale II) yeast

0.25 oz. (7 g) gypsum (optional if using very low-mineral water)

⅔ (130 g) dextrose (if priming)

STEP BY STEP

Mill grains and mix with 10.1 gallons (38.2 liters) of 157°F (69°C) strike water and optional gypsum (see ingredients list) to reach a mash temperature of 149°F (65°C). Hold this temperature for 60 minutes. Vorlauf until your runnings are clear. Collect the first runnings without sparging and top up if necessary to obtain 7 gallons (26.5 liters) of 1.071 SG wort. Boil for 120 minutes, adding hops according to the ingredients list. After the boil, turn off the heat and chill the wort to slightly below fermentation temperature, about 65°F (18°C). Aerate the wort with pure oxygen or filtered air, and pitch yeast. Ferment at 67°F (19°C) for 4 days. Add dry hops and raise to 72°F (22°C) for 3 days. Once at terminal gravity (approximately 7 days total), bottle or keg the beer and carbonate. Age for 6 to 12 months before serving.

EXTRACT WITH GRAINS OPTION: Substitute the 2-row pale malt in the all-grain recipe with 12 pounds (5.4 kilograms) golden liquid malt extract and reduce the caramel malt to 3 pounds (2.4 kilograms). Place the milled grains in a muslin bag and steep in 10 quarts (9.4 liters) of 149°F (65°C) water for 15 minutes. Remove the grain and rinse with 1 gallon (3.8 liters) of hot water. Add water and optional gypsum (see ingredients list) to reach a volume of 5.25 gallons (19.9 liters) and heat to boiling. Turn off the heat, add the liquid malt extract, and stir until completely dissolved. Top up with water if necessary to obtain 6 gallons (23 liters) of 1.082 wort. Boil for 60 minutes. Follow the remaining portion of the all-grain recipe.

BROOKLYN BREWERY
BROOKLYN MONSTER ALE

ccccccc-

**(5 gallons/19 L, all-grain) OG = 1.103 FG = 1.025
IBU = 47 SRM = 15 ABV= 10.2%**

Brooklyn Monster Ale was first brewed in 1997. It is midway between the old British barleywine style and more modern variants. Much of this beer's essential character comes from the use of floor-malted Maris Otter, but the residual sugar is relatively low.

INGREDIENTS

13 lb. 4 oz. (6 kg) Crisp No. 19 Floor-Malted Maris Otter

3 lb. 12 oz. (1.7 kg) Crisp pale ale malt

8 oz. (0.23 kg) caramel malt (60 °L)

3 oz. (85 g) chocolate malt

14 oz. (0.40 kg) cane sugar

9.2 AAU Willamette hops (120 min.) (2 oz./56 g at 4.6% alpha acids)

6.25 AAU Cascade hops (60 min.) (0.9 oz./26 g at 7% alpha acids)

3.5 oz. (99 g) English Fuggle hops (3 min.)

1 tsp. Irish moss (10 min.)

White Labs WLP001 (California Ale) or Wyeast 1056 (American Ale) yeast

⅝ cup (125 g) dextrose (if priming)

STEP BY STEP

Mash the grains at 154°F (68°C) and hold for 90 minutes. Bring mash to 168°F (76°C) to mash out. Sparge slowly and carefully. Collect 5 gallons (19 liters) wort at 1.092 SG. Heat to 205°F (96°C), stir in cane sugar, to reach 1.100. Boil ends at 120 minutes. Adjust volume, if necessary, to 5 gallons (19 liters). Cool to 58°F (14°C), aerate well, and pitch yeast at twice the rate that you would for pale ale. Ferment at 67°F (19°C). After fermentation is complete, cool if possible. If beer must wait more than 1 week after active fermentation has ceased before packaging, transfer to secondary. Age in bottle or keg for no less than 3 months before serving.

PARTIAL MASH OPTION: Reduce the Maris Otter malt in the all-grain version to 2.5 pounds (1.1 kilograms) and pale ale malt to 13 ounces (0.37 kilogram). This recipe also uses 3 pounds (1.4 kilograms) Muntons light dried malt extract and 7 pounds (3.2 kilograms) Muntons light liquid malt extract. Place the crushed grains in a large steeping bag. Place bag inside a 2-gallon (~8-liter) beverage cooler. Stir 5.5 quarts

(5.2 liters) of water at 167°F (75°C) into the grains. Let rest for 60 minutes. The temperature should drop to 154°F (68°C) at the end of the rest. After the mash, vorlauf, and then sparge at 170°F (77°C). Collect 4 gallons (15 liters) or as much volume as your brewpot will handle. Stir in dried malt extract and boil wort for 120 minutes. Add the hops at times indicated in the recipe. Add the table sugar and liquid malt extract in last 15 minutes of the boil. If boil volume dips below 3.5 gallons (13 liters), bring volume back up with boiling water. Follow the remaining portion of the all-grain recipe.

EMPIRE BREWING COMPANY
AMERICAN STRONG ALE

ccccccc-

**(5 gallons/19 L, all-grain) OG = 1.080 FG = 1.016
IBU = 78 SRM = 20 ABV = 8.5%**

This ale is bold, hoppy, and complex, with chocolate and roasted malts adding a full malty character. The strong American hops balance the beer with an aggressive bitterness, followed by a fruity hop flavor and a full hop aroma.

INGREDIENTS

15.5 lb. (7 kg) Thomas Fawcett Maris Otter malt

4 oz. (0.11 kg) Thomas Fawcett chocolate malt (425 °L)

2 oz. (57 g) Thomas Fawcett roasted barley (550 °L)

13 AAU Galena hops (60 min.) (1 oz./28 g at 13% alpha acids)

6 AAU Nugget hops (30 min.) (0.5 oz./14 g at 12% alpha acids)

4.5 AAU Amarillo hops (15 min.) (0.5 oz./14 g at 9% alpha acids)

4.5 AAU Amarillo hops (10 min.) (0.5 oz./14 g at 9% alpha acids)

4.5 AAU Amarillo hops (5 min.) (0.5 oz./14 g at 9% alpha acids)

0.5 oz. (14 g) Amarillo hops (0 min.)

1 oz. (28 g) Galena hops (dry hop)

0.75 oz. (21 g) Amarillo hops (dry hop)

Wyeast 1056 (American Ale), White Labs WLP001 (California Ale), or Fermentis US-05 yeast

1 cup (200 g) dextrose (if priming)

STEP BY STEP

Two or 3 days before brewing, make a yeast starter. (OG 1.015 to 1.020, aerated thoroughly before pitching the yeast. Ferment yeast starter in the mid 70°F/~24°C.) On brew day, mash in at 152°F (67°C) in 20 quarts (19 liters) of water and hold for 60 minutes. Recirculate until wort clears, then begin collecting your wort. Sparge with water hot enough to make the grain bed temperature rise to 170°F (77°C) by the end of wort collection. (Or, mash out to 170°F/77°C and sparge with water hot enough to keep the grain bed at that temperature.) Collect at least 8 gallons (30 liters) of wort (or monitor runnings and stop collecting wort when the specific gravity drops below 1.010). Boil wort for 90 minutes (or until volume is reduced to 5 gallons/19 liters). Add hops at times indicated in the ingredient list. Ferment at 68 to 70°F (20 to 21°C). Dry hop for 2 weeks at 35 to 40°F (1.6 to 4.4°C). Bottle or keg as usual.

EXTRACT WITH GRAINS OPTION: Reduce the Maris Otter malt in the all-grain recipe to 1 pound 10 ounces (0.74 kilogram) and add 4 pounds (1.8 kilograms) Muntons light dried malt extract and 5 pounds (2.3 kilograms) Muntons light liquid malt extract. Steep grains at 152°F (67°C) in 3 quarts (2.8 liters) of water for 1 hour. Boil wort for 90 minutes, adding hops at times indicated. Add dried malt extract at beginning of boil, add liquid malt extract during the final 15 minutes of the boil. Follow the remaining portion of the all-grain recipe.

- - - - - - - - - - - - - - - - - - -

GREAT DIVIDE
BREWING COMPANY
OLD RUFFIAN

{{{{{{{

(5 gallons/19 L, all-grain) OG = 1.103 FG = 1.026
IBU = 90 SRM = 11 ABV = 10.2%

Old Ruffian is a hefty, hop-forward barleywine. The brewery says to expect subtle fruit aromas and complex caramel sweetness at first, followed by aggressive, bold hop bitterness and flavor.

INGREDIENTS

20 lb. (9.1 kg) American 2-row pale malt

0.5 lb. (0.23 kg) crystal malt (75 °L)

0.5 lb. (0.23 kg) Victory malt

0.25 lb. (0.11 kg) flaked wheat

36 AAU Chinook hops (60 min.) (3 oz./85 g at 12% alpha acids)

16 AAU Amarillo hops (30 min.) (2 oz./57 g at 8% alpha acids)

24 AAU Amarillo hops (5 min.) (3 oz./85 g at 8% alpha acids)

White Labs WLP051 (California V Ale) or Wyeast 1272 (American II Ale) yeast (5 quarts/~5 L yeast starter)

⅔ cup (133 g) dextrose (if priming)

STEP BY STEP

This is a very big beer. See below for two options for generating your wort. In all cases, use a single-infusion mash (or steep) at 154°F (68°C), held for 45 to 60 minutes. Add hops as indicated in the ingredient list. Pitch the yeast from your yeast starter, aerate thoroughly, and hold fermentation temperature at 66°F (19°C). Keg or bottle the beer when fermentation is complete and beer has fallen clear. Alternatively, you could try bourbon-barrel aging this beer as Great Divide does, or by adding toasted oak cubes or staves that have been soaked in bourbon. Be sure to taste samples regularly to observe the level of bourbon and oak flavors over time in the beer so they do not overwhelm the nuances of your Old Ruffian clone.

LONG BOIL OPTION: Mash grains listed in the ingredient list with 28 quarts (26 liters) of mash liquor. After mash, recirculate wort until clear. Collect wort until the specific gravity of the final runnings falls below 1.010. (This may be up to 12 gallons (45 liters), depending on a number of variables.) Keep your sparge water heated such that your grain bed temperature creeps up to 168°F (76°C) near the end of wort collection. Boil wort to reduce volume to 6 gallons (23 liters). Add first dose of hops and boil them for 1 hour, aiming for 5 gallons (19 liters) of post-boil wort.

FIRST WORT OPTION: Add enough pale malt to your mash tun so that you can run off 6 gallons (23 liters) of first wort without adding sparge water. For this you will need between 26.75 pounds to 32.5 pounds (12 to 15 kilograms) of pale malt (in addition to the specialty malts and flaked wheat), depending on how much water your grains normally absorb. You will need roughly 9 to 10 gallons (34 to 38 liters) of mash liquor (and 12 to 14 gallons/45 to 53 liters of mash tun space to hold it all). Your 6 gallons (23 liters) of pre-boil wort should have a specific gravity of 1.085 to 1.090. Boil for 1 hour to reduce wort to a volume of 5 gallons (19 liters).

NOTE: You can (and should) sparge the grain bed to collect wort for a second beer.

EXTRACT WITH GRAINS OPTION: Substitute 17 pounds (7.7 kilograms) of the 2-row pale malt in the all-grain recipe with 9 pounds (4.1 kilograms) of extra light dried malt extract. Steep the crushed 2-row and specialty grains in 1 gallon (4 liters) water at 154°F (68°C) for 60 minutes. Remove the grain bag and place in a colander. Slowly rinse the grains with 1 gallon (4 liters) of hot water. Top off the kettle to 6 gallons (23 liters) and stir in the dried malt extract while off of heat. Be sure all the extract is dissolved, then bring the wort to a boil. Follow the remaining portion of the all-grain recipe.

LONG TRAIL BREWING COMPANY
DOUBLE BAG

**(5 gallons/19 L, all-grain) OG = 1.071 FG = 1.016
IBU = 25 SRM = 16 ABV = 7.2%**

This unique recipe is best described as a double altbier. It features a distinct malt presence balanced by a subtle hop backbone that delivers a smooth, complex drinking experience.

INGREDIENTS

13 lb. (5.9 kg) 2-row pale malt

1 lb. (0.45 kg) crystal malt (20 °L)

0.5 lb. (0.23 kg) crystal malt (60 °L)

0.25 lb. (0.11 kg) chocolate malt (350 °L)

0.5 lb. (0.23 kg) wheat malt

5.4 AAU Northern Brewer pellet hops (60 min.) (0.5 oz./14 g at 9% alpha acids)

3.6 AAU Northern Brewer pellet hops (30 min.) (0.25 oz./7 g at 9% alpha acids)

1.6 AAU Mt. Hood pellet hops (0 min.) (0.25 oz./7 g at 6.5% alpha acids)

½ tsp. yeast nutrient (15 min.)

½ tsp. Irish moss (15 min.)

White Labs WLP036 (Düsseldorf Alt) or Wyeast 1007 (German Ale) yeast

¾ cup (150 g) dextrose (if priming)

STEP BY STEP

This is a single-infusion mash. Mix the crushed grains with 4.75 gallons (18 liters) of 170°F (77°C) water to stabilize at 154°F (67.8°C) for 60 minutes. Sparge slowly with 175°F (79°C) water. Collect approximately 6 gallons (23 liters) of wort runoff to boil for 60 minutes. Add hops, yeast nutrient, and Irish moss as indicated. Cool the wort to 75°F (24°C). Pitch your yeast and aerate the wort heavily. Allow the beer to cool to 70°F (21°C). Hold at that temperature until fermentation is complete. Transfer to a carboy, avoiding any splashing to prevent aerating the beer. Allow the beer to condition for 1 week, and then bottle or keg.

EXTRACT WITH GRAINS OPTION: Substitute the 2-row pale malt in the all-grain recipe with 6.6 pounds (3 kilograms) Briess light liquid malt extract and 1.5 pounds (0.68 kilogram) light dried malt extract. Steep the crushed grain in 2 gallons (7.6 liters) of water at 154°F (68°C) for 30 minutes. Remove grains from the wort and rinse with 2 quarts (1.8 liters) of hot water. Add the liquid and dried malt extracts and bring to a boil. Add ingredients as per the schedule, and after the boil is complete, top off to 5 gallons (19 liters). Follow the remaining portion of the all-grain recipe.

PELICAN BREWERY
STORMWATCHER'S WINTERFEST

**(5 gallons/19 L, all-grain) OG = 1.129 FG = 1.032
IBU = 31 SRM = 40 ABV = 13%**

This barleywine is the winner of numerous awards, including a gold medal at the World Beer Cup. It features aromas and tastes of toasted malt, toffee, and caramel, with a warming finish.

INGREDIENTS

15 lb. 9 oz. (7.1 kg) Golden Promise pale malt

7 lb. 7 oz. (3.4 kg) Munich malt

1 lb. 11 oz. (0.75 kg) melanoidin malt

1 lb. 15 oz. (0.88 kg) caramel malt blend (Pelican uses a blend of 4 different caramel malts, ranging from 15 to 120 °L—pick 4 that cover this range and add roughly 0.5 lb./0.23 kg of each)

1 lb. (0.45 kg) torrified wheat

6 AAU Magnum hops (60 min.) (0.50 oz./14 g at 12% alpha acids)

5.6 AAU Golding hops (30 min.) (1.4 oz./40 g at 4% alpha acids)

2.6 oz. (75 g) Hersbrücker hops (whirlpool)

0.88 oz. (25 g) Golding hops (whirlpool)

Wyeast 1968 (London ESB Ale) or White Labs WLP002 (English Ale) yeast

¾ cup (150 g) dextrose (if priming)

STEP BY STEP

Mash the grains at 148°F (64°C) for 90 minutes with a liquor-to-grist ratio of 2.4 to 1. Mash out, vorlauf, and then sparge at 170°F (77°C) to collect wort until runoff extract is about SG 1.040 (10 °Plato). Below that and you are adding too much water (which you are going to have to boil away).

Typical boil times for Stormwatcher's are 4 hours, with an overall evaporation rate of about 35 percent. Add hops at times indicated. Chill, aerate, and pitch yeast at a rate of about 50 to 60 million cells per milliliter. Ferment at 65 to 66°F (18 to 19°C) until complete (at 80 percent apparent attenuation). Remove finishing beer from yeast after first week to ward off autolysis. When finished, carbonate to 2.5 volumes of CO_2. This beer should continue to mature and evolve for months and years.

PARTIAL MASH OPTION: Substitute the Golden Promise malt, Munich malt, and torrified wheat in the all-grain recipe with 8.5 pounds (3.9 kilograms) Coopers light dried malt extract and 5 pounds (2.3 kilograms) Briess liquid Munich malt extract. Place crushed grains in a large steeping bag and steep at 148°F (64°C) for 45 minutes in 5 quarts (4.7 liters) of liquid. Rinse grains with 5 quarts (4.7 liters) of water at 170°F (77°C). Add water to the "grain tea" to make 6 gallons (23 liters). Stir in malt extracts and bring to a boil for 60 minutes. Follow the remaining portion of the all-grain recipe.

- - - - - - - - - - - - - - - - - -

SIERRA NEVADA BREWING COMPANY
BIGFOOT BARLEYWINE STYLE ALE

⋘⋘⋘⋘⋘-

(5 gallons/19 L, all-grain) OG = 1.096   FG = 1.024
IBU = 100   SRM = 14   ABV = 10.1%

First introduced in the winter of 1983, Bigfoot is a cult classic brewed in the barleywine style—meaning a strong, robust bruiser of a beer with the refined intensity of a wine.

INGREDIENTS

18.5 lb. (8.4 kg) 2-row pale malt

1 lb. 7 oz. (0.64 kg) caramel malt (60 °L)

9 AAU Chinook hops (150 min.) (0.75 oz./21 g at 12% alpha acids)

9 AAU Chinook hops (105 min.) (0.75 oz./21 g at 12% alpha acids)

7.5 AAU Cascade hops (60 min.) (1.5 oz./43 g at 5% alpha acids)

3.75 AAU Cascade hops (10 min.) (0.75 oz./21 g at 5% alpha acids)

7.5 AAU Centennial hops (10 min.) (0.75 oz./21 g at 10% alpha acids)

0.25 oz. (7.1 g) Chinook hops (dry hop)

1.25 oz. (35 g) Cascade hops (dry hop)

0.5 oz. (14 g) Centennial hops (dry hop)

Wyeast 1056 (American Ale), White Labs WLP001 (California Ale) or Fermentis US-05 yeast (3.5 qt./3.5 L yeast starter)

1 cup (200 g) dextrose (if priming)

STEP BY STEP

Two or 3 days before brew day, make the yeast starter, aerating the wort thoroughly (preferably with oxygen) before pitching the yeast. On brew day, mash in at 154°F (68°C) in 24 quarts (23 liters) of water. Hold at this temperature for 60 minutes. Raise mash temperature to 170°F (77°C), hold for 5 minutes, then recirculate. Run off wort and sparge with water hot enough to keep the grain bed around 170°F (77°C). Collect 7.5 gallons (28.4 liters) of wort. Boil wort for 150 minutes, adding hops at times indicated. Cool and ferment at 68°F (20°C). Dry hop in secondary for 5 days. Bottle or keg as usual and allow this beer to age.

EXTRACT WITH GRAINS OPTION: Replace the 2-row pale malt in the all-grain with 2 pounds (0.91 kilogram) light dried malt extract and 9.9 pounds (4.5 kilograms) light liquid malt extract. Steep grains at 154°F (68°C) in 3 quarts (2.9 liters) of water. Rinse grains with 2 quarts (2 liters) of 170°F (77°C) water. Add water to brewpot to make at least 3.5 gallons (13 liters) of wort. Stir in dried malt extract and boil wort for 150 minutes, adding hops at times indicated. Keep some boiling water handy and do not let the boil volume dip below 3.5 gallons (13 liters). Add liquid malt extract during the final 15 minutes of the boil. Chill wort and transfer to fermenter. Top fermenter up to 5 gallons (19 liters). Follow the remaining portion of the all-grain recipe.

- - - - - - - - - - - - - - - - - -

TEN

BELGIAN-STYLE ALES

Beer Pictured on Left; see page 144

ALLAGASH
BREWING COMPANY
ALLAGASH TRIPEL

**(5 gallons/19 L, all-grain) OG = 1.078 FG = 1.009
IBU = 28 SRM = 6.6 ABV = 9%**

Allagash Tripel is a complex and delicious version of the Belgian classic. According to the brewery, the beer features herbal notes and passion fruit, with hints of banana and honey.

INGREDIENTS

12.8 lb. (5.8 kg) pilsner malt

1.6 lb. (0.73 kg) sucrose (15 min.)

8 AAU German Tettnang hops (60 min.) (2 oz./57 g at 4% alpha acids)

0.4 oz. (11 g) Hallertau Mittelfrüh hops (whirlpool)

Belgian Ale yeast—Allagash uses a proprietary strain; at home, try Wyeast 1762 (Belgian Abbey Ale II), Wyeast 3787 (Trappist High Gravity), or White Labs WLP510 (Belgian Bastogne Ale) yeast

¾ cup (150 g) dextrose (if priming)

STEP BY STEP

Mash the grains at 153°F (67°C). Mash out, vorlauf, and then sparge at 170°F (77°C). Boil 90 minutes, adding the hops at the times indicated. Add the sucrose for the final 15 minutes. Pitch the yeast and ferment at the high end of the yeast strain's recommended range until final gravity it reached. Bottle or keg as usual.

EXTRACT WITH GRAINS OPTION: Replace pilsner malt with 1.75 pounds (0.79 kilogram) Briess light dried malt extract, 5.75 pounds (2.6 kilograms) Briess Pilsen light malt extract (late addition), and 2 pounds (0.91 kilogram) pilsner malt. Steep crushed malts in 3 quarts (about 3 liters) of water at 153°F (67°C) for 45 minutes. Combine the "grain tea" with the dried malt extract and enough water in the brewpot to make 3 gallons (11 liters) of wort. Boil for 60 minutes, adding the hops at times indicated and the sucrose and liquid malt extract for the final 15 minutes. Chill the wort, transfer to your fermenter, and top up with filtered water to 5 gallons (19 liters). Follow the remaining portion of the all-grain recipe.

ALLAGASH
BREWING COMPANY
CURIEUX

**(5 gallons/19 L, all-grain) OG = 1.073 FG = 1.006
IBU = 30 SRM = 4 ABV = 9.3%**

Curieux is a very complex beer, yet the recipe itself is on the simpler side. The brewery achieves the signature flavor by aging the beer in bourbon barrels and then blending it with a fresh batch of Tripel when bottling.

INGREDIENTS

12 lb. (5.4 kg) 2-row pale malt or pilsner malt

1.7 lb. (0.77 kg) granulated sugar (10 min.)

3 AAU German Perle hops (75 min.) (0.8 oz./23 g at 8% alpha acids)

3 AAU German Spalt hops (10 min.) (0.9 oz./26 g at 4.2% alpha acids)

0.9 oz. (26 g) Styrian Golding hops (0 min.)

½ tsp. yeast nutrient (10 min.)

½ Whirlfloc tablet (10 min.)

Bourbon-soaked oak chips or spirals

Wyeast 3787 (Trappist High Gravity) yeast, White Labs WLP530 (Abbey Ale), Wyeast 1214 (Belgian Abbey), White Labs WLP550 (Belgian Ale), or yeast harvested from Allagash White yeast

¾ cup (150 g) dextrose (if priming)

STEP BY STEP

Mash at 149°F (65°C) for 45 minutes using 3.75 gallons (14.2 liters) of strike water. You can perform a mash-out if you'd like, but it's not necessary. Run off and boil the wort for 90 minutes, adding hops at times indicated in the ingredients list. Add the sugar, yeast nutrients, and Whirlfloc with 10 minutes remaining in the boil. After the boil, chill to 65°F (18°C) and oxygenate. Rack to your fermenter and pitch yeast. You can allow the temperature to rise after a couple days of fermentation. The beer's terminal gravity should be around 1.006. For wood-aging and blending, O'Connor states, "We generally age Tripel in bourbon barrels for 6 to 8 weeks at 55°F (18°C). It is then blended to taste with fresh tripel before packaging. Curieux should have a subtle bourbon character with hints of vanilla and coconut. To replicate this at home, try soaking 1 to 2 ounces of oak chips or spirals in your favorite bourbon for a couple weeks. Then when fermentation is complete, rack into a secondary vessel on top of the bourbon-soaked oak. I recommend tasting the beer every 2 to 3 days. It probably won't take long for the beer to develop the subtle flavors that you're looking for. Oak cubes are also an option, but be aware that the entire process may take much longer when both soaking the oak in bourbon and aging the beer on the cubes. Package the beer as soon as it has developed the desired character. Allagash bottles/keg conditions, but feel free to package the beer any way you choose." If the beer has been aging for several months, you can opt to add extra yeast if you plan to bottle condition this beer.

EXTRACT ONLY OPTION: Substitute the 2-row/pilsner pale malt in the all-grain recipe with 6.5 pounds (3 kilograms) Pilsen dried malt extract. Heat 6.5 gallons (25 liters) water in your brewpot up to a boil. Add the dried malt extract when the water approaches a boil. Stir well then bring it to a boil. Boil the wort for 75 minutes, adding hops at times indicated in the ingredients list. Add the sugar, yeast nutrients, and Whirlfloc with 10 minutes remaining in the boil. Follow the remaining portion of the all-grain recipe.

TIPS FOR SUCCESS

Allagash has their own proprietary strain of yeast. The ingredients list contains several great strains readily available to homebrewers. Michael O'Connor recommends, "If you're feeling adventurous and practice excellent sanitation, you can propagate the Allagash house yeast from a bottle of Allagash White. Our other beers contain an additional yeast strain added just before packaging so a bottle of white is the only way to procure the house strain."

BLACK DIAMOND BREWING COMPANY
WINTER ALE

(5 gallons/19 L, all-grain) OG = 1.067 FG = 1.011 IBU = 21 SRM = 23 ABV = 7.2%

Black Diamond Winter Ale is a classic Belgian dubbel. Perfect for the winter season, it has a deep garnet color that accentuates dark fruity undertones of raisins, dates, plums, and cherries.

INGREDIENTS

10 lb. (4.5 kg) Belgian 2-row pale malt

1.25 lb. (0.56 kg) dark Belgian candi sugar

14 oz. (0.39 kg) Special B malt (120 °L)

8 oz. (0.22 kg) aromatic malt (25 °L)

8 oz. (0.22 kg) caravienna malt (20 °L)

4 oz. (0.11 kg) chocolate malt (350 °L)

5.7 AAU Magnum pellet hops (75 min.) (0.3 oz./9 g at 14% alpha acids)

1 AAU Hallertau pellet hops (10 min.) (0.25 oz./7 g at 4% alpha acids)

1.1 AAU Tettnanger pellet hops (10 min.) (0.25 oz./7 g at 4.5% alpha acids)

½ tsp. yeast nutrient (15 min.)

White Labs WLP500 (Monastery Ale) or Wyeast 3787 (Trappist Style High Gravity) yeast

¾ cup (150 g) dextrose (if priming)

STEP BY STEP

Mix the crushed grains with 3.75 gallons (14 liters) of 168°F (76°C) water to stabilize at 150°F (66°C) for 60 minutes. Sparge slowly with 175°F (79°C) water. Collect approximately 6 gallons (23 liters) of wort runoff to boil for 60 minutes. Add hops and yeast nutrient as indicated. Cool the wort to 75°F (24°C), pitch the yeast, and aerate heavily. Allow the beer to cool to 68°F (20°C) and hold until fermentation is complete. Allow to condition for 1 week, and then bottle or keg as usual.

EXTRACT WITH GRAINS OPTION: Substitute the 2-row pale malt in the all-grain recipe with 6.6 pounds (3 kilograms) Briess light liquid malt extract. Steep the crushed grain in 5 gallons (19 liters) of water at 150°F (66°C) for 30 minutes. Remove grains and rinse with 2 quarts (1.8 liters) of hot water. Add the malt extract and boil for 75 minutes. Follow the remaining portion of the all-grain recipe.

BRASSERIE D'ORVAL S.A.
ORVAL TRAPPIST ALE

(5 gallons/19 L, all-grain) OG = 1.059 FG = 1.006 IBU = 33 SRM = 12 ABV = 6.9%

Orval pours orange-brown with a big, rocky head. The very spritzy level of carbonation and a lightly sour character make the beer feel prickly on the tongue. Orval beer is distinctly dry and has little hop bitterness or flavor, although it is the only Trappist ale to be dry hopped. You'll really taste the pale malt base, so don't use US, German, or English malts.

INGREDIENTS

- 6.25 lb. (2.8 kg) Belgian 2-row pale ale malt
- 2.5 lb. (1.1 kg) Vienna malt (6°L)
- 0.25 lb. (0.11 kg) crystal malt (160°L)
- 1.75 lb. (0.79 kg) cane sugar
- 7.5 AAU Hallertau-Hersbrücker hops (60 min.) (1.9 oz./53 g at 4% alpha acids)
- 2.5 AAU Styrian Golding hops (15 min.) (0.5 oz./14 g at 5% alpha acids)
- 0.33 oz. (9.4 g) Styrian Golding hops (dry hop)
- ¼ tsp. yeast nutrients
- Wyeast 3522 (Belgian Ardennes), White Labs WLP530 (Abbey Ale) yeast (1.5 qt./1.5 L yeast starter), Wyeast 3526 (*Brettanomyces lambicus*), or White Labs WLP650 (*Brettanomyces bruxellensis*) yeast
- 1 cup (200 g) dextrose (for priming)

STEP BY STEP

Mash the grains at 153°F (67°C) in 2.8 gallons (10.6 liters) of water for 60 minutes. Mash out, vorlauf, and then sparge at 170°F (77°C). Boil for 90 minutes, adding the hops at times indicated in the ingredients. Add the cane sugar and yeast nutrients with 15 minutes left in boil. Pitch the Belgian or Abbey Ale yeast and ferment at 70°F (21°C). Rack to secondary when fermentation is complete, adding the *Brettanomyces* and dry hops. Condition for 2 months before bottling. Bottle in heavy-duty bottles.

EXTRACT WITH GRAINS OPTION: Replace the Belgian 2-row pale ale malt, Vienna malt, and crystal malt with 1.75 pounds (0.79 kilogram) light dried malt extract, 2.25 pounds (1 kilogram) light liquid malt extract, 2 pounds (0.91 kilogram) Belgian 2-row pale ale malt, 13 ounces (0.37 kilogram) Vienna malt (6°L), and 0.25 pound (0.11 kilogram) crystal malt (160°L). In a large soup pot, heat 4.6 quarts (4.4 liters) of water to 164°F (73°C). Add the crushed grains to a grain bag and steep around 153°F (67°C) for 45 minutes. While the grains steep, begin heating 2.1 gallons (7.8 liters) of water in your brewpot. When steep is over, remove 1.5 quarts (1.4 liters) of water from the brewpot and add to the "grain tea" in the steeping pot. Place a colander over your brewpot and place your steeping bag in it. Pour the grain tea (with water added) through the grain bag. Heat the liquid in the brewpot to a boil, then stir in the dried malt extract, add the first charge of hops, and begin the 60-minute boil. With 15 minutes left in the boil, add the hops, cane sugar, and yeast nutrients. Turn off the heat and stir in the liquid malt extract. Stir well to dissolve the extract, then resume heating. (Keep the boil clock running while you stir.) Chill the wort, transfer to your fermenter, and top up with filtered water to 5 gallons (19 liters). Ferment at 70°F (21°C), then follow the remaining portion of the all-grain recipe.

BRASSERIE SAINT JAMES
THE WIT ALBUM

(5 gallons/19 L, all-grain) OG = 1.056 FG = 1.011
IBU = 14 SRM = 4 ABV = 5.9%

This Reno, Nevada, brewery's witbier is a cloudy pale yellow, thanks to the addition of wheat malt and flaked oats. It has a spicy, fruity, citrus aroma that's the result of not only the yeast and hops, but also the numerous spice additions.

INGREDIENTS

- 5.5 lb. (2.5 kg) pilsner malt
- 5.5 lb. (2.5 kg) wheat malt
- 0.5 lb. (0.23 kg) flaked oats
- 3 AAU Hallertau hops (45 min.) (0.5 oz./14 g at 6% alpha acids)
- 3 AAU Hallertau hops (15 min.) (0.5 oz./14 g at 6% alpha acids)
- 1.9 AAU Saaz hops (1 min.) (0.5 oz./14 g at 3.8% alpha acids)
- 1.5 oz. (43 g) sweet orange peel (10 min.)
- 0.5 oz. (14 g) coriander, cracked (10 min.)
- 0.5 oz. (14 g) grains of paradise, cracked (10 min.)
- 0.2 oz. (6 g) pink peppercorns, cracked (10 min.)
- 0.2 oz. (6 g) chamomile (10 min.)
- 0.2 oz. (6 g) heather tips (10 min.)
- ¼ tsp. vanilla extract (optional)
- White Labs WLP400 (Belgian Wit Ale) or Wyeast 3068 (Weihenstephan Weizen) yeast
- ¾ cup (150 g) dextrose (if priming)

STEP BY STEP

Mill the grains and mix with 3.3 gallons (12.5 liters) of 165°F (74°C) strike water to reach a mash temperature of 153°F (67°C). Hold this temperature for 60 minutes. Vorlauf until your runnings are clear. Sparge the grains with 3.1 gallons (11.7 liters) and top up as necessary to obtain 6 gallons (23 liters) of wort. Boil for 90 minutes, adding hops according to the ingredient list and Irish moss if desired. With 10 minutes remaining, add the spices loosely in a large spice/hop bag, ensuring that there is sufficient room for water flow. After the boil, turn off heat, whirlpool for 10 minutes, and (optionally) add vanilla extract. Then chill the wort to slightly below fermentation temperature, about

70°F (21°C). Aerate the wort with pure oxygen or filtered air and pitch yeast. Ferment at 72°F (22°C) for 24 hours after the first visible signs of active fermentation. Then decrease temperature and hold at 64°F (18°C) for up to 20 days. Once the beer completes fermentation, bottle or keg the beer, and carbonate to approximately 2.5 volumes. You can cold-crash the beer to 35°F (2°C) for 48 hours prior to packaging to improve clarity.

EXTRACT WITH GRAINS OPTION: Substitute the pilsner and wheat malts in the all-grain recipe with 3.75 pounds (1.7 kilograms) Pilsen liquid malt extract and 3.75 pounds (1.7 kilograms) wheat liquid malt extract. Bring 5.6 gallons (21.2 liters) of water to approximately 162°F (72°C) and hold there while steeping the flaked oats in a grain bag for 15 minutes. Remove the grain bag and let drain. Add the malt extract while stirring, and stir until completely dissolved. Bring the wort to a boil. Follow the remaining portion of the all-grain recipe.

TIPS FOR SUCCESS

Head Brewer Josh Watterson uses rice hulls in the mash to promote the easy flow of wort from the mash tun, so if you have consistent issues with stuck mashes/sparges due to the use of wheat malt, you should follow whatever procedure you would ordinarily use for beers with a high wheat content. He also notes that spicing is essential to witbier, and you should feel free to adjust the spice levels/amounts recommended here to your specific taste. Finally, if the beer seems too "heavy," consider adding a protein rest to your mash schedule to thin out the beer's body without compromising flavor or gravity.

- - - - - - - - - - - - - - - - - - - -

BREWERY OMMEGANG
ABBEY ALE

(5 gallons/19 L, all-grain) OG = 1.075 FG = 1.016
IBU = 22 SRM = 22 ABV = 8.2%

Abbey holds the honor of being Ommegang's first beer. Unsurprisingly, it is closely modeled after classic Belgian dubbels. The goal when you're brewing is to create a deep and rich beer with loads of complexity and a dry finish. The brewery recommends aging and tasting over time.

INGREDIENTS

5.6 lb. (2.54 kg) pilsner malt

2.25 lb. (1.02 kg) Munich malt (10 °L)

2.25 lb. (1.02 kg) amber malt (30 °L)

1 lb. (0.45 kg) Weyermann CaraAroma malt (150 °L)

2.66 lb. (1.21 kg) corn sugar (90 min.)

6.25 AAU Styrian Golding hops (60 min.) (1.25 oz./35 g at 5% alpha acids)

0.33 oz. Styrian Golding hops (0 min.)

0.5 oz. (14 g) sweet orange peel (1 min.)

0.5 oz. (14 g) licorice root (1 min.)

0.25 oz. (7 g) crushed, toasted coriander seed (1 min.)

0.25 oz. (7 g) crushed, toasted cumin seed (1 min.)

0.1 oz. (3 g) star anise (1 min.)

Wyeast 1214 (Belgian Ale), White Labs WLP500 (Monastery Ale), or cultured Ommegang yeast

1⅕ cups (240 g) dextrose (if priming)

STEP BY STEP

Step mash with a 10-minute rest at 113°F (45°C), a 10-minute rest at 144°F (62°C), a 15-minute rest at 154°F (68°C), a 15-minute rest at 162°F (72°C), and a 5-minute rest at 169°F (76°C). Mash out, vorlauf, and then sparge at 170°F (77°C) to collect about 7 gallons (27 liters) of wort. Boil for 90 minutes, adding sugar, hops, and spices as indicated. After the boil, give the wort a stir to create a whirlpool, and let settle for 15 minutes. Cool, aerate, and pitch yeast. Start fermentation cool at 68 to 70°F (20 to 21°C), then allow temperature to rise during fermentation, or ramp up the fermentation temperature until all signs of fermentation are complete. Condition for 2 weeks at 32°F (0°C). Keg and adjust to 3.5 volumes CO_2, or bottle in heavy bottles with dextrose with a target of 3.5 volumes of CO_2.

EXTRACT WITH GRAINS OPTION: Reduce the pilsner malt in the all-grain recipe to 1 pound 2 ounces (0.51 kilogram) and add 3.33 pounds (1.5 kilograms) Weyermann Bavarian Pilsner liquid malt extract. Heat 10.5 quarts (9.9 liters) of steeping water in your brewpot to 124°F (51°C). In a separate pot, heat 7.9 quarts (7.4 liters) of sparge water to 170°F (77°C). Place crushed grains in a large steeping bag and submerge bag in your brewpot. Heat steeping water quickly to 144°F (62°C), stirring occasionally, then turn down heat and slowly raise temperature to 169°F (76°C). It should take about 30 minutes to go from 144°F (62°C) to 169°F (76°C). Remove the grain bag and place in a colander over your brewpot. Rinse grains slowly and evenly with hot sparge water. Heat this "grain tea"—approximately 17.4 quarts (16.4 liters)—to a boil. Boil 60 minutes, adding corn sugar at the beginning of the boil and hops at time indicated. Follow the remaining portion of the all-grain recipe and top off to 5 gallons (19 liters) after cooling.

- - - - - - - - - - - - - - - - - -

BREWERY OMMEGANG
HENNEPIN FARMHOUSE SAISON

(5 gallons/19 L, all-grain) OG = 1.070 FG = 1.011
IBU = 24 SRM = 5 ABV = 7.7%

Hennepin is Brewery Ommegang's Belgian-style golden ale. Brewed with coriander, ginger root, and bitter orange peel, this beer is full-bodied, hoppy, and crisp.

INGREDIENTS

8.75 lb. (4.0 kg) of Belgian pilsner malt

2.5 lb. (1.1 kg) Belgian 2-row pale malt

2 lb. (0.91 kg) light candi sugar

1 lb. 9 oz. (0.7 kg) Belgian pilsner malt

7 oz. (0.20 kg) Belgian 2-row pale malt

6.5 AAU Styrian Golding hops (60 min.) (1.3 oz./36 g at 5% alpha acids)

1.75 AAU Saaz hops (2 min.) (0.5 oz./14 g at 3.5% alpha acids)

1 tsp. Irish moss (15 min.)

1 oz. (28 g) dried ginger root (15 min.)

1 oz. (28 g) bitter orange peel (15 min.)

White Labs WLP550 (Belgian Ale) or Wyeast 1214 (Belgian Abbey) yeast (1 qt./~1 L yeast starter)

¾ cup (150 g) dextrose (for priming)

STEP BY STEP

Brewery Ommegang uses a multiple-step mash starting at 122°F (50°C). Hold at this temperature for 20 minutes. Infuse mash with boiling water or using recirculating heating system to raise the mash temperature to 152°F (67°C). Hold there for 60 minutes. Mash out and collect 6 gallons (23 liters) of wort. Once your wort is collected, add Styrian Golding (bittering) hops and boil for 60 minutes, adding the other ingredients as specified. Pitch the yeast and ferment at 68°F (20°C). [Option: Pitch the yeast to the wort at 64°F (18°C) and let the temperature rise during fermentation, as high as 77°F (25°C).] Bottle or keg your beer, age for 2 to 3 weeks, and enjoy!

EXTRACT WITH GRAINS OPTION: Replace the Belgian pilsner and 2-row pale malts with 0.25 pound (0.11 kilogram) Muntons light dried malt extract and 6.6 pounds (2.97 kilograms) Muntons light liquid malt extract (late addition). Steep the crushed grains in 3 quarts (2.8 liters) of water at 150°F (66°C) for 45 minutes. Rinse the grains with 1.5 quarts (about 1.5 liters) of water at 170°F (77°C). Add water to make 3 gallons (11 liters). Add the dried malt extract and sugar and bring the wort to a boil. Add the Styrian Golding (bittering) hops and boil for 60 minutes, adding the other ingredients as specified. When done boiling, cool the wort rapidly, transfer to a sanitized fermenter, top up to 5 gallons (19 liters) with filtered water, and pitch the yeast. Follow the remaining portion of the all-grain recipe.

- - - - - - - - - - - - - - - - - -

BREWERY OMMEGANG
WITTE

(5 gallons/19 L, all-grain) OG = 1.047 FG = 1.010
IBU = 10 SRM = 3 ABV = 5.2%

This is a traditional, Belgian-style wheat ale. Soft and hazy, it showcases the characteristic phenols from the yeast, along with the gentle taste of coriander and orange.

INGREDIENTS

5.8 lb. (2.6 kg) pilsner malt

2.4 lb. (1.1 kg) white wheat malt

1.1 lb. (0.48 kg) unmalted wheat berries

0.39 lb. (0.18 kg) flaked oats

2.5 AAU Styrian Golding hops (90 min.) (0.5 oz./14 g at 5% alpha acids)

0.35 oz. (10 g) crushed coriander seed (10 min.)

1.2 oz. (34 g) sweet orange peel (10 min.)

Wyeast 3944 (Belgian Witbier) or White Labs WLP400 (Belgian Wit Ale) yeast

1 cup (200 g) dextrose (if priming)

STEP BY STEP

Mash the grains for 5 minutes at 113°F (45°C), 35 minutes at 144°F (62°C), and 20 minutes at 154°F (68°C). Mash-off at 165°F (74°C), collecting about 7 gallons (27 liters) of wort. Boil 90 minutes, adding hops at beginning of boil and spices for final 10 minutes. Cool, aerate, and pitch yeast at 70°F (21°C). Let temperature rise but not above 79°F (26°C). Carbonate to 2.7 volumes of CO_2.

PARTIAL MASH OPTION: Reduce the Pilsen malt in the all-grain recipe to 2.1 ounces (59 grams) and add 4 pounds (1.8 kilograms) Weyermann Pilsner malt extract. In a 2-gallon (7.6-liter) beverage cooler, mash crushed grains in 5.5 quarts (5.2 liters) of water for 45 minutes at 150°F (66°C). While mash is resting, heat 1 gallon (3.8 liters) of water to a boil in your brewpot and another 5.5 quarts (5.2 liters) of sparge water to around 180°F (82°C). Recirculate wort then run off to brewpot. Stir sparge water into grains. Recirculate and run off again. Boil 60 minutes, adding hops and spices at times indicated and liquid malt extract with 15 minutes left in boil. Top off to 5 gallons (19 liters) after cooling and follow the remaining portion of the all-grain recipe.

add 5 ounces (140 grams) Sorachi Ace hops to the wort. After 2 minutes, begin cooling to 64°F (18°C), aerate well, and pitch yeast. Ferment at 71°F (22°C). After fermentation ends and yeast settles, dry hop with Sorachi Ace for 5 to 7 days. Bottle or keg as usual.

EXTRACT WITH GRAINS OPTION: Reduce pilsner malt to 2 pounds (0.91 kilogram). Add 2 pounds (0.91 kilogram) pilsner dried malt extract and 4 pounds (1.8 kilograms) pilsner liquid malt extract. Steep grains at 148°F (64°C) for 60 minutes. Add dried malt extract and boil for 60 minutes, adding hops at times indicated. Add liquid malt extract and sugar during the final 15 minutes of the boil. Follow the remaining portion of the all-grain recipe.

BROOKLYN BREWERY
BROOKLYN SORACHI ACE

(5 gallons/19 L, all-grain) OG = 1.062 FG = 1.007 IBU = 36 SRM = 3 ABV = 7.2%

Brooklyn Sorachi Ace marries the overall structure of the modern saison style with the unique lemon and herbal qualities of the Sorachi Ace hop. Sorachi Ace is used throughout, and very complete attenuation gives refreshing, flinty dryness.

INGREDIENTS

11 lb. (5 kg) pilsner malt

1 lb. (0.45 kg) corn sugar

6 AAU Sorachi Ace hops (60 min.) (0.5 oz./14 g at 12% alpha acids)

6 AAU Sorachi Ace hops (30 min.) (0.5 oz./14 g at 12% alpha acids)

5 oz. (140 g) Sorachi Ace (0 min.)

2 oz. (57 g) Sorachi Ace (dry hop)

Wyeast 1214 (Belgian Ale) or White Labs WLP500 (Trappist Ale) yeast

¾ cup (150 g) dextrose (if priming)

STEP BY STEP

Mash the grains at 122°F (50°C), hold 10 minutes. Raise mash temperature to 146°F (63°C) and hold 60 minutes. Raise mash temperature to 152°F (67°C) and hold 15 minutes, then mash out at 168°F (75°C). Add corn sugar to 5 gallons (19 liters) of collected wort at SG 1.054. Boil for 60 minutes, adding hops at times indicated. Turn off heat and

BROUWERIJ DUVEL MOORTGAT
DUVEL

(5 gallons/19 L, all-grain) OG = 1.061 FG = 1.007 IBU = 30 SRM = 3 ABV = 8.5%

Duvel is the classic Belgian golden ale. Although it's strong, the beer is extremely light in color and dry in taste. The dense, white head that sits above the beer lasts until the beer is gone. The OG for this recipe is based on the beer going into the fermenter on brew day; the ABV is based on the OG plus the dosage sugar addition near the end of fermentation.

INGREDIENTS

11.5 lb. (5.2 kg) Belgian pilsner malt

6 AAU Styrian Golding hops (60 min.) (1.2 oz./34 g at 5% alpha acids)

4 AAU Saaz hops (15 min.) (1 oz./28 g at 4% alpha acids)

0.5 lb. (0.23 kg) dextrose (15 min.)

0.75 oz. (21 g) Saaz hops (0 min.)

¼ tsp. yeast nutrients (15 min.)

¹⁄₁₆ tsp. ("a pinch") yeast nutrients (dosage)

1 tsp. Irish moss (15 min.)

Wyeast 1388 (Belgian Strong Ale) or White Labs WLP570 (Belgian Golden Ale) yeast (3 qt./about 3 L yeast starter)

1 lb. (0.45 kg) dextrose (dosage)

1 cup (200 g) dextrose (for priming)

STEP BY STEP

In your brew kettle, mash in to 131°F (55°C) and heat the mash slowly, over 15 minutes, to 140°F (60°C). Add boiling water to raise the temperature to 148°F (64°C) and hold for 60 minutes. Mash out, vorlauf, and then sparge at 168°F (76°C). (Option: To increase wort fermentablility, mash in at 99°F (37°C) and slowly ramp up the temperature to mash-out temperature. The ramp time can take anywhere from 90 minutes to as long as 3 hours.) Collect enough wort in the brew kettle to compensate for a longer boil. Boil for 90 minutes, adding the hops as indicated in the ingredients list. With 15 minutes left in boil, add the kettle sugar, yeast nutrients, and Irish moss. At the end of the boil, add the last charge of hops, rapidly cool the wort, and transfer it to a sanitized fermenter. The brewers of Duvel pitch at 60°F (16°C) and let the temperature rise to as high as 84°F (29°C) during primary fermentation. If you are not capable of ramping the fermentation temperature, pitch the yeast and then ferment at 68°F (20°C). When primary fermentation is slowing down (3 to 4 days), add the dosage sugar with a pinch of yeast nutrients that have been dissolved in hot water held at 160°F (71°C) for 15 minutes. After final gravity is achieved, rack to a secondary fermenter and allow the beer to condition for 2 to 3 weeks. Bottle when the beer falls clear.

EXTRACT WITH GRAINS OPTION: Substitute the pilsner malt with 2 pounds (0.91 kilogram) pilsen dried malt extract, 3.3 pounds (1.5 kilograms) Pilsen liquid malt extract (late addition), and 3 pounds (1.4 kilograms) Belgian pilsner malt. In a large brewpot, heat 4.5 quarts (4.3 liters) water to 161°F (72°C). Add crushed grains to the grain bag. Submerge the bag and let the grains steep around 150°F (66°C) for 45 minutes. While the grains steep, begin heating 2.1 gallons (7.8 liters) of water in your brewpot. When the steep is over, remove 1.5 quarts (1.4 liters) of water from brewpot and add to the "grain tea" in steeping pot. Place a colander over the brewpot and place the steeping bag in it. Pour the grain tea (with water added) through the grain bag. Heat the liquid in the brewpot to a boil, then stir in the dried malt extract, add the first charge of hops, and begin the 60-minute boil. With 15 minutes left in boil, add the kettle sugar and second charge of hops and Irish moss, then turn off heat and stir in the liquid malt extract. Stir well to dissolve the extract, then resume heating. (Keep the boil clock running while you stir.) At the end of the boil, add the last charge of hops, cool the wort, and transfer to your fermenter. Top off the fermenter with filtered water to make 5 gallons (19 liters). Follow the remaining portion of the all-grain recipe.

BROUWERIJ ST. BERNARDUS NV
ST. BERNARDUS ABT 12 60TH ANNIVERSARY EDITION

‹‹‹‹‹‹‹

(5 gallons/19 L, all-grain) OG = 1.000 FG = 1.017
IBU = 16 SRM = 37 ABV = 11%

While this beer is still in production, the recipe here is for a special sixtieth anniversary edition, which was closer to the brewery's original recipe. Although probably not authentic, the debittered black malt will give you a much smoother beer. It's reported that St. Bernardus uses a different bottling strain than the fermentation strain, so we recommend using Westmalle's yeast.

INGREDIENTS

10.5 lb. (4.8 kg) pale ale malt

3 lb. (1.4 kg) Munich malt (10 °L)

1 lb. (0.45 kg) aromatic malt

0.5 lb. (0.23 kg) Weyermann Carafa Special III malt

2 lb. (0.91 kg) Belgian candi syrup (Dark 2) (15 min.)

1.5 lb. (0.68 kg) cane sugar (15 min.)

3.5 AAU Wye Challenger hops (60 min.) (0.5 oz./14 g at 7% alpha acids)

1.3 AAU Styrian Golding hops (20 min.) (0.25 oz./7 g at 5% alpha acids)

Wyeast 3787 (Trappist High Gravity) or White Labs WLP530 (Abbey Ale) yeast

1 cup (200 g) dextrose (if priming)

STEP BY STEP

Mash with a 15-minute rest at 135°F (57°C), a 35-minute rest at 145°F (63°C), a 25-minute rest at 165°F (74°C), and a 5-minute rest at 172°F (78°C). Collect 6 gallons (23 liters) and boil wort for 60 minutes, adding hops and sugars at times indicated in the ingredient list. Cool wort and aerate. Pitch yeast at 70°F (21°C). Let fermentation temperature rise to around 83°F (28°C). Rack beer to secondary and condition for 6 to 8 weeks at 50°F (10°C). Carbonate to 3 to 3.5 volumes of CO_2.

PARTIAL MASH OPTION: Substitute the pilsner malt in the all-grain recipe with 8 pounds (3.6 kilograms) pilsner liquid malt extract and reduce the Munich malt to 2.5 pounds (1.1 kilograms). Partial mash the crushed grains at 152°F (67°C)

for 45 minutes in 5.5 quarts (5.2 liters) of water. Boil wort for 60 minutes, adding hops and sugars at times indicated. Stir in liquid malt extract with 15 minutes left in boil. After cooling, top off to 5 gallons (19 liters). Follow the remaining portion of the all-grain recipe.

BROUWERIJ WESTMALLE
WESTMALLE TRIPEL

**(5 gallons/19 L, all-grain) OG = 1.081 FG = 1.009
IBU = 39 SRM = 5 ABV = 9.5%**

The quintessential Trappist tripel, Westmalle is very pale, very strong, and wonderfully smooth. One brewhouse technique that makes Westmalle beers unique is the use of direct gas flames on the copper kettles. This creates hot spots that may caramelize the wort slightly, giving a faint burnt-sugar taste to the beers. The beers are also brewed with very hard water, which certainly contributes to the character of the tripel.

INGREDIENTS

12.75 lb. (5.8 kg) pilsner malt

2 lb. (0.91 kg) cane sugar or clear Belgian (rock) candi sugar

9.5 AAU Styrian Golding hops (60 min.) (1.9 oz./53 g at 5% alpha acids)

3 AAU Tettnang hops (15 min.) (0.75 oz./21 kg at 4% alpha acids)

3 AAU Saaz hops (5 min.) (0.75 oz./21 kg at 4% alpha acids)

White Labs WLP530 (Abbey Ale) or Wyeast 3787 (Trappist Style High Gravity) yeast

1⅕ cups (240 g) dextrose (if priming)

STEP BY STEP

Crush your grains and mash in at 131°F (55°C), stirring the grains into 4 gallons (15 liters) of water at around 142°F (61°C), then ramp the mash temperature to 148°F (64°C), stirring as you heat. Quickly boost mash temperature to 168°F (76°C) before transferring wort to your lauter tun. Ramp time (from 131 to 148°F/55 to 64°C) should take at least 1 hour; longer times (up to several hours) will give more fermentable worts and drier, more alcoholic beers. (Westmalle Tripel's apparent attenuation is 88 percent, giving it 9.6 percent ABV.) Collect about 7 gallons (26 liters) of wort and boil for roughly 2 hours total (until you reach 5 gallons/19

liters). Make hop additions as directed in ingredient list. Add sugar at least 15 minutes before end of boil. Cool wort and transfer to fermenter. Top up to 5 gallons (19 liters), aerate well, and pitch yeast. Ferment at 68°F (20°C). Be prepared for final stages of fermentation to proceed slowly. Don't rush, get your beer into bottles, prime with sugar, bottle, and age 8 to 10 weeks. It will improve with more aging, up to about a year. Serve at 50°F (10°C) in a wide-mouthed, stemmed chalice.

EXTRACT WITH GRAINS OPTION: Reduce the 2-row pale malt in the all-grain recipe to 2 pounds (0.91 kilogram) and add 3 pounds (1.4 kilograms) light dried malt extract and 3.9 pounds (1.8 kilograms) light liquid malt extract. Heat 3 quarts (~3 liters) water to 161°F (72°C). Crush pilsner malt and add to liquor. Steep at 150°F (66°C) for 45 minutes. Rinse grains with 1.5 quarts (~1.5 liters) of water at 170°F (77°C). Add water to "grain tea" to make 3 gallons (11 liters), add dried malt extract and sugar, stir well, and bring to a boil. Boil for 60 minutes, adding hops as directed in ingredient list. Stir in liquid malt extract with 15 minutes left in the boil. Follow the remaining portion of the all-grain recipe.

THE BRUERY
SAISON RUE

**(5 gallons/19 L, all-grain) OG = 1.065 FG = 1.001
IBU = 28 SRM = 8 ABV = 8.5%**

Now brewed under their Bruery Terreux label, this beer was actually one of the original beers brewed at the Bruery. It is an unfiltered, bottle-conditioned Belgian-style farmhouse ale that's stood the test of time.

INGREDIENTS

7.5 lb. (3.4 kg) Great Western 2-row pale malt

3.5 lb. (1.6 kg) Weyermann rye malt

4.8 oz. (136 g) Bairds brown malt

1.9 lb. (0.86 kg) dextrose sugar (0 min.)

9.8 AAU German Magnum hops (first wort hop) (0.64 oz./18 g at 15.2% alpha acids)

3.9 AAU Sterling hops (0 min.) (0.55 oz./16 g at 7.1% alpha acids)

0.2 oz. (6 g) dried spearmint leaves (20 min.)

½ Whirlfloc tablet (10 min.)

½ tsp. yeast nutrients (10 min.)

White Labs WLP570 (Belgian Golden Ale) or Wyeast 1388 (Belgian Strong Ale) or the Bruery's house yeast strain (see TIPS FOR SUCCESS)

Your favorite strain of *Brettanomyces bruxellensis*

⅞ cup (175 g) dextrose (if priming)

STEP BY STEP

Mill the grains and dough-in, targeting a mash of around 1.3 quarts of water to 1 pound of grain and a temperature of 150°F (66°C). Hold the mash at 150°F (66°C) until enzymatic conversion is complete. Sparge slowly with 170°F (77°C) water, collecting wort until the pre-boil kettle volume is 6 gallons (23 liters). Add first wort hops toward the beginning of the lauter. Boil time is 60 minutes, adding the mint with 20 minutes left in the boil. Add Whirlfloc and yeast nutrient with 10 minutes left in the boil. At flameout, start a whirlpool and add the whirlpool hops and dextrose. After a 20-minute whirlpool, chill the wort to 65°F (18°C) and aerate thoroughly. Pitch rate is 750,000 cells per milliliter per degree Plato or approximately 2 packages of liquid yeast. Allow the fermentation to raise the overall fermentation temperature to 85°F (29°C). When time to package, pitch 2 million cells per milliliter of *Brett brux* to the bottling bucket and prime to bottle condition. Aim to carbonate the beer to around 2.8 volumes of CO_2 (the conditioning with *Brett* will likely make it higher over time; use sturdy bottles meant to withstand high volumes of CO_2).

EXTRACT ONLY OPTION: Substitute all the malts in the all-grain recipe with 3 pounds (1.36 kilograms) extra light dried malt extract and 3.3 pounds (1.5 kilograms) rye liquid malt extract. Add 6 gallons (23 liters) of water to your kettle and start to bring to a boil. When the temperature reaches about 180°F (82°C), add the first wort hops. When the water comes to a boil, remove from the heat and add the dried and liquid malt extracts, and stir thoroughly to dissolve the extract completely. Turn the heat back on boil for 60 minutes. Follow the remaining portion of the all-grain recipe.

TIPS FOR SUCCESS

The Bruery's Experimental Brewer Andrew Bell states, "Saison Rue is one of the first beers we ever produced. It was batch 4 for us (3/17/2008), and it has changed some over the years. It has always had mint and *Brett*. The malt has always been a blend of 2-row, rye, and a small percentage of some sort of highly toasted malt (we used Special Roast in 2008, but from April 2009 onward we have been using brown malt, usually between 1 to 2 percent). Explore different malt bills in similar percentages! Rye is sticky! Saison Rue is usually not a problem beer for us, but depending on your system, rice hulls would probably be a good idea. We tend to mash on the more acidic side of things. Initially the sugar addition in the whirlpool was a house-made inverted sugar. Since July 2009 we have used dextrose.

"Knockout and fermentation temperatures have changed over time. We used to start with a very cold knockout (50 to 55°F/10 to 13°C) and let it free rise up to 85°F (29°C). The ramping up of temperature during ferment (starting cold) lets our proprietary house yeast produce a more interesting phenol and ester saison profile than if we were to maintain one temperature during fermentation (would just taste more Belgiany). Currently we KO at 65°F (18°C) and allow to free rise to 85°F (29°C).

"Our house yeast that we use for primary fermentation is proprietary but could be harvested from some of our other bottles (fresh Trade Winds or Jardinier or Mischief would be good places to start). White Labs WLP570 is probably the closest commercial example but will probably behave differently. You can experiment with adding *Lactobacillus* (we are experimenting with this with our new Terreux Sour/Farmhouse brand). Personal preference on yeast supplier of *Brett brux* used at packaging. Experiment with other/multiple varieties of *Brett*. Target CO_2 at release is 2.8 volumes, but as it ages it keeps picking up carbonation (well above 3 volumes). Use appropriately thick glass if bottling!

"The mint addition is inspired by several different mildly spiced traditional Belgian saisons (including beers from Brasserie Vapeur). We also use the mint as a self-check mechanism to ensure that we do not release Saison Rue too early. Patrick likes to say that if you can still taste mint over the *Brett*, then it is not ready to release. We usually bottle condition for 6 months prior to release. If using fresh herbs, you would need a higher dosage rate."

HOPFENSTARK
SAISON
STATION 16

(5 gallons/19 L, all-grain) OG = 1.051 FG = 1.002
IBU = 25 SRM = 7 ABV = 6.5%

This is an extremely well-balanced, easy-to-drink saison brewed with the addition of rye. The hops are not the star here; it's all about the spice from the rye, yeast, and the brewer's skill.

INGREDIENTS

8 lb. (3.6 kg) Belgian pilsner malt

2.25 lb. (1 kg) flaked rye

7 oz. (200 g) Weyermann Caramunich III malt (56 °L)

6 oz. (170 g) rice hulls

5.4 AAU German Magnum hops (60 min.) (0.4 oz./11 g at 13.5% alpha acids)

5 AAU German Tettnang hops (10 min.) (1 oz./28 g at 5% alpha acids)

Wyeast 3711 (French Saison) or Lallemand Belle Saison yeast

¾ cup (150 g) dextrose (if priming)

STEP BY STEP

This is a single-infusion mash. Mash the grains and rice hulls at 151°F (66°C) to develop a balanced mouthfeel and light body. Collect 6.5 gallons (25 liters) of wort in the kettle and boil the wort for 90 minutes, adding the first hop addition 30 minutes after the beginning of the boil. With 10 minutes remaining in the boil, add the final hop addition. Chill the wort to 73°F (23°C) and aerate well. Pitch the yeast and fermentation should commence within 24 to 48 hours. Let the fermentation temperature rise up to about 79°F (26°C) over the course of the week, and hold at a warmer temperature until fermentation is complete. After primary fermentation, let the beer condition 1 to 2 weeks before you bottle or keg. Carbonate to 2.5 to 3 volumes of CO_2.

PARTIAL MASH OPTION: Reduce the pilsner malt to 3 pounds (1.36 kilograms), add 3.3 pounds (1.5 kilograms) Pilsen liquid malt extract, and eliminate the rice hulls from the all-grain recipe. Steep the crushed grains in 9 quarts (8.5 liters) of water at 151°F (66°C) for 30 to 40 minutes. Wash the grains with 1 gallon (4 liters) of hot water. Add the malt extract to the wort and top off with water to achieve a boil volume of 5.5 gallons (21 liters). Boil for 60 minutes. Follow the remaining portion of the all-grain recipe.

IECHYD DA BREWING COMPANY
WALLOON BELGIAN DARK STRONG

(5 gallons/19 L, all-grain) OG = 1.080 FG = 1.012
IBU = 30 SRM = 34 ABV = 9.2%

This Belgian dark strong ale is brewed with dark candi syrup and dark malts to create the beautiful dark amber color. It has a complex sweetness with sweet, toffee-like aromas.

INGREDIENTS

11 lb. (5 kg) pilsner malt

2.25 lb. (1 kg) aromatic malt

1 lb. (0.45 kg) Briess Carabrown malt (55 °L)

1 lb. (0.45 kg) Briess Extra Special malt (130 °L)

1.25 lb. (0.57 kg) Belgian dark candi syrup (180 °L)

10 AAU Sorachi Ace hops (60 min.) (1 oz./28 g at 10% alpha acids)

White Labs WLP500 (Trappist Ale) or Wyeast 1214 (Belgian Abbey) yeast

¾ cup (150 g) dextrose (if priming)

STEP BY STEP

Mill the grains and mix with 4.6 gallons (17.3 liters) of 162°F (72°C) strike water to reach a mash temperature of 150°F (65.5°C). Hold this temperature for 90 minutes. Vorlauf until your runnings are clear and lauter. Sparge the grains with 2.7 gallons (10.2 liters) water at 170°F (77°C), stir in Belgian candi syrup until dissolved, and top up as necessary to obtain 6 gallons (23 liters) of wort. Boil for 60 minutes, adding hops according to the ingredient list. After the boil, chill the wort to slightly below fermentation temperature, about 65°F (18°C). Aerate the wort with pure oxygen or filtered air and pitch yeast. Ferment at 66°F (19°C) for 2 days. After initial fermentation begins, allow wort to free rise to 76°F (24°C) until fermentation is complete (a specific gravity of about 1.020). Once the beer completes fermentation, bottle or keg the beer and carbonate to approximately 2.5 volumes. You may want to cold-crash the beer to 35°F (2°C) for 48 hours prior to packaging to improve clarity. Store carbonated beer at near-freezing temperatures for at least 2 weeks before drinking.

PARTIAL MASH OPTION: Substitute the pilsner malt in the all-grain recipe with 7.5 pounds (3.4 kilograms) pilsner liquid malt extract. Bring 5.4 quarts (5 liters) of water to approximately 162°F (72°C) and mix in the crushed grains placed in grain bags for 60 minutes. Remove the grain bags and wash with 1 gallon (4 liters) of hot water. Let the grain bags drain fully. Add liquid extract and Belgian dark candi syrup while stirring, and top off to 6 gallons (23 liters) wort. Stir until everything is completely dissolved. Bring the wort to a boil. Boil for 60 minutes. Follow the remaining portion of the all-grain recipe.

TIPS FOR SUCCESS

Brewer Chip Lewis notes that the initial temperature restraint during fermentation helps with the development of more spicy, peppery phenols relative to the levels of banana and clove. This spicy, peppery note complements the dark raisin, burnt sugar, and pit fruit flavors in the beer beautifully! As Chip also says, this beer is "pretty straightforward." Like so many other Belgian beers, the complexity doesn't have to be complicated.

THE LOST ABBEY
DEVOTION ALE

**(5 gallons/19 L, all-grain) OG = 1.052 FG = 1.006
IBU = 35 SRM = 4 ABV = 5.9%**

This Belgian-style blonde ale is light-bodied and hop driven. It has a low level of yeast phenols. Instead, The Lost Abbey uses aromatic hops to provide a spicy character.

INGREDIENTS

7.25 lb. (3.3 kg) pilsner malt

0.54 lb. (0.24 kg) Crisp crystal malt (15 °L)

1.48 lb. (0.67 kg) dextrose (15 min.)

6.25 AAU Columbus or Warrior hops (90 min.) (0.39 oz./11 g at 16% alpha acids)

1.95 AAU Brewer's Gold hops (45 min.) (0.32 oz./9.2 g at 6% alpha acids)

1.9 AAU Brewer's Gold hops (15 min.) (0.31 oz./8.9 g at 6% alpha acids)

0.81 oz. (23 g) German Tettnang hops (whirlpool)

White Labs WLP530 (Abbey Ale) yeast

¾ cup (150 g) dextrose (if priming)

STEP BY STEP

Crush your grains and mash at 146°F (63°C) for 60 minutes. Mash out, vorlauf, and then sparge at 170°F (77°C) to collect approximately 7 gallons (26.6 liters) of wort. Boil for 90 minutes, adding hops at times indicated and sugar for final 15 minutes. After the boil is complete, add the whirlpool hops, stir, and let sit for 15 minutes prior to cooling. Ferment starting at 66°F (19°C), but allow the temperature to rise without control. Bottle or keg as usual.

EXTRACT WITH GRAINS OPTION: Substitute the pilsner malt in the all-grain recipe with 4.33 pounds (2 kilograms) Weyermann Pilsner malt extract and 1.46 pounds (0.66

kilogram) pilsner malt. Steep crushed malts in 3 quarts (~3 liters) of water at 146°F (63°C) for 45 minutes. Combine "grain tea" with enough water in brewpot to make 3 gallons (11 liters) of wort. Boil 60 minutes, adding hops at times indicated and sugar and liquid malt extract for final 15 minutes. Follow the remaining portion of the all-grain recipe.

NEW BELGIUM
BREWING COMPANY
ABBEY

**(5 gallons/19 L, all-grain) OG = 1.065 FG = 1.011
IBU = 20 SRM = 15 ABV = 7.1%**

Abbey is one of the first beers brewed and released by New Belgium, all the way back in 1991. This recipe is for the original, award-winning beer, which has recently been slightly reformulated.

INGREDIENTS

7.5 lb. (3.4 kg) 2-row pale malt

1.5 lb. (0.68 kg) Munich malt (20 °L)

0.25 lb. (0.11 kg) CaraPils malt

0.5 lb. (0.23 kg) crystal malt (80 °L)

3 oz. (85 g) chocolate malt

2 lb. (0.91 kg) cane sugar (15 min.)

5 AAU Target hops (60 min.) (0.45 oz./13 g at 11% alpha acids)

1.3 AAU Willamette hops (10 min.) (0.25 oz./7.1 g at 5% alpha acids)

1.1 AAU Liberty hops (5 min.) (0.25 oz./7.1 g at 4.5% alpha acids)

Wyeast 1214 (Belgian Ale) or White Labs WLP500 (Trappist Ale) yeast

¾ cup (150 g) dextrose (if priming)

STEP BY STEP

Crush your grains and mash at 150°F (66°C) for 60 minutes. Mash out, vorlauf, and then sparge at 170°F (77°C) to collect approximately 7 gallons (26.6 liters) of wort. Boil for 90 minutes, adding hops and sugar at times indicated. After the boil is complete, cool, aerate, and pitch yeast. Ferment at 70°F (21°C). When final gravity is reached, bottle or keg as normal.

PARTIAL MASH OPTION: Substitute the 2-row pale malt in the all-grain recipe with 1.5 pounds (0.68 kilogram) Muntons light dried malt extract and 3.3 pounds (1.5 kilograms) Muntons light liquid malt extract. Steep grains in 3.5 quarts

(3.3 liters) of water at 150°F (66°C) for 45 minutes. Add water to make 3 gallons (11 liters) of wort, and bring to a boil. Stir in dried malt extract and boil for 60 minutes. Add liquid malt extract and sugar for final 15 minutes of the boil. Follow the remaining portion of the all-grain recipe.

- - - - - - - - - - - - - - - - - -

NEW BELGIUM BREWING COMPANY SAISON BELGIAN STYLE FARMHOUSE ALE

ccccccc

**(5 gallons/19 L, all-grain) OG = 1.058 FG = 1.012
IBU = 25 SRM = 6 ABV = 6.3%**

This retired offering from New Belgium is a classic farmhouse saison. As usual, New Belgium uses an expert hand with the spices. This beer has a balanced and enjoyable amount of cardamom, orange peel, and coriander.

INGREDIENTS

11 lb. (5 kg) 2-row pale malt

10 oz. (0.28 kg) Carapils malt

10 oz. (0.28 kg) crystal malt (20 °L)

4.5 AAU Hallertau hops (60 min.) (1.1 oz./31 g at 4% alpha acids)

4.5 AAU Strisslespalt hops (15 min.) (1.1 oz./31 g at 4% alpha acids)

½ to 2 tsp. cardamom (15 min.)

½ to 2 tsp. orange peel (15 min.)

½ to 2 tsp. crushed coriander (15 min.)

1 tsp. Irish moss

Wyeast 1214 (Belgian Ale yeast), White Labs WLP565 (Belgian Saison I), or Lallemand Belle Saison yeast

¾ cup (150 g) dextrose (if priming)

STEP BY STEP

Mash grains in 15 quarts (14 liters) of water to get a single-infusion mash temperature of 153°F (67°C) for 45 minutes. Sparge with water at 170°F (77°C) and collect 6.5 gallons (25 liters) of wort. Boil for 90 minutes, adding hops as directed. Add the spices and Irish moss with 15 minutes remaining in the boil. After the boil, cool the wort and ferment at 79 to 84°F (26 to 29°C) until complete (3 to 7 days), then leave at that temperature for another 6 days for warm conditioning. Rack into bottle or kegs with corn sugar for a few days, then drop the temperature to 40°F (4.4°C) for 3 to 4 additional weeks.

EXTRACT WITH GRAINS OPTION: Substitute the 11 pounds (5 kilograms) pale malt in the all-grain recipe with 2.5 pounds (1.1 kilograms) light dried malt extract and 4 pounds (1.8 kilograms) light liquid malt extract. Place crushed malts in a nylon steeping bag and steep in 3 quarts (2.8 liters) of water at 153°F (67°C) for 30 minutes. Rinse grains with 1.5 quarts (1.5 liters) of water at 170°F (77°C). Add water to make 3 gallons (11 liters), stir in dried malt extract, and bring to a boil. Add hops at times indicated and liquid malt extract with 15 minutes remaining. Cool wort and top off to 5 gallons (19 liters). Follow the remaining portion of the all-grain recipe.

- - - - - - - - - - - - - - - - - -

ROADHOUSE BREWING CO. SAISON EN REGALIA

ccccccc

**(5 gallons/19 L, all- grain) OG = 1.057 FG = 1.006
IBU = 31 SRM = 4 ABV = 6.7%**

This non-traditional offering may seem like an outlier in this chapter. It's a deliciously novel twist on a saison, with the addition of both peach and apricot at the end of primary fermentation. Need further convincing? Saison En Regalia fetched a silver medal in the Belgian-style fruit beer category at the Great American Beer Festival.

INGREDIENTS

10 lb. (4.5 kg) pilsner malt

1.25 lb. (0.57 kg) wheat malt

4 oz. (113 g) honey malt

4.5 AAU Bravo hops (60 min.) (0.3 oz./9 g at 15% alpha acids)

2.4 AAU Glacier hops (15 min.) (0.4 oz./11 g at 6% alpha acids)

4.4 AAU Zythos hops (15 min.) (0.4 oz./11 g at 11% alpha acids)

2 lb. (0.9 kg) Oregon Specialty Fruit peach puree (added at the end of primary fermentation)

2 lb. (0.9 kg) Oregon Specialty Fruit apricot puree (added at the end of primary fermentation)

White Labs WLP566 (Belgian Saison II) yeast

5 oz. (142 g) corn sugar (if priming)

STEP BY STEP

Mill the grains and mash in 3.9 gallons (14.7 liters) of water at 148°F (64°C) for 45 minutes. Vorlauf until your runnings are clear and sparge the grains with enough 168°F (75°C) water to obtain a 6-gallon (23-liter) pre-boil volume. Boil the wort for 90 minutes, adding the hops at the times indicated in the ingredients list. After the boil, turn off the heat and chill the wort to about 69°F (21°C), transfer the wort to the fermenter, aerate, and pitch the yeast. Allow the fermentation temperature to free rise up to 78°F (26°C), ferment for 10 days, and add the peach and apricot purees. Ferment for an additional 7 days, rack to a secondary fermenter for additional clearing if desired, and then bottle or keg the beer and carbonate.

EXTRACT WITH GRAINS OPTION: Omit the pilsner and wheat malts, and add 6.6 pounds (3.3 kilograms) Pilsen liquid malt extract and 1 pound (0.45 kilogram) wheat dried malt extract. Place the crushed grains in a muslin bag and steep in the brewing water as it heats up. Remove the grain bag when the temperature reaches 168°F (75°C). Add the liquid and dried malt extracts and bring to a boil. Boil the wort for 60 minutes, adding the hops at the times indicated in the ingredients list. After the boil, turn off the heat and chill the wort to about 69°F (21°C), transfer the wort to the fermenter, aerate, and pitch the yeast. Allow the fermentation temperature to free rise up to 78°F (26°C), ferment for 10 days, and add the peach and apricot purees. Ferment for an additional 7 days, rack to a secondary fermenter for additional clearing if desired, and then bottle or keg the beer and carbonate.

TIPS FOR SUCCESS

Roadhouse Brewing Co. utilizes White Labs WLP566 (Saison II) yeast in this beer because they love the fruitiness and subtle tartness it creates in their beer. It also produces a velvety characteristic, which gives it a unique mouthfeel. They are able to coax this profile out of the yeast by giving it a longer primary ferment and allowing the temperature to free rise up to 78°F (25°C). It is important that this yeast be allowed to do its work and reach the proper terminal gravity, as an under-attenuated saison will not have the proper flavor profile. Because of the long fermentation period required, and the sometimes-fickle nature of saison yeast, it's not a bad idea to pitch the yeast as a yeast starter to ensure a good, healthy population of cells. Try using a 0.5-gallon (~2-liter) starter for a 5-gallon (19-liter) batch. Aerate the wort well, and even consider using a pure oxygen setup in the fermenter to be cautious.

ROCKFORD BREWING CO.
ROCKFORD COUNTRY ALE

cccccc-

**(5 gallons/19 L, all-grain) OG = 1.058 FG = 1.007
IBU = 28 SRM = 7 ABV = 6.8%**

This unfiltered French farmhouse-style ale makes an appearance in the spring for Rockford Brewing. The copper/orange-hued beer draws you in, and the combination of toasty malt and fruity apricot esters keeps you coming back for another sip. It's a rustic and refreshing beer.

INGREDIENTS

9.5 lb. (4.3 kg) 2-row pale malt

9 oz. (0.25 kg) Munich malt

6 oz. (0.17 kg) white wheat malt

4 oz. (0.11 kg) Caravienne malt (20 °L)

4 oz. (0.11 kg) Victory malt

3 oz. (85 g) Carapils malt

9.2 oz. (0.26 kg) beet sugar (10 min.)

5.33 AAU Brewer's Gold pellet hops (60 min.) (0.75 oz./21 g at 7.1% alpha acids)

2 AAU Hallertau pellet hops (30 min.) (0.5 oz./14 g at 4% alpha acids)

1 AAU Hallertau pellet hops (10 min.) (0.25 oz./7 g at 4% alpha acids)

½ tsp. Irish moss (30 min.)

½ tsp. yeast nutrient (15 min.)

White Labs WLP566 (Belgian Saison II), Wyeast 3711 (French Saison), or Lallemand Belle Saison yeast

¾ cup (133 g) of dextrose (if priming)

STEP BY STEP

In this single-infusion mash, mix all the crushed grains with 4.9 gallons (18.5 liters) of 168°F (76°C) water to stabilize at 148°F (64°C). This is a medium-thin mash using 1.4 quarts (1.3 liters) of strike water per pound of grain, which is designed to help achieve maximum fermentability. Mash for 60 minutes then slowly sparge with 175°F (79°C) water. Collect approximately 6.2 gallons (23.5 liters) of wort runoff to boil for 60 minutes. While boiling, add the hops, Irish moss, yeast nutrient, and beet sugar as per the schedule. Cool the wort to 75°F (24°C) and transfer to your fermenter. Pitch the yeast and aerate the wort heavily. Allow the beer to cool to 66°F (19°C). Hold at that temperature until fermentation is complete. This may take 10 to 14 days. Gently transfer to a carboy, avoiding any splashing to prevent aerating the beer. Allow the beer to condition for an additional week. Prime and bottle condition or keg and force carbonate to 2.7 volumes CO_2. Allow the beer to age for 2 more weeks to fully develop the flavors.

PARTIAL MASH OPTION: Scale the 2-row pale malt down to 1 pound (0.45 ounce), and add 3.3 pounds (1.5 kilograms) Briess light unhopped malt extract and 2 pounds (0.9 kilogram) light dried malt extract. Steep the milled grain in 2.5 gallons (9.5 liters) of water at 148°F (64°C) for 30 minutes. Remove grains from the wort and rinse with 2 quarts (2 liters) of hot water. Add the malt extracts and boil for 60 minutes. While boiling, add the hops, Irish moss, yeast nutrient, and beet sugar as per the schedule. When the boil is complete, add the wort to 2 gallons (7.6 liters) of cold water in the sanitized fermenter and top up to 5 gallons (19 liters). Cool the wort to 75°F (24°C). Pitch your yeast and aerate the wort heavily. Follow the remainder of the all-grain recipe.

THE SPENCER BREWERY
SPENCER TRAPPIST ALE

⋘⋘⋘-

**(5 gallons/19 L, all-grain) OG = 1.058 FG = 1.010
IBU = 25 SRM = 8 ABV = 6.5%**

Spencer Brewery holds the distinction of being the first American Trappist brewery. Their flagship Belgian-style pale ale is inspired by traditional refectory ales known as *patersbier* ("father's beer" in Flemish). The beer is full-bodied, with a golden hue and a dry finish.

INGREDIENTS

10 lb. (4.5 kg) North American 2-row pilsner malt

2 lb. (0.91 kg) North American 6-row pale malt

4 oz. (0.11 kg) caramel Munich malt (60°L)

6.4 AAU Nugget hops (60 min.) (0.5 oz./14 g at 12.75% alpha acids)

1.2 AAU Willamette hops (10 min.) (0.25 oz./7 g at 4.75% alpha acids)

1 tsp. Irish moss (15 min.)

Wyeast 3787 (Trappist High Gravity) or White Labs WLP530 (Abbey Ale) yeast

¾ cup (150 g) priming sugar (if priming)

STEP BY STEP

Use a step-infusion mash starting at 148°F (64°C) for 75 minutes, then raise to 162°F (72°C) for 15 minutes. Raise the grain bed to 168°F (76°C) to begin the lautering process. Sparge with enough water to collect about 6.5

gallons (25 liters) of wort. Boil for 90 minutes, adding the hops and Irish moss at the times indicated. After flameout, chill the wort down to 65°F (18°C) and pitch the yeast. You can then place the fermenter in a warm space to allow the fermentation temperature to start to rise to 72°F (22°C). Hold at this temperature during active fermentation. When active fermentation begins to settle down (kräusen begins to fall), increase the fermentation to 78°F (26°C) to be sure the yeast ferments to completion. After all signs of fermentation have dissipated and final gravity has been reached, place the wort in cool storage at 50°F (10°C) for approximately 2 weeks. Carbonate to 2.5 to 3 volumes.

EXTRACT WITH GRAINS OPTION: Substitute the 2-row pilsner and 6-row malt with 6.6 pounds (3 kilograms) Pilsen liquid malt extract and 1.2 pounds (0.54 kilogram) Pilsen dried malt extract. Heat 1 gallon (4 liters) of water in a kettle. Place the crushed grains in a muslin bag and soak at 160°F (71°C) for 20 minutes. Place the bag in a colander and rinse the grains with 2 quarts (2 liters) of hot water. Top off the kettle with water to get 6 gallons (23 liters) total. Add the liquid and dried malt extract off heat and then bring to a boil. Boil for 60 minutes, adding the hops and Irish moss at the times indicated in the ingredients list. Follow the remaining portion of the all-grain recipe.

TWO BROTHERS ARTISAN BREWING
DOMAINE DUPAGE

⋘⋘⋘-

**(5 Gallons/19 L, all-grain) OG = 1.059 FG = 1.014
IBU = 24 SRM = 12 ABV = 5.9%**

This French country ale won a gold medal at the Great American Beer Festival, as well as many medals in other competitions. It is amber in color, with a toasty, sweet caramel taste that is balanced by a slight hoppiness.

INGREDIENTS

6.75 lb. (3.1 kg) Vienna malt

5 lb. (2.3 kg) Munich malt

10 oz. (0.28 kg) Weyermann CaraWheat malt (50 °L)

5 oz. (0.14 kg) Caramunich malt (40 °L)

5 oz. (0.14 kg) melanoidin malt

1.8 AAU Northern brewer pellet hops (60 min.) (0.2 oz./6 g at 9% alpha acids)

4.9 AAU Mt. Hood pellet hops (25 min.) (0.75 oz./21 g at 6.5% alpha acids)

6.5 AAU Mt. Hood pellet hops (10 min.) (1 oz./28 g at 6.5% alpha acids)

½ tsp. yeast nutrient (15 min.)

½ tsp. Irish moss (30 min.)

White Labs WLP072 (French Ale) or Wyeast 3725 (Bière de Garde) yeast

¾ cup (150 g) dextrose (if priming)

STEP BY STEP

Mix the crushed grains with 4.25 gallons (16 liters) of 170°F (77°C) water to stabilize at 152°F (67°C) for 60 minutes. Sparge slowly with 175°F (79°C) water. Collect approximately 6 gallons (23 liters) of wort runoff to boil for 60 minutes. Add the hops, Irish moss, and yeast nutrient as per the schedule. Cool your wort to 68°F (20°C), aerate, and pitch your yeast. Hold at that temperature until fermentation is complete. After fermentation, allow the beer to condition for 1 week and then bottle or keg.

EXTRACT WITH GRAINS OPTION: Reduce the Vienna malt in the all-grain recipe to 12 ounces (0.34 kilogram) and the Munich malt to 6 ounces (0.17 kilogram), and add 6.6 pounds (3 kilograms) Briess light malt extract and 4 ounces (113 grams) light dried malt extract. Steep the crushed grains in 6 gallons (23 liters) of water at 152°F (67°C) for 30 minutes. Remove grains from the wort and rinse with 2 quarts (1.8 liters) of hot water. Add the liquid malt and dried malt extracts and boil for 60 minutes. Follow the remaining portion of the all-grain recipe.

- - - - - - - - - - - - - - - - - -

WICKED WEED BREWING COMPANY
RETICENT SAISON

≪≪≪≪≪≪≫

**(5 gallons/19 L, all-grain) OG = 1.052 FG = 1.007
IBU = 26 SRM = 4 ABV = 6%**

Wicked Weed may be best known for its sour and hop-forward beers, but they also brew a wide variety of saisons. Reticent has a complex malt bill to build lots of character underneath the yeast-driven aroma.

INGREDIENTS

5.5 lb. (2.5 kg) pilsner malt

3.125 lb. (1.41 kg) 2-row pale malt

10 oz. (0.28 kg) wheat malt

10 oz. (0.28 kg) rye malt

10 oz. (0.28 kg) flaked oats

4 oz. (0.11 kg) acidulated malt

3.3 oz. (85 g) honey malt

6.3 AAU Warrior pellet hops (60 min.) (0.4 oz./11 g at 15.8% alpha acids)

0.6 oz. (17 g) Tettnang pellet hops (0 min.)

0.8 oz. (23 g) Mosaic pellet hops (0 min.)

0.6 oz. (17 g) US Saaz pellet hops (0 min.)

½ tsp. Irish moss (30 min.)

½ tsp. yeast nutrient (15 min.)

White Labs WLP566 (Belgian Saison II) or Wyeast 3711 (French Saison) yeast

1 cup (200 g) dextrose (if priming)

STEP BY STEP

Mash the grains at 151°F (66°C) with 3.5 gallons (13 liters) of water for 60 minutes. Mash out, vorlauf, and then slowly sparge at 175°F (77°C) to collect approximately 6 gallons (23 liters) of wort. Boil for 60 minutes, adding the hops as instructed. Cool the wort to 68°F (20°C). Pitch the yeast, then keep the beer at 68°F (20°C) for 48 hours before letting it free rise until fermentation is complete. Condition for 2 weeks, and then bottle or keg.

EXTRACT WITH GRAINS OPTION: Replace the pilsner and 2-row pale malt in the recipe with 3.3 pounds (1.5 kilograms) Muntons extra light unhopped liquid malt extract, 22 ounces (0.62 kilogram) light dried malt extract, and 1 pound (0.45 kilogram) 2-row pale malt. Steep the crushed grains in 2.5 gallons (9.5 liters) of water at 151°F (66°C) for 30 minutes. Remove the grains from the wort and rinse with 2 quarts (2 liters) of hot water. Add the malt extract and boil 60 minutes. Add the hops, Irish moss, and yeast nutrient as specified. Increase Warrior pellet hops at 60 minutes to 7.9 AAU (0.5 ounces/14 grams at 15.8 percent alpha acids) to compensate for a smaller boil volume. When done, add the wort to 2 gallons (7.6 liters) of cold water in the sanitized fermenter and top off with filtered water up to 5 gallons (19 liters). Follow the remaining portion of the all-grain recipe.

- - - - - - - - - - - - - - - - - -

BRITISH-STYLE ALES

BEER PICTURED ON LEFT; SEE PAGE 170

21ST AMENDMENT BREWERY AND NINKASI BREWING COMPANY
ALLIES WIN THE WAR

ᗕᗕᗕᗕᗕᗕ

(5 gallons/19 L, all-grain) OG = 1.072 FG = 1.018
IBU = 49 SRM = 23 ABV = 7.1%

This collaboration came to be thanks to 21st Amendment's Shaun O'Sullivan and Ninkasi's Jamie Floyd, who had been friends since brewing together in the 1990s at Steelhead Brewing Company. Both brewers had won GABF medals for their versions of the English strong ale style, and decided to brew one together.

INGREDIENTS

11 lb. 12 oz. (5.3 kg) 2-row pale malt

12 oz. (0.34 kg) English crystal malt (15 °L)

12 oz. (0.34 kg) English crystal malt (45 °L)

12 oz. (0.34 kg) English crystal malt (120 °L)

8 oz. (0.23 kg) English crystal malt (155/165 °L)

12 oz. (0.34 kg) light Munich malt (6 °L)

1.6 oz. (45 g) chocolate malt

6 oz. (170 g) dates (macerated, in the secondary)

8.4 AAU Warrior hops (90 min.) (0.5 oz./14 g at 16.8% alpha acids)

7 AAU Willamette hops (30 min.) (0.9 oz./26 g at 7.8% alpha acids)

0.6 oz. (17 g) East Kent Golding hops (0 min.)

Wyeast 1968 (London ESB Ale) or White Labs WLP002 (English Ale) yeast (3.3 qt./3.3 L yeast starter)

⅔ cup (133 g) dextrose (if priming

STEP BY STEP

For the mash, you will need 4.5 gallons (17 liters) of strike water. Mash at 155°F (68°C) for 50 minutes. Mash out to 168°F (76°C) and hold for 5 minutes. Recirculate and then collect enough wort to boil down to 5 gallons (19 liters) in 90 minutes. Boil wort for 90 minutes, adding hops at times indicated in ingredient list. Chill wort and transfer to fermenter. Aerate well and pitch sediment from yeast starter. Ferment at 68°F (20°C). Rack to secondary and add dates. Bottle or keg after 5 days in secondary.

EXTRACT WITH GRAINS OPTION: Substitute the 2-row pale malt in the all-grain recipe with 2.5 pounds (1.1 kilograms) light dried malt extract and 5 pounds (2.3 kilograms) light liquid malt extract. Place grains in a large steeping bag. In a large (at least 6 quarts/6 liters) kitchen pot, steep grains at 155°F (68°C) for 50 minutes in 3.9 quarts (3.7 liters) of water. Begin heating at least 3 gallons (11 liters) of water in your brewpot as the grains steep. Rinse grains with 2 quarts (1.9 liters) of 170°F (77°C) water and add "grain tea" to water in brewpot. Stir in dried malt extract and bring wort to a boil. Boil for 60 minutes, adding hops at times indicated. Stir in liquid malt extract during the final 15 minutes of the boil. Follow the remaining portion of the all-grain recipe.

TIPS FOR SUCCESS

This recipe contains a lot of specialty grains, including a high percentage of dark crystal malts and some chocolate malt. Darkly roasted grains are, of course, very flavorful, but they are also more likely to give up an excessive amount of tannins if handled improperly. Be careful not to oversparge when collecting wort. If you have a pH meter, monitoring the final runnings and ensuring they don't climb above 5.8 would be a good idea. Also, be sure to make a yeast starter. This yeast strain has a tendency to flocculate early if the pitching rate is too low.

- - - - - - - - - - - - - - -

ANCHOR BREWING COMPANY
ANCHOR SMALL BEER (2ND RUNNINGS)

ᗕᗕᗕᗕᗕᗕ

(5 gallons/19 L, all-grain) OG = 1.032 FG = 1.005
IBU = 30 SRM = 7 ABV = 3.3%

This beer is brewed using the second runnings from a batch of Old Foghorn (page 137). Estimating the efficiency in such a scenario is quite challenging, so be prepared to make some gravity adjustments upward by using dried malt extract or downward by dumping some wort and topping off with water!

INGREDIENTS

22.5 lb. (10.2 kg) 2-row pale malt

5 lb. 3 oz. (2.4 kg) caramel malt (40 °L)

5.9 AAU US Golding pellet hops (60 min.) (0.9 oz./26 g at 6.5% alpha acids)

2.6 AAU US Golding pellet hops (30 min.) (0.4 oz./11 g at 6.5% alpha acids)

White Labs WLP051 (California Ale V) or Wyeast 1272 (American Ale II) yeast

0.2 oz. (6 g) gypsum (optional if using very low-mineral water)

⅔ cup (133 g) dextrose (if priming)

STEP BY STEP

Start with the spent grain bed in the mash tun from a batch of Old Foghorn (recipe on page 137). Sparge with 6 gallons (22.7 liters) of 168°F (75°C) water and top up with water if necessary to obtain 6 gallons (23 liters) of 1.027 SG wort. Add the optional gypsum (see ingredients list) and boil for 60 minutes, adding hops according to the ingredients list. After the boil, turn off the heat and chill the wort to slightly below fermentation temperature, about 65°F (18°C). Aerate the wort with pure oxygen or filtered air and pitch the yeast. Ferment at 67°F (19°C) for 4 days. Add dry hops and raise to 72°F (22°C) for 3 days. Once at terminal gravity (approximately 7 days total), bottle or keg the beer and carbonate.

EXTRACT WITH GRAINS OPTION: Small Beer is brewed using the parti-gyle method of brewing. Because this requires that the wort be made with grains, a true parti-gyle brewed with extract is not possible. This recipe is provided simply for extract brewers who are interested in brewing Anchor Small Beer independently. Substitute the 2-row pale malt and caramel malt in the all-grain recipe with 3 pounds (1.36 kilograms) light dried malt extract and 1 pound 3 ounces (0.54 kilogram) caramel malt (40 °L). Place the milled grains in a muslin bag and steep in 4 quarts (3.8 liters) of 149°F (65°C) water for 15 minutes. Remove the grain and rinse with 1 gallon (3.8 liters) of hot water. Add water and optional gypsum (see ingredients list) to reach a volume of 5.25 gallons (19.9 liters) and heat to boiling. Turn off the heat, add the liquid malt extract, and stir until completely dissolved. Top up with water if necessary to obtain 6 gallons (23 liters) of 1.027 SG wort. Follow the remaining portion of the all-grain recipe.

BIG HORSE BREWING COMPANY
MACSTALLION SCOTCH ALE

(5 gallons/19 L, all-grain) OG = 1.067 FG = 1.015
IBU = 19 SRM = 17 ABV = 6.9%

MacStallion is a deep copper- to brown-colored Scotch ale. Full-bodied, with pronounced malty caramel and roasted malt flavor, this is an ale to savor.

INGREDIENTS

9 lb. (4.1 kg) Golden Promise pale malt

4.5 lb. (2 kg) Maris Otter pale malt

2.5 oz. (71 g) Weyermann Carafa Special II malt (475 °L)

5.2 AAU UK Golding pellet hops (60 min.) (1.1 oz./31 g at 4.75% alpha acids)

½ tsp. Irish moss (30 min.)

½ tsp. yeast nutrient (15 min.)

White Labs WLP001 (California Ale), Wyeast 1056 (American Ale), or Fermentis Safale US-05 yeast.

¾ cup (150 g) dextrose (if priming)

STEP BY STEP

This is a single-infusion mash. Mix all the crushed grains with 4.1 gallons (15.5 liters) of 172°F (78°C) water to stabilize at 155°F (68°C). This is a medium-thick mash using 1.2 quarts of strike water per pound of grain (2.5 liters/kilogram). Mash for 40 minutes, then drain approximately 3 quarts (3 liters) of wort and boil it separately for 1 hour to make a syrup. Be careful not to scorch as the mixture thickens (for cleaning reasons). Slowly sparge with 175°F (79°C) water. Collect approximately 6 gallons (23 liters) of wort runoff. Combine that with your first boiled wort and boil for 120 minutes, adding the hops, Irish moss, and yeast nutrient as per the schedule. After the boil is complete, cool the wort, pitch yeast, and aerate the wort heavily. Ferment at 65°F (18°C). Gently transfer to a carboy, avoiding any splashing to prevent aerating the beer. Allow the beer to condition for an additional week. Prime and bottle condition or keg and force carbonate to 2.4 volumes CO_2. Allow the beer to age for at least four more weeks to fully develop the flavors.

PARTIAL MASH OPTION: Reduce the Golden Promise pale malt in the all-grain recipe to 3 pounds (1.4 kilograms) and replace the Maris Otter pale malt with 3.3 pounds (1.5 kilograms) Muntons light Maris Otter liquid malt extract and 3 pounds (1.4 kilograms) Muntons light dried malt extract. Mash the milled grain in 1.5 gallons (6 liters) of water at 155°F (68°C) for 30 minutes. Remove grains from the wort and rinse with 2 quarts (2 liters) of hot water, then top off to 3 gallons (11.4 liters). Boil for 75 minutes. Top up to 6 gallons (23 liters), add the liquid and dried malt extracts, and boil for an additional 60 minutes. Follow the remaining portion of the all-grain recipe.

BIG ROCK BREWERY
WARTHOG ALE

ccccccc

**(5 gallons/19 L, all-grain) OG = 1.045 FG = 1.011
IBU = 15 SRM = 8 ABV = 4.3%**

Warthog Ale is a crossbreed of a British mild ale and an American cream ale. It's a lighter-bodied beer with a touch of crystal malt for a bit of a malty flavor and relatively low hop bitterness.

INGREDIENTS

8 lb. 14 oz. (4 kg) 2-row pale malt

0.5 lb. (0.23 kg) crystal malt (40 °L)

3.5 AAU Willamette hops (60 min.) (0.70 oz./20 g at 5% alpha acids)

4 AAU Centennial hops (3 min.) (0.44 oz./12 g at 9% alpha acids)

1 tsp. Irish moss (15 min.)

White Labs WLP007 (Dry English Ale) or Wyeast 1275 (Thames Valley Ale) yeast (1.25 qt./1.25 L yeast starter)

¾ cup (150 g) dextrose (if priming)

STEP BY STEP

Mash your grains at 151°F (66°C) for 45 minutes using 12 quarts (11 liters) of mash water. Collect 5 gallons (19 liters) of wort and add 1.5 gallons (5.7 liters) of water. Boil for 90 minutes, adding hops and Irish moss at times indicated in ingredient list. After the boil, chill the wort rapidly to 68°F (20°C). Aerate the wort well and pitch the yeast. Ferment at 68°F (20°C). When the beer has reached final gravity, bottle or keg as normal. Age for 2 weeks before serving.

EXTRACT WITH GRAINS OPTION: Scale the 2-row pale malt down to 1.5 pounds (0.68 kilogram). Add 1.5 pounds (0.68 kilogram) Coopers light dried malt extract and 3.3 pounds (1.5 kilograms) Coopers light liquid malt extract (late addition). Place the crushed malts in a nylon steeping bag and steep in 3 quarts (2.8 liters) of water at 150°F (66°C) for 30 minutes. Rinse the grains with 1.5 quarts (1.5 liters) of water at 170°F (77°C). Add water to make 3 gallons (11 liters), stir in the dried malt extract, and bring to a boil. Boil for 60 minutes, adding the hops at the times indicated in the ingredients list. Add the liquid malt extract and Irish moss with 15 minutes left in the boil. When done boiling, cool the wort, transfer to a fermenter, and top up to 5 gallons (19 liters) with cool water. Aerate the wort and pitch the yeast. Follow the remainder of the all-grain recipe.

COACH HOUSE
POST HORN
PREMIUM ALE

ccccccc

**(5 gallons/19 L, all-grain) OG = 1.050 FG = 1.011
IBU = 38 SRM = 9 ABV = 5.0%**

Coach House was formed in the early nineties following the closure of Greenall Whitley in Warrington, England. Their extra special bitter draws on Maris Otter malt for a classic malt base. It pours a gold color and features a light, floral hop aroma.

INGREDIENTS

9 lb. 10 oz. (4.4 kg) Maris Otter pale malt

8.5 oz. (240 g) crystal malt (40 °L)

7.2 AAU Target hops (90 min.) (0.65 oz./18 g at 11% alpha acids)

2.3 AAU Fuggle hops (90 min.) (0.5 oz./14 g at 4.5% alpha acids)

9 AAU Fuggle hops (0 min.) (2 oz./57 g at 4.5% alpha acids)

1 tsp. Irish moss

White Labs WLP005 (British Ale), Wyeast 1098 (British Ale), or Wyeast 1335 (British Ale II) yeast

⅔ cup (133 g) dextrose (if priming)

STEP BY STEP

Mash the grains at 150°F (66°C) for 60 minutes. Mash out, vorlauf, and then sparge at 170°F (77°C) to collect enough wort to result in 5 gallons (19 liters) after a 90-minute boil. Boil 90 minutes, adding hops at times indicated. Cool, aerate, and pitch yeast. Ferment at 70°F (21°C). After fermentation is complete, bottle or keg as usual.

EXTRACT WITH GRAINS OPTION: Decrease the Maris Otter pale malt in the all-grain recipe to 1.5 pounds (0.68 kilogram), and add 1.75 pounds (0.79 kilogram) Briess light dried malt extract and 3.75 pounds (1.7 kilograms) Briess light liquid malt extract. Steep crushed grains in 3 quarts (3 liters) of water at 150°F (66°C) for 45 minutes. Combine "grain tea," water, and dried malt extract to make 3 gallons (11 liters) of wort. Boil for 90 minutes, adding hops at times indicated and liquid malt extract during the final 15 minutes of the boil. Follow the remaining portion of the all-grain recipe.

CROOKED RIVER BREWING CO.
SETTLER'S ALE ESB

(5 gallons/19 L, all-grain) OG = 1.063
FG = 1.016 IBU = 45 SRM = 14 ABV = 6.2%

This English-style extra special bitter gets an American twist treatment with a big hit of Cascade hops. Don't expect a classic ESB here, but this is a nice bridge between styles for lovers of IPA.

INGREDIENTS

9.5 lb. (4.3 kg) 2-row pale malt

1 lb. (0.45 kg) aromatic malt

1 lb. (0.45 kg) crystal malt (30 °L)

1 lb. (0.45 kg) British crystal malt (55 °L)

9.6 AAU Horizon hops (60 min.) (0.75 oz./21 g at 12.8% alpha acids)

6.75 AAU East Kent Golding hops (30 min.) (1.5 oz./42 g at 4.5% alpha acids)

6.8 AAU Cascade hops (3 min.) (1 oz./28 g at 6.8% alpha acids)

1 oz./28 g Cascade hops (dry hop)

1 tsp. Irish moss

White Labs WLP001 (California Ale) or Wyeast 1056 (American Ale) yeast

¾ cup (150 g) dextrose (for priming)

STEP BY STEP

Mash at 150°F (66°C) for 60 minutes. Vorlauf until your runnings are clear, sparge, and boil for 90 minutes, adding the hops at the times indicated in the ingredients list. After the boil, turn off the heat and chill the wort rapidly to 68°F (20°C). Aerate the wort well and pitch the yeast. Ferment at 68 to 70°F (20 to 21°C). Add the dry hops when the gravity has dropped to about 1.025. When final gravity is reached, bottle or keg as usual. Age 2 to 3 weeks before serving.

EXTRACT WITH GRAINS OPTION: Omit the 2-row pale malt. Add 6.6 pounds (3 kilograms) Muntons light liquid malt extract and 0.25 pound (0.11 kilogram) Muntons light dried malt extract. Steep the grains in 3 gallons (11 liters) of water at 150°F (66°C) for 30 minutes. Add the malt extracts and bring to a boil. Boil for 60 minutes, adding the hops at the times indicated in the ingredients list. After the boil, cool the wort, transfer to a sanitary fermenter, top off with cool water to 5.5 gallons (21 liters), aerate well, and pitch the yeast. Follow the remainder of the all-grain recipe.

ELYSIAN BREWING COMPANY
THE WISE ESB

(5 gallons/19 L, all-grain) OG= 1.061 FG = 1.015
IBU = 32 SRM = 14 ABV = 5.9%

Elysian's recipe for an extra special bitter starts with the British basics but then takes a firm turn toward the Northwest. The IBUs aren't out of line, but the Centennial and Cascade hops make this beer a Seattle-style ESB.

INGREDIENTS

10.5 lb. (4.7 kg) Great Western premium 2-row pale malt

1 lb. (0.45 kg) Crisp crystal malt (77 °L)

1 lb. (0.45 kg) Weyermann Munich malt

4 oz. (0.11 kg) Weyermann Carahell malt

2 oz. (57 g) Special B malt

8.4 AAU Chinook hops (60 min.) (0.7 oz./20 g at 12% alpha acids)

½ oz. (14 g) Cascade hops (2 min.)

½ oz. (14 g) Centennial hops (2 min.)

½ oz. (14 g) Cascade hops (whirlpool)

½ oz. (14 g) Centennial hops (whirlpool)

Wyeast 1056 (American Ale) yeast

⅔ cup (133 g) dextrose (if priming)

STEP BY STEP

Mash the grains at 154°F (68°C) for 60 minutes. Mash out, vorlauf, and then sparge at 170°F (77°C) to collect enough wort to result in 5 gallons (19 liters) after a 90-minute boil. Boil 90 minutes, adding hops at times indicated.

Cool, aerate, pitch attenuative American ale yeast, such as Wyeast 1056 (Elysian uses Siebel BR96, a relative), and ferment at ale temperatures. After fermentation is complete, bottle or keg as usual.

EXTRACT WITH GRAINS OPTION: Substitute the 2-row pale malt in the all-grain recipe with 2.75 pounds (1.3 kilograms) light dried malt extract and 4 pounds (1.8 kilograms) light liquid malt extract. Steep crushed grains in 2.9 quarts (2.8 liters) of water at 154°F (68°C) for 45 minutes. Rinse with 1.5 quarts (1.4 liters) of water at 170°F (77°C). Add water to "grain tea" to make 3.5 gallons (13 liters), stir in dried malt extract, and bring to a boil. Boil for 90 minutes, adding hops according to schedule. Stir in liquid malt extract during final 15 minutes of the boil. Cool wort and transfer to fermenter. Top up to 5 gallons (19 liters). Follow the remaining portion of the all-grain recipe.

FULLER'S BREWERY
ESB
ɕɕɕɕɕɕ-

**(5 gallons/19 L, all-grain) OG = 1.060 FG = 1.014
IBU = 35 SRM = 13 ABV = 5.9%**

If someone says ESB, Fuller's is probably the first brewery that comes to mind! Widely available on both sides of the Atlantic, this beer is still a nice one to have in the keg at home. Note that this recipe is for the bottled version of Fuller's ESB. The cask version in the United Kingdom is a bit lower in alcohol, at 5.5 percent ABV.

INGREDIENTS

11 lb. 3 oz. (5.1 kg) Muntons pale ale malt

1 lb. 2 oz. (0.51 kg) crystal malt (75 °L)

5.25 AAU Target hops (60 min.) (0.53 oz./15 g at 10% alpha acids)

2.6 AAU Challenger hops (60 min.) (0.34 oz./10 g at 7.5% alpha acids)

0.83 AAU Northdown hops (15 min.) (0.1 oz./2.7 g at 8.5% alpha acids)

1.66 AAU Golding hops (15 min.) (0.33 oz./9.4 g at 5% alpha acids)

0.33 oz. (9.4 g) Golding hops (dry hop)

Wyeast 1968 (London ESB Ale) or White Labs WLP002 (English Ale) yeast

⅔ cup (133 g) dextrose (if priming)

STEP BY STEP

Mash grains at 153°F (67°C) in 16.5 quarts (15.5 liters) of water. Mash for 60 minutes. Collect 6.5 gallons (25 liters) of wort. Boil for 60 minutes, adding hops at the times indicated. Cool, aerate, and pitch yeast. Ferment at 70°F (21°C). Rack to secondary when fermentation is complete and add dry hops. Bottle a few days later when beer falls clear.

PARTIAL MASH OPTION: Reduce the pale ale malt in the all-grain recipe to 3.3 pounds (1.5 kilograms) and add 1.3 pounds (0.57 kilogram) Muntons light dried malt extract and 4 pounds (1.8 kilograms) Muntons light liquid malt extract. Heat 3.4 quarts (3.2 liters) of water to 165°F (74°C). Add crushed grains to grain bag. Submerge bag and let grains steep around 154°F (68°C) for 45 minutes. While grains steep, begin heating 2.25 gallons (8.5 liters) of water in your brewpot. When steep is over, remove 1.1 quarts (~1.1 liters) of water from brewpot and add to the "grain tea" in steeping pot. Place colander over brewpot and place steeping bag in it. Pour grain tea (with water added) through grain bag. Heat liquid in brewpot to a boil, then stir in dried malt extract. Add hops at times indicated and the liquid malt extract with 15 minutes remaining in the boil. At the end of the boil, cool wort and transfer to fermenter, adding enough water to make 5 gallons (19 liters). Follow the remaining portion of the all-grain recipe.

HARPOON BREWERY
ENGLISH STYLE
OLD ALE
ɕɕɕɕɕɕ-

**(5 gallons/19 L, all-grain) OG = 1.085 FG = 1.020
IBU = 62 SRM = 17 ABV = 8.6%**

Inspired by the sustaining winter offerings of many English breweries, this complex and malty brew is marked by significant alcohol warmth, balanced bitterness, biscuit and roasted malt undertones, and a sublime mouthfeel.

INGREDIENTS

16 lb. (7.25 kg) 2-row pale malt

7 oz. (0.2 kg) biscuit malt

7 oz. (0.2 kg) crystal malt (30 °L)

6 oz. (0.17 kg) aromatic malt

2 oz. (57 g) chocolate malt

2 oz. (57 g) black malt

16.5 AAU Challenger hops (60 min.) (2 oz./56 g at 8.25% alpha acids)

1.25 AAU Fuggle hops (15 min.) (0.25 oz./7 g at 5% alpha acids)

2.4 AAU East Kent Golding hops (0 min.) (0.5 oz./14 g at 4.8% alpha acids)

½ tsp. yeast nutrient (15 min.)

White Labs WLP007 (Dry English Ale) or Wyeast 1028 (London Ale) yeast

¾ cup (150 g) dextrose (if priming)

STEP BY STEP

This is a single-infusion mash. Mix the crushed grain with 5.5 gallons (20.7 liters) of 172°F (78°C) water to stabilize at 155°F (68°C) for 60 minutes. Sparge slowly with 175°F (79°C) water. Collect approximately 6.5 gallons (25 liters) of wort runoff to boil for 90 minutes, adding hops and yeast nutrient as indicated. Cool the wort to 68°F (20°C). Pitch your yeast and aerate the wort heavily. Hold at 68°F (20°C) until fermentation is complete. Transfer to a carboy, avoiding any splashing to prevent aerating the beer. Let the beer condition for 1 week and then bottle or keg.

EXTRACT WITH GRAINS OPTION: Substitute the 2-row pale malt in the all-grain recipe with 9.9 pounds (4.5 kilograms) Muntons light liquid malt extract and 10 ounces (0.3 kilogram) light dried malt extract. Steep the crushed grain in 5 gallons (19 liters) of water at 155°F (68°C) for 30 minutes. Remove grains from the wort and rinse with 2 quarts (1.9 liters) of hot water. Add the liquid and dry malt extracts and bring to a boil. Follow the remaining portion of the all-grain recipe.

LAKE PLACID PUB AND BREWERY
UBU ALE

cccccc-

**(5 gallons/19 L, all-grain) OG = 1.069 FG = 1.014
IBU = 33 SRM = 23 ABV = 7.2%**

This English-style strong ale is deep garnet red in color. It features dark fruit and roasted malt flavors, with a slightly bitter finish.

INGREDIENTS

11 lb. (5 kg) Maris Otter pale ale malt

1.5 lb. (0.68 kg) wheat malt

1 lb. (0.45 kg) English dark crystal malt

6 oz. (170 g) chocolate malt

1 oz. (28 g) black patent malt

5 AAU Fuggle pellet hops (40 min.) (1 oz./28 g at 5% alpha acids)

5 AAU Cluster pellet hops (20 min.) (0.71 oz./20 g at 7% alpha acids)

4 AAU Mt. Hood pellet hops (0 min.) (1 oz./28 g at 4.0% alpha acids)

1 tsp. Irish moss (15 min.)

Wyeast 1318 (London Ale III), White Labs WLP023 (Burton Ale), or Lallemand Windsor Ale yeast

¾ cup (150 g) dextrose (if priming)

STEP BY STEP

If using one of the liquid yeast strains, 2 to 3 days prior to brewing make a 1.5-quart (1.5-liter) yeast starter. Mash grains at 154°F (68°C) for 60 minutes. Use 18 quarts (17 liters) of mash liquor. Collect 7.5 gallons (28 liters) and boil down to 5 gallons (19 liters), which should take about 3 hours, adding hops and Irish moss as indicated. Cool, aerate, and pitch yeast. Ferment at 70°F (21°C). After fermentation is complete, bottle or keg as usual and allow to age for several weeks.

EXTRACT WITH GRAINS OPTION: Substitute the pale ale malt and wheat malt in the all-grain recipe with 1.75 pounds (0.8 kilogram) wheat dried malt extract and 6.6 pounds (3 kilograms) Muntons light liquid malt extract. Steep specialty grains in 1.75 quarts (1.6 liters) of water at 154°F (68°C) for 45 minutes. Remove grains, rinse with 2 quarts (2 liters) of water at 170°F (77°C), and add dried malt extract. Bring to a boil and boil for 60 minutes, adding hops and Irish moss as indicated. Add liquid malt extract with 15 minutes left in boil. After the boil, top off to 5 gallons (19 liters). Follow the remaining portion of the all-grain recipe.

MARSTON'S PLC
BANKS'S MILD

cccccc-

**(5 gallons/19 L, all-grain) OG = 1.035 FG = 1.008
IBU = 23 SRM = 8 ABV = 3.5%**

The original Banks's beer that made the brand famous, Banks's Mild continues to be the world's bestselling mild. It's a well-balanced, sessionable ale with a perceptible burnt note.

INGREDIENTS

5.5 lb. (2.5 kg) mild ale malt (substitute a 50:50 mix of pale ale malt and Vienna malt, or pale ale malt and light Munich malt, if mild ale malt is unavailable)

0.5 lb. (0.23 kg) flaked barley

0.5 lb. (0.23 kg) crystal malt (40 °L)

0.5 lb. (0.23 kg) light brown sugar

3.5 AAU Fuggle hops (90 min.) (0.7 oz./20 g at 5% alpha acids)

2.25 AAU Kent Golding hops (90 min.) (0.45 oz./13 g at 5% alpha acids)

Wyeast 1318 (London III) or similar yeast

⅔ cup (133 g) dextrose (if priming)

STEP BY STEP

Mash grains in 2.2 gallons (8.3 liters) of 150°F (66°C) water for 60 minutes. Sparge with 168 to 170°F (76°C) water to collect 4 gallons (15 liters) of wort. Add 2.5 gallons (9.5 liters) of water and boil for 90 minutes. Add hops at beginning of the boil and the sugar for final 15 minutes of boil. Whirlpool and cool to 68°F (20°C), pitch yeast, and aerate well. Ferment for 4 to 5 days at 68°F (20°C), then rack to secondary fermenter. Condition for 7 more days or until fermentation is complete and gravity is about 1.008. Prime, bottle or keg, and force carbonate (carbonation will be low compared to most American beers).

PARTIAL MASH OPTION: Add 3.3 pounds (1.5 kilograms) Maris Otter liquid malt extract to the recipe and decrease amount of mild ale malt to 0.5 pound (0.23 kilogram). Steep grains in 3 quarts (3 liters) of water at 150°F (66°C) for 30 minutes. Sparge grains with 2 quarts (2 liters) of 170°F (77°C) water. Add water to "grain tea" to make 5.5 gallons (21 liters) and heat to a boil. Add sugar and malt extract off heat, stirring until dissolved. Follow the remainder of the all-grain recipe.

MIDNIGHT SUN BREWING COMPANY
FULL CURL SCOTCH ALE

〃〃〃〃〃〃〃

**(5 gallons/19 L, all-grain) OG = 1.074 FG = 1.020
IBU = 22 SRM = 15 ABV = 7%**

This beer drinks so much like a traditional Scotch ale, you may forget it was designed by a brewery on the West Coast of the United States! With a sturdy malt bill and minimal hops to get in the way, expect big flavor that's sure to please malt lovers.

INGREDIENTS

14 lb. (6.4 kg) 2-row pale malt

12 oz. (0.34 kg) Special B malt

6 oz. (0.17 kg) crystal malt (30 °L)

4 oz. (0.11 kg) special roast malt

½ tsp. yeast nutrient (15 min.)

6 AAU Perle pellet hops (60 min.) (0.6 oz./17 g at 8.5% alpha acids)

White Labs WLP028 (Edinburgh Scottish Ale), Wyeast 1728 (Scottish Ale), or Mangrove Jack's M15 (Empire Ale) yeast

¾ cup (150 g) dextrose (if priming)

STEP BY STEP

This is a single-infusion mash. Mix the crushed grain with 4.8 gallons (18 liters) of 168°F (76°C) water to stabilize at 150°F (66°C) for 60 minutes. Sparge slowly with 175°F (79°C) water. Collect approximately 6 gallons (23 liters) of wort runoff to boil for 60 minutes, adding hops at times indicated. Cool the wort to 75°F (24°C). Pitch your yeast and aerate the wort heavily. Allow the beer to cool to 68°F (20°C). Hold at that temperature until fermentation is complete. Transfer to a carboy, avoiding any splashing to prevent aerating the beer. Let the beer condition for 1 week, and then bottle or keg.

EXTRACT WITH GRAINS OPTION: Substitute the 2-row pale malt in the all-grain recipe with 6.6 pounds (3 kilograms) Muntons light unhopped malt extract and 2.2 pounds (1 kilogram) dried malt extract. Also, decrease the Special B to 8 ounces (0.22 kilogram), crystal malt to 4 ounces (0.11 kilogram), and special roast malt to 2 ounces (57 grams). Steep the crushed grain in 5 gallons (19 liters) of water at 150°F (66°C) for 30 minutes. Remove grains from the wort and rinse with 2 quarts (1.9 liters) of hot water. Add the liquid extract and bring to a boil. Follow the remaining portion of the all-grain recipe.

MINNEAPOLIS TOWN HALL BREWERY
HOPE & KING SCOTCH ALE

**(5 gallons/19 L, all-grain) OG = 1.063 FG = 1.018
IBU = 22 SRM = 20 ABV = 6.1%**

This exceptionally smooth beer showcases the beauty of malted barley, as notes of caramel, toffee, and toasted chocolate rise from its mahogany depths. Hope & King is true royalty as well, with gold, silver, and bronze medals from the Great American Beer Festival.

INGREDIENTS

11 lb. 4 oz. (5.10 kg) Simpsons Golden Promise malt

6 oz. (0.17 kg) flaked barley

4 oz. (113 g) Munich malt (10 °L)

10.33 oz. (0.29 kg) crystal malt (60 °L)

4 oz. (113 g) US chocolate malt

2 oz. (57 g) UK roasted barley (500 °L)

5 AAU Centennial hops (90 min.) (0.5 oz./14 g at 10% alpha acids)

0.5 oz. (14 g) Kent Golding hops (0 min.)

White Labs WLP005 (British Ale) or Wyeast 1187 (Ringwood Ale) yeast

¾ cup (150 g) dextrose (if priming)

STEP BY STEP

Mash the grains at 153°F (67°C) for 60 minutes. Mash out, vorlauf, and then sparge at 170°F (77°C) to collect enough wort to result in 5 gallons (19 liters) after a 90-minute boil. Boil 90 minutes, adding hops at times indicated. Cool, aerate, and pitch yeast. Ferment at 67°F (19°C). After fermentation is complete, bottle or keg as usual.

PARTIAL MASH OPTION: Reduce the Golden Promise malt in the all-grain recipe to 3.5 pounds (1.6 kilograms) and add 0.75 pound (0.34 kilogram) Northwestern Gold dried malt

extract and 4.88 pounds (2.21 kilograms) Northwestern Gold liquid malt extract. Heat 5 gallons (19 liters) of water to 164°F (73°C), place crushed grains in steeping bag, and steep for 45 minutes at around 153°F (67°C). In a separate pot, heat 2 quarts (2 liters) of sparge water to 170°F (77°C). Rinse grains and bring to a boil for 60 minutes. Follow the remaining portion of the all-grain recipe.

OAKHILL BREWERY
YEOMAN STRONG ALE

**(5 gallons/19 L, all-grain) OG = 1.050 FG = 1.012
IBU = 66 SRM = 9 ABV = 5%**

In 1924, a fire destroyed the original Oakhill Brewery in Somerset, England. The New Oakhill Brewery operated from 1984 until the owner retired in 2004. This beer has been renamed during its history and the information about the original Yeoman Strong Ale recipe is incomplete. Thus, this recipe uses the information available, with some educated guesses to fill in the holes.

INGREDIENTS

9.5 lb. (4.3 kg) Halcyon pale ale malt

11 oz. (0.31 kg) crystal malt (60 °L)

4.35 AAU Challenger hops (90 min.) (0.5 oz./14 g at 8.7% alpha acids)

3.75 AAU East Kent Golding hops (90 min.) (0.75 oz./21 g at 5% alpha acids)

4.13 AAU Bramling Cross hops (90 min.) (0.75 oz./21 g at 5% alpha acids)

4.5 AAU Fuggle hops (90 min.) (1 oz./28 g at 4.5% alpha acids)

1 tsp. Irish moss (15 min.)

Muntons Gervin GV12 Ale or similar English ale yeast

⅔ cup (133 g) dextrose (if priming)

STEP BY STEP

Mash the grains at 152°F (67°C) for 60 minutes. Mash out, vorlauf, and then sparge at 170°F (77°C) to collect about 7 gallons (27 liters). Boil 90 minutes, adding hops at times indicated. Cool, aerate, and pitch yeast. Ferment at 70°F (21°C). After fermentation is complete, bottle or keg as usual.

EXTRACT WITH GRAINS OPTION: Replace the Halcyon pale ale malt with 6.6 pounds (3 kilograms) Maris Otter liquid malt extract. Steep grains in 3 quarts (2.8 liters) water at 152°F (67°C) for 20 minutes. Rinse with 1.5 quarts (1.5 liters) of water at 170°F (77°C). Add water and half of the malt extract to make 3 gallons (11 liters) of wort. Boil 60 minutes, adding hops at the beginning of the boil. Try to keep the wort topped up to 3 gallons (11 liters) during the boil. Stir in the remaining malt extract and add Irish moss for the final 15 minutes of the boil. Cool and top off to 5 gallons (19 liters). Follow the remaining portion of the all-grain recipe.

REDHOOK BREWERY
ESB

**(5 gallons/19 L, all-grain) SG = 1.054 FG = 1.012
IBU = 27 SRM = 11 ABV = 5.5%**

Redhook's flagship beer got its start as a winter seasonal recipe in the mid 1980s and has been brewed continuously since 1987. ESB has a caramel malt sweetness and subtle spice and fruit hop flavors.

INGREDIENTS

9 lb. 14 oz. (4.5 kg) domestic 2-row pale malt

1 lb. 2 oz. (0.51 kg) Weyermann Caramunich malt (60 °L)

0.4 lb. (0.18 kg) Carapils malt

3.8 AAU Willamette hops (60 min.) (0.75 oz./21 g at 5% alpha acids)

5 AAU Willamette hops (15 min.) (1 oz./28 g at 5% alpha acids)

3 oz. (85 g) Willamette hops (0 min.)

0.4 oz. (11 g) gypsum (CaSO$_4$)

1 tsp. Irish moss (15 min.)

Wyeast 1084 (Irish Ale) or White Labs WLP004 (Irish Ale) yeast

¾ cup (150 g) dextrose (if priming)

STEP BY STEP

In kettle, mash in at 150°F (66°C) and add gypsum (CaSO$_4$). Rest for 15 minutes, then add 1 gallon (3.8 liters) of hot water. Heat mash to 161°F (72°C) and let rest for 45 minutes. Heat up to 169°F (76°C) and let rest for 5 minutes. Transfer mash to lauter tun. Sparge with 3 gallons (11 liters) of sparge water to 169°F (76°C). Boil for 60 minutes, adding hops and Irish moss as indicated. Add final hops at knockout (end of boil) and hold for 5 minutes before cooling. Cool wort, aerate, and pitch yeast. Ferment at 68°F (20°C). Bottle or keg as usual.

EXTRACT WITH GRAINS OPTION: Replace 2-row malt with 2.25 pounds (1 kilogram) Coopers light dried malt extract and 3.75 pounds (1.7 kilograms) Coopers amber liquid malt extract. Bring 5.5 gallons (21 liters) of water to approximately 162°F (72°C) and hold there. Steep grains for 15 minutes, then remove bag and allow to drain into the wort. Add malt extracts while stirring and stir until completely dissolved. Boil for 60 minutes. Follow the remaining portion of the all-grain recipe.

STEELHEAD
BREWING COMPANY
WEE HEAVY
SCOTCH ALE

**(5 gallons/19 L, all-grain) OG = 1.105 FG = 1.030
IBU = 25 SRM = 18 ABV = 10%**

A rich, smooth, malty beer that will warm you up as the weather gets cold. This hearty ale is lightly hopped to accentuate the complex malt character.

INGREDIENTS

20.5 lb. (9.3 kg) Great Western premium 2-row malt

10.9 oz. (0.31 kg) Belgian Special B malt

9.33 oz. (0.26 kg) Belgian biscuit malt

2.2 oz. (62 g) Briess chocolate malt

7 AAU Nugget hops (60 min.) (0.53 oz./15 g at 13% alpha acids)

3 AAU Mt. Hood hops (20 min.) (0.5 oz./14 g at 6% alpha acids)

White Labs WLP028 (Edinburgh Ale) or Wyeast 1728 (Scottish Ale) yeast (4 qt./~4 L starter)

¾ cup (150 g) dextrose (if priming)

STEP BY STEP

Heat 6.8 gallons (26 liters) of strike water to 164°F (73°C) and mash grains at 153°F (67°C) for 60 minutes. Mash out, vorlauf, and then sparge at 170°F (77°C) to collect about 11 gallons (42 liters) of wort (specific gravity of pre-boil wort will be around 1.047). Boil for 3 hours (or longer) to reduce volume to 5 gallons (19 liters), adding hops at times indicated in ingredient list. Cool, aerate, and pitch yeast. Ferment at 60°F (16°C). After fermentation is complete, bottle or keg as usual.

EXTRACT WITH GRAINS OPTION: Substitute the pale malt in the all-grain recipe with 5 pounds (2.27 kilograms) Muntons light dried malt extract and 8.13 pounds (3.69 kilograms) Northwestern Gold liquid malt extract. Place crushed grains in a nylon steeping bag. Steep at 153°F (67°C) for 45 minutes in 5.5 gallons (21 liters) of water. Rinse grains with 1 quart (1 liter) of water at 170°F (77°C). Add malt extracts and bring wort to a boil for 60 minutes. Follow the remaining portion of the all-grain recipe.

T&R THEAKSTON BREWERY
OLD PECULIER

**(5 gallons/19 L, all-grain) OG = 1.060 FG = 1.015
IBU = 30 SRM = 30 ABV = 6%**

The beer that made Masham, England, famous, Old Peculier is rich, dark, and smooth tasting, with a character all its own.

INGREDIENTS

9 lb. (4.1 kg) English pale ale malt

0.75 lb. (0.34 kg) torrified wheat (or flaked wheat)

0.75 lb. (0.34 kg) crystal malt (60 °L)

4 oz. (113 g) extra dark crystal malt (150 °L)

5 oz. (142 g) English chocolate malt (450 °L)

3 oz. (85 g) black patent malt

10 oz. (0.23 kg) golden treacle syrup (15 min.)

5 oz. (0.14 kg) black treacle (15 min.)

7 AAU Northern Brewer hops (60 min.) (0.78 oz./22 g at 9% alpha acids)

2.5 AAU Fuggle hops (15 min.) (0.5 oz./14 g at 5% alpha acids)

0.25 oz. (7 g) Fuggle hops (dry hop)

1 tsp. Irish moss (15 min.)

Wyeast 1028 (London Ale) or White Labs WLP026 (Burton Ale) yeast (2 qt./~2 L yeast starter)

¾ cup (150 g) dextrose (if priming)

STEP BY STEP

Heat 14 quarts (13.3 liters) of water to 164°F (73°C) and stir in crushed grains. The mash should settle at 153°F (67°C). Hold mash at 153°F (67°C) for 45 minutes, then begin the lautering process. Collect about 6.5 gallons (25 liters) of wort and bring to a boil. Boil for 90 minutes, adding hops, sugars, and Irish moss at time indicated in ingredient list. Cool wort and transfer to fermenter. Aerate wort and pitch yeast. Ferment at 70°F (21°C). Rack beer to secondary and let beer condition for 2 weeks. Add dry hops 5 days before packaging beer.

PARTIAL MASH OPTION: Reduce the 2-row pale ale malt in the all-grain recipe to 1 pound (0.45 kilogram) and reduce crystal malt to 4 ounces (0.11 kilogram). Add 1.75 pounds (0.8 kilogram) Muntons light dried malt extract and 3.3 pounds (1.5 kilograms) Muntons light liquid malt extract. Place crushed pale ale malt and wheat in a large nylon steeping bag. Heat 4.5 quarts (4 liters) of water to 164°F (73°C) and submerge bag. Mash at 153°F (67°C) for 30 minutes. You can either then add the remaining crushed grains to the first grain bag or utilize a second grain bag. Steep all the grains for 15 more minutes. Rinse all the grains with 4 quarts (4 liters) water at 170°F (77°C). Add water to "grain tea" to make 3 gallons (11 liters), then add dried malt extract and bring to a boil. Add ingredients as indicated and the liquid malt extract with 15 minutes remaining. Cool wort, transfer to fermenter, and top up to 5 gallons (19 liters). Follow the remaining portion of the all-grain recipe.

TIMOTHY TAYLOR BREWERY
BOLTMAKER

**(5 gallons/19 L, all-grain) OG = 1.037 FG = 1.008
IBU = 29 SRM = 9 ABV = 3.9%**

Formerly known as Best Bitter, this classic English bitter was renamed in 2012 but retains its classic copper/amber color; citrusy, fruity hop character; and roasted, malty, bitter finish.

INGREDIENTS

7.75 lb. (3.5 kg) Golden Promise pale malt

5.75 oz. (163 g) crystal malt (120 °L)

3.8 AAU East Kent Golding hops (90 min.) (0.75 oz./21 g at 5% alpha acids)

3.4 AAU Fuggle hops (90 min.) (0.75 oz./21 g at 4.5% alpha acids)

5.4 AAU Styrian Golding hops (0 min.) (1 oz./28 g at 5.4% alpha acids)

1 tsp. Irish moss (15 min.)

Wyeast 1028 (London Ale) or Wyeast 1098 (British Ale) yeast

⅔ cup (133 g) dextrose (if priming)

STEP BY STEP

Mash the grains at 152°F (67°C) for 60 minutes. Mash out, vorlauf, and then sparge at 170°F (77°C) to collect enough wort to result in 5 gallons (19 liters) after a 90-minute boil. Boil 90 minutes, adding hops at times indicated. Cool, aerate, and pitch yeast. Ferment at 68°F (20°C). After fermentation is complete, bottle or keg as usual.

PARTIAL MASH OPTION: Reduce the 2-row pale malt in the all-grain recipe to 1 pound 10 ounces (0.74 kilogram) and add 0.5 pound (0.23 kilogram) Muntons light dried malt extract and 3.3 pounds (1.5 kilograms) Muntons extra light liquid malt extract. Steep crushed grains in 3 quarts (3 liters) of water at 152°F (67°C) for 45 minutes. Combine "grain tea," water, and dried malt extract to make 3 gallons (11 liters) of wort. Boil for 90 minutes, adding hops when indicated and liquid malt extract during the final 15 minutes of the boil. Cool, top off to 5 gallons (19 liters), aerate, and pitch yeast. Follow the remaining portion of the all-grain recipe.

TIMOTHY TAYLOR BREWERY
LANDLORD

(5 gallons/19 L, all-grain) OG = 1.041 FG = 1.010
IBU = 34 SRM = 12 ABV = 4.1%

This sessionable offering from Timothy Taylor is a favorite in the United Kingdom, where it has won both the Brewing Industry Challenge Cup and CAMRA's Champion Beer of Britain Competition numerous times. Expect a complex aroma and flavor for such a small beer.

INGREDIENTS

8 lb. 6 oz. (3.8 kg) Golden Promise malt

2.5 oz. (71 g) debittered black malt

6.75 AAU UK Fuggle hops (60 min.) (1.5 oz./43 g at 4.5% alpha acids)

4.1 AAU UK Golding hops (10 min.) (0.75 oz./21 g at 5.5% alpha acids)

1 oz. (28 g) Styrian Golding hops (0 min.)

Wyeast 1469 (West Yorkshire Ale) or White Labs WLP037 (Yorkshire Square Ale) yeast

¾ cup (150 g) dextrose (if priming)

STEP BY STEP

On brew day, prepare your ingredients: mill the grains, measure your hops, and prepare your water. This recipe uses RO water. Add ¼ teaspoon 10 percent phosphoric acid per 5 gallons (19 liters) of brewing water, or until water measures pH 5.5 at room temperature. Add 1 teaspoon calcium chloride ($CaCl_2$) to the mash. On brew day, mash in the Golden Promise at 152°F (67°C) in 13 quarts (12 liters) of water and hold this temperature for 60 minutes. Add the

black malt to the mash. Raise the temperature by infusion or direct heating to 168°F (76°C) to mash-out. Recirculate for 15 minutes. Fly sparge with 168°F (76°C) water until 7 gallons (26.5 liters) of wort is collected. Add ½ teaspoon of calcium carbonate ($CaCO_3$) to the kettle. Boil the wort very hard for 70 minutes, adding the hops at times indicated in the recipe. After adding the flameout hops, allow the hops to rest in the kettle for 40 minutes as the wort cools naturally. Chill to 66°F (19°C) and rack to the fermenter. Oxygenate, then pitch the yeast. Ferment at 68°F (20°C) until complete. Rack the beer, prime, and bottle condition, or keg and force carbonate.

EXTRACT WITH GRAINS OPTION: Substitute the Golden Promise malt in the all-grain recipe with 5.6 pounds (2.54 kilograms) Maris Otter liquid malt extract. Steep the black malt in 6 gallons (23 liters) of water at 158°F (70°C) for 15 minutes. Remove the grains and let drain. Add the malt extract and stir thoroughly to dissolve, and then bring to a boil. Follow the remaining portion of the all-grain recipe.

TRAQUAIR HOUSE BREWERY
TRAQUAIR HOUSE ALE

(5 gallons/19 L, all-grain) OG = 1.075 FG = 1.019
IBU = 38 SRM = 25 ABV = 7.3%

First brewed in 1965, Traquair House Ale is a deep reddish, full-bodied, and richly flavored ale. It carries a pleasant alcoholic warmth, firm hop bitterness, and a smoky malt flavor from the roasted barley.

INGREDIENTS

14 lb. (6.4 kg) Golden Promise pale ale malt

0.25 lb. (0.11 kg) English roasted barley (550 °L)

6 AAU Kent Golding hops (90 min.) (1.5 oz./42 g at 4% alpha acids)

5 AAU Kent Golding hops (30 min.) (1.25 oz./35 g at 4% alpha acids)

Wyeast 1728 (Scottish Ale) yeast (2.25 qt./2.25 L yeast starter)

¾ cup (150 g) dextrose (if priming)

STEP BY STEP

Heat 19 quarts (18 liters) water to 163°F (73°C), crush grains, mix into liquor. Hold mash at 152°F (67°C) for 60 minutes. Put

the first gallon (3.8 liters) of wort runoff into a heavy pot and heat to a rapid boil, stirring often until reduced to about 1 cup (200 grams) and syrup consistency. Be sure not to scorch, though. This makes a small amount of caramelized wort to be added later. Collect a further 7 gallons (26.6 liters) of wort and begin the boil, which will last about 2 hours. When you have 6.5 gallons (25 liters) of wort (and around 90 minutes left in the boil), add caramelized wort and first addition of Kent Golding hops. Add remaining hops with 30 minutes left in boil. Cool to 68°F (20°C), aerate well, and pitch yeast. Ferment 8 to 10 days at 65°F (18°C), transfer to secondary and condition at 50°F (10°C) for 2 weeks. Bottle or keg, and then age for 8 to 10 weeks.

PARTIAL MASH OPTION: Reduce the pale ale malt in the all-grain recipe to 2 pounds (0.9 kilogram). Substitute in with 3.5 pounds (1.6 kilograms) light dried malt extract and 4.5 pounds (2 kilograms) light liquid malt extract. Steep the pale ale malt and roasted barley in 3.4 quarts (3.2 liters) of water at 152°F (67°C) for 45 minutes. Rinse grains with 2 quarts (2 liters) of 170°F (77°C) water. Add water to "grain tea" to make 3 gallons (11.5 liters), add 2.5 pounds (1.13 kilograms) of the dried malt extract and all the liquid malt extract. Stir until fully dissolved, and bring wort to a boil. At the start of the boil, scoop 4 quarts (3.8 liters) of wort into a heavy pot and boil alongside main wort until reduced to about 1 cup. This will make some caramelized wort to add back later to the larger wort. Stir "mini-wort" often, to prevent scorching. Add water and the remaining dried malt extract back into the big pot to make 5 gallons (19 liters) and bring back to a boil. Add the first hop addition to the larger volume wort at the start of the boil and the second with 30 minutes remaining. With 15 minutes remaining, add the "mini-wort" back into the large pot. Cool and top up to 5 gallons (19 liters). Follow the remaining portion of the all-grain recipe.

TIPS FOR SUCCESS

The ultimate color of this beer will depend largely on the level of caramelization that occurs in the 1 gallon (4 liters) mini-boil. The beer will start at about 17 SRM if very little caramelization occurs and can range up to the upper twenties if you can achieve a high degree of caramelization. But be careful as scorching of the wort can leave you with a bitter, burnt flavor that will change the profile of this beer. Keep a close eye on this boil as the wort changes into a highly viscous syrup.

WELLS AND YOUNG'S LTD
YOUNG'S SPECIAL LONDON ALE

(5 gallons/19 L, all-grain) OG = 1.064 FG = 1.015
IBU = 30   SRM = 11   ABV = 6.4%

Young's Special London Ale is a well-balanced, bottle-conditioned premium bitter brewed with 100 percent British ingredients. Substitute American malt or hops at your own risk!

INGREDIENTS

12 lb. (5.5 kg) Maris Otter 2-row malt

12 oz. (0.43 kg) English medium crystal malt (55 °L)

4 oz. (113 g) carastan malt (35 °L)

7 AAU Fuggle hops (60 min.) (1.4 oz./40 g at 5% alpha acids)

2.5 AAU Kent Golding hops (15 min.) (0.5 oz./14 g at 5% alpha acids)

0.5 oz. (14 g) Kent Golding hops (0 min.)

0.5 oz. (14 g) Kent Golding whole hops (dry hop)

0.5 oz. (14 g) Target whole hops (dry hop)

1 tsp. Irish moss (15 min.)

Wyeast 1768 (English Special Bitter) or Wyeast 1968 (London ESB Ale) yeast

¾ cup (150 g) dextrose (if priming)

STEP BY STEP

Mash grains at 153°F (67°C) in 16.5 quarts (15.5 liters) of water for 60 minutes. Mash out, vorlauf, and then sparge at 170°F (77°C) to collect 6.5 gallons (25 liters) of wort and boil for 90 minutes, adding hops at the times indicated in ingredients list. Cool, aerate, and pitch yeast. Ferment at 69°F (21°C). After fermentation is complete, bottle or keg as usual.

EXTRACT WITH GRAINS OPTION: Replace the Maris Otter malt in the all-grain recipe with 6.6 pounds (3 kilograms) Maris Otter liquid malt extract and 1.5 pounds (0.68 kilogram) Muntons light dried malt extract. Put crushed grains in a nylon steeping bag. Steep at 160°F (71°C) in 5 gallons (19 liters) for 30 minutes. Rinse grains with 1.5 quarts (1.4 liters) of water at 170°F (77°C). Add liquid and dried malt extract and boil for 60 minutes. Follow the remaining portion of the all-grain recipe.

WYCHWOOD BREWING COMPANY
HOBGOBLIN DARK ALE

ϾϾϾϾϾϾ·

(5 gallons/19 L, all-grain) OG = 1.050 FG = 1.012
IBU = 33 SRM = 20 ABV = 5.2%

This ruby-colored English ale delivers a delicious chocolate toffee malt flavor, balanced with rounded moderate bitterness and an overall fruity, mischievous character.

INGREDIENTS

9 lb. (4.1 kg) Maris Otter pale ale malt

1 lb. (0.45 kg) English crystal malt (75 °L)

0.25 lb. (0.11 kg) English chocolate malt

5 AAU Fuggle hops (first wort hop) (1 oz./28 g at 5% alpha acids)

3.9 AAU Styrian Golding hops (30 min.) (0.75 oz./21 g at 5.25% alpha acids)

1.3 AAU Kent Golding hops (10 min.) (0.25 oz./7 g at 5.25% alpha acids)

Wyeast 1187 (Ringwood Ale) or White Labs WLP005 (British Ale) yeast

¾ cup (150 g) dextrose (if priming)

STEP BY STEP

Mash the grains at 151°F (66°C) in 13 quarts (12 liters) of brewing liquor for 60 minutes. Mash out, vorlauf, and then sparge at 170°F (77°C) to collect 6 gallons (23 liters) wort. Add the first wort hops and bring to a boil for 60 minutes, adding the remaining hops as indicated. Cool, aerate, and pitch yeast. Ferment at 69°F (21°C). After fermentation is complete, bottle or keg as usual.

EXTRACT WITH GRAINS OPTION: Substitute the pale ale malt in the all-grain recipe with 2.3 pounds (1 kilogram) Muntons light dried malt extract and 3.3 pounds (1.5 kilograms) Maris Otter liquid malt extract. Steep crushed grains at 151°F (66°C) in 5 gallons (19 liters) of water. Rinse grains with 1.5 quarts (1.5 liters) of water at 170°F (77°C). Add first wort hops and bring to a boil. Add liquid and dried malt extract, and boil 60 minutes. Follow the remaining portion of the all-grain recipe.

CHAPTER TWELVE

EUROPEAN-STYLE ALES & LAGERS

Beer Pictured on Left; see page 179

ABITA BREWING COMPANY
ANDYGATOR DOPPELBOCK

<del>◀◀◀◀◀◀</del>

**(5 gallons/19 L, all-grain) OG = 1.078 FG = 1.017
IBU = 25 SRM = 8 ABV = 8%**

This original high-gravity brew is made with pilsner hops, German lager yeast, and German Perle hops. It features a slightly sweet flavor but ferments to a low enough FG to have a dry finish.

INGREDIENTS

16 lb. (7.3 kg) pilsner malt

6.2 AAU Perle pellet hops (60 min.) (0.75 oz./21.3 g at 8.25% alpha acids)

2.1 AAU Perle pellet hops (30 min.) (0.25 oz./7.1 g at 8.25% alpha acids)

4.1 AAU Perle pellet hops (5 min.) (0.5 oz./14.2 g at 8.25% alpha acids)

½ tsp. yeast nutrient (15 min.)

½ tsp. Irish moss (30 min.)

White Labs WLP830 (German Lager) or Wyeast 2308 (Munich Lager) yeast

¾ cup (150 g) dextrose (if priming)

STEP BY STEP

This is a single-infusion mash. Mix the crushed grains with 5.2 gallons (19.7 liters) of 174°F (79°C) water to stabilize at 154°F (68°C) for 60 minutes. Sparge slowly with 175°F (79°C) water. Collect approximately 6 gallons (23 liters) of wort runoff to boil for 60 minutes. While boiling, add the hops, Irish moss, and yeast nutrient as per the schedule. Cool the wort to 75°F (24°C). Pitch your yeast and aerate the wort heavily. Allow the beer to cool over the next few hours to 65°F (19°C). When evidence of fermentation is apparent, drop the temperature to 52°F (11°C). Hold at that temperature until fermentation is complete (approximately 10 days). Transfer to a carboy, avoiding any splashing to prevent aerating the beer. Condition for 2 weeks at 42°F (5°C), and then bottle or keg.

EXTRACT ONLY OPTION: Replace pilsner malt in the all-grain recipe with 9.9 pounds (4.5 kilograms) Briess pilsen liquid malt extract and 0.75 pound (0.34 kilogram) Briess pilsen dried malt extract. Bring 5.5 gallons (21 liters) of water to a boil and remove from heat as you add the malt extracts while stirring. Stir until completely dissolved, and return to a boil for 60 minutes. Follow the remaining portion of the all-grain recipe.

AVERY BREWING COMPANY
THE KAISER (IMPERIAL OKTOBERFEST)

<del>◀◀◀◀◀◀</del>

**(5 gallons/19 L, all-grain) OG = 1.085 FG = 1.015
IBU = 23 SRM = 11 ABV = 9.3%**

For this beer, Avery took the classic Oktoberfest and turned the volume up! It has a big malty backbone and a luscious deep copper color.

INGREDIENTS

11.5 lb. (5.2 kg) 2-row pale malt

2.1 lb. (0.95 kg) Weyermann Vienna malt

2.1 lb. (0.95 kg) Weyermann Munich Type I malt (7 °L)

1.4 lb. (0.64 kg) Gambrinus dark Munich malt (20 °L)

11 oz. (312 g) Dingemans aromatic malt

4.75 AAU Hallertau Tradition hops (60 min.) (0.6 oz./17 g at 2.7% alpha acids)

4.75 AAU Magnum hops (60 min.) (0.2 oz./6 g at 13.6% alpha acids)

2.5 AAU Sterling hops (30 min.) (0.4 oz./11 g at 6% alpha acids)

0.5 oz. (14 g) Tettnang hops (0 min.)

0.5 oz. (14 g) Hallertau-Hersbrücker hops (0 min.)

Wyeast 2206 (Bavarian Lager), White Labs WLP820 (Oktoberfest/Märzen), or Fermentis Saflager W-34/70 yeast (4 qt./~4 L yeast starter)

¾ cup (150 g) dextrose (if priming)

STEP BY STEP

Mash the grains at 152°F (67°C), using 5.6 gallons (21 liters) of mash liquor heated to 163°F (73°C). Mash in, mix for 20 minutes, then rest for 20 minutes. Vorlauf (recirculate) for 15 minutes. Collect 7 gallons (26 liters) of wort and check specific gravity (SG). If SG is below 1.061, you can either add dried malt extract to make it 1.061 or collect more wort—up to 9 gallons (34 liters)—and extend the boil time accordingly. Boil for 120 minutes, adding the hops at the times indicated in the ingredient list. After the boil, turn off the heat and chill the wort rapidly to 55°F (13°C), aerate well, and pitch the yeast. Ferment at 55°F (13°C) for the first 24 hours, then drop the temperature to 50°F (10°C). When the gravity hits 1.030 to 1.035, let the temperature rise to wherever it can for diacetyl rest. When primary fermentation is complete, bottle or keg as normal.

PARTIAL MASH OPTION: Omit the 2-row malt, scale both the Weyermann Vienna malt and Weyermann Munich I malts to 1 pound 4.2 ounces (0.57 kilogram) each. Add 3 pounds (1.4 kilograms) Coopers light dried malt extract and 6 pounds (2.7 kilograms) Coopers light liquid malt extract (late addition). Heat 5.5 quarts (5.2 liters) of water to 166°F (74°C) and pour into 2-gallon (7.6-liter) beverage cooler. Place crushed grains in a nylon steeping bag and submerge. Stir grains well, tie off bag lightly, and seal cooler. Let partial mash rest, starting at 155°F (68°C), for 45 minutes. (It will most likely drop to around 150°F (66°C) by the end of the mash. This is fine.) While partial mash is resting, heat 0.75 gallon (2.8 liters) of water to a boil in your brewpot and 5 quarts (4.7 liters) of water to 180°F (82°C) in a large kitchen pot. Run off first wort and add to boiling water in the brewpot. Add the 5 quarts (4.7 liters) of 180°F (82°C) water to the cooler, untie bag, stir grains, and let sit for 5 minutes. Run off second wort and add to brewpot. Add dried malt extract and bring to a boil. Add first charge of hops and boil for 60 minutes, adding other hops at times indicated in the ingredient list. With 15 minutes left in the boil, stir in half of the liquid malt extract; add the remaining half at the end of the boil. (Keep the boil clock running when adding extract.) Let the wort sit for 15 minutes before cooling. Cool the wort and top up with enough cool water to make 5 gallons (19 liters), aerate well, and pitch yeast. Follow fermentation and lagering instructions in all-grain recipe.

BOZEMAN BREWING COMPANY
BOZONE HEFEWEIZEN

(5 gallons/19 L, all-grain) OG = 1.049 FG = 1.010
IBU = 21 SRM = 5 ABV = 5.1%

This American take on a classic German wheat beer took home a bronze medal from the North American Beer Awards. Bozeman uses Montana-grown malted pale barley, but if you can't source that, domestic 2-row will work.

INGREDIENTS

5.4 lb. (2.45 kg) 2-row pale malt

5.4 lb. (2.45 kg) wheat malt

0.5 lb. (0.23 kg) acidulated malt

5.5 AAU Cascade leaf hops (60 min.) (1 oz./28 g at 5.5% alpha acids)

4.25 AAU Northern Brewer leaf hops (5 min.) (0.5 oz./14 g at 8.5% alpha acids)

1.87 AAU Saaz pellet hops (5 min.) (0.5 oz./14 g at 3.75% alpha acids)

Wyeast 1056 (American Ale), White Labs WLP001 (California Ale), or Fermentis Safale US-05 yeast

¾ cup (150 g) dextrose (if priming)

STEP BY STEP

Mix the crushed grains with 3.4 gallons (12.8 liters) of water at 161°F (72°C), stabilizing at 150°F (65.5°C) for 60 minutes until conversion is complete. Raise the temperature of the mash to 168°F (76°C) with approximately 2.2 gallons (8.3 liters) of 200°F (93°C) water, and then collect 7 gallons (26.5 liters) of wort to begin a 60-minute boil. The specific gravity of the boil should be about 1.038. Add hops as indicated. There should be about 5.5 gallons (21 liters) of wort remaining after the boil. Cool the wort to 75°F (24°C), aerate, and pitch yeast. Allow wort to cool to 68°F (20°C) for fermenting. When fermentation is complete, wait about 3 more days for a diacetyl rest. Keg or bottle as usual.

EXTRACT WITH GRAINS OPTION: Reduce the 2-row pale malt and wheat malt in the all-grain recipe to 0.5 pound (0.23 kilogram) each and add 3.3 pounds (1.5 kilograms) Briess Bavarian wheat liquid malt extract, 1.5 pounds (0.68 kilogram) Briess Bavarian wheat dried malt extract, and 1 pound (0.45 kilogram) Briess Pilsen light dried malt extract. Steep the crushed malted grain in 5.5 gallons (19 liters) of 150 to 160°F (66 to 71°C) water for 30 minutes, stirring the grain just prior to removing. Remove grains and bring to a boil, adding malt extracts off heat. Boil 60 minutes. Follow the remaining portion of the all-grain recipe.

BRAUEREI AYING
AYINGER CELEBRATOR

(5 gallons/19 L, all-grain) OG = 1.073 FG = 1.021
IBU = 22 SRM = 25 ABV = 6.7%

This massively malty Bavarian dopplebock shows off a distinct chocolaty malt character. The complex fruitiness is balanced by a dry finish. The brewery ages Celebrator for 6 months before release, so you may wish to do the same for a perfect clone.

INGREDIENTS

10.2 lb. (4.6 kg) pilsner malt

2.33 lb. (1.05 kg) Munich malt (10 °L)

2.33 lb. (1.05 kg) Munich malt (20 °L)

0.5 lb. (0.23 kg) Weyermann Carafa Special II malt

6 AAU Hallertau hops (60 min.) (1.5 oz./42 g at 4% alpha acids)

1 tsp. Irish moss (15 min.)

White Labs WLP833 (German Bock Lager) or Wyeast 2487 (Hella Bock Lager) yeast (4 qt./4 L yeast starter)

¾ cup (150 g) dextrose (if priming)

STEP BY STEP

Perform a decoction mash with a 15-minute rest at 131°F (55°C) and a second rest at 158°F (70°C) for 45 minutes. Boil the wort for 90 minutes, adding the hops and Irish moss at times indicated in the ingredients list. After the boil, chill the wort rapidly to 55 to 58°F (13 to 14°C), aerate well, and pitch the yeast. Ferment at 55°F (13°C). When fermentation is complete, allow temperature to rise to 60°F (16°C) for 2 days for a diacetyl rest, then rack to a secondary fermenter and cool to 40°F (4.4°C). Lager for at least 6 weeks, then bottle or keg as normal.

PARTIAL MASH OPTION: Omit the pilsner malt and scale the Munich (10 °L) and the Munich (20 °L) malt additions down to 1.33 pounds (0.60 kilogram) each and the Weyermann Carafa Special II down to 5 ounces (143 grams). Add 2.75 pounds (1.25 kilograms) Pilsen dried malt extract, 5 pounds (2.3 kilograms) Weyermann Bavarian Dunkel liquid malt extract (late addition). In a large pot, heat 4.4 quarts (4.2 liters) of water to 169°F (76°C). Add crushed grains to grain bag. Submerge bag and let grains steep around 158°F (70°C) for 45 minutes. While grains steep, begin heating 2.1 gallons (7.8 liters) of water in your brewpot. When steep is complete, remove 1.5 quarts (1.4 liters) of water from the brewpot and add to the "grain tea" in a steeping pot. Place a colander over the brewpot and place a steeping bag in it. Pour the grain tea (with water added) through the grain bag. Bring the brewpot to a boil, then stir in the dried malt extract, add hops, and begin the 60-minute boil. Try to keep the brewpot topped off to 3.5 gallons (13.2 liters). With 15 minutes left in boil, turn off heat and stir in the liquid malt extract and Irish moss. Stir well to dissolve extract, then resume heating. (Keep the boil clock running while you stir.) At the end of the boil, cool the wort and transfer to fermenter. Add enough cool water to make 5 gallons (19 liters). Aerate the wort and pitch yeast. Follow the remainder of the all-grain recipe.

BRAUHAUS FAUST-MILTENBERGER
FAUST SCHWARZ-VIERTLER

(5 gallons/19 L, all-grain) OG = 1.052 FG = 1.013
IBU = 23 SRM = 27 ABV = 5.2%

This dark-brown lager is hard to track down in the United States, which is all the more reason to brew it instead! It has a solid caramel flavor and a great mouthfeel. It's crisp and flavorful.

INGREDIENTS

7 lb. 15 oz. (3.6 kg) Munich I malt

2 lb. 10 oz. (1.2 kg) pilsner malt

9.1 oz. (0.26 kg) Weyermann Rauchmalz (smoked malt)

2.9 oz. (82 g) Weyermann (dehusked) Carafa I Special

0.64 fl. oz. (19 mL) Weyermann Sinamar

5.9 AAU Perle hops (60 min.) (0.9 oz./27 g at 6.5% alpha acids)

0.1 oz. (2 g) Perle hops (10 min.)

White Labs WLP833 (German Bock), Wyeast 2487 (Hella Bock), or Mangrove Jack's M76 (Bavarian Lager) yeast

¾ cup (150 g) dextrose (if priming)

STEP BY STEP

Two or 3 days before you brew, make a 1-gallon (~4-liter) yeast starter. On brew day, to approximate the mash conditions (and lautering process) used by the brewery, mash in so that you use around 20 quarts (19 liters) of brewing liquor—this is a mash thickness of about 1.8 quarts/lb. (3.7 L/kg), thinner than a typical homebrew mash. Mash in to 113°F (45°C) and give the mash an initial hydration rest of about 30 minutes. Slowly heat the mash to raise the temperature to 149°F (65°C). A rate of just over 1°F (~0.5°C) every minute will mean the temperature ramp will take about a half hour. Rest at 149°F (65°C) for 20 minutes. Then repeat the temperature increase, this time to 154°F (68°C) for a 5-minute rest. The next rest is at 162°F (72°C) for about 10 minutes. To raise the temperature for the mash-out, you have two options: heat the mash as before or boil a decoction, as is done at Faust. For the decoction, draw about ¼ of the mash (a little over a gallon/4 liters) into a large pot and bring it to a boil. Boil for 10 minutes, then return the decoction to the main mash for a temperature increase to 169°F (76°C). Recirculate for about 15 minutes before you collect your wort. Collect all the wort from the grain bed, without sparging. When all the wort is in the kettle, measure the volume. Subtract this from your target pre-boil volume. (The boil is 70 minutes, so 6.2 gallons/23 liters of pre-boil wort would work if you typically boil off 1 gallon per hour.) This is the volume of sparge water you will use. Divide this into 3 aliquots and sparge with each, taking about 30 minutes to rinse the grain bed and collect the wort each time. (If you collected 4 gallons/15 liters of wort, you would need 2.2 gallons/8.3 liters of sparge water separated into three 2.9-quart/2.7-liter aliquots to reach 6.2 gallons/23 liters of pre-boil wort.) Your sparge water should be 169°F (76°C) or hotter if your grain bed temperature has dropped below 169°F (76°C). The boiling time is 70 minutes. Add hops as indicated and the Sinamar about 10 minutes before shutdown. Whirlpool the wort for up to 20 minutes, then chill to the temperature range of your selected yeast, usually to about 50 to 59°F (10 to 15°C) for most Bavarian lager strains.

Ferment the brew like a typical German lager. After primary fermentation (and a diacetyl rest, if needed), rack the beer off the yeast and lager it for 4 to 6 weeks. The optimal lagering temperature would be 28°F (-2°C), but refrigerator temperature (around 40°F/4.4°C) will work.

PARTIAL MASH OPTION: Reduce the Munich I malt to 1 pound 4 ounces (0.57 kilogram) and Rauchmalz to 9.1 ounces (0.26 kilogram). Replace the pilsner malt with 6 pounds 10 ounces (3 kilograms) Munich liquid malt extract. Steep the grains at 149°F (65°C) for 45 minutes in 3 quarts (2.8 liters) of water. Add water to make at least 3 gallons (11 liters), add half the extract, and boil for 70 minutes. Follow the remaining portion of the all-grain recipe.

FLOSSMOOR STATION BREWERY
BLACK WOLF SCHWARZBIER

⟨⟨⟨⟨⟨⟨⟨-

**(5 gallons/19 L, all-grain) OG = 1.055 FG = 1.013
IBU = 30 SRM = 28 ABV = 5.5%**

A GABF medal winner, this German-style schwarzbier from Flossmoor is a lovely dark brown color and features notes of toasted malt and coffee.

INGREDIENTS

9.5 lb. (4.3 kg) pilsner malt

11 oz. (0.32 kg) Munich malt (20 °L)

4.8 oz. (136 g) aromatic malt

11 oz. (312 g) Weyermann Carafa II malt

1.6 oz. (45 g) roasted barley

4.6 AAU German Perle hops (80 min.) (0.6 oz./17 g at 7.7% alpha acids)

2 oz. (57 g) German Hallertau hops (10 min.)

White Lab WLP830 (German Lager), Wyeast 2124 (Bohemian Lager), or Fermentis Saflager W-34/70 yeast

¾ cup (150 g) dextrose (if priming)

STEP BY STEP

Mash the pilsner, Munich, and aromatic malts at 148 to 152°F (64 to 67°C) for 60 minutes. Add the Weyermann Carafa II and roasted barley to the mash just before sparging. (A decoction mash could and should be used if your system allows.) Sparge as normal, and bring the wort to a boil. Boil for 90 minutes, adding the hops at the times indicated in the ingredients list. When the boil is complete, chill the wort down to pitching temperature, transfer to a fermenter, and pitch the yeast. Start the fermentation at 70°F (21°C), and once the initial fermentation starts, lower the temperature to the low 50s°F (~11°C). Ferment to final gravity at 52 to 54°F (11 to 12°C). Lager at 32 to 34°F (0 to 2°C) for 4 to 8 weeks. Then bottle or keg as usual.

EXTRACT ONLY OPTION: Reduce amount of pilsner malt to 3 ounces (85 grams). Add 2 pounds (0.91 kilogram) of light dried malt extract and 4.25 pounds (1.9 kilograms) light liquid malt (late addition). Steep the specialty grains at around 152°F (67°C) in 2 gallons (3.8 liters) of water in a large kitchen pot. Put the crushed grains in a large steeping bag and submerge the bag in the kitchen pot for 30 to 45 minutes. At the end of the steep, remove the bag from the steeping pot and let drip dry for a minute or so. Add the "grain tea" to your brewpot and add the light liquid malt extract. Boil for 60 minutes, adding the hops at the times indicated in the ingredient list. With 15 minutes left in the boil, stir in the liquid malt extract. After the boil, cool the wort, top up with enough cool water to make 5 gallons (19 liters), aerate, and pitch yeast. Follow the remainder of the all-grain recipe.

FLYING DOG BREWERY
TIRE BITE GOLDEN ALE

**(5 gallons/19 L, all-grain) OG = 1.046 FG = 1.012
IBU = 18 SRM = 4 ABV = 4.5%**

This golden-straw colored ale is actually a German-style Kölsch. You'll find it light, grassy, and refreshing. It's a perfect ale for summer.

INGREDIENTS

8 lb. (3.6 kg) 2-row pale malt

1 lb. (0.45 kg) white wheat malt

10 oz. (0.28 kg) Munich malt

4.25 AAU Perle hops (75 min.) (0.61 oz./17 g at 7% alpha acids)

2 AAU Hallertau hops (2 min.) (0.5 oz./14 g at 4% alpha acids)

1 tsp. Irish moss (15 min.)

Wyeast 1007 (German Ale) or White Labs WLP029 (German Ale/Kölsch) yeast (1 qt./~1 L yeast starter)

¾ cup (150 g) dextrose (if priming)

STEP BY STEP

Mash the grains at 153°F (67°C) for 45 minutes. Sparge with hot water of 170°F (77°C) or more to collect 5 gallons (19 liters) of wort. Add 1.5 gallons (5.7 liters) of water and bring to a boil. Boil for 90 minutes total. After the boil is complete, chill the wort down to pitching temperature, aerate the wort, and pitch the yeast. Ferment at 65°F (18°C) until complete (7 to 10 days), then hold the beer at 65°F (18°C) for another 6 days for a diacetyl rest. When the rest is complete, bottle or keg as normal.

PARTIAL MASH OPTION: Scale the 2-row pale malt down to 6 ounces (170 grams). Add 1 pound 10 ounces (0.7

kilogram) light dried malt extract and 3.3 pounds (1.5 kilograms) light liquid malt extract (late addition). Place the crushed malts in a nylon steeping bag and steep in 3 quarts (2.8 liters) of water at 153°F (67°C) for 30 minutes. Rinse grains with 1.5 quarts (~1.5 liters) of water at 170°F (77°C). Add water to make 3 gallons (11 liters), stir in the dried malt extract, and bring to a boil. Add Perle hops and boil for 75 minutes total, adding remaining hops at times indicated in the ingredient list. Add the liquid malt extract and Irish moss with 15 minutes left in the boil. After the boil, cool the wort and transfer to fermenting vessel. Top up to 5 gallons (19 liters) with water. Follow the remainder of the all-grain recipe.

G. SCHNEIDER & SOHN
SCHNEIDER WEISSE ORIGINAL

**(5 gallons/19 L, all-grain) OG = 1.056 FG = 1.014
IBU = 15 SRM = 8 ABV = 5.6%**

With barely any hops, Schneider Weisse Original is a lesson on the complexity you can tease out of a strain of yeast. When it is properly cloned, you'll get aromas of clove, apple, and nutmeg. The beer should finish crisp and almost tart.

INGREDIENTS

7.4 lb. (3.4 kg) Weyermann pale wheat malt (2 °L)

1.85 lb. (0.84 kg) Weyermann Pilsner malt (1.8 °L)

1.85 lb. (0.84 kg) Weyermann Vienna malt (3.3 °L)

0.5 lb. (0.23 kg) Weyermann Caramunich III malt (56 °L)

3.1 AAU Hallertau Mittelfrüh hops (30 min.) (0.74 oz./21 g at 4.2% alpha acids)

4.2 AAU Hallertau Mittelfrüh hops (10 min.) (1 oz./28 g at 4.2% alpha acids)

2 packages of White Labs WLP380 (Hefeweizen IV Ale) or Wyeast 3068 (Weihenstephan Weizen) yeast (1 for primary fermentation, 1 for inoculating Speise)

2 qts. (2 L) sterile wort (for bottle conditioning)

STEP BY STEP

Dough-in at 99°F (37°C) with about 2 gallons (~7.5 liters) of water. This amounts to a 2:1 liquor-to-grist ratio. Allow for a 30-minute rest to thoroughly hydrate the grist, then bring the grain bed gradually to the mash-out temperature of 145°F (63°C) using a hot-water infusion and direct heat. While ramping up, employ a 20-minute protein and beta-glucan rest at 122°F (50°C). Give the grain bed a 60-minute rest at 145°F (63°C) to allow for thorough starch conversion, then recirculate the first runnings until they are clear and sparge while maintaining a stable grain bed temperature. Boil 60 minutes, adding hops as indicated. After flameout, carefully stir the hot wort for 1 minute to create a whirlpool. About 30 minutes into the whirlpool, draw about 2 quarts (2 liters) of hot, sterile wort from the top of the kettle (where there is less trub than below) into a sealable container. Let that wort cool; then store it in the refrigerator during the brew's primary fermentation. You will need this wort later as a priming agent, called Speise, during bottle conditioning. Continue whirlpooling for another 30 minutes, by which time plenty of protein-rich trub should have accumulated in the center-bottom of the brew kettle. Siphon the clarified wort carefully off the debris and heat exchange it into a clean carboy (or bucket for open fermentation) with the pitched yeast. Aerate the wort and ferment it at a temperature of 68°F (20°C) for about 4 days. The brew should now be at the terminal gravity of FG 1.012 and ready for bottle conditioning. On bottling or kegging day, take the Speise out of the refrigerator and let it warm up to room temperature. Because at home you are dealing with just a single batch, you must inoculate your saved "unpitched" wort before using it as a Speise. Thus, pitch the second package of yeast into your Speise, close the container, and shake it vigorously to aerate it. Then pour the Speise into a clean carboy or a keg and rack the fully fermented brew into it for a thorough mix. Transfer the inoculated beer into bottles or keep it in the closed keg. Once mixed with Speise, let the beer condition for about 1 week at a cozy room temperature of 70°F (21°C). This will produce the hefeweizen's spritzy carbonation. Also at this temperature, the flavor of the hefeweizen becomes soft and mellow, with mild banana tones starting to emerge next to clove and phenol notes. Then cool-condition the brew for another 2 weeks at about 45°F (7°C), which is also a good serving temperature.

EXTRACT ONLY OPTION: Substitute all the grains in the all-grain recipe with 8.2 pounds (3.7 kilograms) Weyermann Bavarian Hefeweizen liquid malt extract. Bring 5.5 gallons of water to a boil and stir in extract. Boil for 60 minutes. Follow the remaining portion of the all-grain recipe.

GOOSE ISLAND BREWING COMPANY
SUMMERTIME KÖLSCH

(5 gallons/19 L, all-grain) OG = 1.046 FG = 1.010
IBU = 18 SRM = 4 ABV = 4.7%

Former Goose Island brewmaster Gregory Hall said that his ideal summer beers are session beers that pair well with summertime foods such as grilled sausages. This beer certainly delivers on that front.

INGREDIENTS

7 lb. 11 oz. (3.5 kg) 2-row pale malt

1 lb. 15 oz. (0.87 kg) wheat malt

2.5 AAU Mt. Hood hops (60 min.) (0.5 oz./14 g at 5% alpha acids)

3 AAU Czech Saaz hops (0 min.) (0.75 oz./21 g at 4% alpha acids)

2.5 AAU Mt. Hood hops (0 min.) (0.5 oz./14 g at 5% alpha acids)

Wyeast 2565 (Kölsch) or White Labs WLP029 (German Ale/ Kölsch) yeast

⅔ cup (133 g) dextrose (if priming)

STEP BY STEP

Mash at 145°F (63°C) for 40 minutes, 152°F (67°C) for 45 minutes, and 170°F (77°C) for 10 minutes. Mash pH 5.4 to 5.5. Mash out, vorlauf, and then sparge at 170°F (77°C) to collect enough wort to result in 5 gallons (19 liters) after a 60-minute boil. Boil for 60 minutes, adding the first hop addition as the wort comes to a boil. At the end of the boil, remove from heat, add the last hops addition, and give the wort a stir to create a whirlpool. Let the wort settle for 15 minutes, then chill to yeast pitch temperature. Wort pH = 5.2. Aerate to 8 ppm O2. Pitch rate = 20 million cells per milliliter. Ferment at 56 to 58°F (13 to 14°C).

EXTRACT ONLY OPTION: Replace the 2-row and wheat malts in the all-grain recipe with 3.3 pounds (1.5 kilograms) wheat liquid malt extract and 2.5 pounds (1.13 kilograms) light dried malt extract. Bring 5.5 gallons (21 liters) of water to a boil and remove from heat as you add the malt extracts while stirring. Stir until completely dissolved, and return to a boil for 60 minutes. Follow the remaining portion of the all-grain recipe.

GREAT BASIN BREWING COMPANY
SMOKE CREEK RAUCHBOCK

**(5 gallons/19 L, all-grain) OG = 1.055 FG = 1.016
IBU = 18 SRM = 24 ABV = 5.2%**

This Great American Beer Festival gold medal winner is a deep amber bock made by loading a conventional smoker with malted barley imported from Germany. Great Basin smokes their malts using local mahogany, alder, and cherry wood to add a delightful smoky character to the malt. We recommend trying the same at home as noted in the ingredients and complementing them with a few pounds of rauchmalz.

INGREDIENTS

3.5 lb. (1.6 kg) Weyermann rauchmalz

2 lb. (0.91 kg) Weyermann Pilsner malt (home smoked)

2 lb. (0.91 kg) Weyermann Munich II malt (home smoked)

2 lb. (0.91 kg) Weyermann Munich I malt

1 lb. (0.45 kg) Weyermann Pilsner malt

10 oz. (0.28 kg) Weyermann Caramunich II malt

8 oz. (0.23 kg) Weyermann Carafa Special II malt

4.75 AAU Northern Brewer hops (90 min.) (0.52 oz./15 g at 9% alpha acids)

0.5 oz. (14 g) Hallertau hops (0 min.)

Wyeast 2124 (Bavarian Lager), White Labs WLP830 (German Lager), or Fermentis Saflager W-34/70 yeast

1 cup (200 g) dextrose (if priming)

STEP BY STEP

Infusion mash at 153 to 154°F (67 to 68°C) for 45 minutes. Sparge with water up to 165°F (74°C) and collect 6 gallons (23 liters). Boil 60 minutes, adding hops as indicated. Cool, aerate, and pitch yeast, fermenting 52°F (11°C) until finished. Do a 2-day diacetyl rest at 62°F (17°C) and then cool temperature to lager at 32°F (0°C) for at least 1 month. Bottle or keg as usual.

PARTIAL MASH OPTION: It's hard to do an extract version of a rauchbier because there are no smoked (rauch) extracts available to homebrewers. So, the best we can do is try to get in the ballpark with smoke intensity of a true rauchbier. Some folks will add liquid smoke or peat-smoked malts to up the smoke flavors in an extract rauchbier, but we don't necessarily agree with this tactic. Lovers of a strong peat Scotch whiskey may disagree about adding peat-smoked malt. If you do want to experiment, be sure to start off very conservative with your additions. One ounce (28 grams) of peat-smoked malts or ¼ teaspoon of liquid smoke is noticeable in beers without big flavors to mask them. Swap out the pilsner, home-smoked pilsner, and Munich I malts for 1.7 pounds (0.77 kilogram) Pilsen dried malt extract and 1 pound (0.45 kilogram) Munich dried malt extract. Mash the crushed grains in 2 gallons (7.8 liters) strike water at 153 to 154°F (67 to 68°C) for 45 minutes. Sparge slowly with 2 gallons (7.8 liters) of hot water. Add both dried malt extracts and stir until completely dissolved. Top off to 6 gallons (23 liters) and bring to a boil. Following the remaining instructions from the all-grain recipe.

HEINEKEN INTERNATIONAL
HEINEKEN

**(undiluted base beer = 5 gallons/19L, all-grain)
OG = 1.053 FG = 1.007 IBU = 25 SRM = 5 ABV = 6%
(post-dilution = 6 gallons/23L) virtual OG = 1.045
FG = 1.006IBU = 21 SRM = 4 ABV = 5%**

This classic Dutch lager is available in green bottles across the world. While it's not hard to find, it is a fun cloning challenge—why not try a side-by-side taste test? Believe it or not, the beer is still brewed based on the recipe formulated in 1873.

INGREDIENTS

8 lb. (3.6 kg) 2-row pilsner malt

5 oz. (0.14 kg) Weyermann acidulated malt

4 oz. (0.11 kg) Carapils malt

2.4 lb. (1.1 kg) corn grits

2 tsp. Irish moss

¼ tsp. yeast nutrients

6.6 AAU Magnum hops (60 min.) (0.4 oz./12 g at 16% alpha acids)

0.13 oz. (3.5 g) Saaz hops (15 min.)

Wyeast 2024 (Danish Lager) or White Labs WLP850 (Copenhagen Lager) yeast (3 qt./~3 L yeast starter at SG 1.030–1.040)

2 tsp. polyclar (fining agent)

1 gallon (3.8 L) deaerated water (for blending)

1 cup (200 g) dextrose (if priming)

STEP BY STEP

Heat 12 quarts (11 liters) of water to 142°F (61°C) in your kettle. Set aside corn grits and 1 pound (0.45 kilogram) of pilsner malt. Stir remaining crushed grains into hot water and mash at 131°F (55°C). Make cereal mash by combining 5 quarts (4.7 liters) of water with grits and crushed pilsner malt. While main mash is resting, begin heating cereal mash to 158°F (70°C). Hold cereal mash at 158°F (70°C) for 5 minutes, then heat to a boil, stirring constantly. Boil cereal mash for 15 minutes. After main mash has rested 15 minutes, begin heating it to 140°F (60°F). Stir this mash as well. (If you don't have a brewing partner, save yourself some headaches and make the cereal mash immediately before mashing in the main mash.) Hold main mash at 140°F (60°C) for 15 minutes. Stir cereal mash into main mash and adjust temperature to 152°F (67°C). Hold at this temperature for 45 minutes, then heat to 170°F (77°C). Transfer mash to lauter tun (and rinse out your kettle). Recirculate wort for 20 minutes, then begin running off wort. Heat sparge water to 190°F (88°C) and monitor the temperature of the top of the grain bed. Hold at this temperature for 45 minutes, then heat to 170°F (77°C) to mash out. Sparge with 170°F (77°C) water and collect wort until the specific gravity of the final runnings is below 1.008 or the pH climbs above 5.8. Add enough water so you will yield 5 gallons of wort after a 90 minutes boil—around 6.5 to 7 gallons (25 to 26 liters) for a reasonable evaporation rate. Add a pinch of calcium (CaCl$_2$ or gypsum) at the beginning of the boil. Add hops at times indicated in recipe and Irish moss and yeast nutrients with 15 minutes left in the boil. After boil, cool quickly and transfer to fermenter. Aerate and pitch yeast sediment from yeast starter. Ferment at 53°F (12°C) until terminal gravity is within 3 gravity points of final gravity. Let temperature rise to 60°F (16°C) and let rest until diacetyl is gone. Cool to 30 to 40°F (-1.1 to 4.4°C) and lager for 4 to 6 weeks. Add 2 teaspoons polyclar to beer the night before you keg or bottle it. Dilute 5 gallons (19 liters) of base beer to 6 gallons (23 liters) of finished beer by blending base beer with 1 gallon (3.8 liters) of deaerated water. Package in keg or green bottles.

PARTIAL MASH OPTION: Replace all the malts and corn grits in the all-grain recipe with 2 pounds (0.9 kilogram) 2-row pilsner malt, 13.6 ounces (0.39 kilogram) Laaglander light dried malt extract, 2.5 pounds (1.13 kilograms) Coopers light liquid malt extract, and 1 pound 7 ounces (0.65 kilogram) brewers corn syrup. Reduce Magnum hop addition to 5.4 AAU (0.33 ounces/9.6 grams) and the Saaz hop addition to 0.11 ounces (3.1 grams). Put crushed pilsner malt in a nylon steeping bag. In a 2-gallon (8-liter) kitchen pot, heat 3 quarts (~3 liters) of water to 169°F (76°C), turn off heat, and dunk steeping bag. Steep grains for 45 minutes at 158°F (70°C). While grains are steeping, heat 2 gallons (7.6 liters) of water to 180°F (82°C) in your brewpot. When steep is over, add 2 quarts (2 liters) of hot water from kettle to the "grain tea" in the steeping pot. Remove grain bag and place in colander over brewpot. Pour the diluted grain tea through the grains in the steeping bag. Discard grain bag, add dried malt extract and corn syrup to the liquid in the kettle, and bring to a boil. Once a boil is reached, wait until the foam subsides and then add hops and begin timing the 60-minute boil. With 15 minutes left in boil, add Saaz hops, Irish moss, and yeast nutrients, then turn off heat and stir in the liquid malt extract. Resume heating once the extract is completely dissolved. After the boil, cool wort quickly and transfer to fermenter. Add water in fermenter to make 5 gallons (19 liters). Follow the remaining portion of the all-grain recipe.

IRON HILL BREWERY
BRIDGE ST. BOCK

cccccc

**(5 gallons/19 L, all-grain) OG = 1.076 FG = 1.016
IBU = 24 SRM = 18 ABV = 7.9%**

This bock won a bronze medal at the World Beer Cup. Brewer Tim Stumpf notes that he likes to add a sprinkle of calcium chloride to promote round, smooth maltiness in this beer.

INGREDIENTS

8 lb. (3.6 kg) German pilsner malt

3.6 lb. (1.6 kg) light Munich malt

3.6 lb. (1.6 kg) Vienna malt

10 oz. (0.3 kg) Weyermann CaraAroma malt (130 °L)

6 oz. (170 g) pale chocolate malt (200 °L)

7.5 AAU Perle hops (60 min.) (1 oz./28 g at 7.5% alpha acids)

Wyeast 2000 (Budvar Lager) yeast

¾ cup (150 g) dextrose (if priming)

STEP BY STEP

Mill the grains and mix with 5 gallons (19 liters) of 162°F (72°C) strike water to reach a mash temperature of 150°F (66°C). Hold this temperature for 60 minutes. Vorlauf until your runnings are clear. Sparge the grains with 4 gallons (15 liters) and top up as necessary to obtain 6.25 gallons (24 liters) of wort. Boil for 90 minutes, adding hops according to the ingredient list. After the boil, chill the wort to slightly below fermentation temperature, about 50°F (10°C). Aerate the wort with pure oxygen or filtered air and pitch yeast. Ferment at 52°F (11°C) until about ⅔ of the way through fermentation (when gravity reads approximately 1.036). At that point, allow temperature to rise to 63°F (17°C) to encourage complete fermentation. Once the beer reaches terminal gravity, bottle or keg and carbonate to approximately 2.5 volumes. You may want to cold-crash the beer to 35°F (2°C) for 48 hours prior to packaging to improve clarity. After carbonation is achieved, lager for at least 4 weeks at 35°F (2°C) before drinking.

EXTRACT WITH GRAINS OPTION: Substitute the pilsner, Munich, and CaraAroma malts in the all-grain recipe with 5 pounds (2.3 kilograms) pilsner liquid malt extract and 5 pounds (2.3 kilograms) Munich liquid malt extract. Steep crushed grains at approximately 162°F (72°C) for 15 minutes in 5.8 gallons (22 liters) of water. Remove the grain bags, and let drain fully. Add liquid extract while stirring and top up to 6.25 gallons (24 liters). Boil for 90 minutes. Follow the remaining portion of the all-grain recipe.

- - - - - - - - - - - - - - - -

KODIAK ISLAND BREWING COMPANY
OKTOBERFEST

eeeeee-

**(5 gallons/19 L, all-grain) OG = 1.062 FG = 1.012
IBU = 25 SRM = 12.5 ABV = 6.5%**

This traditional Oktoberfest is a classic take on the German style. It's a malt-lover's beer you should brew well ahead of when you want to drink it. Including lagering, you'll need about 2 months.

INGREDIENTS

- 12 lb. (5.4 kg) Munich malt (9 °L)
- 1.25 lb. (0.56 kg) Victory malt
- 10 oz. (0.28 kg) crystal malt (15 °L)
- 4.5 AAU US Saaz pellet hops (80 min.) (1 oz./28 g at 4.5% alpha acids)
- 2.4 AAU East Kent Golding pellet hops (30 min.) (0.5 oz./14 g at 4.75% alpha acids)
- ½ tsp. Irish moss (30 min.)
- ½ tsp. yeast nutrient (15 min.)
- White Labs WLP810 (San Francisco Lager) or Wyeast 2112 (California Lager) yeast
- ½ cup (100 g) dextrose (if priming)

STEP BY STEP

This is a single-infusion mash. Mix all the crushed grains with 4.6 gallons (17.5 liters) of 168°F (76°C) water to stabilize at 151°F (66°C). This is a medium-thin mash using 1.4 quarts of strike water per pound of grain (2.9 liters/kilograms). This ratio will help to maximize fermentability. Mash for 60 minutes and slowly sparge with 175°F (79°C) water. Collect approximately 6.2 gallons (23.5 liters) of wort runoff and boil for 80 minutes. While boiling, add the hops, Irish moss, and yeast nutrient as per the schedule. After the boil is complete, cool the wort to 65°F (18°C). Pitch your yeast and aerate the wort heavily. Allow the beer to cool to 58°F (14°C). Hold at that temperature until fermentation is complete. This may take 12 to 14 days. After fermentation is complete, gently transfer to a carboy, avoiding any splashing to prevent aerating the beer. Allow the beer to condition for an additional week. Prime and bottle condition or keg and force carbonate to 2.2 volumes CO_2. Allow the beer to age for at least 4 more weeks to fully develop the flavors and enjoy your Oktoberfest clone.

PARTIAL MASH OPTION: Reduce the 2-row pale malt in the all-grain recipe to 18 ounces (0.51 kilogram) and add 6.6 pounds (3 kilograms) Briess Munich liquid malt extract. Mash the milled grains in 2.5 gallons (9.5 liters) of water at 151°F (66°C) for 30 minutes. Remove grains from the wort and rinse with 2 quarts (1.8 liters) of hot water. Top your kettle off to 6 gallons (23 liters) and boil for 80 minutes. Follow the remaining portion of the all-grain recipe.

- - - - - - - - - - - - - - - -

LAKEFRONT BREWERY
EASTSIDE DARK

-ɛɛɛɛɛɛ-

**(5 gallons/19 L, all-grain) OG = 1.060 FG = 1.015
IBU = 20   SRM = 17   ABV = 5.8%**

This Bavarian dark lager uses a blend of 3 specialty grains for a rich and smooth dark beer that anyone can enjoy.

INGREDIENTS

11.25 lb. (5.1 kg) 2-row pale malt

10 oz. (0.28 kg) Briess Munich malt

5 oz. (0.14 kg) Briess chocolate malt

0.75 oz. (21 g) Briess black patent malt

4.5 AAU Mt. Hood hops (60 min.) (0.9 oz./25 g at 5% alpha acids)

1.75 AAU Mt. Hood hops (15 min.) (0.35 oz./10 g at 5% alpha acids)

1 AAU Mt. Hood hops (2 min.) (0.2 oz./6 g at 5% alpha acids)

1 tsp. Irish moss (15 min.)

White Labs WLP830 (German Lager) or Wyeast 2206 (Bavarian Lager) yeast (3 qt./~3 L yeast starter)

¾ cup (150 g) dextrose (if priming)

STEP BY STEP

Mash the grains at 155°F (68°C) for 60 minutes in 15.5 quarts (14.7 liters) of mash water. Collect 6.5 gallons (25 liters) of wort and boil for 90 minutes, adding hops and Irish moss at times indicated. Cool, aerate, and pitch yeast. Ferment at 50°F (10°C). When fermentation is just about complete, let the temperature rise to 60°F (16°C) for 2 days to perform a diacetyl rest, then cool the beer to 36°F (2.2°C) and lager for 2 weeks. Bottle or keg as usual.

EXTRACT WITH GRAINS OPTION: Substitute the 2-row pale malt in the all-grain recipe with 0.5 pound (0.23 kilogram) Briess light dried malt extract, 6.6 pounds (3 kilograms) Briess light liquid malt extract, and 1 pound (0.45 kilogram) pilsner malt. Steep crushed grains in 3 quarts (2.8 liters) of water at 150°F (66°C) for 30 minutes. Rinse grains with 1.5 quarts (1.5 liters) of water at 170°F (77°C). Add water to make 3 gallons (11 liters). Add dried malt extract and bring to a boil. Add hops and Irish moss as indicated and the liquid malt extract with 15 minutes remaining in the boil. After the boil, top off to 5 gallons (19 liters). Follow the remaining portion of the all-grain recipe.

NÄRKE KULTURBRYGGERI
TANNGNJOST & TANNGRISNIR

-ɛɛɛɛɛɛ-

**(5 gallons/19 L, all-grain) OG = 1.071 FG = 1.014
IBU = 27   SRM = 9   ABV = 7.5%**

Berith Karlsson of Närke Kulturbryggeri said that this doppelbock is named after the 2 goats that pulled the wagon of Thor, the god of thunder. Unlike classic versions of the style, this beer has smoked malt and juniper in the recipe.

INGREDIENTS

7 lb. (3.2 kg) smoked malt (Gotland, Viking, or Weyermann)

4.5 lb. (2 kg) Munich malt

1 lb. (0.45 kg) Carapils malt

1 lb. (0.45 kg) wheat malt

13 oz. (0.36 kg) sucrose (15 min.)

7.5 AAU Northern Brewer hops (60 min.) (1 oz./28 g at 7.5% alpha acids)

4.3 AAU Hallertau Mittelfrüh hops (1 min.) (1.3 oz./38 g at 4.25% alpha acids)

4 twigs female (with berries) juniper

White Labs WLP833 (German Bock Lager) or Wyeast 2206 (Bavarian Lager) yeast

⅔ cup (133 g) dextrose (if priming)

STEP BY STEP

Submerge the juniper twigs in about 7 gallons (26.5 liters) of water and bring to a boil for 5 minutes. Remove twigs and use the water for mashing and sparging. Mash the grains at 151°F (66°C) for 60 minutes. Mash out, vorlauf, and then sparge at 170°F (77°C) to collect 6 gallons (23 liters) of wort. Boil for 60 minutes, adding hops and sucrose at times indicated. Cool, aerate, and pitch yeast at 60°F (16°C). Hold until visible signs of fermentation, then slowly chill to 50°F (10°C) and hold for the remainder of fermentation. After fermentation is complete, allow temperature to rise to 55°F (13°C) for 2 days. Then cool to 33°F (1°C) and hold for at least 4 weeks. Bottle or keg as usual.

PARTIAL MASH OPTION: Substitute the smoked malt and Munich malt in the all-grain recipe with 5.5 pounds (2.5 kilograms) Weyermann smoked malt extract and 2.75 pounds (1.25 kilograms) liquid Munich malt extract. Place 4 quarts (4 liters) of water in your brewpot. Toss in the juniper twigs, bring to a boil, and boil for 5 minutes. Remove twigs and cool juniper water to 162°F (72°C). Place crushed grains in a large steeping bag and mash in juniper water at 151°F (66°C) for 45 minutes. Remove bag and rinse with 2 quarts (2 liters) of 170°F (77°C) water. Top up to 6 gallons (23 liters), add malt extracts, and bring to a boil for 60 minutes. Follow the remaining portion of the all-grain recipe.

NESHAMINY CREEK BREWING COMPANY
NESHAMINATOR WHEAT BOCK

(5 gallons/19 L, all-grain) OG = 1.078 FG = 1.017 IBU = 21 SRM = 22 ABV = 8.5%

This is a fairly traditional German wheat bock with a sweet twist. Breaking from tradition, Neshaminy Creek adds orange blossom honey to the boil for additional complexity.

INGREDIENTS

5.5 lb. (2.5 kg) 2-row pale malt

4 lb. (1.8 kg) dark Munich malt (10 °L)

4 lb. (1.8 kg) red wheat malt

1 lb. (0.45 kg) caramel pils/ dextrin malt

0.75 lb. (0.34 kg) crystal malt (60 °L)

0.5 lb. (0.23 kg) chocolate malt (350 °L)

0.25 lb. (0.12 kg) crystal malt (80 °L)

0.5 lb. (0.23 kg) orange blossom honey (60 min.)

5.6 AAU Hallertau hops (45 min.) (1.25 oz./35 g at 4.5% alpha acids)

3.4 AAU Tettnang hops (15 min.) (0.75 oz./21 g at 4.5% alpha acids)

White Labs WLP300 (Hefeweizen Ale) or Wyeast 3068 (Weihenstephan Weizen) yeast

1 cup (200 g) dextrose (if priming)

STEP BY STEP

Mill the grains and mix with 4.8 gallons (18.1 liters) of 168°F (75°C) strike water to reach a mash temperature of 156°F (69°C). Hold this temperature for 60 minutes. Vorlauf until your runnings are clear and lauter. Sparge the grains with 3.3 gallons (12.5 liters) of water, add honey and stir until dissolved, and top up as necessary to obtain 6 gallons (23 liters) of wort. Boil for 75 minutes, adding hops according to the ingredient list. Chill the wort to 63°F (17°C), aerate, and pitch yeast. Ferment at 63°F (17°C) for 3 days. Raise to 68°F (20°C) for 7 more days or until you reach terminal gravity. Then increase to 70°F (21°C) and hold for 3 days for the diacetyl rest before bottling or

kegging. Carbonate to approximately 3 volumes. You may want to cold-crash the beer to 35°F (2°C) for 48 hours prior to packaging to improve clarity.

EXTRACT WITH GRAINS OPTION: Reduce the caramel Pils/dextrin malt in the all-grain recipe to 8 ounces (0.23 kilogram) and replace the 2-row pale malt, dark Munich malt, and red wheat malt with 2 pounds (0.91 kilogram) extra light dried malt extract, 3.3 pounds (1.5 kilograms) Munich liquid malt extract, and 3.3 pounds (1.5 kilograms) wheat liquid malt extract. Bring 5.3 gallons (20.1 liters) of water to approximately 162°F (72°C) and steep grains for 15 minutes. Remove the grain bags and let drain fully. Add liquid malt extract and honey off-heat and stir until completely dissolved. Top up as necessary to obtain 6 gallons (23 liters) of wort. Follow the remaining portion of the all-grain recipe.

NEW BELGIUM BREWING COMPANY
1554 BLACK LAGER

(5 gallons/19 L, all-grain) OG = 1.059 FG = 1.015 IBU = 21 SRM = 35 ABV = 5.7%

This unique dark lager uses a recipe, based on ancient texts, that was destroyed by a flood in 1997. It was re-created through the teamwork of researcher Phil Benstein and New Belgium's brewmaster at the time, Peter Bouckaert.

INGREDIENTS

7.5 lb. (3.4 kg) pale malt

0.5 lb. (0.23 kg) Carapils malt

4 lb. (1.8 kg) Munich malt (20 °L)

10 oz. (0.28 kg) chocolate malt

1 oz. (28 g) black malt

5.8 AAU Target hops (60 min.) (0.53 oz./15 g at 11% alpha acids)

Wyeast 2124 (Bohemian Lager) or White Labs WLP830 (German Lager) yeast

¾ cup (150 g) dextrose (if priming)

STEP BY STEP

Mash the grains at 154°F (68°C) for 60 minutes. Mash out, vorlauf, and then sparge at 170°F (77°C) to collect enough wort to result in 5 gallons (19 liters) after a 90-minute boil. Boil 90 minutes, adding hops at times indicated. Cool, aerate, and pitch yeast. Ferment at 65°F (18°C). After fermentation is complete, bottle or keg as usual.

EXTRACT WITH GRAINS OPTION: Substitute the pale and Munich malts in the all-grain recipe with 3 pounds (1.4 kilograms) light dried malt extract and 3.5 pounds (1.6 kilograms) Munich liquid malt extract. Steep grains in 3 quarts (2.8 liters) of water at 154°F (68°C) for 45 minutes. Add water to make 3 gallons (11 liters) of wort and bring to a boil. Stir in dried malt extract and boil for 60 minutes, adding hops at times indicated. Add Munich malt extract for final 15 minutes of the boil. Cool wort and transfer to fermenter. Top up to 5 gallons (19 liters) with cool water. Follow the remaining portion of the all-grain recipe.

- - - - - - - - - - - - - - - - - -

OCCIDENTAL BREWING COMPANY
DUNKEL LAGER

(5 gallons/19 L, all-grain) OG = 1.054
FG = 1.014 IBU = 27 SRM = 19 ABV = 5.2%

This smooth, malty beer based on the classic Munich style features an assortment of noble hops. Occidental breaks with tradition by using a clean-fermenting ale yeast in place of the lager yeast for additional yeast character and complexity.

INGREDIENTS

12 lb. (5.4 kg) Munich malt (6 °L)

6 AAU Perle pellet hops (60 min.) (0.75 oz./21 g at 8% alpha acids)

2 AAU Hallertau pellet hops (30 min.) (0.5 oz./14 g at 4% alpha acids)

2 AAU Hallertau pellet hops (5 min.) (0.5 oz./14 g at 4% alpha acids)

½ tsp. yeast nutrient (15 min.)

½ tsp. Irish moss (15 min.)

Wyeast 2565 (Kölsch) or White Labs WLP029 (German Ale/Kölsch)

¾ (150 g) dextrose (if priming)

STEP BY STEP

Mash the crushed grains with 4 gallons (15 liters) of 170°F (77°C) water to stabilize at 152°F (67°C) for 60 minutes. Sparge slowly with 175°F (79°C) water. Collect approximately 6.5 gallons (25 liters) of wort runoff to boil for

120 minutes. Add the hops, yeast nutrient, and Irish moss as per the schedule. Cool the wort to 75°F (24°C). Pitch the yeast and aerate heavily. Allow the beer to cool to 65°F (19°C). When evidence of fermentation is apparent, drop the temperature to 52°F (11°C). Hold at that temperature until fermentation is complete. Transfer to a carboy, avoiding any splashing. Condition for 2 weeks at 42°F (5°C), and then bottle or keg.

EXTRACT WITH GRAINS OPTION: Reduce the Munich malt to 2.5 pounds (1.13 kilograms) and add 3.3 pounds (1.5 kilograms) Munich liquid malt extract and 2 pounds (0.9 kilogram) amber dried malt extract. Steep the crushed grain in 3.4 quarts (3.3 liters) of water at 152°F (67°C) for 30 minutes. Remove grains from the wort and rinse with 3 quarts (2.8 liters) of hot water. Add water to make 3 gallons (11 liters), add malt extracts, and bring to a boil for 90 minutes. Add the hops, yeast nutrient, and Irish moss as per the schedule. Top off to 5 gallons (19 liters) after the boil, and follow the remaining portion of the all-grain recipe.

- - - - - - - - - - - - - - - - - -

PAULANER BRAUEREI
PAULANER HEFE-WEIZEN

(5 gallons/19 L, all-grain) OG = 1.053 FG = 1.010
IBU = 18 SRM = 5 ABV = 5.6%

This beer from Paulaner is a well-balanced example of a hefeweizen and a benchmark of the style. Watch your fermentation temperature to get the much-sought-after "breadiness" and the right balance in the banana/clove aroma. Prost!

INGREDIENTS

7.5 lb. (3.4 kg) wheat malt

3.25 lb. (1.5 kg) pilsner malt

4.75 AAU Hallertau-Hersbrücker hops (1.2 oz./34 g at 4% alpha acids)

Wyeast 3638 (Bavarian Wheat) or White Labs WLP380 (Hefeweizen IV) yeast

¾ cup (150 g) dextrose (for priming)

STEP BY STEP

Perform a single decoction mash with a 30-minute rest at 131°F (55°C) and a 45-minute rest at 153°F (67°C).

Mash out, vorlauf, and then sparge at 170°F (77°C). Boil for 120 minutes, adding the hops as instructed. Pitch the yeast and ferment at 68°F (20°C). Rack to secondary when fermentation is complete. Bottle or keg a few days later, when the beer falls clear.

EXTRACT WITH GRAINS OPTION: Replace the wheat malt and pilsner malt with 1.5 pounds (0.68 kilogram) Briess dried wheat malt extract, 3.75 pounds (1.7 kilograms) Weyermann Bavarian Hefeweizen liquid wheat malt extract (late addition), 2.1 pounds (0.95 kilogram) wheat malt, and 0.91 pound (0.41 kilogram) pilsner malt. In a large soup pot, heat 4.5 quarts (4.3 liters) of water to 169°F (76°C). Add the crushed grains to your grain bag. Submerge the bag and let the grains steep around 158°F (70°C) for 45 minutes. While the grains steep, begin heating 2.1 gallons (7.9 liters) of water in your brewpot. When the steep is over, remove 1.5 quarts (1.4 liters) of water from the brewpot and add to the "grain tea" in steeping pot. Place a colander over the brewpot and place the steeping bag in it. Pour the diluted grain tea through the grain bag. Heat the liquid in the brewpot to a boil, then stir in the dried malt extract, add the first charge of hops, and begin the 60-minute boil. With 15 minutes left in the boil, turn off the heat and stir in the liquid malt extract. Stir well to dissolve the extract, then resume heating. Chill the wort, transfer to your fermenter, and top up with filtered water to 5 gallons (19 liters). Follow the remaining portion of the all-grain recipe.

- - - - - - - - - - - - - - - - - - - -

RESURGENCE BREWING COMPANY
OKTOBERFEST

ᒪᒪᒪᒪᒪᒪ

**(5 gallons/19 L, all-grain) OG = 1.053 FG = 1.014
IBU = 25 SRM = 14 ABV = 5.4%**

This upstate New York brewery's oktoberfest is a traditional Marzen-style beer. This means it's lighter in body and color than what some US breweries sell as oktoberfest and it has a biscuity character.

INGREDIENTS

5 lb. (2.3 kg) pilsner malt

2.5 lb. (1.1 kg) light Munich malt (9 °L)

1.75 lb. (0.8 kg) dark Munich malt (20 °L)

1.25 lb. (0.57 kg) Caramunich I malt

0.75 lb. (0.34 kg) biscuit malt

7 AAU Perle hops (60 min.) (1 oz./28 g at 7% alpha acids)

½ tsp. Irish moss

White Labs WLP830 (German Lager) or Wyeast 2124 (Bohemian Lager) yeast

¾ cup (150 g) dextrose (if priming)

STEP BY STEP

Mill the grains and mix with 3.5 gallons (13.3 liters) of 164°F (73°C) strike water to reach a mash temperature of 152°F (67°C). Hold this temperature for 60 minutes. Vorlauf until your runnings are clear. Sparge the grains with 3.8 gallons (14.4 liters) of water at 170°F (77°C) and top up as necessary to obtain 6 gallons (23 liters) of wort. Boil for 60 minutes, adding hops according to the ingredient list and Irish moss if desired. After the boil, chill the wort to 55°F (13°C). Aerate the wort with pure oxygen or filtered air and pitch yeast. Ferment at 55°F (13°C) until fermentation is complete (about 1.014 specific gravity); you may want to increase temperature by a few degrees at the latter stages of fermentation to aid in diacetyl cleanup. Once the beer completes fermentation, bottle or keg and carbonate to approximately 2.5 volumes. You may want to cold-crash the beer to 35°F (2°C) for 48 hours prior to packaging to improve clarity. Store carbonated beer at near-freezing temperatures for at least 4 weeks before drinking.

PARTIAL MASH OPTION: Reduce the light Munich malt in the all-grain recipe to 2 pounds (0.91 kilogram) and replace the dark Munich and pilsner malts with 3 pounds (1.4 kilograms) pilsner liquid malt extract and 1.9 pounds (0.86 kilogram) Munich liquid malt extract. Place crushed grains in 1 or more grain bags. Bring 6 quarts (5.7 liters) of water to approximately 164°F (73°C) and mix grains into the water. Temperature should stabilize around 152°F (67°C). Hold for 60 minutes at this temperature. Remove the grain bags, place them in a colander, and wash with 6 quarts (5.7 liters) of hot water, then let drain fully. Add liquid extract while stirring, and stir until completely dissolved. Top off to 6 gallons (23 liters), then bring the wort to a boil. Follow the remaining portion of the all-grain recipe.

- - - - - - - - - - - - - - - - - - -

SCHNEIDER WEISSE
AVENTINUS

cccccc-

**(5 gallons/19 L, all-grain) OG = 1.076 FG = 1.016
IBU = 10 SRM = 21 ABV = 8.2%**

This wheat-based doppelbock was designed to compete with the true doppelbocks. It has notes of raisins, plums, bananas, cloves, and a touch of chocolate. A decoction mash and extended boil are needed to really bring out the dark malt and caramel flavors.

INGREDIENTS

9 lb. (4.1 kg) wheat malt

4.75 lb. (2.15 kg) pilsner malt

1.5 lb. (0.68 kg) Weyermann Caramunich malt

0.33 lb. (0.15 kg) Weyermann Carafa Special I malt

3 AAU Hallertau-Hersbrücker hops (60 min.) (0.75 oz./21 g at 4% alpha acids)

Wyeast 3068 (Weihenstephan Weizen) or White Labs WLP300 (Hefeweizen Ale) yeast

1¼ cup (250 g) dextose (if priming)

STEP BY STEP

Employ a triple decoction mash. Mash in cold with 2 to 2.5 quarts/pounds (4.2 to 5.2 liters/kilograms) water. Bring up to 95°F (35°C) with direct heat. Pull a third of the mash, and boil for 30 minutes. Add back to main mash to bring temperature up to 131°F (55°C). Repeat the decoction. Add back to main mash, which should be at 146°F (63°C). Repeat decoction, and boil for 45 minutes to 1 hour. Add back to main mash to raise temperature to 166°F (74°C). Let stand a few minutes, then move on to lautering and sparge. Wort boil time is 60 minutes, adding hops at the beginning of the boil. Cool, aerate, and pitch yeast. Ferment at 60°F (16°C). Condition in secondary for 3 to 4 weeks at 42°F (6°C), and then bottle or keg as normal.

EXTRACT WITH GRAINS OPTION: Replace the pilsner and wheat malts with 9.5 pounds (4.3 kilograms) liquid wheat malt extract. Place crushed grains in a nylon steeping bag and steep grains in 3 quarts (2.8 liters) of water at 152°F (67°C) for 45 minutes in a kitchen pot. While steeping, begin heating 2 gallons (7.6 liters) of water to a boil in your brewpot. After steep, place bag in colander over brewpot. Pour "grain tea" through bag, then rinse bag with 1.5 quarts (~1.5 liters) of 170°F (77°C) water. Bring brewpot to a boil, then remove from heat and stir in the liquid malt extract.

Stir until all the extract has dissolved, and return to a boil. Add hops, and boil wort for 60 minutes. Cool wort and top off to 5 gallons (19 liters). Follow the remaining portion of the all-grain recipe

TIPS FOR SUCCESS

Be sure to try to ferment this on the cooler side of the suggested fermentation temperature range. The hefe strain is known to throw some fusel alcohols during more vigorous fermentations, so keeping the fermentation vigor in check through proper temperature control is a good way to keep these unwanted byproducts out of your beer.

SNAKE RIVER
BREWING COMPANY
SEE YOU IN
HELLES

cccccc-

**(5 gallons/19 L, all-grain) OG = 1.048 FG = 1.010
IBU = 16 SRM = 3 ABV = 4.7%**

As Helles is the German word for light-colored, the brewery made sure to deliver with this bright beer. Snake River wanted to keep it as traditional as possible, so this beer has a full body for the ABV and is lightly hopped.

INGREDIENTS

9.5 lb. (4.3 kg) pilsner malt

3.75 AAU Crystal pellet hops (60 min.) (0.75 oz./21 g at 5% alpha acids)

1 AAU Tettnanger pellet hops (15 min.) (0.25 oz./7 g at 4% alpha acids)

½ tsp. yeast nutrient (15 min.)

White Labs WLP830 (German Lager) or Wyeast 2124 (Bohemian Lager) yeast

¾ cup (150 g) dextrose (if priming)

STEP BY STEP

This is a single-infusion mash. Mix the crushed grain with 3.2 gallons (12 liters) of low carbonate water at 168°F (76°C) to stabilize at 152°F (67°C). Hold at this temperature for 60 minutes. Sparge slowly with 175°F (79°C) water. Collect approximately 6 gallons (23 liters) of wort runoff to boil for 60 minutes. Add hops at times indicated. Cool the wort to 75°F (24°C). Pitch yeast, and aerate the wort heavily. Allow the beer to cool over the next few hours to 65°F (18°C). When evidence of fermentation is apparent,

drop the temperature to 52°F (11°C) and allow to ferment for 10 days. Transfer to a carboy, avoiding any splashing to prevent aerating the beer. Condition for 2 weeks at 42°F (5°C), and then bottle or keg.

EXTRACT ONLY OPTION: Replace the pilsner malt in the recipe with 6.6 pounds (3 kilograms) Briess Pilsen liquid malt extract. Add the liquid malt extract to 5 gallons (19 liters) of low carbonate water that has been heated to near boiling. Stir until all the extract has been dissolved. Bring to a boil and boil for 60 minutes, adding hops at the times indicated. Follow the remaining portion of the all-grain recipe.

- - - - - - - - - - - - - - - - - - -

SPOETZL BREWERY
SHINER BOCK

(5 gallons/19 L, all-grain) OG = 1.043 FG 1.010
IBU = 17 SRM = 16 ABV = 4.3%

The best-known beer from the Spoetzl Brewery was originally a seasonal release. That changed in 1973, and fans have enjoyed it year-round ever since. This bock has won all the big awards, including a silver medal at the World Beer Cup and gold medal at the Great American Beer Festival.

INGREDIENTS

3 lb. (1.36 kg) 6-row pale malt

3 lb. (1.36 kg) Vienna malt (4 °L)

2.66 lb. (1.21 kg) corn grits

0.66 lb. (0.29 kg) crystal malt (60 °L)

3 oz. (86 g) roasted barley (500 °L)

4.62 AAU Brewer's Gold hops (0.6 oz./16 g at 8% alpha acids)

1 tsp. Irish moss

⅛ tsp. yeast nutrient

White Labs WLP940 (Mexican Lager) or Wyeast 2247 (European Lager) yeast (4 qt./4L starter)

⅞ cup (175 g) dextrose (if priming)

STEP BY STEP

In a large kitchen pot, mix corn grits and 5 ounces (141 grams) of the 6-row malt with 3.3 quarts (3.1 liters) of 159°F (71°C) water to make a cereal mash. Hold cereal mash at 148°F (64°C) for 15 minutes. While cereal mash is resting, pour the rest of the grains into your brew kettle and mash in to 140°F (60°C). Use about 1.66 gallons (6.3 liters) of water

for an initially thick mash. Heat the cereal mash to a boil, stirring constantly, and boil for 30 minutes. After boiling the cereal mash, add it to the main mash and adjust temperature with water to 152°F (67°C). This should bring your mash thickness into the normal range. Mash for 45 minutes, then heat mash to 165°F (74°C). Stir frequently, and expect the temperature to keep climbing a bit after you shut off the heat. (Any temperature under 170°F/77°C is fine). Recirculate until wort is clear, then collect about 5 gallons (19 liters) of wort, sparging with water sufficiently hot to keep grain bed between 165 to 170°F (74 to 77°C). Add 1.5 gallons (6 liters) of water and boil wort for 90 minutes, adding bittering hops for final 60 minutes. Add yeast nutrient and Irish moss with 15 minutes left in the boil. Cool wort quickly to 54 to 65°F (12 to 18°C), aerate well, and pitch yeast sediment from yeast starter. Ferment at 54°F (12°C) for 10 to 12 days, then let temperature rise to 60°F (16°C) for a diacetyl rest. This should take about 2 days, but taste the beer before cooling. Rack beer to secondary fermenter and cool beer to 32 to 40°F (0 to 4°C). Lager for 30 to 45 days.

EXTRACT WITH GRAINS OPTION: Substitute the 6-row pale malt, Vienna malt, and corn grits in the all-grain recipe with 2.8 pounds (1.3 kilograms) Briess light liquid malt extract, 1.9 pounds (0.86 kilogram) brewer's corn syrup, 0.25 pound (0.11 kilogram) 6-row pale malt, and 1 pound (0.45 kilogram) Munich malt (10 °L). Heat 1.75 gallons (6.6 liters) of water in your brewpot and 3 quart (2.8 liters) of steeping water in a separate 6- to 8-quart (6- to 8-liter) pot. Place crushed grains in a steeping bag. When steeping water reaches 169°F (76°C), turn off heat, and begin steeping grains. The temperature of the steep should drop to around 158°F (70°C). When the temperature of the steeping water falls to 148°F (64°C), remove grain bag from steeping water. Do not rinse grains with water or squeeze bag. Add "grain tea" from the steeping pot to your brewpot and heat to a boil. Once boiling, shut off heat and stir in malt extract. Boil for 60 minutes, adding hops once initial foaming subsides. Add corn syrup for the last 15 minutes of boil, stirring well to avoid scorching. Cool and top off to 5 gallons (19 liters). Follow the remaining portion of the all-grain recipe.

- - - - - - - - - - - - - - - - -

SPRINGFIELD BREWING COMPANY
AVIATOR DOPPELBOCK

ϾϾϾϾϾϾ

**(5 gallons/19 L, all-grain) OG = 1.078 FG = 1.018
IBU = 25 SRM = 18 ABV = 7.8%**

This winter seasonal was brewed by *BYO*'s own technical editor, Ashton Lewis. Springfield Brewing Company says that Aviator drinks like dessert in a glass. Recommended pairings include dried fruits, roasted nuts, and creamy cheeses.

INGREDIENTS

11.6 lb. (5.3 kg) Weyermann Pale Ale malt

2.8 lb. (1.27 kg) Weyermann Munich I malt (6 °L)

1.6 lb. (0.72 kg) Weyermann Munich II malt (9 °L)

2.5 oz. (71 g) chocolate malt (350 °L)

2 oz. (57 g) Weyermann Carafa Special III malt (525 °L)

8 AAU Perle pellet hops (60 min.) (1 oz./28 g at 8% alpha acids)

0.5 oz. (14 g) German Tradition pellet hops (0 min.)

½ tsp. Irish moss (30 min.)

½ tsp. yeast nutrient (15 min.)

White Labs WLP830 (German Lager), Wyeast 2206 (Bavarian Lager), or Fermentis Saflager W-34/70 (or Saflager S-189, if available) yeast

¾ cup (150 g) dextrose (if priming)

STEP BY STEP

Mash the grains at 154°F (68°C) in 6 gallons (23 liters) of water for 60 minutes. Mash out, vorlauf, and then sparge at 175°F (79°C) to collect approximately 6.3 gallons (23.8 liters) of wort. Boil for 90 minutes, adding the hops, Irish moss, and yeast nutrient as instructed. After the boil is complete, cool the wort to 50°F (10°C) or just below, and transfer it to your fermenter. Pitch the yeast and aerate the wort heavily. Allow the beer to ferment at 50°F (10°C) until final gravity is reached. Gently transfer to a carboy, avoiding any splashing to prevent aerating the beer. Chill to almost freezing temperature and allow the beer to condition for an additional week. Prime and bottle condition or keg and force carbonate to 2.1 volumes CO_2. Allow the beer to age for 4 more weeks to fully develop the flavors.

PARTIAL MASH OPTION: Substitute the Weyermann pale ale malt with 6.6 pounds (3 kilograms) Briess light unhopped liquid malt extract and 1 pound (0.45 kilogram) light dried malt extract. Also, bump up the Perle hop addition (60 minutes) to 1.25 ounces (35 grams). Mash the milled grain in 2.5 gallons (9.5 liters) of water at 154°F (68°C) for 30 minutes. Remove the grains from the wort and rinse with 4 quarts (3.8 liters) of hot water. Boil for 30 minutes. Add the liquid malt extract, dried malt extract, and first hop addition, then boil for 60 more minutes. While boiling, add the Irish moss and yeast nutrient as indicated. Chill the wort, transfer to your fermenter, and top up with filtered water to 5 gallons (19 liters). Follow the remaining portion of the all-grain recipe.

THUNDER ISLAND BREWING COMPANY
VITAMIN K KÖLSCH

ϾϾϾϾϾϾ

**(5 gallons/19 L, all-grain) OG = 1.045 FG = 1.010
IBU = 22 SRM = 4 ABV = 4.6%**

This light yellow kölsch is firmly in the German style, despite being brewed in Cascade Locks, Oregon. It's an easy sipper that keeps it interesting—a perfect beer to keep on tap all summer.

INGREDIENTS

8.5 lb. (3.8 kg) 2-row pale malt

8 oz. (0.23 kg) white wheat malt

8 oz. (0.23 kg) Munich malt

6.2 AAU Magnum pellet hops (50 min.) (0.5 oz./14 g at 12.3% alpha acids)

½ tsp. Irish moss (15 min.)

½ tsp. yeast nutrient (15 min.)

White Labs WLP029 (German Ale/Kölsch) or Wyeast 2565 (Kölsch) yeast

¾ cup (150 g) dextrose (if priming)

STEP BY STEP

Mash the crushed grains with 3.5 gallons (13 liters) of 170°F (77°C) water to stabilize at 150°F (66°C) for 60 minutes. Slowly sparge with 175°F (79°C) water. Collect approximately 6 gallons (23 liters) of wort runoff to boil for 60 minutes. Add the hops, Irish moss, and yeast nutrient as per the schedule. Cool the wort to 75°F (24°C). Pitch your yeast and aerate the wort heavily. Allow the beer to cool to 68°F (20°C). Hold at that temperature until fermentation is complete. Transfer to a carboy, avoiding any splashing to prevent aerating the beer. Allow the beer to condition 1 week, and then bottle or keg.

PARTIAL MASH OPTION: Reduce the 2-row pale malt to 2 pounds (0.9 kilogram) and add 3.3 pounds (1.5 kilograms) Muntons extra light liquid malt extract and 0.75 pound (0.34 kilogram) Muntons light dried malt extract. Steep the crushed grain in 2.5 gallons (9.5 liters) of water at 150°F (66°C) for 30 minutes. Remove grains from the wort and rinse with 2 quarts (1.9 liters) of hot water. Add the malt extracts and boil for 60 minutes, adding hops, Irish moss, and yeast nutrient as per the schedule. When done, add the wort to 2 gallons (7.6 liters) of cold water in a sanitized fermenter and top off with cold water up to 5 gallons (19 liters). Follow the remaining portion of the all-grain recipe.

VICTORY BREWING COMPANY
ZELTBIER

(5 gallons/19 L, all-grain) OG = 1.056 FG = 1.014
IBU = 21 SRM = 3 ABV = 5.7%

One of Victory's harder-to-find seasonals, this crisp lager is worth tracking down—or brewing, of course! It's just the thing for fall weather. For best results, use a quality German pilsner malt, and don't stray from the recommended German hops.

INGREDIENTS

11 lb. (5 kg) pilsner malt

0.5 lb. (0.23 kg) Carapils malt

2 AAU Hallertau Tradition hops (60 min.) (0.5 oz./14 g at 4% alpha acids)

2 AAU Hallertau Mittelfrüh hops (30 min.) (0.5 oz./14 g at 4% alpha acids)

4.5 AAU Tettnang hops (15 min.) (1 oz./28 g at 4.5% alpha acids)

Wyeast 2124 (Bohemian Lager) or White Labs WLP830 (German Lager) yeast

⅔ cup (133 g) dextrose (if priming)

STEP BY STEP

This recipe calls for a decoction mash, which Victory does! Infuse the grains with 3.6 gallons (13.6 liters) of water to stabilize the mash at 122°F (50°C). Then raise the mash temperature to 145°F (63°C) and hold for 10 minutes. Pull ⅓ of the mash and decoct, going through a 15-minute rest at 158°F (70°C) before boiling. Mix back into the main mash, hold for 20 minutes, and then raise to 168°F (76°C) for mash-off. Vorlauf until your runnings are clear. Sparge the grains with 3.6 gallons (13.6 liters) and top up as necessary to obtain 6 gallons (23 liters) of wort. Boil for 60 minutes, adding hops according to the ingredient list and Irish moss as desired. After the boil, chill the wort to slightly below fermentation temperature, about 48°F (9°C). Aerate the wort with pure oxygen or filtered air, and pitch yeast. Ferment at 50°F (10°C) until gravity reaches about 1.025, then increase temperature to 54°F (12°C) and hold for 2 days. Once the beer completes fermentation, reduce temperature to 32°F (0°C) over the course of 1 week, and hold there for at least 6 weeks. After cold conditioning, bottle or keg the beer and carbonate to approximately 2.25 volumes.

EXTRACT WITH GRAINS OPTION: Substitute the pilsner malt in the all-grain recipe with 7.5 pounds (3.4 kilograms) pilsner liquid malt extract. Bring 5.4 gallons (20.4 liters) of water to approximately 165°F (74°C) and hold there, steeping the specialty malt in a grain bag for 15 minutes. Remove the grain bag and let drain fully. Add liquid extract while stirring. Bring the wort to a boil. Follow the remaining portion of the all-grain recipe

TIPS FOR SUCCESS

Victory cofounder Ron Barchet recommends, above and beyond anything else, getting your hands on the best possible ingredients, and to look a little deeper into the composition of those ingredients than you ordinarily would. For example, if you can get German pils malt that uses Steffi or Barke barley varieties, you will notice a particularly characterful maltiness. He also notes that it is a good idea for homebrewers to rack the beer off of its yeast cake before cold conditioning to minimize the risk of yeast autolysis and any loss of foam quality. Finally, be sure to pour vigorously (preferably into a proper Isar Krug mug!) to release all the wonderful aromatics in this beer.

CHAPTER THIRTEEN

NORTH AMERICAN ALES & LAGERS

Beer Pictured on Left; see page 200

ANCHOR BREWING COMPANY
ANCHOR CALIFORNIA LAGER

꧁꧂

**(5 gallons/19 L, all-grain) OG = 1.047 FG = 1.012
IBU = 32 SRM = 4 ABV = 4.8%**

California Lager is Anchor's re-creation of a historic lager brewed in California way back in 1876, at a brewery named Boca. It pours a golden color with a creamy head and drinks easy with a smooth finish.

INGREDIENTS

10 lb. (4.54 kg) 2-row pale malt

4.9 AAU Cluster pellet hops (60 min.) (0.65 oz./18 g at 7.5% alpha acids)

2.6 AAU Cluster pellet hops (30 min.) (0.35 oz./10 g at 7.5% alpha acids)

White Labs WLP830 (German Lager) or Wyeast 2206 (Bavarian Lager) or Fermentis Saflager S-23 yeast

0.25 oz. (7 g) gypsum (optional if using very low-mineral water)

⅔ cup (133 g) dextrose (if priming)

STEP BY STEP

Mill the grains and mix with 3.75 gallons (14 liters) of 157°F (69°C) strike water and optional gypsum (see ingredients list) to reach a mash temperature of 149°F (65°C). Hold this temperature for 60 minutes. Vorlauf until your runnings are clear. Sparge the grains with 3.45 gallons (13 liters) of 168°F (76°C) water and top up if necessary to obtain 6 gallons (23 liters) of 1.039 SG wort. Boil for 60 minutes, adding hops according to the ingredients list. After the boil, turn off the heat and chill the wort to slightly below fermentation temperature, about 48°F (9°C). Aerate the wort with pure oxygen or filtered air, and pitch the yeast. Ferment at 50°F (10°C) for 7 days before raising to 60°F (16°C) for 3 days for a diacetyl rest. Slowly lower the beer to 34°F (1°C). Once at terminal gravity (approximately 14 days total), bottle or keg the beer and carbonate. Lager at 34°F (1°C) for approximately 1 month before serving.

EXTRACT WITH GRAINS OPTION: Substitute the 2-row pale malt in the all-grain recipe with 6.6 pounds (3 kilograms) golden liquid malt extract. Bring 5.5 gallons (21 liters) of water and optional gypsum (see ingredients list) to a boil, turn off the flame, and stir in the liquid malt extract until completely dissolved. Top up with water if necessary to obtain 6 gallons (23 liters) of 1.039 SG wort. Boil for 60 minutes. Follow the remaining portion of the all-grain recipe.

ANCHOR BREWING COMPANY
ANCHOR STEAM BEER

꧁꧂

**(5 gallons/19 L, all-grain) OG = 1.050 FG = 1.013
IBU = 30 SRM = 9 ABV = 4.9%**

This beer takes its name from the way beer used to be made in the cool climate of San Francisco. (On rooftops, in the nineteenth century, open containers were used to help cool the beer quickly, releasing an abundance of steam over the skyline.) Anchor Steam is the beer that convinced Fritz Maytag to buy the brewery in 1965 and carry on the brewing tradition that started there in the late 1800s.

INGREDIENTS

9 lb. 2 oz. (4.1 kg) 2-row pale malt

1 lb. 5 oz. (0.6 kg) caramel malt (40 °L)

0.25 oz. (7 g) gypsum (optional if using very low-mineral water)

4.8 AAU US Northern Brewer pellet hops (60 min.) (0.5 oz./14 g at 9.6% alpha acids)

2.4 AAU US Northern Brewer pellet hops (20 min.) (0.25 oz./7 g at 9.6% alpha acids)

0.5 oz. (14 g) US Northern Brewer pellet hops (0 min.)

White Labs WLP810 (San Francisco Lager) or Wyeast 2112 (California Lager) yeast

⅔ cup (130 g) dextrose (if priming)

STEP BY STEP

Mash the grains (with optional gypsum) at 149°F (65°C). Mash out, vorlauf, and then sparge with 3.33 gallons (12.6 liters) of 168°F (76°C) water. Top up if necessary to obtain 6 gallons (23 liters) of 1.041 SG wort. Boil the wort for 60 minutes, adding the hops according to the ingredients list. After the boil, turn off the heat and chill the wort to slightly below fermentation temperature, about 59°F (15°C). Pitch the yeast and ferment at 61°F (16°C) for 7 days before raising the temperature to 66°F (19°C) for 3 days for a diacetyl rest. Once the beer reaches final gravity (approximately 14 days total), bottle or keg the beer and carbonate. Store cold for approximately 2 weeks before serving.

EXTRACT WITH GRAINS OPTION: Substitute 6.25 pounds (2.8 kilograms) golden liquid malt extract for the 2-row pale malt. Place the milled grains in a muslin brewing bag and steep in 3 quarts (2.8 liters) of 149°F (65°C) water for 15 minutes. Remove the grain and rinse with 1 gallon (3.8 liters) of hot water. Add water and gypsum (if using) to reach a volume of 5.6 gallons (21.2 liters), and heat to boiling. Turn off the heat, add the liquid malt extract, and stir until completely dissolved. Top up with filtered water if necessary to obtain 6 gallons (23 liters) of 1.041 SG wort. Follow the remaining portion of the all-grain recipe.

- - - - - - - - - - - - - - - - -

ANDERSON VALLEY BREWING COMPANY
SUMMER SOLSTICE SEASONAL ALE

(5 gallons/19 L, all-grain) OG = 1.049 FG = 1.011 IBU = 5 SRM = 12 ABV = 5%

Anderson Valley describes this summer sipper as a slightly sweet, malty session beer with a creamy mouthfeel and clean finish.

INGREDIENTS

8 lb. 14 oz. (4 kg) 2-row pale malt

13 oz. (0.38 kg) crystal malt (40 °L)

11 oz. (0.30 kg) crystal malt (80 °L)

2.3 AAU Cascade hops (whirlpool) (0.45 oz./13 gat 5% alpha acids)

1–2 vanilla beans (post-fermentation)

Wyeast 2112 (California Lager) or White Labs WLP810 (San Francisco Lager) yeast

⅔ cup (133 g) dextrose (if priming)

STEP BY STEP

Mash the grains at 150°F (66°C). Vorlauf until your runnings are clear, sparge, and then boil the wort for 60 minutes. Add the hops at knockout, stir the wort to create a whirlpool, and let them steep in the whirlpool for at least 20 minutes. After the whirlpool, chill the wort to 65°F (18°C), aerate well, and pitch the yeast. Ferment at 65°F (18°C). Split the vanilla bean lengthwise, then chop. Place in a small bowl and add just enough vodka to cover. Soak for 7 days. When the beer

reaches final gravity, add the vanilla bean tincture and wait another 7 days. Then bottle or keg as normal.

EXTRACT WITH GRAINS OPTION: Scale the 2-row pale malt down to 3 ounces (85 grams), and add 2 pounds (0.91 kilogram) light dried malt extract and 4 pounds (1.8 kilograms) light liquid malt extract (late addition). Place crushed grains in a steeping bag and submerge in 3 quarts (2.8 liters) of water at 161°F (72°C). Steep at 150°F (66°C) for 45 minutes. Begin heating 2 gallons (7.6 liters) of water in your brewpot. After steep, lift grain bag into colander placed over brewpot to collect the liquid. Stir in the dried malt extract and bring to a boil. Boil for 60 minutes. Stir in liquid malt extract with 20 minutes left in the boil. Add the hops at the end of the boil, stir the wort to create a whirlpool, and let them steep for at least 20 minutes. Chill the wort, transfer to fermenter, and top up with cool water to reach 5 gallons (19 liters). Follow the remainder of the all-grain recipe.

- - - - - - - - - - - - - - - - -

BROOKLYN BREWERY
BROOKLYN LAGER

(5 gallons/19 L, all-grain) OG = 1.052 FG = 1.012 IBU = 30 SRM = 13 ABV= 5.2%

Brooklyn Lager is Brooklyn Brewery's flagship beer. It is loosely based on the old Vienna lager style, derivations of which were popular in parts of the United States in the late 1800s. Its bitterness is snappy, with a firm malt core, and the beer is dry hopped.

INGREDIENTS

9 lb. 6 oz. (4.25 kg) American 2-row pale malt

14 oz. (0.40 kg) Munich malt (10 °L)

11 oz. (0.31 kg) caramel malt (60 °L)

4.6 AAU Willamette hops (75 min.) (1 oz./28 g at 4.6% alpha acids)

2.5 AAU Cascade hops (35 min.) (0.33 oz./9.3 g at 7.5% alpha acids)

2.5 AAU Vanguard hops (35 min.) (0.45 oz./13 g at 5.6% alpha acids)

0.5 oz. (14 g) Hallertau Mittelfrüh hops (2 min.)

0.5 oz. (14 g) Saphir hops (2 min.)

0.5 oz. (14 g) Cascade hops (2 min.)

0.75 oz. (21 g) Cascade hops (dry hop)

1.5 oz. (42 g) Hallertau Mittelfrüh hops (dry hop)

White Labs WLP833 (German Bock Lager) yeast

⅔ cup (133 g) dextrose (if priming)

STEP BY STEP

Mash the grains at 118°F (47°C) for 20 minutes. Ramp up to 135°F (57°C) and hold for 5 minutes. To reach the saccharification temperature of 156°F (69°C), there are two methods, depending on your equipment. If your heat source can raise the temperature of the mash rapidly (in 5 to 10 minutes), then do so. If not, add 200°F (93°C) water to the mash, stirring vigorously to avoid hot spots, until you reach the target temperature. (American 2-row pale malt is diastatically powerful, and if the mash isn't heated quickly enough, the resulting wort will be too fermentable.) Hold for 35 minutes at 156°F (69°C), then ramp up to mash out at 170°F (77°C). Vorlauf and then sparge at 170°F (77°C) until you've collected enough wort (gravity should be 13 degrees Plato/1.053 specific gravity). Boil for 75 minutes, adding the hops as instructed. (Brooklyn Brewery's boil is 15 minutes longer, but boiling longer over a direct flame would result in too much color development.) If necessary, adjust the volume to 5 gallons (19 liters). Cool to 55°F (13°C) and pitch the yeast. Once activity has clearly started (approximately 24 hours for lagers), ferment at 52°F (11°C). As activity subsides toward the end of fermentation, allow a free rise to 60°F (16°C) over 48 hours. Once the fermentation is finished, bring the temperature to 36°F (2.2°C) for lagering. After 1 week at 36°F (2.2°C), add the dry hops and hold for 10 days. Bottle or keg as usual.

EXTRACT WITH GRAINS OPTION: Scale the American 2-row pale malt down to 7 ounces (0.2 kilogram), and add 2 pounds (0.91 kilogram) Briess light dried malt extract and 4 pounds (1.8 kilograms) Briess light liquid malt extract to the ingredient list. Place the crushed grains in a steeping bag and steep in 3 quarts (2.8 liters) of water in your brewpot at 154°F (68°C) for 60 minutes. Lift the grain bag and place it in a colander suspended over the brewpot. Rinse the grains with 1.5 quarts (1.4 liters) of 170°F (77°C) water. Add water to the "grain tea" to make at least 3.5 gallons (13 liters), then dissolve the dried malt extract and bring to a boil. Boil for 75 minutes, adding the hops at the times indicated. Stir in the liquid malt extract during the final 15 minutes of the boil. Chill, then top up with filtered water to reach 5 gallons (19 liters). Follow the remaining portion of the all-grain recipe.

EPIC BREWING COMPANY
LOS LOCOS

**(5 gallons/19 L, all-grain) OG = 1.049 FG = 1.012
IBU = 20 SRM = 3 ABV = 4.9%**

Inspired by the Mexican cuisine at chef Troy Guard's Los Chingones restaurant in Denver, Colorado, Los Locos is a sessionable, refreshing lager brewed with corn, natural lime juice, and just a hint of salt. "Los Locos is the spirit of summer in a can—perfect for enjoying on the hammock or with your friends at a raging pachanga," says Kevin Crompton, Epic's brewmaster.

INGREDIENTS

8 lb. (3.6 kg) pilsner malt

1 lb. (0.45 kg) flaked maize

1 lb. (0.45 kg) Carapils malt

15 AAU Amarillo hops (10 min.) (1.5 oz./43 g at 10% alpha acids)

Sea salt (to taste)

Lime juice (to taste)

White Labs WLP940 (Mexican Lager) or Wyeast 2002 (Gambrinus Lager) yeast

⅔ cup (133 g) dextrose (if priming)

STEP BY STEP

Mill the grains and mix with 3.2 gallons (12.1 liters) of 164°F (73°C) strike water to reach a mash temperature of 152°F (67°C). Hold this temperature for 60 minutes. Vorlauf until your runnings are clear. Sparge the grains with 5 gallons (19 liters) of water and top up as necessary to obtain 6 gallons (23 liters) of wort. Boil the wort for 60 minutes, adding hops according to the ingredient list. Chill the wort to slightly below fermentation temperature, about 52°F (11°C). Aerate and pitch the yeast. Ferment at 54°F (12°C) until the completion of primary fermentation, then let the temperature rise to 60°F (16°C) for a diacetyl rest. Add lime juice and salt to taste—you may want to create a salt water solution to aid in adjustment/evaluation. Crash the beer to 35°F (2°C) for 48 hours, and bottle or keg the beer and carbonate to approximately 2.25 volumes. After carbonation, lager at near-freezing temperatures for at least 6 weeks before serving.

EXTRACT WITH GRAINS OPTION: Substitute the pilsner malt and flaked maize in the all-grain recipe with 4 pounds (1.8 kilograms) Pilsen dried malt extract and 1 pound (0.45

kilogram) corn sugar. Bring 5.4 gallons (20.4 liters) of water to approximately 162°F (72°C) and hold there. Steep grains for 15 minutes, then remove bag and allow to drain into the wort. Add dried extract and corn sugar while stirring, and stir until completely dissolved. Boil 60 minutes. Follow the remaining portion of the all-grain recipe.

TIPS FOR SUCCESS

When adding the sea salt and lime juice, start small and build up. They're easy flavors to overdo, and they should be background notes rather than starring players. Also, if you find that you're not getting enough citrus kick out of the Amarillo hops, you can consider adding an additional half-ounce at flame out to boost the tropical/citrus fruit aroma.

FLYING DOG BREWERY
NUMERO UNO

ᒪᒪᒪᒪᒪᒪ

(5 gallons/19 L, all-grain) OG = 1.045 FG = 1.011
IBU = 13 SRM = 4 ABV = 4.5%

Numero Uno is Flying Dog's summer seasonal release. Flaked maize makes up ⅓ of the malt bill and highlights the distinctive corn and cracker flavor traditionally found in Mexican lagers.

INGREDIENTS

6 lb. (2.7 kg) 2-row pale malt

3 lb. (1.4 kg) flaked maize

4 oz. (113 g) Munich malt (10 °L)

1 oz. (30 mL) agave nectar (15 min.)

7 g lime peel (secondary)

2.5 AAU Amarillo hops (60 min.) (0.25 oz./7 g at 10% alpha acids)

4 AAU Saaz hops (5 min.) (1 oz./28 g at 4% alpha acids)

White Labs WLP940 (Mexican Lager) or Wyeast 2002 (Gambrinus Lager) yeast

⅔ cup (133 g) dextrose (if priming)

STEP BY STEP

Mill the grains and mix with 3 gallons (11.4 liters) of 163°F (73°C) strike water to reach a mash temperature of 151°F (66°C). Hold this temperature for 60 minutes. Vorlauf until your runnings are clear. Sparge the grains with 5.5 gallons (20.8 liters) and top up as necessary to obtain 6 gallons (23 liters) of wort. Boil for 60 minutes, adding hops and agave nectar according to the ingredient list. Chill the wort to 54°F

(12°C), aerate, and pitch yeast. Ferment at 54°F (12°C) until gravity reaches 1.024, then let the temperature rise to 60°F (16°C) until fermentation completes for a diacetyl rest. Add lime peel and age to taste (5 to 7 days). Crash the beer to 35°F (2°C) for 48 hours, and bottle or keg the beer and carbonate to approximately 2.25 volumes. After carbonation, lager at near-freezing temperatures for at least 6 weeks before serving.

PARTIAL MASH OPTION: Reduce the 2-row pale malt in the all-grain recipe to 1 pound (0.45 kilogram) and the flaked maize to 1.25 pounds (0.57 kilogram), and add 3.3 pounds (1.5 kilograms) pale liquid malt extract. Bring 1 gallon (4 liters) of water to approximately 163°F (73°C). Place the crushed malt and flaked maize in a muslin bag and submerge in the water. Temperature should stabilize at 151°F (66°C), then hold there for about 60 minutes. Remove the grain bag and place in a colander. Wash the grains with 1 gallon (4 liters) of hot water. Add the liquid extract while stirring, and stir until completely dissolved. Top up to 6 gallons (23 liters), and bring the wort to a boil for 60 minutes. Follow the remaining portion of the all-grain recipe.

TIPS FOR SUCCESS

There are some minor diacetyl concerns with this yeast, so be sure to increase your temperatures once the gravity reaches 1.024. As for the contact time/weight on the lime peel, a lot will depend on your limes and process, so continue to taste throughout the post-fermentation period, and when it's to your liking, package it up.

FLYING FISH
BREWING COMPANY
FARMHOUSE
SUMMER ALE

ᒪᒪᒪᒪᒪᒪ

(5 gallons/19 L, all-grain) OG = 1.045–1.048
FG = 1.010–1.011 IBU = 18 SRM = 3+
ABV = 4.3–4.6%

The crisp, slightly sour flavor of this beer comes from a sour mash with a small portion of the grain. Don't worry—a sour mash is sanitized by the boil so you won't run the risk of "infecting" your system.

INGREDIENTS

8.7 lb. (3.9 kg) of 2-row malt

0.5 lb. (0.23 kg) wheat malt

3 oz. (85 g) Carapils (dextrin) malt

3 oz. (85 g) pale 2-row malt (for sour mash)

1 AAU Styrian Golding hops (first wort hop) (0.25 oz./7 g at 4.0% alpha acids)

3.5 AAU Magnum hops (60 min.) (0.25 oz./1.8 g at 14% alpha acids)

2.1 AAU Styrian Golding hops (30 min.) (0.53 oz./15 g at 4.0% alpha acids)

1.4 AAU Styrian Golding hops (2 min.) (0.35 oz./10 g at 4.0% alpha acids)

White Labs WLP005 (British Ale) or Wyeast 1098 (British Ale) yeast

¾ cup (150 g) of dextrose (for priming)

STEP BY STEP

For the sour mash, start 2 to 3 days in advance. Steep 3 ounces (85 grams) of 2-row pale malt in a pint of 150°F (66°C) water, then cover and let sit for 2 to 3 days. On brew day, mash the grains and sour mash at 152°F (67°C) for 60 minutes. Sparge as normal and collect enough wort to boil for 90 minutes and have a 5.5-gallon (20.9-liter) yield (about 7 gallons or 26 liters). Boil the wort for 90 minutes, adding the hops at the times indicated in the ingredients list. When the boil is complete, chill the wort to pitching temperature, aerate well, and pitch the yeast. Ferment at 68°F (20°C) until final gravity is reached. Bottle or keg as usual.

EXTRACT WITH GRAINS OPTION: Omit the 8.7-pound (3.9-kilogram) portion of 2-row malt. Add 3.3 pounds (1.5 kilograms) Coopers light liquid malt extract and 2.2 pounds (1 kilogram) Briess wheat dried malt extract. Perform the sour mash as described in the all-grain instructions, 2 to 3 days in advance of brew day. On brew day, steep the sour mash along with the wheat and dextrin malt grains in 3 gallons (11 liters) of water at 152°F (67°C) for 30 minutes. Remove the grains from the wort, add the first wort addition of Styrian Golding hops, liquid malt extract, and dried malt extract, and bring to a boil, adding the hops as indicated in the ingredients list. Now add wort to 2 gallons cool water in a sanitary fermenter and top off with cool water to 5.5 gallons (21 liters). Cool the wort, aerate well, and pitch the yeast. Follow the remainder of the all-grain recipe.

GLACIER BREWHOUSE
IMPERIAL BLONDE ALE

≈≈≈≈≈≈-

(5 gallons/19 L, all-grain) OG = 1.081 FG = 1.013
IBU = 25 SRM = 6 ABV = 9%

This light-colored American strong ale from Anchorage, Alaska, is malty, creamy, and smooth. Also known as Ice Axe Ale, it's a rare example of a double-strength blonde.

INGREDIENTS

3 lb. 14 oz. (1.8 kg) 2-row pale malt

8.5 lb. (3.9 kg) Maris Otter pale malt

14 oz. (0.39 kg) pilsner malt

10 oz. (0.28 kg) flaked barley

12 oz. (0.34 kg) Carapils dextrin malt

2.5 lb. (1.13 kg) clover honey (5 min.)

5.25 AAU Centennial pellet hops (60 min.) (0.5 oz./14 g at 10.5% alpha acids)

2.6 AAU Centennial pellet hops (30 min.) (0.25 oz./7 g at 10.5% alpha acids)

5.25 AAU Centennial pellet hops (0 min.) (0.5 oz./14.2 g at 10.5% alpha acids)

½ tsp. yeast nutrient (15 min.)

½ tsp. Irish moss (15 min.)

White Labs WLP001 (California Ale) or Wyeast 1056 (American Ale) yeast

¾ cup (150 g) dextrose (if priming)

STEP BY STEP

Mix the crushed grains with 4.5 gallons (17 liters) of 175°F (79°C) water to stabilize at 155°F (68°C) for 60 minutes. Sparge slowly with 175°F (79°C) water. Collect approximately 6 gallons (23 liters) of wort runoff to boil for 60 minutes. Add the hops, honey, Irish moss, and yeast nutrient as per the schedule. Cool the wort to 75°F (24°C). Pitch your yeast and aerate the wort heavily. Allow the beer to cool to 68°F (20°C). Hold at that temperature until fermentation is complete. Transfer to a carboy, avoiding any splashing to prevent aerating the beer. Allow the beer to condition for 1 week, and then bottle or keg.

PARTIAL MASH OPTION: Reduce the 2-row pale malt in the all-grain recipe to 14 ounces (0.39 kilogram) and replace the Maris Otter pale malt with 6.6 pounds (3 kilograms) Muntons light unhopped malt extract and 2.5 pounds (1.13 kilograms) dried malt extract. Steep the crushed grains in 5.5 gallons (21 liters) of water for 30 minutes. Remove grains from the wort and rinse with 2 quarts (1.8 liters) of hot water. Add the liquid and dried malt extracts and boil for 60 minutes. Follow the remaining portion of the all-grain recipe.

- - - - - - - - - - - - - - -

HEILEMAN'S
OLD STYLE LIGHT

**(5 gallons/19 L, all-grain) OG = 1.037 FG = 1.005
IBU = 14   SRM = 2-4 ABV = 4.0%**

If Old Style Light sounds familiar, that's because this beer has been around for over 100 years. A crisp, fresh, classic American lager, Old Style remains a mainstay in the Midwest—including at Chicago Cubs games.

INGREDIENTS

5 lb. 10 oz. (2.6 kg) 6-row pale malt

1.5 lb. (0.68 kg) rice syrup solids

2.7 AAU Cluster hops (60 min.) (0.38 oz./11 g at 7.0% alpha acids)

1.3 AAU Mt. Hood hops (25 min.) (0.25 oz./7.1 g at 5% alpha acids)

1.8 AAU Sterling hops (0 min.) (0.25 oz./7.1 g at 7.4% alpha acids)

White Labs WLP840 (American Lager) or Wyeast 2272 (North American Lager) yeast

¾ cup (150 g) dextrose (if priming)

STEP BY STEP

Mash the grains 60 minutes at 149°F (65°C). Mash out, vorlauf, and then sparge at 170°F (77°C) to collect 6.5 gallons (25 liters) of wort. Boil 75 minutes, adding hops as indicated. After the boil, collect wort for kräusening. Use the following formula to calculate how much kräusen wort to set aside: Vk (quarts) = 12 * Vw (gallons)/D (sgp), where Vk = volume of wort to set aside for kräusening, Vw = volume of post-boil wort, and D = wort density in specific gravity points. Add approximately 1 pint (500 milliliters) of wort to the calculated volume. This will allow for variations in the degree to which it has fermented before being added to the beer. Freeze and store the retained wort in a sealed, clean container. At this point, cool, aerate, and pitch yeast in the remainder of the wort, and ferment at 53°F (12°C). Two days before bottling or kegging, take out the kräusening wort and add a little water to account for the boiling losses, and then boil for 10 minutes to sanitize. Chill the wort after boiling and pour into a sanitized vessel with enough volume to contain the saved wort

plus an additional 10 to 15 percent. Pitch several grams (approximately 0.1 ounce) of dry, neutral yeast into the sanitized vessel. Stir or agitate well. Cover the vessel loosely with a sanitized lid or aluminum foil and allow it to ferment at room temperature. After 2 days (48 hours), the wort should be actively fermenting (at high kräusen), yet enough sugars should remain to provide carbonation. Add the fermenting kräusen wort in the same manner you would use priming sugar solution for the rest of the beer that is ready for bottling or kegging. You should leave behind most of the trub (sediment) that has settled to the bottom of the vessel used to ferment the kräusen wort. Carbonation should be completed in approximately 7 to 10 days at room temperature.

EXTRACT WITH GRAINS OPTION: Reduce the rice syrup solids in the all-grain recipe to 1 pound (0.45 kilogram), and substitute the 6-row pale malt with 4.25 pounds (1.93 kilograms) American lager liquid malt extract. Bring 5.5 gallons (21 liters) of water to a boil and add extracts. Boil for 60 minutes. Follow the remaining portion of the all-grain recipe.

- - - - - - - - - - - - - - -

INDEED BREWING COMPANY
MEXICAN HONEY
IMPERIAL LAGER

**(5 gallons/19 L, all-grain) OG = 1.078 FG = 1.017
IBU = 17   SRM = 6 ABV = 8%**

This golden-yellow lager with a subtle malt backbone is packed with floral notes of orange blossom and citrus thanks to the use of Mexican orange blossom honey. It has a bright hop flavor to go along with the aroma of graham cracker and honeycomb.

INGREDIENTS

6 lb. (2.7 kg) pilsner malt

6 lb. (2.7 kg) Vienna malt

3 lb. (1.4 kg) Mexican orange blossom honey (whirlpool)

25 AAU Amarillo hops (5 min.) (2.5 oz./71 g at 10% alpha acids)

Wyeast 2000 (Budvar Lager) or White Labs WLP800 (Pilsner Lager) yeast

⅔ cup (133 g) dextrose (if priming)

STEP BY STEP

Mill the grains and mix with 3.75 gallons (14.2 liters) of 164°F (73°C) strike water to reach a mash temperature of 152°F (67°C). Hold this temperature for 60 minutes. Vorlauf until your runnings are clear. Sparge the grains with 3 gallons (11.3 liters) water, and top up as necessary to obtain 6.5 gallons (25 liters) of wort. Boil for 90 minutes, adding hops according to the ingredient list. After removing from heat, stir the wort into a whirlpool, adding/dissolving honey in the process. Let the hot wort settle for 10 minutes. Chill the wort to 48°F (9°C), aerate, and pitch yeast. Ferment at 50°F (10°C) for 7 days, then let the temperature rise to 60°F (16°C) over 7 days. Crash the beer to 35°F (2°C) for 48 hours, and bottle or keg the beer and carbonate to approximately 2.25 volumes. After carbonation, lager at near-freezing temperatures for at least 6 weeks before serving.

EXTRACT ONLY OPTION: Substitute the pilsner and Vienna malts in the all-grain recipe with 4 pounds (1.8 kilograms) Pilsen liquid malt extract and 4 pounds (1.8 kilograms) Briess Goldpils Vienna liquid malt extract. Bring 5.4 gallons (20.4 liters) of water to approximately 162°F (72°C). Add malt extracts while stirring, and stir until completely dissolved. Bring the wort to a boil for 60 minutes. Follow the remaining portion of the all-grain recipe.

TIPS FOR SUCCESS

You may adjust the strength of this beer to your own preference—so long as the ratio of grain to honey is 1 pound of honey for every 4 pounds of grain (0.45 kilogram of honey for every 1.8 kilograms of grain). Also, be sure to tightly control the initial fermentation temperatures. With a large infusion of simple sugars from the honey, fermentation can yield fusel alcohols if not properly controlled. Ferment on the cooler side of the lager range to ensure that the beer doesn't taste "hot."

INDEED BREWING COMPANY
SHENANIGANS SUMMER ALE

(5 gallons/19 L, all-grain) OG = 1.047 FG = 1.009
IBU = 14 SRM = 4 ABV = 5%

Indeed Brewing has been churning tasty brews out of their production facility in Northeast Minneapolis since 2012. With its bold citrus notes, low ABV, and quaffable body, Shenanigans Summer Ale is a fitting ode to the all-too-brief warm summer months.

INGREDIENTS

3.8 lb. (1.7 kg) 2-row pale malt

3.5 lb. (1.6 kg) white wheat malt

14 oz. (392 g) torrified wheat

1 lb. (0.45 kg) raw clover honey (0 min.)

2 mL 85% phosphoric acid 85%

½ tsp. yeast nutrient (15 min.)

Whirlfloc (15 min.)

1.6 AAU Lemondrop pellet hops (first wort hop) (0.32 oz./9 g at 5.1% alpha acids)

5.2 AAU Lemondrop pellet hops (0 min.) (1.5 oz./43 g at 5.1% alpha acids)

Imperial Yeast A15 (Independence), Wyeast 1272 (American Ale II), or White Labs WLP051 (California Ale V) yeast

⅞ cup (175 g) dextrose (if priming)

STEP BY STEP

Mill the grains and mix with 3.1 gallons (11.6 liters) of 167°F (75°C) strike water to reach an infusion mash temperature of 154°F (68°C). Hold at this temperature for 60 minutes. Vorlauf until your runnings are clear. Add the phosphoric acid to your sparge water, and then sparge the grains with 4 gallons (15 liters) of 170°F (72°C) water until 7 gallons (26.5 liters) of 1.033 SG wort is collected in your boil kettle. Boil for 90 minutes, adding hops, yeast nutrient, and kettle finings according to the ingredients list. After the boil, turn off the heat and add the final hop addition and honey. Whirlpool the kettle by gently stirring with a mash paddle for 2 minutes, and then let rest for an additional 13 minutes to achieve a 15-minute flameout steep. Chill the wort to 67°F (19°C), aerate, and pitch yeast. Ferment at 70°F (21°C) until you reach terminal gravity. Crash cool to 33°F (1°C) for the better part of a week, and then package. Carbonate to 2.7 volumes of CO_2.

EXTRACT ONLY OPTION: Substitute the grains in the all-grain recipe with 3.3 pounds (1.5 kilograms) pale liquid malt extract and 2.5 pounds (1.13 kilograms) Muntons wheat dried malt extract. Bring 7 gallons (26.5 liters) of water up to a boil, adding the phosphoric acid and malt extracts during the heating process. The target pre-boil gravity is 1.033. Boil 90 minutes. Follow the remaining portion of the all-grain recipe.

JOSEPH SCHLITZ BREWING COMPANY
SCHLITZ GUSTO

ccccccc

**(5 gallons/19 L, all-grain) OG = 1.046 FG = 1.010
IBU = 30 SRM = 3 ABV = 4.7%**

"The beer that made Milwaukee famous," and the beer that your father probably used to drink. This is a clone recipe of the 60s-era Schlitz, when Schlitz was the largest brewery in the world and before the infamous "reformulation" done in the 1970s.

INGREDIENTS

5.5 lb. (2.5 kg) North American Pilsner malt

2 lb. (0.91 kg) 6-row pale malt

2 lb. (0.91 kg) flaked maize

1.75 AAU Cluster hops (60 min.) (0.55 oz./16 g at 7% alpha acids)

1.75 AAU Cluster hops (10 min.) (1.1 oz./32 g at 7% alpha acids)

¼ tsp. calcium chloride

¼ tsp. gypsum

1 tsp. Irish moss (15 min.)

Wyeast 2035 (American Lager) or White Labs WLP840 (American Lager) yeast (3 qt./~3 L yeast starter)

1 cup (200 g) dextrose (if priming)

STEP BY STEP

This recipe calls for a multi-step mash infusion schedule. Starting with RO water, add the calcium chloride and the gypsum. Dough-in the grains at 113°F (45°C) with 14.3 quarts (13.5 liters) of water. Immediately begin heating mash to 145°F (63°C). Stir mash while heating. Rest for 15 minutes at 145°F (63°C), then heat mash to 154°F (68°C) and rest for 30 minutes (or until iodine test shows negative). Heat to 167°F (75°C) and transfer to lauter tun. Let mash sit for 5 minutes, then recirculate for 20 minutes (or until clear). Sparge with 170°F (77°C) water and collect roughly 5 gallons (19 liters) of wort, then add 1.5 gallons (5.7 liters)

of water and bring to a boil. Boil for 90 minutes, adding hops and Irish moss as indicated. Cool wort to 55°F (13°C), transfer to fermenter, aerate thoroughly, and pitch yeast. Let ferment at 55°F (13°C) until fermentation slows, then allow temperature to rise to 60°F (16°C). After three days (or after sampling the beer and detecting no diacetyl), separate beer from yeast, cool beer to 40°F (4.4°C), and begin lagering. Allow to lager for 6 weeks, then keg and force carbonate to 2.6 volumes of CO_2.

PARTIAL MASH OPTION: Replace the Pilsner malt from the recipe with 3 pounds (1.4 kilograms) Pilsen dried malt extract. Heat 6 quarts (5.7 liters) water to 164°F (73°C) and submerge crushed 6-row and flaked maize in a large steeping bag. Stir and then let partial mash rest, starting at 153°F (67°C) for 45 minutes. While the partial mash is resting, heat 1 gallon (3.8 liters) of water to a boil in your brewpot and heat 5.5 quarts (5.2 liters) of water to 180°F (82°C) in a large soup pot. Recirculate about 2 quarts (2 liters) of wort, then run off first wort and add to boiling water in brewpot. Add the 180°F (82°C) water to the cooler until liquid level is the same as before. Stir grains, let rest 5 minutes, then recirculate and run off wort as before. Add corn sugar and bring wort to a boil. Once hot break forms, add hops and boil for 60 minutes. Follow the remaining portion of the all-grain recipe.

LABATT BREWING COMPANY
LABATT BLUE

ccccccc

**(5 gallons/19 L, all-grain) OG = 1.045 FG = 1.009
IBU = 20 SRM = 5 ABV = 4.5%**

The world's best-selling Canadian beer, Labatt has a distinct hop aroma, delicate fruit flavor, and slightly sweet aftertaste that sets it apart from many of its US counterparts.

INGREDIENTS

6.75 lb. (3.1 kg) 2-row pale malt

3 lb. (1.4 kg) flaked barley

4.4 AAU Hallertau hops (60 min.) (1.1 oz./31 g at 4% alpha acids)

1 AAU Hallertau hops (30 min.) (0.25 oz./7 g at 4% alpha acids)

0.25 oz. (7.1 g) Saaz hops (0 min.)

1 tsp. Irish moss (15 min.)

Wyeast 2272 (North American Lager) or White Labs WLP800 (Pilsner Lager) yeast (3 qt./~3 L yeast starter)

¾ cup (150 g) dextrose (if priming)

STEP BY STEP

Be sure to start with either soft water or mix with reverse osmosis or distilled water to create a low-carbonate water profile. Mash the grains and maize with 12.2 quarts (11.5 liters) of water to get a single-infusion mash temperature of 152°F (67°C) for 45 minutes (or you could also do a step mash with a 15-minute rest at 122°F/50°C and a 45-minute rest at 152°F/67°C). Collect 5.5 gallons (21 liters) of wort, add 1 gallon (3.8 liters) of water, then boil for 90 minutes. Add hops and Irish moss at times indicated. Cool, aerate, and pitch yeast. Ferment at 50°F (10°C), and then lager at 40°F (4.4°C) for 2 to 4 weeks. After fermentation is complete, bottle or keg as usual.

EXTRACT WITH GRAINS OPTION: Substitute the 5.75 pounds (2.6 kilograms) of the 2-row malt in the all-grain recipe with 4 pounds (0.34 kilogram) extra light dried malt extract, and reduce the flaked barley to 1 pound (0.45 kilogram). Place crushed malt and flaked barley in a nylon steeping bag and steep in 3 quarts (2.8 liters) of water at 150°F (66°C) for 45 minutes. Rinse grains with 2 quarts (2 liters) of water at 170°F (77°C). Add water to make 3 gallons (11 liters), stir in dried malt extract, and bring to a boil for 60 minutes. Add hops and Irish moss as indicated, and the liquid malt extract with 15 minutes remaining in the boil. Cool wort to about 50°F (10°C) and transfer to fermenting vessel. Top up to 5 gallons (19 liters) with water, aerate, and pitch yeast. Follow the remaining portion of the all-grain recipe.

LATROBE
BREWING COMPANY
ROLLING ROCK
EXTRA PALE

cccccc-

**(5 gallons/19 L, all-grain) OG = 1.041 FG = 1.006
IBU = 21 SRM = 2 ABV = 4.5%**

Rolling Rock Extra Pale is the rare beer that successfully uses an "off-flavor" to differentiate itself. Yes, Rolling Rock has made a name for itself by brewing a pale lager with a significant amount of DMS (Dimethyl Sulfide) in its flavor

profile. The best way for a homebrewer to get this flavor in your beer is to boil your beer with the lid of your pot covering as much of the kettle as possible without boiling over.

INGREDIENTS

6.5 lb. (3 kg) 6-row pale malt

1 lb. (0.45 kg) flaked rice

1.5 lb. (0.68 kg) flaked maize

5.6 AAU Willamette hops (60 min.) (0.5 oz./14 g at 5% alpha acids)

2.25 AAU Tettnanger hops (60 min.) (0.5 oz./14 g at 4.5% alpha acids)

½ tsp. Irish moss (15 min.)

White Labs WLP840 (American Lager) or Wyeast 2035 (American Lager) yeast

¾ cup (150 g) dextrose (if priming)

STEP BY STEP

Mash grains at 153°F (67°C) for 60 minutes. Mash out, vorlauf, and then sparge at 167°F (75°C) to collect approximately 7 gallons (26.5 liters) of wort. Boil for 90 minutes with the lid on your kettle while being careful not to cause a boil-over. Add hops at times indicated. Chill to 68°F (20°C), aerate, and pitch yeast. Hold beer at 68°F (20°C) until the yeast starts fermenting, and then cool to 52°F (11°C) for the remainder of fermentation. About 3 days after hitting your final gravity, raise the temperature of the beer to about 68°F (20°C) for 3 days for a diacetyl rest. Transfer to secondary and lager the beer at about 35°F (2°C) for another 3 weeks before bottling or kegging.

PARTIAL MASH OPTION: Reduce the 6-row pale malt in the all-grain recipe to 2 pounds (0.91 kilogram), reduce the flaked maize to 1 pound (0.45 kilogram), and eliminate the flaked rice. Add 2 pounds 10 ounces (1.2 kilograms) light dried malt extract and 0.5 pound (0.23 kilogram) rice syrup solids. Steep the 6-row pale malt and flaked maize in a muslin bag in 1 gallon (3.8 liters) of water at 150°F (65°C) for 45 minutes, stirring occasionally. Remove grains from the wort and rinse with 2 quarts (1.8 liters) of 170°F (77°C) water, and then top the kettle up to 6 gallons (23 liters) and add the extracts. Boil for 60 minutes. Follow the remaining portion of the all-grain recipe.

MAGIC HAT
BREWING COMPANY
HOCUS POCUS

cccccc-

**(5 gallons/19 L, all-grain) OG = 1.045 FG = 1.010
IBU = 21 SRM = 4 ABV = 4.6%**

Magic Hat calls this beer "a toast to rays and summer haze." In other words, this beer was made for the lawnmower days and baseball games of summer. As a recommended pairing, try it with an orange wedge.

INGREDIENTS

5 lb. 10 oz. (2.6 kg) 2-row pale malt

3 lb. 6 oz. (1.5 kg) white wheat malt

6 oz. (0.17 kg) acidulated malt

1.5 AAU Cascade hops (60 min.) (0.3 oz./8.5 g at 5% alpha acids)

2.5 AAU Cascade hops (45 min.) (0.5 oz./14 g at 5% alpha acids)

1.5 AAU Cascade hops (30 min.) (0.3 oz./8.5 g at 5% alpha acids)

0.5 oz. (14 g) Cascade hops (0 min.)

0.5 oz. (14 g) Columbus hops (hopback)

Wyeast 1187 (Ringwood Ale) yeast or White Labs WLP005 (British Ale)

⅔ cup (133 g) dextrose (if priming)

STEP BY STEP

Mash the grains at 150°F (66°C) for 60 minutes. Mash out, vorlauf, and then sparge at 170°F (77°C) to collect 6 gallons (23 liters). Boil 60 minutes, adding hops at times indicated. At the end of the boil, turn off heat and add final hops, stir wort to create a whirlpool for 2 minutes, and then cover and allow wort to sit for an additional 18 minutes. If you do not have a hopback, then add this hop addition as a dry hop for 3 days. Cool, aerate, and pitch yeast. Ferment at 70°F (21°C). After fermentation is complete, bottle or keg as usual.

BREWER TIP: "We filter our version of Hocus Pocus bright, but a bit of yeast won't hurt if filtration isn't possible. Also, we run our wort through a hopback prior to the wort chiller to achieve maximum hop aroma. We use rice hulls to aid in the lautering process because of the large percentage of wheat. This will depend on brewhouse design. Be sure to give the brew proper time to condition just in case diacetyl is produced during primary fermentation; a large fermentation with Ringwood (150 barrels) needs 24 hours to reduce the buttery character." Three to 5 days at fermentation temperature is probably good at a homebrew scale.

EXTRACT ONLY OPTION: Replace the grains with 5 pounds (2.27 kilograms) wheat dried malt extract and 1 teaspoon (5 milliliters) of 88 percent lactic acid solution. Add dried malt extract and lactic acid to make 6 gallons (23 liters) of wort, and boil for 60 minutes. Follow the remaining portion of the all-grain recipe.

NORTH COAST BREWING CO.
BLUE STAR
WHEAT BEER

cccccc-

**(5 gallons/19 L, all-grain) OG = 1.046 FG = 1.008
IBU = 19 SRM= 4 ABV = 5%**

Blue Star is an unfiltered American wheat beer that the brewery says was inspired by the style of the American craft beer renaissance. It's a proudly unfiltered beer that's won multiple gold medals at the World Beer Championships.

INGREDIENTS

3.3 lb. (1.5 kg) wheat malt

5.5 lb. (2.5 kg) 2-row pale malt

0.5 lb. (226 g) Carapils (dextrin) malt.

2.9 AAU Cascade hops (60 min.) (0.5 oz./14 g at 5.7% alpha acids)

5.7 AAU Cascade hops (15 min.) (0.75 oz./21 g at 5.7% alpha acids)

2.8 AAU Cascade hops (0 min.) (0.5 oz./14 g at 5.7% alpha acids)

White Labs WLP001 (California Ale) or Wyeast 1056 (American Ale) yeast

¾ cup (150 g) dextrose (if priming)

STEP BY STEP

Mash the grains at 154°F (68°C) for 60 minutes. Mash out, vorlauf, and then sparge at 170°F (77°C) to collect approximately 7 gallons (32 liters) of wort. Boil 90 minutes, adding hops at times indicated. Cool the wort to 75°F (24°C), aerate the beer, and pitch your yeast. Allow the beer to cool over the next few hours to 68°F (20°C), and hold at this temperature until the beer has finished fermenting, then bottle or keg.

EXTRACT WITH GRAINS OPTION: Reduce both the wheat malt and 2-row pale malt in the all-grain recipe to 0.5 pound (227 grams), and add 3.3 pounds (1.5 kilograms) Briess wheat liquid malt extract and 1 pound 14 ounces (0.85 kilogram) Briess light dried malt extract. Steep the crushed malts in 3 gallons (11 liters) of water at 154°F (68°C) for 30 minutes. Remove grains from wort, add the malt syrup and dried malt extract, and bring to a boil for 60 minutes, adding hops at times indicated. Cool and top off to 5 gallons (19 liters). Follow the remaining portion of the all-grain recipe.

ODELL BREWING COMPANY
EASY STREET WHEAT

(5 gallons/19 L all-grain) OG = 1.045
FG = 1.011 IBU = 21 SRM = 7 ABV = 4.6%

Light in color with refreshing citrus undertones, Easy Street is an unfiltered American-style wheat beer. The yeast gives the beer a smooth finish, a slight fruit flavor, and its distinct cloudy appearance.

INGREDIENTS

5 lb. 6 oz. (2.4 kg) wheat malt

4 lb. 6 oz. (2 kg) 2-row malt

0.5 lb. (0.23 kg) Munich malt

2 oz. (57 g) crystal malt (20 °L)

3.5 AAU Cascade hops (60 min.) (0.70 oz./20 g at 5% alpha acids)

3 AAU Saaz hops (2 min.) (1 oz./28 g at 3% alpha acids)

4 AAU Tettnanger hops (2 min.) (1 oz./28 g at 4% alpha acids)

White Labs WLP029 (German Ale/Kölsch) or Wyeast 2565 (Kölsch) yeast (1.25 qt./~1.25 L yeast starter)

¾ cups (150 g) dextrose (if priming)

STEP BY STEP

Mash your grains at 149°F (65°C) for 45 minutes in 12 quarts (11 liters) of mash water. Collect 5 gallons (19 liters) of wort, add 1.5 gallons (5.7 liters) of water, and boil for 90 minutes, adding hops as directed. Cool, aerate, and pitch yeast. Ferment at 68°F (20°C) for 7 to 10 days or until specific gravity remains constant. Bottle or keg as usual.

EXTRACT WITH GRAINS OPTION: Substitute the 2-row malt and wheat malt in the all-grain recipe with 1 pound (0.45 kilogram) wheat malt, 1.75 pounds (0.79 grams) Briess wheat dried malt extract, and 3.3 pounds (1.5 grams) Briess wheat liquid malt extract. Place crushed malts in a nylon steeping bag and steep in 2.4 quarts (2.3 liters) of water at 150°F (66°C) for 30 minutes. Rinse grains with 1.2 quarts (~1.2 liters) of water at 170°F (77°C). Add water to make 3 gallons (11 liters), stir in dried malt extract, and bring to a boil. Add ingredients at times indicated and the liquid malt extract with 15 minutes remaining. Follow the remaining portion of the all-grain recipe, and top off to 5 gallons (19 liters) after cooling.

P. BALLANTINE & SONS
BREWING COMPANY
BALLANTINE XXX

(5 gallons/19 L, all-grain) OG = 1.055 FG = 1.011
IBU = 39 SRM = 5 ABV = 5.7%

Ballantine was founded in New Jersey in 1840, making it one of the oldest brands of beer in the United States. At one time, it was the third largest brewery in the country. In 2014 Pabst Brewing Company bought the brand, but this clone recipe is for the original Ballantine XXX, long the brewery's most popular beer.

INGREDIENTS

8 lb. (3.6 kg) 6-row pale malt

2.5 lb. (1.1 kg) flaked maize (corn)

1 lb. (0.45 kg) light Munich malt

8 oz. (0.23 kg) crystal malt (20 °L)

7 AAU Cluster hops (60 min.) (1 oz./28 g at 7% alpha acids)

4 AAU Brewer's Gold hops (25 min.) (0.5 oz./14 g at 8% alpha acids)

0.75 oz. (21 g) Brewer's Gold hops (5 min.)

1 oz. (28 g) Cascade hops (dry hop)

1 tsp. Irish moss (15 min.)

Wyeast 1056 (American Ale), White Labs WLP001 (California Ale), or Fermentis Safale US-05 yeast (1.5 qt./1.4 L yeast starter)

¾ cup (150 g) dextrose (if priming)

STEP BY STEP

Mash the grains at 150°F (66°C) for 60 minutes. Mash out, vorlauf, and then sparge at 170°F (77°C) to collect enough wort to result in 5 gallons (19 liters) after a 90-minute boil. Boil 90 minutes, adding hops at times indicated. Cool, aerate, and pitch yeast. Ferment at 68°F (20°C). After fermentation is complete, bottle or keg as usual.

EXTRACT WITH GRAINS OPTION: Substitute the 6-row pale malt, flaked maize, and Munich malts in the all-grain recipe with 7.25 pounds (3.3 kilograms) American light lager liquid malt extract and 1 pound (0.45 kilogram) Munich liquid malt extract. Steep grains in 5.5 gallons (21 liters) 140 to 150°F (60 to 66°C) water for 30 minutes. Drain grains and add malt extracts as you bring to a boil for 90 minutes. Follow the remaining portion of the all-grain recipe.

- - - - - - - - - - - - - - - - - -

SHIPYARD
BREWING COMPANY
EXPORT ALE

ᕦᕦᕦᕦᕦ

(5 gallons/19 L, all-grain) OG = 1.052 FG = 1.013
IBU = 31 SRM = 7 ABV = 5.2%

This North American golden ale has a hint of sweetness up front, a subtle yet distinctive hop taste, and a clean finish.

INGREDIENTS

9.75 lb. (4.4 kg) English pale 2-row malt

0.5 lb. (0.23 kg) crystal malt (60 °L)

0.5 lb. (0.23 kg) wheat malt

5.8 AAU Cascade hops (60 min.) (1 oz./35 g at 5.75% alpha acids)

3.75 AAU Willamette hops (15 min.) (0.75 oz./21 g at 5% alpha acids)

4.5 AAU Tettnanger hops (3 min.) (1 oz./28 g at 4.5% alpha acids)

1 tsp. Irish moss (15 min.)

White Labs WLP007 (Dry English Ale) or Wyeast 1275 (Thames Valley Ale) yeast

¾ cup (150 g) dextrose (if priming)

STEP BY STEP

Mash your grains at 148°F (64°C) for 60 minutes. Mash out, vorlauf, and then sparge at 170°F (77°C) to collect enough wort to result in 5.5 gallons (21 liters) after a 90-minute boil. Boil 90 minutes, adding hops at times indicated. Cool the wort to 80°F (27°C), aerate the beer, and pitch yeast. Allow the beer to cool over the next few hours to 68 to 70°F (20 to 21°C), and hold at these cooler temperatures until the yeast has fermented completely. Bottle or keg as usual.

EXTRACT WITH GRAINS OPTION: Substitute the 2-row pale malt in the all-grain recipe with 6.6 pounds (3 kilograms) light liquid malt extract. Steep the 2 crushed grains in 1 gallon (4 liters) of water at 148°F (65°C) for 30 minutes. Remove grains from wort, add malt syrup, top up to 6 gallons (23 liters), and bring to a boil for 60 minutes. Follow the remaining portion of the all-grain recipe.

- - - - - - - - - - - - - - - - - -

SPRINGFIELD
BREWING COMPANY
MUELLER WHEAT

ᕦᕦᕦᕦᕦ

(5 gallons/19 L, all-grain) OG = 1.045 FG = 1.007
IBU = 19 SRM = 3 ABV = 5%

Springfield brewmaster Ashton Lewis says Weyermann pale wheat malt gives a consistent cloudiness that's important to this beer, which has won a gold medal and a bronze in the American-style wheat beer category at the Great American Beer Festival.

INGREDIENTS

3.7 lb. (1.7 kg) Weyermann pale wheat malt

0.7 lb. (0.31 kg) raw (unmalted) wheat berries

4.8 lb. (2.2 kg) Cargill Ida-Pils malt

3.2 AAU Perle hops (70 min.) (0.4 oz./11 g at 8% alpha acids)

2.2 AAU Liberty hops (30 min.) (0.4 oz./11 g at 5.5% alpha)

0.56 oz. (16 g) Liberty hops (0 min.)

White Labs WLP001 (California Ale) or Wyeast 1056 (American Ale) yeast

1 cup (200 g) dextrose (if priming)

STEP BY STEP

Use a mash water volume of 2.9 gallons (10.9 liters) and mash in at 122°F (50°C), rest for 20 minutes, heat to 140°F (60°C), rest for 30 minutes, heat to 154°F (68°C), rest for 30 minutes, and heat to 169°F (76°C) for mash-off. Transfer the mash to the lauter tun, and do a 20-minute vorlauf before sending wort to the kettle. When the top of the grain bed is covered by ~1 inch (~2.5 cm) of wort, begin sparging with 169°F (76°C) sparge water. Measure wort gravity toward the end of collection, and do not collect wort weaker than 1.008. Boil wort for 90 minutes, adding hops at the times indicated. Cool the wort to 64°F (18°C) and aerate. Ferment at 64°F (18°C) until the gravity is no greater than 1.009. Cool beer to 50°F (10°C) and hold for 6 days or until the gravity is no greater than 1.008, and then chill to 32°F (0°C). Bottle or keg and carbonate to a level of 2.8 volumes of carbon dioxide.

EXTRACT WITH GRAINS OPTION: Remove the pale wheat malt and 4 pounds (1.8 kilograms) of the Cargill Ida-Pils malt and replace with 4.25 pounds (1.9 kilograms) wheat dried malt extract. Place the crushed grains in a grain bag and submerge in 1 gallon (4 liters) of water to stabilize at 154°F (68°C). Hold that temperature for 45 minutes. Remove the grain bag, place in a colander, and wash with 1 gallon (4 liters) of hot water. Top up to 3 gallons, and bring to a boil. Remove from heat, and stir in the dried malt extract and the bittering hops. Once all the extract is dissolved, bring back to a boil and boil for 60 minutes, adding the remaining hops as indicated. Follow the remaining portion of the all-grain recipe.

STARR HILL BREWERY
JOMO

ʚʚʚʚʚ

(5 gallons/19 L, all-grain) OG = 1.052 FG = 1.011
IBU = 24 SRM = 11 ABV = 5.4%

This year-round offering from Starr Hill is known for its crisp, clean taste. Its noticeable hop aroma is effectively balanced with a slight malty sweetness. Jomo has won multiple awards, including two gold medals at the Great American Beer Festival.

INGREDIENTS

7.25 lb. (3.3 kg) pilsner malt

1.5 lb. (0.68 kg) crystal malt (20 °L)

1 lb. (0.45 kg) dark Munich malt (9 °L)

1 lb. (0.45 kg) Belgian aromatic malt

6.25 AAU Hallertau Tradition hops (60 min.) (1.25 oz./35 g at 5% alpha acids)

Wyeast 2308 (Munich Lager) or White Labs WLP838 (Southern German Lager) yeast

¾ cup (150 g) dextrose (if priming)

STEP BY STEP

Mill the grains and mix with 3.5 gallons (13.2 liters) of 161°F (72°C) strike water to reach a mash temperature of 149°F (65°C). Hold this temperature for 60 minutes before starting the lautering process. Vorlauf until your runnings are clear. Sparge the grains with 4 gallons (15.1 liters) of sparge water,

and top up as necessary to obtain 6 gallons (23 liters) of wort. Boil for 60 minutes, adding hops according to the ingredients list. Chill to 50°F (10°C), aerate, and pitch yeast. Ferment at 50°F (10°C) for 4 days, or until the beer reaches 1.024 SG. At that time, increase the temperature to 58°F (14°C) for an additional 7 days. Once the beer reaches final gravity, bottle or keg and carbonate to approximately 2.5 volumes. Cold conditioning at near-freezing temperatures can be done prior to or after packaging and should last for at least 6 weeks.

PARTIAL MASH OPTION: Substitute the pilsner malt in the all-grain recipe with 5 pounds (2.3 kilograms) Pilsen liquid malt extract. Place crushed grains in a large grain bag. Bring 1 gallon (4 liters) of water to approximately 162°F (72°C) to reach a mash temperature of 149°F (65°C). Hold this temperature for 60 minutes. Remove grain bag, then wash the grains with 1 gallon (4 liters) of hot water. Let the grains drain fully. Top off to 6 gallons (23 liters) of water, then add the liquid malt extract and stir until completely dissolved. Bring the wort to a boil for 60 minutes. Follow the remaining portion of the all-grain recipe.

TIPS FOR SUCCESS

Starr Hill brewmaster Robbie O'Cain points to three key elements to brewing their Vienna lager: temperature, time, and water. First, mash on the low end of the temperature spectrum (149°F/65°C) to improve attenuation and produce a very fermentable wort with few long-chain sugars.

Second, temperature control is very important for fermenting lagers, as well as for the lagering phase. If you like brewing lagers and haven't already done so, converting an old dorm or full-size refrigerator, or chest freezer, into a fermentation chamber (utilizing a temperature controller) is a great project (there are many design ideas on the Internet for building one of these). Sometimes lager strains can produce sulfur compounds during fermentation that can give off weird odors. If you take your time in the conditioning phase, these should disappear. Also, take your time letting this beer lager at cold temperatures. "This beer is about patience," Robbie says.

And third, Starr Hill brews with very soft water, so if your water has a solid mineral base you might consider diluting your mash or boil water with a distilled water (or at least use something bottled that's softer than yours).

THEODORE HAMM'S BREWING COMPANY
HAMM'S

eeeeeee-

(6 gallons/23 L, all-grain) OG = 1.040 FG = 1.006
IBU = 20 SRM = 3.2 ABV = 4.5%

Hamm's is a classic American lager, so expect a beer that's crisp, refreshing, and very light in color and body. It typically has very high carbonation levels that cover any sweetness that might be present. This beer is brewed with a double mash and is diluted upon packaging. So, if you ferment 5 gallons (19 liters) of base beer, you'll yield 6 gallons (23 liters) for kegging and/or bottling.

INGREDIENTS

7.8 lb. (3.5 kg) 6-row pale malt

3 lb. (1.4 kg) brewer's corn grits

2.4 AAU Hallertau hops (60 min.) (0.6 oz./17 g at 4% alpha acids)

2.7 AAU Tettnanger hops (60 min.) (0.6 oz./17 g at 4.5% alpha acids)

2.4 AAU Hallertau hops (5 min.) (0.6 oz./17 g at 4% alpha acids)

½ tsp. Irish moss (15 min.)

White Labs WLP840 (American Lager) or Wyeast 2035 (American Lager) yeast

⅞ cup (175 g) dextrose (if priming)

STEP BY STEP

Reserve a handful of 6-row malt. Mash in remaining malt with 4.1 gallons (16 liters) of water at 133°F (56°C) and begin mashing at 122°F (50°C) in your kettle. Combine corn with the handful of 6-row malt in 1 gallon (3.8 liters) of water in a large kitchen pot and begin heating it. Rest cereal mash at 158°F (70°C) for 5 minutes, then bring to a boil. Boil for 30 minutes, stirring almost constantly. Heat the main mash, stirring often, to 140°F (60°C) and hold. Combine cooked corn with main mash and adjust temperature—if needed—to 152°F (67°C). Hold at 152°F (67°C) for 30 minutes, stirring often. Heat mash to 168°F (76°C), stirring often, and transfer mash to lauter tun, recirculate, and run off wort. Sparge with water hot enough to keep grain bed at 170°F (77°C). Collect about 5 gallons (19 liters) of wort, add 1.5 gallons (5.7 liters) of water, and bring to a vigorous rolling boil. Boil the wort down to 5 gallons (19 liters) over 90 minutes, adding hops and Irish moss at times indicated. Cool wort to 48°F (9°C) and transfer to fermenter. Aerate wort and pitch yeast from starter. Ferment at 52°F

(11°C), allowing temperature to rise to 60°F (16°C) when fermentation is almost finished. Hold for 3 days at this temperature. Separate beer from yeast and cool to 40°F (4.4°C). Allow to cold condition (lager) for 4 to 5 weeks. When you are ready to keg the beer, boil a little over 1 gallon (3.8 liters) of water for 15 minutes, cool rapidly, and add 3.3 quarts (3.2 liters) to your 5-gallon (19-liter) corny keg. Transfer beer to keg until it is full. You will be left with 3.3 quarts (3.2 liters) of base beer to either dilute to 4 quarts (3.7 liters) with boiled and cooled water or to package as "malt liquor."

EXTRACT WITH GRAINS OPTION: Substitute the corn grits and reduce the 6-row pale malt in the all-grain recipe with 2 pounds (0.91 kilogram) 6-row pale malt, 3.3 pounds (1.5 kilogram) light liquid malt extract, 1 pound (0.45 kilogram) flaked maize, and 0.75 pound (0.34 kilogram) corn sugar. Steep the 6-row and flaked maize in 5 gallons (19 liters) of water at 150°F (65°C) for 45 minutes. Remove grains and rinse with 2 quarts (2 liters) of 170°F (77°C) water. Add the malt extract and boil for 60 minutes. With 5 minutes remaining, add the corn sugar. Follow the remaining portion of the all-grain recipe.

MADE IN GERMANY

SEIT 1817
Bitburger Th. Simon
Privatbrauerei Bitburg / Eifel

Bitte ein Bit

Bitburger®

Premium Beer

INTERNATIONAL TRADEMARK

MIT BITBURGER SIEGELHOPFEN GEBRAUT
NACH DEUTSCHEM REINHEITSGEBOT

GERMANY'S NO.1
DRAFT BEER

CHAPTER

FOURTEEN

PiLSNERS

BEER PICTURED ON LEFT; SEE PAGE 216

BITBURGER BREWERY
PREMIUM PILS

-ᶜᶜᶜᶜᶜᶜ-

**(5 gallons/19 L, all-grain) OG = 1.045 FG = 1.011
IBU = 38 SRM = 3 ABV = 4.5%**

Bitburger makes a classic pilsner that's supremely balanced and a testament to brewing skill. With just two malts and one hop addition, there's not much to hide behind. It's all about achieving a perfect brew day and carefully controlling fermentation for the best results.

INGREDIENTS

8.75 lb. (4 kg) German pilsner malt

0.5 lb. (0.23 kg) CaraFoam malt

8.75 AAU Perle hops (60 min.) (1.1 oz./31 g at 8% alpha acids)

3 AAU Hallertau hops (60 min.) (0.75 oz./21 g at 4% alpha acids)

Wyeast 2007 (Pilsen Lager) or White Labs WLP830 (German Lager) yeast (3 qt./~3 L yeast starter)

⅞ cup (175 g) dextrose (if priming)

STEP BY STEP

Mash the grains in 4.5 gallons (17 liters) at 140°F (60°C). (This is a somewhat thin mash compared to most homebrew mashes.) Hold for 15 minutes, then heat to 150°F (66°C). Hold 45 minutes, then heat to 170°F (77°C) and transfer mash to lauter tun. Collect around 5 gallons (19 liters) of wort, add 1.5 gallons (5.7 liters) of water, and boil for 90 minutes. Add hops at times indicated in ingredient list. Cool wort to 55°F (13°C), aerate well, and pitch yeast. Ferment at 55°F (13°C), then lager at near freezing temperatures. Perform a diacetyl rest (let temperature rise to 60°F/16°C for 2 to 3 days) in between primary fermentation and lagering. With the mash described above, you should achieve a lower FG than that given in the extract recipe. Your all-grain brew should finish around 1.008, yielding a 4.8% ABV beer—the level of alcohol quoted for Bitburger. Bottle condition warm for 2 days, then lager in bottles at 38 to 40°F (3 to 4°C) for 4 to 6 weeks.

PARTIAL MASH OPTION: Scale the pilsner malt down to 1.5 pounds (0.68 kilogram). Add 1.5 pounds (0.68 kilogram) light dried malt extract and 3.3 pounds 1.49 kilograms) light liquid malt extract (late addition). Place the crushed grains in a grain bag and steep in 3 quarts (2.8 liters) of water at 148°F (64°C) for 45 minutes. Pull the grain bag out and drain over the pot in a colander. Rinse the grain bag with 1.5 quarts (~1.5 liters) of water at 170°F (77°C). Remove grains, add water to "grain tea" to make 3 gallons (11 liters), add dried malt extract, and stir well. Bring to a boil. Boil 60 minutes, adding hops at times indicated in the ingredients list. Add liquid malt extract with 15 minutes remaining in the boil. Cool wort to 55°F (13°C), transfer to fermenter, and top up to 5 gallons (19 liters) with cool water. Aerate wort well and pitch yeast. Follow the remainder of the all-grain recipe.

FIRESTONE WALKER BREWING COMPANY
PIVO HOPPY PILS

-ᶜᶜᶜᶜᶜᶜ-

**(5 gallons/19 L, all-grain) OG = 1.046 FG = 1.009
IBU = 40 SRM = 3 ABV = 5%**

When Old World Pilsner goes US West Coast, the result is Pivo Hoppy Pils. Brewed with classic influences from Germany and the Czech Republic, Pivo is then dry hopped to pump up the floral, spicy, herbal, and lemongrass aromatics in German Saphir hops.

INGREDIENTS

9 lb. 6 oz. (4.3 kg) Weyermann Pilsner malt

8.3 AAU German Magnum hops (60 min.) (0.75 oz./21 g at 11% alpha acids)

2.3 AAU German Spalt Select hops (30 min.) (0.5 oz./14 g at 4.5% alpha acids)

0.8 oz. (22 g) German Saphir hops (0 min.)

0.8 oz. (22 g) German Saphir hops (dry hop)

7 g calcium chloride (if using reverse osmosis water)

White Labs WLP830 (German Lager) or Wyeast 2124 (Bohemian Lager) yeast

¾ cup (150 g) dextrose (if priming)

STEP BY STEP

Mash the grains (and calcium chloride, if using) at 145°F (63°C) for 15 minutes. Raise the mash temperature to 155°F (68°C) and hold for 30 minutes. Mash out, vorlauf, and then sparge at 168°F (75°C). Collect 6 gallons (23 liters) of 1.038 wort. Boil for 60 minutes, adding hops according to the ingredients list. Turn off the heat and chill the wort to slightly below fermentation temperature, about 48°F (9°C). Aerate the wort with pure oxygen or filtered air, and pitch the yeast. Ferment at 50°F (10°C). After 4 days of fermentation, add the dry hop addition. After 7 days total, slowly raise the temperature to 60°F (16°C) for 3 days for a diacetyl rest, then slowly lower the beer to 34°F (1°C). Once at final gravity (approximately 14 days total), bottle or keg the beer and carbonate. Lager at 34°F (1°C) for approximately 1 month before serving.

EXTRACT WITH GRAINS OPTION: Replace the pilsner malt with 6.5 pounds (2.9 kilograms) Pilsen liquid malt extract. Bring 5.5 gallons (21 liters) of water and calcium chloride (if using) to boil, turn off the flame, and stir in the liquid malt extract until completely dissolved. Top up if necessary to obtain 6 gallons (23 liters) of 1.038 SG wort. Boil for 60 minutes, adding the hops according to the ingredients list. Turn off the heat and chill the wort to slightly below fermentation temperature, about 48°F (9°C). Aerate the wort with pure oxygen or filtered air, and pitch the yeast. Follow the remaining portion of the all-grain recipe.

MARKET GARDEN BREWERY
PROGRESS PILSNER

(5 gallons/19 L, all-grain) OG = 1.050 FG = 1.008
IBU = 37 SRM = 4 ABV = 5.5%

Progress Pilsner, created in the style of a German Pilsner, is one of three year-round beers at Market Garden Brewery in Cleveland, Ohio. The brewery calls this Great American Beer Festival award-winner a tribute to the spicy, crisp, and clean character of German noble hops.

INGREDIENTS

9 lb. (4.1 kg) Avangard German Pilsner malt

0.5 lb. (0.23 kg) Weyermann Carahell malt (10 °L)

0.5 lb. (0.23 kg) acidulated malt

3.5 AAU Czech Saaz hops (first wort hop) (1 oz./28 g at 3.5% alpha acids)

3.5 AAU Czech Saaz hops (60 min.) (1 oz./28 g at 3.5% alpha acids)

1 AAU Spalter Select hops (30 min.) (0.5 oz./14 g at 2% alpha acids)

3.5 AAU Czech Saaz hops (10 min.) (1 oz./28 g at 3.5% alpha acids)

2 oz. (57 g) Czech Saaz hops (0 min.)

White Labs WLP830 (German Lager) or Wyeast 2124 (Bohemian Lager) yeast

¾ cup (150 g) dextrose (if priming)

STEP BY STEP

This is a multi-step mash. Start with 5 gallons (19 liters) of low carbonate strike water. This is a ratio of 2 quarts per pound of grain (4.2 liter/kilogram) to provide a thin mash with high enzymatic activity. Follow this mash schedule: Start at 131°F (55°C) and hold for 10 minutes for the protein rest. Raise the grain bed to 145°F (63°C) and hold for 30 minutes for beta amylase conversion. Raise the grain bed to 158°F (70°C) and hold for 10 to 15 minutes until starch conversion is complete. Finally, raise the grain bed to 170°F (77°C) for mash-out. Sparge with enough water to collect 7.1 gallons (26.8 liters) of wort pre-boil. Add the first wort hops during the sparge. Bring the wort to a boil, and add the hops according to the ingredients list. Boil for 90 minutes. Chill to 48 to 50°F (9 to 10°C), aerate, and pitch the yeast. Ferment at 52°F (11°C) until around 1.012 SG, then let the temperature rise to 56 to 58°F (13 to 14°C) for a diacetyl rest. After 72 hours at terminal gravity, drop the temperature 2 to 3°F (1 to 1.5°C) per day until you reach 40°F (4°C). Transfer the beer to a secondary and slowly cool to 28°F (-2°C) (or as close to freezing as you can without freezing) for 6 to 8 weeks until clear. Bottle or keg as usual.

EXTRACT WITH GRAINS OPTION: Replace the pilsner and acidulated malts with 6.6 pounds (3 kilograms) Pilsen liquid malt extract and 7 milliliters of lactic acid (88 percent). Steep the crushed malt in 5 gallons (19 liters) as the water heats up. When the water hits 170°F (21°C), remove the grains. Remove brewpot from heat and add the lactic acid, Pilsen liquid malt, and first wort hops. Stir until all the extract is fully dissolved, and bring to a boil. Boil for 60 minutes, adding the remaining hops according to the ingredients list. After the boil, top up to 5 gallons (19 liters) and follow the remainder of the all-grain recipe.

ODELL BREWING COMPANY
DOUBLE PILSNER

(5 gallons/19 L, all-grain) OG = 1.076 FG = 1.015
IBU = 37 SRM = 4 ABV = 8.1%

While lovers of IPAs have flocked to double IPAs, the same has not been true for pilsner. Odell's Double Pilsner gives us a glimpse of what a double pilsner should be, with a surprisingly easy-drinking 8.2 percent beer.

INGREDIENTS

14.5 lb. (6.6 kg) German pilsner malt

1 lb. (0.45 kg) Weyermann CaraFoam malt (2 °L)

4 oz. (113 g) Munich malt (10 °L)

10 AAU Saaz hops (60 min.) (2.9 oz./81 g at 3.5% alpha acids)

5.7 AAU Tettnang hops (1 min.) (1.5 oz./43 g at 3.8% alpha acids)

5.7 AAU Tettnang hops (0 min.) (1.5 oz./43 g at 3.8% alpha acids)

1 tsp. Irish moss (15 min.)

Wyeast 2206 (Bavarian Lager) or White Labs WLP820 (Oktoberfest/Märzen) yeast (4 qt./4 L starter)

¾ cup (150 g) dextrose (if priming)

STEP BY STEP

Use water with a low mineral content. Mash crushed grains with 5 gallons (19 liters) of mash water, heated to 162°F (72°C). Mash at 150 to 152°F (66 to 67°C) for 45 minutes. Recirculate wort until it is quite clear. Collect wort, sparging with 168°F (76°C) water to collect 6.5 gallons (25 liters). (Your SG here should be 1.058. If it's lower than this, add dried malt to reach 1.058 or collect more wort—up to 8 gallons/30 liters—and boil longer). Boil wort for 90 minutes, adding the hops at times indicated. At the end of the boil, turn off heat, add the final hop addition, and stir the wort to create a whirlpool. Allow the wort to settle for 10 minutes. Cool wort, transfer to fermenter, and aerate well. Pitch yeast sediment from yeast starter. Ferment beer at 55°F (13°C). Hold fermentation temperature until beer is finished fermenting. Chill to 34°F (1.1°C) and hold for at least a month. Prime bottles with sugar or keg.

PARTIAL MASH OPTION: Reduce the German pilsner malt in the all-grain recipe to 0.75 pound (0.34 kilogram) and add 2 pounds (0.91 kilogram) Briess extra light dried malt extract and 6.6 pounds (3 kilograms) Briess Pilsen liquid malt extract. Put crushed grains in a nylon steeping bag. In a large soup pot, heat 3 quarts (2.8 liters) of water to 162°F (72°C) and submerge bag. Steep grains at 150 to 152°F (66 to 67°C) for 45 minutes. While grains are steeping, bring 2.5 gallons (9.5 liters) of water to a boil in your brewpot. After steep, put colander over brewpot and place grain bag in it. Pour "grain tea" through grain bag (to filter out the "floaties"), then rinse grains with 1.5 quarts (1.4 liters) of water at 170°F (77°C). Add dried malt extract and boil wort for 60 minutes, adding hops at times indicated. Add liquid malt extract at the end of the boil and let it steep for 15 minutes before cooling. Top off to 5 gallons (19 liters). Follow the remaining portion of the all-grain recipe.

PLZEŇSKÝ PRAZDROJ
PILSNER URQUELL

ᗄᗄᗄᗄᗄᗄᗄ

**(5 gallons/19 L, all- grain) OG = 1.048 FG = 1.015
IBU = 40 SRM = 4 ABV = 4.4%**

Brewed in Plzeň, Czech Republic, Pilsner Urquell is the original pilsner beer. They have held homebrewer competitions to see which skilled homebrewers could re-create this simple but hard-to-perfect classic. Make sure to brew this clone with soft water and carefully monitor your fermentation.

INGREDIENTS

8 lb. (3.6 kg) continental pilsner malt

1 lb. (0.45 kg) Vienna malt

0.5 lb. (0.23 kg) Munich malt (6 °L)

0.5 lb. (0.23 kg) Carapils malt

5.2 AAU Saaz hops (80 min.) (1.3 oz./38 g at 4% alpha acids)

3.2 AAU Saaz hops (45 min.) (0.8 oz./23 g at 4% alpha acids)

3 AAU Saaz hops (25 min.) (0.75 oz./21 g at 4% alpha acids)

1 tsp. Irish moss (15 min.)

Wyeast 2001 (Pilsner Urquell H-strain) or White Labs WLP800 (Pilsner Lager) yeast (3 qt./3 L starter)

¾ cup (150 g) dextrose (if priming)

STEP BY STEP

The traditional Pilsner Urquell utilizes an undermodified pilsner malt that is malted by the brewery. The mash is subsequently triple decocted to help break down the protein matrix that is still present in the undermodified malts. For three reasons we have decided to change up the classic recipe. First, homebrewers don't often have access to undermodified pilsner malts these days. Second, a triple decoction means a long and rigorous brew day for the brewer. Finally, adding in a protein rest could be detrimental to the beer's body and head retention. So, we've simplified the mash procedure and added some malts to help adjust the color and add a slight toasted character that the triple decoction should otherwise add to the beer's profile.

Mash grains with 15 quarts (14.2 liters) soft water at 142°F (61°C) and hold for 30 minutes. Perform a decoction, pull ⅓ thick portion of the mash (~1.5 gallons/5.7 liters), and bring to a boil. Boil for 15 minutes, making sure not to scorch the grain mix. Stir the decocted portion back into the main mash. The main mash should now settle at 155°F (68°C). Hold for a 30-minute rest. Mash out, vorlauf, and then sparge at 170°F (77°C) to collect enough wort to result in 5 gallons (19 liters) after a 90-minute boil. Boil 90 minutes, adding hops and Irish moss at times indicated. Cool, aerate, and pitch yeast. Ferment at 50°F (10°C) until signs of fermentation have slowed considerably. Some diacetyl is noted in Pilsner Urqell, but if there is a strong diacetyl presence at this point, 2 to 4 days at 65°F (18°C) is advised. Rack to secondary, and lager for 4 to 6 weeks at 40°F (4°C). After lagering is complete, bottle or keg as usual.

EXTRACT WITH GRAINS OPTION: Replace grains in all-grain recipe with 1.4 pounds (0.64 kilogram) Pilsen dried malt extract, 3.3 pounds (1.5 kilograms) Pilsen light liquid malt extract, 1.75 pounds (0.79 kilogram) pilsner malt, 0.5 pound (0.23 kilogram) Vienna malt, 0.25 pound Munich malt (10 °L), and 0.5 pound (0.23 kilogram) Carapils malt. In a large soup pot, heat 4.5 quarts (4.3 liters) of water to 169°F (76°C). Add crushed grains to grain bag. Submerge bag and let grains steep around 158°F (70°C) for 45 minutes. While grains steep, begin heating 2.1 gallons (7.8 liters) of water in your brewpot. When steep is over, remove 1.5 quarts (1.4 liters) of water from brewpot and add to the "grain tea" in steeping pot. Place colander over brewpot and place steeping bag in it. Pour grain tea (with water added) through grain bag. This will strain out any solid bits of grain and rinse some sugar from the grains. Heat liquid in brewpot to a boil, then stir in dried malt extract. Boil 60 minutes, adding liquid malt extract with 15 minutes remaining and hops as indicated. Cool and top off to 5 gallons (19 liters). Follow the remaining portion of the all-grain recipe.

SAINT ARNOLD BREWING COMPANY
SAINT ARNOLD SUMMER PILS

(5 gallons/19 L, all-grain) OG = 1.048 FG = 1.008
IBU = 30 SRM = 3 ABV = 5.2%

Saint Arnold's take on a summer quaffer is built like a classic German pilsner but with a heavy hand on the hops. They use noble hops for all additions so the hoppy flavor stays true to the history of the beer.

INGREDIENTS

9.5 lb. (4.3 kg) German pilsner malt

3 oz. (85 g) German Munich malt

7 AAU Hallertau hops (first wort hop) (1.75 oz./50 g at 4% alpha acids)

3.5 AAU Saaz hops (0 min.) (1 oz./28 g at 3.5% alpha acids)

1.3 AAU Hallertau hops (0 min.) (0.33 oz./9 g at 4.0% alpha acids)

1 tsp. Irish moss (15 min.)

White Labs WLP830 (German Lager) or Wyeast 2206 (Bavarian Lager) yeast

¾ cup (150 g) dextrose (if priming)

STEP BY STEP

Mash the grains together at 152°F (67°C) for 60 minutes. A slightly thinner than normal mash will produce a higher degree of fermentability. Collect approximately 7 gallons (26.5 liters) wort, adding the first wort hop addition to the kettle as you collect the wort. Boil 90 minutes, to result in about 5 gallons (19 liters), add the remaining hops at flameout, and let them steep for 10 minutes before cooling. Cool the wort to 75°F (24°C), aerate the beer heavily, and pitch your yeast. Allow the beer to cool over the next few hours to 68°F (20°C), and hold at this temperature until the beer has begun fermenting, normally about 24 hours. Then cool the beer to 48°F (9°C) and hold there for the remainder of the fermentation, probably about 2 more weeks. Bottle or keg when the beer has dropped to its final gravity and fermentation is complete.

EXTRACT ONLY OPTION: Replace pilsner and Munich malts with 6.6 pounds (3 kilograms) Pilsen liquid malt extract. Add water to make 3 gallons (11 liters), and begin to heat. When temperature gets up to about 180°F (82°C), remove from heat and stir in the liquid malt extract and bittering hops.

When all the extract is dissolved, return to heat and bring to a boil. Follow the remaining portion of the all-grain recipe, topping off to 5 gallons (19 liters) after cooling.

SAMUEL ADAMS BREWING COMPANY
NOBLE PILS

**(5 gallons/19 L, all-grain) OG = 1.048 FG = 1.012
IBU = 34 SRM = 5 ABV = 4.9%**

This seasonal from Samuel Adams gets its name straight from its hops; it uses all 5 noble hops (Hallertau, Tettnang, Saaz, Strisselspalt, and Hersbrücker). With a clean lager yeast and a hefty dry hop for a pilsner, the unique character of these hops is on full display.

INGREDIENTS

7.4 lb. (3.4 kg) 2-row pale malt (2 °L)

2.5 lb. (1.1 kg) Bohemian pilsner malt (2 °L)

7.4 AAU Hallertau pellet hops (90 min.) (2 oz./56 g at 3.7% alpha acids)

1.5 AAU Tettnang pellet hops (5 min.) (0.4 oz./11 g at 3.8% alpha acids)

2.3 AAU Saaz pellet hops (5 min.) (0.6 oz./17 g at 3.8% alpha acids)

0.5 tsp. yeast nutrients (15 min.)

1 oz. (28 g) Tettnang pellet hops (dry hop)

0.75 oz. (21 g) Saaz pellet hops (dry hop)

0.5 oz. (14 g) Strisselspalt pellet hops (dry hop)

0.25 oz. (7 g) Hersbrücker pellet hops (dry hop)

White Labs WLP830 (German Lager), Wyeast 2206 (Bavarian Lager), or Mangrove Jack's Bohemian Lager yeast (~3 qts./2.9 L starter or 1.5 sachets dry yeast)

⅔ cup (133 g) dextrose (if priming)

STEP BY STEP

Mix the crushed grains with 3.75 gallons (14 liters) of 165°F (74°C) strike water to stabilize the mash at 153°F (67°C). Hold at this temperature for 45 minutes. Vorlauf for 15 minutes, then begin sparge. Run off into kettle to achieve volume about 6.8 gallons (25 liters) and pre-boil standard gravity of 1.035. Boil for 90 minutes, adding hops and yeast nutrients according the ingredients list. Turn off the heat, give the wort a stir for a minute to create a whirlpool, and let that settle for about 15 minutes. Cool the wort down to 53 to 55°F (12 to 13°C), aerate, and pitch yeast. Ferment at 57°F (14°C) for 2 weeks or until signs of fermentation have died down. Rack to a secondary and lager for an additional 3 weeks at 40°F (5°C). Add the dry hops for the final 2 weeks of the lagering phase. If signs of diacetyl are apparent during racking, then a diacetyl rest is recommended. Give the beer 2 days at 70°F (21°C) to allow the yeast to process any diacetyl before racking over to the secondary vessel. After the lager period is complete, bottle or keg and carbonate to 2.4 volumes of CO_2.

EXTRACT ONLY OPTION: Substitute both of the malts in the all-grain recipe with 3.3 pounds (1.5 kilograms) light liquid malt extract, 3.3 pounds (1.5 kilograms) pilsner liquid malt extract, and 3 ounces (90 grams) extra light dried malt extract. Heat 6.25 gallons (24 liters) soft water in your brew kettle. If you have hard water (>150 ppm calcium carbonate), you can soften by boiling the water for half an hour and decanting off the precipitated chalk or by cutting your tap water with distilled or RO water. Just before the water reaches boil, remove from heat and stir in the malt extract until all extract is dissolved. Boil for 90 minutes. Follow the remaining portion of the all-grain recipe.

WARSTEINER BRAUEREI
WARSTEINER PREMIUM VERUM

**(5 gallons/19 L, all-grain) OG = 1.046 FG = 1.009
IBU = 33 SRM = 3 ABV = 4.6%**

Warsteiner is a well-known German pilsner. This light-colored lager has a more rounded, less crisp malt profile compared to Bitburger (see page 216) despite the lower FG. Treat your yeast well to reach the final gravity of this beer.

INGREDIENTS

9 lb. (4.1 kg) pilsner malt

6 oz. (0.17 g) Carapils malt

7 AAU Magnum hops (60 min.) (0.5 oz./13 g at 14% alpha acids)

2 AAU Tettnang hops (15 min.) (0.5 oz./14 g at 4% alpha acids)

2 AAU Hallertau-Hersbrücker hops (15 min.) (0.5 oz./14 g at 4% alpha acids)

0.25 oz. (7 g) Hallertau-Hersbrücker hops (0 min.)

0.25 oz. (7 g) Saaz hops (0 min.)

1 tsp. Irish moss (15 min.)

Wyeast 2124 (Bohemian Lager) or White Labs WLP830 (German Lager) yeast (4 qt./4 L yeast starter)

⅞ cup (175 g) dextrose (if priming)

STEP BY STEP

Use a multi-step infusion mash with 15-minute rests at 131°F (55°C) and 140°F (60°C) and a 45-minute rest at 149°F (65°C). Mash out, vorlauf, and then sparge at 170°F (77°C) to collect enough wort to result in 5 gallons (19 liters) after a 90-minute boil. Boil 90 minutes, adding hops at times indicated. After the boil is complete, allow the beer to sit covered for 15 minutes before cooling. After cooling, aerate and pitch yeast. Ferment at 55°F (13°C). Rack to secondary when fermentation is complete. Bottle or keg a few days later, when beer falls clear.

EXTRACT WITH GRAINS OPTION: Substitute the grains in the all-grain recipe with 1.4 pounds (0.64 kilogram) extra light dried malt extract, 3.3 pounds (1.5 kilograms) Pilsen liquid malt extract, 1.7 pounds (0.77 kilogram) pilsner malt, and 0.25 pound (0.11 kilogram) Carapils malt. In a large soup pot, heat 3 quarts (3 liters) of water to 167°F (75°C). Add crushed grains to grain bag. Submerge bag and let grains steep around 156°F (69°C) for 45 minutes. While grains steep, begin heating 2.4 gallons (9 liters) of water in your brewpot. When steep is over, remove 1 quart (1 liter) of water from brewpot and add to the "grain tea" in steeping pot. Place colander over brewpot and place steeping bag in it. Pour grain tea (with water added) through grain bag. This will strain out any solid bits of grain and rinse some sugar from the grains. Heat liquid in brewpot to a boil, then stir in dried malt extract. Add hops as indicated and at flameout stir in the liquid malt extract until dissolved. Let hot wort sit covered for 15 minutes before cooling. Top up to 5 gallons (19 liters) and cool. Follow the remaining portion of the all-grain recipe.

SEA DOG

WILD
BLUEBERRY

REFUND ME, MA, VT, CT, NY, IA, OR 5¢ MI 10¢ CA CRV OR

SEA DOG

WILD
BLUEBERRY

BEER WITH NATURAL FLAVOR ADDED   12 FL OZ.

FIFTEEN

FRuiT, SPICE & VEGETABLE BEERS

Beer Pictured on Left; See page 232

ARIZONA WILDERNESS BREWING COMPANY
TRES LECHES

〰〰〰

**(5 gallons/19 L, all-grain) OG = 1.065 FG = 1.016
IBU = 3 SRM = 7 ABV = 6.5%**

This recipe from Arizona Wilderness was a collaboration with Chris Bianco of Pizzeria Bianco. It was brewed to taste like a tres leches cake with additions of lactose, cinnamon, vanilla, and brown sugar.

INGREDIENTS

7.5 lb. (3.4 kg) Maris Otter pale malt

1.3 lb. (0.59 kg) malted oats

1.2 lb. (0.54 kg) flaked oats

1 lb. (0.45 kg) white Sonora Wheat

4 oz. (113 g) Caraamber malt (27 °L)

1 lb. (0.45 kg) light brown sugar (90 min.)

1 lb. (0.45 kg) lactose sugar (90 min.)

0.8 AAU East Kent Golding hops (60 min.) (0.2 oz./6 g at 4% alpha acids)

2.5 vanilla beans

0.4 oz. (11 g) ground cinnamon

White Labs WLP002 (English Ale), Wyeast 1968 (London ESB Ale), or Lallemand London ESB Ale yeast

⅔ cup (133 g) dextrose (if priming)

STEP BY STEP

Seek a mash temperature of 156°F (69°C) and hold that for 60 minutes. Raise to 168°F (76°C) for mashout. Hold 10 minutes. Sparge with about 5 gallons (19 liters) of water to collect roughly 7 gallons (26.5 liters) of wort. Mix in both sugar types and boil for 90 minutes total. Add hops at 60 minutes left in the boil. Cool, pitch yeast, aerate, and ferment with a favorite English ale yeast at 70°F (21°C). When fermentation is complete, add vanilla beans and cinnamon. Says Head Brewer Chase Saraiva, "We provided a rough guideline for amounts, but this should really be done to your taste. Typically, these will be added post-primary based on the profile of the beer. Approximately 2.5 vanilla beans (Madagascar or Tahitian), sliced and seeded, and 0.4 ounces (11 grams) of cinnamon are a good target."

PARTIAL MASH OPTION: Reduce the Maris Otter pale malt in the all-grain recipe to 1.3 pounds (0.59 kilograms). Add 3.3 pounds (1.5 kilograms) Maris Otter liquid malt extract. Place crushed grains in a muslin bag. Mash the grains in 1 gallon (4 liters) water at 156°F (69°C) for 60 minutes.

Remove grain bag and wash with 2 quarts (2 liters) hot water. Top off the kettle to 6 gallons (23 liters) and raise to a boil. As soon as reaching a boil, remove kettle from heat and stir in the liquid malt extract, sugar, and lactose, stirring vigorously until fully dissolved. Once dissolved, return kettle to a boil and add hops. Boil for 60 minutes. Follow the remaining portion of the all-grain recipe.

〰〰〰〰〰〰

BISON BREWING COMPANY
HONEY BASIL ALE

〰〰〰

**(5 Gallons/19 L, all-grain) OG = 1.052 FG = 1.010
IBU = 19 SRM = 6 ABV = 5.5%**

Bison's Honey Basil Ale carefully infuses caramel malts with fresh whole leaf basil and clover honey, creating a herbaceous, floral, and virtually hop-less beer with a soft wisp of honey and just a hint of basil in the aftertaste.

INGREDIENTS

8.75 lb. (4 kg) 2-row pale malt

0.75 lb. (0.34 kg) crystal malt (20 °L)

0.70 lb. (0.31 kg) Carapils malt

0.5 lb. (0.22 kg) honey (5 min.)

0.6 oz. (17 g) scored basil leaves (10 min.)

0.6 oz. (17 g) scored basil leaves (0 min.)

4.6 AAU Cascade pellet hops (60 min.) (0.8 oz./28 g at 5.75% alpha acids)

½ tsp. Irish moss (30 min.)

½ tsp. yeast nutrient (15 min.)

Wyeast 1056 (American Ale) or White Labs WLP001 (California Ale) yeast

¾ cup (150 g) dextrose (if priming)

STEP BY STEP

Mash grains with 3.75 gallons (14 liters) of 170°F (77°C) water to stabilize at 148°F (64°C) for 60 minutes. Sparge slowly with 175°F (79°C) water. Collect approximately 6 gallons (23 liters) of wort runoff to boil for 60 minutes. While boiling, add the hops, Irish moss, yeast nutrient, basil leaves, and honey as per the schedule (before adding basil, score the basil leaves at least five times with a paring knife). Cool the wort to 75°F (24°C). Pitch your yeast and aerate the wort heavily. Allow the beer to cool to 68°F (20°C). Hold at that temperature until fermentation is complete. Allow the beer to condition for 1 week, and then bottle or keg.

EXTRACT WITH GRAINS OPTION: Reduce the 2-row pale malt in the all-grain recipe to 1 pound (0.45 kilogram), and add 3.3 pounds (1.5 kilograms) Briess light liquid malt extract and 2 pounds (0.9 kilogram) light dried malt extract. Steep the crushed grains in 5.5 gallons (21 liters) of water at 148°F (64°C) for 30 minutes. Remove and rinse with 2 quarts (2 liters) of hot water. Add the liquid and dried malt extracts and bring to a boil. Follow the remaining portion of the all-grain recipe.

- - - - - - - - - - - - - - - - - -

BLUEJACKET
MEXICAN RADIO

(5 gallons/19 L, all-grain) OG = 1.076 FG = 1.023
IBU = 32 SRM = 46 ABV = 7.4%

This spiced stout is brewed with oats and lactose, then finished with vanilla beans, ancho chili peppers, cinnamon sticks, and roasted cocoa nibs. It's a truly innovative stout.

INGREDIENTS

5 lb. (2.3 kg) North American 2-row pale malt

5 lb. (2.3 kg) Maris Otter pale ale malt

1 lb. (0.45 kg) flaked barley

1 lb. (0.45 kg) chocolate malt (350 °L)

12 oz. (0.34 kg) crystal malt (80 °L)

12 oz. (0.34 kg) roasted barley

12 oz. (0.34 kg) flaked wheat

4 oz. (113 g) black patent malt

1 lb. (0.45 kg) lactose sugar (15 min.)

7 AAU Millennium hops (60 min.) (0.5 oz./14 g at 14% alpha acids)

2.25 AAU Fuggle hops (60 min.) (0.5 oz./14 g at 4.5% alpha acids)

2.25 AAU Fuggle hops (30 min.) (0.5 oz./14 g at 4.5% alpha acids)

0.15 oz. (4.3 g) cinnamon sticks (10 min.)

2.5 oz. (71 g) cocoa nibs (secondary)

1.25 oz. (35 g) dried Ancho chili peppers (secondary)

3 vanilla beans (secondary)

White Labs WLP001 (California Ale), Wyeast 1056 (American Ale), or Fermentis Safale US-05 yeast

⅔ cup (133 g) dextrose (if priming)

STEP BY STEP

Mill the grains and mix with 4.5 gallons (17 liters) of 164°F (73°C) strike water to reach a mash temperature of 152°F (67°C). Hold this temperature for 60 minutes. Vorlauf until your runnings are clear. Sparge the grains with 3.5 gallons (13.2 liters) and top up as necessary to obtain 6 gallons (23 liters) of wort. Boil for 60 minutes, adding hops, lactose sugar, and cinnamon sticks according to the ingredient list. After the boil, turn off heat and chill the wort to slightly below fermentation temperature, about 65°F (18°C). Aerate the wort with pure oxygen or filtered air, and pitch yeast. Ferment at 68°F (20°C) for 7 days, then drop the temperature to 60°F (16°C) for 24 hours. Add the cocoa nibs, ancho peppers, and vanilla beans, and age for 5 to 7 days. Crash the beer to 35°F (2°C) for 48 hours. After aging the spice addition, bottle or keg the beer and carbonate to approximately 2.25 volumes.

PARTIAL MASH OPTION: Reduce the 2-row pale malt in the all-grain recipe to 2.5 pounds (1.13 kilograms), and add 5 pounds (2.3 kilograms) Maris Otter liquid malt extract. Bring 2.2 gallons (8.3 liters) of water to approximately 164°F (73°C). Place milled grains in grain bags and submerge in the water for 60 minutes. The temperature of the mash should stabilize at about 152°F (67°C). After 60 minutes, remove the grain bags, and let drain fully. Wash the grains with about 1 gallon (4 liters) of hot water, then top off to 6 gallons (23 liters) in your brew kettle. Add liquid extract while stirring, and stir until completely dissolved. Boil 60 minutes. Follow the remaining portion of the all-grain recipe.

TIPS FOR SUCCESS

Mexican Radio adds some complexities to the average stout, in the form of a number of spice additions at two points in the production process. Add the cinnamon in the boil just as you would a hop addition, but add the cocoa nibs, vanilla, and ancho peppers in secondary to limit the amount of oil extraction; to account for the head-killing oils that do get into the beer, the recipe includes a significant addition of flaked wheat and barley to aid in head retention. To prepare the vanilla (go with cheap beans, because the subtleties and nuance of more expensive vanilla will be lost in this beer—but don't use extract!) and peppers, slice lengthwise before adding to the secondary to increase surface area and impact on flavor. You might also consider a vodka tincture, and just add the entire product to the beer. Finally, keep an eye on water. With so much roasted grain, astringency and acidity are a real concern. Consider the addition of a buffer if your water profile is lacking it naturally. Adding ¼ to ½ teaspoon of baking soda to the mash (especially for the partial mash recipe) may be a good idea if you are using soft water.

- - - - - - - - - - - - - - -

BRASSERIE DIEU DU CIEL!
ROSÉE D'HIBISCUS (PINKISH HIBISCUS)

**(5 gallons/19 L, all-grain) OG = 1.055 FG = 1.011
IBU = 15 SRM = 5 ABV = 5.9%**

Very pink, very floral, very crisp, and light bodied—all this adds up to a beer that's very drinkable! This beer's color and aroma are quite eye-catching and aromatic. Look for dried hibiscus flowers at your local food co-op, health food store, or from a local or online dried herb retailer.

INGREDIENTS

5.2 lb. (2.36 kg) Belgian pilsner malt

4 lb. (1.81 kg) wheat malt

1 lb. (0.45 kg) light candi sugar (10 min.)

2.9 AAU Nelson Sauvin hops (50 min.) (0.25 oz./7 g at 11.4% alpha acids)

4.6 AAU Nelson Sauvin hops (10 min.) (0.4 oz./11 g at 11.4% alpha acids)

2–4 oz. (57–113 g) dried hibiscus flowers (5 min.)

0.5 oz. (14 g) coriander seed (0 min.)

Wyeast 3944 (Belgian Witbier), White Labs WLP400 (Belgian Wit Ale), or Fermentis Safbrew T-58 yeast

⅔ cup (133 g) dextrose (if priming)

STEP BY STEP

Mash the grains at 150°F (66°C) for a crisp dry ale. Hold at this temperature for 60 minutes. Mash out, vorlauf, and then sparge at 170°F (77°C) to collect 5.5 gallons (21 liters) of wort in the kettle and boil for 90 minutes. Add hops and other ingredients as indicated. After flameout, allow the beer to sit for 5 minutes. Chill the wort to 68°F (20°C) and aerate. Pitch the yeast and ferment at that temperature. After primary fermentation, let the beer condition for 1 to 2 weeks before you bottle or keg. Carbonate to 2 to 2.5 volumes of CO_2.

EXTRACT WITH GRAINS OPTION: Substitute the pilsner and wheat malts in the all-grain recipe with 6.6 pounds (3 kilograms) wheat liquid malt extract. Heat 6 gallons (21 liters) water to a boil and add the malt extract. Boil for 60 minutes. Follow the remaining portion of the all-grain recipe.

BRASSERIE DIEU DU CIEL!
ROUTE DES ÉPICES (SPICE ROUTE)

**(5 gallons/19 L, all-grain) OG = 1.057 FG = 1.018
IBU = 29 SRM = 17 ABV = 5.3%**

This malty ale plays up the spice of rye with the addition of peppercorns. It features rich chocolate and rye grain flavors, a medium body, and a peppery finish.

INGREDIENTS

8.5 lb. (3.8 kg) English pale ale malt

2 lb. (0.91 kg) rye malt

12 oz. (0.34 kg) Weyermann CaraRye malt (65 °L)

6 oz. (170 g) melanoidin malt

8 oz. (0.23 kg) pale chocolate malt (220 °L)

2.5 AAU Golding hops (60 min.) (0.5 oz./14 g at 5% alpha acids)

6.3 AAU Bramling Cross hops (30 min.) (1 oz./28 g at 6.3% alpha acids)

1 tsp. green peppercorns (0 min.)

1 tsp. black peppercorns (0 min.)

Wyeast 1318 (London Ale III), White Labs WLP023 (Burton Ale), or Lallemand Windsor Ale yeast

⅔ cup (133 g) dextrose (if priming)

STEP BY STEP

Mash the grains at 156°F (69°C) for a rich, fuller-bodied ale. Hold at this temperature for 60 minutes. Mash out, vorlauf, and then sparge at 170°F (77°C) to collect 6 gallons (23 liters) of wort in the kettle, and boil for 60 minutes, adding ingredients as indicated. Allow the beer to sit for 5 minutes after flameout. Chill the wort to 68°F (20°C) and aerate it well. Pitch the yeast and ferment at that temperature. After primary fermentation, let the beer condition for 1 to 2 weeks before you bottle or keg. Carbonate to 2 to 2.5 volumes of CO_2.

EXTRACT WITH GRAINS OPTION: Substitute the pale ale malt and rye malt in the all-grain recipe with 6.6 pounds (3 kilograms) golden liquid malt extract and 1 pound (0.45 kilogram) rye malt. Heat 5.5 gallons (21 liters) water to a boil and add the malt extract. Boil for 60 minutes. Follow the remaining portion of the all-grain recipe.

TIPS FOR SUCCESS

Peppercorns can be added in a mesh bag and pulled before transferring to your fermenter. Or, for more flavor, transfer the peppercorns to the fermenter and rack the beer off them when packaging.

BURNT HICKORY BREWERY
WHITE FLAG THIRD STRIKE APRICOT SAISON

**(5 gallons/19 L, all-grain) OG = 1.069 FG = 1.008
IBU = 38 SRM = 6.2 ABV = 8%**

This Belgian-style wit is brewed with a substantial amount of apricot puree along with the pilsner, white wheat, and rye malts. The goal is to create a medium-bodied but tart saison with abundant fresh fruit aroma.

INGREDIENTS

7.5 lb. (3.4 kg) pilsner malt

3.75 lb. (1.7 kg) white wheat malt

1.25 lb. (0.56 kg) rye malt

12 oz. (0.34 kg) Caravienne malt (20 °L)

8 oz. (0.23 kg) corn sugar (10 min.)

5 lb. (2.27 kg) apricot puree (secondary)

6.1 AAU Citra pellet hops (60 min.) (0.5 oz./14 g at 12.2% alpha acids)

3 AAU Amarillo pellet hops (60 min.) (0.3 oz./8.5 g at 10% alpha acids)

0.5 oz. (14 g) Citra pellet hops (0 min.)

0.5 oz. (14 g) Amarillo pellet hops (0 min.)

½ tsp. Irish moss (30 min.)

½ tsp. yeast nutrient (15 min.)

White Labs WLP566 (Belgian Saison II), Wyeast 3711 (French Saison), or Lallemand Belle Saison yeast

¾ cup (150 g) dextrose (if priming)

STEP BY STEP

This recipe is a single-infusion mash. Mix all the crushed grains with 4.9 gallons (18.5 liters) of 168°F (76°C) water to stabilize at 148°F (64°C). This is a medium thin mash using 1.5 quarts of strike water per pound of grain (3.1 liter/kilogram). Mash for 90 minutes, then slowly sparge with 175°F (79°C) water. Collect approximately 6.2 gallons (23.5 liters) of wort runoff to boil for 90 minutes. While boiling, add the hops, Irish moss, yeast nutrient, and 10-minute corn sugar addition as per the schedule. After the boil is complete, cool the wort to 75°F (24°C). Pitch your yeast, and aerate the wort heavily. Allow the beer to cool to 67°F (19°C). Hold at that temperature for the first 2 days and gradually ramp up to 76°F (24°C) over the next 3 to 7 days. Hold at 76°F (24°C) until fermentation is complete. This may take 10 to 14 days. Gently transfer to a carboy, avoiding any splashing to prevent aerating the beer, and add the apricot puree. Allow the beer to condition for an additional week. Prime and bottle condition or keg and force carbonate to 2.8 volumes CO_2. Allow the beer to age for 2 more weeks to fully develop the flavors.

PARTIAL MASH OPTION: Substitute all the malts in the all-grain recipe with 6.6 pounds (3 kilograms) Coopers light liquid malt extract, 1.75 pounds (0.79 kilogram) pilsner malt, 12 ounces (0.34 kilogram) white wheat malt, 4 ounces (0.11 kilogram) rye malt, and 2 ounces (57 grams) Caravienne malt (20 °L). Steep the milled grains in 2.5 gallons (9.5 liters) of water at 148°F (64°C) for 30 minutes. Remove grains from the wort and rinse with 2 quarts (1.8 liters) of hot water and top kettle off to 5 gallons (19 liters). Add the malt extract and boil for 60 minutes. Follow the remaining portion of the all-grain recipe.

TIPS FOR SUCCESS

If you are unable to locate apricot puree, whole apricots may be substituted in either the all-grain or the partial mash recipe. If using fresh apricots, discard the pit and cut the apricots into small slices. Immerse the slices in 190°F (88°C) water for 2 minutes to sterilize the fruit. Crush the slices and allow them to cool before adding them to the secondary fermenter.

CAPTAIN LAWRENCE BREWING COMPANY
PUMPKIN ALE

**(5 gallons/19 L, all-grain) OG = 1.052 FG = 1.013
IBU = 19 SRM = 11 ABV = 5.2%**

There are a variety of strategies for making pumpkin beers. Captain Lawrence adds fresh pumpkin directly to the mash, while pumpkin pie spices, including nutmeg, cinnamon, and allspice, are added to the end of the boil.

INGREDIENTS

- 10.5 lb. (4.75 kg) 2-row pale malt
- 7.5 oz. (0.21 kg) crystal malt (120 °L)
- 2 oz. (57 g) Fawcett pale chocolate malt (220 °L)
- 4.5 AAU Columbus pellet hops (60 min.) (0.3 oz./8.5 g at 14.8% alpha acids)
- 4 oz. (0.11 kg) fresh pumpkin
- 0.2 oz. (5.7 g) nutmeg (0 min.)
- 0.2 oz. (5.7 g) cinnamon (0 min.)
- 0.2 oz. (5.7 g) allspice (0 min.)
- ½ tsp. Irish moss (30 min.)
- ½ tsp. yeast nutrient (15 min.)
- White Labs WLP001 (California Ale) or Wyeast 1056 (American Ale) yeast
- ¾ cup (150 g) dextrose (if priming)

STEP BY STEP

Finely dice the pumpkin and mix it and the crushed grains with 3.5 gallons (13 liters) of 172°F (78°C) water to stabilize at 154°F (68°C) for 60 minutes. Slowly sparge with 175°F (79°C) water. Collect approximately 6 gallons (23 liters) of wort runoff to boil 60 minutes. Add the hops and spices as per the schedule. Cool the wort to 75°F (24°C). Pitch your yeast, and aerate the wort heavily. Allow the beer to cool to 68°F (20°C). Hold at that temperature until fermentation is complete. Gently transfer to a carboy, avoiding any splashing to prevent aerating the beer. Allow the beer to condition 1 week, and then bottle or keg.

EXTRACT WITH GRAINS OPTION: Reduce the 2-row pale malt in the all-grain recipe to 2 pounds (0.9 kilogram), and add 3.3 pounds (1.5 kilograms) Coopers light unhopped liquid malt extract and 1.75 pounds (0.8 kilogram) light dried malt extract. Steep the milled grains and finely diced pumpkin meat in 5.5 gallons (21 liters) of water at 154°F (68°C) for 30 minutes. Remove grains and pumpkin from the wort and rinse with 2 quarts (1.8 liters) of hot water. Add the malt extracts and boil 60 minutes. Follow the remaining portion of the all-grain recipe.

DOGFISH HEAD CRAFT BREWERY
CHATEAU JIAHU

(5 gallons/19 L, all-grain) OG = 1.088 FG = 1.014
IBU = 10 SRM = ~6 ABV = 10%

This Ancient Ales series beer from Dogfish Head is a re-creation of a nine-thousand-year-old beer originating in a Neolithic village in China. Preserved pottery jars found in Jiahu, in Henan Province, revealed traces of a beverage made with rice, honey, and fruit. In 2005, molecular archeologist Dr. Patrick McGovern helped Dogfish Head brewers create a beer inspired by it.

INGREDIENTS

- 11 lb. 6 oz. (5.2 kg) 2-row pale malt
- 3 lb. (1.4 kg) orange blossom honey
- 2 lb. (0.91 kg) rice syrup
- 1 lb. (0.45 kg) Alexander's Muscat grape juice concentrate
- 0.5 lb. (0.23 kg) hawthorn berry powder
- 0.25 oz. (7.1 g) Simcoe hops (60 min.)
- Wyeast 4134 (Sake #9) yeast (as 1 qt./~1 L yeast starter)
- ¾ cup (150 g) dextrose (if priming)

STEP BY STEP

Mash the grains with 3.5 gallons (13 liters) of water at 149°F (65°C). Rest for 30 minutes. During the rest, heat 4.5 gallons (17 liters) of water to 170°F (77°C) for sparging. After the 30-minute rest, vorlauf until the runnings are clear, and sparge as normal. Collect 6.25 gallons (24 liters) of wort. Once the kettle is full, add the rice syrup and bring to a boil. Boil for 75 minutes, adding the hops at the time indicated in the ingredients list. After the boil, turn off the heat and stir in the honey and hawthorn berry powder, stirring to create a whirlpool. Chill the wort to pitching temperature, aerate well, and pitch the yeast. As fermentation starts to subside, add the Muscat grape juice concentrate. Cool the beer after 12 to 14 days of fermentation. After final gravity is reached, cold condition for 21 days. Bottle or keg as usual. Allow whatever time you deem necessary for proper conditioning and enjoy!

EXTRACT WITH GRAINS OPTION: Scale the 2-row pale malt down to 2 pounds (0.91 kilogram). Add 2 pounds 2 ounces (0.96 kilogram) Muntons light dried malt extract and

4 pounds (1.8 kilograms) Muntons light liquid malt extract. Place the crushed grains in a nylon steeping bag and steep (in a separate pot) in 2.5 quarts (2.4 liters) of water at 149°F (65°C) for 45 minutes. (This is actually a small mash, so follow temperatures and volumes as closely as is feasible.) Bring 2 gallons (7.6 liters) of water to a boil in your brewpot while the grains are steeping. After the steep, place the grain bag in a colander over brewpot. Pour the "grain tea" through the grain bag (to strain out grain husks), then rinse the grain bag with 1.5 quarts (~1.5 liters) of 170°F (77°C) water. Bring this wort to a boil, then add the dried malt extract. Boil for 75 minutes, adding the hops at the time indicated in the ingredients list. Stir in the liquid malt extract with 15 minutes left in the boil. After the boil, turn off heat and stir in honey and hawthorn berry powder. Cool the wort, then transfer to fermenter. Add enough cool water to the fermenter to reach 5 gallons (19 liters), aerate, and pitch the yeast. Follow the remainder of the all-grain recipe.

- - - - - - - - - - - - - - - - - -

DOGFISH HEAD CRAFT BREWERY
KVASIR

ᕙᕙᕙᕙᕙ-

(5 gallons/19 L, all-grain) OG = 1.087
FG = 1.011 IBU = 18 SRM = ~23 ABV = 10.4%

Another beer in Dogfish Head's Ancient Ales series, this beer was inspired by the analysis of a 3,500-year-old Danish drinking vessel. Kvasir includes cranberry juice and birch syrup as well as meadowsweet, yarrow, and myrica gale. The base beer is a red winter wheat, and there are minimal hops for balance.

INGREDIENTS

7 lb. (3.2 kg) wheat malt

5.5 lb. (0.23 kg) Maris Otter malt

0.5 lb. (0.23 kg) caramel malt (40 °L)

0.3 gallons (1.1 L) preservative-free cranberry juice (10 min.)

0.7 lb. (0.32 kg) birch syrup (10 min.)

2 lb. (0.9 kg) honey (10 min.)

0.25 oz. (7 g) meadowsweet (5 min.)

0.1 oz. (3 g) yarrow (5 min.)

10 oz. (283 g) Myrica gale (5 min.)

0.6 lb. (0.27 kg) fresh or frozen lingonberries (0 min.)

0.3 lb. (0.14 kg) fresh cranberries (0 min.)

~5 drops pectinase enzyme

2.64 AAU Hallertau, Spalt, or Tettnang hops (0.6 oz./17 g at 4.4% alpha acids) (60 min.)

0.8 AAU Hallertau, Spalt, or Tettnang hops (0.18 oz./5 g at 4.4% alpha acids) (10 min.)

White Labs WLP011 (European Ale) or Wyeast 1087 (Bohemian Ale Blend) or yeast

¾ cup (150 g) dextrose (if priming)

STEP BY STEP

Twenty-four to 48 hours before brewing, crush the lingonberries and cranberries in 0.5 gallons (1.9 liters) of water and treat with pectinase per the manufacturer's instructions. Heat 4.5 gallons (17 liters) of water to 166°F (74°C). Mash the grains at 153°F (67°C) and hold for 60 minutes. After conversion is complete, start the lautering process. Sparge with just enough water to collect about 6 gallons (23 liters) of wort in the brew kettle. Total boil time is 90 minutes. At 50 minutes into the boil, add the birch syrup, honey, and cranberry juice and the second hop addition. With 5 minutes remaining in the boil, add the meadowsweet, yarrow, and Myrica gale. After 60 minutes have elapsed, turn off the heat and add the lingonberry-cranberry mixture. Give the wort a long stir to create a whirlpool, and let the mixture sit for 15 minutes. Chill the wort to 62°F (17°C) and transfer to a sanitized fermenter. Try to leave most of the fruit behind. There should be about 5 gallons (19 liters) of wort in the fermenter. Pitch the yeast. Ferment at 62°F (17°C). After primary fermentation has completed, rack to secondary fermenter and mature for at least 21 days. Bottle or keg and enjoy.

EXTRACT WITH GRAINS OPTION: Replace all wheat malt and 5 pounds (2.3 kilograms) of the Maris Otter pale ale malt with 7 pounds Bavarian Wheat dried malt extract. Preheat 1.5 gallons (5.7 liters) of water to 154°F (68°C). Place the caramel and Maris Otter malt in a steeping bag in the water. Steep the grains at 153°F (67°C) and hold for 15 minutes. In a second vessel, heat approximately 1 gallon (3.8 liters) of water to 175°F (79°C) for rinsing. After the steeping time has elapsed, place the steeping bag with malt into a colander and let it drain into the brewpot. Rinse the grains with the 175°F (79°C) water and increase the heat. At 200°F (93°C), mix in the dried malt extract and raise to a boil. Add the first hop addition at the start of the boil. Boil time is 60 minutes. Follow the remainder of the all-grain recipe.

- - - - - - - - - - - - - - - - - -

DRY DOCK BREWING COMPANY
APRICOT BLONDE

⟨⟨⟨⟨⟨⟨

(5 gallons/19 L, all-grain) OG = 1.044 FG = 1.013
IBU = 8 SRM = 6 ABV = 4.9%

Dry Dock's Apricot Blonde has long been a popular fruit beer among homebrewers, and it has also taken home a bronze from the Great American Beer Festival. Note that the original gravity is calculated prior to fruit addition while ABV is calculated post fruit addition.

INGREDIENTS

8.5 lb. (3.9 kg) pilsner malt

0.38 lb. (0.17 kg) crystal malt (60 °L)

3.1 lb. (1.4 kg) Oregon Specialty Fruit apricot puree

1–4 oz. (28–113 g) apricot extract

2.3 AAU Cascade hops (60 min.) (0.33 oz./10 g at 7.1% alpha acids)

Fermentis Safale S-04 or Wyeast 1099 (Whitbread Ale) yeast

⅝ cup (125 g) dextrose (if priming)

STEP BY STEP

Mill the grains and mash in 3 gallons (11.3 liters) of water at 150°F (65°C) for 60 minutes. Vorlauf until the runnings are clear, and sparge the grains with enough 168°F (75°C) water to obtain a 6-gallon (23-liter) pre-boil volume. Boil the wort for 60 minutes, adding hops at the times indicated. After the boil, turn off the heat and chill the wort to 68°F (20°C), transfer the wort to the fermenter, aerate well, and pitch the yeast. Ferment at 68°F (20°C). On day 3 of primary fermentation, add the apricot puree. Ferment for an additional 7 days and rack to a secondary fermenter for additional clearing if desired. When fermentation and clearing is complete, transfer the beer to a bottling bucket or keg and add apricot extract 0.5 ounce (14 milliliters) at a time, gently stirring and tasting in between additions until the desired intensity of fruit flavor and aroma is obtained. Carbonate and package the beer as desired.

EXTRACT WITH GRAINS OPTION: Substitute the pilsner malt in the all-grain recipe with 6 pounds (2.7 kilograms) Pilsen liquid malt extract. Add 1.5 to 5 gallons (6 to 19 liters) of water to the brew kettle (the more water, the better). Crush the grain and steep at 150°F (65°C) for 30 minutes.

Add malt extract while stirring, then boil the wort for 60 minutes. Follow the remaining portion of the all-grain recipe.

TIPS FOR SUCCESS

Fruit extracts are an easy and often effective way to add fruit flavor and aroma to a beer, though care should be taken to not overpower the beer by using too much. The intensity of flavor and aroma will vary from one brand of extract to the next, so some experimentation is necessary to obtain the correct balance. Try experimenting with a small amount of your beer and then scaling up when you find the right concentration.

ODELL BREWING COMPANY
PEACH IPA

⟨⟨⟨⟨⟨⟨

(5 gallons/19 L, all-grain) OG = 1.069 FG = 1.013
IBU = 60 SRM = 6 ABV = 7.2%

Odell Brewing Company in Fort Collins, Colorado, brews the majority of its beers on a large system. However, brewers still put to use a 5-barrel pilot system at the brewery week in and week out. This recipe was one of those pilot batches made available at the tasting room (note that it is not the same beer as their seasonal imperial peach IPA, Tree Shaker).

INGREDIENTS

11.7 lb. (5.3 kg) pale ale malt (3 °L)

1.7 lb. (0.77 kg) Vienna malt (3.5 °L)

0.7 lb. (0.32 kg) melanoidin malt (25 °L)

2 tsp. gypsum

4 lb. (1.8 kg) peach puree or crushed peaches (pits removed)

7.8 AAU Warrior hops (60 min.) (0.5 oz./14 g at 15.5% alpha acids)

7.8 AAU Warrior hops (30 min.) (0.5 oz./14 g at 15.5% alpha acids)

8.8 AAU Simcoe hops (0 min.) (0.8 oz./22 g at 11% alpha acids)

4.8 AAU Australian Summer hops (0 min.) (0.8 oz./22 g at 6% alpha acids)

3.2 AAU Crystal hops (0 min.) (0.8 oz./22 g at 4% alpha acids)

1.2 oz. (33 g) Simcoe hops (20 min. into hop stand)

1.2 oz. (33 g) Australian Summer hops (20 min. into hop stand)

1.2 oz. (33 g) Crystal hops (20 min. into hop stand)

1.2 oz. (33 g) Simcoe hops (dry hop)

1.2 oz. (33 g) Australian Summer hops (dry hop)

1.2 oz. (33 g) Crystal hops (dry hop)

½ tsp. yeast nutrients (10 min.)

White Labs WLP001 (California Ale), Wyeast 1056 (American Ale), or Fermentis Safale US-05 yeast

⅔ cup (133 g) dextrose (if priming)

STEP BY STEP

Adjust brewing water by adding 1 teaspoon gypsum per 5 gallons (19 liters) water. Mash in with 1.5 quarts (1.4 liters) strike water per pound (0.45 kilogram) of grist to achieve a mash temperature of 152°F (67°C) and hold for 60 minutes. Sparge with 172°F (78°C) water and collect 6 gallons (23 liters) in the kettle. Boil for 60 minutes, adding hops and yeast nutrients at times indicated. At the end of the boil, add 0-minute hops and stir wort to create a whirlpool. Stir for at least 1 minute, and then let wort settle for a total of 20 minutes. Chill the wort to 170°F (77°C) before adding the "hop stand" hops. Stir for at least 1 minute, then let settle for another 15 minutes. Chill the wort to 68°F (20°C) and aerate thoroughly. Hold at 68°F (20°C) for 3 days or until primary fermentation slows down. Add the peach puree after kräusen has fallen, then wait until fermentation calms back down before adding dry hops. After 5 days on the dry hops, rack the beer to a keg and carbonate or rack to bottling bucket, add priming sugar and bottle. Carbonate to 2.4 volumes CO_2.

PARTIAL MASH OPTION: Substitute the pale ale malt in the all-grain recipe with 8 pounds (3.6 kilograms) pale ale liquid malt extract (7 °L). Place crushed grains in a muslin bag and mash in with 1 gallon (4 liters) water to achieve a mash temperature of 152°F (67°C). Hold for 60 minutes. Wash grain bag with 1 gallon (4 liters) of hot water. Top kettle to 6 gallons (23 liters) water and boil. Once at a boil, remove the kettle from heat and add the malt extract and gypsum. Stir until all the malt extract is dissolved, then return the wort to a boil. Follow the remaining portion of the all-grain recipe.

ROGUE ALES
HONEY KÖLSCH

**(5 gallons/19 L, all-grain) OG = 1.048 FG = 1.010
IBU = 26   SRM = 3   ABV = 5%**

While there's no fruit or spice in this beer, a full pound of raw honey gives it a big flavor. Rogue's twist on the kölsch style has resulted in big-time awards—including a gold medal at the World Beer Championships.

INGREDIENTS

7 lb. (3.2 kg) US 2-row pale malt

1 lb. (0.45 kg) white wheat malt

5 oz. (140 g) dextrin malt

4 oz. (113 g) acidulated malt

1 lb. (0.45 kg) raw wildflower honey (0 min.)

4.1 AAU German Hallertau Hersbrücker pellet hops (60 min.) (1 oz./28 g at 4.1% alpha acids)

9.1 AAU German Hallertau Hersbrücker pellet hops (10 min.) (1.5 oz./43 g at 4.1% alpha acids)

½ tsp. yeast nutrient (15 min.)

Whirlfloc (15 min.)

Wyeast 2575 (Kolsch II) or White Labs WLP003 (German Ale II) yeast

¾ cup (150 g) dextrose (if priming)

STEP BY STEP

Mill the grains and mix with 3.5 gallons (13.25 liters) of 163°F (73°C) strike water to reach an infusion mash temperature of 152°F (67°C). Hold at this temperature for 60 minutes. Vorlauf until your runnings are clear. Sparge the grains with 4 gallons (15 liters) of 170°F (72°C) water until 7 gallons (26.5 liters) of 1.035 SG wort is collected in your boil kettle. Boil for 60 minutes, adding hops, yeast nutrient, and kettle finings according to the ingredients list. After the boil, turn off the heat and add the final hop addition and honey. Whirlpool the kettle by gently stirring with a mash paddle for 2 minutes, and then let rest for an additional 13 minutes to achieve a 15-minute flameout steep. Chill the wort to 60°F (16°C), aerate, and pitch yeast. Ferment at 60°F (16°C) for the first 48 hours, and then free rise up to 64°F (18°C) and hold at that temperature until you reach terminal gravity. Crash cool at 33°F (1°C) for the better part of a week, and then package. Carbonate to between 2.4 and 2.6 volumes of CO_2, then enjoy!

EXTRACT ONLY OPTION: Substitute the grains in the all-grain recipe with 5 pounds (3.2 kilograms) Briess golden light liquid malt extract, 1 pound (0.45 kilogram) Muntons wheat dried malt extract, and 1 teaspoon (5 milliliters) 88 percent lactic acid. Bring 6.5 gallons (24.6 liters) of water up to a boil, adding the lactic acid and malt extract during the heating process. The target pre-boil gravity is 1.035. Boil 60 minutes. Follow the remaining portion of the all-grain recipe.

ROGUE ALES
MARIONBERRY BRAGGOT

くくくくくく-

**(5 gallons/19 L, all-grain) OG = 1.110 FG = 1.025
IBU = 17 SRM = 23 ABV = 11.4%**

A braggot draws on honey as well as malt for a substantial portion of its fermentables. Rogue's braggot uses two of their estate honeys and a handful of Rogue Farms malts, Rogue Farms Rebel hops, and (of course) lots of Rogue Farms marionberries are jam-packed into this flavorful, honey-forward beverage. Use as many of your own local ingredients as possible to make your braggot.

INGREDIENTS

10.5 lb. (4.77 kg) US 2-row pale malt

11 oz. (308 g) Munich malt

11 oz. (308 g) caramel malt (15 °L)

10 oz. (280 g) caramel malt (40 °L)

5.5 oz. (154 g) caramel malt (120 °L)

5.5 oz. (154 g) flaked rye

5.5 oz. (154 g) chocolate malt

6.5 lb. (3 kg) wildflower honey

8 fl. oz. (237 mL) pasteurized marionberry concentrate (fermenter)

8.25 AAU Cascade pellet hops (60 min.) (1.5 oz./43 g at 5.5% alpha acids)

4.1 AAU Cascade pellet hops (0 min.) (0.75 oz./21 g at 5.5% alpha acids)

½ tsp. yeast nutrient (15 min.)

Whirlfloc (15 min.)

Wyeast 1764 (Pacman), Wyeast 1272 (American Ale II), or White Labs WLP051 (California Ale V) yeast

¾ cup (150 g) dextrose (if priming)

STEP BY STEP

Mill the grains and mix with 5.5 gallons (21 liters) of 159°F (71°C) strike water to reach an infusion mash temperature of 148°F (64°C). Hold at this temperature for 60 minutes. Vorlauf until your runnings are clear. Sparge the grains with 4 gallons (15 liters) of 170°F (72°C) water until 6.5 gallons (24.6 liters) of 1.049 SG wort is collected in your boil kettle. Boil for 60 minutes, adding hops, yeast nutrient, and kettle finings according to the ingredients list. After the boil, turn off the heat and add the final hop addition and honey. Whirlpool the kettle by gently stirring with a mash paddle for 2 minutes, and then let rest for an additional 18 minutes to achieve a 20-minute flameout steep. Chill to 68°F (20°C), and transfer into a clean and sanitized fermenter that

already contains the pasteurized marionberry concentrate. Aerate with pure oxygen, pitch yeast, and ferment at 70°F (21°C) until you reach full attenuation. Due to the high gravity and large honey addition, consider oxygenating again (and possibly adding additional yeast nutrient that has been dissolved in a small amount of boiling water and cooled to room temperature) around 18 hours after initial yeast pitch. Crash cool at 33°F (1°C) for the better part of a week, and then package. Carbonate to between 2.2 and 2.6 volumes of CO_2.

PARTIAL MASH OPTION: Substitute the 2-row pale malt in the all-grain recipe with 7 pounds (3.2 kilograms) pale liquid malt extract. Mix the crushed Munich malt and flaked rye with 1.25 gallons (4.7 liters) of 158°F (70°C) strike water to reach an infusion mash temperature of 148°F (64°C). Hold at this temperature for 45 minutes, then add the crushed caramel and chocolate malts to the mash. Steep for an additional 15 minutes. Remove all the grains and wash with 1 gallon (4 liters) of 170°F (72°C) water. Add the liquid malt extract and stir until completely dissolved, then top off until there is 6.5 gallons (24.6 liters) of 1.049 SG wort in your boil kettle. Boil for 60 minutes. Follow the remaining portion of the all-grain recipe.

SEA DOG BREWING COMPANY
WILD BLUEBERRY (BLUE PAW WHEAT ALE)

くくくくくく-

**(5 gallons/19 L all-grain) OG = 1.050 FG = 1.012
IBU = 20 SRM = 4 ABV = 4.9%**

A silver-medal winner at the 2007 World Beer Championships, this wheat beer is all about the aroma and subtle fruit flavor of blueberries. As with any beer that uses flavoring extracts, start with a small amount and then adjust to taste as strength can vary considerably between brands.

INGREDIENTS

6.5 lb. (2.9 kg) 2-row pale malt

3.5 lb. (1.6 kg) wheat malt

4 oz. (0.11 kg) Munich malt

4 AAU Hallertau pellet hops (60 min.) (1 oz./28 g at 4% alpha acids)

2.5 AAU Willamette pellet hops (25 min.) (0.5 oz./14 g at 5% alpha acids)

2 oz. (57 mL) concentrated liquid blueberry extract

½ tsp. yeast nutrient (15 min.)

White Labs WLP005 (English Ale) or Wyeast 1187 (Ringwood ale) yeast

¾ cup (150 g) dextrose (if priming)

STEP BY STEP

This is a single-infusion mash. Mix the crushed grains with 3.2 gallons (13.3 liters) of 168°F (76°C) water to stabilize at 152°F (67°C) for 60 minutes. Sparge slowly with 175°F (79°C) water. Collect approximately 6 gallons (23 liters) of wort runoff to boil for 60 minutes. Add hops at times indicated. Cool the wort to 75°F (24°C). Pitch yeast, and aerate the wort heavily. Allow the beer to cool over the next few hours to 66°F (19°C), and hold at this temperature until the beer has finished fermenting. Transfer to a carboy, and add the blueberry extract while stirring very slowly. Condition for 1 week, and then bottle or keg.

EXTRACT WITH GRAINS OPTION: Substitute the 2-row pale malt in the all-grain recipe with 6.6 pounds (3 kilograms) Muntons unhopped wheat liquid malt extract, and decrease the wheat malt to 4 ounces (0.11 kilogram) and the Munich malt to 2 ounces (57 grams). Steep the crushed grains in 5.5 (21 liters) of water at 155°F (68°C) for 30 minutes. Remove grains from the wort, add the malt extract, and bring to a boil. Follow the remaining portion of the all-grain recipe.

- - - - - - - - - - - - - - - - - -

SMUTTYNOSE
BREWING COMPANY
PUMPKIN ALE

⟨⟨⟨⟨⟨⟨⟨~

**(5 gallons/19 L, all-grain) OG = 1.057 FG = 1.012
IBU = 35 SRM = 8 ABV = 6.1%**

David Yarrington, Smuttynose's brewmaster, says that their pumpkin ale was designed to showcase both the sweetness of the malts and a decent hop presence. Over the years, the brewery has reduced the amount of clove in the beer as that spice most often threw the beer out of balance. When brewing at home, start with just a pinch.

INGREDIENTS

10.75 lb. (4.9 kg) 2-row pale malt

0.9 lb. (0.41 kg) Hugh Bairds light Carastan malt (15 °L)

4 oz. (0.11 kg) crystal malt (60 °L)

4 oz. (0.11 kg) pumpkin puree

5.5 AAU Cascade hops (75 min.) (1 oz./28 g at 5.5% alpha acids)

4.1 AAU Cascade hops (10 min.) (0.75 oz./21 g at 5.5% alpha acids)

3.4 AAU Liberty hops (0 min.) (0.75 oz./21 g at 4.5% alpha acids)

0.14 oz. (4 g) ground cinnamon (0 min.)

0.14 oz. (4 g) ground nutmeg (0 min.)

1 pinch ground clove (0 min.)

Wyeast 1056 (American Ale), White Labs WLP001 (California Ale), Lallemand BRY-97 (American West Coast Ale), or Fermentis US-05 yeast

¾ cup (150 g) dextrose (if priming)

STEP BY STEP

Heat 4 gallons (15 liters) of strike water to achieve a stable mash temperature of 155°F (68°C). Add the crushed grains and the pumpkin puree in the mash, and hold at 155°F (68°C) for 60 minutes. Sparge, and collect 6.25 gallons (24 liters) of wort in the kettle. Boil for 75 minutes, adding hops and spices at times indicated. Give the wort a stir for at least 1 minute, and let the hot wort settle for 15 minutes total. Then chill the wort to 68°F (20°C) and pitch the yeast. Maintain this temperature during active fermentation. Keg or bottle as normal.

EXTRACT WITH GRAINS OPTION: Substitute the 2-row pale malt in the all-grain recipe with 5.75 pounds (2.6 kilograms) extra light dried malt extract. Heat 1 gallon (3.8 liters) of water to 170°F (77°C), and place the crushed grains and the pumpkin puree in a brewing bag. Steep the grains and puree for 20 minutes at 160°F (71°C), then rinse the bag with 1 gallon (3.8 liters) of hot water. Top off the kettle to make 6.25 gallons (24 liters) wort, and boil for 75 minutes. Follow the remaining portion of the all-grain recipe.

TIPS FOR SUCCESS

In the all-grain recipe, you may need to use 0.5 pound to 1 pound (0.23 to 0.45 kilogram) of rice hulls per 5 gallons (19 liters) to prevent a slow or stuck sparge. You can also add a beta glucan rest at 122°F (50°C) for 15 minutes at the beginning of the mash.

- - - - - - - - - - - - - - - - - -

SOUTHERN TIER
BREWING COMPANY
WARLOCK

ᘓᘓᘓᘓᘓᘓ-

**(5 gallons/19 L, all-grain) OG = 1.094 FG = 1.023
IBU = 44 SRM = 37 ABV = 10.1%**

Warlock is a jet-black, high-ABV spice beer. The rich cocoa flavors play well with the residual cinnamon and ginger notes. Complementary flavors include vanilla, nutmeg, and clove.

INGREDIENTS

16.5 lb. (7.5 kg) 2-row pale malt

1 lb. (0.45 kg) Munich malt

1 lb. (0.45 kg) flaked barley

0.75 lb. (0.34 kg) debittered black malt

0.5 lb. (0.23 kg) crystal malt (60 °L)

0.25 lb. (0.11 kg) chocolate malt

1 lb. (0.45 kg) pumpkin puree

12 AAU Chinook hops (60 min.) (1 oz./28 g at 12% alpha acids)

Cinnamon, vanilla, nutmeg, ginger, and clove extracts—to taste

Wyeast 1335 (British Ale II) or White Labs WLP022 (Essex Ale) yeast

⅔ cup (133 g) dextrose (if priming)

STEP BY STEP

Mill the grains and add the pumpkin puree, then mix with 6.25 gallons (23.7 liters) of 163°F (73°C) strike water to reach a mash temperature of 152°F (67°C). Hold this temperature for 60 minutes. Vorlauf until your runnings are clear, and lauter. Sparge the grains with 1.5 gallons (5.7 liters) and top up as necessary to obtain 6 gallons (23 liters) of wort. Boil for 60 minutes, adding hops according to the ingredient list and Irish moss if desired. After the boil, chill the wort to slightly below fermentation temperature, about 66°F (19°C). Aerate the wort with pure oxygen or filtered air, and pitch yeast. Ferment at 67°F (19°C) until wort reaches 1.028 specific gravity, then free rise to 72°F (22°C) until the completion of primary fermentation. Once the beer completes fermentation, reduce temperature to 32°F (0°C) and hold for 10 days. Draw a sample, and add spice extracts to taste, starting with a ratio of approximately 3:1 for the cinnamon to other extracts. Once the exact ratio/intensity is determined, scale up and add to the fermenter. Then bottle or keg the beer and carbonate to approximately 2.25 volumes.

EXTRACT WITH GRAINS OPTION: Substitute the 2-row pale malt in the all-grain recipe with 11 pounds (5 kilograms) pale liquid malt extract. Bring 5.2 gallons (19.7 liters) of water to approximately 165°F (74°C) and hold there, steeping the specialty malts and pumpkin puree in grain bags for 15 minutes. Remove the grain bags, and let drain fully. Add liquid malt extract while stirring, and stir until completely dissolved. Bring the wort to a boil for 60 minutes. Follow the remaining portion of the all-grain recipe.

━ ━ ━ ━ ━ ━ ━ ━ ━ ━ ━ ━ ━ ━

WEYERBACHER
BREWING COMPANY
IMPERIAL
PUMPKIN ALE

ᘓᘓᘓᘓᘓᘓ-

**(5 gallons/19 L, all-grain) OG = 1.080 FG = 1.019
IBU = 21 SRM = 13 ABV = 8%**

Weyerbacher wanted to create the mother of pumpkin ales with this recipe! It dials up the malt as well as the pumpkin and spice. Cinnamon, nutmeg, cardamom, and clove swirl in the glass, making this full-bodied beer an ideal fall night companion.

INGREDIENTS

7.6 lb. (3.5 kg) Muntons pale ale malt (2.5 °L)

5.25 lb. (2.4 kg) Weyermann Vienna malt (3.5 °L)

1.8 lb. (0.8 kg) Weyermann Munich I malt (6 °L)

1.8 lb. (0.8 kg) Weyermann Caramunich II (45 °L)

0.9 lb. (0.4 kg) Weyermann CaraFoam (2 °L)

6.3 AAU Apollo pellet hops (60 min.) (0.35 oz./10 g at 18% alpha acids)

1.6 lb. (0.7 kg) pumpkin puree (10 min.)

0.38 oz. (10.6 g) Vietnamese ground cinnamon (2 min.)

0.2 oz. (5.7 g) ground nutmeg (2 min.)

1 pinch ground cardamom (2 min.)

1 pinch ground clove (2 min.)

Wyeast 1272 (American Ale II), White Labs WLP051 (California Ale V), or Lallemand Nottingham Ale yeast

¾ cup (150 g) dextrose (if priming)

STEP BY STEP

Heat 5.5 gallons (20.5 liters) of strike water to achieve a stable mash temperature of 144°F (62°C). Hold at this temperature until starch conversion is complete, which is at least 60 minutes. Check for complete conversion using

an iodine test before beginning the sparge phase. Collect 6 gallons (23 liters) of wort in the kettle and boil for 60 minutes, adding hops at the beginning of the boil. Add the spices with 2 minutes left in the boil. The pumpkin puree is added directly into the kettle to avoid the stuck mash issue. This means that the yield will be affected downstream as more beer will be lost at each transfer point. Weyerbacher reports that they lose a significant amount of wort in the fermenter. Be careful not to add too much of either the cardamom or the clove, as they can easily overwhelm the beer. After the boil, give the wort a stir for at least 1 minute, and let the hot wort settle for 15 minutes total. Chill to 68°F (20°C), and maintain this temperature during active fermentation. If you can, ramp the temperature up to 72°F (22°C) at the end of active fermentation to assure completion. Bottle or keg as usual.

EXTRACT WITH GRAINS OPTION: Substitute the pale, Vienna, and Munich I malts in the all-grain recipe with 9.5 pounds (4.3 kilograms) Munich liquid malt extract. Heat 1 gallon (3.8 liters) of water to 170°F (77°C), and place the crushed grains in a brewing bag. Soak the grains for 20 minutes at 160°F (71°C), then rinse the grains with 1 gallon (3.8 liters) of hot water. Do not squeeze the bag—let it drip into the kettle. Add water to make 6 gallons (23 liters) of wort in the kettle, and add the liquid malt extract off the heat. Stir until all the extract has dissolved. Bring the wort to a boil for 60 minutes. Follow the remaining portion of the all-grain recipe.

- - - - - - - - - - - - - - - - - -

WYNKOOP BREWING COMPANY
PATTY'S CHILE BEER

꙳꙳꙳꙳꙳

**(5 gallons/19 L all-grain) OG = 1.040 FG = 1.008
IBU = 28 SRM = 4 ABV = 4.2%**

Patty's Chile Beer is aged with Anaheim and ancho peppers, resulting in a golden ale with lots of pepper flavors and aromas. Don't worry, though. Thanks to the pepper varieties there will be just a mild amount of heat.

INGREDIENTS

7.4 lb. (3.4 kg) Golden Promise pale ale malt

7 oz. (200 g) flaked barley

5 oz. (140 g) Weyermann Carahell malt (10 °L)

4.4 AAU East Kent Golding hops (60 min.) (1.25 oz./43 g at 5.25% alpha acids)

1.75 AAU East Kent Golding hops (10 min.) (0.5 oz./14 g at 5.25% alpha acids)

10 oz. (283 g) Anaheim peppers (0 min.)

½ of a medium-sized ancho pepper, roasted (0 min.)

White Labs WLP007 (Dry English Ale) or Wyeast 1098 (British Ale) yeast

¾ cup (150 g) dextrose (if priming)

STEP BY STEP

Mash the grains and flaked oats together at 160°F (71°C) for 60 minutes, and sparge with 175°F (79°C) water. Collect approximately 4.5 gallons (17 liters) of wort, and then add water to make 6 gallons (23 liters). Boil for 60 minutes, adding hops at times indicated. Chop the peppers and add them at flameout. Then cover the kettle and allow the peppers to steep for 15 minutes. Cool the wort to 75°F (24°C) and transfer to your fermenter through a sanitized colander to remove the peppers. Aerate and pitch yeast, and then allow the beer to cool over the next few hours to 68°F (20°C). Hold at this temperature until the beer has finished fermenting. Condition for 1 week, then bottle or keg.

PARTIAL MASH OPTION: Reduce the Golden Promise pale ale malt in the all-grain recipe to 1 pound (0.45 kilogram). Replace with 3.3 pounds (1.5 kilograms) Coopers light unhopped liquid malt extract and 1 pound (0.45 kilogram) light dried malt extract. Steep the crushed grain and flaked oats in 3 quarts (3 liters) of water at 160°F (71°C) for 30 minutes. Remove grains from the wort and wash them with 1 gallon (4 liters) of hot water. Add the liquid and dried malt extracts, bring volume up to 6 gallons (23 liters), and bring to a boil for 60 minutes. Follow the remaining portion of the all-grain recipe.

- - - - - - - - - - - - - - - - - -

WYNKOOP
BREWING COMPANY
TUT'S ROYAL GOLD

ᕦᕦᕦᕦᕦᕦᕦ-

**(5 gallons, 19 L, all-grain) OG = 1.057 FG = 1.009
IBU = 0 SRM = 6 ABV = 7.1%**

This beer was specially brewed in conjunction with *Tutankhamun: The Golden King and the Great Pharaohs*, an exhibit that ran at the Denver Art Museum. Head brewer Andy Brown said the brewery wanted to brew a beer that echoed the beers royals may have consumed in the age of Tut. That said, the brewery did use the advantages they had in regards to an additional three thousand years of brewing science.

INGREDIENTS

6.5 lb. (3 kg) Rahr Premium 2-row pale malt

1 lb. (0.45 kg) coarse-ground ivory teff flour

1.5 lb. (0.68 kg) Simpson's Golden Naked Oats

1.75 lb. (0.8 kg) unmalted wheat

1 lb. (0.45 kg) malted wheat

5 oz. (0.14 kg) rice or oat hulls

5.5 g grains of paradise

4 g Pakistani rose

7 g bitter orange peel

5.5 g tamarind paste

2.3 g ground coriander

1 oz. (28 g) pitted dates

10 oz. (0.28 kg) wildflower honey

White Labs WLP400 (Belgian Wit Ale), or Wyeast 3944 (Belgian Witbier) yeast

⅔ cup (133 g) dextrose (if priming)

STEP BY STEP

Mash the grains and flour at 138°F (59°C) for 30 minutes. (The rice or oat hulls are to assist runoff, which can be problematic with wheat beers; you should add them to the mash along with the other grains.) Add sufficient boiling water to raise temperature to 155°F (68°C) for a further 30 minutes. Run off and sparge to collect 6 gallons (23 liters) of wort, and boil it for 60 minutes. Cool, aerate, and then add spices in a hop or muslin bag to the fermenter as you pitch yeast. Mix the honey and dates with enough boiling water (about 1 pint) to give a pourable slurry and add to the fermenter after the high kräusen has fallen. Rack to secondary after 5 to 7 days, leave 1 to 2 weeks to clarify and reach finishing gravity, then bottle or keg.

PARTIAL MASH OPTION: Replace 5 pounds of the 2-row malt with 2.5 pounds (1.13 kilograms) extra light dried malt extract and remove the rice/oat hulls from the recipe. Place all the crushed grains in a large muslin bag and mix in 2 gallons water at 145°F (63°C) to rest at 138°F (59°C). After 30 minutes, mix in enough boiling water to raise to 155°F (68°C), and hold for another 30 minutes. Remove the grain bag and place in a colander over the brewpot. Wash the grain with 1 gallon (4 liters) of hot water and top off the 3 gallons (23 liters), then bring to a boil. Boil for 60 minutes, adding the dried malt extract with 15 minutes remaining in the boil. After the boil, top off to 5 gallons (19 liters) and follow the remaining portion of the all-grain recipe.

TIPS FOR SUCCESS

The OG stated in the recipe is the gravity that you should shoot for on brew day. The ABV is calculated with the honey and dates added. Teff is a popular grain of Ethiopia and can be found at specialty grocery stores. It is considered the smallest grain in the world, so see if you can find it pre-ground, because crushing a pound of it may be a challenge.

SOUR, WILD & WOOD-AGED BEERS

BEER PICTURED ON LEFT; SEE PAGE 240

ANCHORAGE BREWING COMPANY
A DEAL WITH THE DEVIL

≪≪≪≪≪≪

(5 gallons/19 L, all-grain) OG = 1.164 FG = 1.041
IBU= 40 SRM = 16 ABV = 17%

This massive American-style barleywine from Anchorage Brewing utilizes only one hop variety and loads of malt to ring in at 17 percent ABV. Anchorage ages it for 11 months in cognac barrels.

INGREDIENTS

29 lb. (13.2 kg) 2-row pale malt

1 lb. (0.45 kg) crystal malt (120 °L)

1 lb. (0.45 kg) table sugar

7.3 AAU Galaxy hops (60 min.) (0.5 oz./14 g at 14.6% alpha acids)

18.25 AAU Galaxy hops (15 min.) (1.25 oz./35 g at 14.6% alpha acids)

1 tsp. yeast nutrients (10 min.)

White Labs WLP099 (Super High Gravity Ale)

⅔ cup (133 g) dextrose (if priming)

Lallemand CBC-1 or White Labs WLP099 (Super High Gravity Ale) (if priming)

STEP BY STEP

There are several ways to approach brewing a beer this big. You can perform this as a parti-gyle brew and produce a smaller 3-gallon (11-liter) barleywine and a second more sessionable table beer. You could also use more pale malt to have a higher volume of first runnings. Or you could perform a sparge, which will yield more wort and require a much more extensive boil. Because the extensive boil is what Anchorage Brewing Company does, we'll outline that procedure here and supplement with some sugar to get up to Anchorage's starting gravity.

This is a single-infusion mash, targeting about 1 quart/pound (2.1 liters/kilograms) water to grain mash ratio, roughly 30 quarts (28.4 liters). Mash in at 148°F (64°C) and hold there for 1 hour. Next, recirculate until wort is clear and collect as much wort as you can. Bring this up to a boil as soon as possible. Fill the mash tun back up with 24 quarts (22.7 liters) of water at 180°F (82°C) to raise the mash temperature up to mash out. Stir and then recirculate until wort is clear, and collect as much as you can. Once you have collected all of the wort you can get, try to take a specific gravity reading of

room-temperature wort. The mash should yield approximately 10 gallons (37.8 liters) of 1.078 wort. Add the table sugar and bring wort to a boil until achieving a target volume of 5.25 gallons (20 liters) in your kettle at the end of boil. Anchorage boils A Deal with the Devil for about 5 hours. Depending on your boil-off rate, it may take 5 hours or more to achieve this final volume. Add the majority of the hops at the last 15 minutes of the boil based on the current volume, targeting 40 IBUs. Cool the wort, and add the yeast from either a large starter or repitching yeast from a recently brewed batch of beer. Be sure you have fresh and active yeast, with at least two to three times the usual amount of yeast you'd use for a regular ale. Oxygenate thoroughly, and manage your fermentation by keeping it in the mid-60°F range (~18°C). You may want to hit the wort with a second round of oxygen 24 hours after pitching the yeast. Leave the beer for at least 2 to 4 weeks in the primary fermenter, then you can transfer into a cognac barrel or a secondary fermenter with some French oak chips that have been soaking in cognac for several weeks. This will help emulate the barrel-aging effect. Age to preferred taste; Anchorage ages for 11 months. When ready to package, be sure to pitch a fresh, highly alcohol-tolerant strain of yeast if you plan to bottle condition.

EXTRACT WITH GRAINS OPTION: Substitute the 2-row pale malt and table sugar in the all-grain recipe with 17.75 pounds (8.1 kilograms) extra light dried malt extract. Steep the crystal malt in 1 gallon (4 liters) of water at 168°F (76°C) for about 10 minutes, then remove grain bag and drain well. Top off the kettle to 6 gallons (23 liters) and raise to a boil. As soon as reaching a boil, remove kettle from heat and stir in the dried malt extract. Stir until fully dissolved, then boil for 60 minutes. Follow the remaining portion of the all-grain recipe.

- - - - - - - - - - - - - - -

ANCHORAGE BREWING COMPANY
LOVE BUZZ

≪≪≪≪≪≪

(5 gallons/19 L, all-grain) OG = 1.057 FG = 0.997
IBU = 40 SRM = 8 ABV = 8%

Anchorage beers can be hard to find and they often don't come cheap, yet they have gained many devoted fans. This golden saison has loads of flavor from the yeasts used, including delicious funk from *Brettanomyces*. Admittedly, this is a difficult beer to clone at home.

INGREDIENTS

7.5 lb. (3.4 kg) pilsner malt

3.5 lb. (1.6 kg) wheat malt

12 oz. (0.34 kg) crystal malt (60 °L)

1.3 AAU Simcoe hops (first wort hop) (0.1 oz./3 g at 13.2% alpha acids)

13.2 AAU Simcoe hops (0 min.) (1 oz./28 g at 13.2% alpha acids)

11.7 AAU Citra hops (0 min.) (1 oz./28 g at 11.7% alpha acids)

3 oz. (85 g) Citra hops (dry hop)

1 oz. (28 g) fresh rose hips (0 min.)

0.5 oz. (14 g) fresh orange peel (0 min.)

0.1 oz. (3 g) freshly ground peppercorn (0 min.)

2 oz. (57 g) medium toast oak staves or oak cubes (French oak preferred)

White Labs WLP568 (Belgian Style Saison Ale Yeast Blend) or the Yeast Bay (Saison Blend) yeast

Your favorite strain of *Brettanomyces bruxellensis* yeast

Neutral wine yeast or Lallemand CBC-1 yeast (if priming)

⅞ cup (175 g) dextrose (if priming)

STEP BY STEP

Mill the grains and dough-in, targeting a mash of around 1.3 quarts of water to 1 pound of grain (2.7 liters/kilograms) and a temperature of 150°F (66°C). Hold the mash at 150°F (66°C) until enzymatic conversion is complete, about 60 minutes. Sparge slowly with 170°F (77°C) water, collecting wort until the pre-boil kettle volume is 6 gallons (23 liters). Add the first wort hops early in the sparge phase. Boil time is 60 minutes. Add flameout hops and spicing, then start a whirlpool by stirring wort for at least 1 minute. Let settle. After 30 minutes, chill the wort to 70°F (18°C) and aerate thoroughly. After 3 days, allow the fermentation temperature to rise up to 83°F (29°C). After primary fermentation is complete, transfer to a long-term aging vessel and pitch your *Brettanomyces bruxellensis* yeast. Anchorage Brewing Company ages Love Buzz for eight months in French oak barrels that previously contained pinot noir wine. There are several alternatives. First, you can try to soak oak staves or cubes for several weeks in a sealed bottle of pinot noir (warning: the resulting wine will probably taste more like plywood than wine). Or you can boil the oak then add that along with several ounces of pinot noir directly to the beer. Age until the oak presence is detectable, but you don't want it to overwhelm the beer. Try to taste once a week until this nuance is achieved. At that point, rack the beer off the

oak and add your dry hops. Dry hop for 1 to 3 weeks, then either bottle or keg. Aim to carbonate the beer to around 2.8 volumes of CO_2. If your Love Buzz clone was aging for more than 3 months and you plan on bottle conditioning, we recommend pitching either a neutral wine yeast or brewer's yeast, such as Lallemand's CBC-1.

EXTRACT WITH GRAINS OPTION: Replace the grains in the all-grain recipe with 4 pounds (1.8 kilograms) wheat dried malt extract, 2 pounds (0.91 kilogram) Pilsen dried malt extract, and 8 ounces (0.23 kilogram) crystal malt (60 °L). Place your crushed grains in a grain bag and place in 6 gallons (23 liters) of water in your kettle. Heat until temperature reaches 170°F (77°C), then remove the grain bag and add the first wort hops. When the water comes to a boil, remove from heat and add the dried malt extracts. Stir thoroughly to dissolve, and then return to a boil for 60 minutes. Follow the remaining portion of the all-grain recipe.

TIPS FOR SUCCESS

Unless you invest in oak barrels and don't mind transferring the beer back and forth, the nuances of Love Buzz are going to be difficult to achieve at home. You could try to add the oak when you pitch the saison yeast instead of at the time of pitching the *Brett B*, as this may better simulate the oak-barrel fermentation that Love Buzz undergoes. But this may be a challenge if you need to transfer the beer into another vessel for secondary fermentation. A conical fermenter allowing for a yeast dump would be helpful in this situation. Otherwise, save the oak for secondary fermentation. Also if you are having trouble acquiring the suggested saison blends, you can try making your own blend based on the strains more widely available. Several strains of *Brettanomyces bruxellensis* are now commercially available. Finding the strain that is most appealing to you would be ideal. You could utilize dregs of a favorite beer, but Gabe states that Anchorage Brewing Company pitches a neutral wine yeast strain at the time of bottling, so using the dregs from a bottle of their beer most likely will not get you the results you are after. This recipe calls for fresh rose hips. We would recommend that you first smash the fruit, then freeze the rose hips to help open the fruit up. If fresh rose hip is not available, dried rose hips can be substituted. Cut the quantity by ¼ if you plan to use dried rose hips.

THE BRUERY
MASH

>>>>>>-

(5 gallons/19 L, all-grain) OG = 1.092 FG = 1.016
IBU = 30 SRM = 30 ABV = 11%

The Bruery calls Mash a favorite around the brewery thanks to its intense but balanced character and complex aromas of pear, fig, toasted bread, caramel, vanilla, and toasted coconut. Note that the specifications provided here are all pre-barrel aging numbers. After aging in a bourbon barrel, the beer is above 13% ABV.

INGREDIENTS

17 lb. (7.7 kg) Great Western 2-row pale malt

1.9 lb. (0.86 kg) Briess Bonlander Munich malt (10 °L)

0.4 lb. (181 g) Castle Abbey malt (17 °L)

0.3 lb. (136 g) Castle chocolate malt (340 °L)

13.5 AAU UK Challenger hops (60 min.) (1.4 oz./40 g at 9.6% alpha acids)

½ tsp. yeast nutrient (10 min.)

½ Whirlfloc tablet (10 min.)

Bourbon-soaked oak cubes

White Labs WLP001 (California Ale), Wyeast 1056 (American Ale), or Fermentis Safale US-05 yeast

¾ cup (150 g) dextrose (if priming)

STEP BY STEP

Mill the grains and dough-in targeting a mash of around 1.25 quarts of water to 1 pound of grain (2.6 liters/kilograms) and a temperature of 150°F (66°C). Hold the mash at 150°F (66°C) for 60 minutes. Sparge slowly with 170°F (77°C) water, collecting wort until the pre-boil kettle volume is 7 gallons (26.5 liters). Boil 120 minutes, adding ingredients as indicated. Chill to 65°F (18°C), and aerate thoroughly. The yeast pitch rate is 1 million cells per milliliter per degree Plato. On a homebrew scale, this is approximately 3 packages of liquid yeast. For the wood aging, the Bruery's experimental brewer Andrew Bell says, "After primary fermentation is finished, rack the beer to a CO_2-purged, first-use bourbon barrel (or as an alternative, add bourbon-soaked oak cubes to the beer in a secondary fermenter). Age the beer on the oak until a refined bourbon character is achieved (approximately 1 year on a commercial scale, usually less on a smaller scale depending on the surface area of your oak source). After aging, bottle or keg as normal, carbonating the beer to around 2.5 volumes of CO_2 (forced carbonation would be easier with this high ABV beer)." If you plan to bottle condition, you may consider pitching some fresh yeast at bottling.

PARTIAL MASH OPTION: Reduce the 2-row pale malt in the all-grain recipe to 2 pounds (0.91 kilogram), and add 10 pounds (4.5 kilograms) golden liquid malt extract. Place crushed grains in a large muslin bag. Heat 2 gallons (7.6 liters) water and target a mash temperature of 150°F (66°C). Add the grain bag and hold the mash at 150°F (66°C) until enzymatic conversion is complete, about 60 minutes. Remove the grain bag, and slowly wash the grains with 2 gallons (7.6 liters) of hot water. Add the liquid malt extract, and top off to 7 gallons (26.5 liters) in the brewpot. Follow the remaining portion of the all-grain recipe.

FIRESTONE WALKER BREWING COMPANY
DOUBLE BARREL ALE

>>>>>>-

(5 gallons/19 L, all-grain) OG = 1.051 FG = 1.013
IBU = 33 SRM = 13 ABV = 5%

This beer, also known as DBA, was Firestone Walker's first big hit. It is partially fermented in oak, and the brewery says it stands as an iconic tribute to traditional cask-fermented English ales. Expect toffee, caramel, and toasted oak in the glass.

INGREDIENTS

5 lb. (2.27 kg) US 2-row pale malt

5 lb. (2.27 kg) British pale ale malt

12 oz. (0.33 kg) Munich malt (10 °L)

10 oz. (0.29 kg) crystal malt (80 °L)

3.5 oz. (99 g) crystal malt (120 °L)

1.5 oz. (43 g) chocolate malt (350 °L)

3.5 AAU Magnum hops (60 min.) (0.25 oz./7 g at 14% alpha acids)

5 AAU East Kent Golding hops (30 min.) (1 oz./28 g at 5% alpha acids)

2.5 AAU East Kent Golding hops (0 min.) (0.5 oz./14 g at 5% alpha acids)

2.3 AAU Styrian Golding hops (0 min.) (0.5 oz./14 g at 4.6% alpha acids)

1 oz. (28 g) East Kent Golding hops (dry hop)

1 oz. (28 g) medium toast American oak cubes (in primary fermenter)

½ Whirlfloc tablet

White Labs WLP013 (London Ale), Wyeast 1028 (London Ale), or Lallemand Nottingham Ale yeast

¾ cup (150 g) dextrose (if priming)

STEP BY STEP

This is a multi-step infusion mash. Mix the crushed grains with 3.5 gallons (13 liters) of water to stabilize the mash at 145°F (66°C), and hold for 60 minutes. Raise temperature of mash to 155°F (68°C) and hold for 15 minutes. Raise the mash to 168°F (76°C) and begin to lauter. Collect 6.5 gallons (24.6 liters) of wort to begin your 60-minute boil. Add hops per the schedule in the ingredients list, adding the final hop addition just after turning off the heat. At the end of the boil, you should have 5.5 gallons (21 liters) in your kettle. After the boil, give your wort a stir to create a whirlpool, then let the wort settle for 30 minutes prior to chilling. Cool your wort to 66°F (20°C) for fermenting, aerate well, then pitch your yeast along with the oak cubes. After 7 days, rack the beer into a secondary vessel, then add the dry hops and wait 3 to 4 days. Bottle or keg as usual.

EXTRACT WITH GRAINS OPTION: Substitute the 2-row pale malt, British pale malt, and Munich malt in the all-grain recipe with 2.5 pounds (1.13 kilograms) extra light dried malt extract and 3.3 pounds (1.5 kilograms) Maris Otter liquid malt extract. Place crushed grains in a muslin bag. Begin heating 2 gallons (7.6 liters) of water. Place the grain bag in the water when the temperature hits 160°F (71°C), and hold for 20 minutes. Remove the grain bag and wash with 2 quarts (2 liters) of hot water. If your kettle can hold the water, top off to 6.5 gallons (24.6 liters) and add all the malt extract. If your kettle can only do a partial boil, then add the liquid malt extract during the final 15 minutes of the boil. Total boil time is 60 minutes. Follow the remaining portion of the all-grain recipe.

TIPS FOR SUCCESS

The team at Firestone Walker Brewing Company created one of the only, if not the only, union brewing method in the United States. Inspired by the Burton union systems made popular by the breweries in Burton upon Trent, Firestone dubbed their barrel union the "Firestone Union." Twenty percent of Double Barrel Ale is barrel-fermented in 60-gallon (227-liter) American oak barrels for 6 days before being blended back into the main batch. The remaining 80 percent is fermented in stainless conicals. This system makes it nearly impossible to duplicate the Firestone Union process at home. Instead, homebrewers can opt to add 1 ounce (28 grams) of American oak cubes

in primary fermentation to simulate the barrel fermentation profile. Unfortunately for most of us, the only place to try Double Barrel Ale in its unblended, 100-percent barrel-fermented state is in California at their brewery in Paso Robles or their Taproom Restaurant in Buellton. But that taste (and the rest of Firestone Walker's stellar lineup of beers) is certainly worth a pilgrimage! Matt Brynildson is known for dry hopping his beers prior to the termination of primary fermentation to try to take advantage of biotransformations, which hop oils can undergo in the presence of yeast. The goal is to add the hops with just a few gravity points left in fermentation. Also be aware of "beer volcanoes," as the hops can create a nucleation point to release dissolved CO_2, creating a volcano effect on the beer, which can lead to a significant amount of beer loss and a giant mess.

FUNKWERKS
RASPBERRY
PROVINCIAL

(5 gallons/19 L, all-grain) OG = 1.044 FG = 1.012
IBU = 13   SRM = 3.5   ABV = 4.2%

This Great American Beer Festival gold-medal winner (Belgian-style fruit beer category) started out as a test batch of session summer sour ale, Provincial. When that particular batch didn't quite hit gravity, the Funkwerks brewers decided to experiment! This tart fruit beer features a citrusy, raspberry aroma.

INGREDIENTS

4.3 lb. (1.9 kg) pilsner malt

2.2 lb. (1 kg) wheat malt

0.5 lb. (0.23 kg) Carapils malt

0.5 lb. (0.23 kg) flaked wheat

0.5 lb. (0.23 kg) flaked oats

1.2 lb. (0.55 kg) acidulated malt (20 min.)

3.5 AAU Magnum hops (60 min.) (0.25 oz./7 g at 14% alpha acids)

0.75 AAU Styrian Golding hops (15 min.) (0.25 oz./7 g at 3% alpha acids)

25 oz. (0.74 L) Oregon Specialty Fruit raspberry puree (added at the end of primary fermentation)

White Labs WLP400 (Belgian Wit Ale) or Wyeast 3944 (Belgian Witbier) yeast

½ cup (100 g) dextrose (if priming)

STEP BY STEP

Mash all the grains except the acidulated malt in 3.3 gallons (12.5 liters) of water at 155°F (68°C) for 40 minutes, then add the milled acidulated malt and continue mashing for an additional 20 minutes for 60 minutes total mash time. Mash out, vorlauf, and then sparge at 168°F (75°C). Boil 60 minutes, adding the hops at the times indicated in the ingredients list. Pitch the yeast, ferment at 68°F (20°C) for 4 days, and add the raspberry puree. Ferment for an additional 7 days, rack to a secondary fermenter for additional clearing if desired, and then bottle or keg the beer as usual.

PARTIAL MASH OPTION: Scale down the pilsner malt to 2 pounds (0.91 kilogram), and substitute the wheat malt with 2.7 pounds (1.2 kilograms) wheat dried malt extract. Mill the grains and mash all except the acidulated malt in 1.3 gallons (1.5 liters) of water at 155°F (68°C) for 40 minutes. Once this is complete, add the milled acidulated malt and continue mashing for an additional 20 minutes for 60 minutes total mash time. Rinse the grains with about 1 gallon (4 liters) of hot water. Top off your kettle to 6 gallons (23 liters) pre-boil volume (or as high as you can without fear of boil-over problems). Add the dried malt extract and bring to a boil. Boil the wort for 60 minutes, adding the hops at the times indicated in the ingredients list. Follow the remaining portion of the all-grain recipe.

HAANDBRYGGERIET
NORWEGIAN WOOD

**(5 gallons/19 L, all-grain) OG = 1.060 FG = 1.010
IBU = 28 SRM = 22 ABV = 6.7%**

Jens P. Maudal, head brewer at Haandbryggeriet in Drammen, Norway, says this beer was a re-creation of a traditional farm ale meant for everyday drinking. A stronger version would normally be brewed for the Christmas holiday season. Note the unusual addition of both mash hops and juniper branches.

INGREDIENTS

8 lb. 3 oz. (3.7 kg) Weyermann smoked malt

2 lb. (0.91 kg) Munich malt

19 oz. (0.55 kg) Weyermann CaraAmber malt

18 oz. (0.51 kg) British amber malt

11 oz. (0.31 kg) British pale malt

0.3 oz. (8.5 g) Northern Brewer hops (mash hop)

1.8 AAU Northern Brewer hops (60 min.) (0.2 oz./6 g at 8.5% alpha acids)

5.9 AAU Centennial hops (20 min.) (0.6 oz./17 g at 9.75% alpha acids)

5.6 AAU Cluster hops (0 min.) (0.8 oz./22 g at 7% alpha acids)

2 branches of fresh Juniper (with green berries)

Wyeast 3638 (Bavarian Wheat), White Labs WLP351 (Bavaria Weizen Yeast), or other wheat/wit yeast (2 qt./2 L yeast starter)

¾ cup (150 g) dextrose (if priming)

STEP BY STEP

Mash the grains as well as the juniper branches, and mash hops at 151°F (66°C) for 60 minutes. Mash out, vorlauf, and then sparge at 170°F (77°C) to collect enough wort to result in 5 gallons (19 liters) after a 90-minute boil. Boil wort for 90 minutes, adding hops at times indicated. Cool, aerate, and pitch yeast. Ferment at 70°F (21°C). After fermentation is complete, bottle or keg as usual.

PARTIAL MASH OPTION: Substitute the smoked malt and Munich malt in the all-grain recipe with 5 pounds 14 ounces (2.66 kilograms) Weyermann smoked malt extract and 1 pound 6 ounces (0.62 kilogram) liquid Munich malt extract. Place the crushed malts, juniper branches, and mash hops in with steeping grains, and steep at 151°F (66°C) in 3.75 quarts (3.6 liters) of water for 45 minutes. Rinse the grain bag with 2 quarts (2 liters) of 170°F (77°C) water. Combine "grain tea" and malt extracts along with enough water to top up to 6 gallons (23 liters) and boil for 60 minutes. Follow the remaining portion of the all-grain recipe.

JESTER KING BREWERY
DAS ÜBERKIND

**(5 gallons/19 L, all-grain) OG = 1.038 FG = 0.999
IBU = 12 SRM = 3 ABV = 5%**

Garrett Cromwell, head brewer at Jester King, calls Das Überkind their most versatile barrel-aged beer. The sell it as a stand-alone beer, use it as the base for fruited beers, and they even blend it with fresh, hoppy beer to make Das Wunderkind.

INGREDIENTS

6.8 lb. (3.1 kg) 2-row pale malt or pilsner malt

0.66 lb. (300 g) unmalted wheat

0.33 lb. (150 g) dark Munich malt

0.33 lb. (150 g) flaked oats

3 AAU Golding hops (60 min.) (0.6 oz./17 g at 5% alpha acids)

Wine-soaked oak staves or cubes (prior use is preferred)

Wyeast 3711 (French Saison) yeast

Wyeast 3724 (Belgian Saison) or White Labs WLP565 (Belgian Saison I) yeast

Wild inoculated bugs from local fruits or flowers

¾ cup (150 g) dextrose (if priming)

STEP BY STEP

Mash at 154 to 158°F (68 to 70°C) for 45 minutes using 3 gallons (11 liters) strike water. Mash out, vorlauf, and then sparge at 170°F (77°C) to collect 6 gallons (23 liters). Boil for 60 minutes, adding hops at the beginning of the boil. After the boil is finished, chill the wort and oxygenate well. Rack to your fermenter. Pitch the yeast and bacteria, and ferment at 78°F (26°C) for 2 weeks. For wood-aging, Jester King generally primary ferments in either stainless or an oak foudre before sending it to smaller, 225-liter barrels. Mostly they use neutral wine barrels and find that very subtle oak character complements this delicate beer. You can try to simulate this at home by using oak cubes or staves that have been used once or twice and that have also been soaked in wine. Secondary fermentation takes place at 55 to 62°F (13 to 17°C). Average fermentation/ aging for Das Überkind is 8 to 24 months. Then keg or bottle as you normally would.

PARTIAL MASH OPTION: Reduce the 2-row pale malt in the all-grain recipe to 1 pound (0.41 kilogram), and add 3 pounds (1.36 kilograms) Pilsen dried malt extract. Mash crushed grains at 154 to 158°F (68 to 70°C) for 45 minutes using 1 gallon (3.8 liters) water. Wash the grains with 1 gallon (3.8 liters) of hot water. Top off to 6 gallons (23 liters), and add the dried malt extract. Stir well, then bring to a boil for 60 minutes. Follow the remaining portion of the all-grain recipe.

TIPS FOR SUCCESS

Head brewer Garrett Cromwell has the following bits of advice to add to the mix: "The specialty malts like Munich, and then flaked oats, rotate based on what we have around the brewery. Sometimes we'll use spelt, or Maris Otter, or

malted wheat, etc. For the hops, lately we've been adding aged hops for about 30 percent of our total hop volume with great results. Also, we use 100 percent unaltered well water for all our beer. It's pretty high in bicarbonates, but we absolutely love it. For yeast, we use a mixed culture of different yeast and bacteria for all fermentations. These include Dupont yeast, and Thiriez saison yeast, along with a multitude of yeast and bacteria from flowers around our brewery, spontaneous fermentation slurries, etc. These were all blended together one time and have been evolving as a cohesive culture since being used in our brewery. We maintain this culture in-house. Bottle dregs from any of our beers would be best to approximate the fermentation character we achieve."

JOLLY PUMPKIN ARTISAN ALES
BIÈRE DE MARS

(5 gallons/19 L, all-grain) OG = 1.059 FG = 1.006 IBU = 30 SRM = 19 ABV = 7%

Bière de Mars is a unique take on a bière de garde soured with mixed cultures of bacteria. Jolly Pumpkin brews this beer by blending two batches, which homebrewers can choose to do as well; or brew it in a single batch.

INGREDIENTS

5 lb. (2.3 kg) pilsner malt

3.5 lb. (1.6 kg) wheat malt

14 oz. (0.4 kg) Munich malt (10 °L)

14 oz. (0.4 kg) flaked maize

8 oz. (0.23 kg) caramel malt (40 °L)

1.3 oz. (37 g) black patent malt

1.3 oz. (37 g) acidulated malt

14 oz. (0.4 kg) dextrose sugar (15 min.)

1.9 AAU Styrian Golding pellet hops (60 min.) (0.36 oz./10 g at 5.4% alpha acids)

2 AAU Saaz pellet hops (60 min.) (0.52 oz./15 g at 3.75% alpha acids)

5.2 AAU UK Fuggle pellet hops (30 min.) (1.15 oz./33 g at 4.5% alpha acids)

2 oz. (57 g) medium toasted oak cubes

White Labs WLP550 (Belgian Ale), Wyeast 3522 (Belgian Ardennes), or White Labs WLP515 (Antwerp Ale) yeast

A wild yeast/souring bacteria mixed culture of your choosing (see TIPS FOR SUCCESS)

⅔ cup (133 g) dextrose (if priming)

STEP BY STEP

Mill the grains (flaked maize doesn't need to be milled) and mix with 4.25 gallons (16 liters) of 160°F (71°C) strike water to reach a mash temperature of 150°F (65.5°C). Hold at this temperature for 60 minutes. Vorlauf until the runnings are clear. Sparge the grains with 3.25 gallons (12.3 liters) of 169°F (76°C) water until 6.5 gallons (24.6 liters) of 1.041 SG wort is collected in the boil kettle. Boil for 60 minutes, adding hops and dextrose according to the ingredients list. Recommended pitch rate is 204 billion yeast cells, which can be obtained by using either 1 vial after making a 1-liter stir plate starter, a 2-liter non-stir plate starter, or simply by pitching 2 fresh vials without making a starter. After the boil, turn off the heat and whirlpool the kettle by gently stirring for 2 minutes, and then let it rest for an additional 8 minutes. Next, chill the wort to 64°F (18°C) and transfer into a fermenter. Pitch the yeast, let the temperature free rise up to 67°F (19.5°C), and hold it there for 14 days. Rack to a secondary fermenter, and pitch the wild yeast and souring bacteria mixed culture as per the ingredients list. Allow the beer to condition for 4 to 14 months, depending on how much wild and/or sour character you desire. Regardless of the conditioning time you opt for, the oak cubes should be added 4 months prior to bottling. After secondary conditioning, crash cool the fermenter at the rate of 5°F (2.7°C) per day for 7 days until you reach 32°F (0°C), and then bottle or keg the beer. Carbonate to 2.5 volumes of CO_2 and enjoy!

EXTRACT WITH GRAINS OPTION: Substitute the flaked maize, pilsner, wheat, Munich, and acidulated malts in the all-grain recipe with 1.75 pounds (0.8 kilogram) Pilsen liquid malt extract, 2.5 pounds (1.14 kilograms) wheat liquid malt extract, and 3 pounds (1.36 kilograms) amber liquid malt extract. Place the grains in a grain bag, and then add to 2 gallons (7.6 liters) of 150°F (66°C) water. Allow the grain to steep for 20 to 30 minutes while you continue to heat the water up to no hotter than 170°F (77°C) to avoid extracting tannins. Remove the grain bag, top the kettle up with enough preheated water to reach a total pre-boil volume of 6.5 gallons (24.6 liters), and turn the heat back on. Once you reach a boil, add the malt extract and hops according to the ingredients list. Follow the remaining portion of the all-grain recipe.

TIPS FOR SUCCESS

Jolly Pumpkin makes two batches for this beer; one fermented in a steel fermenter for 1 week with ale yeast, the other with a lager yeast. The batches are then transferred into the same oak foeder, inoculated with house yeasts and bacteria, and conditioned for 1 month. The beer is then racked into standard-sized oak barrels for 3 months of additional aging before being re-blended just prior to packaging. On a homebrew scale, if you have two separate temperature-controlled fermentation environments and want to brew twice, then by all means use two different strains of yeast. If you don't, then the lager-like characteristics of the White Labs WLP515 (Antwerp Ale) offer a good compromise. If you have access to a Bière de Mars, then you can try to utilize the bottle dregs (building them up with a multi-stage stir plate starter is recommended) to gain some of JP's house wild profile. If not, pitch a mixed culture blend into your secondary, such as White Labs WLP655 (Belgian Sour Mix), Wyeast 3278 (Lambic Blend), Wyeast 3763 (Roeselare Ale Blend), East Coast Yeast ECY03-B (Farmhouse Blend Isolate), or East Coast Yeast ECY01 (BugFarm Blend).

JOLLY PUMPKIN ARTISAN ALES
LA ROJA

(5 gallons/19 L, all-grain) OG = 1.062 FG = varies
IBU = 25 SRM = 21 ABV = around 7%

La Roja is one of Jolly Pumpkin's first signature beers. Founder and brewmaster Ron Jeffries says that it is loosely based in the Flanders sour red tradition.

INGREDIENTS

8 lb. 5 oz. (3.8 kg) blend of pilsner and 2-row pale malts

1 lb. (0.45 kg) malted wheat

1 lb. 4 oz. (0.57 kg) Munich malt (10 °L)

13 oz. (0.37 kg) crystal malt (120 °L)

0.5 oz. (14 g) black malt

1 lb. 2 oz. (0.51 kg) dextrose (added to kettle)

4 AAU Hallertau hops or other noble hop (60 min.) (1 oz./28 g at 4% alpha acids)

4 AAU Hallertau hops or other noble hop (30 min.) (1 oz./28 g at 4% alpha acids)

Wyeast 3763 (Roeselare Ale Blend) blend

1 cup (200 g) dextrose (for priming)

STEP BY STEP

Mash the grains at 154°F (68°C) and hold for 60 minutes. Mash out, vorlauf, and then sparge at 170°F (77°C). Boil for 60 minutes, adding the hops at the beginning of the boil and again with 30 minutes remaining. When the boil is finished, chill the wort rapidly to 65°F (18°C). Ferment at 68°F (20°C), then rack to barrel or into a fermenter with oak cubes (or other alternative oak) for aging. Wyeast 3763 (Roeselare Ale Blend) is a blend of lambic cultures, including a Belgian-style ale strain, a sherry strain, two *Brettanomyces* strains, a *Lactobacillus* culture, and a *Pediococcus* culture. Wyeast recommends aging beers brewed with this yeast for up to 18 months to get a full flavor profile and for the acidity to develop. Bottle or keg as usual; heavy-duty bottles are recommended.

EXTRACT WITH GRAINS OPTION: Omit the 2-row pale and pilsner malts. Add 1 pound (0.45 kilogram) Muntons light dried malt extract and 4 pounds 14 ounces (2.2 kilograms) Muntons light liquid malt extract. Steep the grains in 4.6 quarts (4.4 liters) water at 154°F (68°C) for 45 minutes. Rinse with 2.3 quarts (about 2.2 liters) of water at 170°F (77°C). Add water to make 3 gallons (11 liters), add the dried malt extract, and bring to a boil. Boil for 60 minutes, stirring in the liquid malt extract for the final 15 minutes of the boil. Chill the wort, transfer to your fermenter, and top up with filtered water to 5 gallons (19 liters). Follow the remaining portion of the all-grain recipe.

MAGIC ROCK
BREWING COMPANY
SALTY KISS

**(5 gallons/19 L, all-grain) OG = 1.044 FG = 1.011
IBU = 17 SRM = 3 ABV = 4.2%**

Salty Kiss is a tart, fruity, and refreshing gose with a defined saltiness that makes it an excellent accompaniment to many foods. It has taken home the gold at the World Beer Cup.

INGREDIENTS

4.2 lb. (1.9 kg) pilsner malt

3.3 lb. (1.5 kg) wheat malt

1.3 lb. (0.6 kg) acidulated malt

1.34 oz. (38 g) sea buckthorn, dried berries

1 lb. (0.45 kg) gooseberries (frozen and defrost before use)

0.14 oz. (4 g) sea salt

0.8 AAU Cascade hops (60 min.) (0.15 oz./4 g at 6.6% alpha acids)

7.7 AAU Cascade hops (10 min.) (1.4 oz./40 g at 6.6% alpha acids)

White Labs WLP051 (California Ale V) or Wyeast 1272 (American Ale II) yeast

¾ cup (150 g) dextrose (if priming)

STEP BY STEP

Mill the grains and mash in 3.3 gallons (12.5 liters) of water at 149°F (65°C) for 60 minutes. Vorlauf until your runnings are clear, and sparge the grains with enough 168°F (75°C) water to obtain a 6-gallon (23 liters) pre-boil volume. Once you have collected the full volume, remove enough wort to cover the sea buckthorn berries and begin steeping them separately. Boil the wort for 60 minutes, adding the hops at the times indicated in the ingredients list. After the boil, turn off the heat and add the sea buckthorn berries with their steeping liquid, then rest for 20 minutes. Chill the wort to 64°F (18°C), transfer it to the fermenter, aerate, and pitch the yeast. Ferment for 2 days at 66°F (19°C). After 2 days, mash the gooseberries to a pulp and bring them to a boil. Cool the gooseberries to 68°F (20°C) and add them to the fermenter at the peak of fermentation. Ferment for an additional 7 days, then rack to a secondary fermenter for additional clearing if desired. Once fermentation is complete, mix the sea salt into ½ cup (0.12 liter) of boiling water, cool, add to the beer, and then bottle or keg.

EXTRACT WITH GRAINS OPTION: Substitute the 2-row pale malt, wheat malt, and acidulated malt in the all-grain recipe with 4 pounds (1.8 kilograms) wheat dried malt extract, 1 pound (0.45 kilogram) Pilsen dried malt extract, and 0.57 ounce (17 grams) lactic acid (88 percent solution). Bring 5 gallons (19 liters) of water to a boil. Turn off the heat and stir in all the dried malt extract. Once all the extract is dissolved, remove enough wort to cover the sea buckthorn berries and begin steeping them separately. Follow the remaining portion of the all-grain recipe, adding the lactic acid with the sea buckthorn berries at the end of the boil.

TIPS FOR SUCCESS

Dried sea buckthorn berries can be purchased online. Sea buckthorn is a unique, sour-flavored berry that is considered a "super-food," as it is rich in nutrients and phytochemicals, such as vitamin C, carotenoids, vitamin E, amino acids, essential fatty acids, minerals, sterols, and flavonols. Sea buckthorn berries can be used to make pies, preserves, fruit wines, and cosmetics, and their inclusion in this recipe, along with sea salt, will give your beer a unique flavor twist.

MIDNIGHT SUN BREWING COMPANY
ARCTIC DEVIL BARLEY WINE

ccccccc-

(5 gallons/19 L, all-grain) OG = 1.121 FG =1.033
IBU = 25 SRM = 21 ABV = 13.2%

This is an English-style barleywine brewed once each year by Alaskan brewery Midnight Sun. The brewery ages it in oak barrels for several months before releasing it in the fall. Expect to build in a couple months of aging for the clone as well.

INGREDIENTS

21.5 lb. (10 kg) Maris Otter pale ale malt

1 lb. (0.45 kg) Special B malt (138 °L)

6.1 oz. (0.17 kg) Caramunich II malt

15 oz. (0.43 kg) brown sugar

5 AAU Fuggle hops (60 min.) (1 oz./28 g at 5% alpha acids)

3.75 AAU Challenger hops (30 min.) (0.5 oz./14 g at 7.5% alpha acids)

0.9 oz. (26 g) Fuggle hops (0 min.)

0.15 oz. (4.3 g) Challenger hops (0 min.)

8 oz. (227 g) Cascade hops (dry hop)

1.5 oz. (43 g) medium toast American oak chips

Wyeast 1728 (Scottish Ale) or White Labs WLP028 (Edinburgh Scottish Ale) yeast

¾ cup (150 g) dextrose (if priming)

STEP BY STEP

Mash at 148°F (64°C) for 60 minutes. Collect enough wort for a 3.5-hour boil, adding hops during the final hour of the boil per the ingredients list. At the end of the boil, give the wort a long stir and let settle for 15 minutes. Cool, aerate heavily, and transfer to the fermenter. Ferment at 68°F

(20°C) until finished, then transfer the beer into a secondary vessel with the sanitized oak chips. You can sanitize the oak chips by boiling them in 1 cup water for 15 minutes, or you can try soaking these in wine or a spirit of your choice. Midnight Sun will barrel age Arctic Devil for 10 to 12 months in American oak barrels of various origins. We recommend 1 to 2 months on the oak chips, tasting regularly until the desired level of oak flavor is achieved. Dry hop the beer for 10 days, then bottle or keg. Carbonate to 2.4 volumes CO_2.

EXTRACT WITH GRAINS OPTION: Substitute the Maris Otter pale malt in the all-grain recipe with 15 pounds (6.8 kilograms) Maris Otter liquid malt extract. Place the crushed grains in a grain bag and steep in 5 gallons (19 liters) water as it heats up to 170°F (77°C). Remove the grain bag and allow to drain back into the kettle. Bring to a boil and boil for 60 minutes, adding the hops according to the ingredients list. Follow the remaining portion of the all-grain recipe.

NEW BELGIUM BREWING COMPANY
LA FOLIE

ccccccc-

(5 gallons/19 L, all-grain)
OG = 1.062 FG = 1.015 (or lower)
IBU = 20 SRM = varies ABV = 6.0%

French for "the folly," New Belgium's wood-aged sour brown ale spends 3 years in oak foeders to achieve its signature sharp, sour notes of apple, cherry, and plum. While that isn't practical on a homebrew scale, this clone will get you headed in the right direction.

INGREDIENTS

9.75 lb. (4.4 kg) 2-row pale malt

1.3 lb. (0.59 kg) Munich malt

1.3 lb. (0.59 kg) crystal malt (40–80°L, depending on the color you want in the finished beer)

0.65 lb. (0.29 kg) unmalted wheat

5.7 AAU Cantillion Iris hops (1.9 oz./53 g at 3% alpha acids)

Wyeast 1056 (American Ale) or White Labs WLP001 (California Ale) yeast

Wyeast 3278 (Lambic Blend) yeast and bacteria (or individual cultures of *Lactobacillus* and *Brettanomyces*)

1 cup (200 g) dextrose (if priming)

STEP BY STEP

If you treat your water, shoot for 75 ppm of calcium and 50 ppm of chloride. Mash grains at 154°F (68°C) for 30 minutes. Mash out, vorlauf, and then sparge at 170°F (77°C). Add the hops at the beginning of the boil. If you can't find Cantillion Iris hops, try any other low-cohumulone noble hop. Aroma hops are not required, but if you'd like, you could try dry hopping later in the barrel. Ferment with the ale yeast at 77°F (25°C). When primary fermentation is complete, rack to secondary, filtering out as much yeast as possible. You could add some *Lactobacilli* at this stage. Rack to the barrel at any time, again being careful to remove as much yeast as possible. Once the beer is in the barrel, pitch with *Brettanomyces* yeast and *Lactobacilli* (if not already added). A lambic starter culture will also work. Store the barrel in a cool, dry place. After that, it is just a matter of time. Samples can be removed with a siphon or wine thief. Your beer is ready to blend, keg, or bottle whenever you like the taste.

EXTRACT WITH GRAINS OPTION: Replace 2-row malt, Munich malt, and unmalted wheat with 9.4 pounds (4.3 kilograms) liquid malt extract designed for dark German lagers (the extract should include some Munich). Steep the crystal malt at 158°F (70°C) for 30 minutes, then add the extract to the brewpot (stirring well to incorporate), top up to 5.5 gallons (20 liters), and boil, adding the hops at the beginning of the boil. Follow the remaining portion of the all-grain recipe.

- - - - - - - - - - - - - - - - - -

NEW HOLLAND BREWING COMPANY
DRAGON'S MILK

ᙓᙓᙓᙓᙓ

**(5 gallons/19 L, all-grain) OG = 1.096 FG = 1.018
IBU = 31 SRM = 41 ABV = 11%**

First brewed in 2001, New Holland's Dragon's Milk has become a classic. It was an early adopter of barrels, using whiskey and bourbon to add depth to a delicious imperial stout recipe.

INGREDIENTS

- 15 lb. (6.8 kg) 2-row pale malt
- 2 lb. (0.91 kg) Munich malt
- 8 oz. (0.23 kg) crystal malt (80 °L)
- 8 oz. (0.23 kg) crystal malt (120 °L)
- 7 oz. (0.2 kg) Carapils malt
- 10 oz. (0.3 kg) chocolate malt
- 8 oz. (0.23 kg) Weyermann Carafa III malt
- 12 oz. (0.34 kg) flaked barley
- 1 oz. (28 g) oak chips
- 4 oz. (113 g) Jim Beam or similar bourbon whiskey
- 6.8 AAU Nugget pellet hops (60 min.) (0.6 oz./17 g at 13% alpha acids)
- 1.13 AAU Glacier pellet hops (15 min.) (0.75 oz./21 g at 6% alpha acids)
- ½ tsp. yeast nutrient (15 min.)
- White Labs WLP001 (California Ale), Wyeast 1056 (American Ale), or Fermentis Safale US-05 yeast
- ¾ cup (150 g) dextrose (if priming)

STEP BY STEP

This is a single-infusion mash. Mix the crushed grain and flaked oats with 25.4 quarts (24 liters) of 172°F (78°C) water to stabilize at 156°F (69°C) for 60 minutes. Sparge slowly with 175°F (79°C) water. Collect at least 6 gallons (23 liters) of wort runoff to boil for 60 minutes (or more if you want to boil down to help boost your OG), adding hops at times indicated. Cool the wort to 75°F (24°C). Pitch your yeast, and aerate the wort heavily. Allow the beer to cool to 68°F (20°C). Hold at that temperature until fermentation is complete. Soak the oak chips in the bourbon for at least 1 week. Transfer the wort to a carboy, avoiding any splashing to prevent aerating the beer, and add the soaked oak chips. Let the beer condition for 1 week, and then bottle or keg.

EXTRACT WITH GRAINS OPTION: Substitute all the 2-row pale malts and 1 pound (0.45 kilogram) of the Munich malt in the all-grain recipe with 6.6 pounds (3 kilograms) Briess light liquid malt extract, 3.3 pounds (1.5 kilograms) Briess Munich liquid malt extract, and 12 ounces (0.34 kilogram) Briess extra light dried malt extract. Steep the crushed Munich malt and flaked barley in 1.5 gallons (6 liters) of water at 154°F (68°C) for 30 minutes. Add the remaining crushed grains, and steep an additional 15 minutes. Remove grains from the wort and place in a colander, then rinse with 4 quarts (4 liters) of hot water. Add the liquid and dried malt extracts, top off to 6 gallons (23 liters), and bring to a boil. Follow the remaining portion of the all-grain recipe.

- - - - - - - - - - - - - - - - - -

OLD DOMINION BREWING COMPANY
DOMINION OAK BARREL STOUT

**(5 gallons/19 L, all-grain) OG = 1.056 FG = 1.017
IBU = 15 SRM = 42 ABV = 5.3%**

Delaware's Old Dominion has created a sweet stout with a dark malt base. They then infuse it with vanilla beans and oak chips during conditioning—which is much easier to replicate on a homebrew scale than full-on barrel aging.

INGREDIENTS

8 lb. (3.6 kg) 2-row pale malt

1 lb. (0.45 kg) Munich malt

6 oz. (0.17 kg) rauchmalz

6.5 oz. (0.19 kg) wheat malt

6.5 oz. (0.19 kg) Carapils malt

10 oz. (0.28 kg) crystal malt (40 °L)

10 oz. (0.28 kg) chocolate malt

12 oz. (0.34 kg) roasted barley (500 °L)

3.6 AAU Mt. Hood hops (60 min.) (0.6 oz./17 g at 6% alpha acids)

3.6 AAU Mt. Hood hops (5 min.) (0.6 oz./17 g at 6% alpha acids)

2 vanilla beans

2.5 oz. (71 g) oak cubes (medium toast, French oak)

Wyeast 1056 (American Ale), White Labs WLP001 (California Ale), or Fermentis Safale US-05 yeast

¾ cups (150 g) dextrose (if priming)

STEP BY STEP

Mash at 154°F (68°C). Sparge with enough water to collect 6.5 gallons (24.6 liters). Boil for 90 minutes, adding the hops at times indicated. After the boil is finished, give the wort a stir and let settle for 20 minutes. Cool, aerate, pitch yeast, and then ferment at 66°F (19°C). Add vanilla beans (sliced down the center) and oak cubes after primary fermentation has died down. Once you have reached the taste you like, bottle or keg as normal.

PARTIAL MASH OPTION: Substitute the 2-row pale malt in the all-grain recipe with 1.5 pounds (0.68 kilogram) Briess extra light dried malt extract and 3.3 pounds (1.5 kilograms) pale liquid malt extract. In your brewpot, heat 7.67 quarts (7.2 liters) of water to 165°F (74°C). Place crushed grains in a steeping bag and steep at 154°F (68°C) for 45 minutes. Heat 5.75 quarts (5.4 liters) of sparge water to 170°F (77°C)

in a separate pot. Rinse grains and heat wort—of which you'll have about 12.6 quarts (12 liters)—to a boil. Add dried malt extract and hops, and boil for 60 minutes. Add liquid malt extract with 15 minutes remaining. Cool wort, transfer to fermenter, and top up to 5 gallons (19 liters). Follow the remaining portion of the all-grain recipe.

PERENNIAL ARTISAN ALES
DEVIL'S HEART OF GOLD

**(5 gallons/19 L, all-grain) OG = 1.104 FG = 1.024
IBU = 60 SRM = 8 ABV = 11.7%**

Devil's Heart of Gold is a whiskey barrel–aged wheat wine. The name is inspired by the "devil's cut," the portion of the bourbon that is absorbed into a barrel during barrel aging. As this beer absorbs some of the devil's cut, the name fits perfectly.

INGREDIENTS

8.5 lb. (3.9 kg) 2-row pale malt

8.5 lb. (3.9 kg) wheat malt

3 lb. (1.4 kg) golden liquid malt extract

18.9 AAU Magnum hops (60 min.) (1.5 oz./43 g at 12.6% alpha acids)

0.83 oz. (24 g) Columbus hops (0 min.)

Whiskey-soaked oak chips or cubes

2.5 g Yeastex (or equivalent yeast nutrient) (15 min.)

1 Whirlfloc tablet (or similar kettle fining) (5 min.)

Wyeast 1056 (American Ale), White Labs WLP001 (California Ale), or Fermentis Safale US-05 yeast (2-qt./~2 L yeast starter)

¾ cup (150 g) dextrose (if priming)

STEP BY STEP

Mash the 2-row pale and wheat malts at 150°F (66°C) in about 6.25 gallons (24 liters) of water for 45 minutes. Mash out, vorlauf, and then sparge at 170°F (77°C) to collect 6.5 gallons (25 liters) of wort. Boil for 60 minutes, adding the hops, Yeastex, and Whirlfloc at the times indicated in the ingredients list. Rack the wort to your primary fermenter, allowing for plenty of head space. Pitch the yeast, and ferment at 68°F (20°C) for 3 weeks. For wood aging, Perennial brewmaster Phil Wymore states, "You can use whiskey-soaked oak chips or cubes to your preference and aging time. Purge the head space in the bucket or carboy with CO_2 in between samplings. If you can get your hands on a freshly dumped whiskey barrel from a distillery, brew this recipe scaled-up and split over several brew sessions or among brewing companions, enough to fill the barrel. Purge the head space in the barrel with CO_2 if there is any elapsed time between racking batches to the barrel. Despite your possible temptations, let the beer age for at least 10 to 12 months, and don't rack it out until you feel it tastes right." When oak aging is finished, force carbonate the beer in kegs or bottles with priming sugar and fresh pitched yeast, such as Lallemand CBC-1 yeast.

EXTRACT WITH GRAINS OPTION: Substitute the 2-row pale malt and the wheat malt with 3 pounds (1.4 kilograms) golden liquid malt extract and 9 pounds (4.1 kilograms) wheat dried malt extract. Heat 6.5 gallons (25 liters) of water in your brewpot to a boil. Add the liquid and dried malt extract, and stir until all the extract has dissolved. Boil the wort for 60 minutes, adding the hops at times indicated in the ingredients list. Follow the remaining portion of the all-grain recipe.

- - - - - - - - - - - - - - - - - -

RUSSIAN RIVER BREWING COMPANY
TEMPTATION

꿍꿍꿍꿍꿍-

(5 gallons/19 L, all-grain) OG = 1.062
FG = 1.012 (going into the barrel)
IBU = 28   SRM = 4   ABV = 6.8%

Both the ABV and final gravity of Temptation are based on the beer aging in the barrel prior to the souring process. Owner and brewer Vinnie Cilurzo says, "None of our barrel beers are easy to replicate on a homebrew level, as we are matching specific recipes with specific types of wine barrels. For example, Temptation is aged in Chardonnay barrels exclusively. One suggestion for a homebrewer is to add a little bit of Chardonnay into the beer to get the wine character, because they cannot get it from the wood like we do."

INGREDIENTS

11.5 lb. (5.2 kg) 2-row pale malt

10 oz. (0.27 kg) acidulated malt

14 oz. (0.41 kg) dextrin malt

6 AAU Warrior hops (90 min.) (0.4 oz./11 g at 15.0% alpha acids)

1.8 AAU Styrian Golding hops (30 min.) (0.4 oz./11 g at 4.5% alpha acids)

1.4 AAU Styrian Golding hops (0 min.) (0.3 oz./8.5 g at 4.5% alpha acids)

White Labs WLP530 (Abbey Ale) or Wyeast 1214 (Belgian Abbey) yeast

Wyeast 5112 (*Brettanomyces bruxellensis*) or White Labs WLP650 (*Brettanomyces bruxellensis*) yeast

Wyeast 5335 (*Lactobacillus buchneri*), White Labs WLP677 (*Lactobacillus delbrueckii*), or Wyeast 5733 (*Pediococcus damnosus*) bacteria

Oak barrel, staves, beans, or chips

Chardonnay (optional)

1 cup (200 g) dextrose (if priming)

STEP BY STEP

Mash the grains at 158°F (70°C). Boil for 90 minutes, adding the hops at the times indicated. Pitch the ale or abbey yeast, and begin fermentation at 68°F (20°C). Let it free rise to 76°F (24°C). After primary fermentation, drop as much of the yeast out as possible, and move the beer to a wine barrel or secondary fermenter (with oak alternative) where *Brettanomyces* is added. After 8 to 12 weeks of aging with the *Brett*, add bacteria to beer and top the barrel/fermenter with a neutral base beer or Chardonnay. From here, the beer will sit for another 6 to 9 months. After the barrel aging is complete, bottle condition the beer using a wine yeast (such as Scott Labs RP15) and an appropriate quantity of priming sugar to meet your desired CO_2 level (around 3.2 volumes of CO_2). High-pressure-rated bottles are strongly suggested.

EXTRACT WITH GRAINS OPTION: Substitute 6.6 pounds (3 kilograms) light liquid malt extract and 1.75 pounds (0.8 kilogram) light dried malt extract for the 2-row pale malt. Omit the acidulated malt and dextrin malt, and add 0.25 ounce (8 milliliters) 88-percent lactic acid. Add 5 gallons (19 liters) water, extract, and lactic acid to the kettle, being sure to add the liquid malt extract off heat to avoid scorching the clumped extract. Follow the remaining portion of the all-grain recipe.

- - - - - - - - - - - - - - - -

SUN KING BREWING COMPANY
TEQUILA BARREL-AGED FISTFUL OF HOPS

꿍꿍꿍꿍꿍-

(5 gallons/19 L, all-grain) OG = 1.058 FG = 1.010
IBU = 78   SRM = 13   ABV = 6.4%

Sun King Brewing releases Fistful of Hops on a rotating schedule so they can change up the hops every few months. They generally combine 2 to 3 varieties for each release, and this recipe is a typical iteration. Tequila barrel–aging is not as common as whiskey barrel–aging, but it can work quite well for an IPA.

INGREDIENTS

11 lb. (5 kg) 2-row pale malt

10 oz. (283 g) flaked rye

8 oz. (227 g) Weyermann CaraAroma malt (130 °L)

12.5 AAU Warrior hops (70 min.) (0.75 oz./21 g at 16.6% alpha acids)

2.4 AAU Mosaic hops (20 min.) (0.2 oz./6 g at 12% alpha acids)

2.6 AAU Nelson Sauvin hops (20 min.) (0.2 oz./6 g at 13% alpha acids)

1.9 AAU Amarillo hops (20 min.) (0.2 oz./6 g at 9.4% alpha acids)

4.2 AAU Mosaic hops (5 min.) (0.35 oz./10 g at 12% alpha acids)

4.5 AAU Nelson Sauvin hops (5 min.) (0.35 oz./10 g at 13% alpha acids)

3.3 AAU Amarillo hops (5 min.) (0.35 oz./10 g at 9.4% alpha acids)

6 AAU Mosaic hops (0 min.) (0.5 oz./14 g at 12% alpha acids)

6.5 AAU Nelson Sauvin hops (0 min.) (0.5 oz./14 g at 13% alpha acids)

4.7 AAU Amarillo hops (0 min.) (0.5 oz./14 g at 9.4% alpha acids)

0.5 oz. (14 g) Mosaic hops (dry hop)

0.5 oz. (14 g) Nelson Sauvin hops (dry hop)

0.5 oz. (14 g) Amarillo hops (dry hop)

Tequila-soaked oak chips (light toast)

White Labs WLP001 (California Ale), Wyeast 1056 (American Ale), or Fermentis Safale US-05 yeast

¾ cup (150 g) dextrose (if priming)

STEP BY STEP

Mill the grains, and target a mash temperature of 150°F (66°C). Hold at this temperature for 60 minutes. Sparge to collect about 6.5 gallons (25 liters). Boil for 90 minutes, adding the hops at the times indicated. After the boil is complete, turn off the heat, stir in the flameout hop addition, and begin a vigorous whirlpool in your kettle. Let settle for 15 minutes. Chill the wort, aerate thoroughly, and then pitch the yeast. Ferment at 68°F (20°C) until primary fermentation is complete. Add dry hops for 4 to 7 days. To approximate tequila barrel–aging at home, Colt suggests to "get the lightest toasted oak chips you can find and soak them in the tequila of your choice. Now add them to the beer. Taste the beer weekly and pull it off of the chips when it has reached the state where you can taste the wood, the spirit, and beer in harmony. Better still, get a 5-liter oak barrel and fill it with tequila, and let it age a few weeks to a month at a minimum. Next enjoy the tequila you aged, and fill the barrel back up with beer. Make sure to purge out any oxygen from the barrel before filling it with beer." After aging, bottle or keg as normal.

PARTIAL MASH OPTION: Reduce the 2-row pale malt in the all-grain recipe to 1 pound (0.45 kilogram), and add 6.6 pounds (3 kilograms) light liquid malt extract. Place crushed grains in a large muslin bag. Heat 1 gallon (3.8 liters) of water, and target a mash temperature of 150°F (66°C). Add the grain bag, and hold the mash at 150°F (66°C) until enzymatic conversion is complete, about 60 minutes. Remove the grain bag, and slowly wash the grains with 1 gallon (3.8 liters) of hot water. Add the liquid malt extract, and top off to 6.5 gallons (25 liters) in the brewpot. Total boil time is 90 minutes. Follow the remaining portion of the all-grain recipe.

CHAPTER

SEVENTEEN

WINTER BEERS

Beer Pictured on Left; see page 258

AVERY BREWING COMPANY
OLD JUBILATION ALE

≪≪≪≪≪≪-

**(5 gallons/19 L, all-grain) OG = 1.074 FG = 1.014
IBU = 31 SRM = 20 ABV = 8.3%**

Available from October through December, Old Jubilation is a winter strong ale that features a hint of hazelnuts, mocha, toffee, and spice. With those tasting notes, you might expect to find adjuncts in this beer, but no—all the flavor comes from the malt, hops, and yeast.

INGREDIENTS

13.7 lb. (6.2 kg) 2-row pale malt

12 oz. (340 g) Briess special roast malt (50 °L)

12 oz. (340 g) Briess Victory malt

4 oz. (113 g) Briess chocolate malt

0.8 oz. (23 g) black patent malt

5.3 AAU Bullion hops (60 min.) (0.66 oz./19 g at 8% alpha acids)

8 AAU Bullion hops (30 min.) (1.0 oz./28 g at 8% alpha acids)

1.0 oz. Bullion hops (0 min.)

Wyeast 1028 (London Ale) or White Labs WLP013 (London Ale) yeast

¾ cup (150 g) dextrose (if priming)

STEP BY STEP

Mash at 152°F (67°C). Vorlauf until your runnings are clear, sparge, and then boil the wort for 90 minutes, hops as directed in the ingredients list. After the boil, turn off the heat, and chill the wort rapidly to just below fermentation temperature, about 68°F (20°C). Aerate the wort well, and pitch the yeast. Ferment at 70°F (21°C). When the beer has reached final gravity, transfer to a bottling bucket for priming and bottling, or transfer to a keg.

PARTIAL MASH OPTION: Scale the 2-row pale malt down to 1 pound (0.45 kilograms) and add 2 pounds 14 ounces (1.3 kilograms) light dried malt extract and 5 pounds 2 ounces (2.3 kilograms) light liquid malt extract (late addition). Begin by heating 2 gallons (7.6 liters) of water in your brewpot. While that heats, steep the specialty grains at around 152°F (67°C) in 1 gallon (3.8 liters) of water in a large kitchen pot. Put the crushed grains in a large steeping bag and submerge bag in the kitchen pot for 30 to 45 minutes. At the end of the steep, remove the bag from the steeping pot and let drip dry for a minute or so. Add the "grain tea" to your brewpot, and add the dried malt extract and sugar. Boil for 60 minutes, adding the hops at the times indicated in the ingredients list. With 15 minutes left in the boil, stir in liquid malt extract. After the boil, cool the wort, top up with enough cool water to make 5 gallons (19 liters), aerate, and pitch yeast. Follow the remainder of the all-grain recipe.

BOULEVARD BREWING
NUTCRACKER ALE

≪≪≪≪≪≪-

**(5 gallons/19 L, all-grain) OG = 1.072 FG = 1.016
IBU = 32 SRM = 23 ABV = 7.8%**

Boulevard's annual winter warmer is a hearty brew with a deep amber color. The brewery says to expect hints of molasses balanced by the hops.

INGREDIENTS

9 lb. (4.1 kg) 2-row pale malt

1 lb. (0.45 kg) aromatic malt

1 lb. (0.45 kg) English medium crystal malt (50 °L)

1 lb. (0.45 kg) Special B malt

10 oz. (283 g) Carapils malt

6 oz. (170 g) wheat malt

1.25 lb. (0.56 kg) brown sugar

6.5 AAU Magnum pellet hops (60 min.) (0.5 oz./14 g at 13% alpha acids)

1.4 AAU Cascade pellet hops (30 min.) (0.25 oz./7 g at 5.75% alpha acids)

1.4 AAU Cascade pellet hops (0 min.) (0.25 oz./7 g at 5.75% alpha acids)

6.5 AAU Chinook pellet hops (0 min.) (0.5 oz./14 g at 13% alpha acids)

½ tsp. yeast nutrient (15 min.)

½ tsp. Irish moss (15 min.)

White Labs WLP002 (English Ale) or Wyeast 1968 (London ESB Ale) yeast

¾ cup (150 g) dextrose (if priming)

STEP BY STEP

Mash the grains at 152°F (67°C) for 60 minutes. Vorlauf until runnings are clear, and sparge. Collect approximately 6 gallons (22.7 liters) of wort runoff to boil for 60 minutes. Add the hops, Irish moss, and yeast nutrient at the times indicated in the ingredients list. Stir in the brown sugar at the end of the boil. Chill the wort to 75°F (24°C), aerate the wort heavily, and pitch your yeast. Allow the beer to cool to 68°F (20°C). Hold at that temperature until fermentation is complete. Transfer to a carboy, avoiding any splashing to prevent aerating the beer. Allow the beer to condition for 1 week, and then bottle or keg. Allow to carbonate and age for 2 weeks.

EXTRACT WITH GRAINS OPTION: Omit the 2-row pale malt. Add 3.3 pounds (1.5 kilograms) Muntons light unhopped malt extract and 1.8 pounds (0.81 kilogram) light dried malt extract. Steep the crushed grains in 2 gallons (7.6 liters) of water at 152°F (66.7°C) for 30 minutes. Pull the grain bag out and drain over the brewpot in a colander. Rinse with 2 quarts (1.9 liters) of hot water. Add the liquid and dried malt extracts and bring to a boil. While boiling, add the hops, yeast nutrients, and Irish moss as per the ingredients list. Stir in the brown sugar at the end of the boil. After the boil, cool the wort and transfer it to a sanitized fermenter. Top off with cold water up to 5 gallons (19 liters), aerate well, and pitch the yeast. Follow the remainder of the all-grain recipe.

BRECKENRIDGE BREWERY
CHRISTMAS ALE

**(5 gallons/19 L, all-grain) OG = 1.070 FG = 1.019
IBU = 22 SRM = 30 ABV = 7.1%**

Breckenridge Brewery describes this winter warmer as a beer with extra flavor and strength, with a sturdy texture and rich flavors of caramel and chocolate.

INGREDIENTS

13 lb. (5.9 kg) 2-row pale malt

1 lb. (0.45 kg) crystal malt (60 °L)

8 oz. (0.23 g) Special B malt

4 oz. (113 g) chocolate malt

1 oz. (28 g) black patent malt

6.1 AAU Chinook hops (60 min.) (0.51 oz./14 g at 12% alpha acids)

3.8 AAU Mt. Hood hops (15 min.) (0.76 oz./22 g at 5% alpha acids)

Wyeast 1272 (American Ale II) or White Labs WLP051 (California Ale V) yeast

¾ cup (150 g) dextrose (if priming)

STEP BY STEP

Mash the grains at 154°F (68°C). Vorlauf until your runnings are clear, sparge, and boil wort for 90 minutes, adding hops at times indicated in the ingredients list. After the boil, turn off the heat and chill the wort rapidly to just below fermentation temperature, about 68°F (20°C). Aerate the wort well, and pitch the yeast. Ferment at 70°F (21°C). When the beer has reached final gravity, bottle or keg as normal.

EXTRACT WITH GRAINS OPTION: Omit the 2-row pale malt. Add 4 pounds (1.8 kilograms) light dried malt extract and 5.25 pounds (2.4 kilograms) light liquid malt extract (late addition). Begin by heating 2.5 gallons (9.4 liters) of water in your brewpot. In a separate pot, heat 0.50 gallon (1.9 liters) of water to 161°F (71°C). Place crushed grains in a steeping bag and submerge in water, steeping at 150°F (66°C) for 30 to 45 minutes. After steep, remove grain bag and let drip dry into the pot. Add "grain tea" and dried malt extract to the pot, and bring to a boil. Boil for 60 minutes, adding hops at the times indicated in the ingredients list. With 15 minutes left in the boil, stir in liquid malt extract. After the boil, cool the wort and transfer to fermenter. Add enough cool water to make 5 gallons (19 liters), aerate, and pitch yeast. Follow the remainder of the all-grain recipe.

DESCHUTES
BREWING COMPANY
JUBELALE

**(5 gallons/19 L, all-grain) OG = 1.073 FG = 1.021
IBU = 60 SRM = 32 ABV = 7.1%**

Available just around the holidays, Jubelale pours a deep garnet color. In the glass, there are notes of cocoa, dried fruit, and toffee as well as some "spice" from the hops.

INGREDIENTS

12 lb. (5.4 kg) US 2-row pale malt

1.75 lb. (0.8 kg) US caramel malt (120 °L)

1.25 lb. (0.57 kg) US caramel malt (80 °L)

5 oz. (142 g) Briess Extra Special malt (130 °L)

4 oz. (113 g) Carapils malt

3 oz. (85 g) roasted barley (300 °L)

9.75 AAU Bravo hops (60 min.) (0.65 oz./18 g at 15% alpha acids)

3.25 AAU Delta hops (30 min.) (0.5 oz./14 g at 6.5% alpha acids)

1.1 AAU US Cascade hops (30 min.) (0.25 oz./7 g at 4.5% alpha acids)

0.5 oz. (14 g) East Kent Golding hops (0 min.)

0.5 oz. (14 g) German Tettnang hops (0 min.)

Whirlfloc or Irish moss (15 min.)

Wyeast 1187 (Ringwood Ale) or White Labs WLP005 (British Ale) yeast

5 g gypsum ($CaSO_4$) (if using reverse osmosis water)

¾ cup (150 g) dextrose (if priming)

STEP BY STEP

Mill grains, and mix with 4.9 gallons (18.5 liters) of 162°F (72°C) strike water and optional minerals to reach a mash temperature of 151°F (66°C). Hold at this temperature for 60 minutes. Vorlauf until your runnings are clear. Sparge the grains with enough 168°F (76°C) water to collect 6.5 gallons (25 liters) of 1.056 wort. Boil for 90 minutes, adding hops and finings according to the ingredients list. Chill the wort to slightly below fermentation temperature, about 61°F (16°C). Aerate the wort, and pitch yeast. Ferment at 63°F (17°C). Once at terminal gravity, bottle or keg the beer and carbonate.

EXTRACT WITH GRAINS OPTION: Substitute the 2-row pale malt in the all-grain recipe with 8 pounds (3.6 kilograms) golden liquid malt extract. Place the milled grains in a muslin bag, and steep in 7.5 quarts (7 liters) of 151°F (66°C) water for 15 minutes. Remove the grain and rinse with 1 gallon (3.8 liters) of hot water. Add water to reach a volume of 4.5 gallons (17 liters), add optional minerals, and heat to boiling. Turn off the heat, add the liquid malt extract, and stir until completely dissolved. Top up if necessary to obtain 6 gallons (23 liters) of 1.062 wort. Boil for 60 minutes. Follow the remaining portion of the all-grain recipe.

- - - - - - - - - - - - - - - - -

FULL SAIL BREWING COMPANY
WASSAIL

(5 gallons/19 L, all-grain) OG = 1.070 FG = 1.014
IBU = 56 SRM = 18 ABV = 7.2%

This deep mahogany winter warmer has won more than a dozen gold medals in various competitions. The brewery varies the recipe a bit each year, but it has been brewed and released around October each year since 1988.

INGREDIENTS

13.75 lb. (6.2 kg) 2-row pale malt

9 oz. (0.27 kg) crystal malt (60 °L)

2 oz. (57 g) crystal malt (120 °L)

2 oz. (57 g) chocolate malt

1 oz. (28 g) roasted barley

1 oz. (28 g) black patent malt

2.5 AAU Northern Brewer hops (75 min.) (0.36 oz./10 g at 7% alpha acids)

2.5 AAU Styrian Golding hops (75 min.) (0.5 oz./14 g at 5% alpha acids)

3.75 AAU Hallertau-Hersbrücker hops (15 min.) (1.1 oz/30 g at 3.5% alpha acids)

3.75 AAU Styrian Golding hops (15 min.) (0.75 oz./21 g at 5% alpha acids)

7.5 AAU Hallertau-Hersbrücker hops (0 min.) (2.1 oz./61 g at 3.5% alpha acids)

7.5 AAU Styrian Golding hops (0 min.) (1.5 oz./43 g at 5% alpha acids)

Wyeast 1968 (London ESB Ale), White Labs WLP002 (English Ale), or Lallemand Winsor Ale yeast

¾ cup (150 g) dextrose (if priming)

STEP BY STEP

Mash the grains at 150°F (66°C) for 30 minutes. Runoff until the wort clears, sparge, and bring the wort to a boil. Boil for 90 minutes, adding hops as directed in recipe. At the end of the boil, turn off heat and give the wort a stir to create a whirlpool. Let the wort sit for 15 minutes before cooling. Ferment at 68°F (20°C).

EXTRACT WITH GRAINS OPTION: Scale the 2-row pale malt down to 0.75 pound (0.34 kilogram), and add 3.25 pounds (1.5 kilograms) light dried malt extract and 5 pounds (2.3 kilograms) light liquid malt extract. Begin by heating 2.33 gallons (8.8 liters) of water in your brewpot. In a separate pot, heat 0.66 gallon (2.5 liters) of water to 161°F (72°C). Place the crushed grains in a steeping bag and submerge in this water. Steep for 30 to 45 minutes at 150°F (66°C). After steeping, remove the grain bag and let drip dry. Add "grain tea" and dried malt extract to brewpot, and heat to a boil. Boil for 60 minutes, adding hops at times indicated. With 15 minutes left in the boil, stir in liquid malt extract. (Be sure to stir until extract is completely dissolved, or else extract may scorch.) After boil, let wort sit for 15 minutes before cooling. Then, cool wort and siphon to fermenter. Top up to 5 gallons (19 liters), aerate, and pitch yeast. Ferment at 68°F (20°C).

- - - - - - - - - - - - - - - - -

HARPOON BREWERY
WINTER WARMER

(5 gallons/19 L, all-grain) OG = 1.056 FG = 1.014
IBU = 23 SRM = 23 ABV = 5.9%

Since the late 1980s, Harpoon has brewed this New England classic to celebrate the holiday season. Cinnamon and nutmeg dominate the aroma, and the flavor is strengthened by the strong malt backbone. There is a mild sweetness to the finish, along with the lingering flavor of the spices.

INGREDIENTS

9.33 lb. (4.2 kg) 2-row malt

2 lb. (0.91 kg) crystal malt (90 °L)

0.5 lb. (0.23 kg) caramalt (15 °L)

2 oz. (57 g) black barley

6.25 AAU Cluster hops (60 min.) (1.25 oz./35 g at 5% alpha acids)

¼ tsp. cinnamon

⅛ tsp. nutmeg

Wyeast 1968 (London ESB Ale) or White Labs WLP002 (English Ale) yeast

¾ cup (150 g) dextrose (if priming)

STEP BY STEP

Mash the grains at 154°F (68°C) for 60 minutes. Mash out, vorlauf, and then sparge at 170°F (77°C) to collect enough wort to result in 5 gallons (19 liters) after a 90-minute boil. Boil 90 minutes, adding hops at times indicated. Cool, aerate, and pitch yeast. Ferment at 70°F (21°C). After fermentation is complete, add cinnamon and nutmeg in secondary. Bottle or keg as usual 1 week later.

EXTRACT WITH GRAINS OPTION: Reduce the 2-row pale malt in the all-grain recipe to 0.5 pound (0.23 kilogram), and add 1.66 pounds (0.75 kilogram) light dried malt extract and 4.25 pounds (1.9 kilograms) light liquid malt extract. Begin by heating 2 gallons (7.6 liters) of water in your brewpot. Steep specialty grains for 30 to 45 minutes at 154°F (68°C) in 1 gallon (4 liters) of water in a separate pot. After steeping, remove bag and let drip dry for a minute. Then add "grain tea" and dried malt extract to brewpot. Bring to a boil, add hops, and boil for 60 minutes. With 15 minutes left in the boil, add liquid malt extract, stirring well to ensure it dissolves completely. After boil, cool wort and siphon to fermenter. Add water to make 5 gallons (19 liters). Follow the remaining portion of the all-grain recipe.

- - - - - - - - - - - - - - - - - - - -

ODELL BREWING COMPANY
ISOLATION ALE

- - - - - - -

**(5 gallons/19 L, all-grain) OG = 1.061 FG = 1.015
IBU = 29 SRM = 16 ABV = 6.1%**

Odell brews Isolation for the transition of the seasons in Colorado. It's an early-winter beer meant for the excitement of the first "ski, shred, or shoe" of the season. The crisp hop finish and modest ABV (for a winter seasonal) keep the beer refreshing.

INGREDIENTS

4.25 lb. (1.9 kg) Maris Otter pale malt

3 lb. (1.4 kg) Vienna malt

2.75 lb. (1.25 kg) Briess Ashburne mild malt

1 lb. (0.45 kg) Munich malt (10 °L)

0.75 lb. (0.34 kg) crystal malt (90 °L)

0.5 lb. (0.23 kg) crystal malt (10 °L)

4 oz. (113 g) crystal malt (45 °L)

4 oz. (113 g) crystal malt (120 °L)

3.25 AAU Nugget hops (60 min.) (0.25 oz./7 g at 13% alpha acids)

5.5 AAU Cascade hops (30 min.) (1 oz./28 g at 5.5% alpha acids)

Wyeast 1098 (British Ale) or White Labs WLP007 (Dry English Ale) yeast

⅔ cup (133 g) dextrose (if priming)

STEP BY STEP

Mill the grains, and mix with 4 gallons (15 liters) of 165°F (74°C) strike water to reach a mash temperature of 152°F (67°C). Hold this temperature for 60 minutes. Vorlauf until your runnings are clear, and lauter. Sparge the grains with 2.9 gallons (11 liters), and top up as necessary to obtain 6 gallons (23 liters) of wort. Boil for 60 minutes, adding hops according to the ingredient list and Irish moss as desired. Chill to 66°F (19°C), aerate, and pitch yeast. Ferment at 67°F (19°C) for the first 3 days, then allow temperature to rise to 70°F (21°C). Hold there until fermentation is complete (1.015 specific gravity, about 10 days after fermentation begins). Once the beer completes fermentation, bottle or keg and carbonate to approximately 2.25 volumes. You may want to cold-crash the beer to 35°F (2°C) for 48 hours prior to packaging to improve clarity. Store carbonated beer at near-freezing temperatures for at least 2 weeks before drinking.

EXTRACT WITH GRAINS OPTION: Substitute the Maris Otter pale malt, Vienna malt, Briess Ashburne mild malt, and Munich malt in the all-grain recipe with 1 pound (0.45 kilogram) light dried malt extract, 3.3 pounds (1.5 kilograms) Briess Goldpils Vienna liquid malt extract, and 3 pounds (1.4 kilograms) Munich liquid malt extract. Bring 5.4 gallons (20.4 liters) of water to approximately 162°F (72°C), and steep specialty malts in grain bags for 15 minutes. Remove grains, drain, and then add malt extracts and stir until completely dissolved. Boil for 60 minutes. Follow the remaining portion of the all-grain recipe.

- - - - - - - - - - - - - - - - - - -

PYRAMID BREWERIES, INC.
SNOW CAP ALE
⟨⟨⟨⟨⟨⟨-

**(5 gallons/19 L, all-grain) OG = 1.071 FG = 1.017
IBU = 30 SRM = 20 ABV = 7.4%**

This full-bodied winter warmer is brewed in the spirit of British winter ales. Crafted with a flurry of roasted chocolate and caramel malts, and generously hopped, it delivers a smooth finish that makes this beer the perfect cold weather companion.

INGREDIENTS

13.5 lb. (6.1 kg) 2-row pale malt

1 lb. (0.45 kg) crystal malt (80 °L)

0.33 lb. (0.15 kg) chocolate malt

1 tsp. Irish moss (15 min.)

5 AAU Willamette hops (60 min.) (1 oz./28 g at 5% alpha acids)

5 AAU Willamette hops (30 min.) (1 oz./28 g at 5% alpha acids)

1 oz. (28 g) East Kent Golding hops (2 min.)

Wyeast 1728 (Scottish Ale) or White Labs WLP028 (Edinburgh Scottish Ale) yeast

⅔ cup (133 g) dextrose (if priming)

STEP BY STEP

Mash the grains at 155°F (68°C) for 60 minutes. Mash out, vorlauf, and then sparge at 170°F (77°C) to collect enough wort to result in 5 gallons (19 liters) after a 90-minute boil. Boil 90 minutes, adding hops at times indicated. Cool, aerate, and pitch yeast. Ferment at 68°F (20°C). After fermentation is complete, bottle or keg as usual.

EXTRACT WITH GRAINS OPTION: Substitute the 2-row pale malt in the all-grain recipe with 2 pounds (0.91 kilogram) Briess extra light dried malt extract and 6.6 pounds (3 kilograms) Coopers light liquid malt extract. Steep grains in 0.66 gallons (2.5 liters) of water at 155°F (68°C) for 30 minutes. Add water and dried malt extract to make 3 gallons (11 liters) of wort. Boil for 60 minutes, adding hops when indicated. Add liquid malt extract with 15 minutes left in boil. Cool and top off to 5 gallons (19 liters). Follow the remaining portion of the all-grain recipe.

SAINT ARNOLD BREWING COMPANY
SAINT ARNOLD CHRISTMAS ALE
⟨⟨⟨⟨⟨⟨-

**(5 gallons/19 L all-grain) OG = 1.066 FG = 1.013
IBU = 30 SRM = 14 ABV = 7.2%**

Saint Arnold's Christmas Ale is a winter warmer complete with spices . . . or is it? "I would have sworn there were spices before I started working there," says brewmaster Dave Fougeron. However, all that flavor comes from traditional brewing ingredients.

INGREDIENTS

11 lb. (5 kg) 2-row pale malt

13 oz. (0.37 kg) Munich malt

1 lb. 3 oz. (0.54 kg) Caravienne malt (20 °L)

7 oz. (0.2 kg) Caramunich II malt (40 °L)

7 oz. (0.2 kg) Special B malt

10.8 AAU Perle hops (30 min.) (1.5 oz./43 g at 7.2% alpha acids)

3 oz. (85 g) Liberty hops (0 min.)

Wyeast 1968 (London ESB Ale) or White Labs WLP002 (English Ale) yeast

¾ cup (150 g) dextrose (if priming)

STEP BY STEP

Mash the grains at 150°F (66°C) for 60 minutes. Mash out, vorlauf, and then sparge at 170°F (77°C) to collect enough wort to result in 5 gallons (19 liters) after a 90-minute boil. Boil 90 minutes, adding hops at times indicated. Cool, aerate, and pitch yeast. Ferment at 72°F (22°C), which will result in nice, fruity esters. After fermentation is complete, bottle or keg as usual.

EXTRACT WITH GRAINS OPTION: Omit the 2-row pale malt and Munich, and replace with 1 pound (0.45 kilogram) Munich dried malt extract and 6.6 pounds (3 kilograms) light liquid malt extract. In your brewpot, heat 3 gallons (11 liters) of water to 161°F (72°C). Place crushed grains in large steeping bag and submerge in water. Steep for 20 minutes. After steep, remove bag and let drip dry. Add 1.5 gallons (5.9 liters) of water, dried malt extract, and half of the liquid malt extract to brewpot and heat to a boil. (Note: To save time, you can bring the water and the extract up to temperature in a separate pot while steeping.) Add hops as indicated and the remaining liquid malt extract with 15 minutes remaining. Cool and top off to 5 gallons (19 liters). Follow the remaining portion of the all-grain recipe.

SCHLOSS EGGENBERG
SAMICHLAUS

ccccccc-

(5 gallons/19 L, all-grain) OG = 1.139 FG = 1.034 IBU = 28 SRM = 15 ABV = 14%

Once the world's strongest beer, Samichlaus continues to inspire homebrewers. What's not to like about a delicious doppelbock that continues to develop the longer it is aged? It is brewed only once per year, in December, and each year's vintage is released after only 10 months of aging.

INGREDIENTS

21 lb. (9.5 kg) pilsner malt (2 °L)

2 lb. (0.91 kg) Vienna malt (3 °L)

1.5 lb. (0.68 kg) Weyermann CaraBohemian malt (65 °L)

2 lb. (0.91 kg) cane sugar (60 min.)

12.8 AAU Northern Brewer hops (60 min.) (1.5 oz./43 g at 8.5% alpha acids)

2.3 AAU Tettnang hops (15 min.) (0.5 oz./14 g at 4.5% alpha acids)

0.5 oz. Hallertau Mittelfrüh hops (2 min.)

1 tsp. Irish moss (15 min.)

White Labs WLP885 (Zurich Lager) yeast (7 qt./~7 L yeast starter)

½ cup (100 g) dextrose (if priming)

STEP BY STEP

Mash the grains with 8.3 gallons (31 liters) of water at 113°F (45°C). Step mash with rests of 10 minutes at 104°F (40°C), 15 minutes at 122°F (50°C), 45 minutes at 140°F (60°C), and 15 minutes at 158°F (70°C). Collect 13 gallons (49 liters) of wort. Boil to reduce to 5 gallons (19 liters), at least 5 hours, adding hops as indicated. Cool wort, aerate well, and pitch yeast sediment from starter. Ferment for 30 to 45 days at 52°F (11°C). Rack to secondary, add fresh yeast, and let temperature rise to 60°F (16°C), then lager for about 180 days at 38°F (3.3°C). Bottle or keg, shooting for 2.20 volumes CO_2.

EXTRACT WITH GRAINS OPTION: Substitute the pilsner malt and Vienna malt in the all-grain recipe with 10 pounds (4.5 kilograms) extra light dried malt extract and 3.3 pounds (1.5 kilograms) Munich liquid malt extract. Steep grains at 148°F (64°C) for 30 minutes in 5 gallons (19 liters) of water.

Boil wort for 60 minutes, stirring in malt extracts at the beginning of the boil off heat. Follow the remaining portion of the all-grain recipe.

TIPS FOR SUCCESS

The best approach to making a beer of this strength while using a lager yeast is to brew a smaller lager beer and reuse the yeast collected from that batch for pitching into this wort. If you do not have time to brew a full batch, even a small-batch beer would work well. If you end up making a 7-quart (7-liter) yeast starter, be sure to refrigerate the yeast once it has grown up so you can decant the beer off the yeast cake prior to pitching.

SUMMIT BREWING COMPANY
SUMMIT WINTER ALE

ccccccc-

(5 gallons/19 L, all-grain) OG = 1.059 FG = 1.012 IBU = 37 SRM = 28 ABV = 6.4%

First brewed in 1987, this winter warmer exhibits bready, toasted malt flavors with hints of coffee, caramel, black cherry, cocoa, and a dash of hop spice.

INGREDIENTS

10 lb. 14 oz. (4.9 kg) 2-row pale malt

0.75 lb. (0.34 kg) crystal malt (75 °L)

0.5 lb. (0.23 kg) caramel Munich malt (60 °L)

4 oz. (113 g) Weyermann Carafa II malt

4 oz. (113 g) black patent malt

7.5 AAU Willamette hops (60 min.) (1.5 oz./43 g at 5% alpha acids)

2.5 AAU Fuggle hops (15 min.) (0.5 oz./14 g at 5% alpha acids)

2 AAU Tettnanger hops (15 min.) (0.5 oz./14 g at 4% alpha acids)

Wyeast 1968 (London ESB Ale) or White Labs WLP002 (English Ale) yeast

¾ cup (150 g) dextrose (if priming)

STEP BY STEP

Mash the grains at 153°F (67°C) for 60 minutes. Mash out, vorlauf, and then sparge at 170°F (77°C) to collect enough wort to result in 5 gallons (19 liters) after a 90-minute boil. Boil 90 minutes, adding hops at times indicated. Cool, aerate, and pitch yeast. Ferment at 72°F (22°C). After fermentation is complete, bottle or keg as usual.

EXTRACT WITH GRAINS OPTION: Substitute the 2-row pale malt in the all-grain recipe with 2.66 pounds (1.2 kilograms) Northwestern Gold dried malt extract and 4.33 pounds (2 kilograms) Northwestern Gold liquid malt extract. Heat 2.5 gallons (9.4 liters) of water in your brewpot. In a separate, smaller pot, heat 2 quarts (1.9 liters) of water to 164°F (73°C). Add crushed grains to steeping bag and steep at 153°F (67°C) for 30 to 45 minutes in the smaller pot. Add "grain tea" and dried malt extract to brewpot bring to a boil. Boil for 60 minutes, adding hops when indicated. Add liquid malt extract with 15 minutes left in the boil. Cool and add water to make 5 gallons (19 liters). Follow the remaining portion of the all-grain recipe.

RESOURCES

BOOKS

Brew Your Own Big Book of Homebrewing: All-Grain and Extract Brewing • Kegging • 50+ Craft Beer Recipes • Tips and Tricks from the Pros (Minneapolis, MN: Voyageur Press, 2017)

A collection of the best homebrew advice, guides, recipes, and tips from *Brew Your Own* magazine. This book explains the entire brewing process from start to finish with step-by-step photography. Perfect for the first-time homebrewer, the advanced homebrewer, and everyone in between.

Brewing Better Beer: Master Lessons for Advanced Homebrewers, by Gordon Strong (Georgetown, TX: Brewers Publications, 2011)

Three-time Ninkasi Award–winning homebrewer Gordon Strong digs deep into more advanced brewing techniques for those who want to take their brewing to the next level.

Brewing Classic Styles: 80 Winning Recipes Anyone Can Brew, by Jamil Zainasheff and John Palmer (Georgetown, TX: Brewers Publications, 2007)

Longtime *BYO* "Style Profile" columnist (2007 to 2013) Jamil Zainasheff has brewed every style of beer listed in the Beer Judge Certification Program guidelines. In this book, he teams up with *How to Brew* author John Palmer for a solid collection of recipes to get your classic beer styles dialed in.

The Complete Joy of Homebrewing, 4th edition, by Charlie Papazian (New York: William Morrow Paperbacks, 2014)

The classic title written by the founder of American homebrewing.

Designing Great Beers: The Ultimate Guide to Brewing Classic Beer Styles, by Ray Daniels (Georgetown, TX: Brewers Publications, 1998)

A practical, mechanical approach for when you are ready to start concocting your own homebrew recipes.

For the Love of Hops: The Practical Guide to Aroma, Bitterness and the Culture of Hops, by Stan Hieronymus (Georgetown, TX: Brewers Publications, 2012)

Part of the Brewing Elements series of titles from the Brewers Association, this reference is a must-have for any homebrewer interested in understanding hop varieties and hopping techniques.

Homebrew All-Stars: Top Homebrewers Share Their Best Techniques and Recipes, by Drew Beechum and Denny Conn (Minneapolis: Voyageur Press, 2016)

Get expert guidance and tips from some of the biggest names in the homebrewing hobby, including Marshall Schott, Curt Stock, Annie Johnson, and Mike "Tasty" McDole.

How to Brew: Everything You Need to Know to Brew Great Beer Every Time, by John Palmer (Georgetown, TX: Brewers Publication, 2017)

Many homebrewers learned to make beer thanks to John Palmer's comprehensive, step-by-step guide. The original edition is also available online.

Modern Homebrew Recipes: Exploring Styles and Contemporary Techniques, by Gordon Strong (Georgetown, TX: Brewers Publications, 2015)

Gordon Strong explains and explores the newest changes in BJCP style guidelines and shares advice for recipe formulation, adapting recipes to your system, and many recipes.

Project Extreme Brewing: An Enthusiast's Guide to Extreme Brewing at Home, by Sam Calagione (Beverly, MA: Quarry Books, 2017)

Dogfish Head Craft Brewery broke all the rules with many of its beers, and their founder and brewer Sam Calagione generously shares his advice for doing the same in your homebrewery.

Radical Brewing: Recipes, Tales, and World-Altering Meditations in a Glass, by Randy Mosher (Georgetown, TX: Brewers Publications, 2004)

Randy Mosher's style-busting guide to brewing great and artistic homebrews.

Water: A Comprehensive Guide for Brewers,
by John Palmer and Colin Kaminski (Georgetown, TX:
Brewers Publications, 2013)

This title takes the mystery out of one of the least
understood but most important components of
brewing. It's a part of the Brewers Association
Brewing Elements series.

Yeast: The Practical Guide to Beer Fermentation,
by Chris White and Jamil Zainasheff (Georgetown, TX:
Brewers Publications, 2010)

White Labs's founder Chris White teams up with Heretic
Brewing Company's Jamil Zainasheff to explain yeast
selection, storing and handling yeast, and much more
about this crucial brewing ingredient. Also a part of the
Brewers Association Brewing Elements series.

WEBSITES

Brew Your Own magazine: www.byo.com

The online home of *Brew Your Own*, featuring many years
of *BYO* stories, resource guides, charts, photo galleries,
recipes, and more.

American Homebrewers Association:
www.homebrewersassociation.org

Visit the AHA's site for lots of homebrew content,
including joining the organization, events, competition
guidelines, forums, recipes, and *Zymurgy* magazine.

How to Brew: www.howtobrew.com

Check out John Palmer's online version of his book,
How to Brew.

Beer Judge Certification Program: www.bjcp.org

If you want to brew to style, this site is indispensable. It
contains an online directory of the most up-to-date style
guidelines, which are used in homebrewing competitions
around the country (and the world).

Homebrew Academy (formerly known as Billy Brew):
www.homebrewacademy.com

A collection of homebrewing articles and instructions
by Billy Broas, all designed to teach people to make
beer at home.

Brew Science: www.sciencebrewer.com

If you skew toward scientific brewing, check out Jason
Rodriguez's blog detailing his experiments in the science
of brewing beer.

Mad Fermentationist: www.themadfermentationist.com

A log of the homebrewing and fermentational
experiments of the Mad Fermentationist—
a.k.a. Michael Tonsmeire.

Brülosophy: www.brulosophy.com

Marshall Schott, Ray Found, Greg Foster, Malcolm Frazer,
and Matt Waldron share a multitude of homebrewing
experiments in their blog, plus lots of great info on
brewing methods, recipes, and other projects.

Experimental Brewing: www.experimentalbrew.com

Homebrew buddies for life, Drew Beechum and Denny
Conn, share a love for brewing the experimental beers.
Check out their site for a blog, podcasts, books, speaking
dates, and more.

Basic Brewing Radio: www.basicbrewing.com

James Spencer's podcast, which welcomes a wide
variety of homebrewers on a multitude of topics. Features
an archive of shows going back to 2005.

The Brewing Network: www.thebrewingnetwork.com

Home of Beer Radio podcasts and videos including The
Session, The Sour Hour, Dr. Homebrew, Brew Strong,
Brewing with Style, Can You Brew It?, The Jamil Show,
and The Home Brewed Chef.

Beer and Wine Journal: www.beerandwinejournal.com

The current home of *BYO* former editor Chris Colby,
created in conjunction with Basic Brewing Radio's
James Spencer. It features many posts on all things
homebrewing, from techniques, to ingredients, to styles,
to recipes.

TOOLS AND CALCULATIONS

BeerSmith: www.beersmith.com

Home of Brad Smith's brewing software, but also features
tons of information about beer styles, ingredients,
recipes, a podcast, and a forum.

Brewer's Friend: www.brewersfriend.com

An online collection of homebrewing tools, including
calculators, charts, water profiles, brew day sheets
for note taking, water profiles, and much more. (Also
available as an app for both iOS and Android.)

Mr. Malty: www.mrmalty.com

A collection of information and tools created by
Jamil Zainasheff—former *BYO* writer, Ninkasi award
winner, book author, podcast host, and current
brewmaster/owner of Heretic Brewing Company—
back in his homebrewing days.

MESSAGE BOARDS/FORUMS

HomeBrewTalk.com: www.homebrewtalk.com

Reddit /r/homebrewing: www.reddit.com/r/homebrewing

INDEX

Double Agent IPL 59
Double Bag 140
Double Barrel Ale 242–243
Double Chocolate Stout 117
Double Pilsner 217–218
Double Sunshine IPA 54
Dragon's Milk 250–251
Dragon's Milk Brown Ale 87
Draught 107
Dreadnaught 62
Dry Dock Brewing Company: Apricot Blonde 230
Dunkel Lager 189
Duvel 149–150

Eastside Dark 187
Easy Street Wheat 210
Eddyline Brewery: River Runners Pale Ale 16–17
Edmund Fitzgerald Porter 95
Elysian Brewing Company: The Wise ESB 165–166
Empire Brewing Company: American Strong Ale 138–139
English Style Old Ale 166–167
Epic Brewing Company: Imperial Red Ale 67; Los Locos 201–202
Epicenter Ale 72
Epiphany 48–49
ESB: Fuller's Brewery 166; Redhook Brewery 170
Esoterik 132
Everett 95–96
Export Ale 211
Export India Porter 96

Farmhouse Summer Ale 202–203
Fat Tire 69–70
Faust Schwarzviertler 180–181
Fifteen 133
Firestone Walker Brewing Company: Double Barrel Ale 242–243; Pivo Hoppy Pils 216–217; Union Jack 29–30; Velvet Merlin 106; Wookey Jack 47–48
Flossmoor Station Brewery: Black Wolf Schwarzbier 181–182

Flower Power IPA 31–33
Flying Dog Brewery: Gonzo Imperial Porter 92–93; Numero Uno 202; Tire Bite Golden Ale 182
Flying Fish Brewing Company: Farmhouse Summer Ale 202–203
Focal Banger 42
Foreign Extra Stout 107–108
Fort George Brewery: Suicide Squeeze 30
Fort Point Pale Ale 23
Fortside Brewing Company: Black RyePA 48
Foundation Brewing Company: Epiphany 48–49
Founder's Brewing Company: Breakfast Stout 122–124
Frankenlager 61–62
Freetail Brewing Company: La Muerto Imperial Stout 124
Free Will Brewing Company: C.O.B. (Coffee Oatmeal Brown) 81
Full Curl Scotch Ale 168
Fuller, Smith & Turner PLC: ESB 166; Fuller's London Porter 93
Full Sail Brewing Company: Amber Ale 67–69; Wassail 258
Full Suspension Pale Ale 19–21
Funkwerks: Raspberry Provincial 243–245
Furious IPA 37
Fuzzy Kuckles 121–122

Genuine Irish Stout 104–105
ginger: Hennepin Farmhouse Saison 148; Warlock 234
Glacier Brewhouse: Imperial Blonde Ale 203–204
Gluten Free NWPA 15–16
Goddess Porter 90
Gonzo Imperial Porter 92–93
gooseberries: Salty Kiss 248–249
Goose Island Brewing Company: Summertime Kölsch 183
grains of paradise: Tut's Royal Gold 237; The Wit Album 146–147
grapes: Chateau Jiahu 228–229
Great Basin Brewing Company: Smoke Creek Rauchbock 184
Great Divide Brewing Company: Old Ruffian 139–140

Great Lakes Brewing Company: Edmund Fitzgerald Porter 95
Groundhog Imperial Stout 121
Grumpy Troll Brew Pub: Belgian IPA 49–50
G. Schneider & Sohn: Schneider Weisse Original 182–183
Guinness: Draught 107; Foreign Extra Stout 107–108
gur sugar: Dark Lord 130–132; see also sugar; specific types of sugar

H

Haandbryggeriet: Norwegian Wood 245
Hair of the Dog Brewing Company: Blue Dot Double IPA 50
Hamm's 213
Harpoon Brewery: English Style Old Ale 166–167; Harpoon IPA 30–31; Winter Warmer 258–259
hawthorn: Chateau Jiahu 228–229
Hazelnut Brown Nectar 85
hazelnuts 85
Heady Topper 42–43
heather: The Wit Album 146–147
Heileman: Old Style Light 204
Heineken International: Heineken 184–185
Hennepin Farmhouse Saison 148
hibiscus: Rosée d'Hibiscus (Pinkish Hibiscus) 226
Hill Farmstead Brewery: Abner 50–52; Everett 95–96
Hitachino Nest Sweet Stout 108
Hobgoblin Dark Ale 175
Hocus Pocus 209
Holiday Porter 100
honey: Baltic Porter 96–97; Chateau Jiahu 228–229; Gluten Free NWPA 15–16; Honey Basil Ale 224–225; Honey Kölsch 231; Imperial Blonde Ale 203–204; Kvasir 229; Mexican Honey Imperial Lager 204–206; Neshaminator Wheat Bock 188; Shenanigans Summer Ale 206–207; Tut's Royal Gold 237; Wheelchair Barleywine 136
Honey Basil Ale 224–225
Honey Kölsch 231
Hopback Amber Ale 74
Hope & King Scotch Ale 169
Hopfenstark: Saison Station 16 153–154

ACKNOWLEDGMENTS

We would like to thank all the great *BYO* staff who have contributed to our content over the years, as well as the many fantastic freelance writers and technical editors who have made *Brew Your Own* great, including:

Steve Bader	Christian Lavender	Gordon Strong
Glenn BurnSilver	Ashton Lewis	Michael Tonsmeire
Dave Clark	Dave Loew	Joe Vella
Derek Dellinger	Dennis Maciupa	Ward G. Walkup IV
Horst D. Dornbusch	Marc Martin	Mikoli Weaver
Kristen England	Betsy Parkes	Josh Weikert
Terry Foster	Sean Paxton	Anne Whyte
Dave Green	Bill Pierce	Jamil Zainasheff
Garrett Heaney	Scott Russell	Nathan Zeender
Les Howarth	Gretchen Schmidhausler	Paul Zocco
Gabe Jackson	Dawnell Smith	

ABOUT THE AUTHORS

Brew Your Own, launched in 1995, is the largest-circulation magazine for people interested in making their own great beer at home. Every issue includes recipes, how-to projects, and expert advice to help you brew world-class beer. *Brew Your Own* publishes eight issues annually from offices in Manchester Center, Vermont. The magazine's online home, www.byo.com, offers a selection of the magazine's stories, projects, and recipes as well as web-only features. The magazine is available in both print and digital editions.

Editor Dawson Raspuzzi joined *Brew Your Own* in 2013. He is a 2007 graduate of the journalism program at Castleton State University in Castleton, Vermont, and lives with his wife, two children, and two dogs in southern Vermont.